CHAMPS

A Proactive & Positive Approach to Classroom Management

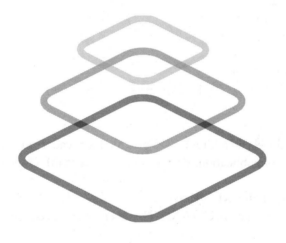

Jessica Sprick, M.S.
Randy Sprick, Ph.D.
Jacob Edwards, M.A., M.Ed.
Cristy Coughlin, Ph.D.

Published in the United States by
Ancora Publishing
21 West 6th Avenue
Eugene, Oregon 97401
ancorapublishing.com

ISBN: 978-1-59909-112-9
Cover and book design by Natalie Conaway

Any resources and website addresses are provided for reader convenience and were current at the time of publication. Report broken links to info@ancorapublishing.com.

Download Reproducible Materials
Go to ancorapublishing.com/CHAMPS3 and enter access code 978-1-59909-112-9

DEDICATION

This third edition is dedicated to the tens of thousands of teachers who have used previous editions to make their classrooms more academically effective, welcoming, and joyful for *all* students. Based on their feedback and on progress in the research community, this new edition strengthens the degree to which this resource can guide veteran and beginning teachers to design and implement a best-practice behavior support plan in their classroom.

TABLE OF CONTENTS

SECTION ONE

Overview of the CHAMPS Approach

CHAPTER 1
Develop a Clear Vision for Your Class and Your Classroom Management Approach

    *Learn about the CHAMPS approach and critical concepts that can help you establish a
    positive and proactive classroom.*

    *Develop an understanding of fundamental behavior management principles so that
    you can make effective decisions and take appropriate actions to help students learn to
    behave responsibly.*

    *Understand how to use your Classroom Management Plan to summarize important
    information, policies, and procedures you will use to motivate students and address
    appropriate and inappropriate behavior.*

SECTION TWO

Preparing: Build Your STOIC Classroom Management Plan

CHAPTER 2
Structure for Success—Behavioral Decisions

    *Develop and plan to actively share guidelines that describe the basic attitudes, traits,
    and behaviors that will help your students be successful in your classroom and
    throughout their lives.*

CHAPTER 4
Teach Students to Meet Expectations

ABOUT THE AUTHORS

Jessica Sprick, M.S.

Jessica Sprick has an M.S. in Special Education. She is a consultant and presenter for Safe & Civil Schools and a writer for Ancora Publishing and ASCD. Jessica has been a special education teacher for students with behavioral needs and Dean of Students. It is these practical experiences that guide her passion for working with educators to create systems of support that allow all students to thrive. She is the author of numerous educational resources, including *School Leader's Guide to Tackling Attendance Challenges*, *Bullying Solutions: Universal and Individual Strategies*, and *Discipline in the Secondary Classroom*. Each year, Jessica works with thousands of educators, providing training and support in how to implement multi-tiered and function-based approaches to improve classroom and school safety and climate and to boost student attendance, motivation, and academic engagement.

Randy Sprick, Ph.D.

Randy Sprick has worked as a paraprofessional, teacher, and teacher trainer at the elementary and secondary levels. Author of a number of widely read books on behavior and classroom management, Randy is former director of Safe & Civil Schools, a consulting company that provides inservice programs throughout the country. Although Randy is largely retired, his Safe & Civil Schools colleagues continue the work of helping large and small school districts improve student behavior and motivation. Efficacy of that work is documented in peer-reviewed research, and Safe & Civil Schools materials are listed on the National Registry of Evidence-Based Programs and Practices (NREPP). Randy was the recipient of the 2007 Council for Exceptional Children (CEC) Wallin Lifetime Achievement Award and was inducted into the Direct Instruction Hall of Fame, along with numerous other awards and honors.

**Jacob Edwards,
M.A., M.Ed.**

Jacob Edwards began his career in education teaching chemistry and biology in the inner city of Los Angeles. Fueled by the belief that all students deserve an equitable, quality education, Jacob became a school leader, where he honed his ability to lead diverse teams of staff and students, improve instructional practices, and establish systems to build positive school culture. Jacob went on to become the founding principal at a middle school in Watts, California, and later led transformation efforts at a middle school in Memphis, Tennessee. Most recently, Jacob joined the Safe & Civil Schools team to continue to improve educational outcomes for all students by working with educators across a variety of school settings.

Cristy Coughlin, Ph.D.

Cristy Coughlin holds a Ph.D. in school psychology from the University of Oregon and an undergraduate degree in psychology from Western Michigan University. Cristy has worked as a school-based behavior consultant and program evaluator for educational projects in the United States, Australia, and Africa. Her areas of expertise are oriented around educational assessment, applied behavior analysis, and translating educational research to practice.

PREFACE

This is the third edition of *CHAMPS*. The first edition of this book was published in 1998. Since that time, research continues to confirm that the proactive, positive, and instructional approaches it advocates are far more effective in managing and motivating students than traditional, authoritarian, and punitive approaches. Teacher effectiveness literature has identified that teachers who are highly successful have classroom management plans that:

- Include high expectations for student success
- Build positive relationships with students
- Create consistent, predictable classroom routines
- Teach students how to behave successfully
- Provide frequent positive feedback
- Correct misbehavior in a calm, consistent, logical manner

Throughout each edition of this book, we have strived to keep content compatible with this seminal teacher effectiveness research as well as capture relevant insights and highlight promising practices from new and emerging research. We have also tried to remain mindful about the daily pressures and current realities teachers face in the classroom to recommend practices, strategies, and tools that will be feasible and contextually relevant in the classrooms of today and tomorrow. This book translates those broad ideas into specific actions you can take to improve your ability to maintain an orderly and respectful classroom in which students are focused and engaged in meaningful instructional activities.

What's New in This Edition?

In this third edition, the content has been reorganized to guide the reader logically and sequentially through the STOIC model (STOIC is explained in more detail in the Introduction and at the beginning of each section):

Structure and organize your classroom.
Teach behavioral expectations.
Observe and monitor students.
Interact positively.
Correct misbehavior fluently.

New content covers:

- How the CHAMPS approach aligns with and supports other school initiatives, including multi-tiered systems of support for behavior (MTSS-B), social-emotional learning priorities, and trauma-informed practice
- Acknowledging and appreciating diversity and improving equity, inclusion, and access by reflecting on existing regularities in discipline planning and identifying better practices that help all students thrive and achieve their full potential

- Centering positive relationships at the foundation of your management approach by using strategies to consciously build and maintain relational trust with students and families
- The importance of maintaining and communicating high expectations for all students, and strategies for doing so
- Procedures for managing partner and cooperative group work and student technology use
- Considerations for developing effective and equitable grading practices
- Considerations for using assigned and flexible seating
- Engaging in ongoing professional development as part of a continuous improvement cycle
- Implementing behavior management practices in the virtual learning environment

CHAMPS as Part of a Behavior Support Continuum

This book fits into a continuum of behavior support products in the Safe & Civil Schools Series, a comprehensive set of resources designed to help school personnel make all school settings physically and emotionally safe for all students. In implementation projects throughout the country, we and our colleagues have learned that when expectations are clear and directly taught to students, much as you would teach writing skills, the vast majority of students will strive to be cooperative and meet those expectations. By implementing the preventive aspects of the Safe & Civil Schools Series, teachers can spend less time dealing with disruption and resistance and more time teaching.

Safe & Civil Schools uses a triangle image to illustrate the methodology behind our training. You may be familiar with the public health model triangle that has universal prevention and intervention at the bottom, selected or targeted services in the middle, and intensive services at the top. In our model, we indicate that good classroom management rests on top of effective schoolwide behavior management practices. Educational practice often results in spending a great deal of time, energy, and money on those individual students who act out most intensely—the tip of the triangle. We hope to stress the importance of placing your time, energy, and money on all students first—the widest part of the triangle. By creating a school and classroom climate that is calm, civil, and structured for student success, individual students will actually require less of your valuable intervention resources.

For information on resources in the Safe & Civil School Series, visit ancorapublishing.com.

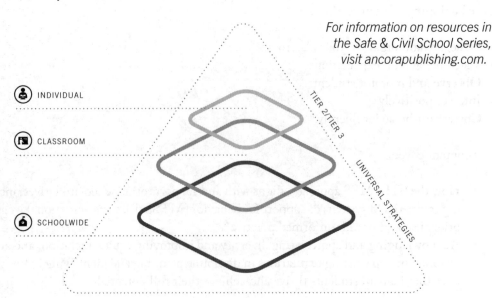

INDIVIDUAL

CLASSROOM

SCHOOLWIDE

TIER 2/TIER 3

UNIVERSAL STRATEGIES

ACKNOWLEDGMENTS

The authoring team wishes to acknowledge all the members of various professional groups who have made this book so much better than we as authors could create by ourselves. In no particular order, this includes all of the Safe & Civil Schools trainers who have used this resource to train countless teachers to construct classroom management plans that are practical and user friendly, and provided us with feedback along the way. Second, the editorial team at Ancora Publishing, including Sara Ferris, Natalie Conaway, and Matt Sprick, were invaluable in helping to ensure that this resource is aligned with and extends the library of Safe & Civil Schools multi-tiered behavior support products. Third, this edition has benefited from the insight and expertise of several contributors and collaborators, including Dr. Jonli Tunstall, Dr. Justyn Patterson, Stephen Minix, Kris Terry-Key, Jeremy Resnick, Jane Wagmeister, Heath Peine, and Billie Jo Rodriguez. Last but not least, we are deeply indebted to the entire support and customer service team at Ancora Publishing: Jake Clifton, Jen Colley, Caroline DeVorss, Jackie Hefner, Carole Mangels, and Nic Roy.

Introduction

This book was conceived and written to help teachers effectively manage student behavior and increase student motivation so they can focus their time and energy on instruction and student success. Discipline problems in school have always been and continue to be a leading frustration for teachers and a drain on instructional time.

Almost half of new teachers leave the profession within a few years (Ingersol et al., 2018). Two of the most common reasons given for leaving are discipline problems and a lack of administrative support for dealing with discipline. Inexperienced and unskilled teachers are often frustrated and sometimes even terrified by students who misbehave and challenge authority. Even skilled, veteran teachers can find themselves pulling their hair out when faced with a particularly challenging group. Or teachers may find they are uncertain how to meet the needs of students as demographics, economic situations, or other factors change within their district. Models for a positive and proactive approach to behavior management, such as CHAMPS, can give teachers in any of these situations the knowledge and skills to be confident and successful in working with students with behavioral or motivational challenges. CHAMPS also provides a powerful framework for evaluating and strengthening classroom management plans across time.

There are many obvious and direct links between academic achievement and student behavior. One disruptive student can negatively affect the learning of all the other students in a class. If students are actively or passively resistant, a seemingly simple transition like moving to lab stations, which should take no more than 2 minutes, can take as long as 10 minutes, wasting large amounts of instructional time. Students who are unmotivated will be less engaged in their work and learn less than if they are excited about the class.

If examples of misbehavior or apathy like these occur every day in every class, you are losing huge amounts of instructional time. By implementing effective management techniques, you can simultaneously increase student engagement and improve academic achievement (Brophy, 1996; Brophy & Good, 1986; Christenson et al., 2008; Gettinger & Ball, 2008; Luiselli et al., 2005; Scheuermann & Hall, 2008; Sprick et al., 2019).

Why bother with a positive approach to discipline?

The educational environment has changed greatly in the last 70 years. The accepted norm for disciplining students used to be punishment, and if the students continued to misbehave, suspension or expulsion. These measures did not necessarily change behavior, but they were easy solutions—the problem seemingly disappeared as the student disappeared from the classroom and eventually the school system. In 1900, high school graduation rates were only 6%, and in 1950, graduation rates were only 59% (Heckman & LaFontaine, 2010). While this may seem like an appalling dropout rate, in the past jobs on farms or in factories were plentiful for those without a high school education.

In the 2017–2018 school year, graduation rates were reported at 85% (NCES, 2020). Schools are doing better than ever in U.S. history at helping students reach graduation. However, imagine looking at a kindergarten class with 20 bright-eyed young five-year-olds. If our current rates of dropout continue, at least three of them will not make it to graduation. Many farm, factory, and other jobs that once allowed someone without a high school diploma to live a comfortable adult life are increasingly being replaced by technology or no longer adequately provide for the individual or their family. It is more important than ever for students to exit school with a high school diploma. We must do better to help all students thrive throughout their K–12 experience and reach graduation. Moreover, we must do more to equip students to be successful outside school, whether they plan to immediately enter the job market or continue on to higher education.

Schools are under tremendous pressure to successfully educate all students, including those who years ago would have left school because of academic or behavioral problems. Effective ways to motivate and encourage positive behavior are vital to serving these students. For students who have struggled in school because of experiences of trauma, poverty, systemic racism, generational difficulties with the school system, or a disability, purely punitive and reactive approaches are unlikely to make a lasting difference. These approaches do not address the needs of the students. We need to do business differently.

Therefore, a proactive and positive approach like CHAMPS is essential. With these strategies you can guide students toward a successful school career, leading in turn to potential success in work and in life.

The CHAMPS Approach

CHAMPS is designed to help you, the classroom teacher, develop (or fine-tune) an effective classroom management plan that is proactive, positive, and instructional. In the last 50 years, a large and varied body of research literature has identified consistent and reliable findings concerning how effective teachers manage student behavior and enhance student motivation. The techniques included in this approach are derived from that literature.

Unlike programs that have set procedures, the CHAMPS approach guides teachers in how to make effective decisions about managing behavior. For example, one of the tasks in Chapter 2: Structure for Success—Behavioral Decisions is about the physical setting. Rather than implying that only one physical setting is correct, we specify factors to take into account when designing the seating arrangement in the classroom. One of the most important factors is your ability to move quickly and directly from any part of the room to any other part. This allows you to supervise by physically circulating throughout the room and to reach and speak quietly with any student in the room—to praise, correct misbehavior, or answer a question.

> *CHAMPS is not a canned program but rather a way of thinking about how to prevent misbehavior and encourage responsible behavior.*

A second factor to consider is the amount of student conversation desired. How much talking will be allowed and during which activities? Some seating arrangements are more conducive to conversation than others. After reviewing the factors to consider, we show different classroom arrangements and delineate the pros and cons of each. However, the teacher always makes the decision: "How can I arrange my room to meet my needs and the needs of my students?"

In CHAMPS, we provide the information you need to make an informed decision—we don't tell you what to do. If you talk about CHAMPS with colleagues, we encourage you to talk about the CHAMPS approach, not the CHAMPS program, because it is not a canned program but rather a way of thinking about how to prevent misbehavior and encourage responsible behavior. It is a model for effective problem prevention and problem-solving. To use a cooking analogy, CHAMPS teaches you how to become an effective cook. Rather than a recipe that you follow in a step-by-step fashion, CHAMPS is like a cooking resource that teaches you how to effectively use different ingredients and cooking tools to create any culinary masterpiece you wish.

CHAMPS, while not a program, does have one absolute rule: Students must be treated at all times with respect, honoring their inherent dignity and rights. Belittling and ridicule have no place in the teacher's repertoire of behavioral practices. You will learn more about some of the foundational principles and practices that guide the CHAMPS approach in Chapter 1.

Is CHAMPS evidence based?

Yes! First, CHAMPS is entirely compatible with more than 50 years of research on how effective teachers manage their classrooms in ways that enhance academic achievement. Second, Safe & Civil Schools has many examples of district-based studies where CHAMPS has been implemented with remarkable results. Improvements include marked reductions in classroom disruptions, office referrals, and in-school and out-of-school suspensions, along with corresponding increases in teachers' perceptions of efficacy and student motivation and behavior.

For information on efficacy data, contact Safe & Civil Schools at safeandcivilschools.com. For more information on how CHAMPS is compatible with classroom management research literature and for summaries of research studies on the CHAMPS approach, see "CHAMPS Resources" below.

CHAMPS RESOURCES

To download research studies, reproducibles, CHAMPS icons, and other materials to help implement CHAMPS in your classroom, visit CHAMPS Resources at ancorapublishing.com/CHAMPS3. Enter the password: 978-1-59909-112-9

How does CHAMPS fit with other initiatives?

CHAMPS is a flexible approach that is highly compatible with many other initiatives and frameworks that may exist within your district. Rather than viewing CHAMPS as a competing approach, consider ways to integrate and merge CHAMPS with effective practices and systems being used in your own practice and across your district. Following are some examples of common initiatives or approaches and how they relate to your work with CHAMPS:

- **Response to Intervention (RtI) and Multi-Tiered System of Support (MTSS).** Response to Intervention (RtI) and Multi-Tiered System of Support (MTSS) are frameworks for ensuring that students experiencing behavioral or academic problems do not go unnoticed, and that once noticed, their difficulties are addressed and supported by school personnel. This process of problem identification matches problem-solving processes and intervention to the needs of the student. RtI and MTSS frameworks focus on providing high-quality instruction and interventions matched to student need, monitoring progress frequently to make decisions about changes in instruction or goals, and applying child response data to important educational decisions (Batsche et al., 2005). RtI and MTSS models often refer to levels of support in three tiers:

  - Tier 1: Universal prevention
  - Tier 2: Targeted support
  - Tier 3: Intensive support

  Within an RtI or MTSS framework, CHAMPS represents a major component in a school or district's behavior support efforts to work toward universal prevention and early-stage problem-solving.

- **Positive Behavioral Interventions and Supports (PBIS).** Positive Behavioral Interventions and Supports (PBIS) is a popular label for behavior management approaches that use long-term strategies to reduce inappropriate behavior, teach more appropriate behavior, and provide contextual supports necessary for successful outcomes (Carr et al., 2002; Horner et al., 1990, Warger, 1999). Traditional behavior management views the individual as the problem and seeks to "fix" them by quickly eliminating the challenging behavior through punitive approaches. PBIS and functional behavior analysis view systems, settings, and lack of skill as parts of the problem and work to change those. According to the U.S. Department of Education, PBIS is a framework to help provide "assistance to schools, districts, and states to establish a preventative, positive, multi-tiered continuum of evidence-based behavioral interventions that support the behavioral competence of students" (A. Posny, personal communication, September 7, 2010). Therefore, rather than a specific program, PBIS is a broad, general term for procedures and techniques designed to help improve behavior through more than just reactive and punitive techniques. The Safe & Civil Schools approach for schoolwide implementation of PBIS is called Foundations. Schools across the nation use the Foundations approach to help improve schoolwide climate and safety. The CHAMPS approach helps educators apply PBIS procedures in the classroom.

- **Trauma-Informed/Trauma-Sensitive Practices.** Trauma-Informed/Trauma-Sensitive Practices are used when educators operate with an awareness and sensitivity to students' experiences of trauma in ways that can help break cycles of trauma, prevent re-traumatization, and best engage a student in learning and the school community. A wide variety of experiences can lead to childhood trauma, such as experiencing or witnessing actual or threatened death, serious injury, or sexual violence; experiencing psychological abuse or neglect; witnessing domestic violence; or living with household members who are mentally ill or suicidal, abuse substances, or are sex offenders (American Psychiatric Association, 2013, Felitti et al., 1998). Children who experience trauma, especially when it is repeated, may experience difficulties in school. They may have trouble paying attention, processing new information, participating in social situations, and forming and maintaining normal relationships. They may also have difficulty learning and reduced ability to regulate and appropriately express emotions (Lubit et al., 2003; Streeck-Fischer & van der Kolk, 2000; van der Kolk, 2003). Trauma-sensitive practices are consistent with the approaches advocated in this book. A trauma-sensitive classroom teacher will anticipate when and where challenges will occur, teach children skills to manage stress and develop awareness, build supports to avoid re-traumatiziation, and encourage healthy, positive teacher-student relationships.
- **Social-Emotional Learning (SEL).** Social-Emotional Learning (SEL) involves helping students learn and develop social-emotional knowledge, skills, and attitudes needed for success in school, work, interpersonal relationships, and personal wellness. When schools engage in effective SEL approaches, students can learn to manage emotions, work toward goals, maintain positive relationships, effectively problem-solve and make responsible decisions, show empathy, and develop a healthy and positive sense of identity (CASEL, 2020). SEL interventions have been shown to increase students' academic performance, improve classroom behavior, reduce student stress and depression, and improve student attitudes (Durlak et al., 2011). The CHAMPS approach advocates for the teaching of SEL and provides some information on teaching these skills in Chapter 4, Task 3. CHAMPS also provides a critical foundation for SEL by establishing a safe, supportive learning environment where students can learn and develop critical social-emotional skills. Rather than competing, these two approaches are both integral to student success.
- **Restorative Practices (RP).** Restorative Practice (RP) is a multi-tiered approach with a focus on community building, increasing respect toward others of different backgrounds, increasing accountability when harm has occurred, and repairing harm to relationships (Smith et al., 2015). Students and staff learn how to peaceably resolve conflicts within the school community by creating opportunities for those involved to listen empathetically to each other's stories, take ownership for their behavior in the conflict, and restore positive relationships. Thus, conflicts and behavioral difficulties in school are seen as opportunities for teaching and modeling nonviolent ways of problem-solving rather than for punishing and excluding students. CHAMPS and RP are complementary approaches that can be used effectively in tandem to improve positive behavior and climate. While CHAMPS has an increased focus on explicit structures and behavior management strategies that teachers can use to set a foundation for a

positive and productive classroom, RP provides a rich array of tools that support building a strong community that uses peaceable ways to mediate and resolve conflict. Safe & Civil Schools approaches and RP work well together to:

- Improve positive school climate.
- Encourage student and parent voices and empowerment in the problem-solving process.
- Reduce suspensions, expulsions, and problematic student behaviors.
- Encourage structure, routines, and effective teaching strategies and behavior management.
- Promote peaceable ways to teach empathy and mediate conflict.
- Reduce incidences of violence and bullying.

How to Use This Book

CHAMPS is organized into four sections and eleven chapters. If you are able to read the book and work through the tasks *before school begins*, read the book sequentially. As you work through each chapter, you will complete a Classroom Management Plan, which is described in Chapter 1, Task 3. The Classroom Management Plan is a succinct document you can use to clarify many of the major decisions you will be making about your classroom approach.

If you begin to use CHAMPS *after the start of the school year*, first read Chapter 9, Task 4: Begin CHAMPS Implementation Midyear. This task will help you map out an approach for reading through priority tasks during the year. You can then tackle the rest of the tasks as you prepare for the next school year.

If you teach in a *virtual learning environment*, skip directly to Section 4: Implementing CHAMPS in a Virtual Learning Environment. While you will read many of the tasks in the first three sections, the content in Section 4 will serve as your guide for applying the CHAMPS strategies, and it will provide additional practical approaches for addressing common concerns in the virtual setting, such as how to improve attendance and engagement.

The acronym CHAMPS reflects the categories, or types, of expectations that you, as a teacher, need to clarify for students about every major activity and transition that occurs in your classroom. If you identify and then teach students precisely what your expectations are for each classroom activity and transition, you will significantly reduce the amount of misbehavior and increase the amount of learning that takes place in your classroom.

Following are brief descriptions of the types of expectations that need to be clarified.

C	**Conversation**	*Can students talk to each other?*
H	**Help**	*How do students get their questions answered?* *How do they get your attention?*
A	**Activity**	*What is the task or objective?* *What is the end product?*

M   **Movement**   *Can students move about?*

P   **Participation**   *What does the expected student behavior look and sound like? How do students show they are fully participating?*

S   **Success**   *If students follow the CHAMPS expectations, they will be successful.*

Bonus Materials. Additional information is provided only as downloadable documents to assist you with your understanding and implementation of CHAMPS. These documents include:

See the copyright page or CHAMPS Resources on page 3 for details on how to download reproducible materials.

- CHAMPS Icons and Reproducible Forms
- Classroom Activity Worksheet Examples
- Is CHAMPS Evidence Based
- List of CHAMPS Reinforcers

Reproducible Forms. More than 150 pages of reproducible forms are available in the download. Reproducible forms are provided in PDF format. They can be printed and filled out by hand. They are also enabled so they can be filled out on your computer and saved electronically. See the document "Using the CHAMPS Files" in the download for detailed instructions on how to fill out forms using Adobe Reader.

Icons. The downloadable materials include six versions of icons (visual representations of different expectations for each CHAMPS category—see the table below) that you can use to teach your CHAMPS expectations. Icons are provided in both PDF and PNG format. See Chapter 4, Task 2 for more information about how to use these icons.

Version 1 Primary, K–2 (B&W)	*Version 2* Primary, K–2 (Color)	*Version 3* Intermediate, 3–8 (B&W)	*Version 4* Pictograph	*Version 5* Sentence Strips	*Version 6* Road Sign
				*Conversation* Talk quietly with anyone in your group.	TALK QUIETLY WITH ONE OTHER STUDENT
				Participation Listen, answer, ask questions, and/or share.	LISTEN, ANSWER, ASK QUESTIONS, AND/OR SHARE

NOTE: Permission is given to administrators and educators who purchase the book to reproduce any form labeled "Reproducible Form" and any CHAMPS icon solely for the purpose of classroom management and teaching CHAMPS expectations. As the owner of this book, you may reproduce as many copies of these icons as you need each year for your own classroom. *Further reproduction of the icons and forms is strictly prohibited.*

Section Descriptions

Section 1 has only one chapter, which introduces foundational concepts that guide the CHAMPS approach. These concepts will be revisited frequently in subsequent chapters as we provide actionable ways to implement these essential but sometimes abstract concepts. It also introduces the Classroom Management Plan, a concise document that you will use to clarify and compile essential information on your vision, classroom organization, and disciplinary procedures. You will fill out each part of the Classroom Management Plan as your work through the *CHAMPS* book. No matter what time of year you begin to read *CHAMPS*, we recommend starting with Chapter 1.

Section 2, Preparing: Build Your STOIC Classroom Management Plan, includes Chapters 2 through 8. This section focuses on essential elements to consider when you are preparing (and later refining) your Classroom Management Plan. In each chapter, we present specific tasks that will help you address that chapter's content. We also offer detailed suggestions about how to accomplish the tasks themselves. These chapters are organized within the STOIC acronym, which is an easy way to remember five main categories of variables proven to be effective in changing behavior and motivation:

S   *Structure (organize) your classroom to prompt responsible behavior.* The way a setting is structured has a huge impact on the behavior and attitude of people in that setting. There are two chapters devoted to the implementation of structural considerations in your classroom.

T   *Teach your expectations regarding how to behave responsibly (i.e., be successful) within the structure that you have created.* Sports coaches provide a great example of teaching behavior and re-teaching as needed to help each individual achieve full potential.

O   *Observe whether students are meeting expectations (monitor!).* In the short run, this means circulate and visually scan the classroom. In the long run, this means collect and analyze meaningful data on student progress.

I   *Interact positively with students.* Provide frequent noncontingent attention to build relationships. Provide frequent, age-appropriate positive feedback to acknowledge students' efforts to be successful. Improve student motivation through positive relationships, feedback, and specific motivational strategies and systems. Two chapters focus on how to interact positively and motivate your students.

C   *Correct misbehavior fluently.* This means briefly, calmly, consistently, immediately, and (as much as possible) privately.

Section 3 contains two chapters on how to implement, sustain, and refine your classroom management plan. Where Section 2 provides practical skills and strategies to help you and your students meet your vision for success, Section 3 gives you information about how to put these skills and strategies into action. Chapter 9: Launch covers how to establish a positive and productive classroom from Day One (and how to launch your CHAMPS approach if you are starting midyear). Chapter 10: Maintain a Cycle of Continuous Improvement discusses how you can use the CHAMPS approach and specific tools to further your professional development and implementation across time. This information in this section will help to ensure that CHAMPS does not become a dusty book on your shelf. Rather, when used within a continuous improvement model, the CHAMPS approach can become a deeply meaningful way to help achieve success with any group of students you work with.

Section 4: Implementing CHAMPS in Virtual Learning Environments contains one chapter that describes how to apply the approaches in the first three sections when you teach students in a virtual learning environment. It provides information about which tasks in CHAMPS can be applied as is, which tasks apply but may need some adaptation, and which tasks are not relevant in the virtual classroom. Throughout this chapter, you will see many samples of specific tools and strategies teachers can use to create a positive and productive virtual classroom experience. This section also provides an increased focus on how to use strategies to increase student attendance and engagement, which many teachers report are their greatest management and motivational challenges with virtual learning.

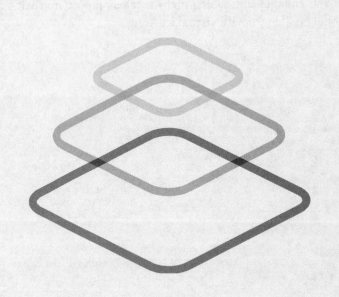

Overview of the CHAMPS Approach

To effectively manage and motivate a class (or classes) of students, you need a clear vision of your ideal classroom—what it should look like, what it should sound like, and what it should feel like to participants in the classroom and to anyone who comes in to observe. Consider the vision and the goals for what students learn academically, socially, and behaviorally as a result of their membership in your classroom. Once you have a clear idea of what you want for your classroom, you can design procedures that will ensure that you achieve those goals. These tasks will also serve as the basis for "enticing" students and families to join you as their guide for how to succeed in your classroom.

Imagine any complex system that you want to be successful within. For our purposes here, think about embarking on an advanced degree. You have narrowed things down to two schools. As you explore the first, you are somewhat disappointed to learn that it is very difficult to determine the nature of program, whether the program will really meet your professional goals, and whether you have the requisite skills to succeed. In addition, as you try to explore these questions, everyone you speak or correspond with acts annoyed and makes you feel hesitant to express questions and concerns. By contrast, with the second school you easily find information about what you will learn in the program, the mission and purpose of the program, and all the requirements for you to enter and successfully complete the degree. The icing on the cake here is that everyone you speak with is helpful and welcoming. Even though the first school might be excellent (but it's also possible that it is not, given its inability to clarify these details), but given a choice, most of us would embark on the journey in which the destination is important, obvious, and attainable, and the road to get there is clearly mapped out in achievable chunks, with every indication that there will be help along the way if you feel you are lost. This section (and the single chapter within it) are designed to help you create a vision, process, and plan to help all your students succeed in your classroom.

CHAPTER 1

Develop a Clear Vision for Your Class and Your Classroom Management Approach

When you know where you are headed, you can guide students to their own success.

Numerous tasks throughout *CHAMPS* will help you define your vision, high positive expectations, and long-term goals. You will continually think about what the ideal learning environment looks and sounds like as you define expectations, plan for your interactions (both positive and corrective) with students, and implement other tasks throughout this book. In this chapter, we present some of the key ideas that guide the CHAMPS approach. These are foundational principles, critical concepts, or pillars for implementation that are essential as you embark on the ongoing journey to implement a positive and proactive approach to behavior management and student support. The concepts in this chapter are critical for developing a clear vision of how to manage student behavior and motivate students in effective ways.

The first two tasks will help you understand some of these fundamental principles of behavior management and motivation. These tasks can also help you to position your work with CHAMPS in the context of other major initiatives and frameworks that exist in your class, school, or district. Task 3 introduces you to the Classroom Management Plan, which will help you summarize your vision, classroom organization, daily expectations, and other major factors you will evaluate and possibly refine as you work through CHAMPS. In this task, you will identify the level of support to put in place in your classroom for students to be successful. The level of support you identify will have significant implications in the decisions that you make throughout this book.

The tasks in this chapter are:

- Task 1: Understand Foundational Principles and Practices That Guide the CHAMPS Approach
- Task 2: Understand How to Shape Behavior
- Task 3: Prepare Your Classroom Management Plan

By attending to each of these three tasks, you can set the foundation for an effective management plan that will help achieve your vision of what your class will look, sound, and feel like, and the goals and accomplishments you and your students will achieve. As you work through these foundational tasks, challenge yourself to carefully examine your own beliefs and practices. Where do you see alignment? Where do these foundational concepts challenge your existing ideas or practices related to behavior, the teacher's role in education, and the potential of your students? Mindsets drive action, so this chapter provides essential information about productive mindsets that will help you effectively manage your classroom so it becomes a productive and positive environment for learning.

TASK 1

Understand Foundational Principles and Practices That Guide the CHAMPS Approach

Learn about the CHAMPS approach and critical concepts that can help you establish a positive and proactive classroom.

● ● ● ● ●

Classroom management is a journey and not a destination. This simple statement is a powerful reminder that self-reflection and a commitment to continuous improvement are integral parts of the educational process. Effective teachers reflect on their own practices to determine what is working for their students (and for themselves!), and they identify those elements of their practice to celebrate and protect. At the same time, effective teachers continually work to identify practices that may need to be changed to address current classroom concerns. The best teachers recognize that change and adjustment are natural parts of teaching. Every student who walks through the door, and every mix of students in the classroom, is different and presents unique strengths and challenges. Thus, effective teachers demonstrate a commitment to flexibility—when something isn't working, they can accept change without judgment and maintain forward momentum toward the vision of success.

Throughout *CHAMPS* you will be challenged to reflect on your current practices: What should be celebrated and protected, and what should be tweaked, changed, or abandoned to increase student success and help you reach your positive vision of the ideal classroom?

This task introduces some of the critical concepts and hallmark practices that serve as the foundation for effective classroom management. As you read this task, challenge yourself to carefully examine how your current practices do or do not reflect these foundational elements.

The concepts we briefly overview here are complex and interwoven, and each has significant implications for your teaching practice. Thus, they will be revisited frequently throughout this book. When an aspect of the book relates closely to one of these foundational principles, you may see a callout box that highlights how the content relates to the foundational principle or practice. For example, if you realize that your classroom practices need to be more carefully aligned to your mission and beliefs, pay careful attention to content in *CHAMPS* that is highlighted with a Mission and Beliefs callout box. There you will find specific tasks and strategies that can help you focus on how to clarify and create a classroom aligned with your mission and beliefs.

Mission and Beliefs: Create an Effective Vision to Guide Your Practice

Mahatma Gandhi once said, "Your beliefs become your thoughts, your thoughts become your words, your words become your actions, your actions become your habits, your habits become your values, your values become your destiny." So, this journey begins with evaluating your beliefs about your students, your educational community, and yourself as a teacher. The process of defining and documenting your beliefs and then using them to inform your practice is an essential element in developing an effective classroom management plan.

> *This journey begins with evaluating your beliefs about your students, your educational community, and yourself as a teacher.*

Begin by reflecting on your mission as an educator. Why did you enter the field of education? What do you hope to accomplish with your students? What do you believe is the purpose of your job? What is your commitment to your school community as a teacher? If your school has a written mission or vision statement, examine this statement and consider whether it reflects the culture of your school and the culture of your classroom. Some examples of good mission statements include:

- *The staff at Franklin Middle School are committed to helping every child develop a love of learning and motivating every child to reach his or her full potential.*
- *Every day, every child in every classroom learns, grows, and feels respected.*

The mission is essential to establish an overarching vision that creates a sense of purpose for all members of the school community. However, it is common for these statements to become empty words. In many cases, staff don't even know what the school's mission statement is! As you reflect on your school's mission or as you create a mission statement yourself, consider daily actions you can take to actively strive to reach the mission. You mission serves as a North Star that you can use to reflect on all aspects of your classroom practice—as in, does this practice, procedure, or approach help me or does it in any way violate my efforts to reach the mission? One way to further refine this process is to define beliefs for yourself about behavior management and discipline.

Your school may already have a set of staff beliefs in the form of a written description of principles related to behavior management and discipline. If so, consider how your own beliefs and actions align with the school's written staff beliefs. Staff beliefs should relate directly to your school's mission—if staff are using practices that align with the staff beliefs, it should help the school achieve its mission. If there are points of disagreement or disconnect, consider how you can begin a conversation with your administrator to better understand the purpose behind certain beliefs or to ensure that staff beliefs match with best practices for behavior management and discipline.

If your school does not have a written set of staff beliefs, consider the following samples and work to write your own set of beliefs to guide a positive and proactive approach to student behavior and motivation.

At Safe & Civil Schools, we have articulated the following:

MISSION: We are committed to providing welcoming and supportive educational settings where all students can thrive.

To accomplish this, we believe:

- Staff behavior creates the climate of the school, and a positive, welcoming, and inviting climate should be intentionally created and continuously maintained.
- All student behaviors necessary for success need to be overtly and directly articulated and taught to mastery. If you want it, teach it.
- All students should have equal access to good instruction and behavior support, regardless of their current skills or backgrounds.
- Clarity of expectations and consistency of application and enforcement of these expectations are essential throughout the school.
- Punitive and corrective techniques are necessary but have significant limitations. Misbehavior presents teaching and learning opportunities.
- Everyone, even students who make poor choices, should be treated at all times with respect and in ways that demonstrate a commitment to helping them reach their positive potential.
- All children have basic human rights that must be honored and upheld by all school personnel, regardless of politics, religion, ideology, or personal beliefs.

Following is a composite of staff beliefs from several different schools (adapted with permission from *Foundations*, by R. Sprick et al., 2014, Ancora Publishing):

All staff members contribute to our school's friendly, inviting environment. We set the tone through our actions and attitudes. We demonstrate continuous support and encouragement for all students in five important ways:

1. We teach students the expectations for responsible behavior in all school settings. We help students strive to exhibit productive habits and attitudes for learning, including:

    *   Being responsible
    *   Always trying their best
    *   Cooperating with others
    *   Treating everyone with respect, including themselves.

2. We recognize that positive relationships with students are foundational to a productive learning environment, and we strive to build positive relationships with every student by learning who they are and fostering their strengths.
3. We provide positive feedback to students when they are meeting expectations and striving to exhibit productive habits and attitudes.
4. We view minor misbehavior as a teaching opportunity, and we respond calmly and consistently to misbehavior with corrections and corrective consequences.
5. We work collaboratively and with a solutions-oriented mindset to solve chronic and severe behavior problems.

To use a bowling analogy, imagine that your mission statement is like the pins at the end of the bowling lane. You must successfully guide your classroom throughout the year to achieve your mission (a strike). Novice bowlers often find their ball veering off course and landing in the gutter of the bowling lane. Similarly, teachers can easily veer off course from their mission when they encounter students with challenging behavior. To help a bowling ball reach the pins, bumpers or guard rails can be placed in the gutter. Your written statement of beliefs about behavior management can serve like bumpers or guard rails to help prevent you from veering off course. Without clarifying these beliefs, you may struggle to evaluate which classroom management practices you should keep, tweak, or abandon across time. However, just as a bowling ball can take many different paths down the lane, even with guard rails in place, your Classroom Management Plan allows you a lot of flexibility and many paths to help your class be successful. As you work through this book, continue to evaluate your beliefs about student behavior and classroom management, and how they relate to your overarching mission. Make efforts to periodically evaluate your Classroom Management Plan and daily actions in relation to your (or your school's) beliefs and mission statement.

Diversity, Equity, Inclusion, and Access: Fulfilling the Promise of Education for All

Effective schools help all students thrive and achieve their full potential. Effective classrooms help all students become increasingly responsible, respectful, motivated, and highly engaged in meaningful instructional activities. Unfortunately, throughout the history of the United States and despite some improvements and earnest efforts of many educators, school systems have not fulfilled the promise of education for all students. Large numbers of students have fallen through the cracks of the system. School systems have struggled to fulfill the promise of an effective education for broad groups, such as Black and Brown students, students identified with emotional and behavioral disabilities, students who struggle from experiences of trauma, and LGBTQ+ students, among others.

Overt and ongoing efforts are needed in all schools (and by all educators within those schools) to nurture Diversity, Equity, Inclusion, and Access (DEIA) to fulfill the promise of education for all. Nurturing DEIA means moving beyond awareness of differences and individual identities into eliminating barriers to access, providing supports that encourage active participation and engagement, and listening to and valuing all perspectives within a community. It requires a commitment from educators to build classroom and school environments that truly support all students and allow them to thrive. DEIA must be a cornerstone commitment for all educators.

DEIA is an important focus within any school community, whether the community is extremely diverse or largely homogenous in terms of race/ethnicity, socioeconomic status, or other factors. Imagine you work in a school with a mix of students from different race/ethnicities, immigrants and refugees from other countries, different socioeconomic circumstances, and different religions. The differences in culture and experiences of students can present unique challenges in meeting a variety of needs, but they also represent wonderful opportunities to learn with and from each other about diverse perspectives. Hopefully, educators working in a school like this have a heightened awareness of the need to consider DEIA throughout their teaching practice.

In a more homogenous community, for example, if 90% of the student and staff population are of one race/ethnicity, it is equally important to commit to and continually reflect on issues of DEIA. However, it can be easy to fall into the trap of not thinking critically about DEIA because one culture or demographic group is so prominently represented. You may make assumptions about your students based on comparison to norms of the population that is most represented. You may not be as aware of the ways in which cultural differences, individual differences, and the backgrounds of your students affect your perceptions of their behavior, motivation, or needs. Regardless of whether you work in a homogenous or a heterogenous community, actively seek to learn about and reflect on DEIA and how you can support all learners.

An effective classroom management approach is one essential element of putting your commitment to DEIA into practice. Effective classroom managers ensure that classroom expectations, disciplinary practices, and everyday interactions are just and equitably applied. They encourage and provide supports needed to all students and continually work to establish a positive and safe learning environment. DEIA should be a primary consideration as you work through the tasks in this book.

In addition, many important school initiatives are designed to help educators nurture specific aspects of DEIA. Cultural competency, trauma-informed/trauma-sensitive care, restorative practices, identifying implicit bias, and other frameworks push educators to analyze existing practices, reveal hidden norms, identify gaps, and consider meaningful supports for students who might otherwise fall through the cracks. When used proficiently, these can be powerful tools to work toward the promise of nurturing DEIA. However, recognize that none of these approaches is a panacea. Effective educators continue to work throughout their career to expand their knowledge and implement practices that will move them closer to fulfilling the promise of education for all.

In their efforts to gain more proficiency in nurturing DEIA, educators typically move through three main phases (or mile markers) of development: Becoming Informed, Increasing Sensitivity, and Changing Practice. Each phase involves increased time, effort, and energy, but also represents getting closer to meeting the goals presented within DEIA.

- **Becoming Informed.** During this phase, educators become aware of potential barriers or gaps that are impacting a student's educational achievement. For example, someone who is trauma informed is aware of research about the negative impacts of trauma and can begin to identify students who may be exhibiting signs of struggle due to experiences with trauma.

- **Increasing Sensitivity.** The second phase involves self-reflection. Educators take a deep look at themselves and how they interact with the world around them in relation to the area of knowledge. This sounds like a simple proposition, but examination of biases and blind spots, and reflection about needed areas of personal growth, can often be difficult. The goal is for teachers to become so well informed that they are now sensitive to barriers to achievement and gaps in supports for students in real time. They can also anticipate underlying issues caused by their own practices or the environment. A teacher who is in the Increasing Sensitivity phase related to issues of implicit bias is not only aware of what biases look like in others and within the educational system, but also has begun identifying her own biases and how they may be impacting her classroom and her students.

- **Changing Practice.** Lastly, educators adopt prevention, early intervention, and responsive support strategies to address the specific issues they were previously informed about and sensitive to. During this phase, their daily actions and efforts become aligned with their knowledge and beliefs—they are living the commitment to DEIA. They demonstrate that their efforts go beyond just knowledge and beliefs. A teacher who delivers culturally competent practice has moved beyond identifying his own cultural values and biases, developing a better understanding of culturally specific knowledge about his students, and having knowledge of institutional barriers that may be preventing some of his students from adequately accessing educational resources. This educator is now mastering skills that allow him to successfully teach students who come from a culture different from his own by integrating his knowledge and sensitivity about cultural competence into the daily actions of teaching.

This progression across phases takes time and requires a commitment from educators to be open to challenging their own assumptions and making changes to existing practices. The actionable and practical skills and strategies in CHAMPS provide one way to help convert sound theory in frameworks related to DEIA into meaningful practice.

Data-Driven Processes: Tools for Continuous Improvement

Data are one of the most powerful tools in any educator's toolbox. When used skillfully, data not only inspire, but can also help you prioritize resources, unpack and clarify complex issues, identify effective remedies, and monitor progress. Two chapters in *CHAMPS* focus heavily on how to use data in your classroom in effective ways (see Chapter 5: Use Data to Monitor and Adjust Your Management Plan, and Chapter 10: Maintain a Cycle of Continuous Improvement).

The relentless pursuit of collecting and analyzing data to inform practice is also one of the most practical tools for establishing a culture that nurtures diversity, equity, access, and inclusion. Some of the questions to ask yourself as you analyze your classroom data include:

- Are certain demographic groups (e.g., race/ethnicity, gender, disability status, students who receive free/reduced lunch) thriving or falling through the cracks?
- Are disciplinary procedures, such as the number and type of corrective consequences, proportional to the subgroups in my classroom?
- Is there any disproportionality in the academic achievement or behavioral success of different groups of students in my classroom?

If differences are identified, that is only the first step. Once you recognize concerns, begin asking the questions that will drive you to make changes:

- If I identify disparities, what can I do to increase parity and representation?
- What can I do to identify the barriers that students may be facing or the needs that must be filled in order for students to reach high expectations of success?
- If I identify disproportionate levels of success and struggle, what is my new course of action, and how do I plan to monitor the new plan to ensure it is working to provide greater equity in supporting all my students to thrive?

As you use data to support efforts toward continuous improvement, be careful to avoid manipulating data to craft a narrative that represents what you think others want to see or that misrepresents the reality of your classroom. If you have to record a video six times to get a clip you feel comfortable coding or having someone else observe, it probably does not represent what is occurring in your classroom on a day-to-day basis! Data should never be used to create a culture of judgment, so there is no need to manipulate data to present a false narrative.

Also be careful not to judge your data in relation to anyone else's in your building: "My classroom is doing better than hers, so I don't need to make changes" or "Look at how much worse my data looks than everyone else's." Rather, judge your data in relation to goals for success with your students. As you look at your data, place your mission statement and beliefs next to the data so you can reflect on where you are now and where you would like to go. Data are simply tools you use to identify what is working and what needs to be addressed as a priority for improvement. Strategies in *CHAMPS* will provide the tools you need to determine what changes to make when you identify a priority for improvement.

Existing Regularities: Evaluate Whether the Way Things Have Always Been Done Is the Best Way to Meet the Needs of the Moment

In many schools, rituals and routines are passed down across the years. When educators within the school are asked where those rituals and routines came from or what the thought was behind doing things a certain way, it is common to find that no one in the school actually knows the history or the purpose! Classroom teachers may adopt a certain practice without much thought because it is what they experienced in school or what their student teaching mentor did in their classroom. Or they may continue using practices in their classroom from year to year without evaluating whether those practices still meet the needs of a changing student population. In other words, these are existing regularities.

> *While it is human nature to do things the way they've always been done, existing regularities post a significant threat to good teaching practice.*

While it is human nature to tend to do things the way they've always been done, existing regularities pose a significant threat to good teaching practice. Historical practices often do not match the current needs and ideals of the educational system. Many common practices historically used in schools were not developed with consideration of critical factors like DEIA, student motivation, and an understanding of how to shape behavior.

A foundational part of the CHAMPS approach is a commitment to continuous improvement, which involves self-reflection about how your current practices are meeting the needs of your current students. As you reflect, we challenge you to look carefully at existing regularities in your practice. Question whether the way you've always done things is still the best way for the students you currently serve. You will likely find that some practices are working just as well now or maybe even better than they did when you began implementing them—the best practices can be timeless! However, you will also likely find that some practices are not helping you reach your vision of success for all students. It may be that your student composition has changed and practices that once supported students are now unintentionally harming them. Or it may be that these practices always had drawbacks, but you are now more informed and sensitive about how to meet the needs of your students. Either way, teachers must be flexible and willing to change when needed. A commitment to continuous improvement means committing to tweaking or abandoning any practice that no longer meets the needs of students.

Although examining existing regularities can happen at any point in the school year, three situations should trigger in-depth evaluation of existing regularities:

- When you identify an ongoing concern with a student, a group of students, or a whole class, carefully look at existing regularities. Reflect on which rituals, routines, and practices are working and which ones may need to be changed or replaced.
- Prior to starting a new school year, do a careful analysis of your Classroom Management Plan, which is the summary document that describes the major considerations and practices in your classroom management approach (see Task 3 in this chapter for how to use the Classroom Management Plan). Consider existing regularities as you examine your plan. Think about what worked well the year before and what you wish was different. Consider whether making changes to any of the existing regularities in your classroom would set students up for greater success. For example, if you have always used the same homework practices but students across the last 2 years have struggled to complete and turn in homework, consider making changes to how you assign, collect, and provide feedback on homework, or even the types or amount of homework assigned. You may wish to do this in-depth analysis of your Classroom Management Plan at least once or twice during the year as well (e.g., before each new term or semester starts).
- When there is a significant change in your student population or in the school environment or community, take some time to think about existing regularities. For example, if you suddenly get an additional group of students added in the second term or if your school has been moved to a temporary location because of a natural disaster, these changes should trigger an evaluation of existing regularities. Consider which rituals, routines, and procedures to keep, tweak, or abandon.

Chapters 5 and 10 provide suggestions for how to use data to identify when a change is needed. Bring the lens of evaluating existing regularities as you identify how to use data for continuous improvement in your classroom.

Locus of Control: Take Control Over Those Factors Within Your Sphere of Influence

Throughout this book, you will be challenged to focus on what is in your locus of control. Locus of control relates to the way you think about the causes of success or failure. If you consider why something is happening in your classroom, you can think about internal causes—things that you have an immediate influence over, such as your own teaching abilities, efforts, and personal actions. You can also think about external causes—things that are not within your sphere of influence, such as luck, students' circumstances outside of school, and the actions of other people. While anything that occurs in a classroom has both internal and external causes, you should spend more time, effort, and energy thinking about and working to address the internal factors that you can influence in meaningful ways.

For example, if students experience high levels of success, internal causes may include things like the organization of your units of instruction, the high levels of participation and interest you prompted through engaging activities and instruction, the study skills you helped students learn, and the safe and supportive class environment you established through effective behavior management. Whether students came into your class with strong academic or behavioral skills and whether families were highly engaged or not (external factors), your efforts and actions (internal factors) contributed in important ways to your students' high levels of success. You should work to celebrate and preserve those aspects of your teaching practice that are within your internal locus of control and that contribute to student success.

If students are struggling, consider changes within your control rather than focusing your time and energy on things that are beyond your sphere of influence. You cannot control your colleagues (administrator, teaching colleagues, other staff) and how they do their jobs. You cannot control who students live with, the circumstances of their lives outside school, or their personal histories. You cannot control whether students enter your classroom with disabilities, experiences of trauma, or past academic or behavioral struggles in school. You *can* control your mindset, your habits, and your actions.

The following are some of the most powerful things that you can control with regard to student behavior:

- Structures you put in place within your classroom to set students up for success
- Teaching expectations explicitly
- Observation and active supervision
- Interacting positively to build positive relationships with students and their families
- Correcting students fluently and with care

These variables make up the acronym STOIC, which is the framework that outlines five main variables that can be used to influence student behavior and motivation. Chapters 2–8 are organized around these five variables.

In addition to the STOIC variables, you can control how you personally feel about yourself as a teacher and what you feel and believe about your students. It is natural at times to question or experience moments of doubt. Change is difficult, behavior management is difficult, and it is easy to become overwhelmed. This can lead to thinking, "This is beyond my control." Sometimes it can lead to blaming others: "If only [*parent/administrator/counselor/special education teacher*] would do their job . . ." Or it can lead to questioning yourself, your students' potential, your beliefs about behavior, and even your overarching mission as a teacher. When you experience these struggles, remind yourself that you are not responsible for everything that happens—many things are beyond your control. You should not try to control those things that are outside your sphere of influence. However, difficult circumstances should never become an excuse for failing to pursue actions that you can control.

You can control *your* response to difficult situations. You control whether you continue to push in a forward direction toward your mission and your positive vision for all students' success. You can control whether you persevere and relentlessly pursue those changes in your classroom that will create the conditions necessary for students' success. You can control your own behavior and attitude as you attempt to work collaboratively with others. We encourage you, as a professional, to take pride and responsibility for the many things that are within your sphere of influence and your internal locus of control. Teachers have a powerful influence on student behavior and motivation, which is why this book is in large part about adult behavior. By continually reflecting on and making changes to those variables within your control, you play an important role in helping all your students experience success in school.

Logic Over Impulse: Recognize the Role of the Amygdala When Dealing With Challenging Behavior

If you have ever experienced serious behavioral concerns with students, such as physically dangerous behavior or serious and ongoing acts of defiance, you likely also experienced certain physiological responses. Did your palms sweat, your muscles tighten, your heart rate increase, or your breathing become shallow? Did you experience some combination of these? If behavioral concerns recurred across time, these physiological responses may have begun to happen before you even entered the environment or activity that triggered misbehavior. Perhaps you experienced these symptoms just by thinking about the student and the misbehavior.

While there is some debate in the scientific community about the specific pathways and processes that cause this effect, the following is a very basic explanation of what occurs in your brain when you experience fear, anxiety, or anger when students misbehave (Ferrara et al., 2020).

A region in the temporal lobe of the brain, called the amygdala, plays a significant role in emotions such as fear, anxiety, and anger. The information that you receive from your senses when you see, hear, smell, and touch converge in your amygdala. Then the amygdala sends messages to the systems involved with emotional reactions and physiological symptoms. If the experience is something you fear, you hate, or you know can hurt you, the amygdala triggers the systems that keep your body safe, such as the adrenal system. Your fight, flight, or freeze response is activated, which means your body rapidly mobilizes energy to deal with the danger. Your body gets ready to fight the threat, run from it, or hide from it.

For example, if you hear or see a snake, and you know from previous experience that this sound represents a serious danger, you might freeze. Your blood pressure and heart rate rise, and stress hormones are released. If you hear a frightening noise, you might quickly run away, and you get a rush of adrenaline that lets you run faster and longer than usual so you can get away from the perceived threat. In a similar way, if you experience something you fear in the classroom (e.g., dangerous behavior from a student or losing control of the class) or something that makes you extremely angry (e.g., repeated misbehavior that drives you nuts), your instinctual reactions may be triggered. Figure 1.1 shows a simplified graphic representation of the processes involved in this sequence.

While these processes were necessary and important from a human evolutionary perspective—they provided a way to stay safe from threats like wild animals or natural disasters—they are actually a major threat to being an effective educator. If student misbehavior triggers instinctual emotional and physiological responses, it can lead to impulsive responses to misbehavior that are likely to escalate negative situations. You risk being reactive and potentially even volatile and explosive with your students. Unfortunately, there are many examples of teachers and other educators who lost control with students who were misbehaving, leading to harmful, unethical, and sometimes even dangerous behavior from the educators themselves.

Even if a teacher does not totally lose control, it is important to recognize that impulsive reactions to misbehavior can be the enemy of your efforts to build relational trust with students. Building positive relationships requires a thoughtful and systematic approach (as described in Chapters 6 and 7) and thus comes from a place of logic and self-control.

> " *It is important to recognize that impulsive reactions to misbehavior can be the enemy of your efforts to build relational trust with students.* "

Figure 1.1 *Fight, Flight, or Freeze Response*

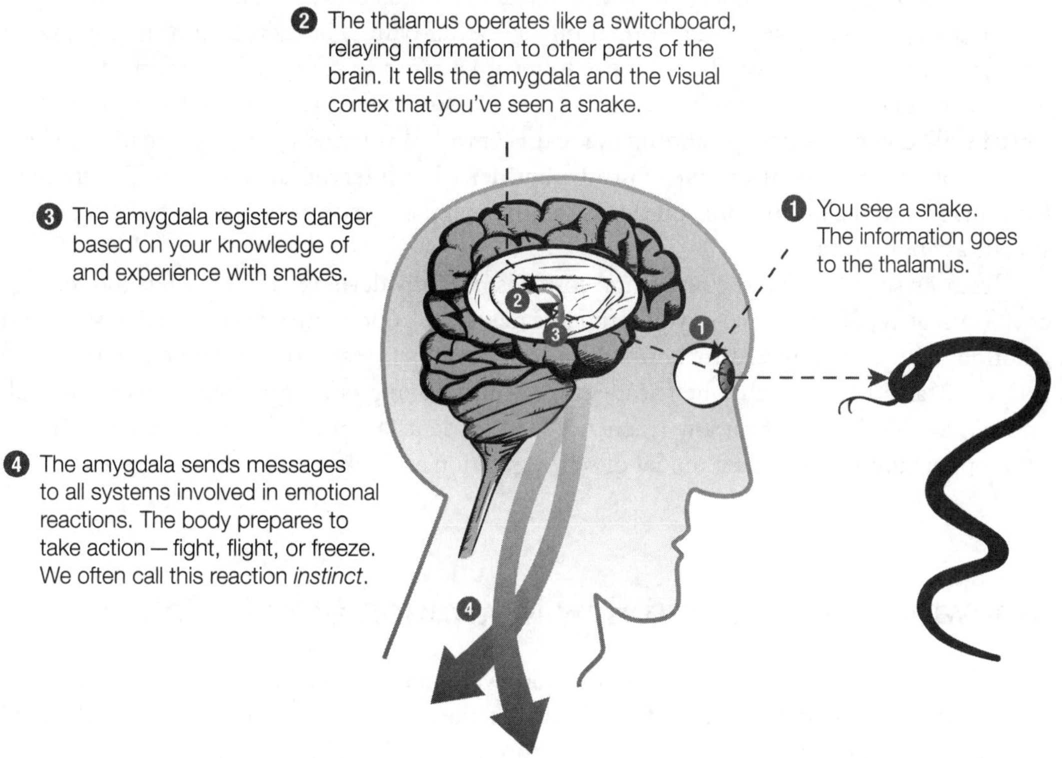

❷ The thalamus operates like a switchboard, relaying information to other parts of the brain. It tells the amygdala and the visual cortex that you've seen a snake.

❸ The amygdala registers danger based on your knowledge of and experience with snakes.

❶ You see a snake. The information goes to the thalamus.

❹ The amygdala sends messages to all systems involved in emotional reactions. The body prepares to take action — fight, flight, or freeze. We often call this reaction *instinct*.

If the amygdala triggers impulsive responses, this is in direct conflict with the ability to use logic and self-control. Educators may find themselves belittling or ridiculing students, snapping angrily at them, screaming and yelling, or engaging in other actions that threaten the positive foundation of relational trust.

Luckily, another area of your brain, the prefrontal cortex, can act as a mediator, taking impulses from the amygdala and allowing you to decide whether or not to act on them. When you recognize that you are triggered, you can coach yourself to use strategies to calm down or slow the negative emotional momentum. Many strategies in this book are designed to help you learn to self-regulate when students engage in misbehavior, such as:

- Use self-talk and tell yourself not to take student misbehavior personally.
- Coach yourself to view misbehavior as a puzzle to be solved and not a threat to be removed.
- Tell the student you need a few minutes to think about how you and the student can move forward in a positive way.
- Adopt an instructional attitude and approach to student misbehavior.
- Engage in positive interactions with other students who are meeting expectations (Chapter 6).
- Prepare yourself to deliver unemotional and fluent corrections to students (Chapter 8).
- Use self-care and mindfulness strategies (Chapter 10).

Evaluate on an ongoing basis whether your prefrontal cortex (logical center) or your amygdala (impulsive center) is in control during times of student misbehavior. The first step is to recognize feelings and physiological symptoms of emotional escalation in the moment. If you notice any symptoms like shallow breathing, sweating palms, or increased heart rate, use a strategy such as one of those listed above to regain a sense of control. In extreme cases, you might need to call another adult to come to your classroom for a short period so you can take a brief walk doing something calming to regain control. If you find recurring situations where your emotions and impulses take control, consider what interventions you can put in place for yourself and seek help from colleagues, family members, friends, and even trained professionals as appropriate.

Research suggests that the prefrontal cortex is not fully developed in children and teenagers (Arain et al., 2013). Some of your students may have poor control over their decisions and emotions, but your more mature brain will allow you to better control your own emotions and actions. Managing yourself when students are misbehaving is within your locus of control, and it is a critical skill set for any teacher. When students are misbehaving, you have a powerful opportunity to provide a model of self-regulation and self-control.

Motivation: Understand How Motivation Affects Behavior

At various points in this book, you will consider ways to boost student motivation, and motivation is discussed in detail in Chapter 7. In this section, you will learn one of the foundational concepts about motivation that is referred to throughout CHAMPS—the Expectancy times Value theory of motivation (Feather, 1982).

Before you learn the basics of this theory, it is important to understand that motivation is not something that you can observe directly (Wentzel & Miele, 2016). You cannot *see* if a student is motivated, but you can infer if a student is motivated from the student's actions and words (e.g., actively engaging with tasks or saying "I want to …"). When a student demonstrates a lack of action with desired tasks (e.g., refusing to engage with tasks, doing the bare minimum, or saying "I don't want to . . ."), you may infer that the student may be struggling with the motivation to engage with the tasks or sustain efforts. In schools, motivation relates to factors such as (Wentzel & Miele, 2016):

- Whether and how a student engages in classroom activities
- Whether and how a student attends to instruction
- Whether the student seeks help when not understanding
- The persistence and effort a student demonstrates when faced with challenging tasks
- A student's choices (e.g., extracurricular activities, courses in high school, or whether to pursue school beyond high school)

Consider a student whose behavior indicates he may be struggling with motivation. The student shows up late to class, sits slumped in his chair, and rarely volunteers to participate. During independent work tasks, the student either does nothing or completes only a small portion of the work. The student appears apathetic and does the bare minimum in class to avoid getting in major trouble, but the teacher continually struggles to get him to engage and participate. It is common to hear teachers describe a student like this as someone who "doesn't care," "doesn't like school," or "doesn't value school."

While a lack of value may be contributing to the student's apathetic behavior, statements such as these fail to acknowledge that the student may struggle with motivation because he does not believe he can be successful. The student may feel unmotivated because he has experienced repeated failure, he knows his skills are far behind his peers, or he has never seen a model of success in school within his family. He may actually highly value being successful in school and desperately want to do well, but because he does not believe it is possible, he is unmotivated.

This example illustrates the Expectancy times Value theory of motivation. This theory explains a person's motivation on any given task as a function of the formula:

$$\textit{Expectancy} \times \textit{Value} = \textit{Motivation}$$

In this formula, *Expectancy* is defined as the degree to which an individual expects to be successful at the task and *Value* is defined as the degree to which an individual values the rewards that accompany that success. In Table 1.1, notice that expectancy and value are each assigned a value on a scale of 0 to 10, with 0 representing no value or no expectancy of success and 10 representing the highest value or expectancy of success. If a person has a value of 10 and an expectancy of success of 10 for a particular task or activity, that person is fully motivated to engage. However, if either expectancy or value is less than 10, the person will not be fully motivated. If either expectancy or value is 0, the person will have no motivation to engage or persist with the task.

Table 1.1 *Expectancy Times Value Theory of Motivation*

Expectancy Rate	×	Value Rate	=	Motivation
10	×	10	=	100
10	×	0	=	0
0	×	10	=	0

Let's go back to the student at the beginning of this section. The teacher in this scenario hopes to come up with a plan that will help the student arrive on time, actively participate in all class activities, and complete classwork. In order to help the student meet these goals, the teacher must consider whether the student fully values the rewards that accompany success but also whether the student believes he can be successful with classroom activities. If the student does not value the rewards that accompany success, boosting motivation will require strategies to boost factors related to value. For example, if the teacher knows that the student doesn't really care about the academic content but really wants his parents to be proud of him, the teacher might increase positive communications with the student's parents when he engages in classroom activities. If, on the other hand, the teacher identifies that the student has a low expectancy of success, she might provide certain accommodations or scaffolds to instruction that allow the student to experience success.

The first step is to determine what is impacting the student's motivation—low value, low expectancy, or both. Compare times when the student demonstrates motivated versus unmotivated behavior. Talk to the student and ask questions that help you understand the student's perspective and beliefs. If you can identify what is affecting the student's motivation, the next step is putting strategies and supports in place to help boost the aspects of motivation that need to be addressed.

Relational Trust: Create the Foundation of Your Management Approach by Consciously Building Positive Relationships

Classroom management and behavior support are about creating the conditions necessary for all students to be responsible, motivated, and highly engaged in meaningful tasks. The goal of an effective classroom management plan is to create a safe, civil, and productive learning environment that reduces barriers to learning. An effective classroom management approach helps all students thrive while meeting high expectations for behavior and academic success. These goals cannot be met without a strong foundation of relational trust with students.

Relational trust occurs when teachers demonstrate respect for students throughout their day-to-day interactions and continually demonstrate that they value students for the unique attributes and experiences they bring to the table (Bryk & Schneider, 2003). Teachers make overt efforts that show they want to understand their students and how best to work with them to maximize their success. Teachers build relational trust when they are consistent with what they say and what they do, and when their actions demonstrate that they have students' best interests at heart.

Think about a great sports coach. Great coaches go through drills and techniques just like any other. But to maximize players' potential, they seek to understand their players. They go beyond just pushing for output, but rather seek to understand how their players process experiences and how best to motivate them. They identify players' strengths and put them in positions that foster those strengths. They put intentional plans in place to help players develop skills needed to address areas of weakness. Players trust that even when the coach is pushing them hard, the coach believes in them and will support them through challenging times. Players try their best because they want to succeed, but also because they want to make their coach proud. If a player is struggling, enough trust has been built that the player can go to the coach and be vulnerable in seeking needed supports. The team is stronger because the coach has established a foundation of relational trust.

Relational trust is critical because no teacher can force their students to behave—nor should they try! While you cannot force someone to behave, you can provide a strong influence to do so when you have built relational trust. Recognize that the student is the one ultimately responsible for making any behavioral changes. If a student does not trust that her teacher has her best interests at heart, she will be much more resistant to doing what the teacher wants her to do. Even if the student can see there might be some benefit in making a change, she might resist because she doesn't want to be compliant to someone she feels is not in her corner.

Relational trust is especially important if the student cannot envision an immediate benefit in making a change requested by the teacher. The student's behavior will be entirely reliant on whether she trusts the positive intentions of her teacher. If she trusts her teacher, she may make the change simply because she knows the teacher wouldn't ask her to do something unless it was important for her success. If the student doesn't trust the teacher, it is unlikely she will put herself in the vulnerable position of trying something new or different simply because the teacher wants it.

Intentional and ongoing efforts to build relational trust are critical when you work with diverse learners who come from a different background than you (e.g., racial, socioeconomic, cultural, linguistic, etc.). Some students may automatically feel a greater sense of relational trust with a teacher who looks like them or who comes from a similar socioeconomic or cultural background. If a student thinks "this person looks or speaks like my mom and dad" or "I know this person came from the same community I grew up in," there may be a feeling of common ground that provides the beginnings of relational trust. The teacher will still have to work to build and maintain relational trust, but the groundwork is already established.

A student who feels that their teacher doesn't look like them or talk like them, or that the teacher speaks from a vastly different background, may not feel the same sense of familiarity or trust at the outset. The teacher will need to do more to build relational trust from Day One so that when the teacher asks the student to do something outside of their comfort zone, the student can trust that the teacher has their best interests in mind.

Beyond recognizing the importance of building relational trust, you can apply some practical skills to do so. Strategies throughout this book provide ways to build and maintain relational trust. These strategies include:

- Interact respectfully at all times with students. When students are engaged in misbehavior, model self-regulation and unemotional ways of addressing misbehavior. Be careful about the way you talk about students to others, including other students, colleagues, and parents, and strive to discuss students in respectful ways that illustrate your belief in their potential for success.
- Explicitly teach your Guidelines for Success, classroom rules, and expectations. If you teach students how and why these behaviors will help them be successful in your class, and you demonstrate integrity by applying these expectations consistently across students, students will learn to trust that you are true to your word.
- Learn about your students' background and interests. Use surveys, interviews, and informal conversations to learn about your students. Ask questions like:

    How many siblings do you have?
    What responsibilities do you have around the house?
    What do you like to do after school?
    Who do you spend your free time with?

- Work to meet students' basic needs for acknowledgment, recognition, attention, belonging, purpose, competence, nurturing, and stimulation and change. Periodically analyze the degree to which students' needs are being met inside and outside of school, and identify ways to implement new programs and practices that help address unmet needs.
- Strive to have more positive interactions with students (e.g., positive greetings, acknowledging efforts and successes) than corrective interactions (e.g., reprimands, corrective consequences). Help students understand that you see them and their strengths, and acknowledge areas of success and growth. Work to establish the understanding that corrections occur so that you can help students learn to be successful in school and beyond, not because you see them as bad kids or that they need to be punished.

The STOIC Framework: Understand Five Main Variables That Can Be Used to Influence Behavior

One of the critical concepts at the heart of CHAMPS is that behavior, no matter how challenging or chronic, can be changed. Some people look at a class of students with challenging behavior and think, "That's just the way the kids are. They'll never change." This book operates off the opposite understanding—if most behavior is learned, it can certainly be changed! And if it can't directly be changed, supports can be put in place that allow you to bypass challenges and barriers. The STOIC framework provides a way to problem-solve using the most effective variables that can facilitate change.

A theme that runs throughout CHAMPS is that all adults who work with kids should be problem solvers. Chronic misbehavior is viewed as a puzzle to be solved (What variables can I manipulate and what strategies can I put in place that might have a positive impact?) rather than a threat that needs to be removed (This student doesn't belong in this class/school). The acronym STOIC provides guidance for fitting the puzzle pieces together, whether you're trying to change the behavior of an individual student or positively affect the collective behavior of a class. STOIC stands for Structure, Teach, Observe, Interact positively, and Correct fluently.

S **Structure your classroom for success.**

The way a classroom is organized (physical setting, schedule, routines and procedures, quality of instruction, and so on) has a huge impact on student behavior. Effective teachers carefully structure their classrooms in ways that prompt responsible student behavior (Epstein et al., 2008; Guardino & Fullerton, 2010; Trussel, 2008; Wannarka & Ruhl, 2008; Weinstein, 1977). They make many decisions outside of their contact time with students to set students up for success, considering factors like how to orchestrate classroom activities and transitions. When students are present, teachers organize the physical environment and instructional activities to help all students be at their best while learning.

T **Teach behavior expectations to students.**

Effective teachers overtly teach students how to behave responsibly and respectfully (in other words, to be successful) in every classroom situation—teacher-directed instruction, independent seatwork, cooperative groups, tests, and all major transitions (Brophy & Good, 1986; Emmer & Evertson, 2009; Trussel, 2008; Simonsen et al., 2008). While many teachers do a fantastic job using effective teaching skills for academic content, they may struggle to apply the same skills to teaching social-emotional skills and behavioral expectations. In CHAMPS, teachers are encouraged to *teach*, not *tell*, when it comes to student behavior.

O **Observe and supervise.**

Effective teachers monitor student behavior by physically circulating whenever possible and visually scanning all parts of the classroom frequently. In addition, effective teachers observe student behavior, particularly chronic misbehavior, in objective ways and use meaningful data to monitor trends across time (Alberto & Troutman, 2012; Brophy, 1983; Colvin et al., 1997; Gunter & Shores, 1995; Kounin, 1970; Scheuermann & Hall, 2008). Teachers monitor data with careful consideration to issues of equity and whether structures are set up in ways to help all students be successful.

I Interact positively with students.

When students have positive relationships with their teachers and feel a sense of trust that their teacher's decisions and actions are in their best interest, they are more likely to communicate, try, and succeed. When students are behaving responsibly, they receive attention and specific descriptive feedback on their behavior. Teachers should focus more time, attention, and energy on acknowledging responsible behavior than on responding to misbehavior—what we call a high ratio of positive to corrective interactions (Brookhart, 2017; Brophy & Good, 1986; Cook et al., 2017; Klem & Connell, 2004; Sutherland et al., 2000).

C Correct fluently.

Teachers must correct misbehavior to help teach students right from wrong and to help them understand how to be successful with each teacher's idiosyncratic classroom expectations. However, corrections should never represent the majority of a teacher's interactions with their students, and they should never violate the students' rights to have others honor their dignity and treat them with respect. When corrections are poorly implemented, they can damage a teacher's efforts in all of the other STOIC variables. Therefore, teachers should preplan their responses to misbehavior to ensure that they respond in a brief, calm, and consistent manner, increasing the chances that the flow of instruction is maintained (Abramowitz et al., 1988; Acker & O'Leary, 1988; Colvin & Sugai, 1988). In addition, with chronic and severe misbehavior, teachers should think about the function of the misbehavior (Why is the student misbehaving?) and build a plan that ensures that the student learns and exhibits appropriate behavior (Alberto & Troutman, 2012; O'Neill et al., 1997).

The acronym STOIC is an easy way to remember these five principles: Structure, Teach, Observe, Interact positively, Correct fluently. Behavior can be changed by continually using and manipulating these five conceptually simple principles. The chapters in Section 2 of this book are organized around the STOIC acronym so that you can learn a wide range of strategies within each of these variables. At first glance, some people may think the word *stoic* implies someone who is cold and unfeeling. However, *Encarta World English Dictionary* gives us a definition of the adjective *stoic* as "tending to remain unemotional, especially showing admirable patience and endurance in the face of adversity." Thus, a stoic teacher is one who is unrattled by student misbehavior and who implements research-based strategies (as found in *CHAMPS*) with patience and endurance.

When you begin to view misbehavior as a puzzle rather than a threat, and when you relentlessly and skillfully manipulate the STOIC pieces of the puzzle, you will find you can change behavior. We have seen it. You can do it!

In this task, you learned some of the critical concepts and foundational principles that guide the CHAMPS approach and are evident in the efforts and practices of educators who are committed to the success of all of their students:

- Mission and Beliefs: Create an effective vision to guide your practice
- Diversity, Equity, Inclusion, and Access: Fulfilling the promise of education for all
- Data-Driven Processes: Tools for continuous improvement
- Existing Regularities: Evaluate whether the way things have been done is the best way to meet the needs of the moment
- Locus of Control: Take control over those factors within your sphere of influence
- Logic Over Impulse: Recognize the role of the amygdala when dealing with challenging behavior
- Motivation: Understand how motivation affects behavior
- Relational Trust: Create the foundation of your management approach by consciously building positive relationships
- The STOIC Framework: Understand five main variables that can be used to influence behavior

As you work through the CHAMPS book, carefully examine how your current practices do or do not reflect these foundational elements and think about whether specific strategies would strengthen your practice in any of these areas.

TASK 2

Understand How to Shape Behavior

Develop an understanding of fundamental behavior management principles so that you can make effective decisions and take appropriate actions to help students learn to behave responsibly.

• • • • •

Every school seems to have some students who appear angry, argumentative, or unmotivated. Frustrated teachers throw up their hands and declare these students lost causes: "They'll never change!" The students often enter a downward spiral fueled by low expectations, constant criticism, and academic failure. Certainly, some tendencies and personality traits seem to be present from birth, but *most human behavior is learned*—which means it can also be unlearned, or shaped into a more desirable form.

Picture Rosa, a responsible and successful fifth-grade student. Imagine that one day, the rewards she receives and values for being a model student evaporate. Instead, she starts getting failing grades, and teachers are critical of her work. The other students laugh at her work and her class participation. They either ridicule her as stupid or ignore her altogether. No one notices when she stays on task, works hard, and is respectful to others. Her parents show no interest in her schoolwork. If this continues day after day, at home and at school, Rosa will probably stop trying to succeed. She may even respond with anger and hostility. If her angry response is rewarded by attention from others, she may find that acting in an antagonistic and aggressive manner gives her a sense of satisfaction or self-preservation. If this were to continue for months or years, Rosa would develop into a very different student from the successful fifth-grader she once was.

Now picture a student, Malik, who often appears argumentative and angry, and as a result has low achievement. Imagine that school personnel create a setting in which he starts experiencing success and good grades, he receives peer recognition for his positive behavior, and he no longer gets so much attention or status for his anger and hostility. If done well, an environment like this can create a powerful positive change in Malik. Behavior can be taught and changed (Alberto & Troutman, 2012; Cooper et al., 2007).

When a student frequently behaves irresponsibly, the student likely hasn't experienced the benefits of responsible behavior enough, or even at all. It's also likely that this student has learned that irresponsible behavior is a more effective or efficient way of getting needs met. The student may get power, control, and perhaps even admiration from peers as a result of misbehavior (Hershfeldt et al., 2010).

> *When a student frequently behaves irresponsibly, the student likely hasn't experienced the benefits of responsible behavior enough, or even at all.*

If a student who was originally well-behaved will probably experience negative behavior changes due to repeated exposure to bad circumstances, a student who was previously struggling has the same probability of experiencing positive behavior changes when repeatedly exposed to good circumstances. The behavior management principles below provide the framework for the rest of this book—that is, exposing all students to the best circumstances can foster positive behavior and high levels of motivation, whether the student previously engaged in mostly good or mostly bad behavior. *Behavior can be changed.*

Behavior Management Principles

Throughout this book, you will focus on the vision of your ideal classroom. Because there will undoubtedly be times when your students behave irresponsibly, your classroom vision should include something about how you will help students learn to behave more responsibly. You can do this by developing an understanding of and skill in using fundamental behavior management principles. Specifically, as a teacher, you need to know why and how to:

- *Structure* your class to promote responsible student behavior.
- Effectively *acknowledge* responsible student behavior.
- Effectively *respond* to irresponsible student behavior.

An overview of the most important principles of behavior management is presented in the following pages. Chapters 2 through 8 provide more detailed information about the principles and specific actions that you can take.

The principles of behavior management are grounded in the assumption that people are constantly engaged in learning and that every life experience adds to a person's knowledge base. Every experience influences a person's subsequent actions, both consciously and unconsciously. In general, behaviors that are rewarded over time are maintained, while those that are not rewarded are typically extinguished. For example, a job seeker who has submitted scores of résumés without any resulting interviews may decide to write a new résumé. He sends out the new résumé and gets multiple interviews. He has learned that the new résumé brings better results, and in the future he will likely use the new résumé instead of the old one. Similarly, if someone goes to a movie that a friend recommends and finds it to be a poor movie and a waste of money, that person will be less likely to trust the friend's movie recommendations in the future.

Scenarios such as these are repeated in each person's life many times each day, in uncountable and interwoven combinations, to create a rich fabric of experiences and learning. Simply put, a person's behavior is influenced by events and conditions they experience. Some experiences encourage that person to engage in certain behaviors, and others discourage that person from engaging in certain behaviors. Figure 1.2 shows a graphic representation of the three main variables that affect behavior.

Figure 1.2 *Variables That Affect Behavior*

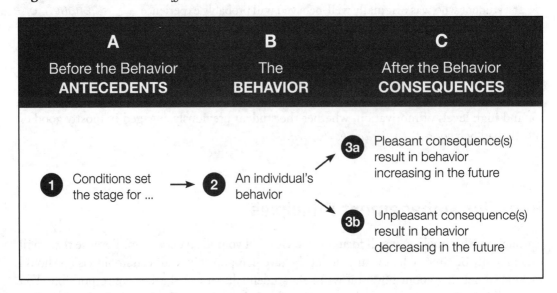

The three variables are:

1. **Conditions:** What is prompting or enabling the behavior?
2. **The Behavior:** What is the person doing?
3. **Consequences:** What is encouraging and sustaining or discouraging the behavior? If consequences that result from a particular behavior are perceived as pleasant, that behavior will increase or occur more frequently. If consequences that result from a particular behavior are perceived as unpleasant, that behavior will decrease or occur less frequently.

Readers with behavioral training will recognize this as a simple antecedent, behavior, consequence model of behavioral theory expressed in commonsense and pragmatic terms. This model provides a useful structure for helping teachers understand basic behavior management principles.

To effectively apply the fundamental principles of behavior management to your classroom, you should keep in mind two essential underlying concepts. These concepts have very important implications for teachers about where to focus their time and energy in terms of managing student behavior. The two concepts are:

- Effective teachers spend more time promoting responsible behavior than responding to irresponsible behavior (Beaman & Wheldall, 2000; Brophy & Good, 1986; Walker et al., 2004).
- Effective teachers recognize that misbehavior (especially any chronic misbehavior) occurs for a reason, and they take that reason into account when determining a response to the misbehavior (Alberto & Troutman, 2012; Cooper et al., 2007; Scheuermann & Hall, 2008).

NOTE: Because the vocabulary typically associated with behavioral theory is so often misunderstood or misused (or both), less technical vocabulary and more commonsense examples are used throughout this book. In addition, although the fundamentals of school-based behavior management are based on a large and comprehensive body of research findings, only that information most useful to teachers is included. As a result, what is presented here reflects a simple understanding of very complex principles.

Promoting Responsible Behavior

You will prevent most misbehavior from ever occurring when you focus the majority of your time and energy on these three major categories of teacher-based actions for promoting responsible behavior.

Modify Conditions

Use effective instruction and set up conditions for students to be successful by prompting responsible behavior and discouraging irresponsible behavior. Specific actions include but are by no means limited to:

- Make sure students understand what the behavioral expectations are.
- Make sure students know how to meet the behavioral expectations.
- Arrange the physical space so that it is more conducive to responsible behavior than to irresponsible behavior.
- Design a fast-paced schedule and provide interesting lessons.
- Run efficient transitions between activities.
- Build positive rapport and relational trust with all students.
- Interact respectfully and positively with all students.
- Show an interest in student work.

Implement Pleasant Consequences for Responsible Behavior

Ensure that students experience appropriate positive feedback when they engage in responsible behavior. Specific actions include:

- Give verbal praise.
- Write positive notes.
- Encourage students to praise themselves.
- Contact parents regarding students' responsible behavior.
- Occasionally reward individuals or the whole class with a special activity.

Remove Any Aversive Aspects of Exhibiting Responsible Behavior

Ensure that students do not experience negative results from exhibiting responsible behavior. Specific actions include:

- Avoid embarrassing students with the way you deliver praise.
- Ensure that no student is the target of laughter for making a mistake during class participation.
- Ensure that no student ever feels like a geek for behaving responsibly.
- Ensure that no one is ridiculed as a teacher's pet for behaving responsibly.

Discouraging Irresponsible Behavior

It is often difficult to understand why a student behaves irresponsibly, especially when the consequences of that behavior seem highly unpleasant. However, whenever a student or group of students exhibits irresponsible behavior on an *ongoing basis*, the behavior is occurring for a reason—it is not completely random (Carr, 1993; Gresham et al., 2001). Therefore, the first thing you need to do is determine the reason for the misbehavior. Likely possibilities are:

- The student doesn't know exactly what you expect.
- The student doesn't know how to exhibit the responsible behavior.
- The student is unaware that they engaged in the misbehavior.
- The student is experiencing some pleasant outcome from exhibiting the misbehavior (for example, she likes the attention she gets from adults or peers).
- The student is successfully avoiding some unpleasant outcome by exhibiting the misbehavior (for example, he is getting out of assigned work).

Many of you may recognize that the previous bulleted list provides an introduction to the concept of *function of behavior*. Once you have a reasonable idea why a chronic misbehavior is occurring, you can take actions to reduce and eventually eliminate it. Again, there are three major categories of teacher-based actions for you to consider.

Modify Conditions

Modify any conditions that may be perpetuating the misbehavior. Specific actions include but are by no means limited to:

- Provide lessons to teach the student how to behave responsibly.
- Assign different seats to two students who talk when they sit together.
- Modify work that is too difficult for a student who is not completing assignments.
- Pace lessons more quickly so students are less likely to get off task.
- Provide something for students to do when they complete classwork so they do not have lots of time to fill with misbehavior.

Remove Any Positive Aspects of Exhibiting Irresponsible Behavior

Remove any pleasant outcomes that might be resulting from the misbehavior. Examples include:

- Ignore misbehavior that is designed to get attention.
- Respond calmly to a student who likes to make adults angry.
- Ensure that a student is not excused from assigned work as a result of the misbehavior.

Implement Corrective Consequences for Exhibiting Irresponsible Behavior

Implement corrective consequences that will make exhibiting the misbehavior more unpleasant for the student. Examples include:

- Use a system of demerits (three demerits result in an after-school detention, for example).
- Take away 15 seconds of recess (or other fun or choice activity) for each infraction.
- Use a classroom point system and institute point fines for particular infractions.

 CASE STUDY

Consider a seventh-grade student, Caleb, who is chronically argumentative with staff, and has been since he entered the middle school. Caleb has been continually sent out of class and regularly assigned to detention. His parents must be called frequently, and he is often confrontational and argumentative with an increasing angry and frustrated school staff.

Imagine you are tasked with developing a plan to help improve Caleb's behavior and increase his likelihood of success in seventh grade. First, you'll need to consider what the student gains from his behavior. There are several possibilities to consider:

- Arguing may give Caleb lots of attention from adults (direct, angry engagement), providing him with a sense of power over adults.
- Caleb may find that getting sent to the office for arguing is more interesting than remaining in the classroom.
- Arguing may give Caleb lots of attention from his peers for appearing strong and powerful enough to fight with teachers.

- Caleb may not know the expectations for respectfully communicating with staff when advocating for himself at school.
- Caleb may be struggling in class and slips into argumentative behavior to avoid doing academic work.
- Caleb may lack the skills to manage anger and frustration, which results in his behavior escalating.

Next, review each of the five action categories and example options for procedures that school personnel might take to influence Caleb's behavior. For each of the possible reasons for misbehavior listed above, select one or two procedures from each category that would make sense to implement with Caleb.

1. Modify conditions (organization, schedule, physical structure, and so on) to encourage more responsible behavior and discourage the irresponsible behavior.

   - Give Caleb a high-status job (to be performed daily) that will increase his sense of power and purpose in the school.
   - Because Caleb seems to behave better during teacher-directed instruction, consider arranging for a greater percentage of his daily schedule to be teacher-directed instruction.
   - To mitigate the possibility that Caleb is misbehaving because he is frustrated by academic difficulties, arrange for him to receive private tutorial assistance in his most difficult subjects.
   - Modify Caleb's academic assignments so that he can succeed.
   - Correct Caleb before he makes an error (for example, privately say to Caleb, "This is the type of work period where you need to try to stay calm and work with me without arguing. Let's have a good day today").
   - Teach particularly difficult assignments to Caleb prior to presenting the assignment to the class.
   - Assign Caleb a different place to sit in the room.
   - Tell all staff to make an effort to give Caleb very clear directions.
   - Remind staff to avoid power struggles with Caleb.

2. Implement pleasant consequences designed to encourage responsible behavior.

   - Tell all staff that whenever Caleb exhibits responsible behavior, they should give him specific praise.
   - Ask all staff members to make an effort to give Caleb frequent, unconditional, positive adult attention.
   - Remind all staff to privately praise Caleb when he follows directions without arguing.

3. Remove any aversive aspects of exhibiting responsible behavior.

- Prearrange times during the day when Caleb can privately ask teachers questions or get assistance so he does not have to do so in front of his peers.
- Remind staff to avoid publicly praising Caleb for following directions.

4. Remove any positive aspects of exhibiting irresponsible behavior.

- Remind staff to avoid engaging in arguments with Caleb. Provide training as necessary.
- Train other students to ignore situations in which Caleb begins to argue.
- Train staff to maintain instructional momentum so Caleb doesn't get attention from peers when he attempts to argue.

5. Implement effective corrective consequences designed to reduce irresponsible behavior.

- Give Caleb a warning when he begins to argue. ("This is an example of arguing.")
- Calmly implement a corrective consequence when Caleb continues to argue after the warning.
- Ignore any further attempts by Caleb to engage in arguing.
- Redirect Caleb to the activity he should be engaged in.
- Keep accurate records of the number of times and the duration of each arguing incident.

Implementing an intervention plan that includes procedures from some or all of these categories increases the probability that staff will be successful in helping Caleb learn to behave more responsibly. An intervention plan may not be effective if staff does nothing to remove the positive aspects of exhibiting the irresponsible behavior, such as the peer and teacher attention the student receives. If getting peer and teacher attention is more valuable to him than anything he gains from the intervention steps taken, the student's behavior will not improve.

• • • • •

In summary, whether you are starting CHAMPS at the beginning of the year or during it, understanding that you, the teacher, can change student behavior—shaping students toward those behaviors that will allow them to succeed—is essential to understanding the CHAMPS approach. Most of the suggestions in the rest of the book assume that you understand the basics of behavior management presented here.

TASK 3

Prepare Your Classroom Management Plan

Understand how to use your Classroom Management Plan to summarize important information, policies, and procedures you will use to motivate students and address appropriate and inappropriate behavior.

• • • • •

By developing a Classroom Management Plan before the school year begins, you set the stage to deal productively with the range of behaviors, both positive and negative, that students will exhibit in your classroom (Alberto & Troutman, 2012; Emmer & Evertson, 2009; Emmer et al., 2003; Scheuermann & Hall, 2008; Trussell, 2008).

An effective management and discipline plan is not a canned program or a static entity. It is a framework that supports a variety of rituals, routines, rules, consequences, and motivational techniques you can use to ensure that students are academically engaged and emotionally thriving. Though your plan should be in place before the school year begins, you will adjust your initial plan to meet the changing needs of the class as the year progresses. Your plan will be somewhat different on the first day of school, on the 20th day of school, on a day a new student comes to class, and on the last day of school.

Some educators are uncomfortable with the term management *when it comes to student behavior. They fear that it connotes a dictatorial approach to force compliance from students. Instead, we urge you to consider what a highly effective, positive manager does in a business setting. A good manager is one who effectively manages time and resources to ensure the business is thriving. The manager considers the strengths and needs of staff members to create the conditions for everyone to be successful. The manager uses effective communication to clearly teach expectations and to determine what the business and employees need so they can all be at their best. Just like an effective manager in business, your job is to design a management plan for your classroom that creates the conditions for student success.*

Let's look at an example from the field of medicine to get a sense of this concept. If you are going into the hospital for surgery, you assume (and hope!) that the surgeon, the nurses, and the lab have a plan in place for how everything is going to work. Without a coordinated plan, the possibility of disaster is high—imagine if they did not have the blood type you need, the equipment was not be sterilized, or there weren't be enough nurses to assist in the operation! A coordinated plan, designed in advance, is essential. However, even with the most organized plan, adjustments may need to be made during the course of the operation. They may need more plasma than originally anticipated, they may need immediate information from the lab about an abnormal growth, or they may find your organs are in a slightly atypical position. With the basic plan in place, it can be adjusted to meet needs that arise during the course of the operation.

Reproducible 1.1 (pp. 42–43) is the Classroom Management Plan. As you proceed through the remaining chapters of CHAMPS, you will complete tasks and fill in different sections of the Classroom Management Plan. A fillable version that you can complete digitally is provided in the downloadable reproducible materials (see p. 3 for download directions). If you prefer, you can print out the form and fill it in by hand. Reproducible 1.2 (shown in Chapter 9, Task 1) is a template that includes bulleted highlights from each chapter to assist you in filling out your version of the Classroom Management Plan. Special thanks to Mike Booher for the idea to provide a template with bulleted explanations.

Identify the Level of Support Within Your Classroom Management Plan for Current (or Incoming) Students

Your Classroom Management Plan may be very tightly or very loosely orchestrated and supported by you as the teacher. This notion of level of support has nothing to do with being friendly or punitive, but simply refers to the degree of orchestration of student behavior and the amount of care you must take when implementing procedures to encourage appropriate behavior. For example, in a highly supported classroom, dismissal may be very organized, with students excused in small groups for a calm, orderly, and quiet exit. In a low-support management plan, the entire class may be excused at once, resulting in a slightly more chaotic feel. The low-support approach requires greater maturity on the part of the class to ensure safe and responsible exiting.

The level of support in your Classroom Management Plan should be based on two factors—your unique personal needs and the collective needs of your students. In this task, you are encouraged to think about these two factors. What are your own unique needs—for example, your tolerance for noise and movement? If a fair amount of noise or movement is not bothersome to you (but remember, you will deal with it all day, every day, for the entire year), you may be able to have less structure and orchestration in your management plan than the teacher with very low tolerance for noise and movement.

> "The level of support in your Classroom Management Plan should be based on two factors—your unique personal needs and the collective needs of your students."

In the first part of this task, you will reflect on your own style and your needs in the classroom. Next, you will consider the collective needs of your students. The class that is collectively less mature and has more behavior problems has a greater need for a high-support management plan—one that is more tightly orchestrated and directed by the teacher—than a class that is collectively mature, motivated, cooperative, and respectful. A group of students in which some (or many) have experienced significant or recent traumas, such as major natural disasters or community violence, will require greater levels of structure and support to create a sense of calm, routine, and safety. Also, a large class usually requires more support than a small class—the class with 30 students typically needs greater organization and orchestration than the class with only 15 students. One way to think about the support you would put in place for a classroom with high needs is *orchestrated care*. Just as an orchestra needs a good conductor to guide and support the musicians to bring out their best as individuals and as a collective, the classroom needs a good classroom manager to bring out the students' best. A classroom teacher can orchestrate the environment to provide the care and support that allows all students to thrive in the classroom community.

The level of support identified in this task has significant implications for all aspects of STOIC. The greater the need for support, the more intentionality you will need to bring into how you structure routines and procedures, teach behavioral expectations and social-emotional skills, and observe student behavior and data. If students need lower levels of support, you may be looser in how you think about providing positive and corrective feedback, but if students require high levels of support, a clear and well-thought-out plan should be put in place for acknowledging appropriate behavior and providing fluent corrections for misbehavior.

Reproducible 1.1 *Classroom Management Plan (pp. 1-4)*

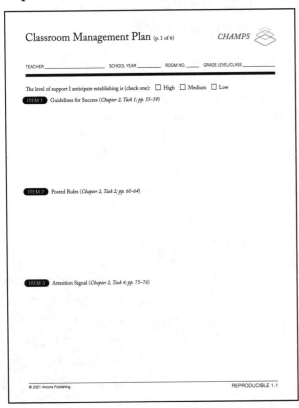

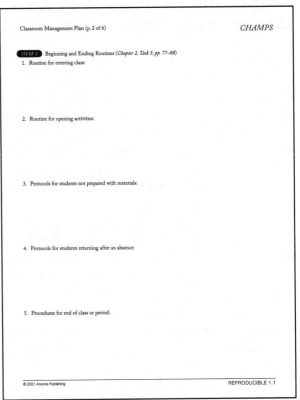

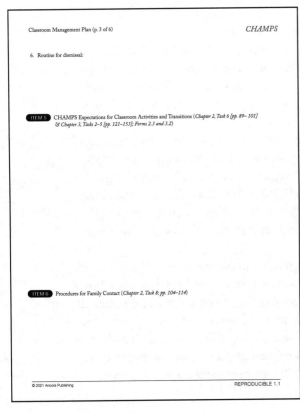

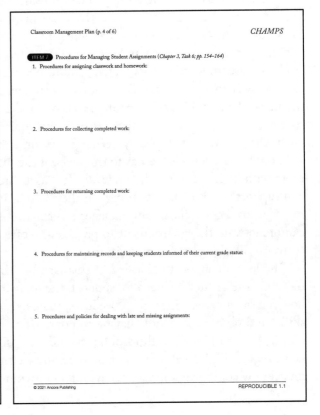

Reproducible 1.1 *Classroom Management Plan (pp. 5–6)*

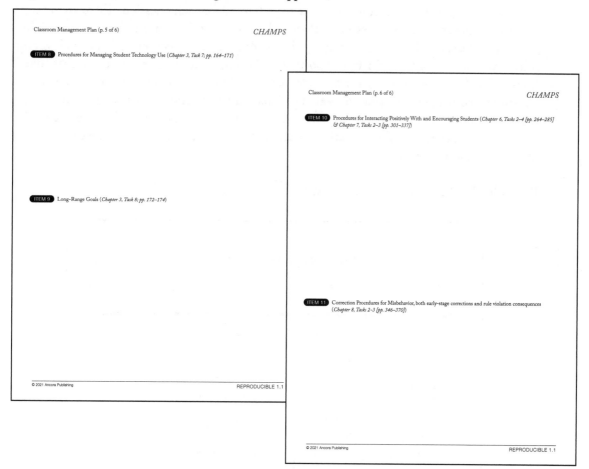

Classroom Management Plan (p. 5 of 6)   *CHAMPS*

ITEM 8 Procedures for Managing Student Technology Use (*Chapter 3, Task 7; pp. 164–171*)

ITEM 9 Long-Range Goals (*Chapter 3, Task 8; pp. 172–174*)

© 2021 Ancora Publishing   REPRODUCIBLE 1.1

Classroom Management Plan (p. 6 of 6)   *CHAMPS*

ITEM 10 Procedures for Interacting Positively With and Encouraging Students (*Chapter 6, Tasks 2–4 [pp. 264–285] & Chapter 7, Tasks 2–3 [pp. 301–337]*)

ITEM 11 Correction Procedures for Misbehavior, both early-stage corrections and rule violation consequences (*Chapter 8, Tasks 2–3 [pp. 346–370]*)

© 2021 Ancora Publishing   REPRODUCIBLE 1.1

Consider Your Needs

Reflect on your personal style. Are there issues that you need to address in order to feel comfortable in the classroom? For example, what is your tolerance for noise? A teacher with a high tolerance for noise still needs to teach students appropriate noise levels but is unlikely to be rattled by a classroom activity in which students are excitedly engaged in cooperative groups and lots of kids are talking at once. On the other hand, a teacher with a low tolerance for noise may find that this type of cooperative group activity—with the voices of 30 students getting progressively louder—has a sense of chaos that leaves the teacher feeling that the class is bordering on out of control. The difference here is not the behavior of the students but the perception of the teacher. In this case, the teacher may need to orchestrate cooperative group activities to ensure that fewer students are talking at one time and to directly teach students to keep noise to a minimum. The teacher must monitor and provide feedback to students about the level of noise that is acceptable. This is especially true during activities such as cooperative groups and active work times such as lab activities.

Review the questions in Part 1 of Reproducible 1.3, Classroom Support Needs Assessment, and assign yourself a score on a scale from 0 to 20 for each question. There are no right or wrong answers to these questions. Plan to be honest with yourself about yourself. This survey is not a scientific instrument, but rather a good way to reflect on the type of classroom setting you need in order to thrive as a positive and energetic force. The answers to these questions will help you determine the issues you need to address in order to be comfortable in the classroom. For example, if you know that you have a low tolerance for background noise, it will be important to develop a management plan that directly teaches students to keep noise to a minimum, especially during activities that can get noisy, such as cooperative groups and independent work times.

Reproducible 1.3 *Classroom Support Needs Assessment (Part 1)*

Classroom Support Needs Assessment (p. 1 of 3) *CHAMPS*

PART 1: TEACHER NEEDS

Read each question and assign yourself a score from 0–20, with 0 representing the answer on the left of the scale and 20 the answer on the right.

Score

1. What is your tolerance for **background noise**?

I love to have conversations in crowded, noisy restaurants.	Holiday music in department stores drives me crazy after about 30 minutes.

   0 1 2 3 4 5 6 7 8 9 10 11 12 13 14 15 16 17 18 19 20 ____

2. What is your tolerance for **individual voices** (volume, pitch, whining, mumbling, etc.)?

No style of voice seems to bother me— even when there are several at once.	Some voices are like fingernails on a chalkboard.

   0 1 2 3 4 5 6 7 8 9 10 11 12 13 14 15 16 17 18 19 20 ____

3. What is your tolerance for **interruption**?

I would be fine working as a receptionist— managing phones, people, and equipment.	When the phone rings twice during dinner, I want to scream.

   0 1 2 3 4 5 6 7 8 9 10 11 12 13 14 15 16 17 18 19 20 ____

4. What is your tolerance for **background movement**?

I thrive on the hustle and bustle of downtown in a large city.	I prefer to relax by the side of a quiet lake.

   0 1 2 3 4 5 6 7 8 9 10 11 12 13 14 15 16 17 18 19 20 ____

5. What is your ability to **multitask** without becoming flustered?

I love to do three things at once.	I do not like to talk to anyone while I am collating papers.

   0 1 2 3 4 5 6 7 8 9 10 11 12 13 14 15 16 17 18 19 20 ____

Teacher Needs Total Score [ ]

0–33 LOW SUPPORT NEEDS	34–66 MEDIUM SUPPORT NEEDS	67–100 HIGH SUPPORT NEEDS
You don't require much structure and will probably be content with a Low, Medium, or High Support classroom management plan.	For you to stay calm and positive, your classroom management plan should involve Medium or High Support.	For you to stay calm and positive, your classroom management plan should involve High Support.

© 2021 Ancora Publishing

REPRODUCIBLE 1.3

After completing the survey, total the scores. Use the scales provided on Reproducible 1.3 to assess your needs and determine the most appropriate level of support for your Classroom Management Plan.

- *Low support needs:* If you scored between 0–33, you may be fine in any type of setting. As long as your students can responsibly handle low supports, you can establish a management plan that is less orchestrated.
- *Medium support needs:* If you scored between 34–66, you probably do best in classrooms that are medium to high support. You require some level of calm, orchestration, and predictability in order to feel that your classroom is running smoothly and under control.
- *High support needs:* If you scored between 67–100, you'll need a high-support plan. If noise, interruption, and multitasking make you nervous or put you on edge, structure your classroom to keep these factors to a minimum so you can stay calm and positive. You may wish to complete the student needs survey simply out of interest, but regardless of the results, plan to implement a high-support management plan.

Consider Your Students' Needs

The second consideration in determining the support level of your Classroom Management Plan is the risk factors of your students.

An example is the number of students in your class—you will probably need a more structured and supported management plan for a class of 30 students than a class of 15. If you have significant numbers of immature or emotionally needy children, the risk factors are probably high, so you need a more tightly orchestrated plan. If your class is composed of predominantly mature and independent students, the risk factors are likely to be low and a looser plan may be perfectly adequate.

If your class has high risk factors and you do not orchestrate activities and transitions tightly enough, student behavior tends to be problematic (Barbetta et al., 2005; Huston-Stein et al., 1977; Martella et al., 2003; Mayer, 1995). For example, beginning instruction immediately when the bell rings is a good idea regardless of the class's risk factors. In a class with high risk factors, however, student behavior may be especially problematic if you do not orchestrate the beginning of class well. If students in such a class have nothing to do for the first 2 minutes of class because you are taking attendance and doing housekeeping activities, they are likely to talk, be out of their seats, and exhibit other misbehaviors. Their behavior, in turn, may make it difficult for you to begin teaching once you finish with attendance and housekeeping. If you begin instruction immediately after the bell rings and then take attendance once students start working on a task, you establish instructional momentum and increase the probability that students will behave appropriately.

Consider the school in which you will be teaching and the class or classes you will have on the first day of school. Review the risk factors listed in Part 2 of Reproducible 1.3 (p. 46) and indicate those items that are relevant for your classroom.

This form is designed to be completed before the school year begins to help you determine the risk factors for your class and the level of support that is most appropriate for your Classroom Management Plan. It can also be used throughout the year to increase your awareness

Classroom Support Needs Assessment (p. 2 of 3)　　　　　　　　　*CHAMPS*

PART 2: STUDENT RISK FACTORS

For each question, circle the number under the statement that best answers the question. If you are unsure about or do not know the answer to a question, circle the middle choice. Add all the numbers circled and enter the total.

Questions 1–6 relate to the population of the entire school.

1. How would you describe the overall **behavior of students** in your school?　　Score

Generally quite irresponsible. I frequently have to nag and/or assign consequences.	Most students behave responsibly, but about 10% put me in a position where I have to nag and/or assign consequences.	Generally responsible. I rarely find it necessary to nag and/or assign consequences.
10	5	0

2. What percentage of students in your school **qualify for free or reduced lunch?***

60% or more	10% to 60%	Less than 10%
10	5	0

3. What percentage of students typically **move in and/or out of the school** during the course of the year?

50% or more	10% to 50%	Less than 10%
10	5	0

4. How would you describe the overall **attitude of students** toward school?

A large percentage hate school and ridicule the students who are motivated.	It's a mix, but most students feel OK about school.	The vast majority of students like school and are highly motivated.
10	5	0

5. How would you describe the overall nature of the **interactions between students and adults** in your school?

There are frequent confrontations that include sarcasm and disrespect.	There is a mix, but most interactions are respectful and positive.	The vast majority of interactions are respectful and positive.
10	5	0

6. How would you describe the **level of interest and support provided by parents** of students in your school?

Many parents are openly antagonistic, and many show no interest in school.	Most parents are at least somewhat supportive of school.	The majority of parents are interested, involved, and supportive of what goes on in school.
10	5	0

*While poverty levels tell you nothing about an individual student, the percentage of students from poverty has an influence on your decision about level of support. Notice that this is weighted the same as at Item 8, the number of students in the class.

© 2021 Ancora Publishing　　　　　　　　REPRODU

Reproducible 1.3 *Classroom Support Needs Assessment (Part 2)*

Classroom Support Needs Assessment (p. 3 of 3)　　　　　　　　　*CHAMPS*

Questions 7–10 relate to students in your class this year. Use your most difficult class, or if you are doing this before the school year begins, simply give your best guess.

7. What **grade level** do you teach?　　　　　　　　　　　　　　　　　　Score

K or 1	6, 7, or 8	Other
10	5	0

8. **How many students** do you have in your class?

30 or more	23 to 30	22 or fewer
10	5	0

9. How many students in your class have been identified as **eligible to receive special education services under the categories of Emotional Disturbance or Autism?** *Note:* This label varies from state to state (e.g., ED, EBD, BD, etc.).

Two or more	One	Zero
10	5	0

10. Not including students eligible to receive special education services, how many students in your class have a reputation for **chronic discipline problems?**

Three or more	One or two	Zero
10	5	0

Student Risk Factors Total Score　[　]

Interpretation: Use the scale below to interpret student risk factors and determine the most appropriate level of support for your classroom.

0–33 **LOW SUPPORT NEEDS**	**34–66** **MEDIUM SUPPORT NEEDS**	**67–100** **HIGH SUPPORT NEEDS**
Your students can probably be successful with a classroom management plan that involves Low, Medium, or High Support.	For your students to be successful, your classroom management plan should involve Medium or High Support.	For your students to be successful, your classroom management plan should involve High Support.

© 2021 Ancora Publishing　　　　　　　　　　　　　　REPRODUCIBLE 1.3

of those aspects of your plan that you should review and revise to increase or decrease the level of support and orchestration in your classroom. You can also judge the appropriateness of your plan's level of support by the frequency and intensity of misbehavior. Very little misbehavior means your plan is about right. Frequent misbehavior is an indication that you need to increase the orchestrated care and support across your management plan.

Use the scales provided in Reproducible 1.3 to assess your students' risk factors and determine the most appropriate level of support for your classroom management plan.

- *Low support needs:* If you scored between 0–33, your students can probably be successful with a Classroom Management Plan that involves low, medium, or high support. The level of support can be defined by your teaching style.
- *Medium support needs:* If you scored between 34–66, your Classroom Management Plan should involve medium or high support for your students to be successful.
- *High support needs:* If you scored between 67–100, your Classroom Management Plan should involve high support. Regardless of your personal preference or style, your students require a detailed, systematic, and organized Classroom Management Plan.

If you teach multiple groups throughout your day (e.g., elementary specials teachers or specialists, and middle school teachers), you will likely need to use a different level of support for different groups. For example, in the morning an elementary music teacher may see a large, boisterous group of kindergarten students who require significant structure and support to be successful. In the afternoon, the same teacher may see a small, highly mature and responsible group of fourth-graders who function well with lower structure and support. In middle school, the classes a teacher sees throughout the day may differ significantly in the number of students and in the maturity and responsibility of these students. The classes may require differing levels of structure and support in order to ensure a safe, civil, and productive learning environment for each group. If you teach multiple groups throughout the day, consider filling out Part 2 of Reproducible 1.3 for the two classes that are most different in terms of student behavior, maturity, and risk factors.

If you do not know enough about the characteristics of your students to complete this questionnaire before the year begins, start the year with higher support. As some classes demonstrate they can handle lower levels of support, you can adjust by relinquishing some of the orchestration of your management plan for those classes.

Putting Your Needs and Students' Needs Together: What Level of Support is Needed?

After completing the questionnaire related to your needs and your students' needs (Reproducible 1.3), determine an appropriate level of support for your Classroom Management Plan.

At the top of the plan (Reproducible 1.1), indicate the higher level of support between your needs and your students' needs. For example, if your needs indicate you are OK with low support but your students require high structure and support, plan to use high support. Similarly, if your students do well with low support but you require more structure and order to function at your best as a teacher, plan to put a high-support plan in place. Once you have determined the level of support, it will guide many subsequent decisions about your Classroom Management Plan, such as organizational routines and whether and how to implement a group-based motivational plan.

Bear in mind that it is always better to err on the side of higher support. When it comes to structural elements in particular, research has shown that classrooms with more structure typically promote increases in appropriate academic and social behaviors (Simonsen et al., 2008). If you personally like and need a highly structured classroom environment, it is all right to plan for that even if the students do not need high structure. However, if you would like a low-structure classroom but the students have significant behavioral and/or motivation concerns, you will need to develop a relatively high-structure, high-support management plan. It is not acceptable to have a low-support approach if the result is chaotic, off-task, or disrespectful behavior from students. Similarly, providing frequent positive feedback and working to establish positive relationships with students will benefit any classroom, but will be of critical importance in classrooms with many students who struggle with academic or behavioral expectations or who require greater levels of support for other reasons.

There are a few additional considerations regarding the level of support.

- **Start the Year With High Support.** As we've already suggested, plan to err on the side of being too highly structured and providing more support rather than less. This rule applies especially to the beginning of the year. By starting the school year with high support, you increase the likelihood that students will engage in high levels of academic engagement and appropriate behavior later in the year (Emmer & Evertson, 2009). In addition, you can easily move to less support if you find your class to be highly responsible. For example, in your end-of-class routine, it is more structured to excuse students in small groups—by rows or tables—than to simply say, "Class, you are excused. See you tomorrow." If, during the first 2 weeks of school, you excuse your class by small groups and find that they are a highly respectful and responsible group, you may then say, "Class, for the last 2 weeks I have been excusing you in groups. You are such a responsible class that, starting today, I will excuse the entire class at once. I know you will handle this responsibly, with no racing to the door. Everyone, remember to respect everyone else's physical safety and to use quiet voices." Now imagine that on the first few days of school you excused the entire class at the same time and they were loud and unruly. It will now be harder to enforce a more highly structured dismissal because the students will expect (and may even look forward to) a loud, unruly end to the day.
- **Make Adjustments as the Year Progresses.** The level of support in your classroom is not static. Structure and procedures may fluctuate during the course of the school year based on students' changing needs. For example, if your students experience a major change or event, such as a major natural disaster or traumatic event affecting the school community, additional structure can help create predictability and a sense of calm and routine. In one school that was implementing CHAMPS, a major hurricane resulted in significant disruptions to local services, displacement of many families, and other impacts on students and families. Teachers in this school collectively recognized that their students required greater levels of support and structure after the storm so that their classrooms were a respite of calm and order from the havoc they were experiencing in other aspects of their lives. Even if students had previously done well with lower levels of support, in the near term high support was necessary to create a sense of order and predictability.

If a new student or students will be moving into your classroom during the year, plan to tweak your management plan and increase structure and support for a few weeks. As many teachers well know, even one individual student can drastically change existing classroom dynamics in ways that warrant greater orchestration by the teacher. This is especially true when you work in a school where high risk factors affect a large portion of the student population and/or the student population experiences high mobility and you predict frequent changes in your classroom composition throughout the year.

You should also work to gradually release responsibility to students across the course of the school year as they demonstrate increased levels of responsibility, maturity, and engagement. If you do not personally require higher structure and see that students are demonstrating capability for increased independence, work to gradually loosen structures while actively teaching students how to handle increased responsibility and independence as the year progresses.

Plan to evaluate students' need for support at various times throughout the year. For example, sometime during the fourth or fifth week of school and again after winter and spring break, evaluate how well students are meeting your expectations (procedures for doing this are discussed in Chapters 9 and 10). If a significant number of students are not meeting expectations, you may need to move to a higher level of support with increased structure and organization (Barbetta et al., 2005; Simonsen et al., 2008). Recognize that during the week before and after each major break and during the last month of school, student behavior predictability deteriorates somewhat. Rather than relaxing your level of support, it is probably better to increase support and structure at that time.

As you read through the subsequent chapters in this book, you will notice references to how various tasks might be implemented differently depending on whether your class has high risk factors or low risk factors. If your students require high levels of support, plan to implement all of the tasks in the next seven chapters of this book. If you students require low levels of support and are highly engaged and responsible, you may implement only those tasks you think might facilitate student engagement with academic tasks or lead to better social-emotional growth in your students, and avoid any procedures that might cut into instructional time. If your students require a medium level of support, plan to implement most of the tasks in this book (except those that seem unnecessary because students are already engaged and motivated without them), but don't worry about implementing the tasks in a highly structured fashion. To summarize, the greater the support needs of your students, the more you as a teacher will need to carefully orchestrate and implement all of the tasks in *CHAMPS*.

Conclusion

In this chapter, you learned some of the foundational principles that guide our work at Safe & Civil Schools and that we hope will guide your approach to the CHAMPS materials and to implementing a proactive and positive management approach. Your Classroom Management Plan is the framework that supports a variety of rituals, routines, rules, consequences, and motivational techniques you can use to ensure that students are academically engaged and emotionally thriving. It may be highly or loosely supported to meet your needs and the needs of your class. You will complete the Classroom Management Plan as you complete each chapter in *CHAMPS* with your current or incoming group of students in mind. Remember to adjust your initial plan to meet the changing needs of the class as the year progresses and from year to year.

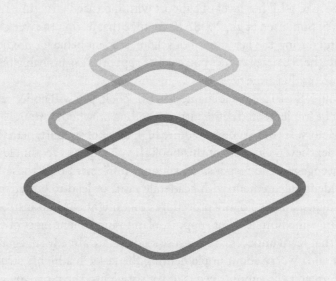

Preparing: Build Your STOIC Classroom Management Plan

Imagine two different college classes . . .

One has an organized professor who starts class on time, uses class time efficiently, clearly states the requirements for assignments and their due dates, and provides detailed and timely feedback on assignments. The other class has a disorganized professor who never starts on time. He is often sorting his notes and presentation slides until 10 minutes into class. Then he takes up class time to talk about things that interest him, not the class topics. His students are never clear on what their assignments are or when they're due, and he rarely offers detailed feedback after grading work. In which of these classes would you do better? Never doubt that a teacher's organization and intentionality affects his students. If he is clear and motivated, his students are likely to be as well.

This section covers the essential elements that you should consider when you are organizing your classroom management approach. Each chapter in this section is situated within the STOIC acronym, which is an easy way to remember the five main categories that have been proven to be effective in changing behavior and motivation:

S **Structure your classroom to prompt responsible student behavior.**

The way a setting is structured has a huge impact on the behavior and attitude of people in that setting. Two chapters are devoted to the implementation of structural considerations in your classroom.

T **Teach your expectations.**

Teach your expectations regarding how to behave responsibly (i.e., be successful) within the structure that you have created.

O **Observe whether students are meeting expectations (monitor!).**

This means circulating and visually scanning the classroom, as well as collecting and analyzing meaningful data on student progress.

I **Interact positively with students.**

This includes offering frequent noncontingent attention to students to develop strong relationships, providing age-appropriate positive feedback to acknowledge students' efforts to be successful, and enhancing student motivation through positive relationships, feedback, and specific motivational strategies and systems. There are two chapters on how to interact positively and motivate your students.

C **Correct misbehavior fluently.**

This means briefly, calmly, consistently, immediately, and (as much as possible) privately.

Within each chapter, a set of tasks will walk you through the process of putting your classroom vision into action by carefully designing a Classroom Management Plan. At the end of this section, you will have developed a concise document that summarizes essential information about your classroom organization, activities, and procedures.

CHAPTER 2

Structure for Success— Behavioral Decisions

The academic and behavioral decisions that you make when developing your Classroom Management Plan define the structure of your classroom.

Imagine you make a reservation at a restaurant. When you arrive at the appointed time, a large number of people are waiting to get in. It takes you 10 minutes to squeeze through the throng of frustrated people to get to a maître d'—who is so frantically busy he does not respond to your polite statements that you have a reservation and instead puts a hand up to indicate you need to wait. After 10 minutes of this, you raise your voice and demand that he pay attention to you. When he finally checks the reservation, he politely but distractedly acknowledges that you did have a reservation, but it was for 15 minutes ago and he cannot possibly seat you now. You state in frustration that you arrived 20 minutes ago and have been trying to get his attention ever since, but he ignored you. He looks apologetic but shrugs in a "what else can I do?" gesture of helplessness. When you are finally seated, you are so agitated that you do not even notice that the food and waitstaff are actually very good.

Now, imagine the same scenario, but on arriving you find that the management is so organized you easily get through to the maître d', who greets you politely and shows you immediately to your table. You find the service, food, and price to be fantastic. Notice how the degree of organization has affected not just your behavior but your attitude toward the setting.

> *Every classroom has a unique structure, and the level of organization and orchestration you use in creating these structures will depend on the support needs of your students.*

Structure relates to the level of organization, orchestration, and predictability of a setting. The academic and behavioral decisions that you make when developing your Classroom Management Plan define the structure of your classroom. This environmental variable has huge implications for student behavior, attitude, and learning. Every classroom has a unique structure, and the level of organization and orchestration you use in creating these structures will depend on the support needs of your students. Each structural decision may be more orchestrated or less orchestrated, but it is important to carefully consider each important element of structure that contributes to student behavior, attitude, and learning. Depending on your needs and the needs of your students, you may design a Classroom Management Plan that takes a low-, medium-, or high-structure approach.

The level of support you identified in Chapter 1 for your class will guide many of the structural decisions you make, including the layout of the physical space and use of a consistent attention signal. The level of support also guides decisions about what your beginning and ending routines look and sound like for the class, and your management of transitions from one activity to another and one location to another. One additional structural variable that is critical to consider is how to establish and maintain family contacts that ensure the greatest likelihood of successful partnerships. Each of these topics appears as a task in this chapter, which is focused on classroom environment and organization. Chapter 3 continues the discussion of structural variables but focuses on tasks related to structure in instructional planning and delivery.

The eight tasks in this chapter are:

- Task 1: Develop and Display Guidelines for Success
- Task 2: Develop and Display Classroom Rules
- Task 3: Design a Positive Physical Space
- Task 4: Select an Attention Signal
- Task 5: Design Effective Beginning and Ending Routines
- Task 6: Design Procedures for Managing Common Transitions
- Task 7: Prepare for Common Areas and Special Circumstances
- Task 8: Establish and Maintain Family Contact

At the end of each task in this chapter, you will update your Classroom Management Plan (Reproducible 1.1).

TASK 1

Develop and Display Guidelines for Success

Develop and plan to actively share guidelines that describe the basic attitudes, traits, and behaviors that will help students be successful in your classroom and throughout their lives.

• • • • •

In addition to academics, teachers need to provide their students with specific information about attitudes, traits, and behaviors that will help them succeed in school and throughout their lives. Every student arrives at school with their own set of guidelines they have learned about how to succeed in the world. However, these guidelines may or may not apply in the school setting. Part of your responsibility as a teacher is to let your students know that everyone can succeed in school and to give them explicit guidelines regarding how. Teachers who don't provide students with explicit Guidelines for Success expect the students to pick up the hidden guidelines present in any setting. Instead, taking the time to identify and teach students exactly what they need to know in order to succeed at school creates a more equal opportunity for all students to grow and thrive in your classroom.

Your Guidelines for Success should reflect broad and—for want of a better word—noble ideals. They should represent what you really hope students will learn from you—not the academic content, but the attitudes and actions that will help them succeed in your class, in classes they will have in the future, in their extracurricular activities, and in life in general. Try to imagine your students as young adults looking back on their elementary or middle school years and thinking, "I remember that my [_____] grade teacher really taught me the importance of [_____]."

Guidelines for Success can help you to communicate the mission and vision for your classroom. If part of your mission is to help your students develop a love of learning, design a Guideline for Success that emphasizes that attitude. If you believe strongly that part of your mission as an educator is to create a classroom environment where each student feels like a valuable part of the community, emphasize traits like teamwork, cooperation, or inclusion in your Guidelines for Success.

The following are some of the guidelines that many CHAMPS teachers have identified over the years:

- Exceptional effort
- Have a growth mindset
- Give your best
- Be persistent
- Be dependable
- Dream big!
- Demonstrate integrity
- Appropriately advocate for yourself and others

- Be curious
- Teamwork
- Respect yourself and others
- Be kind
- Be responsible
- Cooperate with others
- Professionalism

Guidelines for Success are important regardless of the socioeconomic status and learning abilities of the students you teach. Having them is especially critical when your school or class has many students with high needs, whether from experiences of poverty, trauma, disability, disenfranchisement from schooling, or other factors. Students with high needs may not currently have the knowledge or motivation to exhibit traits that educators want, need, or expect students to have. They may struggle to remain focused on a task or meet your high expectations for behavior or participation. They may be less likely to choose a challenging task over a more entertaining one because they may not see a vision of the long-term benefits of a challenging task, or they may believe they are incapable of succeeding. These students can especially benefit from direct teaching of attitudes and traits that will help them succeed (Fairbanks et al., 2007; Gersten & Brengelman, 1996; Gresham, 2002; Howell & Nolet, 2000; Lloyd et al., 1998; Scheuermann & Hall, 2008; Walker et al., 1998). In addition, having these guidelines has been shown to benefit all students and may decrease the number of other supports your students need (Fairbanks et al., 2007).

Some of your guidelines may overlap with your long-range goals (Chapter 3, Task 8 provides ideas on how to develop long-range goals for your classroom), but in general, they should be traits that will help students achieve long-range goals. For example, if you have a goal that students become more proficient writers, ask yourself what attitudes or traits will help your students become proficient writers. Figure 2.1 (on the next page) shows a sample set of Guidelines for Success.

Optimally, Guidelines for Success are developed and used on a schoolwide basis (Sprick et al. 2014). That is, the entire staff creates and agrees to use the same guidelines. Sprick et al. provide suggestions for how to involve staff, students, and parents in developing schoolwide Guidelines for Success. Every teacher in the school should use the school's guidelines. However, teachers may add one or two guidelines that they wish to emphasize within their own classrooms.

Diversity, Equity, Inclusion, and Access

Guidelines for Success are important for working with diverse learners. By clearly communicating the habits, traits, and attitudes that are highly valued in your classroom, you help all learners understand how to be successful in your class. Guidelines for Success can also help foster a sense of community through shared goals and efforts.

If there are no schoolwide Guidelines for Success, consider developing them just for your classroom. When developing your own Guidelines for Success (or Standards for Success, Goals to Strive Toward, or whatever you choose to call them), frame them as brief phrases that describe the attitudes, traits, and characteristics you hope to instill or reinforce in your students. Plan to have no more than five, because you want students to remember them and easily use them as guiding principles for their behavior. If you can use an acronym or rhyme to make them catchy and easier to remember, consider doing so. Guidelines for Success are different from classroom rules. Rules pertain to specific and observable behaviors, and generally have corrective consequences associated with failing to follow them, whereas Guidelines for Success function more like values, goals, and principles. Think of rules as operational and Guidelines for Success as aspirational. Rules relate to the basic requirements for the class to function effectively, while your guidelines reflect your hopes and dreams for who your students can become and what your classroom will feel like throughout the year.

Developing and posting guidelines is just the first step. If students are truly going to learn to exhibit these attitudes, traits, and behaviors, you need to make the guidelines a vibrant part of your classroom. Plan to post the guidelines in a prominent place in your classroom where everyone can see them. You might even consider placing a laminated poster of your guidelines on each wall of your classroom so that the guidelines are visible no matter where you and the students are facing. Also, using vocabulary from the guidelines consistently and regularly will help to keep them familiar. For example, use the guidelines to prompt motivation and get your students excited about striving for excellence. You should also use them as a basis for providing both positive and corrective feedback to students regarding their behavior: "Shelly, you have been getting all your homework completed. Thank you for being so responsible." "Fionna, remember to work quietly. The guideline about treating everyone with respect means you don't disturb others when they are working." Chapter 4, Task 1 provides information on how to teach your guidelines and make them a prominent aspect of your classroom culture.

Remember that when students do not receive explicit information at home about the attitudes, traits, and behaviors that you have identified as important for your classroom, they will default to other learned behaviors. The emphasis that you place on your guidelines may provide critical life lessons that help students become adaptable to different types of environments. If you find that some of your students have had less of a personal context for

Figure 2.1 *Guidelines for Success*

Guidelines for Success

- Be responsible.
- Always try.
- Do your best.
- Cooperate with others.
- Treat everyone with respect (including yourself).

- **Goals**
- **Guidelines for Success**
- **Classroom Rules**
- **Expectations for Routines and Procedures**

Throughout CHAMPS, we refer to goals, Guidelines for Success, classroom rules, and expectations for routines and procedures. One way to keep these different but interrelated concepts clear in your mind is to compare them with driving a car.

Goals and Guidelines for Success are analogous to driving safely and courteously or driving defensively. They are values and goals to strive toward. They are always with you, consciously or subconsciously, and they can always stand evaluation and improvement. This task relates to Guidelines for Success, and Chapter 3, Task 8 provides ideas for developing long-range classroom goals.

Classroom rules and the schoolwide code of conduct are like the enforceable rules of driving—stay under the speed limit, stop at stop signs, and keep in your lane. Information on developing classroom rules is presented in the next task.

Your expectations for classroom routines and procedures, such as where to hand in papers, how to line up for lunch, and how to behave during independent work, can be compared to routines and procedures such as adjusting your seat, keeping your keys in the same place so you can find them, and the different procedures you will need to use when driving different cars that have different features (e.g., automatic vs. manual transmission). Information on expectations for classroom routines is presented in later in this chapter and in Chapter 3. Chapter 4 discusses how to visually display and explicitly teach your expectations to students.

understanding and operating from your guidelines, plan to provide more instruction on how they can implement them and be prepared to give those students more encouragement.

NOTE: Whether you are starting CHAMPS at the beginning of or during the school year, take the time to implement this task. Guidelines for Success give your students critical information about how they can meet expectations and accomplish goals—and this is valuable at any point in the year.

Below is an example of an individual teacher's guidelines from an orchestra class in Jacksonville, Florida.

Mrs. Griffin's Orchestra Guidelines

- Play With Passion
- Take Responsibility for Your Actions
- Do Your Best
- Respect Yourself and One Another
- Be Inspired—"Imagine the Possibilities"

The next example shows how a kindergarten teacher from Hoover Elementary School in Salem, Oregon, used the sample guidelines in Figure 2.1 and adapted them to fit her style.

Mrs. Jones's Guidelines for Success

- Be responsible. (Finish what you start.)
- Always try. (Try, try again.)
- Do your best. (Work hard. This is your job.)
- Cooperate with others. (Be kind. Take turns.)
- Treat everyone with dignity and respect, including yourself. (Remember to say "Please," "Thank you," "Excuse me.")

On the next page are examples of schoolwide Guidelines for Success from elementary and middle schools in Fayette County Schools in Lexington, Kentucky (see Figure 2.2).

UPDATE YOUR CLASSROOM MANAGEMENT PLAN

ITEM 1: GUIDELINES FOR SUCCESS

- List 3–5 Guidelines for Success for your classroom.
- Indicate where and how you will visually post the Guidelines for Success in your classroom.

Figure 2.2 *Schoolwide Guidelines for Success*

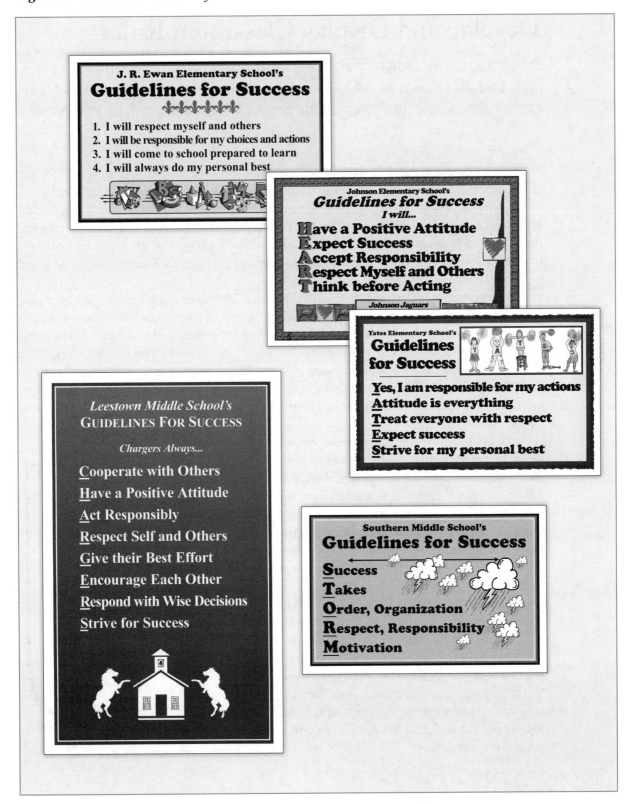

TASK 2

Develop and Display Classroom Rules

Develop a plan for designing and then posting three to six specific classroom rules that will be used as the basis for establishing overarching expectations about behavior and for implementing corrective consequences for misbehavior.

• • • • •

Posted classroom rules communicate specific expectations that are necessary for the classroom to function. Different communities have different rules about what is right and wrong within the community. Therefore, your rules should be as specific as possible so that as you teach the rules, you can provide clear examples of what it means to follow the rule and what it means to break the rule. You should also inform students that unacceptable behaviors (rule violations) will result in corrective consequences (Malone & Tietjens, 2000; McLeod et al., 2003).

It is important to understand that your classroom rules may be similar to rules students have learned in other locations, but they may also be different. In some cases, your classroom rules may be entirely at odds with rules students have learned to function in another community. Different states have different driving laws because of differences in population, geography, and other factors. In a similar way, your classroom community is unique, so your classroom rules are also unique. This doesn't make one set of rules right or wrong, or better or worse than any other. It simply means that you need to identify the rules that are most important for your particular community.

Your classroom rules should serve as the basis for implementing corrective consequences for the most frequent misbehaviors—ideally, if students follow the rules, the most likely misbehaviors will not occur. Before you develop your classroom rules, then, you need to identify the misbehaviors that you think are most likely to occur. Think about your grade level and the typical developmental level of students in your class. Also consider your schedule, your routines, your procedures for managing work, and so on. If your students only rarely struggle with inappropriate language, you may not need a rule addressing this. However, if your class frequently struggles with swearing or "potty language," you might select a rule like: "Use only school- and work-appropriate language and topics." See Figure 2.3 for an example of a typical set of classroom rules.

Figure 2.3 *Classroom Rules*

Classroom Rules

1. Come to class every day that you are not seriously ill.
2. Keep hands, feet, and objects to yourself.
3. Follow directions the first time they are given.
4. Stay on task during all work times.

Four rules is the recommended number, and you should have no more than six. If you have too many rules, students will not be able to keep track of them and you may have difficulty enforcing them (Babkie, 2006; Barbetta et al., 2005; Simonsen et al., 2008). Additionally, a long list of rules sets a negative and adversarial tone when you present the rules to the students. You do not have to have a rule for every possible misbehavior that might occur—only those that are the most likely to occur or those that are likely to create the greatest problems in your classroom, such as physically unsafe behavior, off-task behavior, disruptions, and not having materials.

Decide Who Will Have Input Into the Rules

The first thing to decide is whether you are going to develop the rules yourself or whether you will work them out with your students. This decision is really a matter of style and expediency; both teacher-designed and student-designed rules have high correlations with teacher effectiveness (Emmer et al., 2003; Evertson et al., 2003), and there is currently no clear empirical evidence to indicate whether student-created or teacher-created rules are more effective (Alter & Haydon, 2017).

An advantage of student-developed rules is that the process itself may give students a greater sense of ownership in the classroom (Gathercoal, 1997; Martella et al., 2003; Paine et al., 1983; Salend & Sylvestre, 2005). Proponents of student-created rules argue that the process gives students a way to feel valued and may help establish a positive and collaborative climate. There are disadvantages to student-developed rules, however. Students tend to create too many rules and rules that are overly restrictive (Rhode et al., 2020). When students develop rules, there will be no rules in place for the first day of school, which can be problematic for more challenging groups of students. If you teach more than one class, keeping track of multiple sets of rules will be difficult, and students may not make all the rules you feel you need to have an orderly, well-functioning classroom. If you don't know whether to use teacher-designed or student-designed rules and you have not involved students in rule development before, we recommend designing the rules yourself, at least at first. However, if you like the idea of involving students in rule development and have been successful with the practice in the past, continue to do so.

Be aware that if you allow students to have input in developing classroom rules, you will have to guide the group in developing a manageable number of positively stated rules. You may want to start by having the class brainstorm possibilities, then state each in positive terms (if possible) and select a set of three to six that are the most important.

If you plan to develop rules with your students, you must be willing to follow through with honoring student input; otherwise you may compromise your students' trust in you to accept and use their feedback. Plan some rules or concepts ahead of time that are nonnegotiable for you—those that need to be included in some form. Then you can work with students to develop the wording of the rules that cover those topics, or say something like, "We will include these two rules because they are essential for our classroom to function effectively, and now we will work together to develop the rest."

Relational Trust

Inviting students to participate in developing rules can demonstrate that you value their input and can help build relational trust with your students. However, only use this practice if you are actually willing to take students' input and follow through with student-developed rules.

Another possibility is to brainstorm possibilities with students and tell them that you will take their list and recommendations and make the final decision about which rules to include.

Regardless of whether you involve students in developing rules, explain that rules are in place for the purpose of protecting students' right to learn and enjoy school and for creating a safe and supportive classroom community. While rules should be presented as nonnegotiable boundaries, framing them in terms of creating a positive learning environment in which everyone can be successful can help establish that you are putting student interests first.

Develop Your Rules

Some guidelines to keep in mind when developing your rules are:

- Rules should be stated positively.
- Rules should be specific and refer to observable behaviors.
- Rules must be applicable throughout the entire class period.
- Rules should be posted in a prominent, visible location.

Rules should be stated positively.

Positively stated rules communicate both high expectations and an assumption that students will follow the classroom rules. They set a more positive tone. In addition, clearly stating what you want students to do ensures that students know the expected behavior and sets the stage for student success (Barbetta et al., 2005; Colvin, Kame'enui, & Sugai, 1993; Darch & Kame'enui, 2004; Walker et al., 1996). You cannot assume that when you tell students what not to do, they know what they should be doing instead. One or two of your rules may be difficult to state positively, but make sure that the majority of the rules state what you want students to do. Instead of "no punching or hitting," you could say, "Keep hands and feet to self." Instead of "No food or drinks in the computer lab," you could say, "Leave food and drinks outside the lab."

Rules should be specific and refer to observable behaviors.

Develop rules that describe specific behaviors, not attitudes, traits, or efforts. When stating that rules should be specific and observable, this means that a passing observer could easily mark or tally whether students are following or not following the rules simply by observing student behavior and comparing it to the posted rules. "Arrive on time with all of your materials" is specific and observable, especially if needed materials are visibly posted somewhere in your classroom. "Be responsible" is not. "Stay on task during all work times" is observable. "Always do your best" is not. How can an observer judge whether a student is doing their best? Nonspecific statements like "Be responsible" can have different interpretations to different people.

Statements like "Always do your best" and "Be responsible" are not rules, but if you believe they are important enough to be posted in your classroom, you can include them in your Guidelines for Success. Remember, Guidelines for Success are general, unspecific goals, habits, or attitudes. For example, "Do your best" is a goal you want students to strive toward, not a rule. "Do your best" is too broad, subjective, and open to interpretation to be a rule that has corrective consequences tied to it. While you may have a discussion with a student about your perception that she is not doing her best, you are not going to impose penalties on her for not doing her best. Rules must be specific because infractions of those rules, if observed, have consequences. The rules are specific behavioral expectations that you enforce with reasonable corrective consequences. If a student breaks a rule, it should be clear to everyone that a rule has been broken because the rules will be enforced through the application of corrective consequences (Barbetta et al., 2005).

Teacher Tip—Linking Rules and Guidelines

Some teachers like to link their rules and guidelines. For example, a teacher might use "Be Responsible," "Be Respectful," and "Do Your Best" as Guidelines for Success in the classroom, then link specific rules to each guideline. For example, being responsible in class includes rules like "Arrive on time," "Stay on task," and "Complete your work." A guideline of "Be Safe" could be tied to a rule that students must "Keep hands and feet to self."

Rules must be applicable throughout the class period.

The rules you post must apply throughout the entire class period and never be negated. For example, "Keep hands, feet, and objects to yourself" applies throughout the entire class period. A teacher would never tell students to ignore a rule stating, "Use only school- and work-appropriate language." Some rules that may not apply to the entire class period, such as "Arrive on time with all your materials," can be kept if no portion of the class period invalidates them. Although "Arrive on time with all your materials" focuses only on the beginning of class, it affects the entire class period. If you feel a rule like this is important to have posted, include it on your list.

Problematic rules are those that apply sometimes but not others. "Raise your hand before speaking" may apply only to teacher-directed instruction—you would not expect students to do this when working in cooperative groups. Therefore, "Raise your hand before speaking" should not be posted as a rule, but may be taught as a CHAMPS expectation specific to teacher-directed instruction. (CHAMPS expectations will be discussed later in this chapter and in Chapter 3.)

Rules should be posted in a prominent, visible location.

Posting the rules serves as a visual reminder of your expectations and creates a sense of permanence and importance, more so than simply telling the rules to students (Mayer, 1995; Scheuermann & Hall, 2008; Simonsen et al., 2008). Rules should also be included in your syllabus (Brophy, 1986), but posting the rules allows you to point to them whenever they are discussed. Posting the rules also allows you to be brief in your reminders about minor violations. For example, if students are getting restless and off-task during a teacher-directed portion of a lesson, you can give a quick reminder as you point to your rules: "Class, remember Rule 5. Please stay focused on the lesson."

NOTE: Teachers of very young children may want to provide pictures or graphic images to go along with text-based rules.

When you have to speak to an individual student about a rule violation, point or refer to the rules as you do so. The act of orienting the student's attention to the rules reduces the sense of negative personalization—the sense that you are attacking the student—and implies that you are simply enforcing the classroom rules. Rather than, "Amos, I need you to follow directions the first time," say "Amos, please remember that Rule 1 is to follow directions the first time." In addition, the act of pointing to posted rules decreases intense eye contact between you and the student. This make-eye-contact, break-eye-contact pattern also reduces the possibility that the student will argue with you about the rules.

Subsequent tasks will provide suggestions on what to do when one or more students break a rule. Chapter 8 provides information on when and how to apply corrective consequences for rule violations, and Chapter 9 provides information on how to correct misbehavior during the first several days of school.

Rules should also form the basis of acknowledgment, intermittent or structured celebration, and other positive consequences with students. When you see that your students all immediately followed a direction to transition to a new activity, for example, you might say, "Class, everyone did a fantastic job with Rule 1, follow directions the first time. If we keep this up throughout the week, we might have a little extra time on Friday to play a fun game." Or, when a student who has been struggling with physical horseplay with peers is able to engage appropriately, you might say, "Corrina, all throughout class today you remembered to keep your hands to yourself. Thank you for following our classroom rules and making sure we are all safe!"

UPDATE YOUR CLASSROOM MANAGEMENT PLAN

ITEM 2: POSTED RULES

List 3–6 classroom rules. Double-check that each rule:

- Is stated positively.
- Refers to specific, observable behaviors.
- Is applicable throughout the entire class period (is never negated).

Indicate where and how you will visually post the classroom rules.

TASK 3

Design a Positive Physical Space

Arrange the physical space in your classroom so that it promotes positive teacher-student and student-student interactions and reduces the possibility of disruptions.

• • • • •

Just as the daily schedule of activities can influence student behavior, so too can the physical organization of the classroom (Barrett et al., 2015; Guardino & Fullerton, 2010; Weinstein, 1979). For example, if student desks are arranged in a way that makes it difficult for the teacher to circulate throughout the room, student behavior is likely to be less responsible than when the teacher can easily reach every student. In this task you will read about five aspects of a classroom's physical arrangement that you can address to increase the probability of responsible student behavior and reduce the probability of irresponsible student behavior. Well-designed physical space prevents a wide array of potential behavioral problems (Evans & Lowell, 1979; Simonsen et al., 2008; Weinstein, 1977).

Of course, you do not always have control over the physical arrangement of the space in which you teach. In some cases, you do not teach in your own classroom—for instance, you are a middle school teacher who teaches in a different classroom every period, or you are an elementary music specialist who teaches students in their grade-level classroom. In other cases, tables or workstations in your room are permanently attached to the floor—for example, you are a middle school English teacher whose students must work at lab stations because the science lab is the only classroom available during first period. It is also possible that you have less flexibility in arranging your physical environment because your classroom is small and you have a large number of students.

If any of these scenarios applies to your situation, the suggestions that follow may be difficult to implement. Thus, the basic rule regarding physical arrangements is: Change what you can, and make the best out of what you cannot change. For example, if you teach English in a science lab, you will probably have to put more energy into teaching your students to stay on task than you would if they worked at individual desks. You may also have to take the time to teach students not to play with the sinks and the gas jets. In other words, manipulate those aspects of the physical space that you have some control over. If you have no control over the physical setting, try to address those issues that may arise from the less-than-desirable aspects of the situation. To whatever extent you can control the physical space in which you teach, consider the following suggestions.

If you have multiple classes that require different levels of support and structure, select the desk arrangement that will work best for the group of students with the highest needs. Groups that require less orchestration and support will likely be fine with the higher-structure

Locus of Control

With the physical arrangement of the room, focus on the immediate changes that are within your control so you can structure for success. If there are elements that seem further out of reach, such as different furniture or materials, make a wish list to discuss with your principal at an appropriate time.

desk arrangement, but you can also teach them to quickly rearrange the desks at the beginning and end of particular activities. They will be able to handle the transition and follow your directions to rearrange the furniture. For example, if desks are facing forward in rows (needed for your highly distractable first-period class), but your highly responsible second-period group engages in frequent cooperative group activities, teach the second-period students to quickly move the desks into clusters and then back into rows.

Arrange Student Desks

Arrange student desks to optimize the most common types of instructional tasks that you will use and the amount of desired student-to-student communication. Following are descriptions of five common desk arrangements and their relative pros and cons:

- Desks in rows front to back
- Desks in rows side to side
- Desks clustered in fours
- Desks in U-shape (version 1)
- Desks in U-shape (version 2)

Remember, as you consider what classroom arrangement you want, whether it's one described here or a different one, you need to think about the types of instructional tasks students will be participating in. Also consider the level of support and structure your students require and the level and type of communication that you would like to see between students. For example, in some seating arrangements (e.g., cluster arrangements and U-shape arrangements), students face one another. While some groups of students can handle this well and remain on task during teacher-directed activities and independent work, other students may require an arrangement that does not set them up to be distracted by students seated across from them. In general, the nature of the tasks that students will engage in most frequently is the determining factor for the classroom seating arrangement you select. For example, when students are expected to work independently, research strongly supports seating them in rows (Bennett & Blundell, 1983; Simmons et al., 2015; Wannarka & Ruhl, 2008;). When students are expected to communicate frequently with one another, a group seating arrangement can increase on-task behavior and participation (Marx et al., 1999; Rosenfield et al., 1985).

DESKS IN ROWS FRONT TO BACK
This arrangement, shown in Figure 2.4:

- Is excellent when you schedule frequent whole-class instruction or when students must see a board or screen for tasks.
- Allows for occasional cooperative learning activities. Students can be trained to move quickly from rows into groups of four and back to rows when the cooperative activity is completed.

- Allows students to interact, but the space between desks helps keep off-task conversation down. This arrangement is also helpful when you have students who struggle with physical aggression, horseplay, or keeping the space on their desk organized. Individual desks ensure that students have their own personal space to manage.
- Implies that student attention should be directed to the front of the room.
- Allows you to easily circulate among students.

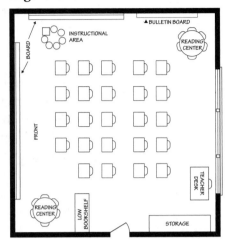

Figure 2.4 *Front to Back Rows*

DESKS IN ROWS SIDE TO SIDE

This arrangement, shown in Figure 2.5:

- Is excellent if you schedule frequent whole-class instruction or if students must see the board for tasks.
- Allows for occasional cooperative learning activities. Students can be trained to move quickly from the rows into groups of four by having one row turn their chairs backwards to face the group behind them. They can then be trained to move quickly back to the rows when the cooperative activity is completed.
- Allows students to interact more easily than Desks in Rows Front to Back, which may result in more off-task conversation than desired.
- Implies that student attention should be directed to the front of the room.
- Maximizes available space in the room so that centers, work areas, and small group instruction can be located around the perimeter of the room.
- May hinder your circulation among students because you must go to an aisleway to get from one group of students to another. Place one or two aisles running perpendicular to the rows to create as much easy circulation as possible.

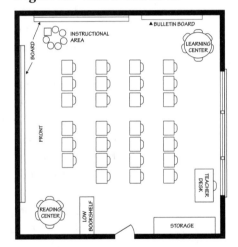

Figure 2.5 *Side to Side Rows*

DESKS IN CLUSTERS

This arrangement, shown in Figure 2.6 (p. 68):

- Allows easy access from any part of the room to any other part of the room, making it easy to circulate among students.
- Is excellent if you schedule frequent cooperative learning tasks.
- Can be problematic when you have students who need less stimulation and distraction. Being a part of a cluster may make it more difficult for them to behave responsibly, and if you separate them at another desk, they may feel excluded.

- Requires students to turn sideways or completely around to see the board or teacher-directed instruction. Because this is uncomfortable, it may lead to less engagement and more distracted behavior during activities that require attention at the front of the room.
- May result in frequent off-task conversation during independent work periods and teacher-directed instruction.
- May prompt too much inappropriate student-to-student interaction for a class with high numbers of immature students.

Figure 2.6 *Clusters*

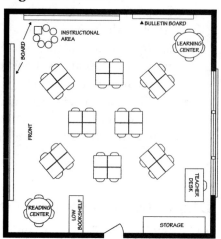

DESKS IN U-SHAPE *(Version 1)*

This arrangement, shown in Figure 2.7:

- Is excellent for whole-class discussions and teacher-directed instruction when you want students to participate with frequent verbal responses.
- Is excellent for classroom circulation—you can quickly reach any student.
- Does not lend itself to cooperative group activities.
- Does not make good use of space (the area in the center of the U is largely unused). May not allow for learning centers, small group instruction space, and so on.
- Is probably not feasible when you have a large number of students (more than about 20).
- Should provide access from the inside of the U to the outside so you and your students are able to cross the room easily.
- Place students who are easily distracted in seats facing the front of the room rather than facing sideways toward other students.

Figure 2.7 *U-Shape (Version 1)*

DESKS IN U-SHAPE *(Version 2)*

A science teacher shared this arrangement with us (thank you, George Garcia). This teacher looked at the suggested arrangements in CHAMPS, considered his own situation (he had tables, not individual desks), and developed a plan that worked for his class. This arrangement, shown in Figure 2.8:

- Is excellent for whole-class discussions and teacher-directed instruction when you want students to participate with frequent verbal responses.

- Is excellent for classroom circulation—you can quickly reach any student.
- Does not lend itself to cooperative group activities.
- May not allow room for learning centers, small group instruction, and so on.
- Is feasible for larger classes (up to 30 students).
- When used with a large class, you may need two rows. With two rows, ensure that the inside U has spaces to access the outside U so you can easily interact with all students.
- Should have enough room around the outside of the U so you and your students are able to move around the room easily.
- Place students who are easily distracted in seats facing the front of the room rather than facing sideways toward other students.

Figure 2.8 *U-Shape (Version 2)*

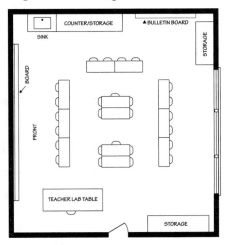

One other consideration for the seating arrangement is whether your classroom has shared tables with two or more workspaces on each table or individual desks for students. While this is often dictated by your school's furniture, if you have a choice in which to use, recognize that shared tables require more maturity and responsibility on the part of the students. If your students are highly immature, struggle to share space, typically have materials sprawled out, or struggle with appropriate peer interactions, individual desks will probably work better for these students.

Ensure Physical and Visual Access to All Parts of the Room

One of the most effective behavior management strategies a teacher can implement is active supervision (Colvin et al., 1997; DePry & Sugai, 2002; Gettinger & Ball, 2008; Schuldheisz & van der Mars, 2001; Van den Bogert et al., 2014). Active supervision includes moving around the room, interacting with students, correcting errors, and providing positive feedback. It requires that you circulate throughout the room as much and as unpredictably as possible. You are more likely to circulate when you can move about the room easily. Thus, regardless of how you arrange student desks, be absolutely certain that you can move easily from any part of the room to any other part of the room.

When students are working independently or in groups, your proximity will have a moderating effect on their behavior. As you circulate, you can provide corrective feedback to students who are off-task, give positive feedback to students who are using the work time well, and answer the questions of students who need assistance. As you are helping one student, you may notice another student who is off task. You should be able to walk to the off-task student so you can have a private interaction to correct the off-task behavior, rather than having to yell across the room. If you have to walk all the way to the outside edges of the classroom and circle the room to reach the off-task student, you are more likely to find yourself frustrated and angry because you have to go out of your way to keep students engaged. You may also find increased levels of off-task and other inappropriate behavior.

The physical arrangement should also allow you to visually scan all parts of the room from any other part of the room (Martin, 2002; Pedota, 2007; Shores et al., 1993). Be careful to avoid screens or bookcases that create spaces you cannot easily see. If you create private spaces for students as "cool down" or mindfulness spaces, or if you create a timeout space, ensure that you can still see the student at all times while creating some sense of privacy for them. You will read about the importance of systematic supervision in Chapter 5—the physical arrangement of the room can make this easy or difficult.

Minimize disruptions caused by high-traffic areas.

There are a number of legitimate reasons why students need to move about the classroom during the day. Yet, whenever students are out of their seats there is a greater potential for misbehavior. Think of the reasons students need to leave their desks and where they need to go. Then arrange the room so that students who are moving about will be less likely to disrupt students who are working at their seats (Evertson et al., 2003; Jenson et al., 2020; Wannarka & Ruhl, 2008). For example, you should keep student desks away from common high-traffic areas where students:

- Get supplies
- Sharpen their pencils
- Turn in their work
- Have small group instruction
- Use learning centers

If you must locate student desks near one or more of these high-traffic areas, you will need to directly teach students how to be in the area without distracting other students. You may also wish to design your seating assignment so that the least distractable and most responsible students are in these higher-traffic parts of the room.

Devote bulletin board or display space to student work.

Save the most prominent display space in your classroom for student work (Pedota, 2007; Trussell, 2008) and for displaying cultural artifacts or visuals that represent students' backgrounds and interests (Gutiérrez, 2008; Hammond, 2014). When student work is prominently displayed, it demonstrates to students that you are proud of their accomplishments and that you want to show others what they've done. Ensure that all students have an opportunity to have work they are proud of displayed throughout the year. When you display representations of student background and interests, you demonstrate that you are interested in and honor your students for who they are. Have students periodically bring in visuals they would like displayed and have them help design the display. Artistic teachers sometimes feel they must have every bit of wall space elaborately decorated. However, when you, the teacher, have done all the decorating, students may get the sense that they are just visitors in "your" room. You also want to ensure that the room is not so covered in artwork, posters, and other materials that it overwhelms students who are easily overstimulated.

Diversity, Equity, Inclusion, and Access

Displaying student work and cultural artifacts and visuals that represent students' backgrounds and interests demonstrates that you are proud of your students and value them as individuals.

If needed, arrange for a timeout and/or cool-down space that is as unobtrusive as possible.

If you plan to send misbehaving students to a quiet space, you need to decide ahead of time where this area will be. When possible, avoid a location where the misbehaving student is on display to students who are at their desks. You might also want to consider having the area somewhat screened off for privacy. Some teachers also create a separate space where students can go if they request a break or if a teacher sees the student is becoming overly anxious or frustrated, or beginning to escalate. In contrast to a timeout space, this area may include some soothing activities such as stress balls, comfort items, and/or a music station.

Determine Whether and How to Assign Seats

In addition to the physical room arrangement, one of the most powerful structural tools at your disposal is the seating arrangement for each group of students you work with. We recommend that all classrooms start with an assigned seating arrangement until you get to know your students. Then consider the level of support your students require when determining whether and how to use assigned seats with your students. If students struggle with peer interactions or remaining on task, or you have students who require more order and predictability (e.g., students who have experienced significant trauma, students with autism spectrum disorder [ASD], students with ADHD), you will need to put careful thought into how you design seating protocols.

Consider benefits of assigned seating.

Assigned seats can provide numerous academic and social benefits. Assigned seats ensure that students go immediately to their seats. Without a seating chart, some students will mill about the room until friends arrive so that they can sit together. One of the main benefits of assigned seating arrangements is that they eliminate the need for attendance roll call. With an assigned seating chart, you can simply look for any empty seats and mark those students absent. This ensures that attendance taking is a quick and efficient procedure so that you can move as quickly as possible into engaging classroom instruction and activities. Assigned seats also allow you to carefully structure productive academic partnerships and groupings. In general, it is beneficial to pair low-performing students with middle-performing students who can help to foster needed skills and understanding, but who are not so high-achieving they will get frustrated with the other learner or simply do the work for them (Archer & Hughes, 2011).

Assigned seats can create a sense of social safety for students. Some students may immediately feel threatened upon entering a classroom environment when they have to seek out a seat at the beginning of class. For example, a student with ASD who requires predictability and ordered routines may struggle in a classroom where students must select their own seats each day. Other students may also have difficulty with or dislike open seating arrangements, including students with anxiety, shy students, students who have few friends in a class, new

Diversity, Equity, Inclusion, and Access

For some students, planful coordinated seating arrangements can provide a sense of predictability and social safety. They can foster inclusion by disrupting cliques and status hierarchies that may occur with open seating arrangements.

students, students with academic or behavioral difficulties, and students who are emerging in English. When teachers are planful about seating arrangements to foster new friendships and promote positive social interaction, there can be less victimization, aggression, and status hierarchies in classrooms (Berg et al., 2012; Gest & Rodkin, 2011).

If you opt to use an assigned seating chart, consider the following recommendations for making an optimal seating arrangement:

- Seat students who are easily distracted far from high-traffic areas of the classroom such as the pencil sharpener and where students turn in or collect work.
- Avoid placing many sociable students together at the back of the classroom. Granstrom (1996) found that students at the back of the classroom tend to interact with each other more frequently than those seated at the front of the room, which can negatively impact time on task and attention to learning activities. Carefully consider which students have the maturity, responsibility, and motivation to remain focused and on task while at the back of the room.
- If students are seated in clusters or other arrangements where some students will have their backs to the teacher or board, ensure that the most responsible and academically engaged students are assigned these seats. This ensures that other students who may require more teacher direction, active supervision, and visual supports are directly facing the teacher or visual references on the board.
- Separate students who are likely to distract one another or who have behavioral problems while ensuring that you are able to maintain visual and physical proximity to these students. You want to make it as easy as possible to provide frequent private positive and corrective feedback to these students. While it may be tempting to place two students who frequently misbehave in the front row on opposite sides of the class, many teachers visually scan these corners of the classroom the least frequently. Consider placing one student in the front row near you and one student a few rows back but in the middle of the classroom where you do the most visual scanning.
- Actively work to separate students who form cliques, and attempt to create diverse groupings of students. It may be beneficial to change the seating arrangement every 3–6 weeks to allow students to experience multiple different social and academic groupings.

If you wish to get student input on where they would like to sit or whom they would like to work with, consider the following procedure that a teacher shared with us. Begin the year with an assigned seating chart. After 3–4 weeks, have students take out a sheet of paper and write preferred seating locations in the classroom and the names of six classmates they would like to sit next to or work with. Share with the students that each time you make a seating chart or groupings for a group activity, you will look at approximately ten students' requests and attempt to pair them with at least one of their requested peers. If a student does not get to sit with preferred peers in one round, you will select a different set of ten students for the next round, and so on. Create a new seating arrangement every 4 to 6 weeks.

One masterful addition that can be used with this procedure is to examine student responses to see which students struggled to write down the names of six peers they want to work with. Also look to see if some students' names did not appear on anyone else's list. These are students who may require additional support in developing friendships or positive working relationships with peers.

If students struggle with behavior, engagement, or positive peer interactions in other areas of your classroom (e.g., small group instruction, carpet), it may be beneficial to assign seats for these activities as well. This can prevent problems such as students arguing over who gets to sit on which carpet square or students selecting seats next to peers who may be distracting.

Consider pros and cons of flexible seating.

Flexible seating is a trend that has gained in popularity in some schools. This can involve allowing students to choose their own location in the classroom and/or replacing standard chairs and desks with a variety of alternatives, such as standing desks, couches or lounge chairs, and exercise balls. Proponents of flexible seating indicate that these practices can increase student engagement and participation while decreasing disruptive behaviors. At this time, we were unable to find peer-reviewed research that supported these positive effects for classrooms as a whole; however, some research indicates that components of flexible seating can have benefits for some students. For example, alternative seating devices such as therapy balls can help students with ADHD, ASD, and other disabilities improve their focus, in-seat behavior, and engagement (Fedewa & Erwin, 2011; Meritt, 2014; Schilling et al., 2003; Schilling & Schwartz, 2004; Wu et al., 2012).

Because research regarding general use of flexible seating is limited, we overview some of the possible pros and cons of these practices and conclude with a set of planning and implementation recommendations if you opt to use flexible seating in your classroom.

Flexible seating can offer students choice and an increased sense of responsibility, which may foster more ownership in the learning environment (Erwin, 2004). One potential advantage of flexible seating options is the opportunity for movement, as a therapy ball or wiggle chair may allow students to move, fidget, and change position while still remaining attentive to class demands. The ability to transition to different seating arrangements or move while in a particular type of flexible seat can accommodate some students' need for physical activity throughout the day (Stapp, 2018). Flexible seating can also be viewed as a culturally responsive teaching practice in some contexts. In the United States, where the dominant culture is individualistic, practices that offer a more communal, collaborative learning approach may be culturally responsive to students from cultures that are more collectivist.

While flexible seating can pose benefits, it can take extra time to facilitate and requires extra organization. For example, in elementary school, it can be easier to manage materials when students have assigned seats because students can store things at their desks. Or clusters of materials can be kept together on a shelf so that a group leader can gather materials for a group rather than having all students get up to get materials. If students are in different seats each day, you will need to get creative with procedures for getting materials in ways that are minimally disruptive to learning. You will also need to teach students lessons on what to do if they do not get the seat they want and provide social-emotional supports for students who may struggle with these responses. Students who arrive earliest at class will be able to select desirable seats first, so you may need to design some structures to create greater equity. Consider creating rules around seats, such as that a students can use a particular seat for up to 1 week but then must allow others to sit there for the next 2 weeks.

Diversity, Equity, Inclusion, and Access

Flexible seating options can provide diverse learners who require more physical activity opportunities to move and fidget. This can help some students focus and engage in class activities.

If you opt to use flexible seating, consider the following recommendations:

- Start the school year with assigned seats so you can gauge factors like students' maturity and the nature of peer interactions. If you have a particularly challenging group, it may be better to maintain assigned seats for the majority of the class and periodically attempt short periods of flexible seating with smaller groups of students. If students are successful in maintaining on-task behavior and appropriate peer interactions, you can gradually try longer periods of flexible seating with larger groups of students.
- Before committing to flexible seating for the whole classroom, try some options for a section of the room or for select activities. For example, create one area of the classroom with a standing desk and plush chairs. Create different times for each group or row to use these options while others remain in their assigned seats.
- Introduce flexible seating by first rotating students through all different seating options on an assigned basis so that all students have an opportunity to experience each option.
- Create expectations for each seating option. For example, if students are allowed to select their own seats, expectations might include: 1) Choose an appropriate spot. 2) If someone is in your preferred seat, select another spot and speak with the teacher if you would like to request using the seat within the next week. 3) Stay focused and on task. 4) The teacher reserves the right to move anyone at any time.
- If students are allowed to select seats at the beginning of the class, have an efficient way to take attendance. See Task 5 for options for taking attendance without losing instructional time with a verbal roll call.
- Recognize that not all students like all flexible seating options. For students who prefer a consistent or assigned seating arrangement, flexible seating can lead to feelings of frustration, worry, or social anxiety. Some students feel more comfortable with a traditional desk and chair or would prefer to have an assigned seat. Periodically seek student input and tell students they should speak with you if some aspect of the seating practices are not working. Also carefully monitor student choice of seats to ensure that cliques or exclusive attitudes aren't emerging and that students have equal access to all choices.
- If students begin to struggle with following expectations with flexible seating, consider assigning seats for a period of time until they consistently demonstrate the ability to follow directions and remain on task.

In summary, the physical space in your classroom should be arranged to prompt responsible behavior from students (Jones & Jones, 2007; Simonsen et al., 2008; Trussell, 2008). While it is not necessary to include a diagram of your classroom arrangement in your Classroom Management Plan, do consider ways to update the physical arrangement of your room if necessary. Make sure that there is easy access from any one part of the room to any other part of the room so that you can circulate unpredictably among students and students can move about without disturbing others. In addition, desks and traffic patterns should be arranged in a manner that takes into account the major types of instructional activities you use and the level of support needed in your Classroom Management Plan. Thinking ahead of time about where to display student work and whether or not you need an in-class timeout space or cool down area will help you ensure the physical space of your classroom is functional for both you and your students. Finally, carefully consider whether and how to use assigned seating or flexible seating options to ensure a positive working environment for all of your students.

TASK 4

Select an Attention Signal

Decide on a signal you can use to get students' attention in any setting. Teach them to respond by focusing on you and maintaining complete silence.

• • • • •

Getting and holding students' undivided attention is an essential management responsibility for all teachers. An orchestra conductor uses a signal, such as tapping her music stand with her baton, to get musicians to pay attention so that everyone can begin playing the music. Like the conductor, you need a signal to get students to interrupt their individual efforts and focus on you so that you can give directions or provide instruction (Carnine et al., 2004; Scheuermann & Hall, 2008).

An attention signal is useful in many situations. Imagine a class of 28 students working in cooperative groups. As the teacher monitors the groups, she realizes that the students do not fully understand their assignment. Using a well-practiced signal, this teacher needs no more than 5 seconds to get students to cease their group conversations and pay attention to her. After briefly clarifying the directions and answering questions, she instructs the students to resume their small group work. Without a well-practiced signal, this teacher would likely spend several minutes to gain student attention. She might even yell over the noise of the groups. It is entirely possible that she would never get all the students to stop talking so that she could clarify the task.

Regardless of the grade level or subject you teach, an attention signal is an important behavior management strategy that you should implement. Whatever level of support your class requires, you need a way to get students to transition from potentially active and noisy activities to activities that demand that everyone's attention be focused on the same subject. An effective attention signal is also critical in the case of an emergency where you need to quickly get all students' attention.

To implement this task, first identify what you will use as a signal. One commonly used and effective signal is to say in a firm (but not strident) voice, "Class, your attention please," while at the same time swinging one arm up in an arcing motion (from 9:00 to 12:00 on a clock face). Then, hold your hand in the 12:00 position (see Figure 2.9). This prompt has been pretaught to students and indicates that they should stop talking, look at you, and raise their hand—holding it up in the air until all students are quiet and looking at you with their hands raised.

This signal has several advantages. First of all, it can be given from any location in the room. Second, it can be used outside the classroom—in the hall or even on a field trip, for example. Third, it has both a visual (the sweeping motion and raised hand) and an auditory (the verbal statement) component. Students who don't hear the signal may see the sweeping arm motion and raised hand, and those who don't see it may hear it. An arcing motion is more likely to be seen peripherally by students, especially those who are not directly facing the teacher, than a simple vertical raise of your hand. Another advantage of

Figure 2.9 *Attention Signal*

this signal (or something similar) is its ripple effect. Even a student who does not hear or see the teacher will find it hard to miss the raised hands of the other students. A final benefit is that having students also raise their hands in response to your signal helps interrupt any other behaviors that might make it take longer to get their attention, and you can easily see when students are paying attention. The most effective attention signals involve some sort of active response from all students, especially for classes that may have more distractible students or those who struggle during transitions.

Other commonly used signals may not offer all the advantages mentioned above. For example, some teachers flick off the lights as a signal for attention. However, this signal requires that the teacher go to the light switch, and it cannot be used at all in the hall or on a field trip. A signal may be ineffective because it must be repeated frequently before students pay attention. For example, if you use a clapping rhythm that students echo back, but you find that you have to use it three or four times in succession before all students stop what they are doing, this signal may waste too much time since you will use it frequently. Any signal that takes longer than 3–5 seconds to gain student attention likely wastes too much valuable instructional time across the course of a term or year.

If you already have a signal that works well for you in all settings, do not bother to change it. However, if you use a signal that has not worked well, or that works well in some environments but not in others, you might want to consider using the signal described above.

Some teachers use multiple signals for variety, or so they have one signal for use in the classroom (e.g., a gong with students responding with a motion or auditory response) and one for outside the classroom (e.g., the arcing hand motion). As long as the different signals do not confuse the students, and as long as each signal is equally as effective as the others in getting the attention of all students, there is nothing wrong with this. It is largely a matter of teacher style.

Regardless of the signal you decide to use, you must teach students what the signal is and how to respond to it from the first day of school. Information on when and how to teach your attention signal is provided in Chapter 9: Launch.

UPDATE YOUR CLASSROOM MANAGEMENT PLAN

ITEM 3: ATTENTION SIGNAL

Describe the attention signal you will use in your classroom. Make sure that it:

- Can be given from any location.
- Has an auditory and a visual component.
- Takes no more than 5 seconds to gain all students' attention.
- (optional but recommended) Involves active participation from students to ensure they are all paying attention.

If you will use more than one signal (e.g., one inside your room and one for activities outside the room), describe each one and when and how it will be used.

TASK 5

Design Effective Beginning and Ending Routines

Design effective procedures for beginning and ending the school day or class period.

• • • • •

The activities and procedures you use to start and end each school day or class period have a significant influence on the climate of your classroom. Effective and efficient beginning and ending procedures create an inviting and supportive environment; they communicate that time is valuable and will not be wasted (Babkie, 2006; Bohn et al., 2009; Emmer & Evertson, 2009; Marshall, 2001; Trussell, 2008). The resulting atmosphere, in turn, makes a difference in student behavior. Consider the following two middle school scenarios.

CASE STUDY

Teacher A begins the day by warmly greeting students as they enter the classroom. She has previously taught students that when they enter the room, they are to immediately take their seats, get out any required materials listed on the board, and begin working on the challenge problem shown on the board. Students who do not have their materials do not interrupt the teacher while she is greeting students because, starting on the second day of school, she taught them specific procedures for dealing with this situation. When the bell rings, the students continue to work on the challenge problem while the teacher uses her seating chart to quickly take attendance. Within 1 minute after the bell rings, Teacher A has taken attendance, secured the attention of the class, and started teaching. Six minutes later, and again 4 minutes after that, a student enters late, but Teacher A does not stop teaching. She has previously taught students her procedures for tardiness (both excused and unexcused), which are designed to ensure accurate record-keeping without disrupting class.

The situation is different in Teacher B's class. As students enter the class, Teacher B is seated at her desk trying to finish up last-minute preparations for the lesson. Some students take their seats, while others socialize in groups of two to five. When the bell rings, Teacher B looks up from her work and acknowledges the students by saying, "Quit talking and go sit down. It is time to begin class." After 2 minutes of nagging and cajoling by Teacher B, the students are finally in their seats and reasonably quiet. The teacher spends 2 minutes completing roll call, then instructs students to get out their materials. She then spends several minutes helping a couple of students who are not prepared (she lets them borrow books and pencils), all the while nagging them to be responsible. Six minutes after the bell rings, Teacher B finally begins teaching. One minute later, and again 4 minutes after that, a student enters late. Both times, the teacher stops teaching to fill out the necessary paperwork and determine whether the tardiness is excused or unexcused.

Note that Teacher A spends only 1 minute on attendance, materials, and tardiness procedures, and even during that minute, students are engaged in an instructional task. Teacher B spends 7 minutes on attendance, materials, and tardiness. Students who arrived on time with all of their materials have been forced to sit and do nothing while the teacher deals with these procedures. In both of these scenarios, a couple of students did not have their materials and a couple of students arrived late—situations that happen occasionally even with the most effective teacher. The difference is that Teacher A has anticipated these common problems and has taught her students procedures for handling them. Her procedures do not usurp teacher time and attention, and do not waste the time of the students who are punctual and prepared.

• • • • •

In this task you will learn how to begin and end your school day or class period with a positive tone and maintain maximum time for instructional activities. We identify six critical times and issues related to beginning and ending the day or class period, provide a goal statement for each that describes optimal outcomes related to that time or issue, and then give suggestions for routines and procedures to achieve the goal. While elementary teachers will find useful suggestions for beginning and ending their school day and for beginning and ending each subject period, this task may be even more critical for middle school teachers who typically have five to seven different classes each day and for elementary specialists (music, PE, computer, art) who may have a new group every 30–60 minutes.

The six critical times and issues are:

- Entering Class
- Opening Activities
- Students Not Prepared With Materials
- Students Returning After an Absence
- End of Day or End of Class Period Activities
- Dismissal

Keep in mind that these suggestions represent just one way of dealing with beginning and ending your day or class. If you already have efficient and effective beginning and ending routines (procedures that adequately address the goal statements shown in each task below), there is no reason to change what you do. If you do not have effective routines, read these suggestions or talk to colleagues (or both), then design beginning and ending procedures for your class that are time efficient and set a positive tone.

ENTERING CLASS

Goal: Students feel welcome and immediately go to their seats and start on a productive task.

Greeting students as they enter your classroom helps them feel welcome, reduces classroom behavior problems, and increases academic success (Allday & Pakurar, 2007; Cook et al., 2018). A brief greeting communicates to students that you are aware of them not just as students but as individuals and that you are interested in them—"Marguerite, how did things go at the choir concert last night?" In addition, greeting students as they enter provides a subtle but powerful message that you are aware of students and what they are doing from the minute they enter the classroom, not just after the bell rings.

In general, you want to greet students at the door. If you are supervising the hall outside your room, you can greet them before they enter your doorway. Although you can greet students inside the classroom (while seated at your desk, for instance), the effect is not nearly as powerful as being at or near the door and greeting them immediately.

Relational Trust

The simple act of greeting students by name each day is a daily ritual that communicates that you see the student, are glad they are there, and look forward to working with them for the day.

Some teachers use a chart on their door that allows students to select their preferred way of greeting the teacher (e.g., high-five, side hug, fist bump, mini dance party, etc.). As students enter the room, they point at the words or picture representing their preferred greeting, then complete the greeting with the teacher. This can be a personalized way to interact with each student as they enter the room. Other teachers will use a simple handshake or a smile and a verbal greeting to ensure each student is welcomed into their classroom.

You should have a task prepared that students can work on when they sit down. The purpose of the task is to keep students busy while they wait for the bell to ring and while you take care of any attendance and housekeeping tasks during the first minute or two of class. Having students work on a daily task like this communicates to them that you value instructional time and plan to use every minute as efficiently as possible.

Keep the task relatively short, requiring 2 to 5 minutes of work from students. It should be a review task that students can perform independently, but it should also be instructionally relevant—not just busy work. For example, math teachers might give a short daily quiz on the previous night's homework assignment. Language arts teachers might have students work in their journals or do a power-writing exercise. A primary teacher might have students work on a handwriting exercise or a practice page of age- and level-appropriate math tasks.

When you finish taking attendance, give students feedback on the correct responses for the task. Have them correct their own papers or trade with a neighbor. Then collect the papers so that later you can enter the score or a check mark in your grading system to indicate that students completed the task. Students need to know that this initial task counts, or they will soon cease to work on the task.

OPENING ACTIVITIES

Across all grades, procedures for opening activities should accomplish the following goals:

- Procedures are efficient and orderly, and keep students instructionally engaged.
- Announcements and housekeeping tasks do not take too much time.
- Procedures for dealing with tardiness are effective.

Goal 1: Opening activities are efficient and orderly, and keep students instructionally engaged while you take attendance.

When the bell rings, and as students continue to work on the assigned task, use an unobtrusive strategy to determine who is present and who is absent. Students should continue to focus on their work while you take attendance. Sitting and doing nothing except for the split second needed to respond to roll call is a very boring way for a student to begin class and can lead to lower engagement and worse behavior throughout the class. A seating chart allows you to quickly identify who is missing for the day by looking for the empty seats in the room. This ensures that attendance takes less than a minute.

If you do not have an assigned seating chart, you can use an oral roll call, but ensure that students continue working while you call out names and mark attendance. Another option is to provide a way for students to indicate they are present as they enter the room. For example, in one classroom a primary teacher created a pocket chart with each student's name on a pocket. As students entered the room, she handed them popsicle sticks, and each student then placed the popsicle stick in their pocket on the chart. While students did a brief daily writing activity, the teacher marked attendance using the pocket chart. Another teacher in middle school gave each student a sticky note as they entered the room. As soon as students were seated, they wrote their names on the sticky notes and began their opening practice task. The teacher then circulated and picked up the sticky notes so he could enter attendance as students continued to work. Then during the period, the teacher used the sticky notes to write and distribute at least one positive comment about their work or behavior to each student.

Regardless of the method you use, ensure that you take attendance each day during time periods that are required by your school so that the school (and thereby families) have an accurate sense of which students are present or absent at any given time. Schools are legally responsible for their students during school hours, so accurate and timely attendance reporting is a critical element of ensuring student safety. If a student is not in school when they are supposed to be, schools must be responsible for identifying this and communicating it to the student's legal guardians.

Goal 2: Announcements and other housekeeping tasks do not take up too much time.

You should begin instructional activities as quickly as possible after the beginning of the period.

In middle school classrooms, try to spend no more than a minute or two on announcements and housekeeping. Activities that are not directly related to the subject of the class (such as school spirit discussions) should be reserved for advisory or homeroom periods as much as possible. If your school does not have an advisory or homeroom period, consider discussing the following ideas with your principal or the team in your school that addresses behavior and climate (e.g., PBIS team, MTSS for behavior team, leadership team):

- Some schools that do not have an advisory or homeroom will select one period during the day that becomes the standard vehicle for schoolwide housekeeping (e.g., information on Spirit Week) and other announcements.
- Some schools will create a rotation of housekeeping announcements. In week 1, all announcements occur during first period. In week 2, all announcements occur during second period, and so on.

In elementary classrooms, opening activities should include recording of attendance, lunch count, and any other housekeeping duties. During these activities, keep students actively engaged. Another goal for opening activities in elementary classrooms is to ease the students into the school day. Effective elementary teachers vary widely in the way they help students settle in through regular morning routines. This variation reflects, among other things, grade level and personal style. For example, some teachers include "sharing" (i.e., students share information about themselves or an item brought from home) as an opening activity, while others do not. Some teachers like to have students do class jobs and take time each morning to assign these jobs. Some teachers conduct calendar and weather activities, and others do not. Because there is no one correct way to start the day, consider the following when planning your opening activities.

Opening activities that take more than a few minutes should have an educational objective. For example, if you take 5 minutes each day to discuss the weather, it should be because one of your science objectives is that students master some basic concepts about weather. Otherwise, don't both with this 5-minute activity. Likewise, if you do a sharing activity, you should have some compelling reasons why you take class time for this activity each day.

Opening activities should keep students actively engaged. If students are expected to sit and do nothing, you will have behavior problems. Think about your typical opening activities. Are students actively engaged and learning? If not, modify your opening exercises. For example, if you have sharing, structure the activity so it does not take too long. Because only one student talks at a time, the activity is largely passive. Students, particularly those at the primary level, will get restless if sharing goes on for more than a few minutes. Consider something like randomly select three students each day to spend about 1 minute sharing.

If your existing procedures for opening activities address the considerations above, there is no reason to change. If they don't, talk to other teachers about what they do first thing in the morning and how much time they take for their opening procedures.

Goal 3: Your procedures for dealing with tardiness are effective and do not cause a loss of instructional momentum.

The following procedures are geared primarily to middle schools where students transition frequently throughout the day and students are tardy when they mill around between classes.

> For students whose tardiness primarily occurs at the start of the day and is often related to parenting practices, be careful when using procedures that apply corrective consequences. If tardies occur through no fault of the student, corrective consequences for the student are inappropriate and may do more damage than good. Consider ways to work with the student and family to create productive home routines and/or alternative transportation options that allow the student to get to school on time.

A procedure for addressing tardies is effective when it:

- Ensures that students who are tardy do not disrupt class or take your attention away from teaching.
- Allows you to keep accurate records of excused and unexcused tardies.
- Lets you assign consistent corrective consequences for unexcused tardiness.

One effective procedure for dealing with tardy students is to have a three-ring binder filled with forms similar to Reproducible Form 2.1, Record of Tardies (p. 82). Place the binder on a table or shelf near the door to the classroom. Each day before students arrive, make sure that a

Reproducible 2.1 *Record of Tardies*

Record of Tardies   CHAMPS

TEACHER _____ DATE _____

Names	Excused Attach the excuse slip from the attendance office or a note from the excusing teacher.	Unexcused
1st Period _____ _____ _____	☐ ☐ ☐	☐ ☐ ☐
2nd Period _____ _____ _____	☐ ☐ ☐	☐ ☐ ☐
3rd Period _____ _____	☐ ☐	☐ ☐

new page is showing with the correct day and date filled in at the top. Attach a couple of paper clips to the page so that students with excused tardies can attach either the excuse slip from the attendance office or a note from the teacher or other school personnel who is excusing the tardy.

During the first week of school, teach your students the procedure to follow when they are tardy, whether it is excused or unexcused. Tell them they are to quietly enter the classroom without interrupting you or any students in the class. They are to go to the tardy notebook, put their name in the box for the appropriate period, indicate Excused or Unexcused, and attach the excuse if they have one. Then they can quietly go to their seat and begin participating in class activities.

When a student enters late, do not stop what you are doing. Visually monitor to make sure that the student who is tardy goes to the notebook and writes something (you can check later to make sure that the student wrote their name). If the student does not go to the notebook, provide a quiet verbal reminder: "Paul, before you sit down, put your name in the tardy notebook and indicate whether you have an excused or unexcused tardy. Now class, what I was saying was . . ."

Later in the period, when the class is engaged in independent work or cooperative groups, check the information on the tardy students in the notebook. Record the information in your grade book or records and follow any schoolwide procedures for reporting unexcused tardies to the attendance office. With excused tardies, look at the note or slip to verify accuracy. If you need to talk to a student about being tardy, do it at this time, while the rest of the class is instructionally engaged. Note that following these procedures prevents tardy students from getting attention and interrupting your lesson.

There should be corrective consequences for unexcused tardies. Most middle schools have a schoolwide tardiness policy that is managed and implemented by the administration. For example, a school's policy for tardies per semester may be:

2 unexcused tardies	=	Family notification (notification occurs for each subsequent incident)
4 unexcused tardies	=	After-school or lunch detention
6 unexcused tardies	=	Saturday school suspension or behavior contract

If your school does not have a tardy policy, develop your own and inform students about it on the first day of school. Avoid any corrective consequences that remove students from classroom instruction and activities, such as in-school suspension or timeouts in the hallway. These types of corrective actions could be rewarding for students whose tardiness is related to disliking the class or learning activities they find difficult. Removal from class can also cause students to fall further behind. A policy similar to the example above can work for you as an individual teacher, although you probably cannot assign something like an after-school detention or Saturday school without administrative approval.

PROTOCOLS FOR RESPONDING TO STUDENTS NOT PREPARED WITH MATERIALS

Goal: Your procedures deal effectively with students who do not have materials or who are not prepared to participate in the class.

To be effective, procedures for dealing with students who are not prepared should:

- Ensure that students can get needed materials in a way that does not disrupt or slow down instruction.
- Establish reasonable penalties that reduce the likelihood that students will forget materials in the future.
- Reduce the amount of time and energy that you, the teacher, spend dealing with this problem.

First, be sure to clearly communicate to students exactly what materials you expect them to have each day in your class (two sharpened pencils, a binder for science class, lined notebook paper, the science textbook, for example). This information should be communicated verbally to students and in writing to students' families as part of a syllabus or notice that goes home on the first day of school. At the end of each class period during the first week of school, remind students what materials they should have when they return to class the next day. If a student does not have access to materials (e.g., students from families living in poverty may not be able to purchase materials), work with the student and/or talk to your administrator and counselor to ensure that the student is able to get the supplies they need when

Diversity, Equity, Inclusion, and Access

Students from families living in poverty may not be able to purchase materials. Talk to your administrator and counselor about your school's processes for helping students get the supplies they need when their family is unable to provide them.

their family is unable or unwilling to provide them. In classrooms where it is anticipated that students will not have access to needed materials, work with your administrator in advance to discuss ways to have materials readily available for students who need them.

Next, develop procedures that allow students who do not bring necessary materials to get what they need to participate in the lesson. If you ask other teachers in your building how they deal with students who do not have materials, you will probably hear about a wide variety of procedures. Some teachers just give away pencils and lend books without any penalty: "I don't make an issue of it. If they need a pencil, I give them one." Other teachers impose penalties: "I think students must learn to be responsible. If they don't bring their textbook and I have to give them one repeatedly, the student owes a lunch detention." There is no one right answer. The important thing is for you to decide in advance how you will deal with this very common occurrence. If you aren't sure whether your planned procedure is fair or appropriate, ask your building administrator for feedback.

If a student simply forgot materials, consider delivering a mild consequence designed to reduce the probability that she will forget materials again. For example, you might inform students that, when possible, they should try to borrow the missing material (such as a pencil or some paper) from another student without involving you or interrupting instruction. And explain that, because borrowing materials from the teacher wastes teaching time, they will owe a short amount of time after class. Assign something like 30 seconds after class for middle school students or a minute off recess for elementary school students.

As much as possible, avoid having students go back to their lockers to get missing materials. Some schools have so many students out in the hallways to get missing materials that it becomes a supervisory and safety hazard in addition to contributing to loss of instructional time. When possible, simply provide a replacement textbook or supplies along with a mild corrective consequence. If students need to go to their lockers to get missing materials (e.g., to get work for an ongoing project), develop procedures that minimize the teaching time lost when you fill out hall passes. For example, you could inform students that if they have to return to their locker for materials after class has begun, it will count as a tardy. Tell them that you will give them a hall pass that they fill out and you sign. While the student is filling out the pass, continue with your other teaching responsibilities. Having the student fill out the pass reduces your involvement with this student from 2–3 minutes to only 30 seconds or so. Some secondary schools implement a schoolwide program titled *START on Time!* to address tardiness. One feature of this program is that teachers do not issue hall passes for the first 10 minutes of class. *START on Time!* by Randy Sprick (2017), is available from Ancora Publishing (ancorapublishing.com).

NOTE: Never let more than one student at a time leave class to go back to their lockers or to use the restroom.

> *It's important that you inform students during the first couple of days of school how you will respond if they do not have their materials.*

It's important that you inform students during the first couple of days of school how you will respond if they do not have their materials. Then, a couple of days into the first week of school, start conducting periodic spot-checks: "As you are working on the challenge problem on the board, I want to check that you came to class with the materials you need. Put your extra pencil, your notebook, and your science book on your desk. While you are working, I'll come around and check." If any students are missing one or more of the required materials, provide a gentle but firm reminder about the importance of being responsible for bringing materials every day. One procedure that can be very helpful in the first few weeks of middle school is to end each class period by having students hold up their writing utensil, then direct them to place it in a specific location (e.g., in a pencil pouch, behind your ear) before heading to their next class. Also ask students to consider what materials they may need to get from their lockers prior to heading to their next class. In this way, you help students develop routines to ensure that they arrive prepared in their next class.

After the first couple of weeks, conduct unpredictable, intermittent spot-checks of materials. Any students who do not have what they need should receive a minor corrective consequence—they lose a point from their participation grade or owe 30 seconds at the end of class, for example. Students who have all materials might receive a bonus point or be released 30 seconds early at the end of class. If you plan to do this, be sure to inform students during the first week of school that you may conduct spot-checks once or twice a week during the first few weeks of school. When a student does come unprepared to class, try not to get upset or frustrated; simply follow through consistently with your stated procedures. Remember, you should implement procedures that do not usurp too much of your time. If you start feeling frustrated because you spend too much time dealing with students who have forgotten materials, ask colleagues for ideas on how to streamline procedures so that you can keep your focus on instruction.

Procedures for When Students Return After an Absence

Goals for when students return from an absence include:

- Welcoming students back to class.
- Allowing students who were absent to find out what assignments they missed and get any handouts and returned papers without consuming much of your time and energy.

Goal 1: Welcome students who have been absent back to class.

Whenever a student returns from an absence, one goal is to ensure that the student feels welcomed back to class and that they were missed during the absence. Many students who are absent do not think people notice or care when they are absent, which can lead to increasing absenteeism across time. One simple procedure is to review the attendance record prior to each day or class to identify which students to welcome back as they enter the classroom. Say something like, "Timothy, we are so glad to have you back in class today!" or "Marnie, when you were absent yesterday we missed your contributions to our class discussion. It's good to have you in class today."

Some teachers use a more structured procedure in which students are prompted to record their own attendance upon returning to class, and the teacher and students can monitor patterns of attendance across time. For example, in one school, students in middle school keep an attendance record within each tab in their binder. Whenever a student returns from an absence, teachers prompt the student to fill out the attendance record for their class during opening activities. In this way, the teacher and student are able to see how many absences the student is accruing across the term or year, which can prompt follow-up conversations when a student's absenteeism may have an adverse impact. A good rule of thumb is that each student should attempt to have fewer than 5% of days absent in any given time period. Assuming a 180-day school year, this would be no more than 3 absences in a trimester, no more than 4 or 5 absences in a semester, and no more than 9 absences in a year.

The Importance of Regular Student Attendance

Regular student attendance is essential for helping all students succeed and for creating a positive and cohesive classroom community. If you have concerns about excessive absenteeism, many of the strategies in this book can be helpful. For example, many absenteeism problems can be prevented when educators clearly communicate the importance of attendance to students and families and use positive procedures to encourage attendance. If you would like specific guidance on how to address this issue, *The Teacher's Guide to Tackling Attendance Challenges* (available at ancorapublishing.com) is another resource written by the authors of *CHAMPS*. This book provides specific classroom-based strategies to prevent and intervene with this critical issue.

Goal 2: Students can find out what assignments they missed and get any handouts and returned papers without consuming much of your time and energy.

Set up two baskets for students to access. Keep the baskets in a permanent location—on a counter, a shelf, or your desk. One should be labeled "Absent—What You Missed" and the other, "Absent—Assignments In." Any time you give students an assignment, a handout (worksheets, reading materials, bulletins, or notices), or graded papers, put that same material in a folder for an absent student. The folder should have the date, the class period, and the student's name on it. Some teachers pair students in a buddy system. When one of the students is absent, it is the responsibility of the partner to copy any assignments, collect any handouts and graded papers, and put that material in a folder labeled with the student's name and the date. A folder should be prepared every day the student is absent and placed in the basket marked "Absent—What You Missed." Teach students that when they return after an absence, they should collect their folder or folders from the basket. This way, they find out all the tasks they must do and get any handouts they need without interrupting you.

The basket marked "Absent—Assignments In" can be used in two ways. When a student returns on Tuesday from an absence on Monday, he turns in any assignment that was due on Monday to the "Absent—Assignments In" basket. At the same time, he picks up his folder from the "Absent—What You Missed" basket. When the student completes the work assigned on Monday (the day he was absent), he turns that work into the "Absent—Assignments In" basket also.

A system like this can save you lots of time and interruptions, but it will work only if you keep the baskets up to date by checking them daily and reminding students to use them when they return from being absent.

Procedures for End of Day or End of Class Period

Goals for developing procedures for concluding the day or class period include:

- Ensuring that students organize materials and clean up the classroom.
- Reserving enough time to give students feedback.

Goal 1: Students organize their materials and complete any necessary clean-up tasks.

Allow enough time at the conclusion of the day, class period, or activity to make sure it ends on a relaxed, positive note. How much time this entails will vary. For example, in a middle school math class, 1 or 2 minutes will probably be sufficient. In a middle school art class, it may take up to 10 minutes to get all supplies put away and the room ready for the next class. Elementary teachers may need 5 to 10 minutes at the end of the day to help students get organized, make sure the room is clean, and make last-minute announcements. If you find that you sometimes lose track of time and the end of the day, class, or activity feels especially rushed or chaotic, set an unobtrusive reminder on your phone, computer, or other device at the time when you would like to transition into closing activities.

At the beginning of the year, elementary teachers especially should plan to allow more time than they think is necessary for wrapping up. Remember that during the first week of school, you may have to take time to help students figure out which bus to take, where their family is going to pick them up, and so on. If the wrap-up and cleanup take less time than you scheduled, you can always use the extra couple of minutes for a discussion, a song, or a word game.

Goal 2: Procedures provide you with enough time to give students both positive and corrective feedback.

When students finish organizing and cleaning up, give the class as a whole feedback on things they are doing well and also on the behaviors and skills that may require more effort on their part. This is especially important during the first 6 weeks of school, but it is also useful intermittently throughout the school year.

> *Class, I want to let you know that the way you have been using class time demonstrates a high level of responsibility. We should be very proud of how well we are all functioning as a group. One thing that a few people need to manage more effectively is remembering homework. Tomorrow, you have a math assignment and a science assignment due. Make a decision right now about when you are going to work on those assignments—this afternoon or this evening. I expect to see two completed homework assignments from each of you. (Bell rings.) Thanks for a good day today. Have a nice evening. You are all excused to go.*

DISMISSAL

Goal: Students do not leave the classroom until you dismiss them. The bell is not a dismissal signal.

On the first day of school and periodically thereafter, remind your students that they are not to leave their seats until you dismiss them. Explain that the bell is a signal to you—you will excuse the class when they are reasonably quiet and when all wrap-up tasks are completed. If you let students bolt for the door when the bell rings, it sets a precedent that your instructional control ends when the bell rings. By reserving the right to excuse the class, you can make judgments about whether you should excuse the whole class at once or by rows or table clusters. As a general rule, primary students should be excused by rows or clusters, and older students can be excused as a class. However, let the older students know that if they rush out of the room or crowd the door, you will start excusing them in a more structured way.

> **"**
> *The beginning and ending of the day or class period play a major role in setting the climate of the classroom.*
> **"**

In summary, the beginning and ending of the day or class period play a major role in setting the climate of the classroom. Opening and dismissal routines that are welcoming, calm, efficient, and purposeful demonstrate to students that you are pleased to see them and that you care so much about class time that not a minute will be wasted.

UPDATE YOUR CLASSROOM MANAGEMENT PLAN

ITEM 4: BEGINNING AND ENDING ROUTINES

Describe your beginning and ending routines. Double-check that your procedures are designed in a such a way that you increase the likelihood students meet the goal listed for each routine. Describe your classroom routines for:

- **How students will enter the room.**
  Goal: Students feel welcome and immediately go to their seats and start on a productive task.

- **How you will conduct opening activities.**
  Goal 1: Opening activities are efficient and orderly, and keep students instructionally engaged while you take attendance.
  Goal 2: Announcements and other housekeeping tasks do not take up too much time.
  Goal 3: Procedures for dealing with tardiness are effective and do not cause a loss of instructional momentum.

- **Responding to students who come to class without necessary materials.**
  Goal: Your procedures deal effectively with students who do not have materials or who are not prepared to participate in the class.

- **When students return from an absence.**
  Goal 1: Students who have been absent are welcomed back to class.
  Goal 2: Students can find out what assignments they missed and get any handouts and returned papers without consuming much of your time and energy.

- **Wrapping up the end of day/class.**
  Goal 1: Students organize their materials and complete any necessary clean-up tasks.
  Goal 2: Procedures provide you with enough time to give students both positive and corrective feedback.

- **Dismissal.** *Goal:* Students do not leave the classroom until you dismiss them. The bell is not a dismissal signal.

TASK 6

Design Procedures for Managing Common Transitions

Define clear behavioral expectations for all common transitions that occur within your class.

• • • • •

Transitions from one activity or location in the classroom or school are frequently problematic times for student behavior. Imagine the following scenario:

As students wrap up a classroom activity, Mrs. Walters tells them it is time to transition to their independent reading activities. Student folders with books are lined up along the side of the wall on top of a bookshelf. The teacher directs her 32 students to get their materials and get to work, and most student begin moving toward the bookshelf. With all students expected to get up at once to gather materials, some students hang back because they know they can't immediately reach their books because of the crowd. These students socialize as they wait. There is jostling as some students grab their materials and then have to push through other waiting students on the way back to their desks. Once students get their materials, some remain standing and continue to socialize until everyone is able to get their materials. The transition takes approximately 5 minutes for everyone to get settled and begin working.

Poorly managed transitions are troublesome because of their potential for student misbehavior and because they end up consuming valuable instructional time (Arlin, 1979; Barbetta et al., 2005; Brophy & Good, 1986; Hofmeister & Lubke, 1990; Martella et al., 2003; Olive, 2004). Transitions may be particularly challenging for some students, including students with disabilities, who may lack skills to transition between activities, and students who have experienced trauma, who may struggle if transitions are unpredictable (Buck, 1999; Souers & Hall, 2016).

> " *Poorly managed transitions are troublesome because of their potential for student misbehavior and they end up consuming valuable instructional time.* "

One type of transition is when students move from one task to another during an activity. For example, math lessons may start with teacher-directed instruction, then students get out their math books and work on several problems as a class, guided by the teacher. Or a transition may occur from one activity to another—for example, when moving from whole class instruction into cooperative groups. When you clearly define and communicate your expectations for transitions, you will have well-managed and efficient transitions.

It is important to recognize that no two teachers have exactly the same set of expectations for their classrooms. Some teachers may indicate that students can talk quietly to one another when lining up or getting materials. Others may indicate that students should be silent during these activities so they remain focused on the goal of getting to the next location or activity. Therefore, specifically defining your expectations is essential if you hope to have a positive and productive classroom.

That is why this task and Task 2 in Chapter 3 are designed to help you define your specific behavioral expectations for students during common transitions and major classroom activities.

Why should I have to teach expectations? Students should just know how to behave in the classroom. Teachers may mistakenly conclude that the teaching of expectations is not really necessary for three reasons. First, an experienced teacher may have such a clear vision of how her classroom should operate that she may not even realize that her room is a unique and idiosyncratic mix of rules, expectations, routines, policies, and procedures. She may, perhaps unconsciously, think that the way she does things is just the logical way all classrooms should operate, and she may not realize how complex her room actually is. "Why should I have to teach the obvious?" she reasons. What this teacher fails to realize is that her familiarity with this complex mix of procedures and routines is based on years of inventing and shaping it, teaching and living with it. However, this mix—this complex world of Room 19—is brand new to students. It's a world they have never experienced before, and they have no preconceived ideas about how to function in it.

The second reason is that teachers—both veteran and new teachers—think that the older the students are, the more they should know how to behave in the classroom. In other words, first graders may need instruction in behavior, but by the sixth grade, students should not need any: "These students have been in school for 7 years. They should already know how to behave. Why should I have to teach them?" While at first glance this statement seems reasonable, the argument against this assumption is much the same as the one above—every classroom is unique. A sixth-grade student has probably experienced at least one teacher with a low tolerance for noise and movement and one with high tolerance, at least one teacher who lets students sharpen their pencils whenever they want and one who requires students to ask permission. In fact, the older students get, the less they know about your unique mix of rules, expectations, routines, and procedures.

The third reason teachers may think that teaching expectations is unnecessary is that they feel many behavioral expectations should be taught at home. However, many teachers quickly learn that children do not necessarily learn the behaviors they need for the classroom at home. In her book *A Framework for Understanding Poverty*, Ruby Payne (2018) insists that educators must have a clear understanding of the hidden rules in any setting. These rules are the unspoken cues and habits of a group and do not necessarily coincide with expectations for students at schools. It is important to understand that each set of rules allows students to be successful in that particular environment, so it is not necessarily a matter of *unlearning* previously learned rules. More importantly, students need to learn how to nimbly shift between environments where different rules are in operation so that they can thrive in any circumstances they may encounter. A term sometimes used for this phenomenon is *code switching*.

Plan to teach students the behaviors necessary to be successful in the school setting, regardless of previous learning or conflicting home or community expectations and without disrespecting student and family backgrounds, values, or beliefs. Understanding the hidden rules that occur in a school and classroom environment will allow teachers to promote successful behaviors among students by directly teaching them all the behavioral expectations that are necessary for success at school. When behavioral expectations differ between school and home or community, it is important to explicitly teach the differences (i.e., code switching) and the rationale for the expectation at school. Avoid labeling behaviors that are inappropriate in school as "wrong" because they may be appropriate in other settings. This information is particularly crucial

Diversity, Equity, Inclusion, and Access

Students come to school with habits and rules they have learned for how to be successful in different environments. While these may not coincide with your classroom expectations, do not label these differences as bad or wrong. Be explicit in teaching students and providing rationale for how to be successful in your classroom.

when working with students and families in poverty situations or who come from different cultural backgrounds than your own.

Remember that your classroom expectations are unique. Your classroom is no less complex than a basketball team. As coaches know, if you want a team to be successful, you have to teach and practice over and over to mastery. This chapter and the next will help you recognize the complexity of your expectations and help you set up a plan to teach the individuals in your class to function successfully as a team.

Be aware that your expectations for student behavior will be different for each major type of instructional activity and transition. For example, your expectations for conversation (whether students can talk or not) in cooperative group activities are probably very different from your expectations for conversation when you are giving a test. During some transitions, you may be OK with students talking to one another, but in others you may prefer that they don't talk so they can focus on transitioning as quickly as possible. Part of the rationale for clearly defining and then teaching behavioral expectations for each major transition and activity relates to the sheer number of idiosyncratic expectations students encounter in the school! If you were to follow a student throughout the day, it is feasible that the student may encounter anywhere from 25 to over 100 different types of behavioral expectations as they move through different settings and activities.

Identify Common Transitions That Occur in Your Classroom

The first step in defining your behavioral expectations for all common transitions is to make a list of the major types of transitions that your students will engage in daily (or on a regular basis). Common transition times include switching from one subject to another, getting textbooks open to a particular page, and trading papers for correction. Use Reproducible 2.2, CHAMPS Transitions List (not shown) to list transitions. Be sure to identify all the specific transitions and categories of transitions for which you will have different behavioral expectations. A list of transitions might include the following:

- Before the bell rings
- Getting out paper and pencils
- Getting a book and opening to a particular page
- Moving to and from a small group location
- Students leaving and entering the classroom (e.g., grade-level teachers grouping across classes for math instruction or students who leave the room for counseling groups or specially designed instructional groups)
- Putting things away (clearing desks)
- Handing in work (e.g., after an in-class assignment or quiz)
- Trading papers for corrections
- Cleaning up after project activities
- Moving as a class to a different, specific location (e.g., library or playground)
- Handing things out (e.g., an assignment sheet or art supplies)
- Opening and dismissal routines (expectations for these transitions were discussed in the previous task)

> *An elementary school teacher who has the same group of students all day will probably have more variety in types of transitions throughout the day than does a middle school teacher.*

Consider Level of Support When Designing CHAMPS Expectations for Transitions

When defining your behavioral expectations, pay close attention to the level of support your students need, and pay careful consideration to structural elements. Remember that structure refers to the level of organization, orchestration, and predictability created by the teacher. The more support your class requires, the more specific and tightly orchestrated you need to make your expectations for transitions. For a low-support class, you probably don't need to specify the routes for students to take to the small-group instruction area. On the other hand, for students who need high support, you should include the expectation that students take the most direct route and that they keep their hands, feet, and objects to themselves so they do not disturb students who are working at their seats (Evertson et al., 2003; Jenson et al., 2020; Jones & Jones, 2007; Shores et al., 1993; Stichter et al., 2004).

In classes that need high support or that are especially large, work to reduce the number of students who are moving at the same time during transitions. It would be preferable to have one student from each cluster or row gather materials for their group while the other students work on a task than to have the whole class move at once. However, for a class with a low need for support, you might allow more students to move at one time as long as they can do so efficiently and without interrupting the instructional momentum of the class.

Also keep in mind that it's always easier to lessen highly structured procedures (gradually!) than to try to implement more structure because students are making bad choices. If students need high structure, it is probably advisable to limit student-to-student talking during transitions at the beginning of the year. However, 2 or 3 weeks into the year, after you've had a chance to see how the students behave, you might revise your expectations. "Class, starting today, once you've lined up at the door, you can have a quiet conversation with the person directly in front of you or behind you until I call for attention to give the next direction."

Clarify Expectations for Voice Levels

One strategy that makes the whole CHAMPS process more efficient is to develop voice levels. This allows you to specify, as part of a clarifying conversation, the voice level students are expected to use during a particular activity.

Below is a sample way to define voice levels using a numbered scale:

0 = **No sound/No talking**
Examples: Taking a test, listening to a concert
1 = **Whisper** (no vocal cords)
Example: Asking another student a question during an independent work time in which conversation is allowed
2 = **Quiet conversational voice** (only people near you can hear)
Examples: Two or three students walking down the hall, four students working in a cooperative group

> **3 = Presentational voice** (an entire class can hear you)
> *Examples: A student giving a report, a teacher teaching a class*
>
> **4 = Outside voice** (you can be heard across a playing field)
> *Example: Cheering at a football game*

Of course, you should modify this list to suit your style. If you are going to use voice levels, plan to make and post a chart that students can easily see from anywhere in the room. Then as you transition into an activity, you can specify to students that the activity is an independent work period, for example, and your voice level expectation is 1. Students can look at your chart and know what is expected.

As you consider what voice level may be appropriate for a particular transition, consider whether students need to talk during the transition and, if so, about what. This relates to the next consideration, which is the amount of time the transition should reasonably take. When students are given permission to talk throughout transitions, it can significantly increase the length of time it takes for them to reach the desired outcome of the transition, especially if you have highly distractible students. You may also have increased concerns with peer conflict or bullying behaviors, as it can be difficult to monitor all peer interactions during transitions that require movement from all students in the room. However, in some transitions, such as cleaning up materials at the end of the day, student talk may be acceptable if the voice level is manageable and students can complete the transition in a reasonable amount of time (see the next item below).

Consider Time to Transition

For each transition, think carefully about how long the transition should reasonably take. While maintaining positive behavior is one major goal associated with your CHAMPS expectations for transitions, an equally important goal is ensuring that transitions do not take up valuable instructional time. Studies on transition time have documented that students may experience as many as 15–20 transitions between activities each day that can collectively consume up to 70 minutes of instructional time (Olive, 2004). If you can design transitions to be as efficient as possible, you can free up additional instructional time or time for other activities designed to strengthen classroom community.

You may have a group of students who are responsible enough to handle the low-structure routine of all students moving at one time to get needed materials. However, if you have more than 15 students in a class, having all students move to get needed materials may likely take several minutes, especially if materials are all located in one part of the room (e.g., a bookcase, art cabinet, computer cart). If a procedure is likely to take up valuable instructional time when conducted with lower structure, consider using higher structure for that particular transition to ensure that it is performed efficiently. For example, while you continue to teach or students work on small group, partner, or independent work, have a "materials manager" who is finished with the work or who needs a bit of a movement break pass out the materials for each student or group. By using this procedure, no instructional time is lost in the transition.

If you are uncertain how long a transition should take, talk with colleagues about how long a procedure takes with their most responsible group of students. For example, you might ask how long it takes their most responsible group of students to line up, hand in work, or get to carpet or lab stations. If a colleague reports a transition time that sounds much quicker than you can envision with your current procedures, ask if they would be willing to share their procedures with you. They could record a video of the transition, or you could find a time to come and observe the class performing the transition if the other teacher is willing.

Complete Planning Forms to Clearly Outline Your CHAMPS Expectations for Common Transitions

The foundation for defining your behavioral expectations is the CHAMPS acronym, which reflects the major issues that affect student behavior. The issues incorporated in CHAMPS and the basic questions to be addressed for each issue are:

C	**Conversation**	*Can students talk to each other?* *If so, about what, and how loudly?*
H	**Help**	*How do students get their questions answered?* *How do they get your attention?*
A	**Activity**	*What is the task or objective?* *What is the end product?*
M	**Movement**	*Can students move about?*
P	**Participation**	*What does the expected student behavior look and sound like?* *How do students show they are fully participating?*
S	**Success**	*Success comes from following CHAMPS expectations. Or, S can stand for Special Considerations—any expectations that do not fit into other categories.*

Reproducible 2.3 is a template of a CHAMPS Transition Worksheet. Download the form and print multiple copies. Then document your behavioral expectations by filling out one worksheet for each major type of transition you identified on the Classroom Transitions List (Reproducible 2.2). These worksheets use the CHAMPS acronym as your guide to defining the important issues for students. See pages 95–100 for samples of CHAMPS Transition Worksheets for lining up and getting needed materials in low-, medium-, and high-support classrooms.

Remember, details are important. The more specific you are in your own mind about what you expect from students, the more clearly you will communicate your expectations to your students. In addition, the more specific your expectations are, the more consistent you are likely to be in enforcing them (Barbetta et al., 2005) and in acknowledging students when they meet your expectations. The completed worksheets will provide the content for your lessons about your behavioral expectations. Specific information on teaching your expectations is covered in Chapter 4.

Reproducible 2.3 *CHAMPS Transition Worksheet (Example A)*

CHAMPS Transition Worksheet

CHAMPS

A
Lining Up,
High Support

TRANSITION __*Fifth grade lining up (high support)*__

CONVERSATION

Can students engage in conversations with each other during this transition?   *No*   Voice level: *0*

If yes, clarify how (so that they are keeping their attention on completing the transition).

Students should line up silently and wait without talking.

HELP

How do students get questions answered? How do students get your attention?

Raise hand silently to ask a question before I give the transition signal or once in line. No questions while moving to line up.

If students have to wait for help, what should they do while they wait?

ACTIVITY

Explain the transition. What will be different afterward (e.g., change in location, use of different materials)? Include time criteria (how long it should take).

Students will go from any location in the classroom to lined up in front of the door (45 seconds or less).

MOVEMENT

Does the transition involve movement? *Yes*   If yes, what kind of movement is allowed for the transition?

Movement from current location to line in front of door.

Can students get out of their seats during this transition for any other reason (e.g., to get a drink or sharpen a pencil)?

Students will be released by rows when I see their desk space is clean. I will ask each row if any students need to get anything (e.g., coat, pencil, lunch) before they line up. Students should only move to another location with permission.

PARTICIPATION

What behaviors show that students are participating in the transition fully and responsibly?

Waiting patiently in seat until row is cued to move. Lined up quickly and silently. Waiting patiently in line for the rest of the class to line up. Keeping hands and feet to self. Ready with needed materials for the activity outside of the classroom (e.g., coat, pencil, lunch box, etc.).

What behaviors show that a student is not participating appropriately in the transition?

Moving before row is released, talking, pushing, rushing to get in line, whining about where they are in line.

SUCCESS

Success comes from following the expectations.

REPRODUCIBLE 2.3

Reproducible 2.3 *CHAMPS Transition Worksheet (Example B)*

CHAMPS Transition Worksheet

CHAMPS

B
Lining Up,
Medium Support

TRANSITION ___*Fifth grade lining up (medium support)*___

CONVERSATION

Can students engage in conversations with each other during this transition? **Yes**   Voice level: **2**
If yes, clarify how (so that they are keeping their attention on completing the transition).
Students should line up silently. Once they are in line, they can talk in a quiet conversational voice to the person in front or behind them until I give the attention signal. They can talk about any school-appropriate topics.

HELP

How do students get questions answered? How do students get your attention?
Raise hand to ask a question before I give the transition signal or once in line. No questions while moving to line up.

If students have to wait for help, what should they do while they wait?

ACTIVITY

Explain the transition. What will be different afterward (e.g., change in location, use of different materials)? Include time criteria (how long it should take).

Students will go from any location in the classroom to lined up in front of the door (45 seconds or less).

MOVEMENT

Does the transition involve movement? **Yes**   If yes, what kind of movement is allowed for the transition?

Movement from current location to line in front of door.

Can students get out of their seats during this transition for any other reason (e.g., to get a drink or sharpen a pencil)?

Students will have the opportunity to get what they need (e.g., sharpen pencil) before we give the signal to line up. No movement to other locations should occur after the signal is given to line up.

PARTICIPATION

What behaviors show that students are participating in the transition fully and responsibly?
Lining up quickly and silently. Talking to the person right next to them about school-appropriate topics. Ready with needed materials for the activity outside of the classroom (e.g., coat, pencil, lunch box, etc.).

What behaviors show that a student is not participating appropriately in the transition?
Running, talking while lining up, talking to people beyond their immediate neighbor, pushing, blurting out questions, taking longer than 45 seconds to line up.

SUCCESS

Success comes from following the expectations.

REPRODUCIBLE 2.3

Reproducible 2.3 *CHAMPS Transition Worksheet (Example C)*

CHAMPS Transition Worksheet

CHAMPS

C
Lining Up,
Low Support

TRANSITION ___*Fifth grade lining up (low support)*___

Conversation

Can students engage in conversations with each other during this transition? **Yes.**   Voice level: **2**
If yes, clarify how (so that they are keeping their attention on completing the transition).
Students can talk in a quiet conversational voice until I give the attention signal. They can talk about any school-appropriate topics.

Help

How do students get questions answered? How do students get your attention?
Students can come to my location to ask their question.

If students have to wait for help, what should they do while they wait?

Activity

Explain the transition. What will be different afterward (e.g., change in location, use of different materials)? Include time criteria (how long it should take).
Students will go from any location in the classroom to lined up in front of the door. Lining up should not take more than one minute.

Movement

Does the transition involve movement? **Yes**   If yes, what kind of movement is allowed for the transition?
Movement from current location to line in front of door.

Can students get out of their seats during this transition for any other reason (e.g., to get a drink or sharpen a pencil)?
Students can get what they need in the classroom if it is necessary for the activity after the transition (e.g., If they need to sharpen a pencil for their specials class, they can do so. If they need to grab their lunch, they can grab it). They should do so quickly and line up.

Participation

What behaviors show that students are participating in the transition fully and responsibly?
Lining up quickly without dawdling. Walking and keeping hands to self. Talking in a quiet voice while waiting.

What behaviors show that a student is not participating appropriately in the transition?
Running, pushing, inappropriate language or comments.

Success

Success comes from following the expectations.

REPRODUCIBLE 2.3

Reproducible 2.3 *CHAMPS Transition Worksheet (Example D)*

CHAMPS Transition Worksheet

CHAMPS **D**
Getting Materials,
High Support

TRANSITION *Third grade getting needed materials (high support)*

CONVERSATION

Can students engage in conversations with each other during this transition? **No** Voice level: **0**
If yes, clarify how (so that they are keeping their attention on completing the transition).
Students at desks should be working on independent work, partner, or small group task. They should follow expectations. Row leader will silently give each member their materials while others are working.

HELP

How do students get questions answered? How do students get your attention? *Students at desks turn up "Help" sign on their desk and keep working. Row leader raises hand to ask question if out of seat.*

If students have to wait for help, what should they do while they wait?

ACTIVITY

Explain the transition. What will be different afterward (e.g., change in location, use of different materials)? Include time criteria (how long it should take). *Students will have needed materials for the next activity. Transition time will be specific for each instance—some will be less than 30 seconds (e.g., getting bucket of student folders) while others might take group leaders multiple trips and take slightly longer.*

MOVEMENT

Does the transition involve movement? **No** If yes, what kind of movement is allowed for the transition? *Students who are not the row leader should not move for any reason.*

Can students get out of their seats during this transition for any other reason (e.g., to get a drink or sharpen a pencil)?
Row leaders should not go elsewhere during the transition. If they need something unrelated to the transition, they can wait for the next activity.

PARTICIPATION

What behaviors show that students are participating in the transition fully and responsibly?

Students at seats continuing to work on current task (no talking unless it is expected for the current activity). Row leaders walking straight to needed materials and back to their group without talking to others. Row leaders get all materials specified on the board for each group member.

What behaviors show that a student is not participating appropriately in the transition?

Students who are not line leaders out of seat. Talking to others outside of the assigned activity. Row leaders withholding materials from peers. Row leaders going to other locations or talking during the transition.

SUCCESS

Success comes from following the expectations.

© 2021 Ancora Publishing

REPRODUCIBLE 2.3

Reproducible 2.3 *CHAMPS Transition Worksheet (Example E)*

CHAMPS Transition Worksheet

CHAMPS

E
Getting Materials,
Medium Support

TRANSITION *Third grade getting needed materials (medium support)*

CONVERSATION

Can students engage in conversations with each other during this transition? *No*   Voice level: *0*

If yes, clarify how (so that they are keeping their attention on completing the transition). *Students will be released by clusters, two at a time, to get needed materials. Teacher will release groups that are working appropriately. Other students should be working quietly on a task at their seats. While getting materials, 0 voice level.*

HELP

How do students get questions answered? How do students get your attention? *Students raise hands at their desks. If they cannot find materials or have a question while out of desk, they should return to their desk, raise hand, and wait to be called on.*

If students have to wait for help, what should they do while they wait?

ACTIVITY

Explain the transition. What will be different afterward (e.g., change in location, use of different materials)? Include time criteria (how long it should take). *Students will have needed materials for the next activity. Each cluster should take no more than 30 seconds to get materials to get back to their seats. Total transition takes no more than 2 minutes, and other students are working while their group is not out of their seats.*

MOVEMENT

Does the transition involve movement? *Yes*   If yes, what kind of movement is allowed for the transition? *Students can ask for permission while other clusters are getting materials for restroom, drink, pencil sharpened.*

Can students get out of their seats during this transition for any other reason (e.g., to get a drink or sharpen a pencil)?

While getting materials, students should not go elsewhere. They should ask for permission when in their seats.

PARTICIPATION

What behaviors show that students are participating in the transition fully and responsibly?

Students at seats continuing to work on current task. Clusters given permission should walk straight to needed materials and back to their group without talking to others. Keep hands and feet to self. Get all materials on board for yourself.

What behaviors show that a student is not participating appropriately in the transition?

Students not in current cluster are out of seat without permission. Talking to others outside of the assigned activity. Clusters getting materials going to other parts of the classroom or talking to peers.

SUCCESS

Success comes from following the expectations.

REPRODUCIBLE 2.3

Reproducible 2.3 *CHAMPS Transition Worksheet (Example F)*

CHAMPS Transition Worksheet

CHAMPS

F
Getting Materials,
Low Support

TRANSITION *Third grade getting needed materials (low support)*

CONVERSATION

Can students engage in conversations with each other during this transition?   **Yes**   Voice level: *I*
If yes, clarify how (so that they are keeping their attention on completing the transition).

Students can talk quietly (whisper voice) to peers while transitioning as long as they are still completing transition expectations.

HELP

How do students get questions answered? How do students get your attention?

Students raise hands to get help. If out of desk, stand in one place with hand raised and wait until called on.

If students have to wait for help, what should they do while they wait?

ACTIVITY

Explain the transition. What will be different afterward (e.g., change in location, use of different materials)? Include time criteria (how long it should take).

Students will have needed materials for the next activity. Students will be released at the same time to get materials. Transition should take no more than 90 seconds.

MOVEMENT

Does the transition involve movement? **Yes**   If yes, what kind of movement is allowed for the transition? *Students can sharpen pencil or get a drink without permission. For restroom, wait until next activity.*

Can students get out of their seats during this transition for any other reason (e.g., to get a drink or sharpen a pencil)?
Yes (pencil, drink).

PARTICIPATION

What behaviors show that students are participating in the transition fully and responsibly?

Moving quickly to get needed materials and back to seat.

What behaviors show that a student is not participating appropriately in the transition?

Dawdling, not getting materials, shouting or talking loudly to peers, distracting others, misusing materials.

SUCCESS

Success comes from following the expectations.

REPRODUCIBLE 2.3

UPDATE YOUR CLASSROOM MANAGEMENT PLAN

ITEM 5: CHAMPS EXPECTATIONS FOR CLASSROOM ACTIVITIES AND TRANSITIONS

- Use CHAMPS Transition List (Reproducible 2.2) to list the common transitions that occur in your classroom.
- Once you have completed CHAMPS Transition Worksheets (Reproducible 2.3) for each transition on your list, attach them or include them in a binder with a paper record of your Classroom Management Plan, and/or include the filled-out digital versions in a file that contains your Classroom Management Plan.

TASK 7

Prepare for Common Areas and Special Circumstances

Identify expectations for student behavior in all common areas and for circumstances like assemblies and substitutes.

Students need to know behavioral expectations for common areas such as hallways, cafeteria, playground, bus waiting areas, and buses, as well as for special circumstances like assemblies and substitutes.

Know Your School's Expectations for Common Areas

If your school has clearly defined behavioral expectations for common areas, ensure that you carefully review the handbook or other material where these expectations are archived prior to the first day of school. In some schools, expectations will be taught during some sort of fair or by other personnel like the counselor and principal. In other schools, you may be responsible for teaching lessons about expectations in these areas. Even if you are not directly responsible for teaching lessons on behavior in common areas, you should be prepared to answer student questions if they arise and provide periodic reminders about expected behavior to students prior to their entering a common area or situation.

If your school has not clarified schoolwide expectations for common areas, including hallways, cafeteria, restrooms, playground, bus loading areas, and buses, ask your principal what you should teach your students about responsible behavior in these settings. See Chapter 4, Task 4 for ideas for teaching common area expectations to students.

Know Your School's Emergency Procedures

Your building should have a defined set of procedures for responding in the event of an emergency, whether that involves a natural disaster (e.g., earthquake, tornado), human-caused threat (e.g., active shooter, bomb threat), or other hazard (e.g., gas leak, fire). A school emergency operations plan (EOP) will specify conditions for when the plan will be activated and describe the actions that students, teachers, and school staff should take before, during, and after emergency events. If your building doesn't yet have a comprehensive school EOP, ask your principal what you should know and communicate to your students about appropriate behavior in these situations.

Classroom teachers need to comply with these emergency plans. To prepare for this:

- Review all school emergency operations plans prior to the first day of school. Make sure you know where evacuation and assembly sites are located, your role and responsibility in each type of emergency, and procedures for ensuring the safety of students. Periodically review these plans throughout the year to ensure that you remember all expected procedures and can automatically follow them in case of an emergency.
- Consider provisions for students with disabilities, visual and hearing impairments, and physical limitations. You may need to identify alternative evacuation routes and shelter for students with limited mobility, or assign a buddy for each student with a disability.
- Consider how to make sure that all students will understand emergency procedures, paying extra attention to students with limited English proficiency.

Prior to scheduled emergency drills, teach expectations for these scenarios with your students. After emergency drills, provide feedback about how well students complied with these expectations and what to work on next time. If your school doesn't have scheduled emergency drills, plan to set aside some time at the beginning of the year to teach expectations and practice procedures for calmly and responsibly responding in the event of different types of emergencies.

Diversity, Equity, Inclusion, and Access

Carefully consider provisions and teaching plans for students with disabilities, visual and hearing impairments, physical limitations, and students with limited English proficiency. As needed, work with your administrator and other service providers to determine appropriate plans.

Prepare Expectations for Upcoming Assemblies

When preparing for assemblies, you will need to clarify how students are expected to line up and enter the assembly, where they will sit during the assembly, where you will sit with your students, and how they will exit. Assemblies are often boisterous and noisy and can lead to highly inappropriate behavior if students are not given clear parameters. Carefully consider the level of support your students need. For classes that require higher support, increase the structure by designing a seating arrangement to ensure that students are successful. For example, separate students who have a high probability of distracting one another. It may be beneficial to fill out a CHAMPS Transition Worksheet (Reproducible 2.3) for entering and exiting the assembly and a CHAMPS Activity Worksheet (Reproducible 3.2) for student behavior during the assembly. For classes that do well with lower support, you can provide less direct orchestration, but still plan to clearly teach your expectations for what student behavior will look and sound like during the assembly. A looks like/sounds like T-chart or discussion about expected behaviors is probably sufficient for students who are generally mature and responsible.

Ensure that you also have a clear plan for quickly gaining student attention during the assembly and during transitions to and from the assembly. If your school uses a schoolwide attention signal—for example, all students know a common signal that is used to gain their attention out on the playground—review and practice this with your students frequently in the week before any assembly. If you school does not have a common attention signal, determine whether your classroom signal will work or whether you need to adapt it or adopt a new one prior to the assembly. For example, using a gong to gain student attention would not be appropriate in an assembly, so design and teach another signal well in advance of your first assembly.

Prepare a Plan for Working With Substitutes

Student behavior is notoriously problematic with substitute teachers, and one study found that students spend up to 5%–10% of the school year with substitute teachers (Varlas, 2001; Vorell, 2011). Many factors can contribute to problematic behavior with substitutes, including disruption to normal routines and different instructional or engagement practices. Some students who have experienced trauma, have behavioral or academic concerns, or are highly anxious may lack a sense of safety with a new adult. Some students may simply be willing to test limits in ways they would not with their usual teacher. Many substitutes have received limited or no training in behavior management techniques, so their responses to student misbehavior may not be terribly effective.

Because all teachers are likely to have absences at some point during the year, it is important to create a plan in advance of when you need a substitute. Your plan should address as many of the procedural and behavioral elements of your classroom as possible. Create a folder that includes a completed copy of your current completed Classroom Management Plan with visuals depicting your CHAMPS expectations for all common classroom activities and transitions. Take pictures of your CHAMPS displays (see Chapter 4 for how to create visual displays of CHAMPS expectations) or use your filled-out CHAMPS Activity and CHAMPS Transition Worksheets. Direct substitutes to follow your CHAMPS expectations for activities and transitions that occur on any day you are absent. This continuity will help many students make better behavioral decisions because they are following the same routines and expectations in your classroom even when you are not present. Your school may have required items that go in a subfolder, such as what to do in case of a lockdown, fire, or other emergency, so include any required items and other information that a substitute needs to know.

If you use an assigned seating chart, consider attaching pictures of each cluster or row to the seating chart, or include student pictures directly on the seating chart so that the substitute can monitor that students are in the correct place. If you do not regularly use a seating chart, it may be beneficial to use assigned seats whenever there is a substitute to create additional structure on those days, especially if you know students tend to behave worse when a substitute is present. If you do so, it may be worthwhile to create a seating chart in advance to use as needed throughout the term or year. Have students periodically practice going to their assigned seat so that they know exactly where to go whenever a substitute is present.

Teachers must take care of their own mental and physical health, and this does periodically require absences from school. However, a temporary teacher can never replace you in terms of knowing your students and the sequence of skills and competencies you build within units of instruction, so it is important to be in school with your students whenever possible. In fact, higher rates of teacher absenteeism are related to lower levels of student performance and increased rates of student absenteeism (Cantrell, 2003; Lee et al., 2015; Miller, 2012).

In summary, prepare plans ahead of time for any common areas and special circumstances that are likely to arise in your classroom. While the Classroom Management Plan does not include designated spaces for common areas, assemblies, or your plans for working with substitutes, you may wish to include a written plan or any documentation for these circumstances in the binder or electronic file that contains your completed Classroom Management Plan.

TASK 8

Establish and Maintain Family Contact

Build positive relationships with your students' families by making initial contact with them at the beginning of the year and maintaining regular contact throughout the year.

• • • • •

There is no question that when school personnel and families work together to help meet the educational needs of students, the probability of effectively educating those students increases tremendously (Esler et al., 2008; Freer & Watson, 1999; Gortmaker et al., 2004; Henderson & Mapp, 2002; Keith et al., 1998; Rones & Hoagwood, 2000; Sheridan et al., 1996). Part of your classroom vision should have your class be a place where you, your students, and your students' families work collaboratively to ensure student success. Building the positive relationships necessary to work collaboratively with families, however, is not always easy. First of all, it requires communication, which takes time—and time can be a problem for both teachers and families. This task will look at how to deliver communication that is helpful, timely, but also manageable for both the teacher and the families.

Making the effort to communicate with your students' families sends a powerful message that you want to include them in what happens at school. In addition, such efforts increase the probability that an

More students than ever live in one-parent households, in foster care, with grandparents, and in other circumstances. It is often inaccurate to refer to the student's parents, and it is cumbersome to continually refer to the student's parent(s), grandparent(s), or guardian(s). Therefore, in most cases the term student's family will be used when referring to a student's primary caregivers.

individual student's family will be receptive should you need to inform them about and enlist their assistance in addressing a behavioral or academic problem (Christenson & Godber, 2001; Miller & Kraft, 2008; Phelan et al., 1994). (Specific information on how to work with families when behavior problems occur appears in Chapter 8, Task 5.) Families should not feel like teachers and the school communicate only when their child is doing something wrong. The more a teacher must communicate with a family about problems at school, the more effort needs to be put into frequent communication for positive things students are doing. The important thing is for families to understand that you see their students as more than just their behavioral problems or academic concerns. Develop a specific plan for making initial contact with students' families at the beginning of the school year and maintaining contact with them throughout the year. A family contact plan increases the likelihood of communicating efficiently and effectively with your students' families.

Understanding Two-Way Communication

As you develop a plan for building and maintaining productive communication with students' families, it is important to understand the distinction between one- and two-way communication. In some schools and classrooms, communication is primarily one sided, with schools providing information to families in a way that does not actively invite their input or participation. The information is presented in an authoritative manner, and parents are treated as passive receivers of this information. Two-way communication, in contrast, treats parents as equals in the collaborative process of educating students. While teachers may have beneficial information about things that can help a student be successful, correspondence is presented in a way that consciously invites parents to bring their questions or provide additional ideas or insights that might be beneficial. Educators actively work to seek feedback and build positive relationships with parents. Throughout CHAMPS, we will provide ideas for ways to strengthen two-way communication.

Positive family contacts are especially important when you have a large number of students with high needs. Unfortunately, the families of these students may be more likely to feel alienated from the school, and some of the students may come from troubled homes. Because it's also possible that contacts will be more difficult to achieve with families of students that have high needs, remember that the greater the needs of your students, the greater the need for you to establish and maintain positive contact with their families.

Many schools have websites that allow you to post class information and assignments. Students and families can find teachers' e-mail addresses and phone numbers as well as general school information. In some schools, e-mail is the most common form of communication between families and teachers. However, you can't be sure that all of your students' families have access to a computer or even the knowledge to send e-mail. Find out if there are other electronic platforms you can use to communicate with families. For example, in some communities applications like Whatsapp are widely used by families, and some families find that social media updates are the easiest way to receive communication from teachers. Whatever method you use to communicate electronically, be sure to also send home on paper all information and messages you post online.

The more personal you can make both initial and ongoing contacts, the more effective you can be in building friendly and productive relationships with your students' families. Face-to-face contacts are more personal than phone calls, phone calls are more personal than notes, and notes are more personal than form letters or social media posts. More-personal contacts generally require more time than less-personal contacts. Thus, although it is critical that teachers establish and maintain contact with their students' families, each teacher will have to determine the nature and amount of contact that is realistically possible. Obviously, a middle school teacher who sees 150 students every day will not be able to have as many or as personal contacts with families as a special education teacher who has 12 students. However, communication remains important for both of these teachers.

If the families of some (or many) of your students are not English speakers or have limited English, you face an additional challenge, but it is essential that you find strategies for communicating effectively with these families. Check with building or district personnel for information about getting assistance in communicating with families in their language. For example, a translator could help with written communications, or an interpreter could be present for telephone calls and at-school events like conferences and Open House. If your school is very diverse and there are many different primary languages, it may not be feasible to make adaptation arrangements for all of the languages. However, if half of your students come from Spanish-speaking homes, for example, arranging for important information to be translated into Spanish demonstrates to families the value you place on communicating with them.

Diversity, Equity, Inclusion, and Access

To communicate with families with limited English, determine supports available in your building or district, and make every effort to provide communication that is accessible. This demonstrates that you place value on communicating with all families.

Initial Contact

Your initial contact with a student's family is their first impression of you, so it's important to make the contact friendly and inviting, yet also highly professional. When possible, try to establish initial contact with families before the first day of school. If that is not possible, make initial contact within the first 2 weeks of school.

The purpose of an initial contact is twofold: to begin establishing a productive relationship with the students' families, and to give the students and their families important information about yourself and your vision for the upcoming school year. Provide the following information during an initial contact:

- A welcome indicating that you are looking forward to an exciting and productive year.
- Your teaching background ("I have taught for fifteen years, with the last three years at the middle school level").
- A statement that you are looking forward to working with the student and getting to know the family.
- Your major goals (academic and behavioral) for the year. In Chapter 3, Task 8, you will work to identify major goals for your classroom.
- When and how the family can contact you when they have questions or want to share helpful information about the student.

- When and how you will maintain ongoing communication with them ("I will be sending home a classroom newsletter every other week, starting next Friday").
- (*Optional*) A copy of your classroom rules, with a slip to be signed by the student and a family member to indicate that they have discussed the rules. You designed or refined your classroom rules in Chapter 2, Task 2.
- (*Optional for middle and high-school teachers*) A syllabus that orients students to some of the detailed expectations for the class, such as homework schedules, routines, and so on.
- Invitation for comments or questions, and a chance for families to tell you how you can contact them.

See Box 2.1 (p. 108) for additional suggestions on working effectively with students and families whose backgrounds are different from yours.

Following are descriptions of four possible strategies for making initial contact with students' families, along with brief discussions of their pros and cons. As you read through them, consider whether one (or some combination) of the strategies might work for you. It's also possible that you already have or will need to develop a strategy that better meets your needs.

Make face-to-face contact prior to the first day of school. Some schools hold an Open House a day or so before school starts so that students and families can meet their teachers and see their classrooms. If there is any possibility of implementing this wonderful idea at your school, you may wish to encourage it. Families of students who are most likely to have trouble—those with a past history of behavioral or academic problems, for example—can especially benefit from attending an Open House. Consider phoning those families to personally invite them to the event and troubleshoot transportation if the family will have difficulty making it to the school. In some schools, buses run the bus routes to bring families who have limited transportation to school, and others offer options such as free public bus passes. Check with your administrator if you learn that a family has a transportation barrier to attending the Open House to determine options for support. In addition, you should prepare a letter that contains the important initial contact information (see Figure 2.10, p. 109) and give it to those students and families who attend the Open House. Of course, you will want to be sure that students and families who do not attend also receive the letter in some other manner.

If you like the idea of face-to-face family contact before school starts but your school doesn't hold an Open House, consider possible alternatives. For example, you might contact the families of students who have had problems in the past (such as a student who is painfully shy or has a history of acting out) and invite those students and families to meet you at school before the first day. Your building principal or counselor can probably let you know which students and families from your class would most benefit from a welcoming contact, if you are not sure.

Contact families by phone prior to the first day of school. If you know who will be in your class, another option is to telephone each student's family. Most families will appreciate this effort to contact them directly. If you prepare an outline of the information you want the students and their families to have, you should be able to make the calls brief while still conveying all the important information they need. (Just make sure that you don't sound like an automated recording by the time you get to the last calls.) Keep in mind that if families take this opportunity to share information about their student with you, this kind of contact can end up taking 10 minutes or so per student. As with face-to-face contact, if contacting all families by telephone is not feasible, you might consider contacting only the families of those

BOX 2.1

Considerations for Cultural Competency When Working With Families Whose Backgrounds Are Different From Yours
(Adapted from "Cultural Competence" by Keba Baldwin and Amalio Nieves)

Child-rearing practices vary from culture to culture. How families feel about their role in working with the school as well as needing and accepting help from others may be different from the school's expectations. In some cultures, families take an active role in their child's school life by assisting with homework, attending meetings, and volunteering. In other cultures, families believe it is not their place to interfere or intervene in the educational process. The educator is the expert. Concurrently, some families may also appear to distance themselves from school because of past negative experiences with their own schooling, fear or misunderstanding of the educational system, job schedules, and/or limited proficiency in English. If families stay away from school, it does not mean they are not interested or involved in their child's schooling. If there is little contact between the school and home, continue to provide information to the home regarding the student's progress and continue to be welcoming. Also recognize that negative judgments about families (e.g., "this student's parents just don't care about school") are highly detrimental to efforts to collaborate with all families, and such judgments are often made with limited or misinformed ideas about family or community circumstances. When families do not appear to engage with the school or may even appear overtly hostile, coach yourself to avoid judgments about the family and continue being consciously welcoming. Over time these efforts may pay significant dividends.

When you work in a diverse community, it is also important to make an honest assessment. Are you currently suited to working with students from different cultures, or do you need to do work to expand your knowledge and abilities? Are you willing to learn from your students so they in turn can learn from you? Are you willing to be overtly and continuously welcoming to all families? Teaching in a school that serves a community very different from your own is not for everyone. A negative or even a helpless attitude can make a lasting negative impact on students. On the other hand, a respectful, supportive attitude can have a lasting positive impact.

One possibility for getting to know a student and their family at the beginning of the year is to invite (but do not require) each family to record a short video or audio recording or write a short essay introducing their child to you. This can be a powerful way to assess the level of support students get at home, the value the family places on committing to an assignment, the family's perception of the student, and their level of writing and language skills. (Thanks to Tricia Huder for this suggestion.) Invite families to tell you anything they wish to about their student, family circumstances, and supports that may be welcomed or needed by the family.

Figure 2.10 *Sample Letter Home*

Dear Families,

Hi! My name is Ms. Emily Veric and I am your child's teacher this year. I am looking forward to a very exciting and productive year. I have been a teacher for 6 years, but this will be my first year teaching fourth grade. As the year goes on, I am looking forward to meeting you and getting to know you and your student.

I want you and your student to know that my major goals for this year are that all students in my class will:

- Develop skills in written expression so they can communicate in both narrative and expository styles.
- Master all basic addition, subtraction, multiplication, and division facts and correctly apply those facts when doing computation and problem-solving.
- Learn to work cooperatively in groups and sometimes take the leadership role.
- Learn to plan long-range projects and bring them to completion, including two major reports and two major projects.
- Speak in front of groups with confidence and style.
- Stay focused on written tasks and bring those tasks to completion.

I will be sending home a classroom newsletter every other week, starting next Friday. In that letter, I will tell you about my Guidelines for Success and my classroom rules. This letter will also be posted on the school website. To read it online, go to www.ourschool.edu and click on the link for "Mrs. Veric's Class."

If you want to speak with me for any reason, please don't hesitate to give me a call. The best time to call is between 3 pm and 4 pm on Monday, Tuesday, Thursday, and Friday at 555-1234. Or call any time between 8 am and 4 pm and leave a message, and I will get back to you. You may also send me an e-mail through the school website.

Please feel free to let me know any information that may help me to be successful with your child, and let me know the best way (and time) to reach you.

Good-bye for now, and let your child know that we will have a great year in Room 17.

Sincerely,

Ms. Veric

Ms. Veric
4th Grade Teacher

students who have experienced academic or behavioral difficulty in the past or families who have previously had limited contact or engagement with the school.

Send a letter home (on the first day of school). A letter sent home with students on the first day of school may be the most common and least time-consuming strategy. However, it also tends to be the least personal. One major drawback is that if no one in the family speaks or reads English, a letter alone will be an ineffective method of communicating and may even make the family defensive. Also, when you send a letter home on the first day of school, it may get lost in a blizzard of other first-day papers, such as bus schedules, immunization information, and lunch menus. Figure 2.9 shows a letter to families from a fourth-grade teacher.

Create a video to send home or post online. Many families today have a computer at home or can access videos via their phone. Another way to make initial contact with your students' families is to make a video introducing you and your classroom and during the first week or two of school send copies home with students on a DVD or a thumb drive and provide links online through email or social media. If your school has a website that allows videos to be posted, you could also make your video available online. A video may give students' families a better sense of who you are and create a greater level of comfort and trust than a letter would. A disadvantage is that it may put a student whose family does not have a computer, DVD player, or smart phone in an uncomfortable or embarrassing position.

Options for recording include recording video on your phone or using a digital camera. Teachers can pair up and help each other make their videos. As one teacher operates the camera, the other can greet her students' families, talk about major goals for the year, and even give a brief tour of the classroom: "And over here is the science learning center. When students are done with their work, this is one of five centers they can choose to spend time in. Of course, they will have to clean up the center after they work here, but we will be working on how to use and take care of the centers during the first 2 weeks of school." Once the first person has finished, the teachers can change roles. If you prepare an outline in advance, filming a video like this should take no longer than writing a letter.

To make sure that each student has the opportunity to take a DVD or thumb drive home during the first 2 weeks of school, you will probably need seven to ten copies. The time, expense, and technological know-how required to make multiple copies of the video may be a disadvantage of this strategy. If needed, check with your district's media department to see if they can help you. If there are many families who speak limited English in your class, look into creating a couple of copies with a voice-over translation.

If you use a video, you will still want to send a letter that goes over your classroom rules and your major goals for the class and have the family sign and return it. The letter also provides a backup form of communication for students who do not have a way to play the video at home.

Ongoing Contact

In addition to making initial contact with your students' families at the beginning of the year, you also need to maintain contact with them during the year. The key is to ensure that families do not feel that you communicate with them only when there is a problem—when families feel that you are really making an effort to keep them proactively informed, they are more likely to work with you should their student have a behavioral or academic problem. Remember that positive communications with families are incredibly important. All parents deserve to hear about areas where their students are doing well or are making positive improvements. It is all too common to hear some parents, especially parents of students with ongoing behavioral concerns, report that they have never received communication from the school about things their student is doing well or efforts their student has made. When teachers contact families only about concerns or when providing report cards, it can lead some families to shut down, and for others it creates excessive worry and stress. For students who struggle in school, you must work to actively identify some of the student's strengths—"catch them being good"—so that you can provide positive feedback to their families.

Suggestions for maintaining ongoing communication include:

Send a short newsletter home on a regular basis. Use a newsletter to keep families informed of major class priorities, activities, and issues. The school website can be a quick, easy way to get information to lots of people; however, the Internet is inaccessible for some and can feel impersonal.

Communicate about class happenings. Share information about what is occurring in the classroom (e.g., information about what will be learned in a new unit) or tips to help their child develop healthy habits (e.g., information about how parents can supervise and teach appropriate technology use). This can encourage families to engage as partners in the learning process. See Figure 2.11 (p. 112) for a sample communication about supervising and teaching about technology use at home.

Some teachers provide families with an outline of their CHAMPS expectations for the class at the beginning of the year, as shown in Figure 2.12 (p. 113). When CHAMPS is implemented schoolwide, such a letter can be sent to all families. Other teachers record videos throughout the year to show students following CHAMPS expectations for various activities. These videos can be shared with families so they help reinforce the teacher's expectations for successful classroom behavior.

Be consciously inviting in seeking parental feedback. At various times during the year, make conscious efforts to reach out to families to seek feedback about what is going well for their student and areas where their child may need additional support. This can be done through a variety of formats, including satisfaction surveys (see Chapter 10, Task 1 for guidance on developing feedback survey that can be used toward the end of a term or school year), letters home inviting families to get in touch if there is anything you need to know about their student's life or progress in your class, and phone calls or conferences. Remember that two-way communication involves shared listening and idea generation and can significantly improve positive relationships with families and opportunities for collaboration.

Keep track of your ongoing contacts with families. Track contacts by using a class list and some form of coding. For example, you might write "9/22, Ph" and "10/4, Conf" next to a student's name to indicate that you made a phone contact on September 22 and had a face-to-face conference at school on October 4. A written method like this lets you monitor how often and in what ways you contact each student's family. You can also see at a glance whether any families have not been contacted.

Strive to make more positive contacts than contacts for problematic issues. As part of your tracking system, you might monitor these contacts by highlighting any positive communication about something the student did well in one color and communication about any problems in another color. This emphasis on the positive will demonstrate to the family that you have the student's best interests at heart and that you want to work with the family to help the student be successful in your classroom. Periodically analyze your color-coded log to see if your communication with each family is weighted to the positive and if any particular family hasn't been contacted in a while. This is especially important with students with the most challenging behavior. Families of students who struggle in school may rarely or even never hear positive feedback about their child. These efforts to acknowledge moments of positive behavior

Figure 2.11 *Technology Tips Newsletter*

Volume 1, Issue 1 - Month 0, 0000

Navigating Today's Digital World

In today's world, our kids are exposed to technology throughout their day. They text, email, use social media, surf the Internet, watch television and movies, and the list goes on. In fact, for many children, technology is one of the main ways they interact with and learn about the world. Over the next several weeks, I'll be sending home some tips I've learned about helping kids navigate this increasingly technological world. I'll be teaching some of these same concepts and skills in our classroom, and it would be extremely helpful if families can teach and reinforce some of the skills we are learning as students use technology at home. If there are other skills or resources you think I should know about, I'd love to learn more!

For today's topic, here are some ideas about safety when dealing with technology.

1. Never share passwords with anyone other than your parents or guardians (even a best friend).

2. Never give out personally identifiable information. This includes your full name and birth date, address, and phone number. If someone is requesting this information, check with your parent or guardian before entering anything.

3. Never give someone your location or agree to meet in person with someone you've met online.

As appropriate, share examples or discuss issues of identity theft, sexual and financial predators, and other risks.

In our next tip sheets, I'll send home ideas about what appropriate and respectful behavior looks and sounds like when communicating through technology, as well as ways to establish effective procedures and rules regarding technology, like how to limit the amount of time or times of day when technology is used. I look forward to partnering with you to build digital citizenship and literacy in our classroom and beyond!

Adapted with permission from Sprick, J., Jenson, W. R., Sprick, R., & Coughlin, C. (2017). *Bullying Solutions: Universal and Individual Strategies*, Ancora Publishing. © 2017 Ancora Publishing

or growth can help build families as willing partners who are more likely to be supportive and who may make efforts to help when the student is struggling.

Create regular routines that prompt you to remember to provide positive communication with families. The key here is to come up with a way to maintain communication without burning yourself out. Some teachers end each day or use a few minutes of their prep period to make one to three positive phone calls home. While communication with families can be time consuming, it is our experience that positive phone calls tend to be quite quick—no more than 30 seconds to 2 minutes—and they often leave teachers in a good mood. Phone calls about concerns tend to take much more time and emotional energy. Another possibility is to plan one day a week to make a certain number of positive calls or send positive notes home via mail, email, or social media private messaging. Rotate through your class roster to ensure that each student receives some positive communication each month.

Figure 2.12 *Sample CHAMPS Letter Home*

Dear Family,

I want to introduce you to my approach to classroom management and discipline issues. The approach is called CHAMPS: A Proactive and Positive Approach to Classroom Management.

Within this approach, the focus is on prevention and on teaching expectations to students. In my classroom, I make every effort to structure for success by creating meaningful activities with frequent variety to engage student interest.

In addition, I directly teach students how to behave responsibly in each major activity and transition. That is where CHAMPS comes in. CHAMPS stands for Conversation, Help, Activity, Movement, Participation, and Success. When students follow the CHAMP expectations, it leads to Success. I encourage you to ask your child if he or she knows about CHAMPS. Ask when and how students in the class can talk, get help, and get out of their seats. Ask how students in my class demonstrate that they are actively participating. If your child doesn't know, encourage him or her to ask me—it will give me a chance to review with students how they can be successful in my classroom.

When students are meeting my CHAMPS expectations, I let them know that they are doing a good job by praising them and occasionally letting the class choose a special game or activity. When a student misbehaves, I try to correct the mistake by telling the student that behavior is unacceptable. I then give the student a chance to do it the right way. If the misbehavior continues, I may impose consequences such as 30 seconds off recess per infraction or a brief in-class timeout. If the problem occurs more than a few times, I will let you know so that we can work as partners to help your child behave responsibly and experience success in my classroom.

If you have questions about any of this, please let me know. By working together, families and teachers can communicate high expectations and ensure a successful experience for all students.

Sincerely,

Mr. Chang
Mr. Chang

One elementary school printed postcards with their school mascot and gave each teacher two stamped and addressed copies of the postcard for each student. The principal asked teachers to ensure that by the end of the first semester, each family received two positive postcards home about their student's strengths or a moment of positive behavior, growth, or effort. The school was shocked to find that some parents called their student's teacher crying because they appreciated the postcard so much. Other parents framed the postcards or shared pictures on social media. The point is that these simple communications were hugely meaningful for many families and may have led some parents to engage in positive and productive ways with those teachers and their child's education.

When family contact is necessary because of a problem a student is having, think about what you want to say and how you are going to say it before making the contact. When family contact is necessary because of a problem a student is having, it's important to pre-think what you want to say and how you are going to say it. This preparation will reduce the chances that you will be misunderstood or inadvertently say something insensitive. Suggestions for handling this type of situation and reproducible templates for making notes prior to contacting a family are provided in Chapter 8, Task 5.

NOTE: If you are developing your Classroom Management Plan in the middle of the school year, hopefully you have already made some contact with families. Moving forward, put your time and energy into maintaining as much positive contact as you can to build relationships with your students' families. Before the beginning of the next school year, plan to develop a specific plan for establishing and maintaining contact with families.

UPDATE YOUR CLASSROOM MANAGEMENT PLAN

ITEM 6: FAMILY CONTACT

Describe your family contact plan, including:

- Procedures for making initial contact with families at the beginning of the school year
- Procedures for maintaining contact with families throughout the year

Conclusion

The tasks in this chapter guide you through organizational decisions in your classroom that can prompt responsible behavior from your students. In the next chapter, we will continue exploring tasks about the structure of your classroom with tasks that focus on how to organize your instructional planning and delivery.

CHAPTER 3

Structure for Success— Instructional Decisions

Organize instructional activities, student assignments, and grading systems to maximize learning and responsible behavior.

As introduced in the previous chapter, structure is the level of organization, orchestration, and predictability of a setting. Now that you have made decisions about how to structure your classroom's physical space, routines, and transitions, this chapter will guide you through decisions about how to structure your instructional activities.

The ten tasks presented in this chapter will help you organize your instructional activities to maximize learning and responsible behavior, manage student assignments and technology use, and develop effective grading systems.

The ten tasks in this chapter are:

- Task 1: Establish an Efficient Daily Schedule
- Task 2: Clarify Expectations for the Common Instructional Activities That Occur in Your Classroom
- Task 3: Design Procedures for Managing Teacher-Directed Activities
- Task 4: Design Procedures for Managing Independent Work Periods
- Task 5: Design Procedures for Managing Partner and Cooperative Group Work
- Task 6: Design Procedures for Managing Student Assignments
- Task 7: Design Procedures for Managing Student Technology Use
- Task 8: Develop Long-Range Classroom Goals
- Task 9: Understand Considerations for Developing Effective Grading Practices
- Task 10: Develop a Grading System That Creates a Relationship Between Student Effort, Growth, and Success

TASK 1

Establish an Efficient Daily Schedule

Arrange or modify your daily schedule to maximize instructional time and responsible behavior and minimize wasted time and irresponsible behavior.

• • • • •

How you schedule subjects across a day and how you schedule tasks within an activity can have a tremendous influence on student behavior (Stronge et al., 2011; Trussel, 2008). For example, the middle school teacher who schedules independent work for the last half or the last period of the day will probably find that students engage in an inordinate amount of off-task behavior. An effective schedule provides enough variety that, at any given time, students won't find it difficult to keep their attention focused on the task at hand. An effective schedule also takes into consideration the maturity level of your students and the degree of skill that you, the teacher, have in presenting various tasks and activities.

The information in this task is designed to help you evaluate (and modify, if necessary) your schedule to ensure that it is more likely to prompt responsible behavior than irresponsible behavior. This task gives specific scheduling suggestions and also identifies the times of day when students are most prone to irresponsible behavior. It includes suggestions for helping students handle those times in a more responsible manner.

Most teachers cannot control all aspects of their daily schedule. For instance, if the teachers at your grade level share students for reading instruction, you must schedule reading for the same time as other teachers. You may have no choice about when your students go to music or physical education—you just have to accept those time slots. The scheduling issues and decisions suggested below will help you arrange those times that have not been predetermined by the schoolwide schedule.

To work through the information in this task, first write down your schedule of daily subjects. Most middle school teachers will have the subject already established, but elementary teachers need to make decisions about when and how long to teach each subject.

Once the schedule of subjects is established, list the activities that occur within each subject, the amount of time spent on each activity, and whether the activity is teacher directed (lecture, discussion, question/answer), independent work (seatwork, lab activities), or a cooperative task (partner work, group work). In other words, outline a typical lesson plan for each subject. While you may deviate from this schedule for particular days or activities, this will help serve as a guide for a typical routine you can set based on students' needs. For example, if you teach math from 9:30 to 10:30, it may look something like this:

5 minutes	Teacher-directed interactive review of previous concepts
10 minutes	Teacher-directed introduction of new concepts
10 minutes	Teacher-directed guided practice, working with students on concepts
25 minutes	Independent work or cooperative tasks (depending on task)
5 minutes	Teacher-directed corrections or guided practice to help students identify errors or misunderstandings
5 minutes	Teacher-directed closing routine

If you teach in 90-minute blocks, pay particular attention to keeping each activity to a reasonable length of time. You should schedule more activities within the period instead of longer activities. For example:

2 minutes	Independent warm-up exercise and attendance
6 minutes	Teacher-directed interactive review of previous concepts
10 minutes	Teacher-directed introduction of new concepts
12 minutes	Teacher-directed guided practice, working with students on concepts
15 minutes	Independent work
5 minutes	Introduction to cooperative exercise
18 minutes	Cooperative group task
5 minutes	Teacher-directed clarification
12 minutes	Independent work
5 minutes	Teacher-directed introduction to homework and closing routine

Once you have written down your schedule of subjects and a sample schedule of activities within each subject, evaluate the variety of activities and times for each activity using the following guidelines:

- Make sure that you have a reasonable balance among the types of activities.
- Within each activity, avoid having any one type of task run too long.
- Schedule independent work and cooperative/peer group tasks so that they immediately follow teacher-directed tasks.

Make Sure You Have a Reasonable Balance Among the Types of Activities

Work to balance the types of activities (teacher-directed instruction, independent seatwork, cooperative/peer group tasks) you use within and across subjects during the day (Simmons, 2020; Stronge et al., 2011; Trussel, 2008).

Your goal should be to balance the kind of tasks students do in a day. In particular, watch for "too much of a good thing"—you may tend to overschedule one type of activity. For example, if you like to have students work in cooperative groups and feel strongly that they learn a lot by working cooperatively, you may have inadvertently allotted a disproportionate amount of your daily schedule or class period to cooperative group tasks. Conversely, if you prefer teacher-directed instruction (lectures, discussions, and demonstrations), you may not schedule enough independent work and cooperative group tasks.

Look at your daily schedule and estimate the approximate percentage of class time (not counting lunch, passing periods, and recesses) that students spend on the various types of tasks. Middle school teachers should think about one particular class over the course of a week. For example, your activities may look something like the following:

- 40% teacher directed
- 35% independent work periods (and, as appropriate, lab activities, or learning centers)
- 25% cooperative groups

There are no absolute rules for creating a balance among major instructional tasks. A technology class, for example, will have far more independent and cooperative work and less teacher-directed instruction than a history class. A class with a large number of immature students who struggle with appropriate peer interactions will have more teacher-directed instruction and independent activities than cooperative activities, at least initially. As the year progresses and you are able to teach students how to work together productively in groups, you can adjust the balance of instructional tasks. To evaluate your schedule, look closely at what type of task takes up the highest percentage of your class time and honestly ask yourself if this might represent "too much of a good thing."

For those teachers who teach multiple groups of students, consider whether different groups require a different balance of activities or sequence of tasks within the schedule.

Within Each Activity, Avoid Having Any One Type of Task Run Too Long

Whenever students engage in one type of task for too long, behavior problems can result (Brophy, 1986; Simmons, 2020; Trussel, 2008). Students tend to become inattentive when teacher-directed instruction is overly long. When students have to sit and do independent work for a long time, they may get bored and stop working. When you have students engage in partner or group work for long stretches without periodically bringing the group back as a whole, students may veer off task or go too far down an incorrect path with their work.

There are no absolute rules about how long is too long (although any activity can be problematic if it runs longer than 30 minutes). In part, it depends on your skills and talents as a teacher. A teacher who designs clear, interesting, fun, and academically appropriate independent assignments can successfully engage students in longer periods of independent work than a teacher who is not as talented in this regard. A teacher whose presentational style is dynamic, organized, and humorous can sustain student attention for longer periods of teacher-directed instruction than the teacher who is less skilled in presenting to the whole class. When a teacher is able to clearly define, teach, and monitor expectations for partner or group work, cooperative activities will remain productive for longer periods. If you have found in the past that student behavior deteriorates as a task progresses (for example, they do well at the start of independent work, but get increasingly off task after about 15 minutes), schedule shorter periods of time for that task.

The length of time for any task is also highly dependent on each group of students because of maturity and skill levels with the task. In general, the younger or less mature your students are, the more you should err on the side of shorter periods for each type of activity, interspersed with another type of activity to provide stimulation and keep the group together. For example, if you have a group of highly immature sixth graders, they may be better able to handle a schedule that moves fluently back and forth between a few minutes of teacher-directed instruction and a short independent practice opportunity or think-pair-share partner activity. Over time, you can work to gradually increase students' capacity to stay focused and productive with different types of activities, but continue to evaluate whether any type of activity runs too long for your students.

Schedule Independent Work and Cooperative/Peer Group Tasks So That They Immediately Follow Teacher-Directed Tasks

Teacher-directed instruction is an excellent way to begin a class period, as it can generate positive energy and momentum and get everyone thinking about the same topic. Beginning a class period with independent work or cooperative work can result in lower rates of on-task behavior. Starting the period by creating a teacher-directed, interactive review of previous concepts, introducing some new concepts or skills, and then moving students into related independent or cooperative tasks allows you to clarify what students should be working on. This technique gives the opportunity for priming background knowledge or creating a rationale for why the learning is important, and it creates a cohesive and clear expectation for on-task behavior, harnessing the power of instructional momentum (Kame'enui & Carnine, 1998; Rimm-Kaufman et al.; 2005; Rosenshine & Stevens, 1986).

There are exceptions to this suggestion. For example, many teachers have students work on review exercises (independently or cooperatively) or a challenge problem as soon as they enter the classroom. During this time, the teacher takes attendance and deals with other housekeeping tasks. This strategy usually involves brief (2- to 5-minute) independent or cooperative activities and is a structured part of the daily routine. Having work ready for students as they enter the classroom can be a very effective practice for encouraging productive behavior from the very beginning of class (Wong & Wong, 2009). Another exception may be a class in which students work mainly on extremely clear, academically appropriate, and highly motivating independent tasks—a computer lab class, for example. As you develop your daily schedule, remember that, in general, teacher-directed instruction is usually the best way to begin class, so avoid starting class with long periods of independent or cooperative group work time.

Implementing the preceding suggestions as you schedule daily subjects is one way to reduce the likelihood of irresponsible student behavior. Another way is to identify and proactively address the specific activities and tasks and the times of day when students typically exhibit the most misbehavior (Park & Lynch, 2014; Scheuermann & Hall, 2008). For problematic times and activities, make a point of diligently teaching how to meet your expectations. Following are descriptions of times that are particularly troublesome for many teachers, along with suggestions for how to mitigate the problems.

After Recess or Lunch

Misbehavior tends to be common right after recess in elementary school and after lunch in middle school. You can decrease misbehavior by directly teaching students how to enter the classroom and settle down. The key is to provide this instruction before every recess and lunch period for the first couple of days of school. You should plan for periodic re-teaching, especially after any long breaks such as winter or spring break. In addition, have a task or activity scheduled immediately after recess that helps students calm down and get mentally ready to pay attention to their work. For example, a primary teacher might have Sharing immediately after recess (rather than first thing in the morning) because it is largely teacher directed but not overly intense. An intermediate or middle school teacher might schedule a few minutes of discussion on current events right after lunch.

Last Hour of the Day

Students (and teachers!) tend to be tired by the end of the day. Students may be more easily distracted and more irritable than they were early in the day, so avoid scheduling too much independent or cooperative group work for the last hour. If you are a middle school teacher who has multiple sections of the same class, this may not seem feasible, but with a little creativity, you can make easy modifications. Let's say you teach two classes of eighth-grade English—one first period and one seventh period. Allowing the first-period class to spend 30 minutes working on a long-range assignment may be reasonable. If you allow the same 30 minutes in the seventh-period class, you will probably have high rates of off-task behavior. You would be better off to begin class with teacher-directed instruction, then have 15 minutes of work on students' projects, then have more teacher-directed instruction and guided practice during the last 20 minutes of class.

Last Five Minutes of a Class Period

This suggestion applies primarily to middle school teachers. Try to end each class period with a few minutes of teacher-directed instruction. If you schedule independent work time during the last part of the class, students may begin to think that once direct teaching is finished, they are free to do their work—or not. By scheduling the last activity as a teacher-directed task, you are making it clear that class time to work on assignments is indeed for the purpose of working on assignments. "Class, you have 15 minutes to work on your assignment, and then I am going to end the class by bringing us all back together to find out if any parts of the assignment need clarification."

It is not very hard to arrange your schedule to end a subject with teacher-directed activities. Say you have students working—individually or in groups—on assignments during the second half of the class period. While they are working, you can monitor individual and group progress, noting common errors, misconceptions, and poor work habits. Then, as the period draws to a close, get everyone's attention and discuss the common errors and poor work habits: "Class, a few things you should keep in mind as you are working on a task like this are . . ."

In addition to giving feedback about the current task, you can use the last few minutes of the period to review homework expectations or remind students about long-range projects and housekeeping details: "Class, do not forget that you should be done with your outline for the projects by Wednesday, and tomorrow is the last day to get your permission slips in for the field trip." Again, if you do not end the class with teacher-directed instruction, students may begin to act as if independent work time is free choice time.

Instructional minutes are valuable. Be careful to spend only a minimum of time on beginning and ending routines and transitions between activities, but allow enough time so that they do not seem frantic or rushed. Also ensure that you start class on time and use bell-to-bell learning as much as possible. There is tremendous variability among teachers—some have no opening or closing rituals at all, whereas others spend so many minutes each day on opening and closing routines that they lose significant instructional time. Again, the key here is to have some balance—but in this case skewed to maximizing instructional minutes.

In summary, a well-designed schedule ensures that students experience a varied but balanced range of activities within subjects. If students are kept engaged with activities that are scheduled for reasonable lengths of time, responsible behavior will likely result. If students are required to engage in the same type of activity too often or for too long, they may become bored, distracted, and even disruptive.

In summary, make sure that your daily schedule:

- Includes a balance of different types of activities (teacher-directed instruction, independent seatwork, cooperative/peer group tasks).
- Avoids having any one type of task run too long.
- Arranges independent work and cooperative/peer group tasks to immediately follow teacher-directed tasks.

TASK 2

Clarify Expectations for the Common Instructional Activities That Occur in Your Classroom

Establish effective procedures for the major instructional activities that occur within your classroom, including teacher-directed instruction, partner work periods, cooperative group work, and independent work periods.

• • • • •

School and teacher effectiveness literature has consistently shown that successful teachers are very clear with students about exactly how they expect students to behave (Brophy & Good, 1986; Epstein et al., 2008; Hattie, 2012; Marzano, 2003; Park & Lynch, 2014; Simonsen et al., 2008). If a teacher doesn't know or doesn't communicate their behavioral expectations to students, the students have to guess at what constitutes responsible behavior. When students must guess how they are supposed to behave, the results are often behaviors such as these, the most common misbehaviors that occur in the typical classroom:

- Students talk too much, too loudly, or about the wrong things.
- Students demand attention by following the teacher around or by calling out to the teacher.
- Students do math when they should be working on science.

- Students socialize when they should be listening to the teacher or working independently.
- Students wander around the room or sharpen pencils when they are supposed to be listening to the teacher.
- Some students monopolize classroom discussions, and others don't participate at all.
- Some students disrupt lessons, and others sit and do nothing during work periods.

You can avoid most, if not all, of these problems by clearly defining for yourself and then communicating to your students how you expect them to behave during each and every classroom activity and transition. If you do not, your students won't know whether it is all right to sharpen their pencils during cooperative group times, to ask other students for help during a work period, or to ask you questions while you take attendance.

Identify Common Instructional Activities That Occur in Your Classroom

In Chapter 2, you defined CHAMPS expectations for major transitions. In this chapter, you will put similar thought into how to provide clarity and consistent expectations for all regularly scheduled activities through your CHAMPS expectations. You will identify the types of structures needed during each work period to ensure that students are highly engaged and responsible throughout different types of instructional activities. In the next chapter, you will learn strategies for clearly conveying and teaching these expectations to your students.

The first step in defining your behavioral expectations for classroom activities is to make a list of the major types of activities that your students will engage in on a daily (or regular) basis. Your list might include activities like:

- Opening/attendance routines
- Class meetings
- Teacher-directed instruction
- Tests/quizzes
- Small group instruction
- Lab activities
- Centers/stations
- Independent work
- Peer tutoring sessions
- Sustained silent reading
- Cooperative groups
- Cushion activities (for students who have finished assigned work before the work period is over)
- Independent tablet or computer work
- Partner or small group tablet or computer work

Try to identify all the specific activities and categories of activities for which you have different behavioral expectations. For example, you may list teacher-directed instruction once because your expectations for student behavior during teacher-directed instruction are the same regardless of subject matter. Or you may separately list teacher-directed instruction in math and reading (because behavioral expectations for both are the same) and teacher-directed instruction in science (because your expectations for science class are different from those for math and reading). Middle school teachers likely have the same basic classroom activities for each subject area they teach (the same activities for all foreign language sections, for example), but different expectations for other classes they teach, such as a science class.

Reproducible 3.1 is a CHAMPS Classroom Activities List form. Stop now. Print the form from the downloadable files (see p. 3) and use it to list each type of classroom activity that will occur in your classroom Classify each as a primarily teacher-directed, cooperative, or independent activity. Your list will probably look similar to the bulleted list above. Most teachers have somewhere between 4–8 activities on their list, although yours may be somewhat smaller or larger depending on the subjects you teach and the range of different instructional activities your students can manage.

Reproducible 3.1 *CHAMPS Classroom Activities List Example*

CHAMPS Classroom Activities List   *CHAMPS*

TEACHER **Ms. Pelayo**   SCHOOL YEAR _____

List each major activity or category of activity that will occur during a typical day in your classroom. Create a separate item for every activity or category during which you will have different behavioral expectations. Classify each item as either a teacher-directed (TD), cooperative (C), or independent activity (IA).

Major activity/category of activity	Type of activity
Teacher-directed instruction	TD
Class Discussion	TD
Small Groups at Seats	C
Small Groups at Centers	C
Independent Work	IA
Tests/Quizzes	IA

Develop Clear Behavioral Expectations for Each Major Instructional Activity

Once you identify your major classroom activities, use the CHAMPS acronym to guide your thinking about important issues you must clarify for your students. Reproducible 3.2 is a template of a CHAMPS Classroom Activity Worksheet. Download this form and print a copy for each major type of activity that you have identified. You will use these forms in the next three tasks.

For each activity, define detailed behavioral expectations for your students in terms of:

C   **Conversation**   *Under what circumstances, if any, can students talk to each other during the activity?*

H   **Help**   *How do students get their questions answered during the activity? How do they get your attention?*

A   **Activity**   *What is the activity? What is its intended objective or end product?*

M   **Movement**   *Under what circumstances, if any, can students move about during the activity? For example, can they sharpen a pencil?*

P   **Participation**   *What does appropriate student work behavior during the activity look and sound like? How do students demonstrate their full participation?*

S   **Success**   *Soar to Success! (Alternatively, some teachers and schools choose to have the S stand for Special Considerations, which can be a catchall for any expectations that do not fit the other categories of the CHAMPS acronym.)*

To answer these questions, you will fill out one worksheet (Reproducible 3.2) for each major type of activity you listed on Reproducible 3.1, CHAMPS Classroom Activities List. These completed worksheets will provide the content for lessons to teach your students about your behavioral expectations across all major instructional activities. In Chapter 4, you will learn strategies for clearly conveying and teaching these expectations to your students.

When completing these worksheets, consider the following:

Create a clear vision of what student behavior should look and sound like in each major instructional activity. If students behaved 100% appropriately, what would your ideal classroom look and sound like? Remember that if you do not clarify and teach exactly what you want from students, some students are likely to make assumptions about what behaviors are acceptable and they are likely to have encountered differing expectations across different teachers.

Carefully consider the level of support you and your students require. The level of support and the corresponding level of structure you identified for your class (or classes) have significant implications for decisions about expectations for behavior and engagement during instructional activities. Remember that:

- Structure can be thought of as "orchestrated care." How much structure do your students need to be at their best, to feel safe and supported, and to engage appropriately in instructional activities and with each other?
- Structure can vary with different groups of students. It may be necessary to alter your expectations from year to year or group to group based on the students' level of maturity and responsibility. Avoid "existing regularities" in which your expectations remain the same across time simply because it is what you have always done or seen.

- Structure can vary across time with the same group of students. If you start with higher levels of structure, you can gradually release responsibility as your students demonstrate the maturity and skills to handle greater levels of independence. You may also find that as you teach students direct skills to become more independent, or if they develop greater levels of intrinsic motivation or maturity across time, you can gradually lessen the structure of routines and activities.

> **Existing Regularities**
>
> *Avoid designing your expectations in exactly the same way each year (or as a first-year teacher, exactly the way your mentor teacher during student teaching designed expectations) simply because that was what was done before.*

However, if you find that behavior is consistently problematic, consider whether higher-structure alterations to the activity might remove many of the current difficulties.

Examine your identity and how your values shape expectations for student behavior. Which behaviors do you consider good, appropriate, and normal? These values are directly influenced by your culture and will vary greatly from person to person. Consider student backgrounds when defining expectations (Leverson et al., 2016). Challenge yourself to explain the purposes of your expectations and ensure that expectations are designed to help all students succeed.

Once you have a vision of the behaviors you want students to exhibit (and correspondingly, the behaviors you do not want them to exhibit), complete Reproducible 3.2, CHAMPS Classroom Activity Worksheet, for each classroom activity.

Pages 126–131 show CHAMPS expectations for a variety of classroom activities. Each activity includes both a high- and low-support example to demonstrate how a teacher might accommodate support needs in designing expectations. These completed examples are provided as models only; there is no intent to imply that you should use the expectations shown on them.

Downloads

Additional examples for independent work while the teacher is with a small group, written tests, and small group reading are available in the downloadable files (see Classroom Activity Worksheet Examples.pdf).

Additional guidance for teacher-directed instruction, independent work periods, and cooperative partner/group activities appears in Tasks 3–5 of this chapter. As you complete CHAMPS Activity Worksheets for these common activities, read through the corresponding task to ensure that your procedures set students up for success in meeting your classroom goals.

UPDATE YOUR CLASSROOM MANAGEMENT PLAN

ITEM 5: EXPECTATIONS FOR CLASSROOM ACTIVITIES AND TRANSITIONS

- On Reproducible 3.1, list all common instructional activities for which you will complete CHAMPS Activity Worksheets.
- Once you complete CHAMPS Activity Worksheets (Reproducible 3.2) for each activity, attach them or include them in a binder with a paper record of your Classroom Management Plan, and/or include the filled-out digital versions in a file that contains your Classroom Management Plan.

Reproducible 3.2 *CHAMPS Classroom Activity Worksheet, Example A*

CHAMPS Classroom Activity Worksheet   *CHAMPS*

A
Teacher Directed, High Support

ACTIVITY *Teacher-directed instruction (high support)*

CONVERSATION

Can students engage in conversations with each other during this activity? *No*   Voice level: *0*
If yes, about what?
With whom?
How many students can be involved in a single conversation?
How long can the conversation last?

HELP

How do students get questions answered? How do students get your attention?
Raise hands silently in the air and keep them up until called upon. For content question, use open hand. For restroom, use closed fist.

If students have to wait for help, what should they do while they wait?
Keep hand raised. Remain still. Wait silently.

ACTIVITY

What is the expected end product of this activity? (Note: This may vary from day to day.)
Working on tasks and activities presented by the teacher. Giving verbal, written, and action responses to teacher-presented opportunities to respond.

MOVEMENT

Can students get out of their seats during the activity? *Yes* If yes, acceptable reasons include: ☒ restroom ☐ drink ☐ pencil sharpener ☐ hand in/pick up materials ☐ other:

Do they need permission from you? *Must have permission for any leaving of seat. Restroom only in emergency.*

PARTICIPATION

What behaviors show that students are participating fully and responsibly?
Looking at teacher, projected display, board, or needed materials on their desk. Answering questions when called on or signaled to. Looking where the teacher directs in the room. Writing as directed by the teacher. Appropriately using a fidget provided by teacher. On-topic comments and questions.

What behaviors show that a student is not participating?
Talking to another student. Passing notes. Doodling. Using fidget inappropriately or having toys or distracting items on desk. Blurting out. Raising hand but waving it wildly in the air. Questions or comments not related to current activity.

SUCCESS

Success comes from following the expectations.

REPRODUCIBLE 3.2

Reproducible 3.2 *CHAMPS Classroom Activity Worksheet, Example B*

CHAMPS Classroom Activity Worksheet   *CHAMPS*

B
Teacher Directed, Low Support

ACTIVITY *Teacher-directed instruction (low support)*

CONVERSATION

Can students engage in conversations with each other during this activity? *No*   Voice level: *0*
If yes, about what?
With whom?
How many students can be involved in a single conversation?
How long can the conversation last?

HELP

How do students get questions answered? How do students get your attention?
Raise hands

If students have to wait for help, what should they do while they wait?
Keep hand raised, wait quietly

ACTIVITY

What is the expected end product of this activity? (Note: This may vary from day to day.)
Working on tasks and activities presented by the teacher. Responding to teacher prompts.

MOVEMENT

Can students get out of their seats during the activity? *Yes* If yes, acceptable reasons include: ☒ restroom ☒ drink
☒ pencil sharpener ☒ hand in/pick up materials ☐ other:

Do they need permission from you? *No. Fill out time out/time in on restroom record and take hall pass.*

PARTICIPATION

What behaviors show that students are participating fully and responsibly?
Looking at teacher. Raising hand with something to say. Answering questions when called on or given signal. Writing when directed.

What behaviors show that a student is not participating?
Talking to another student. Interrupting the talker. Not following directions. Not answering when signaled.

SUCCESS

Success comes from following the expectations.

REPRODUCIBLE 3.2

Reproducible 3.2 *CHAMPS Classroom Activity Worksheet, Example C*

CHAMPS Classroom Activity Worksheet   *CHAMPS*

C
Independent
Seatwork, High
Support

ACTIVITY *Independent Seatwork (high support)*

CONVERSATION

Can students engage in conversations with each other during this activity?   *No*   Voice level: *0*
If yes, about what?
With whom?
How many students can be involved in a single conversation?
How long can the conversation last?

HELP

How do students get questions answered? How do students get your attention?
Put out help sign and mark the question for when the teacher gets to you.

If students have to wait for help, what should they do while they wait?
Keep working. If unable to continue, take out backup work packet.

ACTIVITY

What is the expected end product of this activity? (Note: This may vary from day to day.)
Completing independent work assignment

MOVEMENT

Can students get out of their seats during the activity? *Yes*   If yes, acceptable reasons include: ☒ restroom   ☒ drink
☒ pencil sharpener   ☐ hand in/pick up materials   ☐ other:

Do they need permission from you?
In room—only one student moving at a time. For restroom, get permission and sign out.

PARTICIPATION

What behaviors show that students are participating fully and responsibly?

Looking at own paper. Writing or doing what the task requires. Asking for help from the teacher when it is needed. Continuing to work throughout the work period. If finished, working on other independent tasks to not distract others.

What behaviors show that a student is not participating?

Talking to another student. Getting out of seat multiple times or when another student is out of their seat. Wandering around the room. Leaving the room to use the restroom without permission or signing out. Not doing the task.

SUCCESS

Success comes from following the expectations.

REPRODUCIBLE 3.2

Reproducible 3.2 *CHAMPS Classroom Activity Worksheet, Example D*

CHAMPS Classroom Activity Worksheet *CHAMPS*

D
Independent
Seatwork, Low
Support

ACTIVITY *Independent Seatwork (low support)*

CONVERSATION

Can students engage in conversations with each other during this activity? **Yes**   Voice level: *I*
If yes, about what? *About the task or activity*
With whom? *Only students they sit next to*
How many students can be involved in a single conversation? *Only two students at a time*
How long can the conversation last? *About a minute*

HELP

How do students get questions answered? How do students get your attention?
Ask one or two peers seated next to you (Level I voice). If unable to get question answered, flip textbook up on desk.

If students have to wait for help, what should they do while they wait?
Continue working. If unable to continue, take out reading book.

ACTIVITY

What is the expected end product of this activity? (Note: This may vary from day to day.)
Completing independent work assignment

MOVEMENT

Can students get out of their seats during the activity? **Yes** If yes, acceptable reasons include: ☒ restroom ☒ drink ☒ pencil sharpener ☒ hand in/pick up materials ☐ other:

Do they need permission from you?
Only for the restroom

PARTICIPATION

What behaviors show that students are participating fully and responsibly?

Completing work—writing or doing task. Talking to others only about the work and for no more than a minute. Moving around the classroom only as necessary to sharpen pencil, turn in work, use restroom, or get a drink.

What behaviors show that a student is not participating?

Talking about anything besides the assignment. Talking while moving around the room and distracting others. Not doing the task.

SUCCESS

Success comes from following the expectations.

REPRODUCIBLE 3.2

Reproducible 3.2 *CHAMPS Classroom Activity Worksheet, Example E*

CHAMPS Classroom Activity Worksheet   *CHAMPS*

E
Cooperative Group Work, High Support

ACTIVITY   *Cooperative Group Work (high support)*

CONVERSATION

Can students engage in conversations with each other during this activity?   *Yes*   Voice level: *2*
If yes, about what?   *The assignment*
With whom?   *Only their group members*
How many students can be involved in a single conversation?   *3–4*
How long can the conversation last?   *Throughout the activity or until I signal for attention of whole group*

HELP

How do students get questions answered? How do students get your attention?
Put out Help sign

If students have to wait for help, what should they do while they wait?
Continue working on other parts of the assignment

ACTIVITY

What is the expected end product of this activity? (Note: This may vary from day to day.)
Students will complete as much as possible of the assigned activity in the time given. If finished before time is up, ask me to review the work, then read quietly, work on homework or other unfinished work, or work on independent backup packet.

MOVEMENT

Can students get out of their seats during the activity?   *Yes*   If yes, acceptable reasons include: ☐ restroom   ☐ drink
☒ pencil sharpener   ☒ hand in/pick up materials   ☐ other:

Do they need permission from you?   *Students must have permission for any movement. Movement must be related to assignment.*

PARTICIPATION

What behaviors show that students are participating fully and responsibly?

Everyone in the group contributing—doing their assigned group role, giving ideas. Looking at paper or others in the group. Only talking to your group members and only about the assigned task. Staying with the group until work is finished and approved. Resolving group conflicts using wheel or asking for help from teacher.

What behaviors show that a student is not participating?
Not working with group. Not writing, doing what task requires, or following expectations outlined in job role. Talking to others outside of group. Leaving group when not finished. Arguing with group members. Taking over group work and not honoring others' ideas. Letting others in group do the work and not contributing throughout the task.

SUCCESS

Success comes from following the expectations.

     REPRODUCIBLE 3.2

Reproducible 3.2 *CHAMPS Classroom Activity Worksheet, Example F*

CHAMPS Classroom Activity Worksheet *CHAMPS*

F
Cooperative Group Work, Low Support

ACTIVITY *Cooperative Group Work (low support)*

CONVERSATION

Can students engage in conversations with each other during this activity? *Yes*   Voice level: *2*
If yes, about what? *The assignment*
With whom? *Only their group members*
How many students can be involved in a single conversation? *3–4*
How long can the conversation last? *Throughout the activity or until I signal for attention of whole group*

HELP

How do students get questions answered? How do students get your attention?
"Help manager" can ask question to any other group (move to their table and pose question) before asking teacher (raise hand)

If students have to wait for help, what should they do while they wait?
Continue working

ACTIVITY

What is the expected end product of this activity? (Note: This may vary from day to day.)
Students will complete as much as possible of the assigned activity in the time given. If finished before time is up, students should complete homework or other incomplete work. If all is done, group members can talk quietly at their table.

MOVEMENT

Can students get out of their seats during the activity? *Yes* If yes, acceptable reasons include: ☒ restroom   ☒ drink
☒ pencil sharpener   ☒ hand in/pick up materials   ☒ other: *"Help manager" to talk to one other group at a time*

Do they need permission from you?
No. No more than one or two students should be moving at a time. Get permission for restroom.

PARTICIPATION

What behaviors show that students are participating fully and responsibly?

Looking at paper or others in group. Writing or doing what the task requires. Everyone should contribute throughout the task. Talk only to those in your group unless you are the "help manager" asking another group a question.

What behaviors show that a student is not participating?

Not working. Not collaborating with your group. Talking with others outside of your group. Leaving the group or doing other things before the group work is finished.

SUCCESS

Success comes from following the expectations.

REPRODUCIBLE 3.2

TASK 3

Design Procedures for Managing Teacher-Directed Activities

Establish effective procedures for teacher-directed instructional activities.

● ● ● ● ●

In this task, you will define detailed behavioral expectations for activities that are teacher directed (i.e., any activity where you expect students to primarily direct their attention to you, such as lectures, demonstrations, and direct instruction.) Complete Reproducible 3.2 (CHAMPS Classroom Activity Worksheet) for teacher-directed activities.

Box 3.1 includes guidance and examples to consider in structuring your teacher-directed activities. These suggestions will be particularly relevant if you have a class that requires higher levels of support.

Best Practices for Facilitating Teacher-Directed Activities

Teacher behavior can be a decisive factor in the behavior of students. Students are more likely to pay attention to a teacher who is dynamic, direct, humorous, and enthusiastic in class than to a teacher who talks in a monotone or is confusing or boring. Think back to your favorite teachers in high school and college. How did you feel about their classes? Chances are they were interesting, exciting people who challenged their students. Now think back to your boring teachers. How did you feel about their classes?

A motivational sports coach does more than simply teach players the necessary skills of the game. An effective coach is passionate about the game and about encouraging players to learn, even from their mistakes. Think about the motivational speeches an effective coach gives to a team before a big game and during halftime, and to individual players during the game. After the team has won, the coach might say, "You did great, but don't get overconfident. Next week we face the Cougars, and they may be even tougher." If the team has lost, the coach might say, "Yes, we lost, but you played a great game. We can learn from the mistakes we made. We just need to work even harder next week." The words and actions of the effective coach are designed to inspire the players and motivate them to do their best.

Effective instructional practices are an absolutely integral part of behavior management practices (Gettinger & Ball, 2008; Scheuermann & Hall, 2008). A teacher who implements dull instruction, presents unclear tasks, or assigns work that is consistently beyond the ability of some of the students is likely to have some students who appear unmotivated, disruptive, or hostile. This is true even if the teacher does everything else right in terms of behavior management. Effective instruction can prevent a great deal of misbehavior if only because students who are highly engaged in meaningful tasks do not have time to misbehave. When students are successful, their sense of accomplishment can be so satisfying that they are more motivated to behave responsibly. Educators intuitively understand the link between effective instructional

BOX 3.1

Structuring Teacher-Directed Activities

Conversation: In activities in which students are expected to be quietly working or listening, design expectations that minimize student-to-student conversation. For example, a teacher who establishes the expectation that students can only talk after being called on will likely spend less time talking over students or trying to gain their attention.

Help: Consider methods for seeking help that minimize interruption to instruction. For example, hand-raising can also cause a frustrating lack of instructional momentum during teacher-directed activities if students frequently raise their hands to ask questions like "Can I use the restroom?" and "Can I borrow a pencil?" During teacher-directed instruction, one solution is to teach students two different help signals—one for content-focused questions or comments that other students might benefit from hearing, and one for questions related to personal needs, such as needing materials, restroom, or water. For example, you might teach students to raise their hands into the air with palm open for questions or comments about the content. For questions about individual needs, they can raise their hand in the air with a thumbs-up or closed fist. Thank you to Dr. Anita Archer for this idea! This procedure allows you to signal to a student who has a private question that you see them and will answer their question shortly once you are at a logical pausing point in instruction. Once you reach that logical pausing point, give other students a short active engagement task (e.g., write three examples of the concept, or turn to a partner and describe three important ideas) while you speak with the student with the private question.

Activity: Students tend to become inattentive when teacher-directed activities run overly long. One teacher shared with us that she initially sets a vibrating timer for 3 minutes when her young students are being introduced to seated activities at the carpet. When the timer goes off, she does a quick stand-up-and-move activity. Then she has students sit down again for another 3 minutes of seated instruction. As they demonstrate appropriate behaviors during each 3-minute interval, she expands the intervals to 5 minutes, then 8 minutes, and so on. Her colleagues have expressed disbelief at seeing how well-behaved her students are for long periods of carpet activities. Her response is, "It doesn't start that way, but we work up to it!" This gradual expansion of an activity as students demonstrate increased responsibility is a fantastic practice that can be applied across many different activity structures across all age groups. Additionally, the higher the structure needed for your group, the more carefully you will want to prevent voids in their engagement during any type of activity. Infuse active participation throughout teacher-directed activities.

Movement: Consider all of the reasons why students might need to move during a given activity (e.g., get a drink, use the restroom, sharpen a pencil, get materials from inside class, get materials from outside class [e.g., from a locker], turn in completed work, stand and stretch). As you define your expectations for movement, recognize that free movement (not based on teacher permission) requires more responsibility and maturity on the part of all students. If the expectations for movement are loose, as in "Get up when you need to and take care of your needs," or vague, as in "Movement is minimal," students who struggle with behavior or academic expectations may get up too frequently to avoid working, to distract others, or to engage in other inappropriate behaviors. Students who are attempting to do their work but struggle with attention or are easily over-stimulated may have difficulty remaining focused as other students move about the room. For classes that require more structure and support, consider restricting movement in one of the following ways:

Continued on next page ⟶

Box 3.1 continued

- ***Allow students to move freely for specific reasons but limit the number of students moving in the classroom at one time.*** A teacher might indicate that students can get up to get a drink from a faucet in the classroom at any time during the activity, but the student must first scan the room to ensure that no other students are moving at the same time. If all other students are in their designated areas, the student can move quickly to get a drink.

- ***Require teacher permission for movement within the classroom and to other locations (e.g., restroom, locker).*** This allows you to ensure that only one student is moving at a time and that students are moving for appropriate reasons and at acceptable times during an activity. For example, a student might raise his hand to ask to get a drink in the hallway, but it is right in the middle of an essential portion of the activity. You can tell the student he has permission to get a drink once that portion of the activity is completed.

- ***Indicate that movement for particular reasons is not allowed during a specific activity.*** Some teachers, for example, indicate that students should not request to use the restroom during teacher-directed instruction or partner work because it can be highly disruptive to the instruction or collaborative work. Other teachers may indicate that students may ask to get items from their locker or use the restroom only after the first 10 minutes of class to ensure that students are not congregating with students who are tardy in the halls.

NOTE: Be somewhat careful with restrictions for restroom use. Ensure that there are times available when students can request use of the restroom based on age-appropriate expectations. For example, middle school or upper elementary students may be able to wait for restroom breaks a little longer than students in kindergarten. Also ensure that backup procedures are in place to allow students to get needs met, especially in cases of emergency with the restroom. We heard one terrible story from a teacher whose granddaughter had an incident related to an inhumane restroom policy. One middle school teacher would not allow students to use the restroom during class time and expected students to use the restroom only during passing periods. The granddaughter had a stomach issue one day and despite numerous requests to use the restroom, she was not allowed to leave class. She ended up having an accident in class and was so mortified about the experience that she began refusing to go to school. No policy should be so restrictive that a student cannot access the restroom if they truly need to. If you plan to restrict requests for use of the restroom during particular class times or activities, one highly effective procedure is to tell students they have a certain number of "emergency" restroom passes. If a student has to use the restroom during a restricted time, let them know that you are marking their name down on a chart where you will keep track of students who have used their emergency passes. If the student reaches the limit (e.g., three passes in a term for each period or hour), you will follow up with a planned discussion with the student and involve the student's parents/guardians and the school nurse to determine if there is a physical concern that needs to be addressed.

Participation: The higher the needs of the class for support and structure, the more clearly you will want to define and then teach expectations for participation. What should students look and sound like when they are meeting your expectations for engagement and participation? What common examples can you think of for when students are not appropriately participating? Carefully consider common behaviors that occur in your classroom and determine whether each would be considered on task or off task. For example, if a student is doodling during teacher-directed instruction, do you consider this acceptable participation as long as the student responds to any active participation requests, such as to write something or turn to a partner to explain the concept? Or do students struggle to doodle and attend to your instruction, so you view doodling during teacher-directed instruction as unacceptable? There is no right or wrong answer to these questions, but you should seek to provide as much clarity to your students as possible when providing examples and non-examples of participation.

strategies and high academic achievement; a strong connection also exists between academic failure and disruptive behavior problems in students. Research has shown a clear link between inferior instruction and poor student behavior (Brophy & Good, 1986; Marzano et al., 2003).

It is outside the scope of this program to provide comprehensive guidance on effective instructional practices—the topic is far too broad and complex. However, this task includes descriptions of some elements of effective instruction that can significantly influence student behavior (Gersten & Baker, 2000; Good & Brophy, 2000; Howell & Nolet, 2000; Hudson & Miller, 2006; Kame'enui & Simmons, 1990; Watkins & Slocum, 2004).

Although some teachers will naturally be better presenters than others, every teacher can and should strive to make their presentations as interesting as possible to students. Make sure you vary the tone of your voice and avoid being monotone. (Remember Ben Stein as the teacher in *Ferris Bueller's Day Off*? You don't want to be compared to him.) Vary the intensity of your presentation—sometimes act excited, sometimes act calm and relaxed. Use humor—try to make at least some part of every lesson fun or funny.

Following are several specific strategies you can use alone or in combination as part of your presentation style to increase students' intrinsic motivation. By presenting tasks and behaviors in a manner that generates student enthusiasm, you can drive students forward to succeed.

> **Motivation**
>
> *Effective instructional practices are strongly linked to student motivation. When students appear unmotivated, consider how to strengthen instructional practices to stimulate student interest, increase student success, and actively involve students in instruction.*

Be clear about what students are to learn and explain why the task or behavior will be useful to them.

Most students find it easier to begin and complete an assignment when it has unambiguous directions and clear parameters (Archer & Hughes, 2011; Gersten & Baker, 2000; Hudson & Miller, 2006; Kame'enui & Simmons, 1990; Rosenshine, 1986). Be very direct about the key concepts students need to understand—the more direct your communication, the better. Most people are more motivated to work on a task that has a clear and important purpose than on a task that seems like meaningless busywork. Therefore, whenever possible, tell your students why you want them to work on the tasks you assign. For example, when presenting a new math skill, you might emphasize how the skill will help them solve certain types of problems. Or, when presenting an important historical event, you might emphasize how the event is relevant to the current events in the country you are studying. If you are trying to get your class to work harder toward one of your Guidelines for Success, you can stress how following the guideline will help them individually to be more successful and will make the classroom a better place for everyone.

Obviously, your explanations about why lessons are useful need to be age appropriate. With kindergarten and first-grade students, it may be sufficient to say an activity will be fun or interesting. With eighth-grade students, you need to communicate more precisely what

> **Diversity, Equity, Inclusion, and Access**
>
> *Although clear expectations and explicit instruction are important for all students, they can be especially important for students from diverse backgrounds or English language learners. These students don't always have the same contextual background that other students may have, so you cannot assume they will know why something is important (Doabler et al., 2016; Gersten & Baker, 2000; Gersten & Jimenez, 2002; Rhodes et al., 2005; Richards-Tutor et al., 2016).*

the expected outcome will be and how the task will be useful. It is not necessary to provide this kind of explanation for everything you ask students to do, but you should plan on doing it fairly frequently.

Relate new tasks to previously learned skills.

Whenever you introduce a new skill or topic, tell students how the new skill relates to previously learned skills (Archer & Hughes, 2011; Gersten & Baker; 2000; Hudson & Miller, 2006; Kame'enui & Carnine, 1998; Kame'enui & Simmons, 1990, 1999). Students should not feel that you are presenting hundreds of unconnected, random skills and concepts. They need to understand that what you ask them to do at any particular time relates to what they worked on in the past and will be working on in the future. In this way, students can see how what they have already mastered is useful in understanding new skills or concepts. When you combine this strategy with the previous suggestion (be clear about what students are to learn), you will ensure that students have a sense of continuity about their learning.

Give students a vision of what they will eventually be able to do.

Students should be aware of the long-term benefits of full and active participation in your class. That is, they should know what new skills they will be able to do at the end of the year if they follow your directions and work hard at the tasks you assign. The benefits may involve academic skills, study skills, social skills, or a mix of all three. Your long-range classroom goals (which will be discussed later in this chapter in Task 8) may provide examples of skills that students will be learning. For example, with younger students, you might show them the kinds of books they will be able to read and understand, demonstrate the types of math problems they will be able to complete, and explain how they will learn to keep their attention focused on their work for longer and longer periods of time. With seventh-grade history students, you might share how they will be able to understand current events in new ways and how they will learn to take useful notes and study for tests.

Rally the enthusiasm and energy of students, particularly when asking them to do something difficult or challenging.

Remember, many students will not be easily motivated to do something new or difficult. In this situation, you should make a point of emulating a really masterful sports coach who gives an impassioned speech to the team before an especially challenging game.

EXAMPLES, IDEAS, AND TIPS

The following hypothetical speech might be given 2 days before a unit test in science: "Class, in 2 days we have the unit test in science. This is a tough unit, but I know that you can do it—you can get these important concepts. I want you to do three things in the next 2 days that will really help you get a good score on the test. First, work to pay attention in class. We are going to review the essential information you need to understand, so keep your attention focused.

Second, any time you don't understand something we are reviewing, ask about it. There are no stupid questions. If you aren't sure how to ask a question, just ask me to give more information or to explain the idea again in a different way. Third, decide right now how much you are going to study tonight and how much you are going to study tomorrow night for this test. How many minutes are you going to study? Decide—right now! Now, add fifteen minutes to that number. If you were thinking that you would study zero minutes, add 15 minutes, so you will study at least 15 minutes tonight and 15 minutes tomorrow night. If you planned to study 30 minutes each night, make it 45 minutes. Remember, the more you study, the more you learn—and the more you learn, the better you will do on the test!"

• • • • •

Actively involve students.

Don't talk too much! When you speak for more than a few minutes without getting students involved in some way, many students will tend to tune you out. Ask questions and encourage oral, written, and action responses. Research has shown that giving students lots of opportunities to respond to a teacher's instructional questions, statements, and gestures decreases problem behavior and increases academic achievement (Brophy & Good, 1986; Engelmann & Becker, 1978; Haydon et al., 2012; Sutherland & Wehby, 2001). Frequent student responses provide important immediate feedback to teachers. If students quickly and eagerly answer most questions correctly, you know they are learning the material. Give your students many opportunities to respond (OTRs). To increase your OTR rate, try some of these strategies.

- Ask a question and call on volunteers only sporadically. Attempt to use other types of OTRs that involve all students to increase accountability and allow different voices and ideas to be heard.
- Break complex problems into smaller chunks and have students provide answers to each small part of the problem. Students can write answers on their paper or whiteboard, provide choral responses, or share their response with a partner.
- Ask drill-and-practice questions from note cards and have students provide brief choral or individual answers.
- Provide a question and have the students write the answer on a small whiteboard. They can hold it up to show you when they have the answer.
- Provide students with response cards (e.g., true/false, agree/disagree, A/B/C/D). Ask a question and have students hold up the card that represents their response.
- Mix brief, fast-paced, teacher-directed review of previous material into every lesson. Include group responses throughout the review to ensure that students understand and remember previously learned material. ·
- Ask a question and then draw a student's name from a jar. Once the question has been answered, place the name back in the jar.

As you design OTRs, craft questions that have the appropriate level of difficulty for the students in the class—problems that are not too easy and provide academic challenge.

According to recommendations from research, the optimal rate of OTRs is four to six per minute of instruction on new material with 80% accuracy, and nine to twelve per minute of instruction on drill-and-practice material with 90% accuracy (CEC, 1987; Stichter, 2009). To learn more about OTRs, see Tool 6 in Chapter 10, Task 1. Other strategies for getting students involved in lessons, even teacher-directed lessons, are:

- Use fillable notes in which students write down small amounts of critical content on an outline or note-taking sheet.
- Give students tasks to work on in pairs.
- Present mini tasks for students to work on independently.
- Give mini quizzes.
- Set up role-plays.
- Present guided practice of tasks students will work on later.

Increased OTRs also allow a teacher to provide more immediate feedback to students ("Great answer, Dan," "You really understand the story, Lisa") and keep students on task. When students practice a task, they need to receive information on the parts of the task they are doing correctly and the parts they are doing incorrectly as quickly as possible (Gettinger & Ball, 2008; Good & Brophy, 2000; Hudson & Miller, 2006; Kame'enui & Simmons, 1990). Sincere, age-appropriate praise provides students with personal, immediate feedback as well as positive interactions with the teacher. Increased positive interactions between teachers and students have been shown to decrease misbehavior and lead to increases in on-task behavior (Brophy & Good, 1986; Cook et al., 2017; Walker et al., 2004). Teachers generous in their praise typically experience less off-task or disruptive behavior from their students. A high rate of OTRs and praise go hand in hand—OTRs provide lots of opportunities to praise correct academic responses and appropriate manners of response. Students need to know about their mistakes as soon as possible if they are going to learn from those mistakes. During an oral class exercise, you should provide this kind of performance information to students immediately. Likewise, feedback about correct and incorrect responses during guided practice in class should be immediate.

Have clear objectives.

You should always know exactly what you want your students to know or be able to do as a result of the lessons you teach and the tasks you assign. Think about classes you have taken in which the teacher's classroom lessons had nothing to do with the tests and assignments. Preparing for tests probably became guesswork, and going to class seemed like a waste of time. Most people would get pretty discouraged by this situation.

Plan your lessons by first thinking about how you will evaluate students' mastery of the content. For example, before you begin a 2-week science unit, create the test students will take at the end of the unit (or review it, if you are using a published test that goes with your textbook). By creating or looking at the test first, you will know the key vocabulary words, concepts, and operations that you need to directly teach during instruction. You can then make sure that any tasks you assign will help students practice those vocabulary words, concepts, and operations. For those who question this as "teaching to the test," consider that a test should cover the material you want students to learn, and so should your instruction. In fact, a clear and consistent match between instruction and evaluation is a hallmark of effective teaching (Fuchs et al., 1985; Fuchs & Fuchs, 1986; Gresham, 2002; Howell & Nolet, 2000; Hudson & Miller, 2006; Shinn & Bamonto, 1998; Ysseldyke & Christenson, 1988). To learn more about effective grading systems, see Tasks 9 and 10 later in this chapter.

Ensure high rates of success.

Students learn faster when they get predominantly correct answers on both oral and written tasks. While it is true that students should be challenged with difficult tasks, it's also true that students will get discouraged over time when they are constantly presented with tasks that are too difficult. When tasks are too difficult, students make many errors, often learn a lot of incorrect information along the way, and become more likely to engage in misbehavior (Fisher et al., 1978; Martella et al., 2003; Rosenshine, 1997). Try to provide clear enough instruction and frequent enough practice opportunities to ensure that students will get approximately 90% correct on most tasks.

In situations where you know that students are likely to make many errors, you should plan to provide more teacher-directed instruction—whether you work with students in small groups (while the other students work independently) or with the whole class. Consider the following example involving a whole-class math lesson.

EXAMPLES, IDEAS, AND TIPS

Your original plans call for about 15 minutes of teacher-directed instruction and 30 minutes of independent work time for students to work on the assignment. During the teacher presentation portion you realize that many students are confused and do not seem to understand the assignment. If you stick with your plan, many students are likely to make lots of errors, and some will become discouraged. Several students may seek your help during the independent work period. Because many students are confused, a better approach would be to change your plan.

Instead of giving 30 minutes of independent work, you might say, "Class, since this is such a difficult assignment, I am going to walk you through the first ten problems. Anyone who wants to work ahead may do so, but I invite anyone who is still confused to do the problems with me. Watch me do problem 1, then copy what I have done."

Data-Driven Processes

A reasonable goal to set for yourself is to be a slightly better presenter every year. Pick one or two of the suggestions in this task to focus on this year. Ask colleagues and administration to visit your classroom to observe and help you with your presentation style. Record your teaching on audio or video and then analyze your instructional style and look for improvements you can make.

Provide guided practice before releasing students to work on independent or cooperative tasks and assignments.

Guided practice increases the chance that students will have the skills or knowledge needed to complete the task successfully, and also create behavioral momentum. That is, when you guide students through the first part of a task, a portion of the task is already completed by the time you say, "Now do the rest of the assignment on your own." Without guided practice, students face a blank piece of paper when you say, "Get to work on your assignment."

For many students, the hardest part of doing assigned tasks is getting started. Guided practice increases work completion because it ensures that students have started their work, and likely understand it, before the independent part of the class period begins (Archer & Hughes, 2011; Rosenshine, 2012).

For example, when teaching a math lesson, you might start by reviewing previously taught concepts, then introduce the day's new concept, then work through the first several exercises of the math assignment, and finally turn students loose to work on the remainder of the assignment independently or in groups.

If the assignment has 30 problems, you might model and lead students through the first six: "Watch me do the first two problems on the board and copy what I do." Then demonstrate and explain. "On the next two problems, I'll do the first half, and you do the second half." You demonstrate the first part and let students do the second part. Correct problems and answer student questions, or re-teach based on student mistakes. "Now do the next two problems on your own. Stop when you finish problem 6 so we can correct." Let all students do two problems while you monitor their performance. Then model or have individual students demonstrate the correct answer. Answer questions and provide any additional instructions.

If students are doing well, you can then assign the remaining problems as independent work. If many students are having problems, continue to work through the problems together until you are sure they understand the concepts and processes.

The support needs of your group should determine how often you use guided practice. The greater the need for support, the longer you should guide the work before letting your students work independently.

In summary, these tips will ensure that your teacher-directed activities are appropriate and effective:

- Be clear about what students are to learn and explain why the task or behavior will be useful to them.
- Relate new tasks to previously learned skills.
- Give students a vision of what they will eventually be able to do.
- Rally the enthusiasm and energy of students, particularly when asking them to do something difficult or challenging.
- Actively involve students.
- Have clear objectives.
- Ensure high rates of success.
- Provide guided practice before releasing students to work on independent or cooperative tasks and assignments.

TASK 4

Design Procedures for Managing Independent Work Periods

Establish effective procedures for facilitating independent work periods.

• • • • •

In this task, you will define detailed behavioral expectations for all independent work periods (i.e., any activity where you expect students to work alone with limited teacher direction and guidance). As you did in the previous task with teacher-directed activities, you will complete Reproducible 3.2, CHAMPS Classroom Activity Worksheet, for each activity you've classified as an independent work period.

Box 3.2 (pp. 142–143) includes additional guidance and examples to consider in structuring your independent work activities. If you have a class that requires higher supports, review these suggestions closely.

Best Practices for Facilitating Independent Work Periods

When students are expected to work without direct teacher supervision, off-task behavior can easily result. There is more potential for off-task behavior—which can lead to inappropriate horseplay and disrespectful interactions among students—when students are working independently than during most other types of activities. Your goal should be to keep students on task and actively engaged in their work. The following suggestions can help minimize off-task behavior during independent work periods.

Be sure that any independent work you assign can be done independently by students.

If you assign students tasks that they cannot complete independently, you set them up to fail. When students have to do work that is beyond their ability, they are likely to:

- Do the work but fail because of excessive errors.
- Not do the work and fail because they didn't complete the assignment, and/or act out or disrupt others while they are not working.
- Do the work but deal with feeling and looking helpless because they ask for help day after day from you or peers.

Motivation

Remember that motivated behavior is more complex than whether a student values the rewards that accompany a task (e.g., learning, good grades, etc.). If tasks are designed in such a way that a student has little or no expectancy of success, or if a student has experienced repeated failure with similar tasks across time, the student is unlikely to be motivated to complete the task. To boost motivation and participation, ensure that work is at a student's independent level (where the student can reasonably complete the task with 90%–95% accuracy without assistance).

> ## BOX 3.2
>
> # Structuring Independent Work Activities
>
> **C**onversation: In activities in which students are expected to be quietly working, design expectations that minimize student-to-student conversation. For example, during independent work, a teacher who has an expectation of 0 voice level (no talking) is likely to see much more productive and focused work than a teacher who allows students to talk quietly with their peers as long as they are still able to finish their work. For students who finish early, you will want to include backup activities or extension activities to keep them engaged while they remain quiet and allow peers to finish their work.
>
> **H**elp: Consider methods for seeking help that limit student-to-student conversation and movement (e.g., to write their name on the board). You can limit these distractions by doing the following:
>
> - ***Introduce a specific procedure for students to use when raising their hands to recruit your attention.*** Traditional hand-raising procedures can become problematic during independent work time for the following reasons: a) it is physically difficult to keep a hand in the air for the 3 to 5 minutes it may take you to respond, b) the student is necessarily off task while waiting for your help, and c) hand-raising tends to draw more attention to a student, which may discourage some students from asking for help. To avoid these pitfalls, establish procedures that allow students to continue working once you have seen and acknowledged their raised hand. While you are circulating or assisting other students, periodically scan the room to look for students who have their hands raised. Some teachers carry a clipboard or sticky notes so that they can write down names of students who need help. Try to ensure that hands are not raised for more than a minute or two before you see the student and write their name down. Once a student's name is written down, signal that the student should put their hand down and continue working until you can provide assistance. If multiple students have requested help, go to them in the order you wrote them down on the clipboard or sticky note. With this procedure, you will need to teach students seeking help to skip the portion with the question and continue to other parts of the work. If they are unable to continue, ensure that students always have backup work or silent reading/drawing they can do so they remain engaged while waiting for your assistance.
> - ***Teach your students how to use an alternative visual signal to recruit your assistance.*** Instead of hand-raising, another option for a visual signal for help is to have students put an upright book (not the book they need for the assignment) or a flag or sign on the corner of their desk. Figure 3.1 on the next page shows an example of how a sign can be used. One side of the sign says, "I'm fine." Another side says, "Please help!" The third side says, "Make note of your questions and keep working." Reproducible 3.3, Student

Work Status Display (not shown), is a premade sign that you can print and fold for students to use. (This idea was originally suggested by Paine et al., 1983.)

Another option is shown in Figure 3.2. Get two paper or plastic cups, one green and one red, and tape the open ends together. All students have a taped-together pair of cups on their desk. When a student, partnership, or group is doing OK, the green cup is on top. When help is needed, the student(s) turn the cups over so that the red cup is on top. To ensure that cups are not rolling around the room, attach Velcro to the desk and bottom of each cup so student can fasten the cup in place when turning it over.

- **_Provide clear expectations for seeking help from peers._** If you plan to allow students to ask one another for help before asking the teacher, be sure that students understand that talking is permitted only to get needed help on assignments. Specify who the student can talk to when seeking help (e.g., ask the person directly to your left or right). Also provide clarity on the expected voice level and for what topics (e.g., ask a question directly related to the activity or needed materials). However, if students struggle to remain on task and you find yourself having to correct for too many students talking to each other or too loudly, you may need to increase structure by using help methods that involve the teacher rather than other students.

Figure 3.1 *Help Sign*

Figure 3.2 *Cups as Signal*

Activity: If students struggle to focus on independent work for long periods of time, plan activities so that they are interspersed with short periods of teacher-directed instruction. If students struggle to remain seated for long periods of time, ensure that seated activities are relatively short or interspersed with opportunities to wiggle and stretch. Ensure that all students have something to work on, even once they've finished their work.

Movement: For classes that require more structure and support, consider restricting movement by limiting the number of students moving in the classroom at one time, requiring teacher permission for movement within the classroom and to other locations, or indicating that movement for particular reasons is not allowed during independent work.

Participation: High-support classes require you to put extra effort into clarifying and teaching expectations for participation. Carefully consider the wide range of behavior that occurs in your classroom during independent work time. Which behaviors indicate full participation and which behaviors do you consider off-task?

Over time, many students slip into the second option because when they do nothing, act out, or disrupt, at least they look tough or bored instead of stupid and helpless. Following are suggestions for steps you can take to ensure that the independent work you assign can be completed by all students (Archer & Hughes, 2011; Babkie, 2006; Barbetta et al., 2005; Gettinger & Ball, 2008; Howell & Nolet, 2000).

- Modify assignments to meet the needs of the lower performing students in the class. For example, highlight important ideas or provide a study guide for the student to follow when reading independently.
- For some of the students, provide alternative assignments that focus on prerequisite skills or that offer more accessible content but similar skill practice or application.
- Work together on the assignment with a few students in a small group while the rest of the class works independently (Ysseldyke et al., 1990). Or, if you have a paraprofessional supporting the classroom, have them work the small group while you circulate through students who are working independently.
- Have students work in pairs or cooperative groups so they can help each other (Johnson et al., 2008; Spencer, 2006). Do not overuse this strategy or your higher performing students may get tired of helping others do their work. Also ensure that you preteach students with higher levels of skill or speed in completing tasks to prompt their peers without taking over and simply completing the assignment themselves.
- Use computer-assisted instruction or practice (Cheng & Lai, 2020; Escueta et al., 2017; Silver-Pacuilla & Fleischman, 2006).
- Provide students with guided notes (Konrad et al., 2009; Sweeney et al., 1999).
- Have students who may struggle check in with you more frequently (e.g., after completing every one or two steps in a ten-step assignment) to ensure that they are on the right track. If students complete an entire assignment or project before identifying errors, they will have to redo all of the work and have also practiced errors, increasing the likelihood of future difficulty.

Consider physical organization factors that may improve student focus.

During independent work, the room arrangement can play a significant role in whether students are able to remain on task or not (Wannarka and Ruhl, 2008). If the desk arrangement has students facing one another, this inadvertently prompts social interaction for a highly social group of students. If your students struggle to remain focused during independent work times, consider whether elements of your room arrangement could be altered to maximize student success.

For example, if students are seated in clusters but talk excessively during independent work, consider solutions like:

- Rearranging desks into rows so that all students face one direction rather than each other.
- Using cardboard trifold desk dividers to create a work cubby for each student. These are sometimes used in classrooms during tests to prevent students from looking at others' work but could easily be used during independent work periods.

- Having some students move to other locations in the classroom (e.g., to a small group table or spaced out along the wall with clipboards) to reduce the number of students at each cluster table.

Schedule independent work times in a way that maximizes on-task behavior.

The subject of scheduling to maximize on-task behavior and minimize off-task behavior was discussed in Task 1 of this chapter. The following information summarizes suggestions on how to improve student engagement during independent work periods.

- Do not schedule long periods during which students are expected to stay on task while working independently. There is no magic rule about how long students can stay focused, but in general, having students work on the same task for more than 30 minutes without some change in routine will result in high rates of off-task behavior. Even 30 minutes can be far too long for primary-grade students or highly immature older students unless you have built up to that amount.
- Do not schedule lengthy independent work periods to immediately follow high-excitement times such as recess or assemblies. Some teachers use a short (2–5 minute) independent activity to calm students when they return to class, but schedule longer work periods some distance from these high-excitement times.
- Do schedule independent work periods to follow some form of teacher-directed instruction.
- Arrange for the independent work periods that occur at the end of the day to be shorter than independent work periods that occur at the beginning of the day.

Provide timely feedback for any independent work that is assigned.

As previously indicated, students need to receive timely feedback about what they are doing correctly and what they are doing incorrectly. If you have students do an assignment on a new math concept, but you take a week or more to return their corrected papers, they will learn little. When you assign written tasks to be done independently, be sure to correct the papers within 1 or 2 days and then go over the corrected papers when you return them: "Class, look at the papers I just handed back. Quite a few people had trouble with question number 5. Let's look at why you had trouble. When you do a problem like this, keep in mind that . . ."

In summary, the following tips will ensure that your independent work activities are appropriate and effective:

- Be sure that any independent work you assign can be done independently by your students.
- Consider how the physical space can be rearranged to improve student focus.
- Schedule independent work times in a way that maximizes on-task behavior.
- Provide timely feedback on any independent work you assign.

TASK 5

Design Procedures for Managing Partner and Cooperative Group Work

Establish effective procedures for facilitating partner and cooperative group activities.

• • • • •

In this task, you will define detailed behavioral expectations for all partner and cooperative group activities (i.e., any activity that involves students interacting together to accomplish specific goals or develop end products related to the classroom content).

As you did in the previous tasks, you will complete Reproducible 3.2, CHAMPS Classroom Activity Worksheet, for each activity you've classified as a partner or cooperative group activity.

If you have a class that requires higher support, consider the additional guidance and examples shown in Box 3.3 in structuring your partner and cooperative group activities.

Best Practices for Facilitating Partner and Cooperative Work Periods

Cooperative learning, which includes both partner and small group activities, involves students interacting together to accomplish specific goals or develop end products related to the classroom content. Cooperative learning includes everything from informal tasks that last for a few minutes to an entire class period to more formal learning where students work together for up to several weeks to complete specific tasks and achieve shared learning goals.

Cooperative learning is beneficial for a variety of reasons. When well designed, cooperative work encourages the students to reorganize and clarify material, recognize misconceptions, internalize and acquire new strategies and knowledge, and develop new perspectives and understanding (Bargh & Schul, 1980; King, 2002; Saxe et al., 1993). In explaining their problem-solving processes, students think about the salient features of the problem, which develops their problem-solving strategies as well as their metacognitive awareness of what they do and do not understand (Cooper, 1999).

Cooperative group work has additional benefits. It gives students the opportunity to work with and learn from their peers, develops critical interpersonal social skills, and provides an increased variety of activities. For students who prefer interpersonal learning settings, cooperative activities can be a powerful motivating factor. Students who struggle academically can learn from more capable peers. For students emerging in English, partner and small group activities provide opportunities to engage in structured academic talk that can drive language and concept development and build linguistic confidence (DePalma, 2010; Gersten et al., 2007; Harmer, 2007; Tuan & Nhu, 2010).

BOX 3.3

Structuring Partner and Cooperative Group Activities

Conversation: In partner or small group activities, provide clear parameters for who students can talk to and about what topics. For example, if students are expected to work in partners, indicate that students are allowed to speak with only their designated partner about the assigned topic. Specify a voice level that will allow partners to hear one another but will maintain a sense of calm in the classroom, such as a Level 2 Quiet Conversational voice. Note that whispering can be very difficult to decipher (especially with young children!), and if responses are longer than a sentence, whispering can be difficult to maintain for long periods. Rather than a whisper voice, we recommend a quiet conversational voice (only people near you can hear you) for partner and small group activities.

Help: As with other instructional activities, establish procedures for seeking help that limit noise and movement as much as possible. The more noise and movement occurring in the classroom, the more difficult it will be for some students to focus on instructional activities. Students who struggle with behavior and engagement are also more likely to talk about other things or move around for reasons other than to get help when the expectations allow for more noise or movement. Instruct partners or groups to use a predetermined visual signal to recruit your assistance, or provide clear expectations for how students can seek help from other groups (e.g., one person can go speak with one person from a nearby group).

Activity: If students are highly immature and struggle with appropriate peer interactions, schedule shorter periods of partner and group work with very clearly defined targets and explicitly taught social skills. As students gain skill in working collaboratively, you can gradually expand the time and range of activities that are done with partners or small groups

Movement: For classes that require more structure and support, consider restricting movement by assigning one partner or group member to gather or return materials or by limiting or requiring teacher permission for movement within the classroom and to other locations during cooperative work activities.

Participation: Provide as much clarity to your students as possible when providing examples and non-examples of participation. What does participation in group discussions look and sound like? For example, during partner work, you may teach students to "Look, lean, and whisper," as recommended by Dr. Anita Archer.

However, cooperative learning can present significant behavioral challenges, such as students getting each other off task, bullying behaviors, and placing too great a burden on some students to carry the bulk of the work while others are left out of meaningful learning. These concerns can be minimized through careful orchestration of structural elements such as group composition and size, developing and teaching norms and structures to guide partner and group interactions, selecting appropriate tasks to support cooperative work, and developing appropriate strategies for discussion and rich learning of content (Barron & Darling-Hammond, 2008, Lou et al., 1996, Webb et al., 1997).

Establish effective cooperative partnerships and small groups.

When designing partnerships and small group learning opportunities, carefully consider the size of the grouping and which students will work well together. In general, smaller groups are preferable, especially with younger students and those not used to group work (Blatchford et al., 1999, Lou et al., 1996). The smaller the size of the group, the greater each student's individual accountability may be to participate and contribute. When groups get too large, it can be difficult to equally distribute conversation and workload. It may be difficult to work towards consensus on tasks that require group agreement. Groups of two to six are generally recommended, with groups consisting of three members exhibiting some of the best performance with problem-solving types of tasks (Heller & Hollabaugh, 1992; Johnson et al., 2008). Consider starting primarily with partner work and gradually moving to larger groups for particular activities once students are successful at following expectations, exhibiting necessary social skills, and producing the desired learning outcomes.

We do not recommend allowing students to select whom they work with, as this can reinforce social divisions such as students separating by social status, race/ethnicity, or gender. This practice can be highly isolating for children who are not chosen by their peers. Assigning groups also ensures that the teacher can separate students who are likely to distract one another or engage in other negative behavior. Assigning partners or groups can help reduce anxiety for some students, whether they be shy, slower processors, worried about other students' feelings, or new to the school.

Diversity, Equity, Inclusion, and Access

Assign students to groups to reduce social divisions and ensure that students do not feel anxious about having to find a group.

If you would like students to have some voice in whom they get to work with, consider the procedure described in Chapter 2, Task 3, in which students periodically list 3–5 students they would like to work with sometime during the year. Each time you create cooperative work groups, select five to ten students who you will work to match with one of the peers on their list. Over time, work to accommodate each student with at least one request. To reduce grumbling about assigned work groups, it can be beneficial to have students brainstorm the advantages of working with peers other than their closest friends.

Each time you assign students to partnerships or groups, consider which grouping structure will provide the best support in leading to desired task outcomes. Possible grouping methods include:

- Random grouping
- Homogenous ability grouping based on similar levels of achievement in the task

- Heterogenous ability grouping—distributing students of differing abilities to different groups to ensure all groups have similar representation of high-, middle-, and low-performing students
- Grouping based on other factors like shared interests, personal relationships, or mixed gender and ethnicity

Different tasks may warrant different grouping structures to facilitate particular learning or interactional outcomes. For example, you might use homogenous ability grouping in some tasks to provide extended learning activities for groups whose abilities are above the majority of the class and scaffolded activities or greater teacher direction for small groups whose skills are below the majority of the class. In other cases, you might distribute students based on other considerations, such as shared interests in different topics for the group work (e.g., students interested in researching mammals are in one group, while students researching reptiles are in another). In yet other cases, you might use a random grouping strategy so that students have the opportunity to connect with many different students.

An example of a commonly used random grouping strategy is *clock partners*. Give each student a diagram of a clock face. Have students form a partnership by giving a direction such as "find a partner who is wearing the same color shirt as you. If you can't find someone, look for someone with the same color shoes or pants." Once all students have found a partner, have them write their partner's name in the 1 o'clock space. Give another direction for students to form a new partnership. "You are going to find a new partner. Hold up the number 1 if you prefer dogs, and a 2 if you prefer cats. Find someone who is holding up the same number." Once students are in their new partnerships, have them write their new partner's name in the 2 o'clock space. Continue giving students different types of directions to find new partners until all 12 spaces have been filled. Tell students that they cannot be with the same partner twice. Then, whenever you want students to get into a random partnership, tell them an hour on the clock face and to stand next to or sit with that partner. We recommend that you have students turn their clock faces in to you after each use or keep them stapled in a consistent place in their binders so they do not get lost.

When considering how to design effective ongoing partnerships that will be used across a period of weeks or for a longer project, in general match up students who will work well together but have somewhat different ability levels. Group students with lower ability in the task with students with medium ability rather than with peers with lower ability, who may struggle to work together to achieve learning outcomes, or those with the highest ability levels, who may get frustrated or simply do the work for their partner. For students who are English language learners, mixed-ability pairs are recommended to improve positive academic outcomes (Baker et. al., 2014), provide opportunities for language and concept development (DePalma, 2010), and create the opportunity for native and non-native English-speaking students to learn from different perspectives (Helfrich & Bosh, 2011). In collaborative learning groups, as with pair work, select students carefully to ensure they can work productively; not all students are able to work to their full potential in this situation.

Diversity, Equity, Inclusion, and Access

Mixed-language pairs are recommended when working with English language learners to allow for language and concept development. Both members of the partnership can benefit as they learn to appreciate different perspectives that come from different cultural backgrounds.

Additional factors to consider when designing partnerships and small groups include:

- If there are multiple highly distractible or immature students in the class, seek to distribute them so they are not working near each other or in the same group. Place them in partnerships and groups with more focused and responsible peers.
- If students will be in the same cooperative groups or partnerships for longer periods (e.g., a month or more), it may be necessary to move students with significant behavioral challenges to new groups or partnerships more frequently (e.g., once a week or every 2 weeks) to ensure that other group members do not get overly fatigued by these students.
- Consider whether your seating arrangement is conducive to easy and productive transitions to and from partner or group work. If transitions to getting into groups are chaotic and require things like moving desks and lots of students moving around the classroom, consider ways to restructure the desk arrangement, seating arrangement, or transition expectations to ensure a smooth transition. For example, if you plan to use frequent partner activities, consider desk arrangements and a seating chart that places partners directly next to each other. See Chapter 2, Task 3 for ideas on designing a positive physical space, and Chapter 2, Task 6 for ideas for designing procedures for these types of transitions.

Teach interactional skills necessary for the cooperative task.

One strong rationale for use of cooperative learning activities is that they provide opportunities for students to learn and practice essential social skills that they will need both in school and outside of school in work settings and personal relationships. However, this is also one of the main challenges in facilitating cooperative learning! Many students need guidance and support in how to engage appropriately with peers. Teachers must be prepared to teach students interpersonal and small group skills such as how to communicate accurately and unambiguously, how to share responsibility for the task by accepting and supporting one another, and how to manage conflicts constructively (Johnson & Johnson, 1991). Teachers also play a critical role in helping students get to know one another and trust each other, which is an essential foundation for productive cooperative learning. For each cooperative activity you plan to have students engage in, create a list of needed social skills. For example, for a partner brainstorming activity, necessary social skills might include:

- Actively listen to your partner's ideas.
- Each person contributes ideas.
- Validate and compliment your partner's ideas.
- Provide a gentle correction or disagreement for an idea that might not fit (e.g., "You know, Ali, I think that might be a reptile, not an amphibian. Should we put a question mark next to it?").

Identify common problems you have encountered with the social aspects of cooperative activities and list them as social skills you will need to directly teach students. Chapter 4, Task 3 provides guidance on how to teach social and interactional skills.

Provide clear objectives and accountability structures for cooperative work.

For each cooperative task, carefully explain the task and expectations for completing it. Explain the group's task, including goals for academic achievement and social interaction. Clarify responsibilities for each group member, such as to try, ask questions, listen to group members, praise good ideas and participation, and be present. Group objectives and responsibilities might also be posted on the board and/or at the top of any informational materials provided to the students about the task.

Give careful thought to how to structure the task so that the individual members of the partnership or group feel a sense of responsibility for the success of the other members in their group. This concept is called *positive interdependence*, in which students' individual success is linked with the success of their partner or group members (Johnson & Johnson, 1989, 2005). No individual can succeed with the task unless their group members are also successful.

A teacher can create positive interdependence through well-designed structures that require all students to participate in and contribute to the activity. For example, you might provide each group member with only part of needed materials for the task so that group members need to combine resources to reach the group goal. Or you might establish specific group roles that are complementary and interconnected so the group needs to work together in their roles to complete the task. Some possibilities for group roles include (Heller and Hollabaugh, 1992; Johnson et al., 2008):

- **Facilitator:** Keeps group on task and encourages participation from all.
- **Recorder:** Takes notes and summarizes main points.
- **Reporter:** Shares summary and speaks for the group.
- **Materials Manager:** Collects, distributes, and puts away materials.
- **Time Keeper:** Keeps track of time and reminds group how much time is left.
- **Checker:** Checks written work for accuracy.

Other group roles could include Skeptic, Educator, Mediator, Editor, and Praiser. There are many possibilities for combinations of roles. Determine which grouping of roles will be most beneficial for structuring shared accountability and participation.

In addition to shared accountability structures, include individual accountability structures so that each student in the partnership or small group knows that they will be required to demonstrate their own knowledge or understanding gained through the group learning process. If students know that they will be individually responsible for their learning, it increases the likelihood that all students participate. Some possibilities for individual accountability include:

- Inform students in advance that each student is responsible for knowing and being able to explain each part of the group's work, then periodically ask individuals to explain portions of the work to you.
- Have students teach another student who was not in their group or partnership what was learned or share what was developed in the cooperative task.

- Randomly call on a few students to share the outcomes of the cooperative group task with the whole class.
- Give individual tests.
- For written work, require that each student's handwriting appear on the group work.

Monitor group interactions closely throughout partner and group activities.

Classroom teachers play a critical role in establishing and modeling practices of productive group learning processes and conversations (Barron & Darling-Hammond, 2008). This can occur through well-thought-out instruction prior to the activity, but it also occurs through careful monitoring and in-the-moment feedback as students engage in cooperative tasks.

While students are working cooperatively, continuously circulate and scan so that you can monitor group interactions and learning. Pay attention to how frequently each group member contributes to the group's work and gently prompt groups that may need assistance: "I've heard some great ideas from Simone and Julian. Tanya, can you share your thinking for the next problem, and Lee, you are up for the one after that." Listen to student discussions to get insight on how well they understand the concepts and material. If multiple groups are having difficulty, bring the whole group back together so you can provide additional instruction on the task or areas of misunderstanding. If an individual group is struggling, assist that group while continuing to listen and periodically scan the room to monitor how other groups are doing.

Assess student understanding and partner/group functioning.

It is important to decide in advance how you will assess both students' learning outcomes from cooperative tasks and how well the partnerships or small groups functioned. These activities bring closure to the lesson or activity and allow you to evaluate what has been learned in regard to content objectives and how to work with others in the class. There are many possibilities for how to assess cooperative learning outcomes. Examples include (Barron & Darling-Hammond, 2008):

> " It is important to decide in advance how you will assess both students' learning outcomes from cooperative tasks and how well the partnerships or small groups functioned. "

- **Rubrics.** Provide specifics about how levels of progress will be evaluated for different aspects of the task. For example, a project might be evaluated on content mastery, organization, and creativity or design. An oral presentation might be evaluated on posture/tone, originality of ideas, structure/organization, pronunciation/enunciation, and preparedness. When designing a rubric, consider essential goals that students should learn and demonstrate through the task.

- **Performance assessments.** Use short individual or group assessments to see how students apply their newly acquired knowledge in a new context. Performance assessments include written or oral assessments such as quizzes and short projects to demonstrate understanding.
- **Written journals.** Have students maintain an ongoing record of their experiences, reflections, and problem-solving throughout a project. Some journal entries may be content specific (e.g., write how your group chose to complete Step 3) or describe aspects of the group's functioning (e.g., write about a challenge your group has encountered with communication and how you are working to overcome that challenge).
- **Portfolios.** Have students compile a collection of their work over time. Periodically include activities that will have them highlight their progress and reflect on their personal growth or learning.
- **Weekly reports.** Use weekly written responses to simple questions about the cooperative group work throughout the duration of an ongoing project. These questions can ask about content or how the group is working together.
- **Self-assessments.** Have students evaluate their own work using a rubric or focus questions.
- **Peer review.** Have students consider the level, value, or quality of a product produced by peers. With this type of assessment, it may be most helpful to have students provide detailed descriptive feedback about strengths and areas of improvement rather than a specific grade or numerical evaluation. Peer review can also be used to have students evaluate the level, value, or quality of member contributions in their own group. Group members identify how well they are achieving their goals and maintaining effective working relationships. They describe member actions that were helpful or unhelpful and what actions could be helpful to continue or change. You can use peer reviews to make decisions about skills that need to be taught or reviewed with the whole group or individual students. They can also be used to help guide discussions in which groups process how to continuously improve their working relationships during cooperative activities.

As students engage in cooperative activities, emphasize the importance of continuous improvement. Design tasks that encourage students to celebrate the hard work of their group members and recognize areas of accomplishment or improvement. Have students reflect on the process of learning together and what could be improved, both in their individual contributions and interactions and within the overall group functioning. These activities encourage students to apply a growth-oriented approach to cooperative learning.

In summary, use the following recommendations to maximize the effectiveness of your partner and cooperative group activities.

- Establish effective cooperative partnerships and small groups.
- Teach interactional skills necessary for the cooperative task.
- Provide clear objectives and accountability structures for cooperative work.
- Monitor group interactions closely throughout partner/group activities.
- Assess student understanding and partner/group functioning.

TASK 6

Design Procedures for Managing Student Assignments

Determine how you will assign, monitor, and collect student work.

• • • • •

An all-too-common frustration for most teachers is dealing with students who do not complete assigned classwork or homework. Students who do not complete assignments often do not get the practice necessary to achieve mastery of essential instructional objectives. In addition, without seeing students' completed assignments, you may not have sufficient information to determine whether they have mastered skills or whether they need more practice. Anything that you can do to increase the likelihood that students will complete assignments is worthwhile because you will significantly increase the rates of student learning and significantly decrease your level of frustration. In this task, you will read about procedures and routines for managing student assignments. Implementing well-designed and well-organized strategies for assigning, monitoring, and collecting student work can alleviate much of your potential frustration. Good strategies for managing assignments accomplish the following:

- They let students know that you put a high value on completing work.
- They prompt more responsible student behavior regarding assigned tasks.
- They help you effectively manage student assignments without taking unreasonable amounts of time.

You will consider five major areas related to managing student work: assigning classwork and homework, collecting completed work, returning graded work to students, keeping records and providing feedback, and addressing late and missing assignments. This task covers the kinds of decisions you should think about for each area as well as strategies you might implement.

Assigning Classwork and Homework

One of the first things to consider in this task is implementing a system that allows students to easily find information about assignments. While in class, students should have a specific place to look, such as the board or an assignment sheet, to find out what they are assigned. It is not enough to simply tell students the assignments or to include them on a slide during lessons. These methods do not create a permanent place for students to check to see what they need to do. When there is no set place where students can check their assignments, a student who forgets what the day's homework or is not sure what classwork to turn in has no choice but to ask you or another student for the information. When assignments are written and left on the board or recorded on an assignment sheet hung in a particular place in the classroom, the student can simply look at the board or assignment sheet.

Figure 3.3 shows how you might use board space for recording assignments. An alternative to using board space or assignment sheets is to use a flip chart. You can also put a large sheet of paper on the bulletin board and write each day's assignments on one page. Middle school teachers might use one page for each class period for a full week. Each day, you can flip over (or add) a new page for that day's assignments. This system has the additional advantage of providing easy access to information about previous assignments. A student who has been absent can simply go to the flip chart or bulletin board, find the pages for the days he was absent, and copy down what he needs to do. Because a class with high risk factors is likely to have frequent student absences, having a permanent record of daily assignments is especially useful.

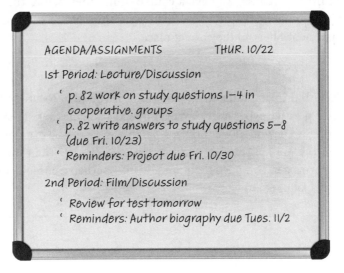

Figure 3.3 *Sample Assignments on Board*

AGENDA/ASSIGNMENTS   THUR. 10/22

1st Period: Lecture/Discussion

' p. 82 work on study questions 1–4 in
  cooperative groups
' p. 82 write answers to study questions 5–8
  (due Fri. 10/23)
' Reminders: Project due Fri. 10/30

2nd Period: Film/Discussion

' Review for test tomorrow
' Reminders: Author biography due Tues. 11/2

If you give both short-term daily assignments and long-term assignments (a term paper, for example), be sure to note both types of assignments on the board or assignment sheet. Daily reminders about a long-term task will help students remember to work on the task on an ongoing basis rather than put it off to the last minute. Written reminders can also prompt you to let students know what parts of a long-term assignment should be done at certain points in time: "Remember that your projects are due in one week, so by Monday you should have your outline and your first draft completed." If students are fairly responsible and consistently meet deadlines, these suggestions are probably sufficient. If, however, your students struggle with completing long-term assignments on time, consider ways to break the assignment into smaller chunks that are due on a regular basis. For example, for a ten-page paper, have students submit two pages each week, or have them first submit an outline, then the introduction, then the body of the paper, and so on.

As part of your plan for assigning work, determine how you expect students to organize materials and monitor assignments. That is, when you give an assignment, where will students keep a record of it? One effective strategy used in many schools is to have students keep a three-ring binder with dividers for various subjects and an assignment sheet for each subject that includes classwork and homework. If your school has adopted a specific schoolwide study skills curriculum, you should follow the organizational strategies suggested in that curriculum.

One reason to have students keep a record of assigned classwork and homework is so that when they get home, they know what they need to do. Many teachers use electronic methods, such as a class website or shared spreadsheet, for students and family members to check on assigned work and homework. However, we also recommend teaching students to copy the assignments onto a sheet of notebook paper and keep it in a consistent place in their notebook. This ensures that students learn organizational skills for keeping track of their own work. It also increases equity for students who may not have consistent access to Internet-connected devices in the home and for students who struggle with technology or organizational skills with user names and passwords for logging in when at home. If you give out a weekly assignment sheet, teach students to keep the assignment sheet in a consistent place in their notebooks. Be specific—tell students exactly how and where to record the information. Show them a model and, especially at the beginning of the year, monitor whether they are following through: "Class, we have a couple of minutes before the bell. Open your notebooks to the page immediately after the divider for this class. I want to see that you have the Weekly Assignment Sheet in the correct place."

> With primary students in particular, if you plan to assign homework, strive to make it a positive experience. For example, if students do not have support at home for getting homework done (perhaps parents work in the evening or no one speaks English in the home), you can suggest that students use the time before class begins in the morning to complete their homework—perhaps with older students available to assist the younger students.

Collecting Completed Work

Another issue to consider is how students turn in completed homework and in-class work. Some assignments are submitted physically in class while other assignments may be submitted electronically (e.g., via an app or email). See the following considerations for each of these approaches.

Use procedures that promote student responsibility with work submitted physically in class.

Whenever possible, collect work personally from each student: "Class, put your homework on the upper right-hand corner of your desk. While you are working on the challenge problem on the board, I will come around and collect it. If you were unable to complete the homework, please be prepared to discuss with me your plan for when you will finish it and what you need to make that happen." The biggest advantage to this procedure is that you know immediately which students have not completed the work (and students know you know). If a student does not have their work completed, you can take that moment to emphasize that work completion is an important aspect of responsible behavior in your class. Do not listen to excuses, but let the student know that they can speak to you later if they need support to get the work done. When you use this procedure, the class should be doing something worthwhile while you collect their work. If they are doing nothing, it is a waste of potentially productive time.

This procedure is especially important for collecting homework. Students they will have to face you when they don't have their homework. If you have worked at building relationships with your students, they will not want to disappoint you. You send a powerful message about responsibility when you stand right beside a student and provide positive feedback on the student's demonstration of responsibility or express concern at their lack of homework. You should collect student work personally if you have determined that your students need a high-support Classroom Management Plan. This procedure does have the disadvantage of being time and labor intensive for the teacher. If your class requires only low or medium support, you may prefer another procedure.

Procedures that are less time intensive include:

Relational Trust

When you have worked to build relational trust with your students, they will work more diligently to complete work so as not to disappoint you. They will also be more likely to talk with you and work collaboratively with you to come up with solutions when they are facing challenges that make homework or classwork difficult to complete.

- Have students hand in their work by rows or tables.
- Have a student helper collect it.
- Have students put their work in a designated basket.

These procedures lack the interpersonal contact and immediate feedback advantages that you get from collecting work directly from each student. Students don't actually see you handling their homework and class assignments, and until you grade the papers you don't know who has completed the assignment and who has not. Thus, any feedback (positive or corrective) is delayed until the next day or even longer. If you used one of these methods in the past and were unhappy with your students' rate of work completion, try experimenting with collecting work directly from students and see whether work completion improves. If you plan to use one of these methods, ensure that you mark which students turned in the work as soon as possible (i.e., before the next day's class) and provide positive feedback to students who completed the work while checking in with students who did not. This also ensures that students who completed the work but forgot to turn it in are prompted to get their work submitted in a timely manner. See the last section of this task, Procedures to Address Late and Missing Assignments, for additional ideas to increase work completion rates.

Use procedures that promote student responsibility with work submitted electronically.

When students submit assignments through an app, website, or email, give some thought to how to check in with students about whether they electronically submitted their assignments. One possibility is to use a modification of the procedure described above for work submitted physically in class. While the class is engaged in independent work, check in with each student about the work that was due. For example, you might ask each student to indicate on a sticky note a + if the work was completed and submitted or a − if the work was not submitted. Or open the site where students submit work and use it to provide positive feedback to students who submitted the work and check in with the students whose work was not submitted: "Class, as you work on the challenge problem, I'll come around and we can check off whether your essay was submitted to my email."

Consider having students check off completed tasks.

If you give students a daily or weekly assignment sheet or have them use an assignment notebook, consider adding checkoff boxes so students can indicate that they have completed a task. Another option is to have students check off completed tasks on a wall chart (similar to Reproducible 3.4, Completed Assignments Checklist). If you use some kind of wall chart in an elementary classroom, include on it all the major daily tasks and plan on putting up a fresh copy (with student ID numbers on it) each day. In middle school, you can probably put up one sheet per class for the whole week. Note that an assignment checkoff sheet like this is not an official record and does not take the place of or supersede your grade records. It is simply an opportunity for students to put closure on tasks.

Once you have taught students how to use a checkoff procedure, you can also teach them to self-reinforce in an age-appropriate manner. For example, with middle school students you might say, "When you check off your completed math assignment, tell yourself, 'I am choosing to be successful in this class because I am responsible for completing my work.'" You might even consider posting the statement above the chart so students can read the statement as they check off each completed task. It is no accident that the major time-management systems used by adults include checkoff boxes on the list of daily tasks so each one can be checked off when it's completed. Self-reinforcement and closure on tasks can be achieved using this simple but powerful idea of a checkoff procedure.

Motivation

Teaching students to self-monitor and self-reinforce by checking off completed assignments and tasks is a beneficial motivational strategy that can serve them well in school and beyond.

Reproducible 3.4 *Completed Assignments Checklist Example*

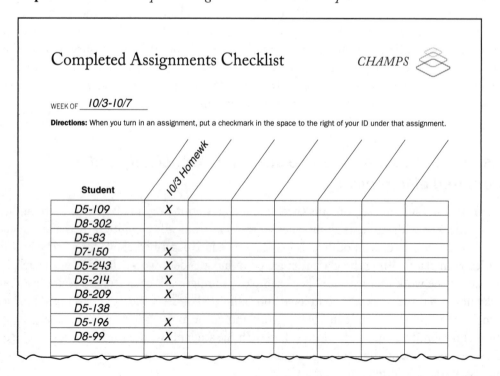

Completed Assignments Checklist   CHAMPS

WEEK OF __10/3-10/7__

Directions: When you turn in an assignment, put a checkmark in the space to the right of your ID under that assignment.

Student	10/3 Homewk						
D5-109	X						
D8-302							
D5-83							
D7-150	X						
D5-243	X						
D5-214	X						
D8-209	X						
D5-138							
D5-196	X						
D8-99	X						

Returning Graded Work to Students

Just as students are expected to be on time turning in their work, you must be timely with grading it and returning it to them. For simple homework and in-class assignments, return it the next day whenever possible. This will keep students actively aware of their progress and allow them to work on problem areas when the tasks are still relatively fresh in their minds. In addition, timely return gives students a chance to learn what they are doing wrong before moving on to more advanced work, which often builds on previous work.

Because you expect a reasonable level of neatness from your students on their written work, you must hold yourself to the same standard. Anything that is complex or difficult to communicate should be covered in person, not in a note you write in the margin. Legibility is essential as well; feedback serves no purpose if students can't read it.

It is vital that grades be kept as confidential as possible. Do not post grades with student names on the check sheet or anywhere else public. Your students will find out about each other's grades quickly enough without your help. Respect the fact that some of your students will not want to share their grades or may be embarrassed. Put letter grades on the back pages of assignments or return work face down. To facilitate the latter, write each student's name on the back of the papers where you can see it.

Finally, do not waste class time by having students wait while you return graded work. Have them do some in-class work or talk about the assignment you are returning. This is a perfect time to address problems that most of your students had trouble with or to answer questions that were raised by the work.

Keeping Records and Providing Feedback

An important yet often overlooked aspect of managing student assignments is providing regular feedback to students on their completed work and current grade status. While many teachers no longer use a physical grade book and instead keep electronic records, experienced teachers know that an accurate and complete grade record is an essential part of a well-run classroom. This information is critical for monitoring and evaluating student performance. Many teachers with complete and comprehensive grade books, however, do not have procedures for keeping students informed of their current grade status. Students who aren't aware of their grade status in the middle of a term may not realize that they need to improve. You can design a form that includes the range of assignments and tests you will use during each grading period (see Task 10 for details on how to do this).

If a student is falling behind by the second week of school, you should immediately inform the student and her family that she is not making adequate progress and collaborate with the student and family to come up with a plan for success. In addition, you should have a standard policy to send notes or make phone calls (or both) to families of students who have more than a certain number of missing assignments (five, for example). Regular and gentle nagging will increase rates of work completion, and students need to learn that they are still accountable for completing assignments even when they are

Data-Driven Processes

Just as regular data collection and analysis can be beneficial for teachers in guiding their process of improvement, having students regularly analyze their own data (e.g., rates of work completion, classroom grades) can help students set goals and make improvements.

past due. The opposite of this is also true in that you will want to plan for positive communication in the form of a quick email, postcard, or phone call home periodically for students who regularly complete their work on time or whose grades indicate that they are making adequate progress. This positive feedback will also be a powerful motivating factor and help students and families see that you value their responsibility and efforts.

In primary classrooms, regularly informing students of their grade status may not be useful or appropriate, although you should still provide timely feedback to parents when students are demonstrating difficulty with completing classwork or submitting homework. Middle school teachers should definitely have a system for keeping students updated weekly on their current grade status. Descriptions of two such systems follow. Consider implementing the one that best fits your personal style.

1. **Use a grade book program on a computer and print out a weekly report for each student on each subject.** Most school districts use an electronic system for recording student grades. If you don't already keep your grade records in an electronic system, consider doing so. In addition to saving time when you have to figure grades at the end of the term, these program allow you to print out a grade record for every student each week. The printout shows any missing assignments or tests, the score possible and the score earned on each assignment, the total points accumulated, and the current grade.

2. **Have students complete a Student Grade Record.** Even if you have access to a computer grading program, there are some benefits to having each student keep their own records. Rather than simply handing students their grade record each week, have each student record their scores on a personal recording sheet. This increases student awareness about how grades work and increase some students' accountability for getting work completed and putting in their best effort. You can design a form that includes the range of assignments and tests you will use during each grading period (as described in Task 10).

Each time you hand something back to students, have them get out their record sheet and enter the score they received in the appropriate space (such as a 92% on Test 2). About once a week, have students total the points they have earned. As students add up their points, you can put a breakdown of the point range for each letter grade on the board.

The major disadvantage of using a student grade record rather than a computer-generated printout is that it is more time consuming. You will need to be very direct about how to complete the grade record and take class time to have students record their scores every time you hand back graded work. We do not recommend that the student grade record take the place of your own electronic records, but rather that this procedure can supplement your own record-keeping to improve students' sense of responsibility and awareness about grades.

Provide extra feedback if your class needs a boost.

In addition to ensuring that all students receive regular and ongoing feedback about their current grade status, you may be able to increase rates of work completion by providing feedback to the class as a whole on the classwide percentage of completed work. For example, you might use a large wall chart (or a projected slide if wall space is not available) to record the daily percentage of homework or classwork handed in. Simply take the number of completed assignments and divide it by the number of students present that day to create a chart like the one shown in Figure 3.4.

An advantage to using a charting procedure is that it provides a daily opportunity for you to discuss the importance of being responsible for completing work. In addition, it may create a bit of peer pressure to complete work because each student's work completion, or lack thereof, affects the class percentage. If you wish, you can tie small-scale rewards to achieving certain goals: "When the class percentage is 92% or higher, the class earns the last 5 minutes of class as choice time." See Chapter 7 for additional ideas for using a structured reinforcement system for classes that need additional support and motivation to submit work in a timely way.

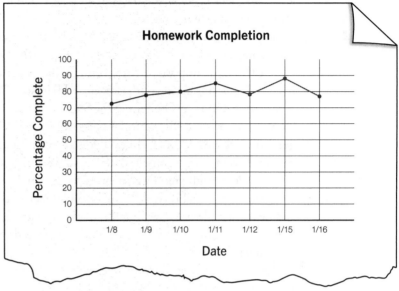

Figure 3.4 *Sample Homework Completion Chart*

Procedures to Address Late and Missing Assignments

The last major consideration regarding managing student assignments is how to handle late and missing assignments. Some teachers choose to have no penalty for late work (students can hand in anything, anytime, and there is no cost), while others do not allow students to turn in any assignment late (a late assignment equals zero points).

Some middle ground between these two extremes is recommended. When there is no penalty or emphasis on timely work completion, some students turn in everything late, possibly even handing in all assignments on the last day of the term. If students are allowed to do this, it is unfair to you (you should not have to stay up all night at the end of every grading period) and it is unfair to the students (they learn that they do not really have to pay attention to due dates, which can be a difficult habit to break). It can also lead to students putting everything off to the last minute and missing out on needed practice and teacher feedback, and students may do lower quality work due to rushing. Some students fall so far behind with missing assignments that they are unable to catch up at the end of the term.

However, an extreme "If it's late, it's a zero" policy does not take into account that an occasional late assignment is likely for even the most responsible student. It also does not accommodate for the fact that many students have circumstances that make on-time work completion, and especially homework, far more challenging. Imagine the student who is expected to provide childcare for younger siblings in

Diversity, Equity, Access, and Inclusion

Be careful to avoid policies that provide extreme penalties for late or missing assignments (e.g., zeros for late work). These policies do not accommodate for the fact that many students have circumstances that make on-time work completion far more challenging. Consider supports that may help students overcome barriers and challenges to completing work on time.

the evenings while parents work. Even penalizing grades (e.g., 10% reduction for each day an assignment is late) can adversely impact students whose late work is due to circumstances largely beyond their control.

If you do not wish to use a penalty for late work but need to prompt timely work completion, consider ways to teach the importance of this habit. Provide lessons that emphasize that one of the most important things in any job is completing work on time, so this will be an essential expectation in your classroom. Help students make connections between their work completion and your Guidelines for Success: "Class, remember that two of our guidelines are 'Never give up' and 'Strive for success.' One of the ways we can meet these guidelines is to get our work turned in on time. If you are ever having difficulty getting your work in for any reason, I want you to come talk to me so we can figure out a plan together."

Provide periodic reinforcement to students who complete their work on time to acknowledge their responsibility. Also plan to connect with any students whose work is late so you can hear their plans for getting the work completed. If a student begins to exhibit a pattern of late work, you may need to put a more structured plan in place with the student and involve the student's family.

One effective procedure for students who do not complete their assignments by the due date is to have them fill out a Missing Assignment Slip (see Reproducible 3.5). By filling out the slip, they are acknowledging that they did not turn in their work. It eliminates the problem of a student saying, "I did that assignment—could you have lost it when you were grading the papers?" You hold onto the Missing Assignment Slip. If the student hand in the assignment later, you can give the slip back to them. The accumulation of these Missing Assignment Slips will be a written, signed record of every missed assignment, and this can be powerful evidence to show at family conferences or to use when having an early-intervention phone call with a family about your concerns about work completion.

Reproducible 3.6 is a No Assignment Form shared by a high school teacher. Students complete the form when they don't submit homework or classwork by the deadline. This teacher found that the excuses written by students came in handy during subsequent family conferences because some students blamed family members for their missing homework. Once students understood that their family would see these No Assignment forms when they came for a conference or when the teacher contacted them about missing homework, it had a positive impact on the rate of homework completion.

If you plan to use a policy with a penalty for late work (e.g., a 10% reduction of points on an assignment for late work, or not accepting late work after a certain amount of time), emphasize to students your understanding that some of them have circumstances that can make it more difficult to turn in work at certain times. Communicate repeatedly to students and families that if a student is having difficulty with work requirements or timelines, they should come talk to you as early as possible so that you can work out a plan together so their grade is not affected. You will also need to ensure that your policy is clearly communicated to students and families so that they understand how late work can affect a student's grade across time, and work to intervene as early as possible when you notice a pattern of late work.

> Details of and criteria used in a late and missing work policy will reflect the decisions of individual teachers as well as any district policies. It is of critical importance that when you develop a policy, you inform students and their families about the policy at the beginning of the year or term.

Reproducible 3.5 *Missing Assignment Slip*

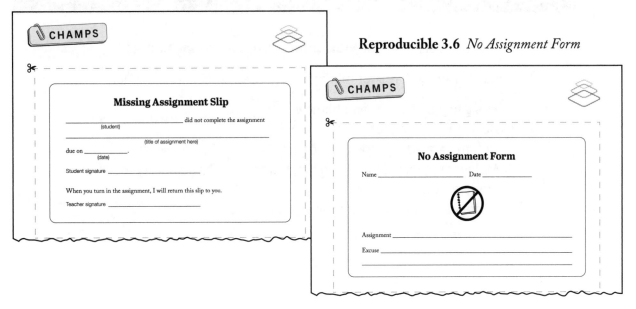

Reproducible 3.6 *No Assignment Form*

Figure 3.5 shows a sample policy that might be implemented by a middle school science teacher, along with ways to alter the expectations slightly to provide increased understanding and emphasis on the importance of communication.

Figure 3.5 *Sample Late Assignments Policy*

> ### Late Assignments Policy
>
> 1. Any assignment that is turned in late will receive an immediate 10% penalty unless you communicated with the teacher in advance why you would need more time. This will be considered on a case-by-case basis.
> 2. Late assignments will not be accepted in the final week of the grading period.
> 3. I will inform the family of any student who has more than three late or missing assignments, and we will work out a plan for you to complete the assignments before or after school or during lunch.

In most classrooms, a large percentage of student time is spent working on tasks that will be submitted to the teacher. The way you manage assignments and work periods has a big impact on how much responsibility students take for managing and completing their tasks. If you effectively manage student assignments, students are more likely to complete that work, thus giving them the practice they need on essential instructional objectives. In addition, when students complete their work, you can see whether they are achieving mastery of those objectives and can make judgments about whether additional instruction is necessary.

UPDATE YOUR CLASSROOM MANAGEMENT PLAN

ITEM 7: PROCEDURES FOR MANAGING STUDENT ASSIGNMENTS

Describe your procedures for managing student assignments, including:

- Assigning classwork and homework
- Collecting completed work
- Returning graded work to students
- Maintaining records and keeping students informed of their current grade status
- Addressing late or missing assignments

TASK 7

Design Procedures for Managing Student Technology Use

Design efficient and effective procedures for when and how students use technology in the classroom, as well as clear procedures for when technology will not be used.

• • • • •

While technology such as computers, tablets, and other devices can provide numerous benefits and possibilities within the classroom, they also pose significant management challenges. Students may visit inappropriate websites, use devices to cyberbully, get distracted by content unrelated to course material, or cause damage to expensive devices due to rough play or a lack of understanding about how to use technology appropriately. Schools and teachers often have differing expectations about use of personal devices, which can lead to a lack of clarity or students who push boundaries with phones. Careful consideration of structural elements and explicit teaching of expectations and procedures when using technology can reduce many of these concerns.

Teachers should take care to ensure that use of devices doesn't replace meaningful non-technology-based activities. Especially for younger children, health agencies have repeatedly warned against early and excessive exposure to computer technology, both inside and outside of school (Walsh, 2018). However, periodic moderate use of technology in the classroom can provide opportunities to teach students important digital skills necessary for the workforce and for engaging in responsible digital citizenship. Moderate technology use in the classroom varied with face-to-face activities such as discussion, hands-on learning activities, journaling, and other device-free activities has also been shown to have a positive association with academic performance outcomes (Bouygues, 2019).

When planning for use of technology in the classroom, consider how to define your expectations, procedures, and structures for two types of technology use:

- What are your policies and protocols for use of shared devices provided by the school (e.g., tablets, computers)?
- What are your policies and protocols for students' personal devices?

Considering Student Privacy

Be aware of student privacy issues. Two major federal laws, the Family Educational Rights and Privacy Act (FERPA) and the Children's Online Privacy Protection Act (COPPA), protect student privacy and lay out clear definitions for what information is protected, who can access or share it, and when. In many states, state and local laws also apply (e.g., SOPIPA in California). In addition to federal policies, also make sure that you are using any safeguards that your district and/or school has already put in place, which may include a list of approved apps to use in the classroom, an Internet filter that blocks student access to risky apps that might be collecting students' data or lack effective platform and content moderation, or an established policy or set of guidelines for using apps, including social media. Common Sense (commonsense.org) has set up a rating system to summarize different educational technology's privacy practices and offers basic training for teachers in protecting student privacy.

Define Expectations for Use of Shared Devices in Class

Think through when and how you expect students to use school-provided devices in your classroom. Will school devices be used periodically for activities where students retrieve devices from a mobile cart and use them across a few days for a specific project? Will students use devices for short periods on a daily basis for additional practice on particular concepts or specific activities? Do you have one-to-one access to devices, will students need to share devices within a class or between classes, or will you need to use a computer lab outside of the classroom? Responses to these questions about when and how you plan to have students use devices can help you think about structures you will need to put in place and expectations you will need to teach.

For whatever scenario you envision, plan to define and then teach CHAMPS expectations for technology-based activities and transitions. If you have not done so already, use Reproducible 2.3 to respond to questions about how to have students transition to and from use of devices in the classroom, and use Reproducible 3.2 to respond to questions about expectations for student behavior and participation during the technology-based activity. As you define your expectations, consider the following tips.

If students will retrieve devices from a cabinet or mobile cart, consider staggering this transition to reduce the number of students getting or returning devices at one time. No more than three or four students moving with devices at a time is recommended. You might use a procedure where you release students with laptops numbered 1–4 to retrieve their devices first, then 5–8, and so on. Or you might assign a few students the job of passing out and collecting the devices while other students are working on another task or receiving instruction. If you number the devices and have the students use the same device each day, this can streamline the time it takes students to get started and help them treat "their" device responsibly. If devices are numbered, you might also number the slots in the storage cabinet or cart and teach students to return their device to its numbered location to speed up the transition process.

Define expectations for holding and using devices during transitions that require movement with a device. Provide clear directions and model with examples and non-examples. "Hold the closed computer with two hands, one on each side of the computer, when you are walking to and from your desk. Don't hold it in one hand. Keep it closed until are seated at your desk." You will also want to teach students to handle devices gently when using them, including while opening and closing, typing, and clicking.

If students will be expected to use closing procedures like shutting a tablet down or plugging in a mobile laptop when ending a technology-based activity, ensure that these expectations are built into your end-of-activity CHAMPS expectations.

Establish an electronics policy and teach students about acceptable use of technology in the classroom.

Before students use electronic devices in class for the first time, spend time teaching them about acceptable uses of technology. Students should be clear on expected behavior. Establish an electronics policy that will be shared with students and their families. You may wish to have students sign a technology contract that indicates they agree to follow the electronics policy. For each agreement in the policy or contract, explicitly teach what is acceptable versus unacceptable behavior. The following are sample agreements that could be included in an electronics policy:

- Use of electronic devices is a privilege, not a right. If I abuse the use of technology, I will be restricted from this privilege for a period of time (TBD) in the classroom, and/or I may be expected to conduct service within the school if devices are damaged.
- I will treat electronic devices carefully and as if they are my own.
- I will treat my classmates with respect at all times when using technology. I will never use technology to cyberbully, spread rumors or gossip, harass, or fight with my peers.
- I will not share any personal information when doing classroom activities online. I will never give out my last name, phone number, address, or school name unless this is approved by my teacher.
- I will only search for things or say or do activities online that I would do if my teacher were sitting right next to me.
- I will never take or send a picture or video of anyone without that person's and my teacher's permission.
- I will not delete the history on the computer unless I am directed by the teacher to do so. I understand that my teacher will access this history periodically to ensure that I am using technology appropriately in the classroom.

- When researching or using online images or media, I will credit any sources I use and not plagiarize.
- I will never use technology to be hurtful or mean to someone else.
- When it is time to put devices away, I will not argue or try to negotiate for more time.
- I will only use electronic devices for approved classroom purposes and will remain engaged in the activity given by my teacher until I am given permission to do something else.

Preplan logical consequences for students who violate the electronics policy. If a student is using applications or browsing the Internet in ways that are unrelated to schoolwork or your electronics policy, the simplest response is to take the student's device away for the duration of the class. If they are using it to take notes, tell them to use pen and paper. If they are using the device for research on a topic, provide an encyclopedia or other print resource related to the topic. If they are creating a presentation, have the student write out their plans on paper and plan to transfer the information to their presentation at home or in the next class period. If a student repeatedly struggles to use devices appropriately, restrictions from technology may need to extend for a longer period, such as the duration of a project or a week or two.

Also plan to teach digital citizenship skills as you introduce web-based activities or use technology for classroom interactions. Most students don't automatically know how to navigate the Internet safely or communicate effectively and respectfully, and many parents struggle with these skills as well. It is never too early to start teaching digital citizenship skills such as how to engage respectfully with others online, issues of Internet privacy and security, and how to evaluate online sources. Numerous sources offer more information about teaching digital citizenship skills. Common Sense Education (commonsense.org), for example, provides a K–12 digital citizenship curriculum for each grade level that includes teacher tutorials, materials, and lessons for every classroom.

> *Plan to teach digital citizenship skills as you introduce web-based activities or use technology for classroom interactions.*

Evaluate whether your attention signal will quickly get all students' attention when working with technology.

In Chapter 2, Task 4, you designed an attention signal that would allow you to get all students' attention quickly and effectively. Consider whether this same attention signal will work when students are working with technology or if a different or adapted signal is needed. If students are engrossed in a project or activity and are focused on the screens of a computer or tablet, you may find it is harder to get their full attention in a timely manner. Or you may find that you get their initial attention but some students struggle to maintain that attention after the initial signal because they want to return to working on the device. Using an attention signal that prompts students to flip over their tablets, lower their laptop screen, or turn away from a desktop computer can alleviate some of these concerns. For example, if your typical signal is to clap out a rhythm and have students repeat the rhythm, you might use this initial procedure and then prompt students to turn their tablets over on their table. It can also be beneficial to give students a 2-minute warning before a transition to help prevent last-minute requests to stay on the device for a longer period or a last-minute frenzy to complete something.

Provide clear instructions and learning objectives for the task before students begin using devices.

Tie student technology use to clear learning objectives. While educational technology can have a positive effect on student achievement, the content, design, and use of the technology makes a tremendous difference (Tamim et al., 2011; Zheng et al., 2016). Consider the content objectives for the activity along with any objectives related to learning to use technology for conducting research or designing a presentation, or to practice specific skills like typing. These objectives should be clearly conveyed to students and help you design instruction for how students can use the technology to meet learning objectives.

For ongoing projects that will take multiple instructional periods, identify and communicate both long-term objectives for the whole project and shorter-term goals or steps for each work period. Students need a reference for what they should attempt to complete each day. These shorter-term goals also allow you to see which students are getting stuck or falling behind so you can provide timely support. In one English Language Arts class, we observed a teacher who had students use computers to select a song of their choice with a narrative plot. They then mapped out the storyline using presentation tools and finally presented to the class. During the first work period, some students had selected a song within the first 10 minutes and began creating their presentation. Other students took an entire period to find a song. Two students had not yet selected a song by the end of the third work period. These students ended up failing the assignment because they had not reached the initial objective within a reasonable amount of time and were unable to make up the lost time in the remaining work periods. After this experience, this teacher provided a short-term objective indicating that any student who had not selected a song by the end of the first work period would have a song assigned to them. This prevented students from falling too far behind and provided greater focus and clarity within each work period.

Because some students struggle to listen to directions once devices are in their hands or at their desks, provide instructions and learning objectives before students get their devices or before they turn them on. This can help ensure students understand their assignments and prevent distractions before their tasks begin. It also allows you to reinforce your expectations for student behavior and your electronics policy before they begin working.

If students are creating a presentation, video, or other product using digital technology, you may wish to have them establish an outline or template for the assignment before they begin working on the computer. This can help them stay more focused on the overarching goals of the project and keep them from getting stuck or sidetracked by something like finding the right picture for one part of the project.

When you have a limited number of computers or handheld devices and students will be expected to share, determine whether you will have some students work on a paper-pencil task while others use the devices, or whether the activity is conducive to a partner or small group activity with students sharing a device. If the latter, consider assigning specific roles beforehand to the group members. For example, who will do the typing and clicking, and who will read directions and keep the group focused on each step of the directions or outline? For prolonged activities, allow students to alternate roles. If someone other than the assigned person wants to type or click, teach them to first get permission from you and the current user. For groups of more than two, you may need to model and have students practice physical positioning of the device so that multiple students can see the screen while giving each other adequate personal space. Groups larger than three may be difficult because not everyone will be able to see the screen.

Observe students' technology use and provide feedback.

Unstructured and unsupervised computer use can lead to lower levels of student engagement, attention, and performance (Carter et al., 2016). Carefully monitor students as they use computers, tablets, or other devices. Walk around the classroom and look over students' shoulders to confirm that they are on task, including checks for minimized windows and open apps that could be causing distractions. Move in an unpredictable manner. We recall observing one classroom in which the teacher moved predictably from one side of the room to the other. As the teacher moved to the right side of the classroom, students on the left began doing activities unrelated to the learning task. As the teacher moved back to the left side of the room, these students quickly switched back to the assignment while the students on the right side opened unrelated windows. Students are far less likely to play games or access social media if they know that at any moment their teacher will appear behind them. The layout of the classroom can make this easier—desks should be organized so you can move around easily, without climbing over book bags and cables to reach different parts of the classroom.

Periodically monitor browser history as well. You can prevent students from clearing browser history by using tools such as GoGuardian (goguardian.com) and Securly (Securly.com). Some software tools have been developed to be an "all-seeing eye" on student devices. For example, GoGuardian allows teachers to view, take control, and freeze student devices from a single teacher control panel. You can also teach students that they are not to erase their history. If you check it and find it has been erased, the student will lose device privileges for the remainder of the work period and possibly the next day devices will be used.

Provide in-the-moment positive feedback to students who are focused, using technology appropriately, and demonstrating progress with learning objectives. Consider building in time for periodic one-on-one teacher check-ins with each student so you can acknowledge what the student is doing well and areas of growth regarding technology-based activities. You can also use this time to ask questions about challenges the student faces using technology and create a plan for support or intervention as needed.

Define Expectations for Use of Personal Devices in Class

As of 2020, Pew reports that 95% of teens have access to a smartphone and 45% say they are online on a near-constant basis. Common Sense Media reports that by age 12, more than two-thirds of students (69%) have their own smartphone. Educators have widely differing views on whether and how students should be allowed to use these personal devices in classrooms, with advocates of banning phones citing reasons like:

- Research has shown that limiting phone use in schools decreases distraction and directly correlates with achievement (Beland & Murphy, 2016; Kuznekoff & Titsworth, 2013).
- Reduced screen time can reduce the impacts of social media (which can often have negative effects) and reduce cyberbullying.
- Banning phones can reduce the likelihood of phone theft or damage at school.

Others say that banning phones is problematic if not impossible. Schools can spend significant time and resources trying to figure out corrective consequences for students who violate a cell phone ban. Many claim that having phones can be helpful for students who need to stay in touch with their parents, and with issues of school violence such as school shootings, many parents advocate for their children to have phones so they can get in touch in case of an emergency. Proponents of cell phones in the classroom also say that managing phone use is an essential 21st century skill and that schools can play a powerful role in helping students learn to be self-sufficient learners, use devices in prosocial ways, and use modern tools that may be helpful to them in a workplace or in daily life.

If your school or district has a policy banning cell phones from the school or from use during class times, it is essential that you follow existing policy. It is highly problematic when seven or eight out of ten staff members follow a schoolwide policy but some do not. This sends a very confusing message to students. Some will get confused about when and where they can use their devices and may unwillingly violate a teacher's expectations simply because they are not clear about the policy. It can also lead to friction within the school as some students begin pushing back with teachers who are following the schoolwide policy or believing that some teachers are "nice" because they give students more leeway while other teachers are "mean" because they follow the school's expectations. If you believe that devices should be allowed, consider taking this request to your administration or schoolwide team responsible for evaluating issues of policy, but follow the school's stated policy in the interim.

Some schools with cell phone bans have used structure elements to make it easier to enforce this schoolwide policy. For example, the *Guardian* (Ho, 2019) reported that in the 2019/2020 school year, over 1,000 schools were rolling out use of magnetically locking pouches. Students keep their phones with them, but at the beginning of the day, they place their phone inside a pouch that magnetically locks. At the end of the day, they tap the pouch on an unlocking station. Trials of this technology in San Francisco indicated that the pouches worked well to improve student concentration and discourage students from using their phones throughout the day. A middle school in Fresno, California provides traditional paper envelopes at the beginning of each day and students seal their cell phone in an envelope. At the end of the day, teachers conduct spot checks of students' envelopes. If their envelope are still sealed at the end of the day, students are rewarded with a raffle ticket for a daily drawing.

If your school does not have a policy or allows each teacher to define their own policies when students are in class, clearly define your own policy and post it somewhere visible in the classroom. For example, if phones will never be used in class and you expect that students do not use them for any reason, consider including this as one of your classroom rules (see Chapter 2, Task 2 for information about developing and posting classroom rules). Your rule might be, "Cell phones must be put away at all times." Some teachers also use something like a pocket chart as students enter the classroom. Students place their phones into the chart as they enter class, and the teacher locks the chart in a cabinet until the end of class to ensure no devices are stolen.

If phones will be used at certain times for class purposes but are generally expected to be put away, clearly define when they can be used versus when they should be out of sight. For example, one teacher uses a poster with an image of a cell phone printed on a green side and a red side. The poster stays on the red side for most of class, but whenever an activity occurs when cell phones can be used to look up information or respond to a poll, the teacher flips the poster to the green side.

Another teacher (Cardenas, 2017) describes using a cell phone charging station to incentivize responsible behavior, telling students:

> *This is how cell phones work in our class: I don't want to see them out and being a distraction during class, but I also want you to learn how to control your own behavior and be able to use them at appropriate times. If you know that you can't handle the distraction during class, drop your phone off at the charging station. Plug it in, turn the ringer off, and just forget about it for the class period. If you choose to hang on to your phone, I'll give you one reminder if I see it out during class; the second time I see your phone I'll simply ask you to walk it over to the charging station and store it there until the end of class.*

If you plan to periodically allow cell phone use, consider sharing research about cell phone use, distraction, and multitasking (i.e., research indicates we are not as good at multitasking as many of think we are!) to help students learn to make informed decisions about their cell phone use. Also indicate that this use is a privilege, and if students abuse it by using cell phones inappropriately or during times when you have indicated they are not allowed, you will have to adopt a more restrictive policy that phones are not allowed at any time during class. Some teachers find that allowing periodic times for tech breaks, during which students can check their devices for 30 seconds to a minute, can cut down on students trying to sneak peeks at their phones during class learning activities.

Whatever your policies and procedures regarding technology, including shared devices and personal devices, doing work in advance to precorrect for any anticipated behavioral challenges can go a long way toward ensuring that these devices enhance rather than detract from learning. Consider how to clearly define and then teach procedures regarding use of technology. See Chapter 4 for information on how to explicitly teach students behavioral expectations and social-emotional skills.

UPDATE YOUR CLASSROOM MANAGEMENT PLAN

ITEM 8: PROCEDURES FOR MANAGING STUDENT TECHNOLOGY USE

Describe procedures for managing student technology, including:

- Expectations for use of shared devices in class
- Expectations for use of personal devices in class
- How you plan to monitor student technology use and provide feedback

Once you have developed a written electronics policy to share with students, attach a copy of it to your Classroom Management Plan.

TASK 8

Develop Long-Range Classroom Goals

Identify several major goals—instructional and behavioral—that you wish to accomplish with all of your students by the end of the year.

• • • • •

Without a destination in mind, you may arrive at a place you don't want to be. Although this is a seemingly obvious statement, it illustrates why it is so important to determine, before school begins, what you hope to accomplish with your students by the end of the school year. If you envision your goals, you are more likely to achieve them—and not end up achieving other, undesirable goals! Identify four to seven major goals that summarize why being in your classroom will be a worthwhile experience for your students. Specifically, identify what your students should know or be able to do differently at the end of the year that they didn't know or were unable to do on the first day of school.

Long-range goals can be instructional or academic, behavioral or social, or a mixture. Instructional goals focus on what students will be able to do differently as a result of the academic content you teach. Behavioral goals focus on the attitudes or traits you hope to instill in your students. Your goals may be predominantly behavioral or predominantly academic—it is entirely up to you.

Long-range goals help you plan and make decisions on a daily basis throughout the year. For example, if one of your goals is for students to learn how to plan long-range projects and bring them to completion, you should devote instructional time to several long-range projects over the course of the year. On the other hand, if planning and completing long-range projects isn't a goal, you would plan for students to engage in more short daily activities and spend less time and energy on long-range projects.

Mission and Beliefs

Take the time to think about and then write down your long-range goals for your class. Use your mission and beliefs and your Guidelines for Success to help you identify the most important long-term behaviors, attitudes, and academic goals you hope to accomplish with your students.

Your goals should also help you make decisions about the behaviors and attitudes you want to emphasize with students. If a goals is that students will "learn to study independently and stay on task," you need to make an effort throughout the year to discuss, model, and provide feedback about students' on-task behavior. A teacher who does not have this goal may emphasize a different behavior, such as to work collaboratively with peers or advocate appropriately for yourself.

If you are starting CHAMPS during the school year, implementing this task may be a relatively low priority simply because it requires time for reflection and careful planning—time that you may not have during the school year. However, before the next school year begins, give careful thought to what your long-range goals for that year will be.

Sharing your goals with your students and their families at the beginning of the year lets them know what you feel is important for students to learn, both academically and behaviorally, and how you hope to guide students toward accomplishments. Detailed information about how to share goals with students and their families is discussed in Chapter 4.

Keeping your long-range goals in mind is particularly important as you move further into the school year. We all know how easy it is for teachers to get so busy and so immersed in daily details that they lose sight of the big picture—the set of skills, knowledge, and behaviors they want their students to have by the end of the year. With long-range goals in mind, you can keep your eyes on the prize and periodically ask yourself whether what you are doing on a daily basis is aiding (or hindering) your efforts to help students reach these goals.

To develop your own long-range goals, start by considering these suggestions:

- Ask yourself what you want students to know and be able to do at the end of the year that they may not be able to do now. What knowledge, processes, attitudes, behaviors, and traits do you hope to instill in your students? What do you want students to remember about their year with you?
- Find out the building-, district-, and state-level goals for the grade level or subject you teach. Your goals should probably reflect some of these.
- Talk to other teachers at your grade level or above about the goals they have for their students. If you teach third grade, for example, ask fourth-grade teachers what skills, knowledge, and behaviors they think new fourth-grade students need to be successful. If you are an eighth-grade teacher, connect with teachers at the high school to find out how you can best prepare your students for the transition to ninth grade.

Following are examples of major long-range goals for different grade levels and subject areas. You may want to post your goals in the classroom. These samples are included to prompt your thinking. You should not necessarily adopt them as your own long-range goals.

Kindergarten—All students will:

- Treat everyone with courtesy and respect.
- Learn to listen and follow directions.
- Learn to cooperate with others.
- Learn to stay on task and finish assignments and activities.
- Develop basic decoding and comprehension skills (for example, alphabet letter names and sounds, blending, segmenting, and rhyming).
- Develop basic math concepts (for example, numbers 1–20 and shapes).

(This example was provided by Shelley Jones, Hoover Elementary, Salem, Oregon)

Fourth Grade—All students will:

- Master all basic addition, subtraction, multiplication, and division facts and be able to use those facts accurately when doing computation and problem-solving.
- Learn to work cooperatively in groups and sometimes take the leadership role.
- Develop writing skills that allow them to communicate in both narrative and expository styles.
- Learn to plan long-range projects and bring them to completion (including two major reports and two major projects).
- Learn to speak in front of their peers with confidence and style.
- Learn to stay focused on written tasks and bring them to completion.

Eighth-Grade U.S. History—All students will:

- Memorize ten key events in U.S. history (including the year the Constitution was ratified, the beginning and ending years of the Civil War, and the year the United States entered World War II) and be able to explain the importance of the event in the context of U.S. history and current events.
- Be able to describe and apply five essential concepts in the U.S. Constitution (including the three branches of government and the First Amendment right of free speech).
- Be able to learn something new about U.S. history and analyze that event using the timeline events and constitutional concepts noted above.
- Learn to take notes from lectures, films, and readings and use those notes to analyze and synthesize information on tests and projects.
- Learn to study independently and stay on-task during class and when working on homework.

UPDATE YOUR CLASSROOM MANAGEMENT PLAN

ITEM 9: LONG-RANGE GOALS

List 4–7 long-range goals for your class.

TASK 9

Understand Considerations for Developing Effective Grading Practices

Learn about grading reforms and reflect on your current grading practices.

• • • • •

We would like to thank Jeremy Resnick and the Ventura County (California) Office of Education for this contribution on how to evaluate whether your current grading practices are effective. In this section, Jeremy summarizes many of the current reforms in grading practices that seek to address some of the pitfalls of traditional grading systems.

Teacher grading practices often fall into the category of existing regularities, in which we fall into the trap of doing things the way they've always been done. The question to ask yourself is whether your current approach to grading is helping you accomplish classwide goals or is it inadvertently undermining other efforts to support students' success.

The purpose of this task is not to advocate for one grading practice over another but rather to raise some questions for you to consider as you explore the explicit and implicit connections between grades and behavior, and vice versa.

Examine the Existing Regularities of Your Grading System

Grading practices are often are akin to the water that fish swim in; fish don't understand that they are actually *in* water because it is all they know. As with many practices in education, educators, like the fish, often do not take the time to examine the "water we are living in" and simply accept it as is. This often leads educators to adopt the practices that they experienced themselves as children—the very cycles of punitive behavior practices that this book attempts to overturn. This can be especially true with grading practices: Educators often adopt the method of grading that they experienced as students without pausing to consider if there is another, perhaps better, way. As with classroom management approaches, many educators also take grading practices personally—a teacher has invested much time and energy into devising them, so they become intertwined with the teacher's professional, perhaps even private, persona. It is important to again take a *stoic* approach to remove personal feelings on the matter and to simply and objectively consider whether current grading practices may be contributing, directly or indirectly, to some of the behavioral issues you wish to address. Indeed, given the current system of education, grades and behavior are inextricably linked.

> **Existing Regularities**
>
> *Educators often adopt grading methods that they themselves experienced without pausing to consider if a different way might better serve the needs of their students. Consider the purpose of grades and whether your current grading methods help to accomplish classroom goals.*

Consider this scenario: Marcus had a rough start to the beginning of the first term of sixth grade. He had found elementary school relatively easy and, if he did his work in class, he tended to do well. He paid attention in class, participated as much as he could, and was generally liked by both staff and students. "A pleasure to have in class" was the most frequent comment on his progress reports. However, as the content of his classes increased in difficulty and more demands were placed on his time, he struggled to find a routine and successful study habits. He missed the due date on a couple of assignments and did not perform well on some initial assessments. About halfway through the term, he had a conversation with the school counselor and was able to set some goals and establish some habits that resulted in fewer missed assignments and greater confidence and performance on important assessments, which indicated he was progressing at grade level.

Meanwhile, Cynthia had a different experience as she entered sixth grade. She had always needed some extra structure to ensure her academic success and so had a strong foundation as she entered the new school year. Often quiet but generally focused, she dutifully turned in her assignments on time and tended to perform relatively well on tests. Unfortunately, Cynthia's family experienced some hardships midway through the term, and her time and energy now had to be spent on some nonacademic priorities. As a result, she began missing some assignments and not paying as much attention in class. Her assessments indicated that she was missing some key concepts and skills.

At the end of the term, the grade book entries for Marcus and Cynthia looked like this:

	Assignment			Test	Assignment		Test	Final grade
	#1	#2	#3	#1	#4	#5	#2	
Marcus	0	40%	0	60%	75%	85%	90%	?
Cynthia	90%	80%	90%	70%	0	0	20%	?

What final grade would you give each student and why?

Generating a mean average (and assuming no weighting of grades), Marcus and Cynthia would have the exact same grade, 50% or F according to most grading systems. If we give added weight to the tests, say 70% of the total grade, then Marcus would earn a 57% whereas Cynthia would now have 49%. Whether we weight the grade book entries or not, do either of these final grades for these students seem appropriate to you? Why or why not?

Obviously, there are more complexities and nuances involved in the grading process, but Marcus and Cynthia's examples help to highlight that assigning grades to students can be quite subjective. Indeed, research indicates the greatest sources of variability in education occur from classroom to classroom at the same school rather than between schools or districts (Rowan et al., 2004). In other words, what one teacher deems an A another teacher may deem a C. One teacher may give a student additional points or credit for effort and behavior, whereas another teacher does not. One teacher may allow test retakes without penalty while another does not. One teacher may choose to ignore earlier, poorer grades in order to allow for improvement while another teacher simply averages the grades as we did above. Without a clear understanding of what grades are for and what they represent, we risk miscommunicating our expectations to students as well as conflating behavior and academic achievement.

Consider the Connection Between Grades and Motivation

Let's return, for a moment, to the concept of motivation provided in Chapter 1—the Expectancy times Value theory of motivation as represented below.

Expectancy Rate	×	Value Rate	=	Motivation
10	×	10	=	100
10	×	0	=	0
0	×	10	=	0

The Expectancy times Value theory of motivation proposes that students' motivation to engage in any behavior is related to the degree to which they value the rewards of that behavior and their expectation of succeeding at it. Consider now that grades are the thing that students do or do not value. If a student does not value good grades, they will not be a motivating factor for that student, even if the student is perfectly capable of the work. Inversely, if a student does value grades but does not have the skills to get good ones, grades may, in fact, be a demotivating factor because the student does not expect that they can be successful. Regardless, we must ask ourselves an even more important question: If grades do, in fact, motivate a student, should they? This leads to an even broader essential question: What is the purpose of grades?

Unless we clarify the intended purpose of grades, they run the risk of becoming simply another commodity that savvy students learn to manipulate and that can lessen a student's internal motivation to learn for the sake of learning, instead promoting "an attitude toward learning as an *end* rather than a means" (Zimmerman, 2020). Grades, in essence, are a giant token economy. While such systems can be valuable when there is little to no motivation to begin with, it is always the intent to fade such systems so as to not degrade internal motivation once it is fostered. We cannot fade grades, so students may begin to see school "as a game they play for grades—a game that at best treats learning as incidental, and at worst distracts students from making meaning" (Winger, 2005).

The primary purpose of grades is to provide information to a student, their parents/caretakers, and educators working with that student about what the student knows and can do. In districts and schools that have adopted standards-based grading, the purpose is even more finite—grades communicate whether a student has mastered the standards or not. Standards-based grading (SBG) and mastery-based grading (MBG) systems involve teachers assigning grades based on students' final mastery of learning activities such as projects, tests, essays, presentations, and so on. Students are often assigned grades on these activities based on a rubric such as:

> 4 = exceeds expectations
> 3 = meets expectations
> 2 = partial mastery of expectations or can perform with assistance
> 1 = little or no mastery or cannot meet expectations even with instructor assistance

A failing grade should indicate that a student has not mastered course objectives. Students who master the objectives should receive a C or a low B, and students who exceed the objectives should earn a high B or an A.

Motivation	

Some teachers use grades to try and motivate students to succeed. However, if a student does not value good grades, this approach doesn't work. If a student does value good grades but has little expectancy of success, grades are often demotivating. Consider using grades to communicate about what the student knows and can do while using other strategies to boost motivation.

Reflect on Common Grading Practices and Reforms

What follows is a list of some of the more frequently and recently discussed reforms in grading practices. They are presented with the hope that they will lead to reflection and discussion among you and your colleagues in order to make decisions that will be best for your students while remaining compliant with any guidelines and regulations put forth by your state, district, and school.

To support your reflection on the considerations presented below, you can use Reflection on Grading Practices (Reproducible 3.7, p. 178) to organize your thoughts around your current grading practices and potential next steps using the STOIC acronym that organizes the other concepts in this book.

Reproducible 3.7 *Reflection on Grading Practices*

Reflection on Grading Practices   *CHAMPS*

STOIC component	Reflection Questions	Current Practice	Potential Next Steps
Structure	How is your grading system structured? Do you use a 0–100 scale, a 0–4 scale, or something different? Do you weight the different types of assignments in your grade book? How do you calculate a final semester grade? Are your grades standards based? Is behavior and/or effort factored into your grades? If so, at what percentage?		
Teach	Do students and their parents/guardians know how you calculate grades? If so, how is that information communicated? Do you provide rubrics and/or exemplars for students prior to an assignment? Do you teach students how to monitor their own academic data and set goals?		
Observe	Do you engage in the formative assessment process to clarify learning goals, elicit evidence from students, interpret that evidence, and then act on that evidence to modify your teaching practices and activities?		
Interact	Do you provide positive as well as corrective feedback on students' academic work?		
Correct	Do you provide frequent, specific, actionable feedback centered on the specific knowledge and skills students need to work on to demonstrate mastery?		

© 2021 Ancora Publishing   REPRODUCIBLE 3.7

Consider whether zeros make mathematical and ethical sense in your grading system.

With a typical 100-point scale, a zero in a grade book, even a well-deserved one, is mathematically devastating to a student's final grade. The zero, often given for missing work, has an overwhelming impact on a student's grade when there is a 10-point range for an A, B, C, or D yet a 60-point range for an F. Given a 100-point scale, consider making 50 the lowest grade you assign.

Suppose for a moment that you firmly believe that grades can and should be used as rewards and punishments. If you give 50 on a 100-point scale, what would happen? A 50% is still a failing grade. Even if a student turned in no work and demonstrated no effort, you could "punish" them with all 50s and they would still fail the class. However, a student with 50s who rallies at the end of the grading period (like Marcus in our opening scenario) has a fighting chance to earn a passing grade rather than give up in the face of the mathematical impossibility that a stack of zeros creates. Had Marcus received 50s as his lowest scores, he would have ended with a weighted grade of 68%, which allows him to pass the class and gives him credit for the improvements he demonstrated during the second half of the grading period. Making a 50 your lowest assigned score is not "giving" students a 50 (Reeves, 2004); they are still receiving a failing grade that is appropriate yet not demoralizing or demotivating.

In contrast, most grade reformers agree that a zero does make mathematical and ethical sense if you use a point scale in which grades are equally distributed (e.g., a 4-point mastery scale where an A is worth 4 points, a B is worth 3 points, etc., or a system in which each grade is the equivalent of 20%: A is 81–100%, B is 61–80%, C is 41–60%, and so on; Dueck, 2014; Feldman, 2019; Marzano & Heflebower, 2011; O'Connor, 2017; Reeves, 2004). With this type of scale, there is an equal span between each subsequent grade; therefore a zero is no longer the mathematical black hole that it is with a 100-point scale.

Eliminate the use of curved grading systems.

If the main purpose of grades is to reflect each student's mastery of course objectives, grading on a curve does not accurately communicate this information. Instead, grading on the basis of mastery of objectives means that every student has the opportunity to pass. In contrast, if you grade on a standard curve, you distribute grades according to predetermined percentages, such as:

> 2% of students receive an A
> 14% of students receive a B
> 68% of students receive a C
> 14% of students receive a D
> 2% of students receive an F

The common practice of curving grades results in norm-referenced grading in which a student's performance is evaluated against the performance of their peers. Norm-referenced assessments are excellent for diagnostic tests or universal screeners but not for communicating how a student is progressing against a set criteria, such as state standards. Grading on a curve also takes all incentive away from lower-performing students. They soon realize that their grade has little to do with how well they master course content and that they have to beat higher-performing students to succeed. No matter how hard they work, their performance will always be evaluated relative to other students in their class. If instead they know they can pass a course because they have mastered course objectives, they will soon learn that they can succeed regardless of their relative position to other students. Your goal should be to provide instruction that gives all students what they need to get a C or better. You are not giving away passing grades, but rather are giving them to any student who has earned them by mastering course objectives.

Criterion-referenced grading, which involves comparing a student's progress to a set of criteria like state or district standards, helps educators and students to focus on what matters:

the learning. Indeed, most researchers agree that the most valid, effective, and meaningful grade is criterion referenced (Bureau of Exceptional Education and Student Services, 2006; Guskey, 2002). If a student demonstrates mastery of a standard, their grade should reflect that fact regardless of how their peers performed. Curving grades is, quite simply, unfair.

Consider using homework and other formative assignments for progress monitoring outside of your grading system.

There is general consensus among most grade reformers and researchers that homework and other formative assignments should not be included in a student's grade (Dueck, 2014; Feldman, 2019; O'Connor, 2011; Winger, 2005). Anything that is formative is intended to provide the teacher with insight into how students are performing for the purposes of modifying learning activities in order to improve student learning. Therefore, by its very nature, anything that is formative should not receive a grade.

In addition, homework completion may not always be an accurate reflection of what a student knows and can do. There is no way to know whether a student received external help with work or if they copied it entirely from a peer. If a teacher assigns a grade for homework completion, they may be inadvertently contributing to the idea of viewing grades as a commodity. Even worse, they may actually be assigning a grade based on privilege that does not account for a student's home life (Feldman, 2014). When students receive grades for homework, it can inadvertently reward students who have privileged home conditions, such as highly educated family members who can assist, private tutors, or access to reliable Internet or other beneficial technology and materials, while punishing students who do not have access to these privileges.

This is a good time to mention that "grading" and "providing feedback" are not necessarily the same thing. The suggestion here is that, yes, a teacher should go over the homework and provide specific and actionable feedback to students, but assigning a grade to that work, even if just for completion in an earnest effort to build students' responsibility, may be at cross purposes.

Rather than grading homework as a means to incentivize completion, you might consider using one of the classwide systems for motivation presented in Chapter 7. For example, you could monitor homework completion across all students and offer a reward when the class meets or exceeds a certain criterion (e.g., when 90% of students turn in their homework, the class earns a point toward a larger reward).

Allow retakes and redos.

Offering students retakes or redos on any assignment helps to communicate that learning is what is valued, not a (sometimes) arbitrary letter grade. Just as it is unreasonable to expect students to behave perfectly at all times, it is also unrealistic to expect them to not make mistakes with their schoolwork. In fact, through observing student mistakes a teacher gets a glimpse into how students are processing their learning and so can make course corrections along the way. Not allowing retakes or redos sends the message that mistakes are to be avoided at all costs, including cheating. Offering retakes and redos is about redemption and improvement. It sends the message to students that their teacher believes they are capable and that everyone deserves a chance to try and do better. Again, the goal is learning, not a letter or a number.

One strategy that can elevate the practice of allowing retakes and redos, and also provides a mild incentive for students to try their best the first time, is to require students to submit a written or verbal (e.g., audio recorded) comparison of their original and redone work. The student should describe what they learned or did differently so that they can demonstrate their increased mastery.

Let students monitor their own progress.

More powerful than any grade a teacher can give a student is empowering a student to monitor their own learning. Self-reported grades, wherein a student assesses the quality of their own work, have been shown to have a massive effect on student learning (Hattie, 2008). Allowing students to reflect on their current progress, set a goal based on where they are, and make a plan on where they want to go is a practice that prioritizes learning over a grade. Just as goal-setting can be a valuable practice for a student struggling with behavior, this simple strategy can be used with students academically. Through rubrics and exemplars, teachers can help students gauge where they are and identify steps needed to progress to the next level of mastery. Refer to goal setting in Chapter 7, Task 2, for other ideas on how to help students monitor their own learning.

Consider whether incorporating behavior (and/or effort) into a grade still provides an accurate reflection of students' level of mastery.

As with the other items in this section, there is no concrete right or wrong when it comes to including behavior or effort in a student's grade. However, there are important factors to consider in deciding what is best for your students and school community. If you return to the premise that grades are meant to reflect a student's attainment of knowledge and skills, including behavior has the potential to miscommunicate a student's progress. If, for example, a student is extremely well behaved, courteous, and kind, and tries really hard, but still struggles academically, an inflated grade to reward the student for good behavior detracts from a potentially serious academic issue. One educator shared a troubling example of this phenomenon. A student had straight As throughout high school, but when she reached the ACT exam, she was unable to score high enough to get into a good college. Because her grades were largely based on participation and good behavior, they covered up the fact that she was struggling academically. This is why some parents become alarmed or upset when a student gets good grades on report cards but performs poorly on standardized year-end assessments. Likewise, if a student has a poor grade in math and struggles with behavior, for example, the family and others have no idea if it is the student's behavior or the math (or both) that are the issue.

It does students no favors when teachers artificially inflate their grades based on good behavior and effort. Conversely, if a student demonstrates mastery of the academic content and skills but behaves poorly, giving them a lower grade as punishment detracts from their academic abilities. The implicit bias of interpreting behavior makes grades reflective of that interpretation rather than a representation of what students know and can do. Of course, this is not advocating that you ignore poor or good behavior or effort; it is suggesting that grades might not be the best way to address behavioral and motivational issues.

If you do plan to include behavior and/or effort in your grading system, you can reduce the likelihood that these portions of the grade create an inaccurate representation of students' mastery of learning objectives. For example, you may wish to report academic and nonacademic grades separately (Winger, 2005). The next task discusses how to include behavioral grading components that do not adversely affect the reflection of students' academic understanding, knowledge, and skills.

In summary, the primary purpose of grades should be to provide information to the student, their parents/caretakers, and educators working with the student about what the student knows and can do. Grades should not be rewards and punishments used to motivate students. This is not to say you cannot use other methods of motivating students, but to use grades for motivation belittles the primary purpose of grades (i.e., to communicate a student's progress) and may inadvertently contribute to an "unconscious curriculum … of compliance" (Winger, 2005). One goal of education should be to create engaged and self-motivated students, not merely compliant ones. Even if you follow all of the other suggestions in this book with fidelity and clarity of heart and vision to "develop a loving, supportive school culture, it won't mean a thing if the way we grade dispirits students" (Feldman, 2014). Therefore, the ideas presented in this task are not intended to serve as a list of "musts" but rather "maybes"—possibilities to consider to ensure that the time and effort you put into your behavior management system is not undermined by your grading practices.

TASK 10

Develop a Grading System That Creates a Relationship Between Student Effort, Growth, and Success

Design a grading system that aligns evaluation with course objectives.

• • • • •

This task is most relevant for teachers in middle school. If you work in the upper grades of elementary school, skim through this section to determine if any of the content might help address grading issues in your classroom.

As a teacher, it is easy to make the assumption, "But Caitlan and Antonio just don't care about their grades. I wish all my students cared about their grades like Janelle." In some classes, you may even assume that over half the students in class don't care about grades. We urge you to consider a different position. Specifically, that an individual student's beliefs regarding grades have a lot to do with past success or failure with learning tasks and past success or failure in understanding how systems work. Let's take two examples, Janelle and Caitlan, to represent two groups of students—those who make connections between their effort and grades and those who do not seem to care about their grades and exhibit little effort.

Janelle has learned that "if I do my best, complete assignments, and study for tests or other assessments, it is *very* probable that I can pass, and probably get an A or a B. This is within my ability to control the outcome." Also recognize that students like Janelle, who have been successful in the past, are probably motivated by a combination of the rewards of getting a good grade with the avoidance of the consequences of getting a bad grade. Phrased differently, students who are already successful with the whole school experience know that through hard work and past learning they can be successful with the task requirements, earn a good grade as recognition, and avoid the disappointment (including the disappointment of their parents) that comes from a bad grade. This is probably true for Janelle, as long as the teacher's system is reasonably easy to understand.

Caitlan, on the other hand, has had an entirely different experience with school. From her perspective, "no matter how hard I work, no matter what I try to do, I always get an F, so why should I even try?" For Caitlan, the possibility of passing or getting an A or B seems *impossible*—truly not within her ability to control. She has experienced so many Ds and Fs that she has become inured to the disappointment of failing (including any disappointment from home). In these circumstances, Caitlan is very unlikely to put much effort into avoiding a bad grade because she views it as inevitable and outside her ability to control. Caitlan will not be motivated unless the instructional and evaluation system (that you, the teacher, establish) is structured so Caitlin learns what Janelle already knows—"If I try my best, complete assignments, and study for tests, I can master learning objectives and even get a good grade." Students who have experienced failure need to learn that learning and getting a good grade are within their ability to control.

This task provides suggestions on how to make decisions about evaluation methods and the process you use to verify that students are learning what you teach them. The goal of this process is to clearly show the links between doing work and participating, learning, and receiving a passing grade. The task concludes with information about how to design grading systems if you plan to include a behavior or effort component and how to communicate with students regarding their grades.

> " *Students who have experienced failure need to learn that learning and getting a good grade are within their ability to control.* "

Communicate Important Course Objectives and Align Evaluation with These Objectives

In order to increase motivation and success for all of your students, especially those who typically struggle, you need to clarify your instructional objectives and then evaluate students on the basis of only those objectives (Archer & Hughes, 2010; Kame'enui et al. 2002).

Some teachers view all information and concepts they teach as equally important. When this is the case, evaluation may consist of a random sampling of that information to determine student mastery. Consider an extreme (but true) example of what can happen if a teacher designs an evaluation based on this kind of random sampling.

CASE STUDY

In an undergraduate history course, a college instructor assigns 1,200 pages of reading. Every 3 weeks, students are to be tested on a 400-page section of the reading and on 3 weeks of lecture. The final grade is based entirely on the three tests. Prior to the first test, students receive no information that will help them prepare for it. When they ask what information from the text will be important, the teacher tells them, "Everything is important."

The first test is a single essay question covering a topic that was not mentioned in class and was discussed on only three pages of the text. Out of 50 students, one receives an A, 3 receive Bs, 14 receive Fs, and 32 receive Cs and Ds. Students complain that the test was unfair: "How could we know which three pages were important? There is no way to memorize 400 pages of text!"

The instructor replies, "I tested you on those three pages not because they were the most important but because anyone who knew those three pages would have learned the material on the other 397 pages." On hearing this reply, half the students drop the class before the second test. Think about the probable attitude and motivation of the students who remain. Remember the Expectancy times Value theory of motivation introduced in Chapter 1: Even if value is high, how many of the remaining students have a strong expectancy of success in this class? If this course is not essential for a student's major, how many students would give it a strong enough value to do the extra work needed to memorize 400 pages of text for the next exam? It is more likely that many students would do the bare minimum needed to get a C in the class.

This example demonstrates how a course can seem impossible to some students when important objectives are not made clear to them and when the evaluation methods are not clearly aligned with the instructor's important course objectives. Even sophisticated college students may choose not to try when the odds against knowing what they should learn or what to study seem overwhelming. The instructor made an error in assuming that it was the students' responsibility to identify what content was important. He felt that his job was only to *give* information. This misconception not only made it impossible for students to know what to study, but also decreased their expectancy of success and so reduced their motivation.

• • • • •

One skill many academically successful students have is the ability to determine critical learning objectives. If testing is on random information, higher-achieving students still have a chance to succeed because they start with more background knowledge, are more likely to be adept at remembering information, and are probably more skilled at guessing what the teacher will choose to include on a test. Less capable students will have difficulty sorting out critical objectives and less chance of remembering unconnected information. If mastery of objectives is evaluated based on a long-term project and the teacher has not clearly communicated the objectives on which students will be evaluated, students may spend too much time focusing on aspects of the project that are ancillary to the learning objectives (e.g., a beautiful design) rather than on the purpose of the project (e.g., demonstrating critical thinking about course concepts).

One of the benefits of organizing your grading system around specific objectives is that students do not have to second-guess what they are supposed to learn (Woodward, 2001). Many students do not know enough about a given subject to identify the most important material or concepts to learn, so trying to second-guess their teacher is impossible. When students understand a class's objectives, they will know what they are supposed to study. This knowledge increases the likelihood that they will make the effort and so make it easier for you to evaluate their performance. Consider the suggestions below for turning your established goals into meaningful units of evaluation and instruction.

Break down course content into one- or two-week units of instruction. If you think of the long-range goals you established in Task 8 as the final destination of a learning journey with your students, your units of instruction will be the steps you take to reach that destination. Divide the content you intend to teach over the entire term, semester, or year into logical units. Depending on how you build your class, this may be defined for you by curriculum guides or the structure of a professional learning community (PLC) you are working with. If you plan on giving formal midterm exams, divide the semester or term in half, and then divide each half into one- or two-week units.

Prior to designing instruction, for each unit identify the essential objectives that you want your students to master and retain for the rest of the semester. What are you going to hold students accountable for knowing and understanding, not just for this unit but for the remainder of the semester or year? If you will give some sort of summative exam like a final, or a learning project where the student displays cumulative learning, what are the critical components from each smaller unit of instruction that you expect them to retain and integrate across time? These essentials may be facts, higher-order processes or operations, critical thinking or problem-solving skills, or some combination of these.

One way to identify essential objectives is to begin the process of designing your units of instruction. Start by determining your method of performance evaluation. In some cases, this may be a test. In other cases, the essential objectives may be evaluated through a product, in which case your first step is to determine the criteria by which you will evaluate the product. By settling on your evaluation tool (test or product) first, you can identify exactly what you want students to know or be able to do and then determine the essential content you will need to teach. If you are using predesigned tests from a district curriculum, textbook publisher, or PLC, this step means examining what is on that test, editing it as allowed to match with your essential objectives, then considering essential content to teach.

Break your essential objectives into a manageable number of concepts that are essential for literacy in the subject. If you are basing instruction on a textbook, you may find that many texts present only a few essential concepts and lots of embellishments with interesting but nonessential information. Do not worry if your essentials make up only a small percentage of the content of a given chapter of the book. Plan to teach these essential objectives directly and provide multiple practice opportunities through daily assignments and homework to ensure that students reach mastery of this core content.

The essential competencies for a unit of instruction should comprise the majority of the point value for tests, major assignments, and projects—if you use a traditional 100-point grading scale, we recommend allocating about 80% of the total point value possible to assessing essential competencies. This organizational structure allows you to communicate that you will directly teach everything students need to know to get a passing grade for the class. For students who have experienced academic failure in the past, you can use this concept to let them know that you will do everything possible to help all students pass—not by giving away grades but by being direct in telling them the essential objectives and by creating lots of practice, feedback opportunities, and any needed support to help them get there. One common concern that some teachers express is, "But I don't want to tell students what will be on the test." However, remember that the point of a test is to evaluate whether students are learning essential competencies.

Furthermore, if essential competencies make up only 80% of the point value on the test, in a traditional A through F grading system you are letting students know everything they need to get a high C or the very lowest possible B. If you are using a mastery- or standards-based grading system, you are letting them know everything they need to meet proficiency standards.

Students who wish to earn higher grades (As or exceeds standards) will need to go beyond basic objectives. This is another benefit of directly teaching the essential competencies. You create a challenge for students who want to earn an above-average grade or demonstrate advanced proficiency. You will not need to teach the remaining 20% of point value on tests and major assignments. To gain this content, students will need to read the textbook carefully, extend their own knowledge, or otherwise go above and beyond. They will need to demonstrate above-average mastery of the subject. You can inform students that while you will directly teach and support what is needed to get a high C or low B, they will have to demonstrate performance above and beyond that to earn a higher grade. Thus, about 20% of the point value of tests or major assignments can be based on advanced objectives—perhaps content from the textbook, lectures, video, or other academic tasks that students were exposed to but that you did not emphasize or teach as directly as the core objectives.

The 80/20 approach prevents the problem in which a teacher views their job as covering 100% of the content and testing to see what students have learned. In most subjects, much of the content is not absolutely essential to literacy in the subject. Read any chapter from any science, health, or social science book and you will notice that much of the material is not essential to understanding the really important concepts, or "big ideas," and is probably not essential to understanding later chapters of the book. Some teachers actually label test items as essential and as advanced objectives to demonstrate to students a direct connection to what they do in class and being able to pass the class.

Build cumulative review of essential objectives into subsequent units of instruction. After the first unit is completed, provide a one- or two-page summary of the essential objectives covered in that unit. Let students know that the second unit test or project evaluation will have a review section or project component on the essential objectives from Unit 1. Here is one way to do this if using regular tests to assess student learning:

Unit 1
- 80% of the point value covers essential objectives from Unit 1.
- 20% of the point value covers advanced objectives from Unit 1.

Unit 2
- 60% of the point value covers essential objectives from Unit 2.
- 20% of the point value covers advanced objectives from Unit 2.
- 20% of the point value covers essential objectives from Unit 1.

Unit 3
- 60% of the point value covers essential objectives from Unit 3.
- 20% of the point value covers advanced objectives from Unit 3.
- 20% of the point value covers essential objectives from Units 1 and 2.

Unit 9
- 60% of the point value covers essential objectives from Unit 9.
- 20% of the point value covers advanced objectives from Unit 9.
- 20% of the point value covers essential objectives from Units 1 through 8.

If you are using projects or another evaluation method, consider how to incorporate objectives from previous units in a similar way to ensure that students are retaining and strengthening their knowledge and skills in essential objectives across time.

When you follow this structure, students can be taught to study the review sheets you give out at the completion of each unit. Or it will help them consider what core competencies they need to review, seek help with, or continue to work on in subsequent units. If they are correct or demonstrate mastery of most of the essential objectives for the current unit and the essential objectives for past units, they will get a high C or passing grade. If they want an A or B or evaluation of advanced proficiency, they will have to demonstrate mastery of advanced objectives from the current unit. Do not include review items that cover advanced objectives from previous units. You want to demonstrate that you hold students responsible only for keeping track of the essential objectives.

One huge advantage of this cumulative review strategy is that students will likely perform better on finals and statewide tests, and they are also more likely to retain core content objectives across time. Because they have been reviewing the essential objectives with each new unit, the information stays fresher in their minds and is more likely to transfer into their long-term memory. Most adults do not remember their locker combination from when they were sophomores in high school. You knew this information very well at one time and throughout the year successfully opened that lock hundreds of times. Why don't you remember it now (assuming you are not one of those rare individuals who can remember)? Because it has been years since you needed to use that information. Through lack of use, that information has faded from your memory. Do not let that happen with your essential objectives. Keeping the information fresh in students' minds throughout the semester or the entire year will allow your students to retain the information and understanding much better and for much longer. If you have done a good job of aligning your essential objectives with school and district objectives for mastery in each grade level, this cumulative review of what students learn in your classroom will help them transfer their knowledge and understanding into their subsequent classes.

Consider Whether to Include a Behavioral Grading Component

If your district has policies about whether a percentage of the grade will be based on behavior, effort, and participation, obviously follow your district's policies. If there are no district or building policies, you will need to decide whether behavior or participation should have an impact on grades. As mentioned in Task 9, some experts discourage the use of behavioral grading procedures on the grounds that a grade should reflect only students' mastery of standards. However, for some students, including a small behavioral grading component can provide important feedback that helps them understand that hard work, dependability, and appropriate behavior can help them master learning objectives. As you reflect on whether and how to include a behavioral grading component, carefully consider whether the portion of the grade you include for behavior, effort, or participation contributes to or detracts from communication about students' mastery of the course standards.

Highly motivated and academically successful students have learned that their daily performance has a cumulative effect on their grade. They understand that each day's work affects how much they learn, which in turn affects their test performances and their final grade. Academically motivated students can take the long view that their daily efforts affect their future schooling options and even job opportunities. Less mature and lower-performing students often do not understand these relationships. These students may not realize that the reason they are not passing is that they do not work or listen during class.

CASE STUDY

Mr. Nakamura teaches a geometry course that he has designed to include lectures, class discussions, and assignments Monday through Thursday. Each Friday, students take a quiz on the week's material. The class discussions and lectures typically focus on the previous day's homework. Mr. Nakamura has designed his schedule to allow students to work on problems independently and then to resolve any difficulties as a group.

During class activities, not all of the students work diligently. Some students work hard each day and take each assignment seriously, and some do not seem to care whether they learn to solve the problems. The students who goof off during class work times do not get out of hand, but they also do not learn the content they are expected to master, and so they perform poorly on quizzes and tests. As the end of the term approaches, many of these students seem legitimately shocked and panicked that their grades are so low. At this point, they are too far behind to catch up their grade, and they may have significant difficulty in learning the necessary concepts for success for the remainder of the school year.

• • • • •

Many grading systems in middle school are structured like those in college. Attendance and behavior do not in themselves affect the grade. The grade is usually based solely on assignments, tests, and quizzes. In this type of system, there is no immediate accountability for goofing off. By the time a student fails a test, it is too late to make improvements. For students with less maturity, the delayed consequence of an end-of-term grade may be too weak to be effective, and these students may need more frequent reinforcement to stay on task.

The benefit of including a behavior component in the academic grade is that it places ongoing emphasis on how effort and appropriate participation will influence course mastery and the grade earned. Without this immediate, daily feedback, many students do not connect the impact of poor behavior with negative school outcomes until it is too late to turn their grade around, earn necessary credits, and learn important academic concepts. If you do not include behavior in grading, you will need to carefully consider how to communicate to students and families how the student's poor behavior or lack of participation is likely to eventually impact mastery of learning objectives.

One possibility if you do not wish to include behavior or participation as part of the academic grade is to create a separate grade for "citizenship" or "employability skills." Or you can run a parallel system of providing a weekly behavior and effort score that affects the academic grade only when a student is just below the cutoff for receiving a higher grade. For example, the behavioral grade would come into play only when a student is no more than 2% below the cutoff for the next higher grade. You might establish criteria like the following:

- If you are 1% or less away from the next highest grade but have 80% or more of the behavior and effort points, you move up to the next grade.
- If you are 2% or less away from the next highest grade but have 90% or more of the behavior and effort points, you move up to the next grade.

Another possibility is to partly base a grade on behavior by saying that your class objectives involve teaching students the overall behaviors they need to be successful in any educational setting. For example, in a chemistry class, the abilities to stay on task, follow directions, and follow safety rules are critical factors for success. This same argument can be used to justify grading on behavior and effort in more traditional academic classes like English and history. By including behavior and effort as part of grading, you demonstrate to students that learning independent study skills, knowing how to listen, and taking responsibility for assignments and materials have a direct relationship to success and good grades. These behaviors are necessary for all of their future educational and professional endeavors and are therefore important objectives. Because these behaviors represent sound educational objectives, it is reasonable to base a percentage of each student's grade on them. We recommend basing no more than 10%–20% of a student's grade on behavior or participation in academic classes and periodically evaluating whether students' grades still accurately reflect their mastery of course objectives.

If even this moderate influence of behavior and effort on grades is unacceptable in your district or you are concerned that it does not accurately communicate student mastery, you can still implement systematic feedback on behavior and effort like the system described in the remainder of this task. Instead of affecting student grades, however, behavior and effort points will have to count toward something else. To reinforce these ideas, there must be a positive motivator and a negative motivator—for example, evenings without homework or free time for the positives, and extra homework or loss of a privilege for the negatives. The planning steps that follow are provided if you plan to base a small percentage of the academic grade on behavior and effort. Adapt these procedures as necessary to ensure that you follow the policy guidelines of your district.

NOTE: Some teachers track verbal participation in class. For example, each time a student speaks up in class by participating in a discussion or verbally answering a question, the student gets a point added to their academic grade for the day. This type of system, however, can be unfair to shy, quiet students. In addition, it can encourage each student to say something each day just to get checked off for speaking in class. The system described in this chapter for evaluating behavior and effort is different: Students are given points both for the degree to which they follow the rules and for demonstrating significant effort. These effort points could be for verbal participation, but could also be given for cooperating, demonstrating respect, actively participating in activities, and so on.

One problem with many behavioral grading systems is that they are somewhat arbitrary and subjective. If you are considering using a behavior or effort grading component, read through the following suggestions on how to implement or modify such a system to ensure that it is effective, applied fairly and justly across students, and clearly communicates what students must do to earn a good behavioral grade.

PLANNING STEP 1
Establish a grade percentage for classroom behavior or effort.

To teach students that daily effort affects their final grade, establish a set percentage of the final grade for classroom performance. The exact percentage may vary from class to class according to several factors:

- *Subject.* Some subjects must have grades that are based heavily on competency. For example, students in a writing class must demonstrate competency in basic writing skills to pass the course. If too high a percentage of the grade is based on behavior and effort, a student could potentially pass the class without demonstrating mastery of the basic course objectives. For this type of class, do not allocate more than 10% of the total possible points for behavior and effort. In a chorus class, it might be appropriate to base somewhat more of the grade on behavior and effort. Consider how a student would demonstrate mastery of learning objectives in your class even if they are not exceptionally talented. In a basic chorus or PE class, for example, it may be appropriate to give higher levels of credit to students who work hard and follow expectations, even if they do not possess much natural talent.

- *Course level.* The level of student experience with a given subject should affect how much of their grade is based on behavior and effort. Students beginning a new skill should have a higher percentage of the grade based on classroom effort than those with experience, whose grade may be based more on mastery of course content. When students acquire a new skill, effort will determine whether they move beyond the beginning stages. It is during this time that students need the most encouragement. As they gain proficiency in any skill area, that skill becomes more intrinsically reinforcing. For example, beginning string students need encouragement as they learn to read and play notes. Advanced string students are able to enjoy their own ability to play complex pieces and interpret music.

Determine in advance what percentage of the final grade your students can earn for daily behavior and effort in class. Throughout the term, you will need to monitor and record student behavior. Be sure to inform students about the behavioral grading component at the start of the semester, rather than after problems occur, so students know what to expect. Also, communicate with students regularly about their behavioral grade and how it is affecting their overall grade. If you implement this procedure without letting students know that their class behavior has an impact on their academic grade, it becomes an unfair and arbitrary system.

PLANNING STEP 2
Determine the approximate number of total points students may earn during the term.

Count the units of study you hope to cover during the term, working from the district text or a district curriculum guide. Next, using this number, estimate the number of tests, assignments, and projects students will be doing during the term. Although you are projecting what you hope to accomplish during the term, these preplanning steps should not lock you into a system. By estimating the number of tests, assignments, and projects students will be graded on, you can prepare the students for how you plan to evaluate them. You do not have to plan the assignments or write out your tests in advance. You can adjust the number of assignments and tests as you work to meet the needs of your students.

Assign point values to the tests, assignments, and class projects. The point value of each type of work will vary according to the organization of your course and how you want to balance the points for different tasks. Once you have assigned approximate point values, add them together to get an approximate number of work points that students may earn during the term.

Planning for a history class might look something like this:

Nine Units Covered in the Nine-Week Term

8 unit tests (100 points each)	800 points
8 quizzes (25 points each)	200 points
Final exam	200 points
1 term paper	200 points
Total work points	**1,400 points**

PLANNING STEP 3
Determine the approximate number of total points based on behavior and effort.

Using the total work points from Step 2 and the percentage of the grade that will be based on behavior and effort from Step 1, determine the approximate number of points possible based on behavior. Using the history example, there are 1,400 work points. If this teacher wants the behavior portion of the grade to have about a 10% influence on the grade, she takes 10% of 1,400 to find that approximately 140 points should be possible for behavior and effort. She could then divide this number by the number of weeks in the term to determine how many behavior points are possible for each week—in this case, 15.56. Because she does not want to bother with fractional points, she will round up or down. This teacher will inform students that they can earn up to 16 points each week for behavior and effort. This information should be included in your syllabus. See the example below.

Nine Units Covered in the Nine-Week Term

8 unit tests (100 points each)	800 points
8 quizzes (25 points each)	200 points
Weekly behavior/effort (16 points each)	144 points
Final exam	200 points
Term paper	200 points
Total points possible	**1,544 points**

NOTE: You may note that in the example above, the teacher wanted behavior and effort to be about 10% of the grade, but she ended up with 1,544 possible points and 144 for behavior and effort, which is less than 10%. There are formulas for doing this more accurately that you can figure out on your own, but in most cases, it is perfectly acceptable for the point values for behavior and effort to be slightly less than the original percentage you estimated for this category.

PLANNING STEP 4
Design an efficient system for monitoring and recording daily classroom behavior points.

To understand that daily performance affects their final grade, students need to see that their daily behavior is being monitored and recorded.

The Behavior Record (Reproducible 3.8) provides space to record each student's behavior during the week. It can be used to note attendance, assignments, behavior, classroom performance, and weekly point totals.

Reproducible 3.8 *Behavior Record Example*

Behavior Record
(Weekly by Student Name)

CHAMPS

DATE __10/14__ REMINDERS _____

Name	Fri.	Mon.	Tue.	Wed.	Thu.	Total
Jeno, Kaleesi	dd	CC	dA	d		11
Bendix, Frank	C	C	AA	B	B	16
Bignoia, Brad	o		A		A	13
Collins, Rosa	t	Btt	ttt		CB	9

CODES: o = off task; t = tardy; d = disruptive, A = doing your best (effort);
B = be responsible, C = respect/cooperation

© 2021 Ancora Publishing

REPRODUCIBLE 3.8

At the bottom of the form is a place for a code. For this, first identify three or four positive traits or behaviors you wish to encourage at a classwide level. These will likely have several points in common with your Guidelines for Success. Then identify three or four particular misbehaviors that represent rule violations you wish to reduce at a classwide level. For each positive and each negative behavior, assign a code that you will use to record occurrences of that behavior on your record sheet. The chart in Figure 3.6 shows an example.

Once you complete the codes, enter an alphabetical list of student names for each class you teach. Thus, if you teach five classes, you will have a different sheet for each class. Notice that the form begins with Friday of one week through Thursday of the following week. That

Figure 3.6 *Sample Codes for Behavioral Grading*

Misbehavior	Code	Positive Trait	Code
Off task	o	Doing your best (effort)	A
Tardy	t	Be responsible	B
Disruptive	d	Respect/Cooperation	C

way, you can calculate and post the grades on Friday to show your students how they did on the previous five days. Posting these grades on Monday may be too much of a delay and can reduce the interest of some of the less mature students in the behavior and effort score.

Keep the behavior record form readily accessible at all times, especially when you are circulating throughout the classroom monitoring student behavior during independent work and cooperative group activities. Some teachers keep forms for each class on a clipboard; others use a notebook. Throughout the period, students should see you using the record form. If a student comes in late, you can quickly mark a t for tardy. If a student needs to be reminded to get to work, note an o for off-task next to the student's name. Immediate notation of these negative behaviors will teach students that they are immediately accountable for their actions every day.

When students excel, you can record an A for effort or a C for cooperation on the form. You will have to determine when you start using this system how publicly you wish to acknowledge student behavior. In general, reserve public feedback for when the whole group receives a positive mark. When an individual student receives an A, it is usually best to tell the student privately, either in the moment or at a later time. (For additional information on giving students positive feedback without embarrassing them, see Chapter 6.) Consistently using the behavior record form during class will allow you to record behavior grades as they happen without cutting into your class time.

NOTE: If you are working with low-performing students in a remedial setting of any kind, consider giving behavior and effort points daily instead of weekly. This increased immediacy in feedback will help motivate students who may have given up. The major disadvantage to this is the amount of time required. Therefore, use daily grades only with smaller classes. With a smaller class, assigning and recording daily performance grades should take only 2 or 3 minutes at the end of each period. A system of this type can also be incorporated into any behavior plan a student may have, such as a daily behavior card.

Each time you record a positive behavior, add 1 point to that student's current total for the week. Each time you record misbehavior, subtract 1 point from that student's current total. Because you are unlikely to be able to give each student enough positive marks to get all of them into the A or B range, determine a number of points that each student will start with at the beginning of each 5-day period. This should be approximately mid-C level—in our example, 12 points. Inform students that every week they start with 12 points and will move up or down from there based on the marks they receive during the week. In the Reproducible 3.8 example, if you start with 12 and subtract 1 point for each lowercase letter and add 1 point for each uppercase letter, you come out with the total in the far-right column. The one exception in the example is Frank Bendix. He has six positives but receives only 16 points—not 17. Inform your students that no matter how many positive marks they receive, they will not get more points than the total possible, in the same way that if an essay is worth 100 points, they won't get a score of 110 no matter how many positive comments are written in the margins.

PLANNING STEP 5
Determine the impact of excused and unexcused absences on your grading of behavior and effort.

Determine how you will deal with students who are not in class. Obviously a student who is not in class cannot be evaluated on behavior and effort. However, you do not want your system to penalize students who have legitimate absences. Below are some recommendations to consider:

- *Unexcused absences.* An unexcused absence removes the student from the learning environment, causes them to fall behind, and can distract other students. There must be a negative consequence equal to all the points the student could have earned if present. Thus, if 20 points are possible for the week, students should be penalized 4 points for each day they have an unexcused absence.
- *Excused absences.* Students who have an excused absence will be allowed to earn back the credit they missed. Note that they will not automatically earn performance points on the days they are gone. Instead, they will have an opportunity to do extra credit to make up the lost class time. This procedure is not designed to penalize students who are ill; rather, it is designed to demonstrate how valuable class time is. When students miss class time, they also miss learning. Thus, a small extra-credit assignment must be completed to compensate for the lost time. Students will learn that they are accountable for making up missed time. This procedure also applies to students who miss class because of involvement in sports, student government, and other extracurricular activities. You are not discouraging students from participating in other activities; you are holding them accountable for class time. A student who is pulled out regularly for special services of some type, such as English language learning or speech therapy, should not be required to make up the missed participation points.
- *Sent out of class.* A student who is sent out of class has lost the opportunity to earn performance points for the class period and will lose points based on the remaining amount of class time missed. A student who misses half the class will lose half the behavior points for that day, in addition to any other behavior coding recorded before the removal. Be careful not to penalize the student more than the points lost for that day. For example, if a student was sent out close to the beginning of one class but returned for the remainder of the week, she should not lose all 20 points for the week, even if she exhibited highly inappropriate behavior. When she returns to class, she should have the opportunity to earn full points for the remainder of the days in the week.

PLANNING STEP 6
Assign weekly performance points and provide feedback to students.

At the end of every Thursday, your behavior record form will have all the information you need to determine students' weekly performance points. Simply follow these steps:

1. Begin with the number of points students can earn for average performance.
2. Add the appropriate number of points for each notation of excellence.
3. Subtract the appropriate number of points for each notation of inappropriate behavior.
4. Record the total number of points earned on the Behavior Record (Reproducible 3.8).

The first few weeks will be a period of adjustment as you get used to regularly noting performance, but as you continue, the task will become automatic. After some practice, you will be able to scan the performance sheet and quickly take in totals. Noting behavior in class should not take extra time once you get used to it, and totaling and awarding the points each week should take no more than 5 minutes.

When students enter class on Friday, give them their weekly performance points for the previous 5-day period and inform them that the new 5-day period has just begun. If they do not receive the point totals before they go home for the weekend, the mental connection between their performance and their grades will weaken. Students need frequent and consistent feedback, especially with the implementation of a system to encourage them to follow the rules and give their best effort. There are several ways to give individual students information about their points while maintaining an element of confidentiality:

> *" The first few weeks of regularly noting performance will be a period of adjustment, but as you continue, the task will become automatic. "*

- If you are using a computerized grading program, print out and distribute current grade status reports to each student, using student numbers for confidentiality.
- If you have a class with more behavioral concerns or class size is small, the best way to give feedback is a personal form for each student that breaks down the totals of the weekly performance points. This provides students with the most immediate and direct information. It also keeps the process private for each student. The drawback is that it will take longer than 5 minutes to prepare these for every student in your class.

Some teachers prefer to post the sheet on which they totaled the previous week's points and use a coded number to cover the student names on the far left. This method is not recommended. Some students may share their numbers with each other, and if some students struggle more with behavior and effort, they may be easily identifiable by their peers, which defeats the goal of confidentiality.

When you have logged the performance score in your grade book, file the Behavior Record Form. Keeping these records can be useful for several reasons, the most important being to provide answers to any questions about a student's grade. The record sheets provide detailed information about a student's behavior and motivation. This information is useful in conferences with students, parents, and administrators. It can also be helpful in determining a special education placement or in any formal hearings or meetings about a particular student.

Keeping the Behavior Record Forms on file can also provide you with valuable information about revising your teaching methods with a particular group. For example, if you are concerned about off-task behavior in your seventh-period class, you can look at the record forms for the past 4 weeks to track the problem. If there are many o's (for "off task") marked on the sheet, you should be concerned and make a plan of action. You may want to consider giving your class more structure. Explore any steps in this book that you have not yet taken. Talk with colleagues who may have a similar group of students and find out what steps they have taken. You should be able to use the record sheets to get a sense of how your class is doing as a whole, not just to evaluate students on their own.

EXAMPLES, IDEAS, AND TIPS

An exciting variation on behavior and effort grading comes from the Academy of Irving Independent School District (Texas). The academy is a high school in which students are graded on employability skills (ES). The following information was provided by Patrick Martin, lead special education teacher, and Robin Wall, principal. The academy is a school of choice where entrance selection is based on a lottery system; a student who fails to maintain the required grade could potentially be returned to his or her home campus. The ES grade is based on a rubric developed in conjunction with business leaders. The skills measured are:

- Keeps appointments on time
- Completes assignments on time
- Exhibits professionalism in the areas of courtesy, appropriate language, and dress
- Works toward achieving individual and group goals
- Adheres to the ethical use of technology in regard to property, privacy, and appropriateness

The grading scale for these five areas runs from 1 ("rarely does any of these") to 5 ("always does these"). Each of the five areas is graded individually. Let's say that a student receives a 3 in each of the five areas. At this point, the total score is 15. That number is then multiplied by 3 to arrive at 45, and then added to 25 for a graded score of 70. Each grade level has a passing score that must be achieved in order for the student to be invited back the next academic year. The score is 70 for freshmen, 80 for sophomores, and 85 for juniors and seniors.

At the beginning of the school year, each parent and student receives a briefing regarding the academy's expectations and performance criteria. What they have noted is that the grades in academic subjects closely parallel the ES grade. It is unusual for a student to have a high ES grade and be low academically. The underlying philosophy for the program is that the skills needed to succeed in academics are the same skills employers want and employees need for success in the adult working world.

Ensure That Students Receive Regular Feedback on Behavior, Academic Performance, and Current Grades

This recommendation is obvious but difficult: Get graded work back to students as quickly as you can. The longer a student waits between completing a task and getting feedback on it, the less the student will apply the feedback academically. The longer the delay, the less impact (good or bad) a grade will have. In addition, you want students to know their current status in your class at all times. It is imperative that students be able to track their own grades so that they can measure the effect their effort has on their grade performance. If you are using a computerized grade program, you can and should easily print out current grades and assignment status on a weekly basis.

If you are not using a computerized system, you can teach students to keep a grade sheet. While time consuming, it can also be beneficial to teach students to track and calculate their own grades so that they have a deeper sense of how different assignments and their scores impact their final grade. Two different options are shown below.

Give students a grading sheet with spaces for them to record points for each scored piece of work in your class. Earlier in this task, you identified the approximate number of tests, assignments, and class projects students would complete during the term and the number of points each would be worth. List this information on a student grading sheet with spaces for students to record work points, weekly performance points, and point totals. A sample is provided as Reproducible 3.9.

The benefit to this grade-tracking method is that students have a visual idea of what tests, quizzes, assignments, and participation will be given throughout the term and how much each is worth. By prompting students to use the Student Grading Record each time you return an assignment, you are reminding them about what is coming next and can prompt them if they have missing scores. The downside is that students do not have a cumulative record of their grade until all of the scores have been given. Students will not have an overall sense of their letter grade or percentage until the end of the grading period unless you also use another method. For some students, this inability to see how their grade changes daily or weekly removes some

Reproducible 3.9 *Student Grading Record Example*

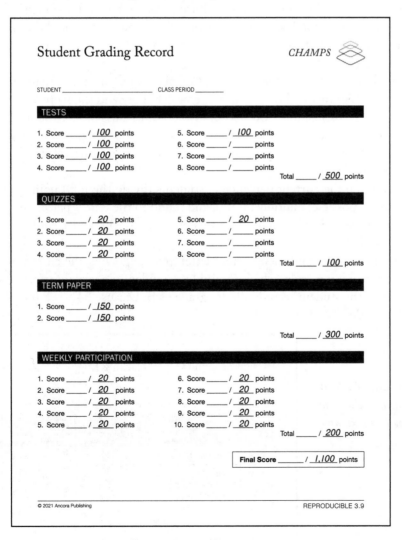

of their understanding about their current grade status until it is too late and they realize the grade they want is unattainable.

Give students a record to calculate their cumulative grade. The Assignment and Grade Tracking Log (Reproducible 3.10) provides a running record of scores for all assignments as they are returned to students. Students calculate their cumulative grade and can easily see how each score affects their percentage and letter grade.

You will need to demonstrate and teach students how to record scores on this form using the following steps:

1. For each assignment you return, students record the date the assignment was due and the assignment name.

2. In the Points Earned and Points Possible column, students record the grade they received on the individual assignment. For example, if the assignment had a total of 15 points possible and the student earned 13 points, the student would record 13/15.

3. In the Total Points Earned column, students record the accumulated points they have earned throughout the semester. They then add the score from the previous Total Points Earned (one row above) to the Points Earned for each new assignment. For example, the student had 38 total points earned from all previous quizzes and then records scores for an essay in which she earned 25 points. She records a new Total Points Earned score of 63 (38 + 25 = 63).

4. In the Total Points Possible column, students record the accumulated points possible for all assignments throughout the semester. They add the score from the previous Total Points Possible (one row above) to the Points Possible for the new assignment. For example, the total points possible from all previous quizzes was 45, and the essay assignment had 30 points possible. The student records a new Total Points Possible value of 75 (45 + 30 = 75).

5. To determine the current percentage, students divide the total points earned by the total points possible, multiply by 100, and round to the tenths place. For example, the student divides 63 by 75, multiplies this number by 100, and records a Current Percentage of 84%.

6. Finally, students record their current letter grade, applying the current percentage to your letter-grading scale, which should be provided in a visual format somewhere in the room. The student records a letter grade of B, because 84% is a B on her teacher's grading scale.

Reproducible 3.10
Assignment and Grade Tracking Log Example

Assignment and Grade Tracking Log   CHAMPS

STUDENT _____ HOMEROOM _____ SUBJECT _____

Due	Assignment	Points earned/ Points possible	Total points earned/ Total points possible	Current percentage	Current letter grade
9/15	Quiz: Unit 1	13 / 15	13 / 15	87%	B
9/20	Quiz: Unit 2	10 / 15	23 / 30	77%	C
9/25	Quiz: Unit 3	15 / 15	38 / 45	84%	B
10/1	Essay	25 / 30	63 / 75	84%	B

The maturity and level of sophistication of your students will serve as a guide for determining how much prompting you must give them to record their grades. Students will need to be taught how to keep this sheet in an easy-to-find place in their notebook and how to track their grades. Each time they receive a grade, they should record it. It may be necessary to warn students that you will conduct periodic spot checks to be sure they have kept their grading sheets up to date. If many students in the class have low skills, motivation, or maturity, you may need to reinforce students by awarding bonus points for keeping their sheets up to date.

If your students are fairly sophisticated (with low support needs), the grading sheet may simply be a useful tool for them. Hand out the sheet at the beginning of the term, and let students know that you will occasionally check to see if they are properly recording their grades. A grading sheet will be a useful tool for all students, especially because you can use it to illustrate your grading plan. You may need to make some minor adjustments if you decide to add or remove assignments as the term progresses, but the students will have a clear outline of their activities and the relative grade values for different assignments.

Some students, especially those less proficient in math, may need ongoing assistance in using this tracking log. Each time you return an assignment, demonstrate and guide the recording of scores until all students are able to perform this procedure with ease. By doing this as a teacher-directed group activity, you will also prompt all students to participate and view grade tracking as a routine part of classwork. If you fade the guided portion of this procedure once students are proficient, be sure to continue to circulate and periodically check how individual students are doing with completing the log. This will ensure that students are following through with tracking grades and are using the appropriate steps to complete the log.

In summary, if you communicate important course objectives, align evaluation with these objectives, and ensure that students receive regular feedback on behavior, academic performance, and current grade status, your grading system can become more than a simple evaluation tool. It will become a systematic monitoring device that demonstrates to students that they are accountable for their efforts each day and that their efforts will result in a better grade at the end of the term. If you opt to incorporate behavior into your grading system, plan to do a periodic deep dive to consider whether students' grades still accurately communicate mastery of learning objectives and standards. If you find that the behavior and effort grade is masking or overwhelming how students are doing academically, you will need to reevaluate your system and make changes for subsequent groups you work with.

Conclusion

The tasks in this chapter presented a series of structural variables to consider in planning and facilitating instructional activities with your students. By developing a daily schedule, behavioral expectations for all common instructional activities, procedures for managing student work and technology use, and grading systems and goals that clearly relate to your regular instructional activities, you will set your students up for the best chance of succeeding in your classroom. In the next chapter, we will discuss how to teach students these expectations and procedures.

CHAMPS Notes

CHAPTER 4

Teach Students to Meet Expectations

When your expectations are clear, students never have to guess how you expect them to behave.

Once you have structured your classroom for success, the next step is to directly teach students how to behave successfully in your classroom (Barbetta et al., 2005; Evertson & Emmer, 1982; Moskowitz & Hayman, 1976; Simonsen et al., 2008). Teaching expected behavior involves far more than simply telling students what you expect on the first day of school. You will teach students to strive toward your vision for the classroom and your Guidelines for Success. You will also teach them the details of how to function successfully in your classroom with expectations for activities and transitions. Finally, you will teach common social-emotional or behavioral skills that students need to be successful, both in school and beyond.

Imagine you decide to participate in a team sport that you have never played before. At the first practice, the coach covers all the information about how she expects the team to function—from big-picture items like sportsmanship and teamwork to the plays and patterns the team will run on the field to the specifics of each position on the team. After presenting this massive amount of information, the coach informs the team that she will not be going over any of this information again—everyone is expected to know and operate from this information for the rest of the season. Even when the team does badly, the coach refuses to review or practice. She reasons, "I taught my expectations on the first day of practice. What is wrong with this team?"

Now imagine a coach who, at the first practice, covers some big-picture items like sportsmanship and teamwork, but at every practice refines and extends the details of those goals. At first, the coach mainly focuses on conditioning and one or two specific plays. As each new play is introduced in subsequent practices, the coach models the play, has the team practice, provides positive and corrective feedback, and then reruns the play until the team reaches mastery. Then the team practices previously taught plays to ensure that they are integrating new expectations with the basics. At every practice the coach provides more leadership, inspiration, and opportunities to practice to mastery all the skills that are required to make the best team possible.

Which team would you like to join?

Specifically defining your expectations is essential if you hope to have a positive and productive classroom. However, defining your expectations is not in and of itself sufficient to achieve that goal. You also must effectively communicate your expectations to your students (Brophy & Good, 1986; Simonsen et al., 2008; Sulzer-Azaroff & Mayer, 1991; Trussell, 2008). Thus, the tasks in this chapter cover designing lessons to teach students the guidelines, rules, and expectations you defined in Chapters 2 and 3.

Teach Expectations No Matter When You Start

Even if you are starting this program partway into the school year, it is essential to attend to the tasks in this chapter. In particular, clarify and teach expectations for any activities or transitions during which student behavior has been consistently problematic.

The five tasks presented and explained in this chapter are:

- Task 1: Teach Your Guidelines for Success and Classroom Rules
- Task 2: Prepare Visuals and Lessons to Communicate Your CHAMPS Expectations
- Task 3: Teach Behavioral and Social-Emotional Skills
- Task 4: Clarify Behavioral Expectations for Common Areas and Special Circumstances
- Task 5: Clarify Behavioral Expectations With Parents and Guardians

TASK 1

Teach Your Guidelines for Success and Classroom Rules

Prepare to teach and reinforce your guidelines and rules to students at the beginning of the year.

• • • • •

When teaching your students, remember that teaching is not the same as telling. Use good instructional techniques when teaching the guidelines and rules (Epstein et al., 2008; Park & Lynch, 2014; Rosenshine, 2012; Simonsen, 2008), such as:

- Use age-appropriate lessons to introduce and re-teach as necessary.
- Provide a rationale for each guideline and rule.
- Demonstrate enthusiasm and passion for how the guidelines and rules can help the class community and individual students.
- Provide examples and non-examples of what it looks and sounds like when a student is and is not following the guidelines or rules.
- Help students make connections between the guidelines and rules (e.g., "You can demonstrate our guideline of 'being responsible' when you arrive to class on time and follow directions").
- Emphasize the guidelines and rules throughout the year through positive and corrective feedback, celebrations of progress, weekly or monthly themes, and other activities.

Figure 4.1 (pp. 204–207) shows a sample lesson from *Foundations* (Sprick et al., 2014) on teaching the Guideline for Success "Excel."

NOTE: Whether you are starting CHAMPS at the beginning of or during the school year, take the time to implement this task. Guidelines for Success and classroom rules give your students critical information about how they can meet expectations and accomplish goals—and this is valuable at any point in the year.

As with your long-range goals, share Guidelines for Success and classroom rules with students' families. Task 5 in this chapter provides more information about communicating expectations for your classroom to students' families.

Incorporate Guidelines For Success

Keep guidelines alive by using them frequently in the classroom. For example, if "Strive for Excellence" is one of your guidelines, you can reference this in situations where you want to prompt motivation: "Remember to do your best, neatest work on these posters. We want to show the rest of the school that our class strives for excellence." You should also use the guidelines as a basis for providing both positive and corrective feedback to students about their behavior.

Figure 4.1 *Sample Lesson from Foundations for Teaching Guidelines for Success*

Module C, Presentation 2

Scripted Lesson

Page 1 of 4

Guidelines for Success
Lesson 2 • KEYS for Success: Excel

KEYS for Success: Excel

OBJECTIVES

- Students will explain how to excel in a subject or activity.
- Students will describe how to apply these qualities and decisions to school.

MATERIALS

- Document camera, interactive whiteboard, or PowerPoint
- Student copies of the Student Worksheet for Lesson 2—Keys for Success: Excel

Introduction

1. Review the Guidelines for Success and key points from Lesson 1. Have students fill in the missing words.

   (Know): Seek (knowledge) and be active in your own learning.

   Excel: Do your best. Try your hardest and strive for excellence in all you do.

   Yearn: Desire to be successful. Set goals and work hard to accomplish them.

   Serve: Work with others. Give of yourself, your time, and your talents.

   Point to each guideline as you read it. You may have students read them chorally with you or do cloze reading by having students complete the last half of the sentence. Have them fill in the blanks on their worksheet.

   (**Know**): Seek (knowledge) and be (active) in your own learning.

   (**Excel**: Do your best. Try your hardest and strive for excellence in all you do).

   Yearn: Desire to be successful. Set goals and work hard to accomplish them.

   Serve: Work with others. Give of yourself, your time, and your talents.

2. Introduce the lesson objectives and provide the rationale for why this skill will help students be successful.

   In today's lesson, we are going to focus on the guideline Excel. Experts in every field do certain things so that they excel and set themselves apart from everyone else. They have positive and productive attitudes, make good decisions, and develop healthy habits and routines that allow them to rise

Foundations: A Proactive and Positive Behavior Support System

Figure 4.1 *Sample Lesson from Foundations for Teaching Guidelines for Success*

Module C, Presentation 2

Scripted Lesson

Page 2 of 4

Guidelines for Success
Lesson 2 • KEYS for Success: Excel

to the top of their field. Examining what these experts do and think will help you learn what you need to do to excel in school and any other field or area in which you desire to do well!

Lesson Body

1. Demonstrate filling out the How to Excel chart on the student worksheet for a specific field (musician, athlete, engineer, writer, etc.) Talk aloud and explain your thinking as you fill out the chart. Have students write responses on their worksheet.

Let's look at what an expert in the field of music might need to do in order to excel. I'm going to think about a classical musician, but we could also break this down for a pop star, rock musician, or some other expert in the music industry.

What does a musician do, or what effort does a musician put in to become the best in the field and excel? Well, I know that professional musicians have to practice, practice, practice. When they are younger, they take lessons. All musicians that I know set goals for practice and performance, such as practicing 6 hours a day or continuing to practice one passage until it is perfect. Then they stick to those goals. I'm going to write these things down in the "Things they did/Effort" box.

Now, what kinds of attitudes or mindsets do musicians need so that they excel? They . . .

How to Excel: Musicians

Things they did/Effort	Attitude/Mindset
Practice, practice, practice Take lessons Set goals and stick to them	Don't give up—strong Confident Positive
Relationship skills	**Things avoided**
Respectful Willing to work with others Show humility Help others and accept help	Distractions—certain people, certain activities Naysayers

Ask additional examples in each box. Have students share one idea with a partner first, then randomly call on students to share their partner's response.

Foundations: A Proactive and Positive Behavior Support System

Figure 4.1 continued *Sample Lesson from Foundations for Teaching Guidelines for Success*

Module C, Presentation 2

Scripted Lesson

Page 3 of 4

Guidelines for Success
Lesson 2 • KEYS for Success: Excel

2. With students, develop a list of topics or fields in which someone may excel. For example:

   - Sports (have students select specific sports)
   - Science
   - Art
   - Business
   - Technology
   - Chess
   - Medicine

3. Divide students into partners or groups, then have each partnership or group select a topic from the list generated in Step 2. Direct students to think of things that leaders in the field they selected had to do in order to excel and get to the top. Students will brainstorm and write their answers on the How to Excel Chart on their worksheets.

4. When students finish brainstorming, randomly call on groups to share something from each box. Add their ideas to your original How to Excel Chart.

5. Have a class discussion about how each of the listed efforts, attitudes, skills, and things avoided will help them be successful at Ben Franklin Middle School. Also discuss the following points:

   > The second part of the guideline Excel says, "Do your best. Try your hardest and strive for excellence in all you do." What things listed on your How to Excel chart are similar or have the same meaning? Do you think that experts in the field you chose follow this guideline—doing their best, trying their hardest, and striving for excellence?

   > The point is not to be the best at everything but to do your own best in whatever you do. This is about *personal best*. Strive for excellence and excel, not in comparison with other people, but to be the best you can be. Many musicians, athletes, public speakers, writers, etc., are not trying to beat anyone else. Their goal is to create their personal best and excel.

   > Notice that most of what is on the How to Excel Chart doesn't have to do with talent, IQ, or something you are born with. It has to do with how hard you try, how well you work with others, and the choices you make.

Foundations: A Proactive and Positive Behavior Support System

Figure 4.1 *Sample Lesson from Foundations for Teaching Guidelines for Success*

Module C, Presentation 2

Scripted Lesson

Page 4 of 4

Guidelines for Success
Lesson 2 • KEYS for Success: Excel

Conclusion

- Summarize and review what students should do to excel at Ben Franklin Middle School.

- Explain that students can apply these same efforts, attitudes, relationship skills, and positive decisions to become successful in any endeavor—classes, a job, relationships—so that they excel in life.

- **Exit Ticket:** Have students complete Items 2 and 3 on their worksheets—identify an area in which they would like to excel and list at least five things they can do to excel.

"Hakeem, when you pick up litter in the classroom without being asked, it is a great example of being responsible." "Fiona, you need to work quietly. The guideline about treating everyone with respect means you do not disturb others when they are trying to work." Work to embed Guidelines for Success within the daily routines of your class as often as possible.

Guidelines for Success can also be used as the basis for celebrations of progress (such as class awards at the end of the week), monthly themes for your classroom (October is Be Responsible Month), and writing assignments and class discussions. Some teachers create songs, raps, or pledges about the guidelines that can be recited each day or a few times a week. Other teachers award mystery raffle tickets to students who are demonstrating a "Guideline of the Day." At the end of the day or week, students guess which guideline was being acknowledged, and the teacher reveals the Guideline of the Day. The important thing to remember is to make the guidelines a vibrant and ongoing part of your classroom culture.

Remember, if some students do not receive information about or modeling of these kinds of attitudes, traits, and behaviors at home, the emphasis that school personnel place on their guidelines may provide critical lifelong lessons. If you find that some of your students have less of a context for understanding and operating from your guidelines, plan to provide more instruction on how students can implement them and be prepared to give students more encouragement and pep talks about their benefits.

> **Motivation**
>
> *Guidelines for Success can be used to motivate your students through shared goals, positive feedback, and celebrations of progress.*

Plan to Teach Your Rules Using Positive and Negative Examples

It is also important to teach and reinforce your classroom rules so that students understand the behaviors necessary for the classroom to function in a safe and effective way. The best way to help students understand your rules is to demonstrate specific examples of following and not following the rules. Through the use of both positive and negative examples, you teach students to understand your interpretation of the rule and how you will make judgments about whether a particular behavior follows or breaks a rule (Gresham, 1998; Kame'enui & Simmons, 1990; Sugai & Lewis, 1996). Students may not know what working during work times looks like. This may require teaching some behaviors that you feel are unnecessary, but it is better to overteach than to underteach. You might sit at a desk and show your students what not paying attention looks like, to contrast it with what paying attention looks like. This can help make an abstract concept concrete and more easily understood. Plan to teach your rules each day for at least the first 5 to 10 days of school.

Following are other suggestions for ways that you might teach or clarify your rules, as well as suggestions for providing a rationale for each rule.

Create scenarios of some behaviors that follow the rules and some that violate the rules. Place them on a worksheet or activity cards. Have students work individually, in partners, or in groups to discuss whether each scenario is an example or non-example of following the rules. If it is a non-example, ask them to explain why it violates a rule.

Role-play positive examples and negative examples of following the rules. Have students give a thumbs-up for positive examples or a thumbs-down for negative examples. Make sure to demonstrate extreme behaviors as well as ones that are subtler and require more consideration and judgment from the students. For example, to illustrate the rule "Follows directions without arguing," you might role-play a student's reaction to a direction to sit in their assigned seat in a variety of the following ways:

- Says, "Make me," and doesn't go to his seat.
- Goes to his seat but scowls and doesn't say anything.
- Goes to his seat after saying "OK."
- Begins going to his seat but takes the longest route and says "hi" to others on the way.
- Goes to his seat and within a minute gets out again.
- Mutters "stupid teacher" and walks to his seat.
- Asks, "Why can't we sit somewhere else today?"

Use real-life examples to provide a rationale for why rules are necessary. Explain to students that they will encounter rules throughout their lives. When they are driving, one common rule is to drive on the right side of the road. Ask students why this rule is important. They will likely come up with responses like "to keep people safe," "so people don't run into each other," or "because if everyone just drove on either side, traffic would be even more crazy than it already is." Explain that your classroom rules are like the rule of driving on the right side of the road. They are designed to keep people safe, make sure that no one is interfering or getting in the way of someone else's learning, and keep the instruction and class activities running as smoothly as possible.

For each rule, have students create a list of reasons why it is important in the classroom and in other aspects of their lives. This can be done individually, in partners, in small groups, or with the whole class. For example, ask students to brainstorm why the rule "Come to class every day that you are not seriously ill" is important for class and for later life. Guide students to think about things like: "It is important so we don't miss important information in class." "If you skip or are absent a lot in a job, you will get fired. We are developing habits for work."

In summary, teach and incorporate your Guidelines for Success and classroom rules using effective instructional techniques such as rationale, positive and negative examples, and frequent positive and corrective feedback.

TASK 2

Prepare Visuals and Lessons to Communicate Your CHAMPS Expectations

Develop a preliminary plan and prepare lessons for teaching your CHAMPS expectations to students.

• • • • •

In Chapter 2, Task 6 and Chapter 3, Task 2 you learned how important it is to define exactly how you expect students to behave during various classroom activities and transitions. But identifying expectations alone is not enough. If students are going to be able to meet your expectations, you need to communicate those expectations to students clearly and thoroughly (Brophy & Good, 1986; Simonsen et al., 2008; Sulzer-Azaroff & Mayer, 1991; Trussell, 2008). Teaching expectations is the first step in a three-step process for effectively communicating expectations to students:

1. Teach expectations.
2. Observe student behavior during activities and transitions.
3. Give students feedback about their implementation of the expectations.

This three-step process is summarized in Figure 4.2 (p. 210). As shown, the first step in the communication process is teaching your expectations to students. To teach effectively, you need to prepare lessons that communicate your expectations during the first week of school or whenever there is a major change in the design of classroom procedures or routines. Detailed information on the second and third steps in the communication process—observing student behavior and giving students feedback on their implementation of expectations—is presented in Chapter 9.

Your plan for how you will teach your CHAMPS expectations should be based on the complexity of your expectations, your own teaching style, the age and sophistication of your students, and the level of structure and support you plan to establish in your classroom. For example, in settings with mature and responsible students (a class that needs only a low-support

Figure 4.2 *Three-Step Process for Communicating Expectations*

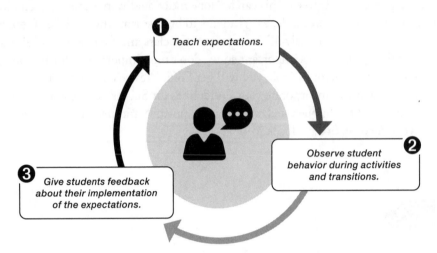

management plan), it may be sufficient to verbally describe your expectations on the first day of school and provide a simple list on a flip chart of the three or four major considerations. Then provide short verbal reviews on the second and third days, and thereafter use only occasional reminders. On the other hand, with students who need higher support, you should probably plan to teach your expectations—using visual displays, demonstrations, and actual practice—every day for at least the first 10 days of school. For primary-level students, especially kindergarten and first grade, you will probably extend this instruction on behavioral expectations for at least the first month and, if needed, throughout the first quarter of the year—a strategy also instrumental in addressing the needs of English language learners and students with special needs in your classroom. If your classroom experiences high mobility (i.e., many students moving in and out of the classroom as they transfer between schools), create a plan for how to teach incoming students the expectations while reinforcing the expectations for the rest of the class. Task 4 later in this chapter covers more details for the special circumstance of new students.

When developing your teaching plan, you need to make decisions about how to organize the content and then how to display the expectations for the students. Following are examples of how to apply these concepts of lesson organization and use of visual displays for high-support, medium-support, and low-support lessons.

Use the CHAMPS Acronym

For classes (or teachers!) that require high support, you should use the CHAMPS acronym as the basis for teaching your expectations and creating visual displays to communicate that information to students. Classes that do not need as much support can also benefit from use of the acronym to create consistency and clarity, but it is critical with groups of students who have higher needs or may struggle to meet expectations. A number of district-based CHAMPS trainers have said that when a teacher does not use the CHAMPS acronym for a high-support class, the students are not clear about the teacher's exact expectations.

The acronym is a useful way to communicate that there is consistency in what students have to know to behave responsibly. Although the specific expected behaviors may be different between, for example, cooperative groups and teacher-directed instruction, students learn that the headings (Conversation, Help, Activity, Movement, Participation) are the same from one activity or transition to another. Students also realize that you have definite thoughts about each classroom activity and transition. Without the acronym as an anchor, students may feel that there are just thousands of unconnected expectations. Another advantage to using the CHAMPS acronym is that the content is already neatly organized for you—all you have to do is use your CHAMPS worksheets. See Box 4.1 (pp. 212–213), CHAMPS Adaptations, for examples of how some teachers have adapted the CHAMPS acronym for younger and older students.

Prepare Visual Displays of CHAMPS Information

Decide whether your visual displays will be text or picture based. The reproducible materials provided for download on the CHAMPS Resources web page (see p. 3) include 396 visuals for you to choose from—six different icons for 66 different CHAMPS expectations such as "CONVERSATION: Talk quietly with anyone in your group" and "PARTICIPATION: Listening/Answering/Asking" (see the sample icons in Figure 4.3). The six different versions of the icons associated with each expectation are:

Version 1: **Primary (B/W).** Line drawings that young students (K–2) can color
Version 2: **Primary (Color).** Full-color illustrations aimed at young students (K–2). Note that thumbnails are shown in black and white, but the images provided in the downloadable materials are in full color.)
Version 3: **Intermediate.** Black and white drawings for older students (3–8)
Version 4: **Pictograph.** Black and white graphic symbols
Version 5: **Sentence strip.** Text-only icons
Version 6: **Road sign.** Text-based street signs in different shapes and colors

Figure 4.3 *Sample CHAMPS Icons*

Version 1 Primary, K–2 (B&W)	Version 2 Primary, K–2 (Color)	Version 3 Intermediate, 3–8 (B&W)	Version 4 Pictograph	Version 5 Sentence Strips	Version 6 Road Sign
				Conversation Talk quietly with anyone in your group.	TALK QUIETLY WITH ONE OTHER STUDENT
				Participation Listen, answer, ask questions, and/or share.	LISTEN, ANSWER, ASK QUESTIONS, AND/OR SHARE

BOX 4.1

CHAMPS Adaptations

For Young Children

If you teach very young students (pre-kindergarten or kindergarten) or students with cognitive deficits, you may wish to simplify the CHAMPS acronym.

For example, Ray Roth and Suzanne Hays implemented CHAMPS in a preschool setting. CHAMPS was shortened to MAC: Movement, Activity, and Conversation. Susan Schilt, of the Pinellas County Public Schools in Florida, used this concept to develop "Mr. MAC" as shown in Figure 4.4.

Another example of adapting the CHAMPS concept for young children comes from the Read Well beginning reading curriculum by Marilyn Sprick and Shelley Jones. They developed TEAM: Talk, Effort, Ask, and Move. Figure 4.5 is an example of how this can be applied to independent work periods.

Figure 4.4 *Mr. Mac Poster*

T	**Talk**	Talk quietly about reading and writing only to the person next to you.
E	**Effort**	Think about reading and writing. Do your personal best handwriting and spelling.
A	**Ask**	Put your question card up, but keep working.
M	**Move**	Stand or sit at your desk, in your personal space.

Figure 4.5 *Sample Expectations for Independent Work*

For Older Students

Another adaptation is ACHIEVE—Activity, Conversation, Help, Integrity, Effort, Value, Efficiency. Susan Banks and Leslie Salmon of the Adult Education Center in West Palm Beach, Florida, used this acronym with students whose ages range from 17 to 70. The ACHIEVE acronym is from *Discipline in the Secondary Classroom* (4th ed.; Sprick et al., 2021), which is essentially CHAMPS for grades 9–12.

Figure 4.6 *Sample ACHIEVE Posters for an Adult ELL Class*

Each of these 396 icons is available in PDF and JPG formats so you can size the graphic to meet your needs. Note that Versions 1 and 2 are essentially the same. Version 1 icons are line drawings that students can color. Version 2 icons are full color but can be printed in either black and white or full color, depending on your printing capability.

Once you have selected the icons appropriate for your class (artistic teachers may wish to design their own), determine how you will use them to create classroom displays.

Poster. One of the easiest options is to create a poster-size version of each of your major instructional activities and major transitions (use the CHAMPS worksheets you filled out in Chapters 2 and 3 for guidance) and paste the icons in an appropriate place. A chart stand, as shown in Figure 4.7, is a good way to display your expectations in poster form. Another way is to mount all the posters above your board space in the front of the room—this eliminates the need to flip to the correct poster each time you change activities.

Figure 4.7 *Chart Stand*

Projector. You might put the expectations on standard paper for display with a document camera or use a projector and load the icons into PowerPoint or Keynote presentations. The downside of this method is that if you need to use the document camera or a slide presentation for other aspects of the activity, you will need to remove the visual display. Only use this method if you can keep the expectations posted for the entirety of the activity or transition, or if your students are highly responsible and do not need the continuous visual display. If you use this method and find that students are struggling to meet expectations, consider transitioning to a visual display that remains posted throughout the entirety of the activity or transition.

Bulletin board display. Some teachers devote an entire bulletin board to a CHAMPS display, using push pins to display the relevant icons for each type of activity (Figure 4.8). Or you might use a magnetic board with magnets to hold the icons in place. Clerese Sprague from Hood River, Oregon, shares that she made a large chart to display her CHAMPS expectations. Clear pockets are attached to the chart next to each letter. Just before she begins a new activity or transition, she places the appropriate icons in the appropriate pockets on the chart. At the beginning of the year (and periodically thereafter), she explains what each icon means as she places it in the pocket.

If you prefer to use text-based displays, the Version 5 icons are sentence strips that work well for pocket charts. They can even be printed as magnetic strips for use on a magnet board. Because the icons are provided in PDF format, you can electronically size them to fit your needs.

If you want to create your own text-based versions of your expectations, you can use Reproducible 4.1, CHAMPS Expectations, a fillable form provided in the reproducible materials. This form is a version of a CHAMPS chart that allows you to fill in the activity or transition and then type in the content that you want for each part of the CHAMPS acronym. You can also cut and paste CHAMPS icons into these templates. The default print size is 8.5" x 11", but you can rescale to print at poster size if your computer and printer have that capability. Ask your school's technical experts for assistance with this, if needed.

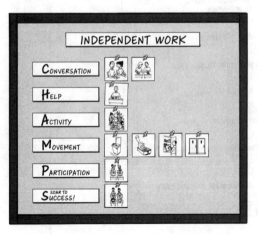

Figure 4.8 *Bulletin Board Display*

Visit CHAMPS Resources (see p. 3) for fillable activity worksheets and templates for the MAC and ACHIEVE acronyms (Reproducibles 4.2A–B and 4.3A-B, respectively) described in Box 4.1, CHAMPS Adaptations.

Prepare Lessons for Teaching Your CHAMPS Expectations

When developing your plan for teaching expectations—that is, deciding how detailed your lessons will be, anticipating how many days you will actively teach the expectations, and choosing how you will organize the content—it is better to overplan than to underplan. For classes with higher needs, plan to err on the side of more lessons and more detail than you think you might need. It's always easier to condense or eliminate some lessons than to scramble to create new lessons once school has begun.

High-Support Lessons

If your students require higher levels of support and clarity of expectations, plan to implement the following steps:

1. Tell students the type of activity that is coming next.
2. Tell students what you expect and show the visual with your CHAMPS expectations.
3. Model the behaviors you expect to see, with particular emphasis on Participation.
4. Ask some students to demonstrate the expectations.
5. Model some non-examples of behaviors you don't want to see.
6. Model the correct way one more time.
7. Verify that students understand the expectations: Model behavior, and have students identify whether you are exhibiting appropriate or inappropriate behavior.
8. Review all the positive expectations and re-model the right way.
9. Have students get started on the activity or transition.

Some aspects of behavioral expectations may be clearer to students if they are demonstrated. One way to do this is to model (act out) both positive and negative examples of what you expect (Gresham, 1998; Sugai & Lewis, 1996). For example, when teaching students what participation should look and sound like during independent work periods, model the right way and the wrong way to participate in the activity. You can even exaggerate behaviors to make it more interesting for students. If you use modeling, it's a good idea to first provide a couple of positive models (the right ways to demonstrate participation), then give the negative models (the most probable wrong ways students might behave). Finally, briefly demonstrate the positive models again. By beginning and ending with positive models, you reduce the chance that students will mistakenly view the negative models as the right way to do things (Bandura, 1977; Kame'enui & Simmons, 1990).

With transitions and activities that are complex or potentially problematic, students will not really understand what is expected of them until they experience the transition or activity. One way of addressing this problem is to have the class practice the actual behavior. For example, washing hands and lining up for lunch tends to be a complex set of expectations for primary-age students. Therefore, sometime before lunch on the first day of school, have students actually practice the behavior. At the intermediate grade and middle school levels, you could have students practice getting out materials and heading a paper within a reasonable period of time (30 seconds, for example). Other expectations that can benefit from practice include entering the room in an orderly fashion from recess or at the beginning of class, appropriate noise level within cooperative groups, getting quiet when the attention signal is given, moving quickly and quietly to and from small groups or lab stations, moving desks into and out of cooperative group activities, and so on.

You may also wish to involve students when modeling expectations. Many students at both the elementary and middle school levels enjoy participating in role-play situations in which student volunteers demonstrate (model) one or more aspects of the expectations. The advantage of involving students in role-play situations is that it gets them more actively involved in the lesson and gives them an opportunity to practice the expected behaviors you are teaching (McGinnis & Goldstein, 1994; Walker et al., 2004). Ask for a couple of volunteers and have them demonstrate a positive model of one or more aspects of your expectations. Then you can model some examples of the wrong way to behave and end by asking different students to demonstrate the positive expectation. Notice that with modeling, the students should always model the positive behaviors—the teacher is the only one who models the negative ones. You don't want to give the students extra chances to practice the wrong ways of doing things!

Diversity, Equity, Inclusion, and Access

Be considerate if ELL students or other students are uncomfortable modeling in front of the whole class. An alternative approach is a buddy system that allows each student to comfortably model the expectations with a peer.

As you move into subsequent days of school, you may be able to reduce the amount of modeling substantially, but continue to review expectations and check for understanding. Plan to ask students a few questions about the expectations before you start the activity or transition. The answers students give (or fail to give) will help you determine whether you have adequately explained the essential information. If students can answer your questions, you are probably ready to start the activity or transition. If students seem unsure of their answers or are unable to answer the questions at all, you should go over the information again more thoroughly. Plan on re-teaching the expectations until students know them.

When checking for understanding of expectations, avoid asking for volunteers to answer the questions. Students who do not know the answer are unlikely to volunteer, so you will not get accurate information about whether all students understand the expectations. A more effective approach is to ask the question first, give everyone time to think, and then assign one individual student to answer or have the entire class hold up a whiteboard or fingers to indicate their response.

Everyone, get ready to answer a few questions. During the time we will be working in cooperative groups, can you get out of your seat for any reason? If so, what are the reasons? (Pause for students to think.) Jared, please answer.

Everyone, think about whether you can get out of your seat without permission to sharpen your pencil or get needed materials during teacher instruction. Give a thumbs-up if you can get out of your seat without getting permission first. Give me a thumbs-down if you need to get my permission first.

You are going to show me from 0–4 on your fingers what voice level you can use during the transition to stations. Think for a moment. Now hold up the number from 0–4.

For classes that need higher levels of support and structure, you will probably want to teach expectations for at least the first 10 days of school, then begin fading to every other day, then every third day. Students should be able to effectively meet your expectations for an activity or transition for at least 3 days before you begin fading from direct teaching to brief reminders and infrequent prompts. You will likely want to re-teach (some teachers say "re-CHAMP") the expectations at least every 3 to 4 weeks. You will also want to plan for re-teaching at times of the year (immediately after a long break or before a field trip, for example) that you know are likely to be more difficult for students (Mayer, 1995; Scheuermann & Hall, 2008).

Note that if you do not re-teach when students repeatedly fail to meet your expectations, there is a tacit implication that what they did the day before was perfectly acceptable. Therefore, any time that student behavior is slipping, return to teaching your expectations before the activity in subsequent days until students again meet them for 3 consecutive days. Although this may feel frustrating or redundant, remind yourself that your expectations are unique to your classroom, so it may take students some time to become automatic with your routines and procedures. Also remind yourself that some things that are not acceptable in your room may be acceptable or even encouraged by a teacher that some of your students have in the class period before coming to you. By taking enough time to teach your expectations, you will save time, energy, and frustration in the long run by not having to constantly respond to misbehavior.

Medium-Support Lessons

For classes with a medium- or low-support management plan, you may choose not to go into the full details of implementing the CHAMPS acronym. A slightly less structured approach is to develop T-charts for your major instructional activities and transitions. They are called T-charts because they look like a capital T with "Looks Like" on one side of the T and "Sounds Like" on the other side (see Figure 4.9, p. 218). An advantage of T-charts is their simplicity, but a disadvantage is that they do not provide specific information on the details of Conversation, Help, Activity, Movement, and Participation. However, for a medium-support class, they may provide sufficient information. T-charts can be graphically displayed in all the same ways that CHAMPS charts can be displayed—posters, projected, bulletin board, and so on.

With medium-support classes, you may be able to teach expectations more quickly and with fewer steps. For example, the following steps may be sufficient:

1. Tell students the type of activity that is coming next.
2. Tell students what you expect and show the T-chart.
3. Model the behaviors you expect to see.
4. Have some students demonstrate the expectations.
5. Review all the positive expectations and re-model the right way.
6. Have students get started on the activity or transition.

In addition, with classes that can handle less support, you may be able to phase out teaching expectations before activities and transitions as early as the second week of school, and simply review expectations at the beginning of the week for a few weeks.

Figure 4.9 *T-Chart for Expectations During Teacher-Directed Instruction and Discussion*

LOOKS LIKE	SOUNDS LIKE
• Eyes on speaker, overhead, or your own notes • Everyone looks as if they are listening to the speaker • Hands raised before speaking • Notes being taken on essential points • Everyone in seat except speaker • If someone disagrees, they raise hand to become the speaker—no nonverbal expressions of disagreement	• Only one voice at a time can be heard • Presentation voice used when you are the speaker • Questions and comments from the speaker relate to the lesson • No noise other than writing or turning a page of your notes if you are not the current speaker • All verbal participation sounds are respectful, even when you are disagreeing

For primary-level students, you can use pictures on each side of the T-chart instead of sentences.

Low-Support Lessons

For classes with a low-support management plan, you may not even need to prepare T-charts. It is possible that you need to delineate only three or four specific expectations for each major activity or transition. If this is the case, print the expectations for each activity and transition onto 8.5" x 11" paper in landscape format. Add a tabbed divider to each page that labels the activity or transition so you can quickly flip to the correct page. Put these pages into a tabletop display portfolio (available at art supply stores), as shown in Figure 4.10. These may also be known as presentation displays or easel binders. A notebook taped to stay upright like a tent will work, too (see Figure 4.11).

The advantage of a display portfolio or notebook is its simplicity. The disadvantage is that on an 8.5" x 11" paper you will be able to display only a few sentences that can be seen from across the room, so you can't incorporate as much information as you can with T-charts and CHAMPS posters.

If low-support lessons work with your students, you may not even need to prepare any lessons—you can just have your CHAMPS worksheets handy as you show the expectations on the display portfolio. Then talk students through your expectations and explain what it takes to be

Figure 4.10 *Display Portfolio*

Figure 4.11 *Notebook*

successful in your classroom. Plan to do this for at least the first 2 or 3 days of school. If students are behaving well and meeting your expectations, you can fade out instruction on your expectations quickly. Decide whether or not the flip chart is still helpful to students. If it is, you can simply flip to the appropriate page of the folio (without instructing students) whenever you move from one transition to another.

Remember that the level of support is also about the teacher's needs, not just the needs of the students. If you are bothered by noise, lots of movement, and interruptions, you should probably implement the suggestions for medium- or high-support lessons. Detailed CHAMPS lessons give students the specific information they need to meet your expectations for a calm, orderly classroom.

See Chapter 9 for additional information about teaching and reinforcing your expectations with the three-step communication cycle. In Chapter 9, you will learn how to start on day one and plan for implementation on days two through 20.

TASK 3

Teach Behavioral and Social-Emotional Skills

Be prepared to teach behavioral and social-emotional skills that are essential for school and life success.

• • • • •

Students must be able to exhibit a wide range of behavioral and social-emotional skills to be successful in school and beyond. In addition to being able to follow directions and listen to their teacher, students must be able to interact appropriately with peers, seek help when needed, persist through challenges, and appropriately communicate frustration. Many students do not know how to exhibit these or other needed skills, and other students may not understand why these skills are beneficial for their success. If you plan to teach explicit lessons and reinforce these skills across time, you help your students learn skills for success in your classroom and for future learning situations they will encounter.

See Box 4.2 (p. 220) for more on how social-emotional learning (SEL) and classroom management complement each other.

Prior to school starting, when you don't yet know your students, consider which skills tend to be difficult for students in the age group and student population you work with. Start the year with focused lessons on these skills. For example, a first-grade teacher might identify "learning to accept no" as an important skill that should be emphasized toward the beginning of the school year. This teacher might also identify that students may need to learn how to share or seek help when they are in conflict with another student. A middle school teacher, in contrast, might identify that middle school students have become overly proficient with eye rolling and annoyed-sounding responses when given a direction or correction. These students may need lessons on how to respond appropriately to corrections and directions from adults. List the behavioral and social-emotional skills you think would be beneficial for the student

BOX 4.2

Understanding the Relationship Between Effective Classroom Management and Social-Emotional Learning

Unfortunately, in some schools and districts, effective classroom management and multi-tiered systems of support for behavior (MTSS-B) have been viewed as competing with social-emotional learning (SEL) initiatives. We encourage you to view these as critical and interrelated efforts rather than as competing initiatives. They are both essential for students' immediate and long-term success.

A well-designed classroom management plan provides the necessary structures to teach and reinforce social-emotional competencies effectively and efficiently (Bear et al., 2015). As described throughout CHAMPS, effective classroom managers establish classroom structures and supports to help their students thrive at whatever level of current social-emotional functioning the students exhibit. They teach clear expectations to eliminate hidden norms while also reinforcing and motivating students through positive relationships and positive feedback about students' efforts and growth. If students are highly responsible and mature, teachers can reduce some of the orchestration of the classroom environment. They will still teach social-emotional skills, but the skills they teach may be more sophisticated and students may require less support in order to practice and demonstrate those skills. In contrast, a classroom of students who are collectively less mature or struggle more in school will require different skills and more support in using and applying these skills.

If students struggle to meet a teacher's expectations for any number of reasons (e.g., trauma, disability, prior struggles in school, cultural differences, etc.), it is important to help them learn and develop the social and emotional competencies necessary for school success but also for their broader relationships and eventual employment. However, without support from the teacher or a predictable, orderly classroom environment, the classroom may be so chaotic and disruptive, or relationships between students or between students and staff may be so fraught, that students are unable to practice the SEL skills they are learning. For example, imagine a teacher who has many students who struggle with emotional regulation, so when students are frustrated, they are likely to yell, hit, or otherwise escalate. If the teacher tries to teach students to identify their emotions and manage emotional upsets but the classroom feels out of control, students will likely feel constantly overstimulated and unable to practice new self-regulation skills. By manipulating aspects of the classroom environment (i.e., STOIC variables), the teacher helps provide a solid foundation of support for students. When the classroom feels calmer and less stressful, students will be better able to practice and apply new social-emotional skills.

One way to easily incorporate social-emotional competency instruction into your classroom is to directly link social-emotional skills to your Guidelines for Success. Identify behaviors associated with social-emotional competencies that fall under each Guideline for Success. For example:

- **Be Responsible:** Identify your own feelings, use positive self-talk, set goals
- **Strive for Excellence:** Ask questions, learn from mistakes, seek help when needed
- **Care for Others:** Consider others' feelings, avoid gossip, respond to conflict with "stop, think, plan"

These connections will provide you with a common language and increased opportunities to teach, practice, and reinforce skills.

population you work with. As the school year progresses and you learn your students' areas of strength and weakness, periodically evaluate your list and determine which skills and competencies you should focus on through explicit lessons and integration into instructional activities.

When determining which social-emotional skills to teach, a powerful framework is "the CASEL 5," a social-emotional learning framework based on five competencies designed to foster student knowledge, skills, and attitudes that are important for students' learning and development. The five areas of competence, according to CASEL (2020), are:

- "Self-awareness: the abilities to understand one's own emotions, thoughts, and values, and how they influence behaviors across contexts." Included within this competency are skills such as integrating one's personal and social identity; identifying personal, cultural; and linguistic assets; identifying one's emotions; and demonstrating honesty and integrity, among others.
- "Self-management: the abilities to manage one's emotions, thoughts, and behaviors effectively in different situations and to achieve goals and aspirations," which includes capacities to delay gratification and manage stress as well as feel motivation and agency for personal and collective goals. Skills such as using stress management techniques, setting personal goals, and using planning and organizational skills are included in the self-management competency area.
- "Responsible decision-making: the abilities to make caring and constructive choices about personal behavior and social interactions across diverse situations." Students who exhibit this competency are able to consider ethical standards and safety concerns, use reasoned judgment to evaluate benefits and consequences of different actions, and reflect on their role in promoting personal, family, and community well-being.
- "Relationship skills: the abilities to establish and maintain healthy and supportive relationships and to effectively navigate settings with diverse individuals and groups." Students must be able to clearly communicate, actively listen, cooperate, work collaboratively to problem-solve and negotiate conflict constructively, navigate settings with different social and cultural demands and opportunities, provide leadership, and seek or offer help when needed.
- "Social awareness: the abilities to understand the perspectives of and empathize with others, including those from diverse background, cultures, and contexts." Students who exhibit this capacity are able to take others' perspectives and demonstrate empathy and compassion, are able understand diverse social norms for behavior in different settings and identify unjust ones, and recognize situational demands and opportunities.

Reproducible 4.4 (pp. 222–223) provides a sample list of lessons that could be designed to address different aspects of these five competencies. Consider checking or highlighting skills and competencies that may be beneficial to directly teach and reinforce with your students. Add additional ones that are not listed but would be beneficial for your students. We have grouped the five competencies into the categories of Personal Development (self-awareness and self-management), Social Development (social awareness and relationship skills), and Character Development (responsible decision-making).

Sample SEL Lessons (p. 1 of 4)

CHAMPS

CLASS _____ DATE _____

Personal Development: Self-Awareness and Self-Management

Topic	Possible Lesson Focus
Identifying emotions	• Self-awareness of emotional tendencies • Identifying one's own habitual responses • Identifying triggers to emotional responses • _____ • _____
Identifying barriers to success	• Focus versus distractibility • Flexibility versus rigidity • Organization/drive versus procrastination • Self-confidence versus anxiety • Delayed gratification versus immediate gratification • Humility versus arrogance • Working hard and putting in your best versus being lazy or doing the bare minimum • Developing a sense of identity versus following the crowd • Optimism versus pessimism • _____ • _____
Strategies to overcome barriers to success	• Know/identify your core principles and values • Positive self-talk and attribution • Learning self-discipline and impulse control • Goal setting • Organizational skills • Self-advocacy • Stress management techniques (e.g., deep breathing, relaxation, positive self-talk) • Developing grit/resilience/perseverance • _____ • _____

Reproducible 4.4 *Sample SEL Lessons (pp. 1–2)*

Sample SEL Lessons (p. 2 of 4)

CHAMPS

Social Development: Social Awareness and Relationship Skills

Topic	Possible Lesson Focus
Communication skill	• Active listening skills • Identifying/reading other forms of communication (body language, tone, facial expression, gestures) • Relating to others through empathy and paraphrasing • Presenting your own ideas to others (balancing confidence with humility) • Common conversational skills • _____ • _____
Handling conflict (with adults or peers)	Preventing or avoiding conflict • Identifying assumptions and stereotypes • Avoiding gossip • Avoiding teasing • Appropriate immediate responses to negative behaviors from others • _____ • _____ Responding to conflict • Using a strategy of "Stop, Think, Plan" • Using another conflict resolution strategy (e.g., Kelso's choices, when to seek help) • _____ • _____

Working with authority figures	• Understanding social hierarchies
	• Following directions/rules
	• Look at it from their perspective
	• Accepting feedback appropriately
	   – Correction/consequence
	   – Compliment
	• When and how to communicate concerns to another person/level of the hierarchy
	• Making a good impression
	   – Communication with authority
	   – Presenting good work ethic
	   – Presenting good habits (punctuality, dress, materials)
	   – Appropriate conversation/interaction
	
	• _____
	• _____

REPRODUCIBLE 4.4

Sample SEL Lessons (p. 3 of 4)   *CHAMPS*

Topic	Possible Lesson Focus

Peer interactions in school/work/social settings	• Cooperation
	• Contributing to the group
	   – How to introduce/enter
	   – Participate without taking over
	   – Constructive criticism/respectful disagreement
	• Friendship skills
	• Understanding and appreciating diversity
	• Understand power dynamics of groups
	   – Harassment and bullying
	   – Understanding the roles of victim, bystander, perpetrator and what to do
	     if you find yourself in one or more of these roles
	   – Ensure everyone belongs
	• Responding to pressure (passive, aggressive vs. assertive)
	• _____
	• _____

Seeking help	• Asking questions, advocating for self and others • Growth mindset • Finding expectations and hidden norms • Choosing/evaluating friends and support systems • Learning from mistakes • _____ • _____

Reproducible 4.4 *Sample SEL Lessons (pp. 3–4)*

Sample SEL Lessons (p. 4 of 4)   *CHAMPS*

Character Development: Responsible Decision-Making

Topic	Possible Lesson Focus
Self-awareness	• Know your own ethical and performance principles • _____ • _____
Using problem-solving skills in real life	• Predicting cause and effect (outcome of decision) • Determining fact versus opinion • Evaluating internal versus external locus of control • Determining safe versus unsafe behaviors • Determining appropriate versus inappropriate behaviors • _____ • _____
Keeping doors open	• Evaluating options and action steps • Time management and personal responsibility • Following rules and guidelines • Making realistic plans • Developing perseverance • Developing flexibility • Setting short-term and long-term goals – Other employability skills • _____ • _____

REPRODUCIBLE 4.4

If you will be designing your own lessons, create an outline of the skills to be covered and remember to apply good teaching practices (Gresham, 2002; Gueldner & Merrell, 2019), such as:

- Provide a rational for the importance of each skill.
- Model skills.
- Offer opportunities for students to practice and role-play skills.
- Check for student understanding.
- Provide immediate feedback.
- Use examples relevant to your students.
- Maintain a high positive to corrective ratio of interactions with your students.
- Maintain high student expectations.
- Highlight examples with sociocultural relevance.
- Integrate the information and skills throughout the day.

Also work to find ways to emphasize these skills on an ongoing basis through positive and corrective feedback, celebrations of progress or classroom themes, or special activities like guest speakers.

There are many programs and published curricula that can be used by individual classroom teachers or a whole school to teach social-emotional skills. CASEL provides evaluation guides on the effectiveness of a variety of social-emotional programs to help schools identify promising programs for implementation. A few programs to consider are included in the resource box below.

RESOURCES FOR TEACHING SOCIAL-EMOTIONAL SKILLS

Burrow-Sanchez, J. (2013). *ADAPT: Advancing Decision Making and Problem Solving for Teens.* Ancora Publishing.

ADAPT is a small group intervention for middle and high school students who are at risk for substance use, aggression, truancy, poor school performance, and depressive moods.

....

Carrizales-Engelmann, D., Feuerborn, L., Gueldner, B. A., & Tran, O. (2016). *Merrell's strong kids: Grades 3-5: A social and emotional learning curriculum* (2nd ed.). Paul H. Brookes Publishing.

Carrizales-Engelmann, D., Feuerborn, L., Gueldner, B. A., & Tran, O. (2016). *Merrell's strong kids: Grades 6-8: A social and emotional learning curriculum* (2nd ed.). Paul H. Brookes Publishing.

Whitcomb, S. A., & Damico, D. M. P. (2016). *Merrell's Strong Start—Pre-K: A social and emotional learning curriculum.* Paul H. Brookes Publishing.

Whitcomb, S. A., & Damico, D. M. P. (2016). *Merrell's Strong Start—Kindergarten-Grade 2: A social and emotional learning curriculum.* Paul H. Brookes Publishing.

Merrell's Strong Kids programs teach social and emotional skills, promote resilience, and increase children's and adolescent's coping skills. Lessons address emotion education (including learning about the interactions among thoughts, feelings, and behaviors), understanding other people's emotions, finding ways to manage anger, dealing with interpersonal conflict, reducing stress, and setting and attaining goals. Lessons are scripted and intended to be easy to use in the time frame of one 45- to 60-minute class period over the course of 12 weeks (one lesson per week).

Channing-Bete Company (n.d.). *PATHS (Promoting Alternative Thinking Strategies) program.* Author.

PATHS is a classroom-based SEL curriculum designed to teach students to resolve conflicts peacefully, empathize with others, and make responsible decisions. Modules are available for Pre-K through grade 6. The program includes lessons, supplementary activities, posters, and family contact and support materials.

....

Committee for Children (n.d.). *Second Step.* Author.

The *Second Step* program is a Tier 1 classroom curriculum that teaches social-emotional and self-regulation skills to students from pre-K through grade 8. The research-based lessons include videos, individual and group exercises, and practice scenarios. It can also be used in small groups to complement the classroom program and to teach Skills for Learning (listening, focusing attention, calming down, etc.).

....

Jenson, W. R., Bowen, J., Clark, E., Block, H., Gabrielsen, T., Hood, J., Radley, K., & Springer, B. (2011). *Superheroes Social Skills.* Ancora Publishing.

Superheroes Social Skills is an evidence-based small group program that enhances the social competence of elementary students with autism spectrum disorders (ASD), behavioral disorders, or developmental delays, though it can accommodate any student who needs to learn to interact appropriately with peers and adults. This program is appropriate for students in grades K–6 who have autism spectrum disorders, as well as any student in grades K–2. Superheroes teaches 17 critical social skills, such as following directions, taking turns, responding to questions and requests, and solving problems. The program uses video animations and comic books to teach the skills. Other program elements include peer modeling videos, practice scenarios, and the Power Charge motivation system.

Morningside Center for Teaching Social Responsibility. (2001). *The 4Rs (reading, writing, respect, & resolution): A teaching guide.* Author.

The 4Rs (Reading, Writing, Respect and Resolution) Program integrates a focus on social and emotional development into the language arts curriculum for children in grades pre-K through 5. The program provides read-alouds, book talks, and sequential, interactive skills lessons to develop social and emotional skills related to understanding and managing feelings, listening and developing empathy, being assertive, solving conflict creatively and nonviolently, honoring diversity, and standing up to teasing and bullying.

....

Mulkey, S., & Sprick, M. S. (2010). *SMART Kids: Social Grace, Manners, and Respectful Talk.* Ancora Publishing.

SMART Kids provides students in grades K–1 with instruction in social skills, manners, and respectful talk. Skills covered include giving compliments, making friends, accepting "No" for an answer, apologizing, solving problems, and more. Lessons include direct instruction and age-appropriate activities and games. *SMART Kids* includes 18 five-day lesson plans, with each lesson running about 15 minutes. Lessons can be adapted for small group use.

....

Sheridan, S. M. (2010). *The Tough Kid social skills book.* Ancora Publishing.

For students in grades 3–7, *The Tough Kid Social Skills Book* teaches the learned behaviors that students need to get along successfully in a majority of social situations. Skills covered in the 12 lessons include joining in, playing cooperatively, solving problems, dealing with teasing, and accepting "No." The book also includes assessment and data collection tools for identifying students in need of social skills training. The book can be used for small group, classroom, and schoolwide social skills training; it includes tips for implementing the program in each environment.

TASK 4

Clarify Behavioral Expectations for Common Areas and Special Circumstances

Be prepared to teach your CHAMPS expectations for common areas. Also be prepared to teach expectations to any new students who enter your class and for any unique events that may occur.

• • • • •

We have emphasized the importance of defining and teaching your expectations, observing student performance, and giving students feedback on your expectations for their behavior. In addition to the information presented thus far, you should address four other situations involving behavioral expectations:

- Students must be taught the expectations for common areas in the school, such as hallways, cafeteria, with specialists, bus and car loading areas, and buses.
- Students must be taught expectations for school emergency situations.
- Students may enter your class after you have taught your expectations (students who enter your class after the first few weeks of school).
- Students may participate in unique events, such as field trips, assemblies, and having a classroom guest speaker.

Teach Common Area Expectations

Common areas can provide some of the greatest behavioral challenges in school. Many of them are less structured or have less supervision than students may have in a classroom environment, which can lead to significant concerns with student misbehavior. Common areas include locations such as hallways, lockers, restrooms, cafeteria, playground, bus waiting areas, buses, and parking lots. As with any other location in school, students benefit from clear and explicit expectations and instructions on how to behave and engage with others in each of these environments.

At the beginning of the year, follow your school's process for teaching students expectations for common areas. In some cases this may involve viewing a series of videos, going to a "fair" that parades students to different locations to learn expectations, or providing a series of classroom-based lessons on each location. However, if all of the common area expectations are taught at one time, some students are likely to struggle to remember many different sets of expectations. These lessons will be far more effective if some instruction or review occurs just before students enter any common area, there is a process for observing student behavior in the setting, and students receive feedback immediately after they were in the location on how well they met the expectations.

Provide mini lessons each day for the first week or two of school just prior to students entering any common area location. For example, just before students go to the cafeteria, review the expectations for waiting in line, then for sitting and eating. Before students are released to go to their buses, review expectations for hallway behavior, bus loading areas, and buses. Let students know that you will periodically check in with the supervisors in these locations to find out how students are doing with the expectations, and that you expect students to treat all common areas and common area supervisors with respect. You may wish to tie your Guidelines for Success to student behaviors and attitudes exhibited in common areas to further reinforce how the positive culture you and your students have built in your classroom should extend to other areas of the school as well. "You can show you are working towards our Guidelines for Success of teamwork when you are respectful and polite to each adult who is working in the cafeteria. They are an important part of our team." Whenever you receive feedback that your students are struggling in common areas, and during times of the year when behavior is predictably more difficult (e.g., the week before and after any major break, the days surrounding holidays like Halloween and Valentine's Day), plan to spend a little bit of extra time preparing them to transition to common areas by reviewing and reinforcing the expectations for the area.

One powerful tool we have seen some teachers use is a binder ring with 3" x 5" or 5" x 7" cards printed with visuals of the expectations for each common area (see Figure 4.12). Laminate the cards, if possible, and hang them inside the door to your classroom. Just prior to any transition to a common area, pull up the card for the common area and review expectations with students.

If you teach in an elementary school with specials teachers (e.g., music, PE, art), or if students have pull-out instruction with specialists, grade-level teachers can play a pivotal role in setting up these teachers as well as their students for success. Specialists and specials teachers can provide copies of the CHAMPS posters or filled-out CHAMPS worksheets so that other teachers are aware of the expectations students are to follow when they transition to these different environments. Grade-level teachers then remind students of the expectations in these other classrooms prior to the transition to increase the likelihood that students will transition into these environments successfully. These settings can create a significant challenge because students are often in them for a limited time (e.g., 30 minutes), which may constrain specials and specialist teachers' time for teaching behavioral expectations. Students may go to these special classes only once or

Figure 4.12 *Teacher Copy of Common Area Expectations on Binder Ring*

twice a week, so it can be difficult for students to gain fluency with the expectations. If grade-level teachers help review the expectations and indicate that they will be communicating with the specialists/specials teachers about how students are doing, this can provide great support and continuity across classrooms.

Teach Expectations for School Emergency Situations

Your building should have a defined set of procedures for responding in the event of an emergency, whether that involves a natural disaster (e.g., earthquake, tornado), human-caused threat (e.g., active shooter, bomb threat), or other hazard (e.g., gas leak, fire). These procedures will specify the conditions for when the plan will be activated and describe the actions that students, teachers, and school staff should take before, during, and after emergency events.

At the beginning of the year, follow your school's process for teaching students procedures for emergency situations. This may involve watching a video, discussing procedures during homeroom or a defined period, or participating in practice drills. Prior to any scheduled emergency drills, go over procedures and expectations for these scenarios with your students. After each drill, provide feedback about how well students complied with these expectations and what to work on next time.

It's a good idea to post or store critical emergency information in an easily accessible location in your room so that you can quickly reference procedures, the location of evacuation and assembly sites, and escape routes. Periodically review these plans throughout the year to ensure that you remember all expected procedures and can automatically follow them in case of an emergency.

If you have any students with visual and hearing impairments or mobility limitations, plan to individually teach them alternative evacuation routes or assembly locations. You might also assign a buddy for each student with a disability.

Diversity, Equity, Inclusion, and Access

Whenever you have students in your classroom with limited mobility, visual or hearing impairments, or other special needs, consider whether alternative evacuation routes or specialized plans may be required to keep students safe in emergency situations. Plan to individually teach and provide opportunities to practice alternative procedures.

Teach Expectations to New Students

The first 2 weeks of school are the most important time for teaching behavioral expectations and classroom routines. However, most teachers will experience some degree of flux in your student population over the course of the year. That is, you will have at least one student leave and at least one new student enter your class. Many schools have such high student mobility rates that less than half of the students in a class at the beginning of the year are still there at the end of the year. When a new student enters your classroom, some form of orientation (similar to what you provide for all students during the first 2 weeks of school) will be essential to get the student off to a successful start. You should plan in advance how you will do this. In fact, the higher you expect your student mobility rate to be, the more prepared you need to be to teach your expectations to new students.

The more structured and well-managed your classroom is, the easier it will be for new students to learn expectations because the expectations will be consistently modeled by other students and reinforced by you. A student who enters a poorly managed class has more difficulty understanding the expectations because they are not clearly modeled or consistently enforced.

To help you develop a plan for teaching your expectations to new students, review the following strategies that you can implement at a classroom level.

Teach the new student individually.

The most common and basic method of orienting a new student to your class is to simply teach the new student your expectations yourself. For the first several days to a week, meet with the student for a couple of minutes immediately before each major activity and transition. Tell the student what will be happening and explain your CHAMPS behavioral expectations for that activity or transition. At the conclusion of the activity or transition, let the student know how he did and orient him to the next activity or transition.

The advantage of this approach is that it generates frequent contact between you and a new student during the student's first week in class. The disadvantage is that it requires a great deal of your time. If you are likely to get only one to three new students during the year, pairing this approach with Re-teach the Entire Class is probably both reasonable and effective. However, if you have many new students during the year, it is impractical, and a disservice to the rest of the class, to take that much time with each new student.

Re-teach the entire class.

If you have to orient a new student to your class, take the opportunity to go over the CHAMPS expectations for all activities and transitions with the entire class. For one day, immediately before each activity and each major transition, ask students to volunteer to share some information about expected behaviors and procedures. "Please raise your hand if you can tell one of the important expectations for independent work periods during math class." Call on students until all the important information has been reviewed. If students leave out something essential, add it yourself.

This procedure has several advantages. The new student gets important information, and the information is reviewed and reinforced for the other students. Having students present the information communicates that the expectations are shared by the class, not just by the teacher. Finally, taking a couple of minutes to do this before each activity and transition makes a statement that you believe that student knowledge of correct behavior is important enough that you will use class time to re-teach it.

The main disadvantage of re-teaching the entire class is that if you must do it more than once every 4 to 6 weeks, it takes too much class time. In addition, students may get tired of discussing the same expectations over and over. Therefore, if you re-teach for one new student and then get another new student 2 weeks later, do not repeat the procedure.

Another disadvantage is that when you use this procedure by itself, a new student gets only one day of orientation. You will not want to take the entire class's time to orient a new student for more than one day, but the typical class has so many expectations and routines that the student is not likely to remember all the details on the second day at a new school. So if you use this procedure, use one of the other procedures (Teach the New Student Individually or the Buddy System) as well.

Teach with the Buddy System.

With this procedure, you give individual class members the responsibility of orienting new students to the routines and procedures of the class.

> *Paul, this is Rico. Rico is a student who really understands and follows the procedures that will help you be successful in this class. Throughout the day (or class period), you two have permission to quietly talk—even at times when talking is usually not allowed. Paul, if you have a question about how we do things, you can ask me or quietly ask Rico. Rico, anytime during the next week that something is going on that may be new to Paul, please quietly explain what we are doing and why.*

If you plan to use this procedure and are likely to have a lot of new students during the year, take time in the second or third week of school to talk to the entire class about how you may call on them individually to help orient a new student. Be sure you don't always use the same student as the buddy—call on different students as the year progresses.

The advantage of this approach is that it takes pressure off you to spend class (instructional) time with a new student. In addition, it communicates your expectation and belief that your students fully understand and implement your expectations.

A possible disadvantage is that you won't have enough contact with a new student for that student to feel a real connection with you. If you use the Buddy System, make a point of frequently interacting with and getting to know any new student (checking on her work, asking how she is doing, seeing if she has any questions, and so on). The buddy concept also makes the class member who is orienting the new student feel very special—they become invested in the classroom rules.

Create a "Welcome to Our Class" video.

If you anticipate a high rate of student mobility, it may be worth taking time to have your students develop an orientation video at the beginning of the year. The amount of time required to plan and direct this activity will vary depending on your own style and preferences. Some teachers may assign the task to a small group of students and give them only a broad outline of topics to cover. Other teachers may guide the entire process and involve class members only as actors to demonstrate procedures. If you think this might be a reasonable option for you, plan to produce the video in about the third week of school. By then, procedures and routines should be well established, and developing the video can help solidify and reinforce the important expectations for the class.

An advantage of this procedure is that it can help create a sense of class pride and unity—and it's also great fun to make and potentially very entertaining. New students can view the video at school (with a school counselor or a peer buddy) or take a video home to view with their families. If your community has a significant number of families who speak a particular language other than English, see if you can get district personnel or a community volunteer to help you produce a version of your video in that language. A video can help families get a feel for your classroom rules and expectations and may serve to prevent miscommunication between school and home that may occur with written information, especially if the family is not fluent in English.

The major disadvantage of an orientation video is that it can be time consuming to develop and, without monitoring and guidance, some students may get overly silly during the production process. Use your own judgment regarding the trade-off between time spent up front developing such a video and time saved later in welcoming and orienting new students.

Teach Expectations for Unique Events

In addition to knowing the behavioral expectations for major classroom activities and common transitions, students need to know how they are expected to behave during any unique events that occur, such as field trips. If you have not taught your class the expectations for a particular event, misbehavior may be likely—not because students are willfully disobedient, but because they do not have the knowledge and skills to behave in a manner that you consider responsible.

Imagine taking your unprepared third-grade students to an assembly to hear a speaker. If your class is one of the first to arrive, students may have to wait 5 to 10 minutes. Some students may start conversations with friends two or three rows away; others may get bored and start pushing and shoving each other. As the assembly begins, many of the students may continue their inappropriate behaviors. You try to get them to quiet down and listen to the speaker, but soon the situation feels out of control. Now imagine that 1 to 2 weeks before the assembly you defined and started teaching how you expected students to behave during the assembly. Students would then know that they are allowed to quietly converse only with someone no more than a "12-inch voice" away and that they need to stop talking and pay attention once the principal walks to the microphone.

As soon as you know that your students will be participating in a special event that calls for new behavioral expectations, plan to start defining and then teaching your expectations.

Because each special event will be unique, at least in some ways, the first step should be to identify the specific types of situations students are likely to be engaged in during the event. You may need to do some advance research to find out about the nature of the event and the types of experiences students will encounter. Figure 4.13 shows the kind of event analyses you might come up with for two different events—an assembly and a field trip to a hydroelectric dam.

Once you identify the major situations for the special event, the next step is to use the CHAMPS acronym to define your behavioral expectations for each of those situations. Then start communicating your expectations to students. For each situation you identified, teach students the CHAMPS expectations so that they know exactly what constitutes responsible behavior. Keep in mind that simply telling students your expectations is not as effective as modeling, role-playing, and discussion.

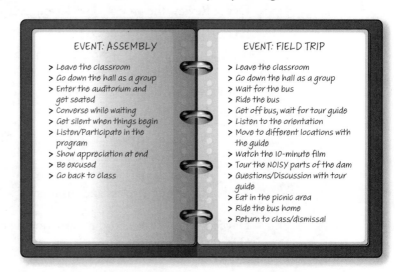

EVENT: ASSEMBLY

> Leave the classroom
> Go down the hall as a group
> Enter the auditorium and get seated
> Converse while waiting
> Get silent when things begin
> Listen/Participate in the program
> Show appreciation at end
> Be excused
> Go back to class

EVENT: FIELD TRIP

> Leave the classroom
> Go down the hall as a group
> Wait for the bus
> Ride the bus
> Get off bus, wait for tour guide
> Listen to the orientation
> Move to different locations with the guide
> Watch the 10-minute film
> Tour the NOISY parts of the dam
> Questions/Discussion with tour guide
> Eat in the picnic area
> Ride the bus home
> Return to class/dismissal

Figure 4.13 *Sample Event Analyses*

The greater the complexity of the event or the more problems that have been associated with that type of event, the more days you should rehearse the appropriate behavior. For a simple situation—a guest speaker, for example—a brief orientation the day before and a short review immediately prior to the event is probably sufficient. However, if students had a problem the last time they engaged in a similar event, plan on teaching and reviewing expectations for at least 4 or 5 consecutive days.

If the situation or your expectations are complex, if the event involves potential danger, or if there are many different components to the event (as in the field trip in Figure 4.13), you definitely should plan to teach your expectations for at least 5 days. Don't try to teach all your expectations every day; break them down so that each day you introduce a few of the expectations.

Teaching expectations for an event like the field trip example in Figure 4.13 might be organized as follows:

Day 1: Take about 10 minutes to discuss and practice the CHAMPS expectations for the following:

- Leaving the classroom
- Going down the hall as a group
- Waiting for the bus
- Riding the bus
- Getting off the bus and waiting for the tour guide

Day 2: Review content from the previous day and introduce expectations for:

- Being silent while the guide is providing orientation
- Moving to different locations with the guide
- Watching the 10-minute film

Day 3: Review the previous two lessons. Introduce and mentally prepare students for staying calm and keeping their voices down (no shouting) while:

- Touring the NOISY parts of the dam

Day 4: Review content covered in the three previous lessons and introduce expectations for:

- Asking questions and discussion with the tour guide
- Eating in the picnic area
- Riding the bus home
- Returning to class and dismissal

Day 5: Put all of the above information together and introduce the learning objectives for the event—that is, what you want students to learn from the trip.

TASK 5

Clarify Behavioral Expectations With Parents and Guardians

Communicate with families about what their students will be learning and doing in your classroom.

• • • • •

One definition of family engagement is "an intentional and systematic partnership of educators, families, and community members . . . who share responsibility for a student's preparation for school, work, and life, from the time the child is born to young adulthood" (Weiss et al., 2010). There is no doubt that when educators and families engage in such a planned partnership, student outcomes are likely to improve (Epstein, 2018; Fan & Chen, 2001; Hattie, 2012).

As you work to teach your guidelines, classroom rules, expectations, and behavioral and social-emotional skills to your students, provide communication to families about what their students will be learning and doing in your classroom. Many families benefit from understanding the social and emotional skills that students are developing at school, and they may even reinforce them at home. We have even seen examples where families use the CHAMPS acronym to clearly teach their kids the expectations for behavior in a restaurant, in the car, or when playing at home! Regular communication can also help parents understand circumstances that may be occurring at school that they can help their child navigate, such as how to maintain peer relationships or how to talk with a teacher or other adult at school if they are struggling academically or otherwise.

Figure 4.14 (p. 234) is a sample communication telling families about a teacher's Guidelines for Success.

Determine the Best Method of Communication

While it may be simplest to just give students a paper copy of your communication with parents to take home, many families are unlikely to receive the communication through this method. If you plan to send home paper-based communication about expectations and social-emotional skills in students' backpacks or binders, consider an additional method such as a weekly email update, social media posts, or a print mail version. If you can provide this information on a regular basis (e.g., every week or every other week on Monday), families will learn to look for this information and may pay more attention to it. This also allows you to keep each message relatively short and focused.

Be considerate of the reading level and language requirements in any written communication to families. Decide whether it would be beneficial to record a short video clip instead, or record an audio clip of yourself or a student reading the communication. As much as possible, provide materials that are translated into parents' primary language.

Figure 4.14 *Sample Letter Home About Guidelines for Success*

Dear Families,

I am excited to tell you about one of the most important parts of our classroom: our Guidelines for Success. The guidelines highlight some of the habits and attitudes that will help students be successful in my class, and they are an important basis of our positive classroom community. I also hope they can help students outside of my classroom, in future classes and jobs, and in their relationships.

The Guidelines for Success are:

- Have a good attitude.
- Be kind and help others.
- Give your best effort.
- It's OK to get things wrong. Learn from it!
- Always respect others and yourself.

I hope you will hear your student talking about these guidelines at home. We will be referring to them frequently in class. We will have monthly themes related to them and will be working on some projects to show our efforts to grow with each guideline. This month will focus on ways that students can show a good attitude (more information on this next week!).

If you are interested, it is hugely helpful when we can create links between what we are doing at school and what you are doing or what you see at home. This helps students see that these habits and attitudes are important and can be beneficial outside of school, too. If you want to find ways to work the Guidelines for Success into your interactions with your student, simple encouragement goes a long way: "You've had such a great attitude when you were working on homework this week!" If you see efforts from your student that match the Guidelines for Success, I'd love to hear about them so I can acknowledge the student.

Please let me know if you have any questions or concerns about the Guidelines for Success. I look forward to working with your students to strengthen these habits and attitudes across this year.

Sincerely,

Ms. Veric

Ms. Veric
Fourth-Grade Teacher

Seek Family Input on Expectations and Social-Emotional Skills

Work to build two-way communication and trust by periodically asking families to weigh in on the behavioral and social-emotional skills that they hope to see taught at school. You can also ask if there are specific skills families are working on at home that you can reinforce in the classroom. Or, if families notice children using the skills they are learning at school, ask parents to notify you so you can reinforce their student at school.

Some families may have different expectations for behavior at home, so clear communication helps families understand what will help their child be successful at school. However, ensure that communication about your expectations at school never indicates that differing expectations in the home are somehow bad or wrong. In your communication to families about your expectations, indicate that you hope to understand these differences so that you don't inadvertently negate parental lessons for how students should behave when outside of school. Help families to understand that the different social norms and expectations in your classroom can help their child learn to be flexible with differing environments. This flexibility can open doors to the child in the future.

For example, in one classroom where students were frequently swearing, the teacher shared with us that one parent was initially resistant to the teacher's efforts to try to teach his student not to swear at school. He felt that this language was fine for his son at home, so his son shouldn't be forced to use different language at school. When discussing his frustrations with the teacher, the parent indicated that he is able to swear at his workplace without any repercussions. However, once the teacher probed a little further, she learned that the parent could swear around his coworkers, but when his bosses were around, he knew he needed to turn off the swearing so he could keep his job. By explaining that the teacher's job was to help his child learn this same "on/off" switch so that swearing was not habitual, the parent then agreed with the teacher's plan. The teacher was able to include this example in her lessons to the students, honoring that swearing is considered acceptable in some environments and social situations. At school, she needed to teach them to turn it off as it is not appropriate in many work environments.

> **Relational Trust**
>
> *To build relational trust with students' families, work to establish two-way communication that provides clear information on your expectations but that also invites families to bring questions, ideas, and insights about their child and behavioral or social-emotional skills that families believe are important.*

Conclusion

Your students will never know what you expect of them until you find a way to communicate it to them. Once your students understand what you expect them to achieve, you will be a big step closer to helping them succeed. Making sure that your expectations are achievable and well communicated are the first two steps in making this happen. When it does, you will find yourself working with your students instead of working against them.

CHAMPS Notes

CHAPTER 5

Observe—Use Data to Monitor and Adjust Your Management Plan

Circulate and scan your classroom for opportunities to both praise positive behavior and correct misbehavior. Observing student behavior also includes collecting and using data to assess the effectiveness of your Classroom Management Plan.

Chapter 5 addresses the O in STOIC—Observe student behavior. You have already Structured your room for success and set up a plan to Teach students to behave successfully. Now you will learn the importance of Observing student behavior as well as how to observe effectively. This chapter begins by providing information on how to circulate and scan, how to make judgments about when and how to provide positive interactions and praise, and when to correct student misbehavior. The chapter then goes on to suggest ways to use data to assess the effectiveness of your management plan so you can make adjustments to facilitate responsible behavior from your students.

The act of observing affects the behavior of the people being observed (Kazdin, 1977; Repp et al., 1988). This is more true in the classroom than almost anywhere else. You probably remember a teacher who seemed to "have eyes in the back of her head." She never missed any rule violation, and there was very little misbehavior in her classroom. You also probably remember a teacher (maybe the same one with that multidirectional vision) who you liked and admired so much that you never wanted to disappoint her. Perhaps you also remember a classroom where large numbers of students misbehaved because the teacher was so oblivious she never noticed either positive or negative behavior—she just went through the motions of teaching as though students were not even in the room.

This chapter has three tasks:

- Task 1: Scan All Sections of the Classroom Continuously and Circulate Whenever Possible
- Task 2: Understand Why and How to Use Data for Continuous Improvement in Your Classroom
- Task 3: Use Data Snapshots to Monitor and Adjust Your Management Plan

The first task covers strategies and techniques for effectively observing your students' behavior. The second teaches you about the utility and benefits of periodic data collection to determine whether your Classroom Management Plan is working as well as you hope. The third task includes a calendar plan with suggestions for times during the year to conduct checkups and mine your data.

TASK 1

Scan All Sections of the Classroom Continuously and Circulate Whenever Possible

While teaching, observe students for behaviors to praise and misbehaviors to correct.

• • • • •

The importance of observing students by circulating and scanning was identified in the very early research on how effective teachers manage the classroom. Kounin (1970) described effective teachers as having both "with-it-ness" and "in-touch-ness." By circulating throughout the room as much as possible and by using visual and auditory scanning (fancy term for keeping your eyes and ears open) whether you are circulating or not, you can stay in touch with all parts of the classroom. "With-it-ness" really means that you are not just circulating, looking, and listening, but you are also mentally paying attention to that information.

 CASE STUDY

You are circulating around the room during a cooperative group activity. You notice (you get sound and visual cues) that a group across the room—Group A—is getting a bit agitated. You know the maturity level of the students, and you want to see if they can work out the problem by themselves, without your intervention. So rather than rushing over to Group A, you move to Group B about halfway across the room. You look as if you are listening and interacting with Group B (and you are), but part of your senses and mind are actually focused on Group

A. If Group A solves the problem, you go over and give positive feedback on their ability to disagree, stay respectful, and resolve the difference in a mature and responsible manner. But if you notice that the intensity of group A's agitation is increasing, you leave Group B and go directly to Group A—not to scold them, because you arrive before there is any major problem, but rather to guide them through a process for resolving the difficulty in a respectful and responsible way. A teacher who does not scan may not notice that Group A is having a problem until it becomes a loud argument or fight, a situation that then requires the teacher to impose a corrective consequence.

• • • • •

Keep in mind that you are not just observing for problems, but also for opportunities to give the class and individuals positive feedback. When you scan early in an independent work period and notice a student working hard—someone who in the past has tended to get off task— go to that student immediately and provide a positive interaction, such as descriptive praise, in a manner that will not embarrass the student (more on this in Chapter 6). In other words, scan for problems, but also scan for opportunities to provide meaningful positive feedback.

Visual Scanning

Regardless of what you and the students are doing, you should have a clear line of sight to all students and visually scan all settings in the classroom frequently (Emmer et al., 1980; Scheuermann & Hall, 2008). For example, when you are circulating, don't just look at the students nearest to you—visually sweep any place students are present, even a learning center across the room. When you are conducting a whole class activity, visually scan the back rows and the front corners. When you are helping an individual student with their work, plan to occasionally stand up and look around the room. When you are teaching a small group, look up from the group periodically and observe students who are working at their seats.

> *Regardless of what you and the students are doing, you should have a clear line of sight to all students and visually scan all settings frequently.*

As you scan, look for any misbehavior that requires correction. If a student is engaged in a misbehavior, go to the student and issue a gentle reprimand or assign an appropriate consequence. Also look for opportunities to acknowledge and encourage responsible behavior. Go to students who are following expectations or demonstrating the Guidelines for Success and provide age-appropriate positive feedback.

Finally, use visual scanning to identify students who may have questions or otherwise need your assistance. During independent work periods especially (when you are not engaged with a small group), look for students who have signaled that they need assistance. If you ask students to use a flag or open book as a signal for help (see Chapter 3, Task 4), you need to show students that the signal actually works. If students find that you don't respond when they signal, they will stop using the signal and will come to you or call out to get your attention instead.

Auditory Scanning

In addition to looking to all parts of the classroom, you should listen to all parts of the classroom. Within your management plan there will emerge a baseline, or normal, level of background noise in your room—though this level may be quieter or louder than the normal level of other teachers in your building. Whenever you notice a change in the baseline level of background noise, turn up your level of "with-it-ness"—that is, analyze whether the change is a problem. The noise level may increase because students are very excited and engaged about the assigned cooperative task, and they may just need a gentle reminder to keep their conversations quiet enough so that the noise does not disturb the class next door. Or the noise level may suddenly decrease because students become aware of a conflict brewing between two students in the back of the room and stop what they are doing to see what is going to happen.

Circulating

Whenever possible, circulate throughout the classroom in unpredictable patterns. Do not spend the majority of your time in any one part of the room, and avoid a walking pattern that may let students know that you will not be near them for a significant amount of time. This is especially important during independent work periods and cooperative group activities. Your proximity communicates your concern for and interest in the students. It also communicates that if someone chooses to engage in misbehavior, you will likely notice it.

> *"Whenever possible, circulate throughout the classroom in unpredictable patterns."*

Obviously, there are times when circulating is difficult—for instance, when you are teaching a small group or presenting to the class and writing on the board. However, whenever you can, try to move about the room. For example, about 10 or 15 minutes into teaching a 30-minute small reading group, you might give the students in the group a short task to perform independently while you quickly circulate among the other students. Then you can resume instruction with the small group. Or, while teaching a math lesson to the whole class and writing on the board, you might give students a couple of problems to work on and then circulate through the room. After looking at students' work, you can return to the board and continue with the teacher-directed portion of the lesson.

Remember, as you circulate, give positive feedback to students who are meeting your expectations, answer any questions students may have, and provide gentle reprimands or consequences to students who are not meeting expectations (Colvin et al., 1997; De Pry & Sugai, 2002). And always try to avoid staying too long in any one place.

In summary, actively observe your students by circulating in unpredictable patterns whenever possible and by using both visual and auditory scanning consistently. You will use the information from this continuous observation process to make judgments about when to prompt students to solve a problem before it has escalated, when to capitalize on reinforceable opportunities, and—whenever rule violations are observed—when to apply corrective consequences consistently, calmly, and immediately.

TASK 2

Understand Why and How to Use Data for Continuous Improvement in Your Classroom

Learn about the importance of using data in your classroom, the types of data you should collect, and how to feasibly incorporate data collection efforts into your teaching practice.

• • • • •

When you go to the doctor for a physical examination, one of the first things that happens is the collection of data: weight, height, pulse, and blood pressure. Sometimes additional data are collected, such as respiration, cholesterol levels, and so on. Then your doctor objectively evaluates the information she has gathered, along with your subjective reports about how you feel, and makes a judgment about your overall health. She may decide you are just fine. If a concern is identified, she may decide that she has enough information to recommend a certain course of treatment. Or she may decide that more data are needed so that informed decisions can be made about a logical course of treatment. Without both objective data and informal conversations with you about any concerns, the doctor would be less able to accurately assess your overall health and make useful recommendations about your health care options.

In a similar way, good teachers use informal and formal data collection methods to identify and make informed decisions about their management plan. Periodically use some simple data tools as described in Chapter 10, Task 1 to determine whether your management plan is working as effectively as you would like. You may use data to consider:

- Which aspects of your Classroom Management Plan are going well and should be maintained as is.
- Whether there are one or more problem areas that indicate you need to make adjustments to your management plan.
- Whether the level of support you are currently using should be maintained or revised.

The phrase "Let's collect data!" can conjure different reactions from individuals. For some (e.g., many school psychologists!), data collection is viewed as an exciting and essential part of the educational process. For many others, data collection is at best viewed as a tedious but important part of their job role, and at worst it can be viewed as hoops to jump through and a waste of valuable time. However, data collection is actually an important part of our daily lives, and we do it in many locations and situations. In our homes, we use data to monitor and make decisions about a variety of everyday things, such as which services and service providers to use, or how well those services are meeting current needs. Let's look at one example of the power of data collection and analysis in daily life.

Data-Driven Processes

Good teachers use multiple methods of data collections to identify strengths and weaknesses in their current management approach and then make informed decisions about changes to their Classroom Management Plan. Use data to continuously improve and make gains toward your long-term goals and classroom mission.

Consider your cell phone bill. If you see a significant spike in costs one month, you may do some additional digging to determine the cause of your increased bill. For example, you might want to check to see if one of your children is making purchases without permission. Or you might check in to see if your partner had to make purchases that impacted the bill. If neither of these explanations are the case, you would probably contact the service provider to find out if you were inappropriately charged.

If you find the spike was related to your children's misuse, you will likely consider what should be done differently to deal with your children's cell phone use, and many of these solutions neatly fit into the STOIC acronym.

- **Structure.** If you put more restrictive parental safeguards on the devices, reset passwords, or limit your children's use to certain hours or times when you can more adequately supervise, these are structural solutions.
- **Teach.** You might teach your children how their use is costing the family more money and teach them about appropriate uses on the phone (i.e., teaching expectations).
- **Interact Positively.** You might look for ways that your child can earn permission to purchase apps, such as helping out with additional chores or saving up points as part of a positive reinforcement system.
- **Correct Fluently.** You may require your child to repay any charges through work at home or in the community, or you may implement other corrective consequences by restricting them from using devices for a period of time.

Whatever you eventually decide to do, monitoring the data of your cell phone bill (the Observe in STOIC) was the starting place for making informed decisions about what needed to be done differently to eliminate the problem in the future.

Understand the Purpose of Data Collection

To understand why it is important to collect data at the classroom level, consider some of the ineffective but all-too-common ways that educational decisions are made in many classrooms. Data help us avoid making decisions based on:

- Subjective feelings, which are influenced by emotions, preconceptions, distractions, and simply being busy with teaching.
- Instinct or overreaction to a single piece of information, such as one behavioral incident or parent complaint
- Custom, tradition, or existing regularities— the "the way we are doing it is the way it's always been done" mentality.

Existing Regularities

Collecting data is an essential step for identifying practices in your classroom that may have worked in the past but are not currently meeting the needs of your students. Use data to identify ineffective existing regularities so you can tweak or abandon practices that are not helping students meet your vision for success for all students.

- Power, influence, or politics—in some schools very vocal staff members can make other staff members think they have to do things a certain way, even when those strong suggestions may not apply to another teacher's style or classroom situation.

Let's go back to the cell phone analogy. Perhaps you realize that your cell phone plan is too expensive or you do not think you are getting enough data or adequate coverage in your current plan. Rather than relying on subjective feelings, limited information based on a TV commercial, just sticking with your current plan because you've always had it, or going off of one recommendation from your vocal brother, most people will probably collect some data so they can make informed decisions. Perhaps you do some research and find that your current provider has another plan that better meets your needs. Or you might compare service providers and find another company and plan that is better for you and your family. In some cases, you may even realize that your current plan is still the best option. Whatever you decide, data collection and analysis played an integral part in your making informed decisions about what actions to take.

Using multiple sources of data in your classroom allows you to make informed and effective decisions based on solid information about your improvement priorities, current behavior management practices, and the current behaviors occurring in your classroom. During the decision-making process, you'll ask questions such as:

- What parts of my classroom and my management plan are working well and should be celebrated and protected?
- What is working adequately but could be improved or tweaked?
- What is not working and should be substantially modified or eliminated?
- Have newly implemented changes in my Classroom Management Plan resulted in positive or negative results, or has there been no change?

Data serve a critical role in decision making and solving student behavior problems. In a problem-solving process, data are systematically collected and used in (a) problem identification, (b) problem definition, (c) intervention design, (d) monitoring of intervention effects, and (e) evaluation of outcomes and solutions (Deno, 2005; Tilly, 2008). One of the most compelling reasons to collect, analyze, and summarize data on an ongoing basis is that incremental but significant changes may otherwise go unnoticed (Alberto & Troutman, 2012). Ongoing data collection will enable you to see trends before and after making changes to your Classroom Management Plan.

Data serve a critical role in decision making and solving student behavior problems.

Data can also inform how to respond when there are significant changes in your classroom. For example, imagine if several new students joined your class across the course of the first trimester. Your data sources indicate that the classroom dynamic has shifted since the beginning of the year, and you realize that you may need to change some aspects of your management plan that were in place earlier in the year. These data will help you make logical decisions about what changes are needed.

Overcoming Common Barriers to Collecting Data

If you find yourself struggling to make data collection a part of your classroom practice, ask yourself if you are currently facing any of these common barriers or roadblocks.

Data collection is frustrating because we are asked to collect data but nothing is ever done with it!

In schools, we have to be very careful about collecting data just for the sake of data collection. It just becomes noise. We are reminded of an editorial cartoon showing two busy professionals. One says to the other, "Get all the information you can. We'll think of a use for it later." The act of collecting data is very frustrating if nothing meaningful is then done with these data. It can also be frustrating if data are collected and analyzed but we view it only from a perspective of saying whether a goal was achieved or not (e.g., "did we meet the target?"). If it does not inform meaningful future changes, this type of review can feel meaningless.

In this book, we advocate for collecting and analyzing data for the overarching purpose of driving continuous improvement in your classroom. We also recommend focusing your data collection efforts on specific student outcomes, using tools at different times of year to create a snapshot of student behavior. For example, at one time of year you might monitor rates of student misbehaviors to determine trends across types of misbehaviors, identify which students are engaging in misbehavior, and pinpoint times of day or types of activities that are associated with increased rates of misbehavior. At another time of year, you might observe for rates of on-task behavior, and at another time of year, monitor your ratios of positive to corrective interactions with students. The point of all this data collection is to inform ongoing decisions you make in adjusting your Classroom Management Plan throughout the year. In the next task, we provide suggestions for creating a yearly schedule of data collection and analysis so that you collect a variety of types of data about different aspects of your classroom and can scope out the planning time needed to analyze trends.

Data collection is anxiety producing because it may be used to make judgments about me as a teacher or my classroom practices.

It can certainly cause anxiety when data is used to make judgments about whether a teacher is "good" or "bad," especially if observations and data are used infrequently. This is analogous to high-stakes testing or an end-of-term summative exam as the only method of determining student success. One benefit in collecting your own data in the classroom is that it allows you to approach these data without worrying about outside judgment or accountability. The data are your own to view, and you get to make decisions about how to use them to inform your classroom practice.

As you collect and reflect on your classroom data, work to continually remind yourself that data collection is a tool for improvement and not a judgment on your character. If you notice a concerning trend, talk yourself into viewing it not as an indictment, but as a puzzle or challenge to be solved. Look at the concerning trends and use this information to set a goal for improvement. Work to identify aspects of your management plan and STOIC variables that may make a difference in helping you and the class reach those goals. The more often you collect and analyze your data for decision-making, the less anxiety-producing this process will become.

Data collection feels impossible because of the thousands of other responsibilities I have to juggle while teaching!

Most teachers did not receive training on how to collect behavioral data in their teacher preparation programs. Just like any other part of your teaching practice, you will need to learn certain skills and strategies to make data collection a part of your toolkit. The data collection tools provided in this book are designed to be approachable for veteran teachers and new teachers alike. In the remainder of this chapter and in Chapter 10, Task 1, we provide information about how to use a variety of different classroom-based data collection strategies and tools. We focus on ways to make data collection manageable as you balance other teaching requirements, as well as how to analyze and use the collected data for making effective decisions about improvements for your classroom.

Understand Types of Data

There are a variety of different types of data that you can collect in your classroom, including both subjective and objective data. With subjective data, such as anecdotal notes, surveys, interviews, and rating scales, you are seeking someone's (e.g., your own, students, other adults) subjective perception about variables in the classroom. Observational data involve real-time coding of events in the environment and can include frequency tallies and timing the latency or duration of events. You may also analyze historical or longitudinal data sources, including behavioral referrals, attendance or tardy rates, and student grades, to see what happened in the past and/or compare trends across time. Specific types of data you can collect include:

- **Anecdotal notes.** Note-taking after specific times, activities, or events will help you keep an informal record of events. As much as possible, focus anecdotal notes on what you can see and hear (e.g., "Rudy was talking frequently—at least 10 out of 20 minutes—throughout the independent work task and said he didn't want to do it"). Make note of questions you would like to follow up about (e.g., "I need to investigate whether Rudy is struggling with the reading requirements for these tasks"); however, avoid judgments about students (e.g., "Rudy is unmotivated and doesn't care about school"). Remember that these notes could be subject to subpoena if there is ever any legal action regarding the student. Ensure that your notes are written so that you would feel comfortable with others seeing them.

    While anecdotal notes should not be used on their own as data for decision making because they are highly subjective, they can be used to help identify other more objective data you may wish to collect (e.g., "I should count each of Rudy's incidents of talking out of turn on a daily schedule to see if time of day makes a difference"). Anecdotal notes may also be used in conjunction with more objective sources like observational data to give context about specific events or environmental variables that might be important when planning changes for improvement. For example, if a frequency tally of on-task/off-task behavior shows that students struggle to remain on task during independent work activities, you might keep anecdotal notes for a week during those activities about your observations. For example, "Table 1 and Table 4 seem to be having the most difficulty staying on task. I had to provide numerous redirects to keep the students at these tables on task each day this week."

- **Surveys.** Surveys are a relatively easy way to get information from the whole class (and parents too). You can keep them confidential for those who may feel uncomfortable without anonymity. It might be appropriate to use anonymous surveys to get feedback on students' or parents' perceptions about aspects of the classroom such as peer-to-peer relationships, levels of motivation, effort, and engagement with academic tasks, or their perceptions of how fair and respectful you are to students. However, recognize that surveys measure perceptions and not objective facts, so you should interpret results cautiously and attempt to verify findings through other data sources to avoid inaccurate conclusions. See Chapter 10, Tool 7: Family/Student Satisfaction Survey, for a sample survey you can use to determine how satisfied students and families are with your classroom either during the year or at the end of the year.

- **Interviews.** Interviews or focus groups can be more time consuming than surveys to implement but are more open ended and can lead to deeper understanding about what is going on in your classroom. If data from other sources are confusing or not interpretable, have discussions with students or families to gather more in-depth information. For example, if you notice that your students frequently come back from the lunch or recess period upset and unable to productively engage in academic tasks, you might pull several small groups of students for a discussion about what is happening outside of the classroom. Or if survey results indicate that many students in your class are concerned about bullying behavior and you were unaware of bullying concerns, you might interview a random sampling of students to see if you can find out what led to the concerning responses. See Reproducible 9.2 (p. 423) for a sample interview that can be used to determine if students understand your behavioral expectations.

- **Rating scales.** Rating scales involve awarding a variable number of points based on a prespecified criterion or rubric. Teachers can rate how well students met expectations during a transition or activity, quality of participation or on-task behavior, or levels of respect. For example, a teacher might rate student participation as:

  > 0 = Most of the class struggled with participation
  > 1 = Several students in the class struggled to participate
  > 2 = One or two students struggled to participate
  > 3 = All students participated appropriately

  Students can be asked to use rating scales to self-monitor factors like engagement, motivation, or how well they are meeting classroom objectives (e.g., "Today, I followed directions: 0 = not at all, 1 = somewhat but needed reminders, 2 = independently and without reminders"). Students can also be asked to rate other classroom variables, such as how the class is doing as a whole with respect or participation, or how you are doing as teacher with positive versus corrective interactions or providing support to students when needed. See Chapter 10, Tool 1, CHAMPS Versus Daily Reality Rating Scale, for a sample rating scale that a teacher or students can use to rate how well they met the posted expectations for particular transitions or activities.

- **Observational data.** Observations provide a unique opportunity to reflect about current practices. When you focus on specific aspects of behavior for your observations, you often see and hear things that may have previously gone unnoticed. One caution with observational data is that it represents a snapshot in time, so you'll need to remember to reflect on whether the data collected in an observation is representative of the overall behavior of your students during similar times and activities. When possible, collect observational data across numerous days (typically 3–5 days) during similar times and activities to see the overall trend. Types of observational data include:

  - *Frequency count or tally.* Mark tallies for each instance of observed behavior. You can tally the frequency of a positive behavior, a negative behavior, or both. Examples of frequency counts include tallying the number of times students blurt out or talk out in a period, marking whether students followed directions or did not follow directions, and counting how many incidents of students helping one another or giving compliments were observed. See Tool 2: Ratio of Interactions Monitoring Form, Tool 3: Misbehavior Recording Sheet, Tool 5: On-Task Behavior Observation Sheet, and Tool 6: Opportunities to Respond Observation Sheet in Chapter 10 for samples of classroom frequency counts.
  - *Duration data.* Duration data are used when you need to record the length of time students engage in a particular behavior. For example, you may want to collect data about how long a transition takes. Use a stopwatch and start the time when students are given a direction to transition, or write down the time you gave the direction. When students have finished the transition, stop the stopwatch or write down the time and calculate the number of minutes that transition took. You can keep using this procedure throughout the day or period and calculate the total minutes spent in transition at the end of the day.
  - *Latency data.* Sometimes it is helpful to record how much time it takes for a particular behavior to begin. For example, if you give a direction and it takes a long time for students to get started, you can record the length of time between the start of the direction to when students begin engaging in the expected activity.

- **Momentary time sampling.** Momentary time sampling involves periodically observing the class and recording whether they are engaged in a target behavior at that exact point in time. For example, you may want to monitor classroom volume. You might set your watch to vibrate every 5 minutes and record the volume of the class at that moment (0 = no sound/no talking, 1 = whisper level, 2 = quiet conversational voices, 3 = loud voices). At the end of the work period, you will have an approximate record of classroom volume.
- **Existing historical and longitudinal data.** Use historical data to determine trends and patterns across time. Historical data can include incident reports or referrals, attendance and tardy rates, injury reports, grade book analysis, and other academic reports. You can use these reports to determine whether individual students are exhibiting chronic problems and to make judgments about the progress of the class as whole across time. See Chapter 10, Tool 4: Grade Book Analysis Worksheet for ways to compile and analyze

existing data on absenteeism, tardiness, work completion, and assignment failure to determine if any individual student or the class a whole would benefit from changes in your management plan or an individualized support plan.

Getting Creative With Data Collection Techniques

If collecting observational data like a frequency count or monitoring duration feels onerous, the following ideas are creative ways we've seen teachers collect data in real time:

- Use paper clips or pennies in your pocket to conduct a frequency count. Put a collection of small items in one pocket, and each time you notice the behavior you are counting, move one item to the other pocket. At the end of the activity, count the number of items you moved.
- Carry around sticky notes and use them to record data and to provide students with positive or corrective feedback.
- Purchase a golf counter to keep frequency data.
- Purchase a stopwatch and hang it around your neck as you teach if you are taking duration or latency data.

Use Your Classroom Goals to Guide What Data You Collect

The goals for your classroom should guide you throughout the process of data collection and analysis, as should the broader goals of your school and district. Without clear goals, it is impossible to answer questions about the effectiveness of any given practice.

For example, if you do a web search for "professional train pusher Japan," you will find a variety of videos showing tightly packed trains and platforms during rush hour in Japan. As the doors begin to close, professional personnel work to wedge as many passengers as possible into the train cars, pushing on passenger's backs to get more people into the train, stuffing articles of clothing sticking out of the doors into the train car, and finally pulling the doors shut. If someone were to ask you, "Is this effective?" without specifying the goal, your response would be based purely on your subjective perceptions or feelings about what you viewed in the video. If you are claustrophobic or concerned about being too close to other people because of germs, your response would likely be, "No, this is not effective!" However, if you were told, "The goal is to get every passenger onto the train," and then asked, "Is this effective?" the response changes. This practice does in fact get as many people as possible off the platform onto the train. Your view of the situation is guided by the lens we bring about what is considered effective.

In relation to your classroom, data collection should be guided by your long-term goals. Most teachers collect frequent academic-related data and use a variety of sources to determine how students are doing in mastering academic goals. The same should be done in monitoring behavioral or social-emotional goals. If one of your goals is for students to learn to listen and follow directions, periodically collect and monitor data that will allow you to objectively determine how well they are making progress toward that goal. If one of your goals is for students to learn to work cooperatively in groups and sometimes take a leadership role, plan several times during the year when you will collect data related to these goals. Review the long-term goals you developed in Chapter 3, Task 8, and use these goals as you work through this task to identify a plan for data collection.

Mission and Beliefs

Data collection should be guided by your long-term goals and your overarching mission and beliefs. As you consider each piece of data you collect, remember to use your mission like a North Star, reflecting on whether the data indicate that current practices and procedures are helping reach your mission and goals or whether they are in any way leading you and students away from that vision of success.

Use Hallmarks of Effective Classrooms to Guide Data Collection

In addition to your own classroom goals, there are some aspects of the classroom that should be monitored in every classroom. Reviews and summaries of classroom observation research have consistently found that a number of classroom behaviors significantly relate to students' achievement and success in school (Brophy & Good, 1986; Reyes et al., 2012; Rosenshine & Stevens, 1986; Stronge et al., 2011;). These findings have informed the development of classroom observational tools and data collection approaches (Hilberg et al., 2004; Hintze et al., 2008).

These hallmarks are defining features of effective versus ineffective classroom environments and relate to three broad categories:

- Student behavior
- Student engagement
- Teacher behavior

NOTE: The following information on hallmarks of effective classrooms are overviewed in this task to give you a general sense of recommended types of data that should be collected throughout the year. In the next task, you will work on a calendar plan of when to collect data snapshots using the data tools referenced here.

Student Behavior

Monitoring student behavior helps you ensure that students are generally on task, respectful, and meeting your posted or pretaught expectations. The following recommended data collection efforts fall under this category:

- Periodically monitor students' on-task versus off-task behavior. This can be as simple as scanning the room to identify any students who appear to be off task and marking the approximate percentage of on-task behavior at that moment in your classroom: "I can see that three out of my thirty students are visibly off task. I'll mark 90%." This informal tracking can be monitored across time and across different activities to determine if off-task behavior is generally a problem in your classroom. We recommend using a more formal process at least a few times a year for tracking on-task versus off-task behavior as described in Tool 5 in Chapter 10, Task 1.

- Monitor whether students are behaving respectfully to you and other supervising adults who may be in your room. This might involve using a simple tally of disrespectful comments and actions across several days. The Misbehavior Recording Sheet, Tool 3 in Chapter 10, Task 1 provides guidance on how to collect data for a specific misbehavior like disrespect. You can also tally incidents of disrespect between students. However, recognize that many disrespectful and bullying types of behaviors are covert, so a direct observation method may cause you to underestimate incidents of peer-to-peer disrespect. Consider using additional methods, such as an anonymous survey, whole group discussions, and one-on-one discussions with students, to get a better sense of student-to-student respect.

- At various times during the year, use data to determine how well students are complying with your posted or pretaught expectations. One method is to use a rating scale to indicate how well students are meeting your CHAMPS expectations for each major activity or transition (see the CHAMPS Versus Daily Reality Rating Scale, Tool 1 in Chapter 10, Task 1). An alternative is to use a tally of misbehaviors related to your posted expectations or classroom rules. For example, list your classroom rules on a piece of paper. For several days, each time you address a rule violation with a student, mark a tally next to that rule on your monitoring sheet. At the end of the week, analyze how many rule violations occurred and which rules are causing students the most difficulty.

Student Engagement

Use data to get a sense of students' connection to instruction and other academic activities by monitoring opportunities to respond, percentage of correct responses, and any other instructional variables that have been a focus of staff development.

- Monitor opportunities to respond during teacher-directed instruction. This helps you ensure that students are not passive recipients of information. Frequent opportunities to respond provide useful information about how well students are attending to your instruction and whether they are understanding what you are doing and saying. Monitor your opportunities to respond by tallying how often you ask students to participate, whether verbally (e.g., chorally responding or answering a question), in writing (e.g., take a note, draw a picture), or through an action (e.g., thumbs up/down). While the amount of responding may differ depending on the type of teacher-directed activity (e.g., a whole group discussion will have different response rates than a fast-paced interactive review of previously learned facts), there should be many opportunities for every student to respond during any instructional period. See Tool 6, Chapter 10, Task 1 for more guidance on monitoring opportunities to respond during teacher-directed activities.

- During non-teacher-directed activities, it may be less feasible to monitor opportunities to respond, but plan to track engagement in other ways. Use on-task/off-task monitoring, check-ins with individual students, and other methods to observe independent and partner and group activities. For example, during group work, you might circulate around the room observing each group and marking a tally for each group member who is visibly participating in the activity. After several passes around the room, you should see tallies next to each student's name.

- Keep track of the percentage of correct responses in opportunities to respond in teacher-directed instruction and independent tasks. The goal is for students to be responding correctly at least 80% of the time during initial instruction and 90% of the rest of the time so they are not practicing errors and losing motivation due to lack of success. You can collect these data during teacher-directed tasks by making a tally for correct responses and a minus for incorrect responses. If there is a whole group response like a choral response or writing on whiteboards, mark the approximate percentage of correct responses for each opportunity to respond. During independent seatwork, walk around, examine students' work and mark pluses or minuses for each student. During cooperative activities, your observation will be more subjective, but if you notice that two out of six groups are frequently way off base (not off task but conceptually struggling), make notes about your observations and use this information to inform subsequent planning for small group activities.

- Periodically ask your students about their feelings and perceptions toward school and the instructional content, assigned work, and activities that you use in your classroom. When students feel that school is relevant and important to their lives, they are more likely to experience positive learning outcomes and feel motivated to succeed in your classroom (Fredericks et al., 2004). This feedback can help you adjust instruction to be more engaging and meaningful to your students. You might gather feedback by conducting a focus group, administering a brief survey, or asking students individually about their perceptions.

- Observe for any other instructional variables that have been a focus of staff development in your school or district. Use any recommend data-tracking methods associated with priority initiatives rolled out in your school or district. If data collection methods were not provided as part of staff development, consider how you can best monitor your students' or your growth toward the goals of the initiative.

Teacher Behavior

Effective teachers observe student behavior by physically circulating and visually scanning the classroom. They also maintain a healthy ratio of positive to corrective interactions and provide fluent corrections, which you will learn more about in Chapters 6–8. The following methods can help you monitor these critical teacher behaviors:

> *Effective teachers observe student behavior by physically circulating and visually scanning the classroom.*

- *Active supervision.* Monitor your active supervision of students in different activities and transitions. Reflect on questions such as:

  - Do you circulate to all parts of the classroom in unpredictable patterns?
  - Do you use visual and auditory scanning to quickly identify students who need assistance or possible problems/misbehaviors in the classroom?
  - Do you make frequent eye contact with your students, regardless of the instructional activity?

Consider periodically using video recordings and subsequent analysis, or have a peer observe you and provide information about your use of circulation and scanning to actively supervise.

- *Ratio of positive to corrective interactions.* One of the most important pieces of data to monitor in your classroom is the ratio of positive to corrective interactions you maintain with your students. Monitor the frequency of positive feedback and positive noncontingent interactions with your students in comparison to the frequency of corrective interactions. The goal is to maintain at least a 3:1 ratio of positive to corrective interactions. This positively skewed ratio is important because, in every classroom, some students are starved for attention. If a teacher is, on average, paying more attention to students when they are misbehaving than when they are engaged in desired behavior, students learn that it is easier to get attention by annoying the teacher than by trying to meet the teacher's expectations. When interactions are skewed to the corrective, some students shut down while others tend to challenge the teacher more because they feel the teacher dislikes them or they enjoy the sense of power and control they get from frustrating the teacher. These data can be collected in an objective way with a simple

The Benefits of Video When Collecting Data

We would like to thank Safe & Civil Schools consultant and author Tricia Skyles for the following contribution on the benefits of video for getting a clear picture of current practices and classroom conditions.

When educators are aiming to improve classroom management, an accurate assessment of their current reality is essential for making positive changes. However, educators often rely on what some refer to as the educator's cardiac assessment—"In my heart, I feel the students are behaving better" or "It feels like we aren't making any progress."

This is where video comes in. To make good decisions that will benefit students, teachers need accurate information about their classroom management skills and a clear picture of their practice. One of the major ways that video is so useful is that it helps teachers see exactly what their current practice looks and sound like. In some cases, teachers are thrilled to see their Classroom Management Plans are working; in others, teachers may be disappointed in what they learn.

Anyone who has stepped foot in a classroom recognizes the complex dynamics involved in the setting. There is so much happening at any given moment that many teachers may develop an incomplete picture of what is going on in the classroom. Video helps teachers see the unseen—that is, practice that may remain hidden among the hustle and bustle of teaching. When used with any of the data collection tools presented in CHAMPS, video allows them to truly and accurately home in on specific measures of their Classroom Management Plans.

While video may not be for everyone, for teachers who choose to use this tool it can be like adding fuel to the fire. Teachers may find themselves improving faster and more likely to sustain changes to their practice. Video can be used to get a clear picture of reality and to set goals and measure progress toward those goals across time. Further, for teachers receiving any kind of coaching assistance, video can be used as a focal point for those conversations. When video is recorded and analyzed throughout the year, teachers are likely to make significant improvement in the way they manage their classrooms to impact student learning.

tally of positive interactions versus corrective interactions. Guidance about how to code interactions and analyze and make effective decisions about these data are included in Chapter 10, Task 1, Tool 2.

- *Corrections.* Evaluate whether your corrections are delivered fluently, which means they are consistently applied, unemotionally delivered, and as brief as possible. At various points during the year, reflect on whether you are achieving the goal of maintaining fluent corrections with all of your students. You may wish to take quick anecdotal notes after corrective interactions with students, observe video or audio recordings, have a colleague observe your classroom and mark tallies for fluent versus nonfluent corrections, or deliver a feedback survey to your students.

In summary, using data to monitor what is going on in your classroom is critical for assessing whether your management plan is working throughout the year. The type of data you collect should capture both your long-term goals and hallmarks of effective classrooms, including information about student behavior, student engagement, and teacher behavior. To help you collect data, this book includes a variety of tools for collecting and evaluating information about your classroom (see Chapter 10). The next task will help you develop a plan to collect and use data as part of an ongoing process of refining your Classroom Management Plan.

TASK 3

Use Data Snapshots to Monitor and Adjust Your Management Plan

Develop a plan to collect and use data as part of an ongoing process of refining your Classroom Management Plan.

• • • • •

Remember that data should never be collected purely for the sake of collecting data! Data are meaningless unless connected to meaningful analysis, decision-making, and adaptations to your Classroom Management Plan based on what you observe. This is where the Improvement Cycle comes in. One thing that separates great teachers from those who are good or simply OK is whether they continually strive to improve aspects of their classroom from day to day and year to year. The best teachers do this by using an ongoing cycle that involves reviewing data, prioritizing goals for improvement based on that data, revising aspects of their Classroom Management Plan to address those goals, and implementing new plans while monitoring the efficacy of any changes. This Improvement Cycle is shown in Figure 5.1 (p. 254).

In Chapter 10, we will discuss how to use data as part of a cycle of continuous improvement. In this task, you'll make a plan for collecting data snapshots that will help you understand the current conditions in your classroom. These efforts will accomplish the **Review** portion of the

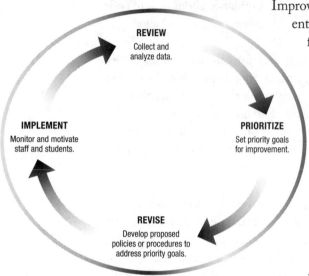

Figure 5.1 *Improvement Cycle*

Improvement Cycle, where you will collect and analyze different types of data that will then be used to identify priorities for improvement in your classroom.

There may be times where informal data or your subjective perceptions guide you to collect data on one or more aspects of your classroom. For example, if you feel like the amount of misbehavior is increasing as you near a major break, you might begin tallying misbehaviors and tracking trends to see if your management plan needs adjustments. While this kind of review of a specific data source can occur at any time, we also recommend using data snapshots to provide a picture of your classroom at a specific point in time during the school year. These snapshots should take place with some regularity in your classroom. At minimum, plan to collect and analyze data focusing on one aspect of student behavior, student engagement, or teacher behavior once or twice a month.

Schedule When to Collect Data Snapshots in Your Calendar

You are much more likely to stick to a plan to collect and analyze data when you build implementation into your schedule. Therefore, stop right now and use the prompts below to create a schedule for data collection in your planning calendar. Write each prompt on or near the suggested date. Make sure to avoid specific dates that are already scheduled for other major activities, such as field trips or schoolwide testing.

The tools listed below are described in detail in Chapter 10, Task 1. As the year progresses and you come to a particular prompt on your calendar, go to the specified pages in this book and follow the directions for collecting and analyzing the data.

Recommended Data Snapshot Calendar

Week 3	Student Interviews or Quiz (Task 3 in Chapter 9)
Week 4 or 5	CHAMPS Versus Daily Reality Rating Scale (Tool 1)
Second Month (early)	Ratio of Interactions Monitoring Form (Tool 2)
Second Month (late)	Tool of your choice*
Third Month (early)	Misbehavior(s) Recording Sheet (Tool 3)
Third Month (late)	Grade Book Analysis Worksheet (Tool 4)
Fourth Month (early)	On-Task Behavior Observation Sheet (Tool 5)
Fourth Month (late)	Tool of your choice*
January (early)	CHAMPS Versus Daily Reality Rating Scale (Tool 1)
January (late)	Opportunities to Respond Observation Sheet (Tool 6)
February (early)	Ratio of Interactions Monitoring Form (Tool 2)
February (late)	On-Task Behavior Observation Sheet (Tool 5)

March (early)	Grade Book Analysis Worksheet (Tool 4)
April (after spring break)	CHAMPS Versus Daily Reality Rating Scale (Tool 1)
May	Tool of your choice*
Last Two Weeks	Family/Student Satisfaction Survey (Tool 7)

Tool of your choice: These dates have been left open for you to select a data tool that is relevant based on what you have observed in your classroom. For example, if you are concerned that students are not fully engaged during instruction and you realize that you are not scheduled to monitor opportunities to respond for a number of months, select the Opportunities to Respond Observation Sheet. You might also opt to collect data on an aspect of your classroom that does not correspond to one of the tools provided in CHAMPS. For example, you might take data on how well you circulate and scan in the classroom or provide fluent corrections. Or use a method such as anonymous surveys to get an understanding of students' perceptions of whether peers are treating each other respectfully in the classroom.

If you are a middle school or high school teacher and know that you will have different groups of students in different terms or semesters, you may need to adjust the calendar schedule. We recommend using the following tools with each group of students you work with throughout the school year:

- Student Interviews or Quiz (Task 3 in Chapter 9),
- CHAMPS Versus Daily Reality Rating Scale (Tool 1)
- Ratio of Interactions Monitoring From (Tool 2)
- Grade Book Analysis Worksheet (Tool 4)
- Family/Student Satisfaction Survey (Tool 7)

If you teach multiple groups of students, you might plan to schedule data snapshots for targeted classes to keep your data snapshot plan manageable. For example, you might identify two classes that require lower and higher support needs to gather information about how your classroom management plan is working across groups of students with different levels of need. These tools include:

- Misbehavior Recording Sheet (Tool 3)
- On-Task Behavior Observation Sheet (Tool 5)
- Opportunities to Respond Observation Sheet (Tool 6)

Mine Your Data

Once you have collected the data using a particular data tool, plan to spend time analyzing the data as objectively as possible. Avoid subjective judgments about what data mean at this point, but rather focus on precise descriptions of what you are seeing in the data. Use specific, observable terms, such as, "The data show that students are on task an average of 80% of the time." Ask yourself whether the time period you observed represents an anomaly or the norm. If you took data and felt that student behavior was significantly better (or worse!) than it is on a daily basis, consider taking data for a few more days to get a broader view of the students' behavior across time.

Once you have collected representative data, spend some time looking for trends in the data that are positive indicators (e.g., "During cooperative activities, on-task behavior is high at an average of 93%"). These will be aspects of your plan that should be preserved and celebrated. Then look at any red flags that appear in the data and whether there are perceived problems (e.g., "During independent work, on-task behavior is only averaging 66%").

Mine your data looking for specific trends or areas of concern. Ask yourself questions like:

- Does the data show that concerns are occurring across the whole classroom?
- Are there certain students who are significantly contributing to the percentage of misbehavior, off-task behavior, etc.?
- Is the data similar across times, days of the week, and activities, or are there differences in the data that correspond to a particular pattern or trend?

Pay careful consideration to mining your data with an equity lens—as in, does the data show that all my classroom students are thriving or struggling at similar rates, or does the data show differences across demographic groups? For example, if you monitor ratios of interaction and discover that your ratio of interactions with White students is 3:1, but your ratio of interactions with Black and Latino students is only 1:1, highlight this as an area of concern that needs to be addressed. Again, avoid making judgments about what the data mean at this point in the process. Simply make note of what is evident in the data. When you reach the Prioritize and Revise steps of the Improvement Cycle (in Chapter 10), you can then use this information to follow up with questions such as, "What are the barriers in my classroom or supports needed to allow all of my students to access the same levels of success on this data point?"

In summary, collecting data snapshots will help you understand the conditions in your classroom throughout the school year. As the first step in the Improvement Cycle, these data snapshots will drive the priorities for improvement that you identify and the revisions that you make to your Classroom Management Plan. Scheduling when to collect data snapshots will help you plan to allocate enough time for data collection and analysis in your busy teaching schedule.

Diversity, Equity, Inclusion, and Access

Mine your data with an equity lens. Break down your data to see if there are different rates of success or struggle across demographic groups (e.g., gender, race/ethnicity, disability status, LGBTQ+, religion, and so on). When you work to revise aspects of your management plan, you will work to determine if there are barriers in your classroom or additional supports that are needed to help all students achieve high levels of success.

Conclusion

Even the most carefully thought-out classroom management plan needs to be monitored and adjusted based on the needs of any particular class. By using a variety of methods to collect data on student behavior at different times of the year, you can metaphorically take the temperature and pulse of the class and make decisions about the health of your management plan. If you find your plan is working well, carry on; after all, if it isn't broken, don't fix it! However, if you find areas that need improvement, you can tweak any number of variables to facilitate more responsible student behavior.

CHAPTER 6

Interact Positively—Build Positive Relationships and Provide Positive Feedback

When you build positive relationships and provide frequent positive feedback, you motivate students to demonstrate their best behavior.

The I in STOIC is addressed in the following two chapters about how to strengthen positive relationships with students and boost student motivation. While observing student behavior, you are looking for opportunities to increase your students' motivation to continue behaving responsibly and to try to behave even better in the future. Over time, the positive relationship you build with your students increases their trust in you, which allows them to open up, seek help, and work with you to overcome barriers and challenges. In this chapter, you will learn how to use attention and praise as a tool to increase motivation. Chapter 7 provides information on using goal-setting strategies to increase the motivation of classes who are largely responsible and require fewer supports for motivation. It also discusses how you can use whole class extrinsic reinforcement systems with classes that need medium or highly supportive tools to increase motivation.

As early as 1977, O'Leary and O'Leary wrote that "teacher attention is perhaps the most basic of all influences on student behaviors, and the systematic use of attention should characterize every teacher's classroom repertoire." In 1996, Sheets and Gay wrote that "the causes of many classroom behaviors labeled and punished as rule infractions are, in fact, problems of students and teachers relating to each other interpersonally. Intentionally working to build positive relationships and providing frequent positive feedback help teachers and students relate to one another and are critical for effective classroom management.

An extensive body of research literature confirms the importance of teacher-student relationships: When the teacher-student relationship is positive and respectful, students are more

Relational Trust

To use a gardening metaphor, think of the positive relational trust you build with your students as planting a seed in rich, fertile soil. The positive feedback you give students on a regular basis for growth, effort, and achievement is like providing the necessary water and sunlight for the plant to grow.

likely to behave appropriately, work hard to meet the teacher's expectations, internalize positive school-related values, and succeed in school (Appleton et al., 2008; Blum, 2005; Hamre & Pianta, 2001; Klem & Connell, 2004; Pianta et al., 2003; Roorda et al., 2011; Wentzel, 2002). Studies have also shown that students tend to work more diligently when they receive higher rates of positive feedback than when they do not (Bain et al., 1991; Beaman & Wheldall, 2000; Ferguson & Houghton, 1992; Hall et al., 1968; Harrop & Swinson, 2000; Merrett & Wheldall, 1987; Nafpaktitis et al., 1985; Pergande & Thorkildsen, 1995). These findings have been consistent from preschool to high school.

While the research is impressive, you do not need a research base to realize that this concept is true. From your own experience, you probably know that most people will work harder for a teacher or boss who is personable and respectful, and treats students or employees like a person—not like a number in the grade book. Most people also work harder when they receive positive feedback and are recognized for strengths, rather than only getting attention for things they are doing wrong.

The six tasks presented and explained in this chapter are:

- Task 1: Strive to Provide a High Ratio of Positive Interactions
- Task 2: Build Positive Relationships With Students With Noncontingent Attention
- Task 3: Provide Positive Feedback With Contingent Attention
- Task 4: Provide Intermittent Celebrations
- Task 5: Maintain a Positive Ratio of Interactions with Parents and Guardians
- Task 6: Maintain Positive Communication with Colleagues

TASK 1

Strive to Provide a High Ratio of Positive Interactions

Plan to interact at least three times more often with each student when they are behaving appropriately than when they are misbehaving (that is, at least a 3:1 ratio).

• • • • •

In some classrooms, teachers circulate through the room acknowledging students who are focused, working appropriately with peers, and engaging in other appropriate behaviors. These teachers notice when students put in their best effort, and let students know when they demonstrate growth toward learning outcomes, expected behaviors, or social-emotional skills. These teachers greet students by name and authentically welcome them back from absences. Students feel that these teachers are genuinely glad to have them in class each day. They feel seen and know that these teachers see their strengths and positive contributions, even if they sometimes or often struggle in school.

In other classrooms, teachers spend far more time interacting with students when they are doing something inappropriate. They may forget to greet some students, or their first interactions are reprimands or corrections for misbehavior. Some students may feel like the teacher sees them only for their faults or mistakes because the teacher frequently provides reprimands or corrective consequences but rarely interacts with the students otherwise. Some students may feel like the teacher never really even knows if they are there because they are not reprimanded for negative behavior, but they also aren't acknowledged for positive behavior.

Your attention is a valuable commodity. In fact, it is one of the most important and limited commodities in any classroom. Each time you interact positively with a student, whether by greeting them, commenting on one of their interests, or providing positive feedback for something the student was doing right, your attention is like putting one dollar in the bank. Each time you must correct a student or give them your attention when they are misbehaving is like withdrawing three dollars. Why are corrective interactions more costly than positive interactions? The simple reason is that it is human nature to react more deeply to corrections and negative interactions than positive ones (Baumeister et al., 2001). Think about your response to performance evaluations. If you are thinking about your evaluation on the way home, do you think more about the positive aspects of the evaluation or the critical aspects? If you are like most people, you probably spend more time reflecting on and criticizing your own performance (or the person who was evaluating you).

To further understand why it is so important to increase efforts to ensure positive interactions with your students outweigh corrective interactions, consider the following:

- Some students are starved for attention. Most teachers have direct experience with students who demand attention, and most have seen the desperate measures some students will take to get attention.
- For the student who is truly starved for attention, the form of attention may not matter. A reprimand for misbehaving may satisfy this student's desire for attention just as much as positive feedback for behaving responsibly (Alberto & Troutman, 2012). In fact, the scolding may be even more satisfying because it probably lasts longer and involves greater emotional intensity from the teacher. Some students have also learned they are far more skilled in getting negative attention from adults than positive.
- With students who are starved for attention, the behavior you reinforce with attention is the behavior that you will begin to see more often (Skinner, 1953). When you have more interactions with students when they are behaving appropriately (positive interactions), you will see an increase in positive behavior over time. On the other hand, when you have more interactions with students when they are behaving inappropriately (corrective interactions), you will see an increase in negative behavior over time.

The behavior management strategy of providing a high ratio of positive interactions (RPI) is one of the most powerful tools in our classroom management tool box. Research confirms that high rates of positive interactions can simultaneously increase student engagement and decrease inappropriate behavior (Caldarella et al., 2020; Cook et al., 2017; Downs et al., 2019;

Reinke et al., 2013; Sutherland et al., 2000; Trussell, 2008). Achieving a high ratio of positive interactions means making the conscious effort to interact with every student more frequently (at least three times more frequently) when the student is behaving appropriately than when they are behaving inappropriately. At a minimum, effective teachers give at least three times more attention to students for growth, effort, positive behavior, or by simply showing interest in them than for inappropriate behaviors or failure to meet expectations. This strategy is one of the most essential but also one of the most difficult to implement.

Understand the Difference Between Positive and Corrective Interactions

Note that your interactions with students are considered positive or corrective based on the student's behavior at the time you attend to them. For example, if a student is off task and you say, "Wanda, you need to get back to work or you will not complete your assignment," it is considered a corrective interaction even if you made the request very pleasantly and your intention was to help the student. It is a corrective interaction because the student was engaged in an inappropriate behavior (being off task) when you initiated the interaction, and the purpose of your interaction was to change or correct Wanda's current behavior. Some teachers mistakenly believe that when they are nice to a student, it is a positive interaction and when they are acting hostile or sounding angry, it is a negative or corrective interaction.

To give an even more overt example, some teachers give very skillful corrections that almost sound more like compliments than corrections. These interactions are easily mistaken as positive interactions because they are so skillfully delivered. Imagine that a student is not working during a work time. If the teacher walks over and says, "Hakim, you did a fantastic job on the responses yesterday. I can't wait to see what you do today." Is this positive or corrective? If you indicated that it is corrective, you are absolutely right! Remember, whether something is a positive or corrective interaction is based on whether the student was engaged in appropriate behavior or inappropriate behavior at the time of the interaction. In this case, the purpose of the teacher's interaction was to prompt Hakim to get started. It is a fantastic correction because it is fluent (Chapter 8 describes the features of fluent and effective corrections), and for many students, this simple prompt increases the likelihood that they will get started over an angry direction to "get to work!" The risk is that if Hakim is a student who is starved for attention, he might engage in the same behavior the next day purely so that the teacher will come over and interact with him again.

It's also important to realize that just because an interaction is corrective does not mean it is wrong. It may, for example, be the most useful way to get a student back on task at the time. However, understand that unless you make an effort to interact with this same student when she is on task, she may learn that it is actually easier to get your attention (which may be what she wants) for being off task than for behaving well. Remember, each time you give attention to a student, you may be reinforcing the behavior you are paying attention to—whether the behavior is appropriate or inappropriate (Alberto &

Locus of Control

Some students are starved for attention due to circumstances outside of your classroom. While you likely cannot control these outside circumstances, it is within your locus of control to ensure you maintain a positive ratio of interactions with these students. These efforts can help students feel a sense of belongingness and meet their needs for attention, acknowledgment, and recognition.

Troutman, 2012; Carr et al., 2000; Skinner, 1953). Thus, you should pay at least three times more attention to students when they are exhibiting positive behavior than when they are exhibiting negative behavior.

Avoid the Criticism Trap

Unfortunately, achieving this 3:1 positive to corrective ratio is not always easy. In fact, observational studies regularly show that most teachers pay significantly more attention to students' misbehavior than to their positive behavior (Floress et al., 2018; Jenkins et al., 2015) In 1986, Dr. Wes Becker wrote about a set of studies he conducted with teachers who were trying to reduce out-of-seat behavior during work periods. He encouraged the teachers to reprimand students more immediately and more consistently: "Don't miss a single student who gets out-of-seat at the wrong time." The teachers assumed this would decrease the behavior. In fact, the number of students getting out of their seats at the wrong times actually increased.

Dr. Becker called this phenomenon the Criticism Trap. Although the teachers thought they were doing something effective (reprimanding or issuing a consequence for an inappropriate behavior), the students, who were starved for attention, were getting out of their seats at least in part to get their teachers to look at them and talk to them. The students' need for attention was satisfied when their teachers told them to get back in their seats—and they typically did sit down, at least initially. When students took their seats, the teachers were reinforced for reprimanding. "Ah, now I can teach." But before long the students realized, consciously or unconsciously, that they were not getting attention when they did what the teachers wanted, so they got out of their seats again. The teachers reprimanded again, giving the desired attention, and the students were again reinforced for getting out of their seats.

A scenario like the above example becomes a destructive pattern in which all parties involved get what they want in the short run. The students get attention when they violate the teacher's expectations. The teacher gets momentary compliance each time he reprimands. However, when this cycle is allowed to continue, no one gets what they want in the long run. Over time, students behave less and less responsibly, and the teacher gets more frustrated, negative, and corrective. The only real way out of the Criticism Trap is to have more interactions with students when they are behaving responsibly than when they are misbehaving.

 CASE STUDY *Example From the Field*

The concept of RPI has surprising power, but it is easy to forget. In presenting this concept to a group of educators in a large urban district, Randy (founder of the CHAMPS approach) had a powerful conversation with a veteran teacher. Kathy, the teacher, described her third- and fourth- period classes at the secondary school as the toughest groups she had ever taught in her decades-long career. She felt as though these classes were always on the verge of being out of control. After learning about RPIs, Kathy went back to her school and immediately began implementing a plan to increase her positive interactions with students. In an email to Randy, Kathy wrote:

"Randy, I could cry. As they entered the classroom, I greeted the students in my classes with big smiles for each *individual*. The kids smiled back and said that I seemed to be in a good mood. (Wow, if they see the difference that quickly, I *have* been grouchy.) I started them on the first assignment with enthusiasm and told them how this particular assignment would benefit them relative to the subject I'm teaching. While students worked, I walked around the room with a pad of sticky notes. When I found a student working or asking questions or cooperating with other students to understand the process, I wrote a personal, specific note thanking him or her for that behavior.

"I am amazed. My students are working and happy. I am happy for the first time in a long time in these classes. Thank you. Thank you. Thank you!

"I felt so hopeless. I know it won't always be this good every day, with every class, and with every kid, and I will constantly come up with new ways to show the positive, but I'm so encouraged that I can do this. When you explained the positive-to-corrective ratio yesterday afternoon, I could hear my own voice saying, 'Stop that.' 'Don't do that.' 'Sit down.' I had to think long and hard to find any positive things I say to my class.

"This concept has truly touched my heart, and if I can hold on to it, I know that I can truly say at the end of the day that I did the right thing. RPI is a remarkably powerful strategy. If my words help spread this message to others, please feel free to use them."

Randy and Kathy have kept in touch, and Randy says that they remind each other about how they—and everyone—need to be constantly vigilant about keeping those positive interactions at a high level. Although Randy has known this concept for decades, he still says he needs to remind himself!

• • • • •

If you think you have fallen into the Criticism Trap, or if you believe that your RPI with students is less than 3:1, implement strategies to increase your positive interactions with students. Tasks 2–5 provide many practical ways you can increase your positive relationships, such as:

- Each time you interact with a student engaged in inappropriate behavior, tell yourself that you owe that student three positive interactions.
- Identify specific times during each day that you will give students positive feedback on some aspect of their individual behavior or class performance. For example, you might decide that at the beginning of each math period, you will compliment five or six students.
- Schedule individual conference times with students to compliment them on their behavioral or academic performance or growth.
- Periodically scan your classroom, specifically searching for important reinforceable behaviors that you can acknowledge to students.
- Identify particular events that occur during the day (for example, a student getting a drink of water) that will prompt you to observe the class and identify a reinforceable behavior.
- Reduce the amount of attention (that is, the time and intensity) a student receives for misbehavior and increase the amount of attention the student receives when not engaged in misbehavior.

- Devote 15 seconds at the end of each day to identify one or two students who had a rough day—lots of corrective interactions. Write their names on a sticky note and place the note in your plan book for the next day. Use that note as a reminder to pump up the RPI with those students. By focusing on positive attention the next day, you can usually prevent yourself from falling into a Criticism Trap spiral. (*Thanks to a teacher in Guilford County Schools, North Carolina, for sharing this idea.*)

In Chapter 10, we provide suggestions for how you can periodically monitor your RPI by using Tool 2: Ratio of Interactions Monitoring Form (Reproducibles 10.4, 10.5, and 10.6) to determine if you have fallen into the Criticism Trap. For now, just be aware that the behaviors you pay the most attention to are the behaviors that are likely to occur with the most frequency as the year progresses. Consequently, we urge you to make a concerted effort to interact with every one of your students more frequently when they are engaged in positive behavior than when engaged in negative behavior.

Relational Trust

Students often believe that if the teacher corrects their behavior, the teacher does not like them. Even high school teachers report that students have this misconception. By providing noncontingent attention or specific praise as soon as possible after correcting a student's misbehavior, you send the message that you still care for the student and dissolve the tension the student may feel. This helps maintain the relational trust you have worked to develop with the student.

Level of Support and Ratio of Positive to Corrective Interactions

The higher the level of support necessary for your students, the greater the probability that at least some of them are starved for attention or will need more positive feedback to overcome barriers and challenges they are faced with. Students who are starved for attention are likely to try to get their attention needs met through misbehavior, potentially leading you into a pattern of frequent nagging and reprimanding—the classic spiral into the Criticism Trap. Students who struggle academically will need increased positive feedback so that they know they are making growth and persist through challenges. Students who face challenges such as anxiety, depression, or adverse experiences outside of school will need your positive attention to ensure that they trust you enough to talk with you when they are struggling and need more support. Your positive attention can also be a powerful motivating factor that helps students who doubt their own abilities (i.e., you can help increase their expectancy of success), but also in increasing their sense that their efforts in school are valuable. Therefore, the greater your class's need for support, the more you need to make an effort to maintain positive interactions at a very high level. This task is absolutely essential for classes that need high support. You may even need to strive for a 5:1 or, with a few of the individual students who exhibit the most at-risk behavior, even a 9:1 RPI. Maintaining a 3:1 RPI is also important with classes that can manage low support, but it is generally easier to accomplish because there tends to be less misbehavior in these classes.

If you implement the strategies in this chapter and find it is still difficult to maintain a 3:1 RPI because of the numbers of misbehaviors you must correct with your students, revise your Classroom Management Plan to provide increased structure and focus on teaching of

STOIC Framework

If it is difficult to maintain a 3:1 ratio of positive to corrective interactions because of excessive misbehaviors, adapt structures in your classroom to increase the likelihood students engage in appropriate behavior, and explicitly teach expectations, social-emotional, and behavioral skills.

expectations and behavioral skills. The S and T of STOIC can be powerful in reducing the numbers of misbehaviors you see from your students, allowing you more opportunity to provide positive feedback, and ensuring that you are able to maintain high positive ratios of interaction.

In summary, strive to maintain at least a 3:1 ratio of positive to corrective interactions with your students. This is important for each class as a whole, but also for each individual student. The next tasks in this chapter provide practical ways that you can boost your positive interactions with students, creating a more positive classroom environment and strengthening your relationships with students.

TASK 2

Build Positive Relationships With Students With Noncontingent Attention

Create a positive relationship with each student by using every opportunity possible to provide each student with noncontingent attention.

• • • • •

Imagine three different students in a hypothetical classroom. The first is a highly talented, good-looking, socially adept student. The second student struggles academically and behaviorally and is not particularly liked by peers. The third is an average student. Each of these students, and all the others in the room, should feel equally valued and respected by you not because of what they accomplish or how they behave, but just because they are one of your students. All of these students have strengths and deserve to have educators who work with them recognize, acknowledge, and foster those strengths. So, how do you give each of these students the kind of attention they need to feel valued and respected?

In this task, specific suggestions are offered for how to build positive relationships with students. The focus is on noncontingent attention—a fancy way of saying that you will give some time and attention to each student regardless of how that student behaves or performs academically. Mike Booher, a former Safe & Civil Schools trainer, refers to noncontingent attention as *reach outs*, because you are in essence reaching out to make a connection with every student, regardless of their performance, circumstances, or efforts.

It is very important for you to make an effort to provide every student with attention that is not contingent on any specific accomplishment. Contingent positive attention (as described in Tasks 3 and 4) involves interacting with and giving feedback to students when they have accomplished or demonstrated improvement on important behavioral or academic goals (O'Leary & O'Leary, 1977; Sheuermann & Hall, 2008). Noncontingent attention, on the other hand, involves giving students time and attention not because of anything they've done, but just because you notice and value them as people (Alberto & Troutman, 2012; Carr et al., 2000). Simple daily ways of giving noncontingent attention include greeting your students as they enter your room and showing an authentic interest in the thoughts, feelings, and activities of each student.

The benefits of noncontingent attention are fairly obvious. Like all of us, students need to be noticed and valued. When they feel noticed and valued, they are more likely to be motivated to engage in appropriate behaviors and try their best. They are also more likely to feel comfortable being vulnerable, making mistakes in learning, or coming to you in a time of need. The benefits to you include the following:

Relational Trust

Noncontingent interactions are important for building relational trust with your students. When you invest in your students through these types of positive interactions, students are more likely to view your actions and efforts as having positive intent, and they are more likely to want to act in a spirit of cooperation with you.

- You will feel more connected to your students.
- Students will have a model of pleasant, supportive social interactions—you!
- Student behavior and effort will improve.
- Each day will be much more pleasant, resulting in an improved classroom climate for you and the students.

You may wonder how simply saying "hello" and making an effort to talk to students can improve their behavior. Dr. Vern Jones (2007), a leading expert on student discipline and motivation, explains noncontingent attention with the bank analogy. Each time you interact with a student and show an interest in them as a person, you make a deposit. When you have invested enough (had enough of the right type of interactions so that the student feels valued by you), the student is more likely to want to follow your rules and strive to achieve your Guidelines for Success. In addition, if you make enough deposits, there will be reserve capital for those times when you may have to make a withdrawal because of student misbehavior. Whether the withdrawal consists of a gentle reprimand, a discussion, or a corrective consequence designed to help improve the student's behavior, the more you have invested in the student, the more likely they are to understand that you are trying to help them by correcting them. Students who struggle with chronic misbehavior will also recognize that you see them as more than just the sum of their faults because they know you have gotten to know them beyond their misbehaviors or struggles at school.

"Mrs. Jacobsen cares so much about me that she is taking the time to help me learn to be responsible. I want to do what she is asking me to do." When nothing has been invested, the student may feel that you are simply trying to control their behavior. "Mrs. Jacobsen wants me to sit down and be quiet because she doesn't like me. Well, the heck with her. I'll do whatever I want, whenever I want. She can't make me sit down." Noncontingent attention helps you build a spirit of cooperation between yourself and your students. In addition, by building a relationship with your students, you increase the likelihood that they will feel connected to you and to their school. This connectedness has been shown to correlate with long-term student success (Centers for Disease Control and Prevention, 2009; Klem & Connell, 2004: Thapa et al., 2013).

Showing an interest in students and acting friendly does not mean you should try to be a friend or a peer. You are the teacher, and you do not want to be so friendly that you seem to be an equal or that you do not hold high expectations for all of your students (paired with any needed supports). You are the person in charge of the classroom and the one who needs to intervene if there are rule violations. However, as the person in authority, you want to continuously find ways to communicate that you value and are interested in every one of your students as individual people.

Ways to Build Positive Relationships With Students

This next section provides detailed explanations of some ways to give your students noncontingent attention.

Greet students.

This is the simplest but one of the most important ways to provide noncontingent attention. As students enter your room first thing in the morning or at the beginning of class, provide a friendly greeting. "Hello, Jonathan. Good morning, Will. Francine, how are you today? You know, I'm tired this morning, too. You and I may have to nudge each other to stay awake in class. Maria, Jacob, Tyrone, good to see you." You may not be able to greet every student each day, but you should try to greet enough students each day so that over the course of a week every student has been greeted at least a few times.

Elementary teachers should greet their students throughout the day—greet a few students when they come in from recess or after music class or when they return from lunch. Middle school teachers should attempt to greet at least five to eight students per class as students enter the room. You can also make a point of greeting your students when you see them in the hall. They may barely respond (some students will be self-conscious if they are with friends), but they will notice if you don't take the time to acknowledge them.

Some teachers get creative in the ways that they personalize their greetings with students. As mentioned in Chapter 2, Task 5, some teachers use a personalized handshake with each student or a chart that allows students to select their preferred greeting (e.g., handshake, salute, dance party, fist bump). However, even if your routine is simply smiling at the student and greeting them by name, this moment of connection is a powerful way to start each day or class in a positive way.

Learn how to correctly identify your students.

As you begin learning your students' names, take extra care to learn the correct pronunciation of each name. Although this is of vital importance to demonstrate that you honor and value your students, many teachers do not make this simple effort. We've heard many examples where teachers have even made jokes about what a name sounds like, which should never occur. When teachers are not familiar with the pronunciation of a student's name, they may be less likely to call on that student or engage with them in class. Further, when teachers consistently mispronounce names, students are at risk for feeling shamed, anxious, or embarrassed (Kohli & Solórzano, 2012; Wan, 2017).

Let your students know on the first day of school that it is important to you that you learn to call them by their preferred name and that you want them to help you learn to say it the correct way. You may wish to record your students introducing themselves and their names. For any names that are difficult for you to pronounce, listen to the recording each day and repeat the pronunciation until you have acquired it. For older students, it's also a good idea to also ask students their gender pronouns (he/his, she/hers, they/theirs). If you aren't sure of a student's pronoun, you might ask them directly at a private moment or refer to them by name only. You might inquire by sharing your own: "I use the pronouns he, him, and his. I want to make sure I address you correctly, so if you use specific pronouns, please let me know or correct me if I use one incorrectly." Another option is to pass around a sign-in sheet at the beginning of the year and ask students to indicate their preferred name and pronoun in writing.

Diversity, Equity, Inclusion, and Access

Each student deserves to have teachers who learn and use the correct pronunciation of their name and the pronoun they use to reflect their gender identity. This simple effort demonstrates that you honor and value the student's individuality and background.

Show an interest in students' work and other interests.

During independent work periods, when no one needs immediate assistance, go to individual students or cooperative learning groups and look at student work or have a quick discussion to learn more about the students. Taking a few moments to look at what a student is doing demonstrates that you are interested in the student and their work. Sometimes you may offer praise in this context; other times you can simply say something like, "I am looking forward to reading this when you are finished, Tammie." You can also ask about what students are working on or learning in other classes or in activities outside of school, such as sports or music. Having students share things they are proud of or excited about can provide an important point of connection.

Learn more about students' cultures and other aspects of their personal identities they would like to share.

Invite students to share with you or the class about aspects of their cultural identity or family background. Explore the rich differences of your students and show that you value them beyond just academic considerations. Showing this interest can benefit whether they were born in another country or region of the United States, have particular racial or ethnic backgrounds that inform how they view their identity, or view their urban or rural background as important to who they are.

Diversity, Equity, Inclusion, and Access

Invite but do not require students to share about their cultural identify or family background. These efforts demonstrate that you are interested in your students and that you value their diverse experiences and perspectives, and can help you better understand students' needs and interests.

As described in Chapter 2, Task 3, use some display space in the classroom to display art, artifacts, and information that reflect students' unique interests and identities. Ask students who speak another language in their home setting to share some common greetings or phrases, like "please" and "thank you," and work to incorporate these into your interactions with students and their families.

Recognize that sharing about family or personal identity may be uncomfortable for some students, such as those who have difficult home lives, live in foster care, or struggle with issues of self-worth. Provide opportunities for those who would like to share, but do not force students to engage in these activities. For example, if you have a writing project where students can research and write about an aspect of their family background or culture, provide an alternative writing prompt that does not put these students in an uncomfortable position. For example, you could provide an option for students to write about a personal interest or to research and write about another culture they are interested in.

Use "trust generators" to build rapport with students.

Psychological research has identified a set of actions that people can use to develop more authentic, vulnerable, and trusting connections with others (Brafman & Brafman, 2010). Reciprocal self-disclosure—sharing information about yourself with your students and encouraging your students to share information about themselves with you—can enhance trust and strengthen relationships (Cayanus & Martin, 2008). Zaretta Hammond, author of *Culturally Responsive Teaching and the Brain*, calls these self-disclosure acts *trust generators*. Use the following trust generators to help build rapport with your students (Hammond, 2014):

- *Selective vulnerability.* Share your own vulnerable moments—for example, discuss a personal challenge you've overcome, lesson you've learned, or mistake that you've made in the past. Your students will be more likely to respect and connect to you.
- *Familiarity.* Make a point of regularly crossing paths with your students in the school and community. For example, attend community or sports events that you know are popular with your students. People naturally develop a sense of familiarity with someone who they see often in a particular setting on a regular basis.
- *Similarity of interests.* Share hobbies, sports, or other things you like to do that are similar to a particular student's interests. Also share social causes that you are passionate about, such as caring for the environment or advocating for equity.
- *Concern.* Show concern and personal regard for issues and events important to your students. Ask follow-up questions about recent events, such as births, illnesses, or other life transitions.
- *Competence.* Demonstrate competence by conveying genuine willingness to make sure students understand important concepts. Take efforts to make learning less confusing, more exciting, and more successful.

Identify students' strengths.

Every student has strengths and deserves to have educators who work with them identify and celebrate those things that the student does well. For some students, their strength may be in a specific subject or activity, while others may exhibit strengths with particular habits, attitudes, or skills.

There are many benefits when teachers actively work to identify student strengths. Students are more likely to feel connected to their teachers when they believe they are seen as more than the sum of their faults or challenges. They may be more likely to work hard and persist through challenges when they are bolstered by feelings of accomplishment and pride in who they are or what they can do. You can think of this like a snowball effect—once the ball gets rolling in a positive direction, it will keep building momentum and rolling.

A few times each year, consider listing a few strengths for each of your students. Make efforts to find ways to acknowledge the student for those strengths or create situations where the student can demonstrate the strengths. When identifying student strengths, reflect on questions such as:

Motivation

When teachers actively work to identify and foster student strengths, this can be a powerful motivating factor that helps the student persist through challenges and try new things.

- *What positive qualities does the student bring to the classroom?* (Yasin is conscientious of other students and is always willing to share.)
- *What skills or talents are you aware of?* (Glenn is talented at building structures and figuring out how machines work.)
- *What special efforts do you notice from the student on a regular basis?* (Bailey is often eager to help other students fix their mistakes when revising assignments.)
- *Is there a particular area of content that the student is drawn to?* (Micah loves learning about anything to do with animals, while Jan is obsessed with baseball statistics.)

Remember that some students may have strengths that are typically unrecognized or undervalued in the traditional classroom. For example, a student may have a strong connection to their spiritual belief system and may be very knowledgeable about and committed to regular practice of their faith. Another student may have amassed a lot of knowledge about car maintenance and repair from spending time with and learning from an older sibling.

See Figure 6.1 for an example of how a teacher listed student strengths and identified ways to connect to or build on those strengths.

Figure 6.1 *Student Strengths*

Student	Strengths	Ways to Acknowledge or Build Upon
Marcella A.	• Comes to class on time every day • Helps peers when they are frustrated or don't understand something	• Send a postcard to family thanking them • Give Marcella a class job as a peer helper
Eleanor V.	• Puts careful thought and effort into work • Fantastic volleyball player	• Ask Eleanor to select some work she is proud of that we can display • Ask her questions about her volleyball practice/games
Dante O.	• Wants to learn new things • Avid reader	• Have Dante write extension questions and connect to those in lessons • See if Dante wants to read to students in younger classes
Talia R.	• Has strong opinions and beliefs • Great organizational skills	• Invite Talia to join the debate club and speak to her strengths • Ask Talia to describe to me how she keeps herself so organized so that I can provide some examples to the class

If you are a specials or secondary teacher and are unable to create such a chart for all of your classes due to the number of students you see each day, consider just focusing on the students who are struggling behaviorally or academically in your classes. Also consider focusing on students who are quiet or average-performing and might have a tendency to get less overall attention from you—positive or corrective.

If you find it difficult to list strengths for any of your students because they currently have many visible challenges or have made classroom life particularly difficult, recognize that these are the students who most need you to try and learn about their strengths. Unfortunately, some students rarely or never have their strengths acknowledged at school because their struggles are so visible. Unless someone makes a conscious effort to find their strengths, the student may begin to feel everyone in the school is against them or may even begin to doubt they have strengths. Find times to meet with the student and interact noncontingently, learning more about what the student likes to do outside of school or things they take pride in. You can also try to see if you can reframe current areas of challenge into potential areas of strength if they are channeled in a particular direction. A student who currently struggles with noncompliant and argumentative behavior may have a strength of having strong opinions and convictions. If this student learns to use these convictions in socially appropriate ways, they might end up being a fantastic lawyer or activist for good causes. Examples of common challenges reframed as strengths include:

- Constantly wiggling and out of seat → Lots of energy and athleticism
- Talks to peers during inappropriate times → Has lots of friends and loves social interaction
- Shuts down when struggling academically → Cares deeply about doing well in school
- Blurts out in class → Likes to participate and contribute to discussions

Reframing challenges into potential strengths may help you view the student's behavior in a different light. While the behavior may still be challenging, you can begin finding ways to help channel the student in a more positive direction.

Invite students to ask for assistance.

Occasionally, find private times to ask individual students how they are doing in class. If anyone indicates that they are having trouble, arrange a time for that student to get some additional help from you. For those who say they are doing fine, let them know that if they ever have trouble, they should not hesitate to come see you, and that this is true for academic and non-academic concerns. If you make an offer of assistance to every student in the first couple of months of school, you communicate that you are aware of them as individuals and that you are available to help them.

It may be beneficial to put reminders in your calendar every few months to make efforts to be consciously inviting to students and parents about reaching out to you for assistance whenever needed. You should also advertise information about other adults in the school who are available to help students if they are ever struggling and don't feel comfortable coming to you. For example, every few months provide the names and emails of the principal, counselor, and social worker, along with where to find their offices in the school and any other relevant information. Invite these staff members to come and speak to your class periodically so that students are aware of who they can go to if they need assistance.

Whenever time permits, have a conversation with a student or group of students.

Having a conversation with students demonstrates (more so than just greeting them) that you are interested in them—in their experiences and their ideas. Brief social interactions create an emotional connection between you and your students, and they are not hard to do. For example, if three students enter your middle school classroom at the beginning of the passing period, you can casually chat with them as you stand at the door and greet other entering students. As you are escorting your second-grade class to lunch, you might talk quietly with a couple of students as you go down the hall (unless students are not supposed to converse in the halls). Find out your students' individual interests and ask about them—ask a student about his soccer game the previous evening, for example. Periodically share something about yourself. "My son played goalie for his team in college. What position do you like to play?"

Make a special effort to greet or talk to any student you've recently interacted with regarding a misbehavior.

This kind of gesture on your part communicates that past corrective interactions with the student are now just that—past—and that you do not hold a grudge. It also lets the student know that you are prepared for a fresh start. For example, if immediately before lunch you had to talk to a student about being disruptive, that student should definitely be one of the five or six students you greet when the class comes back after lunch: "Aaron, good to see you. How are you doing?" A greeting in these circumstances actually decreases the probability that the student will misbehave in the next instructional activity. Be careful to avoid statements like, "Aaron, good to see you. I hope we're going to have a better afternoon than we did this morning." While this might seem like an acceptable greeting, it can actually send the student spiraling into a more negative space. It also indicates that you have not really hit the reset button. If you need to speak with the student about how to move forward from a problematic behavioral incident, try to do this before the student's reentry into the environment. Then authentically greet and welcome the student back to class without mentioning the previous negative behavior.

Level of Support and Noncontingent Attention

This task is one of the few tasks in CHAMPS that is not optional based on whether students need more or less support. Whether your students need high, medium, or low support, you owe it to every individual to build a positive relationship by interacting with them as frequently as possible in a manner that is friendly, inviting, and personable. However, recognize that if your students require higher levels of support and/or you find yourself having to correct students more often for misbehaviors, increasing your noncontingent attention can be an important way to ensure that you maintain a positive ratio of interactions. For students who have previously struggled in school or who may view the educational system as stacked against them due to issues like systemic racism, overt and ongoing efforts to get to know these students and show that you value them as individuals are essential so that you demonstrate you want to work with the student to overcome any barriers to their thriving in the educational system.

UPDATE YOUR CLASSROOM MANAGEMENT PLAN

ITEM 10: INTERACT POSITIVELY

List specific ways you plan to provide noncontingent attention to students (e.g., learn to pronounce each student's name correctly, greet at least six students at the door each period, etc.).

TASK 3

Provide Positive Feedback With Contingent Attention

Give students a variety of positive feedback on their progress and success in meeting behavioral and academic goals.

• • • • •

Among the most important practices of an effective teacher is giving feedback—letting students know about their behavioral and academic progress and success (Brophy, 1981; Brophy & Good, 1986; Hattie & Timperley, 2007; Simonsen et al., 2008). Giving positive feedback is a powerful way to encourage responsible behavior. When done well, positive feedback confirms for students that they are on the right track and increases the probability that they will strive to demonstrate the same behaviors in the future (Kazdin, 1980; Skinner, 1953). It also helps students learn to identify things they are doing well, boosting their sense of self-efficacy and expectancy of success across time. Positive feedback is the main way to boost positive interactions with students so you can maintain at least a 3:1 RPI.

Qualities of Effective Feedback

In this task, we discuss six hallmarks of effective positive feedback. If you incorporate these suggestions into the positive feedback you give your students, you can significantly increase the probability that your feedback will encourage and motivate students to behave responsibly in the future.

Feedback should be accurate.

Effective positive feedback is related to a behavior or set of behaviors that did in fact occur. When an individual receives positive feedback about something they did not actually do, the feedback is meaningless. If you comment verbally or in a note to a student that his accuracy in completing math assignments is improving, be sure that the student's accuracy really is improving. If you note that a student demonstrated improved self-control by staying in her seat during an entire instructional period, be sure that the student actually did stay in her seat. Students should receive a clear, consistent message about why they are receiving your positive attention (Alberto & Troutman, 2012; O'Leary & O'Leary, 1977). Your feedback should be especially frequent and immediate if the skill is new for the student or has been difficult in the past (Dishion & Stormshak, 2007; Scheuermann & Hall, 2008).

Feedback should be specific and descriptive.

When giving positive feedback, be sure to tell students exactly what it was they did (Brophy, 1981; Martella et al., 1995). Feedback should be full of information—confirming for a student what the behavior or task was and what was important or useful about it. If you want to let a cooperative group know they have done well, describe the specific behaviors that were exhibited. When writing a note regarding a student's paper, identify the specific things the student did that contributed to the quality of the paper.

> *Feedback should be full of information—confirming for a student what the behavior or task was and what was important or useful about it.*

Specific descriptive feedback lets students know which aspects of their behavior you are commenting on. Behavior-specific praise has been consistently shown to have a positive effect on on-task student behavior in general and special education (Bain et al., 1991; Cameron & Pierce, 1994; Ferguson & Houghton, 1992; Hall et al., 1968; Houghton et al., 1990; Sutherland et al., 2000). Simply writing "excellent" or giving an A at the top of a paper, with no other notes, does not give the student any information about what aspects of the paper led to your positive reaction. Was it the effective use of figurative language? The organization? The creative use of the overall idea? The student has no idea what was particularly good about the paper, so will not necessarily use those writing skills again. The next paper the student writes may not include any of the good qualities of the first one because the student doesn't know what those qualities are.

Finally, when possible, link positive feedback to a student's goals, general class rules, or Guidelines for Success. When specific behavior is linked to goals or to classroom rules, students will begin to understand how their actions are related to more global or sophisticated expectations. Students need to know how their specific actions translate into being responsible, on task, polite, and so on.

Following are some common mistakes teachers make when providing positive feedback. All of them can be avoided by providing specific descriptions of student behavior.

The "Good Job" syndrome. It's easy for teachers to fall into a simple repetitive phrase that they use over and over and over to give positive feedback. There are two problems with this. First, most simple phrases such as "Good job," "Nice work," "Yes," and "Fantastic" provide no specific information—what exactly the student did that was useful or important. Second, when a particular phrase is overused, it becomes background noise, and students will cease to hear it. If you use such a phrase, follow it up with "because . . .," "doing . . .," or "when you . . . " For example:

- "You did a great job during that activity *because* you listened carefully to the directions."
- "Great job *doing* the steps exactly as we practiced."
- "Your paragraph was fantastic *when you* organized your thoughts on the planner first!"

Making judgments or drawing conclusions about the student. Be very cautious about reinforcing by stating or implying that a student is "good," "smart," "talented," or "brilliant," especially when praising correct answers or positive behavior. When a student answers a difficult question, it can be tempting to say something like, "Allison, you are so smart." The problem is that a statement like this not only doesn't provide specific information about what the student did, but it may imply to the student that if she had not come up with that particular answer, you might not think of her as smart.

Statements like "you are so smart" or "you've got so much talent" also refer to internal aspects of the student that are difficult to change. Because most people believe that talent and IQ are relatively stable and unchangeable aspects of themselves, if a student is praised for talent or smarts and then begins to struggle, he may believe he has maxed out his natural abilities and then give up.

Motivation

Avoid praise that focuses on internal attributes of the student like talent, smarts, or IQ. Instead, help your students understand how persistence, effort, and other changeable factors like increased studying or time on task help them reach their goals.

According to researcher Carol Dweck, there are two types of mindsets: a fixed mindset and a growth mindset. Students with a fixed mindset believe that they are born with certain basic abilities, intelligence, and talents—and that's all they have. In contrast, students with a growth mindset believe that their abilities, intelligence, and talents can be developed with time, experience, effort, and persistence (Dweck, 2008). Teachers have the power to influence and change a student's mindset. With a growth mindset, students can see the connection between effort and success and are more likely to put in the work to achieve their goals. To help foster a growth mindset among all your students, focus on praising effort, work ethic, and persistence. Instead of saying "You're so smart," you might say, "I can see that you studied hard and were prepared for that test."

Calling attention to yourself. Some teachers praise by saying, "I like the way you . . . " Even if you finish the sentence by specifically describing the student's behavior, a student may inadvertently take that initial phrase to mean that they should behave to please you. In fact, what you are working toward is for students to behave in particular ways because it will help them be successful learners. Another problem with an "I like the way you . . ." kind of phrase is that some students might get the idea that you like them when they are behaving appropriately, which in turn implies you don't like them when they are not. Keep the focus of your feedback on students and what they did, not on your likes and dislikes.

If you want to use a lead-in phrase when delivering your descriptive praise, consider using variations of "You should be proud of how well you . . ." This keeps the focus on the student, not on you. The one exception is when a student does something particularly helpful. In that circumstance, feel free to let the student know that you appreciate their help. For example, if you drop some papers and a student helps you pick them up, it is reasonable and logical to say something like, "Thank you for helping me pick those up. I appreciate having such a thoughtful student."

Feedback should be contingent.

Contingent feedback is positive feedback on a student's growth, effort, or achievement, and it can be based on academics or behavior. Contingent delivery of feedback allows the student to see a direct relationship between their behavior and your positive attention. You provide the positive attention only when the student demonstrates the target behavior that you want to increase or maintain (Alberto & Troutman, 2012; Cooper et al., 2007; O'Leary & O'Leary, 1977; Scheuermann & Hall, 2008). Contingent feedback has been successfully used to increase academic and social behaviors as well as to decrease problem behaviors (Hattie & Timperley, 2007; Simonsen et al., 2008).

If you are going to provide feedback to a student about a target behavior, be sure the behavior has some level of importance. It should not be an overly simple behavior for the person who demonstrated it. To understand why, imagine that someone you know and respect (a favorite college professor, your minister, your boss) sees you drive into a parking lot. As you step out of your car, he comes over to you and says, "Excellent left turn into this parking lot. You used your turn signals, you checked your blind spot, and you controlled your speed as you pulled into the parking space to ensure that you did not scratch the car on either side of you." This feedback may be accurate and descriptive, but it is also at best meaningless and at worst insulting to you. It implies that these driving behaviors are something special when, to an experienced driver, making a left turn into a parking lot is really no big deal. You would probably wonder why the person was being so gushy and excited about something that you have done successfully many times. It's even possible that receiving this meaningless (or insulting) feedback reduces your respect for that person.

There are three major circumstances when using contingent positive feedback may be especially beneficial.

When learning a new skill. The first is when the feedback occurs while someone is learning a new skill or behavior. If you had a good teacher when you were first learning to drive, that person may have occasionally given you positive feedback similar to the statements in the previous paragraph. The difference is that because you may have driven only once or twice before, those statements were probably not at all insulting or meaningless because they provided specific and descriptive confirmation of what you did correctly.

When increasing a behavior that requires effort. Contingent feedback is also important when you want to increase a behavior that requires effort, whether or not it is a new behavior. For example, imagine you have been making a concerted effort to be more helpful around the house because your partner has been carrying more than their fair share. If your partner expresses gratitude for the extra help and shares appreciation that the household chores are more equally divided, that positive feedback is unlikely to be meaningless or insulting to you. The behavior isn't new or particularly complex—after all, putting socks in the hamper is not exactly rocket science—but it does take effort to change a bad habit. Feedback that acknowledges effort is likely to be valued by the person receiving the feedback and can lead them to maintain or increase the frequency of the behavior in the future.

When taking pride in the behavior. Finally, positive contingent feedback is important when a person is proud of their behavior or set of behaviors or if the thing being praised was particularly difficult or complex. For example, think about a term paper you wrote—one you felt was especially well written. When you got the paper back, you probably looked at the grade and then went through the paper page by page to see if the instructor had written any comments. For most people, any positive comments received in these circumstances are not viewed as meaningless or insulting. In fact, it is quite likely that you will be pleased by the comments, particularly if the instructor described which parts of the paper were well thought out or well written.

Feedback should be age appropriate and nonembarrassing.

It is important that feedback is sincere and meaningful (O'Leary & O'Leary, 1977; Scheuermann & Hall, 2008). The feedback you give to a kindergarten student will be presented somewhat differently from the feedback you give to an eighth-grade student. For example, with primary students, you may find that they like public praise. Below are two examples of praise statements that may be very meaningful and highly reinforcing to younger students.

- *Rosa, what beautiful handwriting! You did a great job using Theo Bear's guidelines. This is your personal best.*
- *Everyone, look at Jamal. He is being polite and respectful. Jamal, you get to show the class how to be a good partner.*

> " It is important that feedback is sincere and meaningful. "

With older students, you can use more sophisticated vocabulary to describe behavior. And in terms of being contingent, with older students it is more appropriate to focus on advanced behaviors and combinations of behaviors. At the same time, be careful not to embarrass older students when you provide positive feedback. Middle school students, in particular, may feel a great deal of peer pressure to fit in and be cool. Think about the thousands of messages students get that suggest that being good is geeky. If you provide feedback in a way that embarrasses a student, it not only won't be positive or encouraging, it may actually discourage the student from behaving responsibly in the future. For example, many students avoid behaving responsibly when they are praised in a way that makes them look like a teacher's pet. If a student seems to be embarrassed when you give positive feedback, consider experimenting with one or more of the following suggestions. See Box 6.1 (pp. 278–279) if students react negatively to positive feedback.

Use a quiet voice when providing feedback to individual students. If a student feels you are putting them on public display, it may increase the possibility that they will feel embarrassed in front of their friends. Be especially careful to provide private positive feedback when the student is working on something that is difficult for the student but has already been successfully performed by peers.

Be brief. If you go on too long, accepting the praise graciously may be difficult for the student.

Be somewhat businesslike. Simply state the positive behavior(s) the student exhibited. If you sound too excited or pleased when you praise, it can make a student think, "I pleased the teacher—goody, goody."

Avoid pausing and looking at the student after you praise. A pause can imply that you expect the student to respond, and this puts a student in an awkward position—"Should I smile? Should I say thank you?" Smiling or saying "thank you" in front of peers can be socially embarrassing, especially to students who value their tough image. A tough student will often make a smart-aleck comment or engage in misbehavior to reassert their image to peers.

Feedback should be given immediately.

Immediacy is important because students need to know when they are doing something correctly. In addition, students who are starved for attention may start demanding attention through misbehavior if they get none for meeting expectations—they may feel that attention for behaving badly is better than none at all. Positive feedback is most effective when it occurs very soon after the behavior you are trying to encourage. With primary students in particular, waiting until later to give the feedback does not help to solidify the desired behaviors. By the time you praise them, the students have forgotten exactly what it was they did. Students who are starved for attention may also turn to negative behavior quickly if you do not deliver positive feedback in a timely way.

Feedback should fit your style.

There is no one right way to give positive feedback. You can incorporate these suggestions for giving effective positive feedback and still have plenty of room for your individual style. A teacher who has a businesslike personality can and should employ a more businesslike style of providing positive feedback. A teacher who tends to be excited and energetic may be more like a cheerleader when giving feedback. A soft-spoken teacher's feedback will probably be quieter than a boisterous teacher's feedback. In most cases, if you are comfortable with your style of giving feedback, your students are probably comfortable as well. Remember, it is important that praise is delivered and received sincerely (O'Leary & O'Leary, 1977), and this is difficult to do if you don't deliver praise in a manner that is comfortable for you and your students. If your students are responding to your current style with embarrassment, consider our suggestions about age-appropriate and nonembarrassing feedback.

Level of Support and Positive Feedback

Research has demonstrated that teachers of students with high rates of behavioral difficulties rarely use praise and communicate disapproval more often than approval (Henricsson & Rydell, 2004; Jenkins et al., 2015; Sutherland et al., 2000). This tendency is troubling in that the students who most desperately need lots of positive feedback and encouragement are the least likely to receive it. With the strong research linking positive feedback and teacher-student relationships with improved outcomes, it is especially important that teachers of students with many at-risk factors work to provide a well-structured and supported classroom with high rates of positive feedback for appropriate behavior (Stormont et al., 2007).

Within the CHAMPS approach, the more risk factors your class has, the more you need to manage student behavior with positive, not punitive, means. With a class that can handle lower levels of support, you may be able to get away with relatively low rates of positive feedback and still have students behave responsibly. We do not recommend this, but you can probably give relatively little positive feedback and students will be fine. If your students come from stable situations and their families give them encouragement to work hard and behave responsibly, they may work hard and behave well without getting much positive feedback from you, although they probably will not experience high levels of motivation.

BOX 6.1

When Students Respond Negatively to Positive Feedback

Some students may respond negatively to a teacher's efforts to provide positive feedback. For example, shortly after being told that he is behaving in a mature and responsible manner, a student may exhibit his worst behavior, leading a teacher to decide that the student should no longer receive positive feedback or acknowledgment. The student who misbehaves after receiving positive feedback is a relatively common phenomenon, with several possible explanations. Fortunately, there are techniques you can try to reduce the probability that a student will continue to react badly to positive feedback.

One reason a student may misbehave immediately after receiving positive feedback is that he is embarrassed by the feedback. If you suspect this is the case, try modifying your feedback as suggested earlier in this task. See whether making the feedback more private, stating it in a more businesslike or brief way, or eliminating pauses after you provide positive feedback results in the student reacting more positively. Or provide the positive feedback by writing it on a sticky note and handing it to the student without comment. Also think about whether the feedback is age appropriate, or if other students have already acquired the skill.

The other reasons a student may respond negatively tend be more complex and slightly harder to remedy. The student may have an image of himself as a tough guy and feels he has to uphold that image. The student may feel peer pressure to maintain his bad image. Or the student may have trouble handling success. When you provide feedback to someone who has one or more of these issues, the feedback won't fit her image of herself and can make her feel uncomfortable—terrified by her own success. Exhibiting misbehavior helps a student like this return to feeling like a troublemaker or a loser. She may believe she is incapable of being successful,

and she must show you that the success was an aberration. In addition, the misbehavior takes some pressure off the student—"See? You can't expect me to be successful all the time." Regardless of the reason for a student's misbehavior after receiving positive recognition, you can try experimenting with one or more of the following suggestions.

Treat the misbehavior (the downturn after receiving positive feedback) as a momentary interruption in the student's success.

You praise a second-grade student for the quality of an assignment he completed, and he then tears up the paper and throws it on the floor while you are handing papers to other students. You might say something like, "Jamie, please pick up that paper and put it in the trash before you go out to recess."

Try not to communicate anger or disappointment at this misbehavior. Keeping your emotions under wraps can be tough. When a student falls apart after you acknowledge his success, it is natural to feel angry or disappointed. You may want to say something like, "Jamie, you were doing so well and now you're throwing paper on the floor. I just don't understand, and I am very disappointed." Statements like these may feed into the student's need to feel like a tough guy or a loser, and they definitely take the pressure off the student to continue to succeed—it's clear the teacher has once again seen the worst the student has to offer.

At a neutral and reasonably private time, talk to the student about her tendency to misbehave after getting positive feedback.

See if the student can give you any insights into the reason for her negative response to your positive feedback. Ask her if she has any suggestions for ways you can give positive feedback that will reduce the chance that she will misbehave afterwards. Tell the student that part of your job is to help students know when they are doing well, so it is important for you to provide positive feedback; however, you want to do this in a way that works for the student. Try experimenting with any reasonable suggestions the student makes. If the student cannot come up with any strategies for you to try, ask her what she thinks about some of the suggestions included in this task, such as the one below about giving feedback more privately.

Find a way to give the positive feedback more privately.

The student may prefer to get a note rather than public praise. He may prefer to have you give the feedback at the end of the period rather than during it. He may prefer that you use a signal that only he knows (scratch your forehead, for example) to tell him he is behaving responsibly.

Switch from giving specific descriptive feedback to simply interacting with the student when she is behaving responsibly.

Say "hello" to the student as she enters class. If she is on task during independent work, don't specifically praise her, but do go over and ask if she has any questions or needs any help. If she has behaved responsibly throughout the morning, don't praise, but ask her if she would be willing to distribute handouts to the class. At the end of the day, tell her to have a nice evening. This contingent attention, given when she is behaving responsibly, may reinforce the appropriate behavior even though you are not providing specific descriptive positive feedback (Skinner, 1953).

If eliminating the positive feedback is successful (the student handles the attention as long as no praise is included), continue to withhold praise for a few weeks while continuing to provide attention to the student. If the student's behavior is improving, gradually introduce subtle praise. Once a day or so, make a matter-of-fact statement about something the student has done. Don't gush or be overly enthusiastic—just make a comment:

- *Thank you for getting that assignment in on time.*
- *That was a creative contribution you made to your cooperative group.*

If you see a downturn, back off and return to attention without praise. However, if the student is handling it, gradually increase the frequency of specific descriptive feedback.

However, when students need high support (that is, the class has many risk factors), frequent positive feedback is essential. The many benefits (increased academic engagement, improved social behavior, decreased problem behavior) of positive feedback, especially feedback that is specific and contingent, have been well demonstrated in the literature (Brookhart, 2017; Hattie & Timperley, 2007; Kluger & DeNisi, 1996; Sutherland et al., 2000).

Without feedback, some students will not know when they have met your expectations—when they have behaved or performed a task as you requested. Furthermore, when students try to meet your academic and behavioral expectations and do not receive any feedback—any indication that you notice their efforts—some of them will cease striving to meet the expectations (Dishion & Stormshak, 2007). "I try to do what she wants, and she never even notices. Why should I bother?" The greater the number of students with high needs, the greater the need for you to provide frequent positive feedback that follows the recommendations within this task (Barbetta et al., 2005; Beaman & Wheldall, 2000; Chalk & Bizo, 2004; Sutherland et al., 2000).

Tips for Prompting Yourself to Remember to Deliver Positive Feedback

To help you remember to provide lots of positive feedback, consider the following ways to prompt yourself throughout each class period:

Set a frequency goal.
On a sheet of paper, tally each instance of positive feedback you provide. Alternatively, use a golf counter or transfer manipulatives such as paper clips or bingo chips from one pocket to the other each time you deliver a positive feedback statement.

Set a watch or mobile device to vibrate at set intervals.
Whenever you notice the signal, deliver one positive feedback statement to the whole group and provide positive feedback to three individual students.

Create a visual reminder.
Determine a visual cue to prompt you to deliver feedback. For example, every time you look at the clock or notice a student sharpening their pencil, pause and provide some form of positive feedback to your students.

UPDATE YOUR CLASSROOM MANAGEMENT PLAN

ITEM 10: INTERACT POSITIVELY

In summary, feedback should be:

- Accurate
- Specific and descriptive
- Contingent
- Age appropriate
- Given immediately
- Given in a manner that fits your style

It may be beneficial to add these general principles for delivering positive feedback to the Interact Positively section of your Classroom Management Plan. If you identify that any of these are particularly challenging for you, make some notes in your management plan about how to deliver effective positive feedback.

TASK 4

Provide Intermittent Celebrations

Periodically reward both individual students and the whole class with a celebration that acknowledges their progress and success in meeting behavioral and academic goals.

• • • • •

Intermittent celebration means giving a reward on some, but not all, occasions when a student or group demonstrates a particularly important behavior. An occasional celebration of progress and success can be especially useful for motivating immature students, students with a long history of behavior problems, and students who need to make major behavioral changes. Those of you familiar with behavioral theory may recognize this concept as an intermittent reinforcement schedule (Skinner, 1953).

The essential idea behind intermittent celebrations is that when a student or a group of students makes a significant academic or behavioral improvement, you give them more than simple verbal praise. Provide some form of positive feedback that lets them know they have accomplished something special. Create a sense of celebration about what they accomplished. The key is to use these celebrations as sparingly as possible but as frequently as necessary (and always unpredictably!) to keep students proud and excited about their achievements.

Rewarding behavior is not bribery, although some people equate the two. Bribery is the inducement to do something illegal, unethical, or immoral. Providing intermittent rewards for students who have exhibited desired behavior more accurately reflects an attempt by school personnel to recognize and celebrate students' progress and success. To understand the power of this kind of feedback, imagine a second-grade student who has written a story that really impresses the teacher. The teacher shows the story to the principal, who in turn calls the student into the office to congratulate him. The principal also calls the student's mother to let her know what a special skill the student demonstrated. This student will remember these events for the rest of his life. (*I know, because it happened to me. —Randy Sprick*)

Use more frequent intermittent celebrations of success when students are in the early stages of learning a new skill or improving an existing skill, or whenever they are working on a behavior that is difficult for them (Scheuermann & Hall, 2008). For example, if you are trying to motivate students to increase their rates of work completion, you might occasionally (say, an average one out of three times—but be unpredictable) reward the class when 100% of the students complete their daily assignments by playing music during the next day's work period. As the level of work completion improves, you reduce how often you give a reward (for example, an average of one out of six times—remaining unpredictable). Please note that making the delivery of rewards unpredictable keeps them special and reduces the likelihood that students will become bored with them (Alberto & Troutman, 2012).

Rewards that are meaningful to your students will be most effective (Dishion & Stormshak, 2007; Scheuermann & Hall, 2008). The

Motivation

Using frequent intermittent celebrations of success is especially important to boost students' motivation to try and help them persist through challenges when they are in the early stages of learning a new skill or when they are working on a skill that is particularly difficult for them.

more academically successful or socially mature the students, the greater the chance that some sort of informational feedback will suffice. For example, most successful students in grades 4 and above appreciate a specific descriptive note indicating what they did well on a paper. On the other hand, the younger the class or the less academically successful and socially mature the students, the more likely it is that they need a more extrinsically valuable reward in order to be excited about the celebration. And, of course, with primary students and even some secondary-level students, adding some sort of a sticker or stamp can make a note even more meaningful.

Be creative about the kinds of intermittent celebrations you use in your classroom—have fun in a manner that fits your personality and your style. Some people may think that students will not respond well to intermittent reinforcement unless it has a monetary value or involves food. Not true! If you use intermittent rewards wisely and understand the concept, you can make almost anything work.

EXAMPLES, IDEAS, AND TIPS

Mike Booher shared the following examples from high school teachers. If high school students liked these rewards, elementary and middle school students will be sure to like them as well if their teachers have fun with them.

- My daughter's high school AP calculus teacher (65 years old) performs what the students call the Wally Wiggle. When the class grasps a new concept or does well on a particular concept, he does a quick John Travolta dance from *Saturday Night Fever*. The students love watching him dance. Getting him to do a Wally Wiggle is a big deal—and these are AP students!
- Gloria Bozeman from C.E. Byrd High School in Shreveport, Louisiana, says, "I blow a kiss with a smile for intermittent celebrations—the students love it!" This nonverbal reward would also work as a noncontingent reward.
- Another Shreveport high school teacher says that her students love it when she places stickers on their foreheads as an intermittent celebration.

• • • • •

The reproducible materials that come with this book include a variety of awards, certificates, notes to students, and notes to parents. Figure 6.2 shows a few examples of the awards and certificates (Reproducible 6.1A–6.1N), daily report cards (Reproducibles 6.2A–6.2B) that can be sent home, and badges and buttons (Reproducible 6.3).

You can print these reproducible forms and write in the information. Or you can type the student's information directly into the electronic file for a more formal and professional appearance. Thumbnails of all the reproducible files are provided in the downloadable materials. See CHAMPS Resources on page 3 for download details.

Downloads

Reproducibles 6.1A–6.1N and Reproducible 6.3 are provided in color. Reproducible 6.3 can be printed on Avery label #5294 and used as stickers. Stickers can be placed on student work or worn on student clothing as badges for the day.

Figure 6.2 *Examples of Reproducibles for Students*

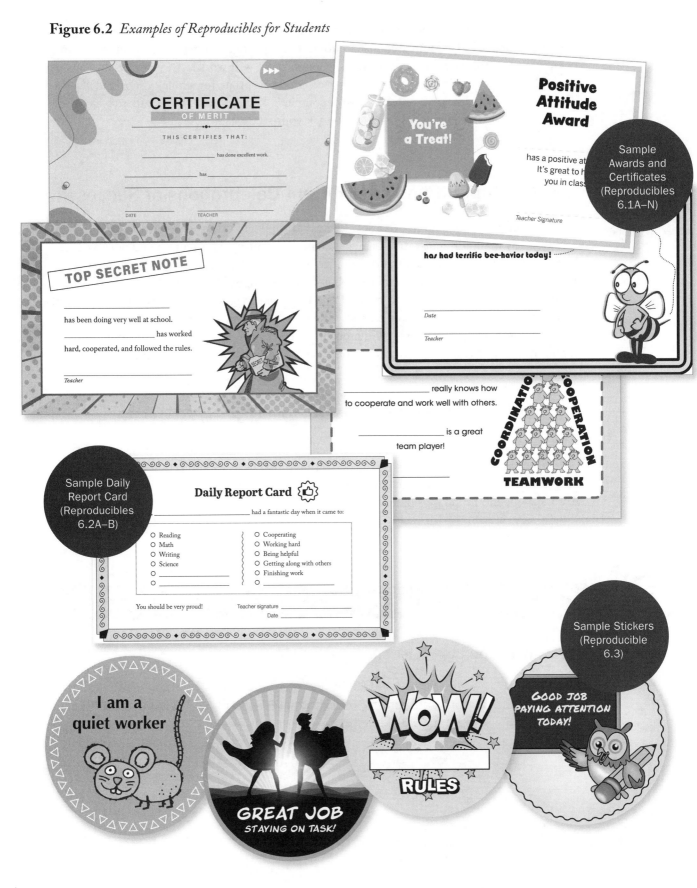

Figure 6.3 shows a variety of ideas for intermittent celebrations of success. The suggestions in the left-hand column are most appropriate for younger students. Those in the middle column are appropriate for older students, though most will work with younger students as well. The suggestions in the right-hand column are appropriate for whole groups and classes. These lists are by no means comprehensive or complete. For additional ideas, talk to colleagues, read other books, and—the best idea of all—ask your students.

Level of Support and Intermittent Celebrations of Success

For students in a classroom needing lower levels of support (a class with few risk factors), you can probably maintain motivation primarily with noncontingent attention and positive feedback. If you wish, you can use intermittent celebrations for variety, for a sense of change, or just to infuse a bit of fun into your class—but do so sparingly. With a medium-support classroom, occasional celebrations can be used as a way to keep students striving to be successful and to keep things interesting and exciting. If your students have many risk factors and need a high-support management plan, it will probably be essential for you to use intermittent rewards regularly, along with noncontingent attention and positive feedback (Barbetta et al., 2005).

> ### *Extra Motivation May Be Needed for High-Support Classes*
>
> For a class that needs high support, even this combination of procedures may not be sufficient to keep students motivated. You may also need to implement one or more of the reinforcement systems suggested in Chapter 7 in order to maintain responsible behavior and high levels of enthusiasm.

UPDATE YOUR CLASSROOM MANAGEMENT PLAN

ITEM 10: ENCOURAGEMENT PROCEDURES

List ideas for how you plan to intermittently reinforce individuals and groups of students who demonstrate growth, effort, or achievement (e.g., give at least two certificates of achievement to students every month, play a funny 2–3 minute video when the class makes improvements on a goal they are working on, etc.).

Figure 6.3 *Intermittent Celebrations of Success*

Ideas for Younger Students (Grades PreK–4)	Ideas for Older Students (Grades 3–8)	Ideas for the Group
• Let student choose a story. • Let student be first in line. • Let student use piano, computer, etc. • Let student dictate a story that someone types and prints for the student to illustrate. • Let student earn extra minutes of recess for entire class. • Let student wear a sign or badge. • Let student work near a class pet or have hamster or other caged pet on desk for the day. • Let student sit in your chair. • Let student perform for the class. • Have class give student applause. • Identify student as "Special Student of the Day." • Allow student to keep a special trophy or stuffed animal on desk for the day. • Give student a gift certificate for free ice cream or french fries. • Congratulate student in front of class. • Take student's picture and post it. • Draw stars on back of student's hand. • Invite student to eat in room with you. • Give student a paper crown to wear. • Post banner or poster with student's name and accomplishment.	• Let student teach a portion of the lesson. • Let student tell a joke to the class. • Let student supervise or tutor younger students. • Let student repair a broken desk or replace batteries in a calculator. • Let student choose a modified or independent assignment. • Let student choose a peer with whom to play a board game or computer game. • Let student leave class a few minutes early. • Give student a Certificate of Achievement. • Publicly congratulate (but be careful not to embarrass) student. • Congratulate student in front of another adult. • Give or lend student a book that was special to you at the same age. • Give student a job or responsibility. • Give student a ticket to school dance or sporting event. • Ask the principal or counselor to call student in and congratulate student on classroom success. • Send student or family a letter via the mail. • Shake student's hand and congratulate in a very adult-to-adult manner. • Give student a Free Homework Pass. • Write a positive note to student. • Call student at home to congratulate for classroom success.	• Let class listen to recorded music during an independent work period. • Let class select a theme for one day, such as Talk-Like-a-Pirate Day, Dress-up Day, Backward Day, Opposite Day, Hat Day. • Let class invite someone to come to class to see completed projects or assignments. • Let class work outside. • Let class redecorate classroom. • Have a class party. • Give everyone in class food or a beverage, such as popcorn, fruit, crackers, or juice. • Go to recess or lunch with class. • Have class applaud for themselves. • Tell a joke to class. • Give class a new freedom or more responsibility (for example, increased freedom to move about the room). • Give everyone in class a special pencil or other school supply item. • Read to class. • Give class additional recess or break time. • Invite parents to come and watch class demonstrate a particular skill or competency. • Set up a competition with another class. • Have a pizza delivered to classroom. • Teacher wears funny clothes to class. • Schedule a field trip.

TASK 5

Maintain a Positive Ratio of Interactions with Parents and Guardians

Plan to interact with families more often when students are behaving appropriately than when they are misbehaving.

• • • • •

Imagine being a parent of a student who has behavioral challenges in school. Imagine anticipating a weekly, if not daily, phone call or email from the school indicating that the student exhibited some sort of inappropriate behavior. What if these problems persisted across multiple years of the student's school experience? What if, despite your best efforts to provide corrective consequences or talk to your student about expectations at home, the student continues to struggle at school? Over time, it would be understandable if you became disheartened and perhaps fearful about regular communication from the school. Some parents might even begin to screen the school's phone calls. Some parents might become defensive and begin to blame the school for not providing the supports needed for the child to be successful. In the end, sometimes a school's attempts to maintain an active partnership with the parents by communicating concerns result in frustration, resistance, and the loss of an important educational partner.

Now imagine being a parent of a quiet, shy student who does all of his work but is somewhat average academically. For years, the parent never hears anything from the school, either positive or negative. In seventh grade, the student's English teacher becomes concerned that the student is almost painfully shy and makes a phone call to express these concerns to the parent. After years of hearing nothing from the school, this one communication carries too much weight, sending some parents into a frenzy of concern. Others may dismiss this communication because they are disconnected from the school. They may think this teacher is just overreacting or doesn't like their child.

In Chapter 2, Task 8, you learned about the importance of communicating with parents not just about expectations and concerns, but also about areas of improvement and things that students are doing well. Now that you are familiar with the concept of maintaining a 3:1 ratio of positive interactions with your students, prompt yourself to maintain a positive ratio of interactions with all parents and guardians. Keep a color-coded communication log, as described on page 111, or find another way to record your parent communications.

Periodically analyze your log to ensure you are maintaining at least a 3:1 RPI with each family. Look carefully for families who have not yet received any communication from you. If this is the case, set a goal that you will make at least three positive contacts in the next month or two. Also look carefully at those students for whom you have made more contacts about behavioral problems or other concerns. For example, if you have a student who has been frequently absent, and you know you have called home twice to talk about these concerns, check that you have also had at least six positive communications

Relational Trust

It is important to build and maintain relational trust with your students' families as well as the students themselves. Making intentional efforts to provide positive feedback, maintaining at least a 3:1 ratio, can go a long way in helping families trust that you are positively invested in their student.

about things the student is doing well in class in a similar time frame. If you are finding it difficult to maintain this positive ratio with some of your students, examine the possibilities below for ways to increase positive feedback to parents.

Ways to Provide Positive Feedback to Parents

There are many different ways you can communicate positive feedback to parents. Communicate growth and achievements of the whole class and acknowledge individual student efforts. Recognize that positive feedback about the whole class will be less impactful and personal than feedback about an individual student. However, group feedback can also contribute to your positive ratio.

Positive feedback about the whole class might include:

- Send a form letter about the class's accomplishments
- Send a group email about the class's growth or efforts
- Update newsletter, social media, or website
- Share a graph or chart representing the class's progress toward behavioral goals
- Send a picture of the whole class (with parent permissions to share student images)
- Send a video demonstrating something the class has learned or accomplished
- Ask the principal or another staff member to send a letter, email, or robocall congratulating the class
- Invite families to join a class celebration

Positive feedback about an individual student can be provided in these ways:

- Postcard or letter home
- Personal email
- Positive phone call
- Ask parent if they can come for a brief positive conference
- Send a certificate of achievement
- Share a graph or chart representing the student's progress toward behavioral goals
- Send a picture of the student's work
- Send a picture of the student engaged in something in class
- Send a video demonstrating the student's efforts or talking about something the student has accomplished
- Ask the principal or another staff member to contact the parent (e.g., give a positive behavior referral)
- Share something positive about the student in a newsletter, social media post, or website (with the student and parent's permission)

If you have to communicate with parents about concerns, and the student or group makes improvements after you talk to parents about your concerns, make every effort to provide positive communication to parents updating them and thanking them for any part they played in helping their student. For example, if you talk to a parent about a student repeatedly being

If you have students rank preferred options for reinforcement, you may find that positive communication to parents is ranked as one of the most preferred, especially by those students most at-risk. While it may seem counterintuitive, students who have a somewhat difficult relationship with their parents often want their parents to know when they are doing well in school.

late to school, and the next day the student arrives on time, send a brief thank-you email or note in the student's backpack acknowledging the student for being on time. If the student receives a referral for disruptive behavior, and the next day the student engages appropriately during class, make every effort to communicate this improvement to the parents that same day.

In summary, maintaining positive working relationships with parents and guardians requires making efforts toward positive communication, not just calling on them when there is a concern. Your efforts to provide positive feedback to family members can strengthen your partnership with families and increase family engagement with the school system. It also reinforces to the student that you are acknowledging their strengths and efforts, which can in turn lead to better behavior and improved effort.

TASK 6

Maintain Positive Communication With Colleagues

Contribute to a positive staff environment by bringing positive communication skills to your interactions with colleagues.

• • • • •

The daily behavior of staff set the tone for the overall climate of any school. This climate can be positive and inviting or negative and uninviting, or somewhere in between. When staff members make conscious efforts to construct a positive and welcoming climate through respectful interactions, efforts to build positive relationships, and delivering positive feedback, student outcomes and student connection to school improve (Klem & Connell, 2004; Thapa et al., 2013; Wang & Degol, 2016). However, it is not enough to work to consciously construct this positive climate only with students. Another important consideration that is often overlooked is how a positive staff-to-staff climate is constructed and maintained.

Some of the signs of a healthy staff environment include (Deal & Peterson, 2010; Jarzabkowski, 2002; Shah, 2012):

- Engaging in noncontingent interactions, such as greeting one another by name in the hallway and common areas and learning about other staff members' interests and families
- Avoiding the creation of cliques and gossip about other staff members
- Actively welcoming new staff members by inviting them to join in staffroom conversations and staff meeting discussions and activities
- Collaboratively problem-solving about classroom concerns

- Seeking help from colleagues when personally or professionally struggling, while maintaining a level of professionalism with colleagues
- Acknowledging colleagues' efforts, growth, and accomplishments

In this task, you will consider ways to maintain healthy and positive communication with staff colleagues. Note that the following recommendations for creating a positive staff environment apply to how you interact with all staff members, not just other teaching staff. Ask yourself if you consistently interact positively and professionally with the custodial and lunchroom staff, instructional assistants, nursing staff, counselors and social workers, and administrators.

Let Your Guidelines for Success Be Your Guide

As a general rule, your own behavior and interpersonal interactions should model those same behaviors and social-emotional skills you want your students to learn. Your Guidelines for Success can provide a powerful set of guiding principles. Periodically use your guidelines to analyze your own behavior and interactions with other staff, with students, and with families. For example, if you have a guideline to Strive for Excellence, do you do this in your own teaching practice by following a cycle of continuous improvement (as described in Chapter 5, Task 2) and by engaging in productive, collaborative problem-solving with colleagues? If you have a guideline to Always Treat Others With Respect, are your interactions with colleagues and parents you don't particularly like still respectful and pleasant? Do you avoid gossip or negative conversations about your students, families, and colleagues? If your guideline is to Include Others and Show Appreciation for Diversity, do you make frequent efforts to reach out to have positive interactions and seek ideas from classified staff members and those from a different race/ethnicity than your own? Model the same behaviors, traits, and attitudes you believe are important for your students.

Engage in Noncontingent Positive Interactions With Staff Colleagues

Make an effort to learn the names of all staff members in your school. A simple friendly greeting each time you see the custodian, counselor, or a teaching colleague is the simplest step that can be taken to begin consciously constructing a positive climate. Saying something like, "Good morning, Anabelle. I hope you had a good weekend" is not just polite and respectful, it provides a model for students about appropriate social interactions. This greeting demonstrates to students that staff members know and respect one another and work collaboratively. Even in the absence of students, simple greetings can go a long way in helping all staff feel they are an important part of a cohesive school unit.

Although finding time is always a struggle in schools, find small moments when you can engage staff colleagues and learn more about their interests and lives outside of school. This can occur in the staff room or before staff meetings, but it can also happen passing in the hallways or when you stop in the cafeteria to say hello to your students. If you realize you do not know anything about a certain staff member, set an intention to find that person several times across the next month to engage them in casual conversation.

Avoid Exclusive Interactions With Colleagues

Most staff members in a school have one or more colleagues whom they gravitate toward. You may bond with another staff member who has kids your own age, or with a staff member who shares your passionate support for a particular sports team. One staff member may share your self-professed geeky love of data collection! Another may be going through the same licensing or accreditation process as you are, and you bond over your mutual struggles to complete particular assignments.

While it is perfectly acceptable and even desirable to have friendships with other staff members. it is also very easy for some friendships to turn into clique-ish and exclusionary behavior. If you find yourself consistently gravitating toward colleagues who are close friends, prompt yourself to make intentional efforts to broaden your circle and invite others in. For example, if you always sit with the same group at a staff meeting or professional development opportunity, ask a few other colleagues to join your table. Or sit with a different group every other staff meeting. Each month, make an effort to engage with and get to know a few different colleagues who are not a part of your usual circle. While you may not become friends with every staff member, having ongoing friendly and collegial interactions will make the overall work environment more pleasant and improve staff communication.

Welcome New Staff Members

Entering into a new school can be an intimidating process as you learn to navigate a new building and set of procedures and routines. New staff members must get to know the culture of a school and determine norms for behavior and interaction. If you are already a settled member of the staff, make a conscious effort to make this process as comfortable as possible for new staff members who join your team. No new staff member should ever feel uncomfortable entering the staff room or a staff meeting because they are unsure where to sit or if they are interrupting. Invite new staff members in, as in, "Hey, do you want to join us?"

If your school does not have a formal process for orienting new staff members, determine if there are times when you can volunteer to get to know a new staff member and show them the ropes. You could take the new staff member on a tour of the school or introduce them to other staff members. Give them your phone number or email in case of any questions. Invite them to join you once or twice a month for a few minutes before or after school for an informal chat to see how things are going.

First-year teachers often go through a period of isolation, feeling overwhelmed, and sometimes even serious depression or anxiety. These feelings typically peak in the fall and early winter. Think about what you can do to help a first-year teacher through their first, most difficult year. Also recognize that many first-year teachers are hesitant to ask questions or for help because they fear it will be viewed as a sign of weakness. While you want to be careful not to be overbearing or interfere, try to be as approachable as possible and periodically reach out to see if the new teacher needs any support.

 CASE STUDY *Example From the Field*

During my first year of teaching, I really struggled in the October/November first-year slump. I felt like I wasn't doing anything right and seriously questioned leaving the profession. One staff member, Martha, randomly brought a small bouquet of flowers to me and told me how much she appreciated my being on the staff. It happened to be on a day I was launching a theme for my class on Random Acts of Kindness. My students thought I staged her entrance, but it was just a coincidence! That simple act of kindness allowed me to open up about how much I had been struggling. With support from her and others in the school, I was able to make it through those difficult months. My assistant principal, one of the school counselors, and a few veteran teachers reached out a lot through that winter to see what supports I needed. They also reassured me that I was doing great and that it would continue to get better. By March of that year, I knew that I wanted to devote the rest of my life to education. I owe a large part of that to Martha, John, Ezra, Carrie, and Sara, who made me feel welcome and helped me through those tough times.

—Jessica Sprick

Adopt a Collaborative Problem-Solving Approach With Colleagues

Collaboration among school professionals is associated with numerous positive outcomes, including staff members feeling less isolated and having improved motivation and morale, and improved educational outcomes for students (Lomos et al., 2011; Ronfeldt et al., 2015; Vangrieken et al., 2015). This collaboration can be formal, through activities such as a Professional Learning Community (PLC) or a formal problem-solving team like a Student Support Team. It can also be informal, as in a discussion between two teachers about an educational concern. Through communication with colleagues, teachers can expand their teaching or classroom management toolkit and identify ways to provide more inclusive practices and meet the needs of diverse learners. If a teacher is struggling to implement what they know are best practices, they may be able to find help from a colleague who has success.

Staff communication and collaboration is only positive and effective when staff members bring a productive mindset and communication skills to the conversation. Consider the difference between venting and problem-solving. Venting is a natural part of life when we need to find a pressure release valve about something that greatly concerns us. Classroom management issues, and especially chronic misbehavior of individual students, can cause immense frustration and angst. It is natural to want to vent about these issues to colleagues who may understand what you are going through because they see the same students.

However, it is very easy for venting to turn unproductive. Venting can embed negative perceptions about the student, family, or group of students. Consider what happens when colleagues spend too much time agreeing with each other about negative aspects of the student or situation. "She's never going to learn how to behave." "Yeah, I don't know why they don't just send her to a behavioral school. We're all in the same boat." "Yep, we all know it's going to happen eventually." These types of conversations can easily result in teachers believing that there is no hope for change or that it is not worth trying other things within their management plan to improve the situation.

Rather than venting with school colleagues, adopt a problem-solving approach. When you have a concern that you would like to talk about, seek out colleagues who have the skills to help you generate some new ideas. It may be tempting to go to the teacher who is most negative about their students so you have someone to commiserate with, but recognize that this is likely to pull you down rather than lift you up. This teacher is unlikely to offer meaningful supports and solutions. Seek out those colleagues who appear to still love teaching and are willing to continue learning and improving throughout their career.

If a colleague comes to you and is beginning to cycle into unproductive venting, we recommend saying something like, "That sounds like a really difficult situation. I can see why you are frustrated. Would you like to sit down and brainstorm some ideas? I might not have the solution, but we can see what we can come up with together." If the teacher says no, then shift the conversation to another topic. You have made it clear that you are there as a support for problem-solving. You have also signaled that you do not want to get sucked into a negative black hole of unproductive venting.

If the teacher says yes, consider whether you have time to brainstorm at that moment or if you should make an appointment for some time in the next day or two. You want to ensure that you have enough time (at least 15 minutes of uninterrupted time) to have a relaxed discussion with your colleague.

Even with family members or individuals outside of your school, try to be careful about unproductive venting. If you find yourself cycling over the same phrase or set of concerns without looking for new solutions, seek out colleagues at school to help you with problem-solving.

Evaluate the Language You Use About Students and Families

While most staff members are careful about using respectful and inclusive language in front of students and families, some may be less careful around professional colleagues. The language that staff members use about students and families helps define the culture of the school, so it is important to carefully evaluate whether your language reflects the climate and culture you want in your school.

Avoid labeling students. Labels like *behavioral kid*, *Tier 3 student*, *bully*, *victim*, or *homeless student* are dehumanizing and can lead to further marginalization of students who face challenges in school. It identifies the student as a concern or a deficit. These labels also put the student in a fixed position. A student may *have* some significant behavioral concerns, but if behavior is changeable, they are not a behavior kid, they are a *student with behavioral challenges*.

Educators who have a special-education or mental health background are familiar with this concept of *person-first* language. You identify the person as a person, rather than the label of their disability or a trait, as in "the child with a developmental disability" rather than "the developmentally disabled child." He is a child first. He has a developmental disability, but that developmental disability is not who he is. Some examples of changing from negative identification language to person-first language include:

- Tier 3 student → the student who receives Tier 3 supports
- Bully → child who engages in bullying behavior
- Victim → student who was targeted
- Homeless student → student who is unhoused

Also evaluate whether the secondary descriptor is relevant to the context of your conversation. If, for example, knowing that the student is currently without a stable home is relevant for providing an idea of the challenges that may be leading to the student's behavioral or motivation concerns, referring to the student as one who is unhoused may be appropriate. Or, if the student's identified learning disability is relevant for helping others understand the supports the student needs, you can refer to the student as having a learning disability. If these descriptors do not provide needed context, there is no reason to include them in the conversation.

In summary, periodically evaluate whether you are maintaining positive and professional communication with colleagues. In Chapter 10, we provide more information on maintaining professionalism across other aspects of your teaching practice and interactions.

Conclusion

Building positive relationships and providing adequate rates of positive feedback will often be challenging, but the rewards will be worthwhile. When you have a highly motivated class due to these efforts, you will see higher rates of on-task behavior; experience decreased disciplinary problems, fewer referrals, and less absenteeism; and find that you have more lesson time to devote to the "good stuff." Different students must be reached on different levels, but if you are diligent, you will find a way to inspire each of your students. Make sure each student is aware that you are expecting their success because you know they can succeed. Make the same effort to reach each student on more than one level by building a positive relationship with them, by acknowledging their growth and efforts, and by using positive communication with their families and your professional colleagues. Inspire your students through your positive interactions, and you may just find that they return the favor.

CHAMPS Notes

CHAPTER 7

Interact Positively—Motivational Strategies and Systems

Classwide strategies and systems can increase students' motivation to behave responsibly and strive toward goals.

Chapters 3 and 6 suggested some basic strategies for promoting student motivation—using effective instructional practices and giving students meaningful and relevant positive feedback on their behavioral and academic progress. This chapter extends those suggestions by explaining concepts about how to understand motivation, and when and how to implement a classwide system or systems to increase student motivation to behave responsibly and to strive to achieve goals such as your Guidelines for Success (see Chapter 2, Task 1). A *classwide system* is an organized and systematic set of procedures designed to have a positive impact on all the students in your class (Fairbanks et al., 2008; Hawkins, 2010). Using a classwide system to enhance motivation is appropriate for many circumstances and may even be necessary in cases such as:

- The behavior of many students in your class is challenging in many different ways—for example, not following directions, wasting class time, and showing disrespect.
- Students are for the most part responsible, but quite a few students have a problem with one specific behavior, such as work completion or talking during work periods.
- Your class behaves responsibly enough, but students have grown somewhat apathetic.

This chapter provides information on how to decide which basic kind of system (non-reward- or reward-based) to use. It also discusses how to implement, maintain, and fade a reward-based system. In addition, a menu of easy-to-implement classwide systems is provided—you can choose one or more most appropriate for your particular situation.

The tasks in this chapter include:

- Task 1: Understand Motivation
- Task 2: Use Non-Reward-Based Strategies to Increase Motivation and Responsible Behavior
- Task 3: Effectively Employ One or More Classwide Reward Systems to Increase Motivation and Responsible Behavior

TASK 1

Understand Motivation

Learn about how motivation is a product of both how much a person wants rewards that accompany success and how much they expect to be successful.

• • • • •

The word *motivate* can be defined as "to provide an incentive, to move to action, to drive forward." Understanding motivation will enhance your efforts to implement effective motivational procedures with your students—that is, to move them to do their best academically and exhibit responsible and successful behavior. When you implement effective instruction as presented in previous chapters, along with building positive relationships with students and delivering frequent positive feedback (discussed in Chapter 6), you motivate students to demonstrate their best behavior. The concepts presented here can help you maintain the motivation of students who already follow the rules and do their best on assignments, increase the motivation of students who do nothing or only enough to get by, and motivate responsibility in students who tend to misbehave.

Most Repeated Behavior Is Motivated

The first concept to understand is this: Behavior that is repeated is almost always motivated by something—behavior doesn't tend to reoccur when there is no motivation (Katzell & Thompson, 1990). This concept holds true regardless of what individuals may think or say about their own behavior. For example, Ruben may repeatedly complain about his job and even say that he is unmotivated to work, but if he goes to work regularly, he shows that he is in fact motivated in some way to work. Similarly, Tawnee may say she is motivated to paint as a hobby, but if she never gets out her paints and brushes, she is not truly motivated to paint. This does not mean that Ruben will never lose his motivation to go to work or that Tawnee will never regain her motivation to paint, but their current behavior belies their words.

Teachers must realize that the student who repeatedly misbehaves is, at the moment, more motivated to misbehave than to behave. Likewise, the student who does nothing is more motivated to do nothing than to work. This means you, as the teacher, need to increase these students' motivation to behave responsibly and complete assignments while working to decrease the factors that motivate the student to misbehave, such as gaining attention or avoiding work.

> **Motivation**
>
> *If your efforts to increase students' motivation to engage in desired behaviors are not effective, you will also need to work at decreasing their motivation to engage in the undesired behaviors.*

Foster Motivation With a Mix of Intrinsic and Extrinsic Factors

A second important concept is this: Most people are motivated to engage in a particular behavior by a complex mix of intrinsic and extrinsic factors. A person is intrinsically motivated when the pleasant consequences of a behavior are natural, or directly related to the essential nature of that behavior. Thus, a person who is intrinsically motivated to read reads because he likes to learn new things, enjoys a good story, and finds curling up with a book relaxing. The person who is intrinsically motivated to ski does so because she finds the speed exhilarating, the fresh air pleasant, and the feeling of exhaustion at the end of a challenging day gratifying.

Extrinsic motivation occurs when someone engages in a behavior because of pleasant consequences that are not directly related to the essential nature of the behavior. For example, babies tend to utter "mama" and "dada" more frequently than other sounds because of the reactions (smiles, tickles, praise) these sounds elicit from the most significant people in their lives. A college student continues to attend and write papers for a class that she does not like because she wants a certain grade and because doing well in the class will move her toward her desired goal of a degree. A six-year-old child makes his bed to get lavish praise from his mom and dad regarding how responsible, hardworking, and helpful he is.

While some people believe that the only valid kind of motivation is intrinsic motivation and that teachers should not give students praise and rewards of any kind, this book does not adhere to that principle. This mistaken belief is addressed in more detail later in this chapter, but it is enough to say that the line between intrinsic and extrinsic motivation is not as distinct as it may seem. Motivation for most behaviors is usually a mix of intrinsic and extrinsic factors. Although the person who reads a lot may do so for the intrinsic rewards of the task, he may also enjoy the compliments he gets for his wide knowledge. The frequent skier may find that in addition to the exhilaration of skiing itself, she also enjoys having others comment on her skill. The baby learning to talk makes "mama" and "dada" sounds because he enjoys making noise, not just because of the reactions of his parents. The college student who attends class and writes papers does so not only because of the grades, but also because sometimes the class is genuinely interesting.

So if motivation is usually both intrinsic and extrinsic, this means that when you have students who are unmotivated to work or to behave responsibly, you need to try to enhance both their intrinsic (make a science lesson more engaging, for example) and extrinsic (write an encouraging note on returned homework) motivation. The key implication is that in the

> **You may need to use extrinsic motivation more heavily at first when a student is learning something new or difficult.**

early stages of learning something new or when learning something difficult, some students (particularly those who have experienced frequent past failure) are not likely to be intrinsically motivated to engage in the behaviors necessary to learn (Jovanovic & Matejevik, 2014). The student who has struggled with reading for years is unlikely to have a "love" or "joy" of reading, at least at first. You may need to use extrinsic motivation more heavily at first when you are providing remedial reading services. As the student becomes more proficient, plan to fade the use of extrinsic motivators in favor of more natural consequences. As the student is able to read more proficiently, work to find reading materials they will find interesting so that they begin to experience the enjoyment of reading for reading's or learning's sake. If you do not fade the extrinsic rewards, the behavior is unlikely to be sustained because the teacher will not always be around to provide the extrinsic incentives. You can find suggestions for both intrinsic and extrinsic motivators throughout this chapter.

Consider Both Expectancy and Value

A third important concept has to do with the relationship between a person's motivation to engage in a task and that person's proficiency at that task. A skilled woodworker is more likely to find spending time in a workshop rewarding than the person who has never learned to use tools. Similarly, the skilled musician is more likely to find daily practice enjoyable than the person who has played for only 3 weeks. In addition, an individual who has experienced success at learning many different skills in the past is more likely to be motivated to try learning something new in the future than someone who has experienced repeated failure (Howell & Nolet, 2000; Jacobsen et al., 1986). The student who has had a lot of academic success is more likely to feel excited about the challenge of a tough course than the student who has failed at similar academic pursuits in the past.

This concept relates to the Expectancy times Value theory of motivation, which we discussed in Chapter 1, Task 1. This theory explains a person's motivation on any given task as a function of the formula:

$$Expectancy \times Value = Motivation$$

The first variable, *Expectancy*, is how successful a person thinks they will be at a given task. A straight-A student will have a high expectancy for success with academic tasks. A student who struggles academically year after year will have a low expectancy of success with academic tasks.

The second variable, *Value*, is how much a person wants something. Value relates to the question, "Does the student want to do the task, and why?" (Schunk et al., 2012). Value can be intrinsic—a sense of accomplishment for a job well done or the reward of learning. Value can also be extrinsic—how much someone wants a good grade, an award, money, or attention. If a student values a task, that value can be extrinsic, intrinsic, or a mix of both.

Table 7.1 *Expectancy Times Value Theory of Motivation*

Expectancy Rate	×	Value Rate	=	Motivation
10	×	10	=	100
10	×	0	=	0
0	×	10	=	0

Regardless of the type of value involved, if the expectancy of success is low, motivation will be low. Remember this table from Chapter 1—if the rate for either expectancy or value is zero, the other factor's rate won't matter—the resulting motivation rate will always be zero.

The expectancy factor is just as important as the value factor in determining motivation. Many teachers, when trying to ascertain why a student is unmotivated to behave responsibly or complete assignments, tend to ascribe the lack of motivation to issues involving the value component of the formula only:

> *Nothing seems to motivate him. He doesn't care about getting good grades. He takes no pride in his accomplishments. He doesn't care about free time or stickers or positive notes home. I tried to put him on a point contract where he could earn time to play a game with a friend or computer time, but he said he didn't really care about games or computers. I guess there's nothing else I can do.*

What these explanations fail to take into account is that if students don't *believe* that they can succeed at behaving responsibly or completing assignments (they have a low expectancy rate), their motivation will be very low or nonexistent as a result. A person may actually place a very high value on a task, but if they try it and experience failure, especially if failure is repeated, they are unlikely to be motivated to continue trying (Schunk, et al. 2012).

Another aspect of the theory is that the rates for both expectancy and value are defined by what a *student* believes, not what you, the teacher, may believe. You may know that a student is absolutely capable of being successful if he would simply try. However, if the student has a low expectation of success, his motivation will also be low. Or you may believe that students love pizza and so a pizza party will be motivating. However, if the students regularly eat pizza at home, this may be less valuable to them than something like a positive phone call or note home.

Whenever a student has no motivation or little motivation to do something (complete work, participate in class discussions, behave more responsibly), you should try to determine whether the lack of motivation stems from a lack of value (intrinsic and extrinsic), a lack of expectancy, or a lack of both. If a student has no motivation to complete academic tasks, for example, one of the first things to do is determine whether or not the student is capable of being successful at the tasks. If not, you may need to modify the tasks so that the student will be able to succeed. See Chapter 3, Tasks 3 and 4 for some recommendations for best practices for ensuring high rates of success in teacher-directed and independent work periods. In addition to these modifications or accommodations, efforts should be made within the school to determine academic interventions needed to build the student's skills across time so that eventually the student can be successful without modifications. Going into depth on modification and remediation of academic tasks is outside the scope of this book, but there are people in your district who can help with additional strategies to bring success within such a student's reach.

The Expectancy times Value theory can be a particularly useful way for teachers to think about behavior and motivation. To develop your understanding of this theory, periodically take the time to analyze activities you are motivated to do and those you are not motivated to do. When thinking about something you are highly motivated to do, identify the value you place on engaging in and completing the activity, and the expectancy of success you have before engaging in it. When you think about an activity that you are not motivated to do, see if you can determine what is low—the expectancy rate, the value rate, or both. Try to identify any activities that offer rewards you value but that you avoid doing because your expectancy of success is low. Analyzing your own motivation (or lack of motivation) will help you develop a deeper understanding of your students' motivation. As you work through subsequent chapters and analyze your students' motivations, keep the following concepts in mind:

- Your students' behavior will let you know what they are motivated and not motivated to do. You will have to work on increasing their motivation to engage in positive behavior and possibly on decreasing their motivation to engage in negative behavior.
- Use procedures that address both intrinsic and extrinsic motivation and that are naturally related to the desired outcomes when trying to increase positive student behavior (Haring et al., 1986; Scheuermann & Hall, 2008; Stokes & Baer, 1977).
- Students' motivation to engage in any behavior is related to the degree to which they value the rewards of engaging in that behavior and their expectation of succeeding at it.

Cost as an Inverse Variable

One additional factor that can reduce the value component of a student's motivation is the perceived cost of engaging in the task or expected behaviors (Wigfield & Eccles, 1992). Even if the student has a high expectancy of success and values the rewards that accompany success, if the perceived cost of engaging is high, it can negatively impact the student's motivation and behavior. Costs can be related to the amount of effort the student thinks they will have to put into the task, having to give up something in order to engage with the task, or potential psychological or emotional costs (e.g., anxiety about performing well or fearing failure). Imagine the student who does well academically and personally loves learning, but who realizes that doing well in school is not perceived by peers as "cool." Her motivation and behavior may be negatively impacted as she wrestles with the competing social cost. If a student realizes he can demonstrate academic competencies and get good grades, but it requires that he stop spending time after school doing an activity he loves so that he can study more, he may struggle to be academically motivated. When a student appears to be unmotivated, consider whether potential costs may be weighing on the student.

In summary, understanding some of the basic concepts of motivation can provide you with a roadmap for thinking about how to enhance your students' motivation to reach academic competencies, achieve long-range goals, and demonstrate responsible behaviors in your classroom. In the next two tasks, you will consider strategies that can be used to boost your students' motivation and build off the critical concepts in this task.

TASK 2

Use Non-Reward-Based Strategies to Increase Motivation and Responsible Behavior

Stimulate student interest and employ effective goal-setting strategies to encourage students to demonstrate responsible behavior.

• • • • •

You likely already use many strategies to enhance your students' motivation. Use of effective instructional techniques like those described in Chapter 3 can provide significant boosts to motivation as students understand why the work they are doing is important and experience higher rates of success and engagement. Creating a strong connection with your students, providing lots of positive feedback for efforts and growth, and using intermittent rewards to acknowledge success as described in Chapter 6 can be powerful motivating forces for many students. In this task, consider some additional ways to boost your students' motivation by stimulating student interest and using goal-setting strategies. These strategies can be applied for whole classes or targeted for specific students who struggle in your class with motivation, behavior, or academic success.

Stimulate Student Interest

One way to enhance student motivation is to seek ways to stimulate and foster student interest. Interest occurs when a student likes and demonstrates willful engagement in an activity (Schraw & Lehman, 2001). Interest relates to a person's effort, concentration, and affect when engaging in a current activity, but also to one's motivation to re-engage and strengthen one's knowledge or deepen one's experience across time (Wentzel & Miele, 2016).

Triggering situational interest. Student interest may be initially triggered by posing interesting questions designed to hook the students or create an element of surprise in class. Most people can remember a science teacher who used a riveting example of a chemical reaction (e.g., some sort of explosion!) to gain students' attention and foster their enthusiasm for a new unit. Using interesting and varied materials such as video, text, audio, art works, and source materials can trigger interest. A well-liked teacher who demonstrates enthusiasm and interest for a particular topic can also be a powerful force in stimulating students' interest. Using engaging participation strategies throughout instruction can help maintain students' attention and interest.

In each of these examples, interest is dependent on contextual factors like the teacher, text, or mode of presentation. This type of context-based interest is called *situational interest*. While situational interest is an important way to help students enjoy their classes and may increase their effort and concentration within a particular task or activity, it is also important to recognize that this kind of interest is somewhat fragile (Schraw & Lehman, 2001). If the students move to a different teacher or the teacher stops using engaging strategies, students' interest, engagement, and motivation for the topic may wane.

Cultivating personal interest. Compared to situational interest, *personal interest* is a more enduring and stable form of interest (Schiefele, 2009). It is characterized by students seeking to deepen their own understanding and re-engaging with content or a topic because they like it or wish to learn more. Think of the student who signs up for additional biology classes after getting hooked in a great introductory class, or the student who begins extending her knowledge outside of class by checking out library books and watching videos. Even the most skilled teachers are unlikely to ensure that every student develops a deep personal interest in every subject or unit. However, teachers who consistently work to generate situational interest are more likely to have students who eventually develop deeper personal interest in the content or topics.

Teachers can also tap into students' existing personal interests (not necessarily directly related to the class topic or content) to foster motivation in class. Observe and listen to your students to determine what they like and demonstrate interest in. Have conversations and use interest inventories or surveys to learn about students' interests. Connect to their personal interests by providing some activities in which students can choose a topic based on a personal interest and by building on their personal interests within existing lessons and units (Schunk et al., 2014).

Use Goal-Setting Strategies

> *Learning to set and achieve realistic goals is a lifelong skill that allows students to develop purpose and control.*

Goal setting is another powerful way to enhance motivation. Goal setting involves helping students learn to strive for positive goals they can achieve (Rader, 2005). Goals can be academic, behavioral, or a mix of both, and can include short-term and long-term goals. Goal setting encourages students to think about what they hope to accomplish now and in the future and involves identifying immediate, specific actions that can be taken to reach those goals. When students have a specific goal that is challenging but attainable, and when students are able to experience progress toward a goal, they are more likely to put in effort and persist with challenges (Wentzel & Miele, 2016). Use goal setting to enhance students' motivation and boost their sense of self-efficacy when they demonstrate positive improvements.

Goal setting is a useful strategy for motivating students to take the steps necessary to change just about any behavior. Many students with frequent behavior problems struggle with a lack of direction and sense of purpose. Although they might know that they need to "try harder" or "be more responsible," they often don't know what specific actions are needed to reach these broad and amorphous goals. Over time and with repeated struggles, they may begin to view themselves as "bad" and incapable of success. Learning to set and achieve realistic goals is a lifelong skill that allows students to develop purpose and control. For students who do the bare minimum to get by or demonstrate a sense of apathy, goal setting can help them identify longer-term goals and aspirations and connect them to necessary daily, habitual behaviors and attitudes. It can also help them take pride in day-to-day accomplishments and efforts.

The process of goal setting with students also provides a great opportunity for you to clarify behavior expectations and communicate your high and positive expectations for each student.

By acknowledging accomplishments and recognizing each student's progress toward their goals, you help students learn to take pride in working toward their goals. When errors and setbacks occur, the process of goal setting allows you to work with a student to identify challenges and needed supports, and to help the student get back on track for success. Goal setting can represent a joint agreement between a teacher and student to invest effort in achieving the goal.

Throughout goal-setting processes, consider the following recommendations (Boekaerts, 2002; Rader, 2005; Wentzel & Miele, 2016):

- Set specific goals that can be tracked or measured (e.g., remain on task 95% of the time), not general goals (e.g., do your best).
- Encourage students to participate in setting their own goals. The goal provides a point of connection between teacher and student as they agree to jointly invest effort into achieving the goal, and a mutually agreed-upon goal has a better chance of being accomplished.
- Use moderately challenging goals. Consider setting short-term goals within longer range or more challenging goals so that students experience success.
- Identify both the specific actions that students need to take to reach the goal and strategies to overcome the obstacles that might be in the way. When students are aware of specific actions and how to overcome possible obstacles, they are more likely to achieve their goals.
- Avoid performance-based goals in which ability is demonstrated in comparison to others. Focus on mastery goals, in which students focus on self-improvement and improving competence toward something that is personally challenging.
- Give feedback on students' progress throughout the goal-setting process, providing support when students are struggling to make progress and providing positive feedback and intermittent rewards when students make growth towards their goals.

Implement a Classwide Goal-Setting System

Goal-setting systems can be beneficial for any class. If a class is for the most part behaving responsibly, by definition a significant amount of intrinsic motivation is being demonstrated. When this is the case, goal-setting procedures can often extend and channel that intrinsic motivation in productive directions. If a class exhibits frequent misbehavior, there may not be sufficient intrinsic motivation among the students for goal-setting procedures to have much of an impact without additional incentives. If you choose to use goal setting, consider combining it with one or more of the reward-based systems described in the next task.

In the following systems, the first level of implementation involves the teacher setting goals for each student and sharing them with the individual students. Once students understand the concept of striving to achieve a goal and are motivated to do so, you can teach them to set their own goals and goals for the class as a whole.

You should work with a class for at least one full month before implementing any goal-setting system so that you are able to get a clear sense of students' habits and needs. Following are descriptions of three effective goal-setting procedures.

The teacher sets goals for students. To use this procedure, go through your class list student by student and think about each one—what attitude, behavior, or habit would help each individual student be more successful? Examples of goals you might identify for different students include:

- Complete more work.
- Write more neatly.
- Follow directions without arguing.
- Get along better with other students (listen to others and take turns).
- Be willing to take more risks—accept more challenges.
- Have a more positive attitude—complain less.
- Accept and learn from mistakes.
- Stay focused on work during class.
- Talk only at appropriate times.
- Demonstrate more self-control (use anger management strategies).
- Master basic multiplication and division facts.
- Become more independent and self-reliant by trying things first before asking for help.
- Interact more with other students (be less shy).
- Be willing to try new things.
- Persist when working on something challenging.
- Arrive on time.

You can use Reproducible 7.1, Goal-Setting Form, to record goals for each student in your class. Write the name of each student on the form. Then take 15 to 30 seconds per student and think about what that student most needs to learn. Think about the lasting legacy you want to leave with this student. "If I could help Tina learn only one thing, it would be . . ." Leave the Priority column blank for now. If you can't think of a goal for a particular student, skip that student and come back to them later. When you go back to that student, try to identify why you could not come up with a goal. Perhaps the student is already hard working and responsible—if this is the case, you could set the goal that the student continue to be highly motivated ("Continue to do your best and continue to be a hard-working, creative, and cooperative student"). If you do not know a student well enough to identify a goal, do not set a goal for the student, but set one for yourself to get to know that student better. This task of identifying a goal for each student (and going back to the students who require more thought) should take between 15 and 30 minutes for an entire class. For teachers who teach multiple classes, consider using this process with a different class each month.

Once you identify a goal for each student, identify the level of priority for each student. You need to determine which of the students' goals have an element of urgency to them and which represent goals that are merely desirable. You should plan on committing greater time and attention to helping the students who may not be successful in school and life if they do not achieve their goal or learn the skill or trait. If a goal is less urgent (the student will probably do fine whether or not they improve in this particular skill or trait), it will not require as

Reproducible 7.1 *Goal-Setting Form*

Goal-Setting Form		CHAMPS
Student Name	**Goal**	**Priority** 1+, 1, 2, 3
Alison, Keith	Keep up good work!	3
Bhatt, Vang	Participate more	1
Cedeno, Rosa	Manage her temper	1+
Draper, Melissa	Neatness	2
Ericson, Joe	No more late work	2
Jackson, Rain	Finishing work	1
Green, Maya	Stop bullying	1+

much time or attention from you. This step of prioritizing students' goals is essential because even the best teacher cannot do everything at once.

You will notice that the Priority column on the Goal-Setting Form calls for rating each student's goal with a priority of 1+, 1, 2, or 3. Figure 7.1 is a guide for determining which rating is most appropriate and identifying the corresponding action you should take to help the student achieve the goal.

Figure 7.1 *Guide for Setting Goal Priorities*

	Urgency for the Student	Action by the Teacher
1+	The student must immediately learn to meet this goal in order to succeed in my classroom and in the future.	I will meet with the student and family, fill out a goal contract, provide frequent positive feedback, and may set up an individual contract.
1	This student would benefit greatly from learning to meet this goal.	I will meet with the student, fill out a goal contract, and provide frequent positive feedback when the student strives to meet the goal.
2	This student might benefit from learning to meet this goal.	I will provide frequent positive feedback when the student strives to meet the goal.
3	This student is going to be fine whether they learn to meet goal or not.	I will provide occasional positive feedback when the student strives to meet the goal.

Be careful about identifying too many goals as priority 1+. For goals with priority 1+, you will arrange to have a student/family conference concerning the goal. If you identify eight or more students with priority 1+ goals, the class probably needs a reward-based motivation system (see Task 3 in this chapter).

Once you identify a goal for each student and specify priorities for all the goals, determine how to make students aware of the goals you hope they will achieve (Fuchs et al., 1985; Johnson et al., 1997). One way is to have a conference with each student to discuss the goal and provide the student with a written description of the goal. With very young students, use a pictorial description. Many readers are probably now thinking (or shouting!), "I don't have time to meet with every student! I have 30 students!" Or, if you are a secondary or specials teacher, "I have 180 students!" Prioritizing will help the potentially overwhelmed teacher through this procedure. You should definitely plan to meet with the students who have the highest priority goals, the 1+s. In fact, for students with 1+ goals, you should try to meet with the individual student and their family. For students who have priority 1 goals, you should also meet with the student, but you do not need to involve the family. You can hold off scheduling meetings for the students who have priority 2 and 3 goals. In fact, it's fine if you meet with these students only if you can find the time.

When you meet with a student or the student and family, complete a Goal Contract (see Reproducible 7.2). To fill out a Goal Contract, first identify the overall goal—it will probably be what you wrote for the student on the Goal-Setting Form. However, if your goal for the student is framed in terms of something the student should *not* do, transform the goal into a positive statement of what the student *should* do (for example, "stop being disruptive" becomes "participate responsibly in lessons and study times"). Then list *three specific ways* the student can demonstrate that they are striving to achieve the goal. It is very important to tell the student that he can exhibit tangible, objective behaviors to show you he is working toward his goal. You should also have a rationale in mind that you can present to the student about how striving to achieve this goal will help him. Also include tangible ways that you can help the student reach the goal, such as by providing positive feedback, changing a structural element like the student's seating arrangement, and so on. You might seek the student's input to see if there are things the student needs from you to help him meet the goal. Work with the student to identify any anticipated barriers or obstacles that you and the student will need to put strategies in place to overcome. Express your enthusiasm and belief that the student can accomplish the goal. Convey your commitment to helping the student in any way necessary to reach the goal. Communicate all of this information to the student during your conference.

Reproducible 7.2 *Goal Contract*

Goal Contract	CHAMPS

STUDENT __Caden Martinez__   DATE ___9/30___
TEACHER ___Mr. Williams___   GRADE/CLASS ___7___

My personal goal is ___to earn a 2.0 GPA for the next grading period and to get along with others—including the teachers.___

I can show that I am working on this goal by ___1) Turning in all homework, 2) Studying for tests, 3) Not arguing with teachers, 4) Being friendly and acknowledging others.___

Student signature ___Caden Martinez___

....

I can help you reach this goal by ___1) Getting you into the Homework Club, 2) Helping you set up a system for tracking your assignments and grades, 3) Helping you set up a system for studying for tests, 4) Setting up some sessions to practice dealing with anger-provoking situations.___

Teacher/Mentor signature ___Mr. Williams___

Another way you can share your goals with students is by having mini-conferences—take time during independent work periods to briefly inform individual students of the goals you hope to see them strive to achieve. You might use mini-conferences with students who have priority 2 and 3 goals.

Finally, you can communicate your goals for students somewhat indirectly by looking for and capitalizing on opportunities to give each student positive feedback related to the behavior or trait that you hope to help them achieve. This method of communication works even if you have not yet had a goal conference or a mini-conference with the student. When a student exhibits behavior that reflects the identified goal, comment on it.

EXAMPLES, IDEAS, AND TIPS

Your goal for a student is for him to "talk only at appropriate times," and he participates appropriately while a guest speaker is in the room. You might say, "Jerron, while our guest artist was here this morning, I noticed that you gave him your full attention. You talked only during the times that he wanted you to discuss things at your table and when you raised your hand to be recognized. That demonstrated a great deal of respect for the speaker."

Whether or not you've had a goal discussion or completed a Goal Contract with a student, feedback of this nature will help the student realize that this is a behavior that you are monitoring and that you feel is important for them to learn. Providing this type of contingent, descriptive, and immediate positive feedback is also extremely valuable after you have conducted a goal conference with a student. Periodically look at the Goal-Setting Form that you completed for the class so you can remember what behaviors to acknowledge for each student.

Elementary teachers who teach one class should go through this entire goal-setting process once a month. Middle school teachers and elementary specials teachers should also plan to use the process once a month, but for a different class each month so that you end up thinking about goals for each of your classes once or twice a year. Remember, whether you are a middle school or elementary teacher, wait to use goal setting until you have worked with your students for at least a month. As you repeat the goal-setting process, your goal for a particular student may vary from time to time. If a student has not made progress on the goal or has made some progress but still has more to go, maintain the same goal. If the student has met your goal, consider setting a new goal. Each time you go through the process, you should restate the priorities and conduct conferences with students who have priority 1+ and 1 goals and mini-conferences when possible with students who have priority 2 and 3 goals. For all students, give positive feedback when you see them taking steps toward their goals.

RESOURCE: INDIVIDUALIZED GOAL SETTING

Intervention E: Goal Setting in *Early -Stage Interventions: Behavior Strategies for Every Teacher* (Sprick et al., 2020) provides more guidance on identifying individualized short- and long-term goals with students, as well as how to track progress and evaluate efforts in working toward these goals. Intervention E is particularly relevant for students who begin to show signs of chronic behavior problems. By teaching goal-setting strategies as skills, you not only help students change their current behavior patterns, but also set them on a path for developing more agency over their future aspirations and successes.

The teacher guides students in setting goals. Once students understand the concept of striving to achieve a goal, you can conduct one or more lessons to teach them how to set their own goals. If students are involved in their own goal setting as opposed to the teacher setting goals for them, they may be more likely to work harder (Boekaerts, 2002). Motivation also increases when students genuinely feel that they control what occurs in their lives (Decintio & Gee, 1999). Teaching students to set and monitor their own goals also teaches them a powerful lifelong skill that can help them develop purpose and control.

Begin by discussing the importance of goal setting. Remind students that they have been working hard to achieve the goals that you set for them. Then explain that learning to set goals and striving to meet them is a beneficial skill that can help them succeed in school, in work situations, and in life.

Have students identify and discuss some short-term goals they want to achieve for themselves. Short-term goals help the student establish a target to achieve in the near future, generally between one month and a year. Encourage students to focus on school-based goals—however, let them know that setting goals in areas outside of

Motivation

Foster student motivation by teaching them to set and monitor their own goals. Motivation is enhanced when students feel a sense of control over their lives, and goal setting is also a beneficial lifelong skill.

school, such as sports and hobbies, can also be very useful. You may want to put some sample goals on the board to provide ideas for students who have trouble coming up with goals of their own. Help students focus on specific goals that are relevant to the student's success.

Relational Trust

Model completing a Goal Contract for yourself and ask your students to help you be accountable for working to achieve your goal. Relational trust is built when students see that you are working along with them to reach high expectations for success.

Pass out copies of the Goal Contract (Reproducible 7.2). Have each student write an overall goal and three ways to demonstrate that they are trying to achieve the goal. If you complete a contract for yourself as students do the activity, you validate them for their efforts. Once students complete their Goal Contracts, tell them to keep a copy of their goal on their desk or on the front cover of a notebook so they will be reminded frequently of the goals they are striving to achieve.

For a couple of days after this session, try to meet with each student to discuss their Goal Contract. If a student has set an unreachable goal, help her to make the goal more realistic. Record each student's goal on a blank version of the Goal-Setting Form (Reproducible 7.1) so that you have a summary of all the students' goals on one or two pages. Once you sign all the contracts and summarize all of the students' goals, watch for any opportunity to give students positive feedback on their efforts to achieve their goals (as you did when you set the goals for students). If this process proves useful—behavior is improving, motivation is increasing—repeat the activity once each month.

The teacher guides students in setting a classwide goal. Consider guiding your students in the process of setting a classwide goal. The goal might involve reducing a classwide problem (eliminate teasing), increasing a positive behavior (improve classroom climate through increased positive interactions), or participating in a service project (work regularly in the community or school garden). Put a reasonable time limit on achieving the goal so that you and the class will have a specific date to evaluate their success.

You may find it is beneficial to actively count and chart progress toward the classwide goal. For example, if students are working to reduce teasing, you can tally each incidence of teasing that occurs in the classroom. At the end of the period or day, tell students how many incidents of teasing were observed and record the number on a chart or graph. Compare from day to day and discuss what will be needed for students to meet the goal identified by the class. Even without rewards, this process of graphing progress in a visual way can motivate the class to reach its goals.

Establishing and actively working toward a common goal as a group is a powerful way to increase students' sense of purpose and belonging (Rader, 2005). It can build classroom pride and create a powerful sense of community.

Help Students Engage in One or More Long-Range Goal-Setting Activities

Discussing long-range goals can help spur students' thinking about aspirations and the future. This is especially important for older students who struggle to remain motivated in middle school. Some students struggle to envision a positive future, while others may be unmotivated to demonstrate the effort needed to reach their long-range goals because they do not see how their short-term efforts relate to their longer term aspirations.

With planning for long-range goals, have students start at a desired end result or outcome and then have them work backwards to think about what they need to develop or accomplish in order to reach their desired result. For example, if students are 12 or 13, you might ask them to consider where they would like to be in 10 or 15 years. Do they want to be self-sufficient and living on their own? What kind of job would they like to be working, and/or do they envision being in college? What kind of transportation do they want to be using—a personal vehicle, public transportation, bike? What do they want their personal life to be like in terms of family, friends, and how they spend their free time? Students could write answers to these questions, develop a picture map with drawings or cutouts from magazines, or record a video discussing their envisioned future.

If a student has ideas about the type of lifestyle they would like in the future, determine whether the student has any idea of the cost and effort it will take to attain the vision. If not, provide some assignments for the student to collect information. For example, if a student identifies wanting to live on their own and drive their own car, but is unable to identify what they would like to do to generate income, provide examples of possible careers that would allow the student to accomplish the other goals.

If a student's long-range goals seem unrealistic, acknowledge their goals while encouraging the student to include other possibilities. For example, if the student identifies a lavish lifestyle and says they will be a star athlete or rock star and make millions of dollars, prompt them to think about what doors they could keep open if they were injured or something unexpected happened—what other jobs would allow them to live the lifestyle they identified?

If a student says they have no aspirations or can't identify what they want in the future, learn about the student's interests and try to help the student explore job and lifestyle options that capitalize on those interests. For example, ask the student to describe the kinds of people they wish to spend time with as an adult. If the student doesn't know where to begin, generate a list of options: "Let's make a list of the characteristics of people we know. Then you can look at that list and identify words that describe the kind of people you would like to spend time with when you are older."

Once students identify responses to these questions, have them work backwards to think about what they need to do in the shorter term to reach this vision of success. Ask questions like: "To get to the job you identified, what kind of education will you need? Do you need a high school or college diploma? Will you need to do an apprenticeship or volunteer work to gain experience?" Keep working backwards and asking guiding questions until you reach present-day circumstances. Have students set one or more short-term goals needed for them to begin working toward their long-term vision.

UPDATE YOUR CLASSROOM MANAGEMENT PLAN

ITEM 10: ENCOURAGEMENT PROCEDURES

List ways you plan to motivate your students using non-reward-based methods. Describe specific ways you plan to stimulate interest and/or use goal-setting strategies with your students.

Effectively Employ One or More Classwide Reward Systems to Increase Motivation and Responsible Behavior

Classwide systems can increase student motivation to behave responsibly and strive toward goals.

• • • • •

Classwide motivation systems generally fall into one of two categories:

- Non-reward-based systems potentially improve students' desire to behave responsibly and achieve goals by enhancing their intrinsic motivation.
- Reward-based systems use extrinsic reinforcers to increase student motivation to behave responsibly and strive for goals.

If your students are for the most part behaving responsibly, completing most of their work, and exhibiting cooperation, they do not need extrinsic rewards to be motivated. In a class that is functioning this well, students demonstrate daily that they are intrinsically motivated to meet classroom expectations. With such a class, a non-reward-based system, such as one of the goal-setting systems described in the last task, is perfectly reasonable. In fact, goal setting can be a very effective strategy for not only maintaining but also enhancing already acceptable levels of motivation (Locke & Latham, 2006; Tubbs, 1986). Goal-setting procedures are designed to give students something to strive for so they do not fall into patterns of going through the motions in the classroom.

If you do not need a reward-based system for your students because the class is already behaving responsibly, you may decide to skip the remainder of this task for now. Return to it if your student population changes and your students require an extra boost of support and motivation, or review this chapter if you find that your students are not responding as well as you would like to goal-setting procedures.

On the other hand, if you are frustrated by the amount of student misbehavior or the lack of student productivity in your class, your students are demonstrating that they are not intrinsically motivated to behave responsibly. Implementing a system in which students can earn extrinsic rewards for responsible behavior may be just what is needed to encourage them (Chaffee et al., 2017; Maggin et al., 2017; Stage & Quiroz, 1997). A reward-based system may provide the incentive needed to light a fire under students and get them moving in a more positive and productive direction.

If your class is made up of predominantly highly responsible students, but just one or two students exhibit behavioral or motivational challenges, it is probably best to use goal-setting procedures as your whole-class approach to improving motivation and set up individualized reward systems with those challenging students. For example, you could set up individual behavioral contracts with each student. However, if you have three or more students with behavioral challenges, plan to set up a reward-based classwide system. Managing too many individualized systems is much more work than managing one classwide system. The classwide system may improve the behavior of all but one student, and then you could work on an individualized intervention with that student.

Note About Rewards and Reinforcers

While *reward* and *reinforcer* are often used interchangeably, there is an important distinction between the two terms.

A *reinforcer* is defined by its effects on future behavior. A reinforcer is something that, when presented after a behavior, increases the likelihood that behavior will occur again in the future in the given situation. In contrast, a *reward* is not defined by its effects on behavior. Rewards are generally assumed to be positive, but they may not actually increase future behavior (Alberto & Troutman, 2012; Skinner, 1953).

We use the term *reward* throughout this book to refer to tangible items, special privileges, access to preferred activities, and points or tokens that are delivered after desired behavior occurs. Praise and specific feedback are examples of social rewards. These tangible and social rewards are only *hypothesized* reinforcers until they effectively increase the likelihood of future desired behavior. If behavior doesn't improve, the rewards you selected may not be reinforcing, so you may need to revisit and adjust your list of possible rewards.

If you have any doubts about whether your class would benefit from a reward-based system, use one or more of the monitoring procedures in Chapter 10 (such as the CHAMPS Versus Daily Reality Rating Scale or the Misbehavior Recording Sheet) to help you confirm the need for a motivational system based on extrinsic rewards. If you have tried to manipulate other elements of STOIC and have been unsuccessful in prompting sufficient levels of appropriate behavior, a reward-based system may be beneficial to jump start students' motivation and success in meeting behavioral goals. Even if you determine that your class needs or would benefit from a reward-based motivation system, you may find yourself reluctant to implement a system that depends on extrinsic rewards. Some people have concerns about the use of rewards and reward-based systems to improve student behavior. Box 7.1 (p. 312) provides answers to some of the most commonly raised questions about using rewards. The information provided should help you understand how a reward-based system (or systems) can be incorporated usefully and effectively into your Classroom Management Plan.

The remainder of this task walks you through the processing of designing and implementing a classwide motivation system and aligns with the three steps presented in Develop and/or Revise Your Classwide Motivation System (Reproducible 7.3, see sample on pp. 313–314):

Step 1: Identify problems, goals, level of support needed, and the type of system you will use.

Step 2: Select a system (one or more) and prepare to implement it—choosing, designing, and implementing a reward-based system.

Step 3: Determine how to maintain, modify, and fade a reward-based system.

BOX 7.1 | # Common Concerns About Using Rewards

Despite their potential benefits for students, reward-based systems can raise several common and legitimate concerns from educators that need to be addressed.

Shouldn't students behave appropriately without rewards? Students should behave appropriately, and they should be motivated to be successful. However, some students need to be taught to value appropriate behavior. When misbehavior becomes a problem across the classroom, teachers are left with two options: (a) let students continue to engage in inappropriate behavior, or (b) implement a classwide system to motivate students to change the pattern of behavior as quickly as possible. Classwide systems that use rewards as extrinsic motivators allow students to earn particular prizes, praise, and so on for demonstrating appropriate behavior. While some people believe the only valid kind of motivation is intrinsic—students should want to learn simply for the value of knowledge—for students who have experienced little academic success or have behavior problems, you may initially need to use tangible rewards to spark students' motivation. The reality is that longer misbehavior goes unchanged, the more deeply ingrained it becomes and the more likely it is to worsen.

Won't students stop working as soon as the rewards are removed? If you overuse reward systems, students may learn to work only for tangible rewards and fail to learn the value of working hard, getting along with others, being cooperative, taking pride in a job well done, and other intrinsic rewards in school and life. However, with carefully planned steps, you can fade a structured reward system that assists in the initial process of making a behavior change. If a system is removed suddenly, the student may stop working. A carefully designed system is a long, involved process that gradually teaches the student to value success even once the reward is removed.

Why should students who misbehave get extra rewards or privileges? Students probably shouldn't get extra rewards and privileges as a result of misbehavior. In an ideal world, everything would be equal and fair. However, students do not enter school as equals. Therefore, *equal* treatment cannot mean the *same* treatment when working with students of different backgrounds and abilities. Some students bring background knowledge and values that support cooperation, responsibility, and hard work. These students have already learned to value the attitudes and behaviors that bring success in a school setting. Reinforcement for these students is inherent in the natural school environment and

in their homes without external rewards. Students who bring challenging behavior to the classroom environment have more to learn. They may be discouraged by or suspicious of efforts to help them change. These students may need additional incentives to learn how to behave responsibly at school.

Shouldn't we avoid reinforcing students and focus more on encouraging them and facilitating learning? In education, we often get wrapped up in words. The distinction between *reinforcement* and *encouragement* is largely semantic. If a student is working hard and the teacher stops to engage in a friendly interaction, one person might say, "The teacher is facilitating learning by encouraging the student's interest." Another person might say, "The teacher's attention is rewarding the on-task behavior." In both cases, the teacher does the same thing; only the words describing the situation are different. Regardless of semantics, reward procedures can be either implemented carefully to support and encourage students or implemented poorly so students do not learn to value effort and accomplishment.

Will students become the kind of people who always ask, "What will you give me if I do that?" If reward systems are not handled carefully, this potential drawback may become a reality. All adults involved in this intervention must carefully focus on the accomplishments that lead to the reward versus the reward itself. If adults systematically focus interactions on student accomplishments, eventually students develop a sense of satisfaction that takes the place of the actual reward. For example:

Ms. Mayberry: *Class, you've earned 5 minutes of free time at the end of class today. Can someone tell me what you did to earn it?*

Student: *We turned in our homework.*

Ms. Mayberry: *Yes, 95% of the class turned in completed homework assignments this week. You must be exceptionally proud of yourself. You are becoming stronger, more responsible students with this kind of practice.*

If possible, students should be encouraged to make improvements through positive interactions and strategies that honor hard work, cooperation, kindness, and responsibility. However, there are times when some students won't understand or be motivated by less structured interventions. A high-powered classwide system may be necessary to get these students moving in the right direction.

Reproducible 7.3 *Develop and/or Revise Your Classwide Motivation System Example*

Develop and/or Revise Your Classroom Motivation System (p. 1 of 2)

CHAMPS

TEACHER *Ms. Garcia*   GRADE *5*   ROOM *31*   SCHOOL YEAR _____

STEP 1   *Preparation*

1. What problem(s) are you trying to solve?

   Call-outs, interruptions during instruction (jokes, burping noises), disrespectful comments, horseplay, poor-quality work, missing assignments, foul language

2. Describe the goal(s) of your system; limit your objective to one major category of behavior (e.g., reduce disruptions and name-calling, increase work completion, or decrease apathy—increase motivation).

   Decrease disruptions: call-outs, interruptions during instruction, disrespectful comments, horseplay, foul language

3. At the present time, the level of support my students need is: [X] High   [ ] Medium   [ ] Low

4. Decide whether you need a non-reward-based or a reward-based system. (See pp. 310–311 to help with this decision.)   [ ] Non-reward-based   [X] Reward-based

---

STEP 2   *Select a system (one or more) and prepare to implement it*

1. Read through the different systems to find one that is appropriate for the level of structure your class currently needs. The system I will implement (one from the *CHAMPS* book or something else) is:

   Whole-Class Points (Time Interval)

2. Describe the system.

   For each 20 minutes I will set the timer. When the timer goes off, I will award the class 0 to 3 points.

   > *3 = no disruptions/everyone worked hard*
   > *2 = no disruptions*
   > *1 = only a few disruptions*
   > *0 = too many disruptions*

3. Identify materials needed to monitor behavior and record progress (e.g., tickets, charts, Mystery Behavior Envelopes).

   I will use the CHAMPing the Way to Success charts. For the first chart, I will use the 20-point CHAMPS chart. I will also need a timer to remind me of the 20-minute intervals.

Continued on next page ⟶

REPRODUCIBLE 7.3

Reproducible 7.3 continued *Develop and/or Revise Your Classwide Motivation System Example*

Develop and/or Revise Your Classroom Motivation System (p. 2 of 2)

CHAMPS

Step 2 continued

4. Identify the rewards to be used. If you will involve the students in generating the list of rewards, describe how.

   Initially the reward will be 10 minutes for the whole class to play a game. I know they like this. After the class has earned this reward 2 or 3 times, I will conduct a brainstorming session to get additional ideas for rewards and activities to work toward.

5. Identify when and how you will explain the system to the students and the date for implementation.

   During Friday morning welcome/announcement, I will explain the chart, the reward, the timer, and the 0–3 points per interval. I will do practice runs during the day from 10:00 to 10:30 and at 2:00 to 2:30 (times the class typically does well). If they do well, I will put points on the chart. We will start the full system on Monday.

STEP 3   *For reward-based systems, identify how you will maintain, modify, or fade the system*

1. How will you keep your energy and excitement about the system at a high level?

   After each interval in which they do well (2 or 3 points), I will express how proud they should be and emphasize teamwork. If they do poorly (0 or 1 point), I will keep the focus on what they can do during the next interval to get to 3. I will stay focused on even small improvements.

2. How will you make the system more challenging as the class reaches a high level of consistent success?

   I will continue at the 20-point level, using different themed charts until the class is getting 2 or 3 points at each interval. I will let the class know that the next chart will have 25 points, and the next will have 30 points. Then I will change the time interval to 30 minutes, but go back to the 20-point chart. Then I will make the interval 60 minutes and use a 15-point chart, eventually getting to half-day intervals and a 20-point chart.

3. Once the system is fairly lean, how will you move to increasingly intermittent rewards?

   While still using the 20-point chart and a half-day interval, I will intermittently give other rewards and activities. After demonstrating this intermittent concept, I will encourage the class to realize that they do not need the time interval system any longer.

4. When appropriate, fade the system by having a discussion with students about abandoning the system and/or switching to goal-setting systems.

   After using the intermittent system for several weeks, and if positive behavior continues and students seem proud of their success, I will implement individual Goal Contracts. We will then have discussions about whether or not the class still needs the reinforcement system.

REPRODUCIBLE 7.3

Following this procedural information are descriptions of different types of classwide motivation systems—what the system is designed to accomplish, the level of classroom support (high or medium) for which it is most appropriate, and specifics on how to use it. The menu of classwide systems begins on page 323.

 ## CASE STUDY

Mr. Harn's third-grade class was bordering on out of control. Before the year began, he thought a medium level of support would be appropriate for his students. By the third week of school, it was clear that the initial procedures he had set up were not sufficient. He began using the daily Misbehavior Recording Sheet (see Chapter 10, Task 1). From his data he determined that he needed to revise his level of classroom support to high and implement a classwide motivation system appropriate for a high-support class to further encourage students to behave responsibly. After reading the descriptions of the various systems in the menu, he decided that the Whole-Class Points (Time Interval) system would work well for his students and fit his own personal style.

With this system, Mr. Harn awarded one point to the class for each 15-minute period during which all the students behaved appropriately. For each point the class earned, Mr. Harn filled in a circle on the whole-class point chart. When the class earned ten points (10 circles were filled in), the students got 5 minutes of extra recess and Mr. Harn posted a new coy of the point chart with all the circles empty. Once the system was implemented, Mr. Harn noticed significant improvement in the students' behavior. Periodically he would change the theme of the chart—going from a penguin theme to a race car theme to a speedboat theme. Over time, he also gradually added more spaces on the chart before students got their reward and increased the time students were required to behave appropriately. After the students had earned a number of rewards and were demonstrating consistent improvements in their behavior, Mr. Harn held a class meeting and together he and the class decided to switch to an intermittent type of system using Classroom Lottery Tickets.

STEP 1 — *Identify problems, goals, and level of support needed.*

Begin by answering the following questions about the goals of your classwide motivational system. These considerations correspond with Step 1 of Reproducible 7.3, Develop and/or Revise Your Classwide Motivation System.

What problems are you trying to solve? Begin by thinking about behavioral and motivation concerns. Brainstorm a list of your concerns. Does it seem that a significant number of students do just enough to get by? What misbehaviors occur fairly frequently? These are the types of concerns you should list here. If you are addressing this question before the year begins but have taught in this school in the past, use the last couple of years as a guide to the types of problems you may encounter. If you have not taught in this school before, talk to your new colleagues who have taught this population of students. The issues you list will guide you toward the objectives of your system.

What are the goal(s) of your system? Based on your brainstormed list of concerns, decide what you want to achieve by implementing a classwide system. If you have many problems listed, you may need to limit the focus of the system. For example, you may prioritize and say that initially the system will focus on reducing disruptions (callouts, disrespect, name-calling) and later, after disruptions are under control, you will modify the system or build a new system that focuses on increasing work completion and quality of written work.

What level of support do your students require? Think about your class's current need for support. If you are thinking about this task before the year begins, base this decision on the Classroom Support Needs Assessment that you completed in Chapter 1 (Reproducible 1.3). If you are thinking about your class's support needs during the year, base this decision on your subjective perception of the behavior and motivation of the class. Also consider any objective data you have, such as one or more of the tools in Chapter 10, Task 1. If there are periodic problems or minor but consistently annoying issues, a medium-support system is probably fine. If many students misbehave on a very frequent basis, you probably need a high-support plan.

STEP 2 — *Select a classwide system and prepare to implement it.*

To select a system, you will read through all of the systems described for the level of support your class needs to identify the option that will best accomplish your goals, fit your style, and meet the needs of your students. However, before you review the menu of suggested systems, read through the following general information on using a reward-based system. It's important to carefully choose, implement, maintain, and eventually fade the system or systems you use. In fact, the effectiveness of a reward-based system, like all other aspects of your management plan, is dependent on how well you facilitate it.

Following are tips on how you can effectively choose and implement a reward-based system, keep it running well, and eventually fade it altogether.

Consider whether to use a regular or intermittent system. As you choose your system, keep in mind that some systems are regular and highly systematic in terms of how students earn the rewards ("If you do _____, then you earn _____"), while others give students rewards intermittently and unpredictably. Intermittent systems are not so regular ("Sometimes when you do _____, you might earn _____").

Regular systems tend to be more appropriate when you are trying to motivate a class that needs high support or when students are in the early stages of trying to learn or do something highly difficult or complex for them. These systems can also be harder to maintain and fade than intermittent or unpredictable systems.

For medium-support classes, or once students have begun demonstrating some success with something difficult or complex, intermittent reward systems are often sufficient. From a technical standpoint, intermittent systems are actually the most powerful (Cooper et al., 2007; Skinner, 1953). All gambling is based on intermittent reward schedules. People are motivated to keep putting money in the slot machine because they never know when they are going to win.

However, in the initial stages of teaching and motivating a high-support class, you may need a systematic and regular system (Alberto & Troutman, 2012). The regular system is important for teaching and getting students to buy in because it encourages students to practice the skill regularly and allows them to receive a high rate of reinforcement (rewards, positive feedback). Once students are consistently successful with a regular system, one step on the way to fading to intrinsic rewards is to switch to an intermittent system.

Make sure the system is appropriate for and interesting to students. In addition to deciding whether students need a regular or an intermittent reward-based system, be sure the system is one that the students find compelling. For example, the Whole-Class Points (Time Interval) system described in the menu can be made visually stimulating and exciting to primary students (see the examples on p. 325), but it is probably too babyish for most middle school classes. Conversely, if you try to use the Behavioral Grading system with a first- or second-grade class, many of the students probably won't understand how the system works because grading is a somewhat abstract concept to them. The goal is to design a system that students are drawn to and find exciting.

Make sure the rewards students will be working toward are highly motivating. If students don't care about or don't want to earn the reward they are working toward, your system is not likely to be effective. Initially, you should use high-power rewards—rewards that students want so badly that they are motivated to try to meet your expectations to earn it. Therefore, you need to identify a range of rewards that the whole class will want to earn. Examples include free time, extra recess, getting out of class 2 minutes early, and a reduction in the number of problems or questions assigned for homework. You should also be prepared to vary the rewards so that students don't become bored or satiated with one reward (Hall & Hall, 1980).

It is usually helpful to work with students to decide on the rewards for the class (McCurdy et al., 2020; Skinner et al., 2009). For example, you might conduct a brainstorming session and ask students to identify rewards that they as a class can get or do when all students demonstrate responsible behavior. During a brainstorming session, write down any suggestion that any student makes, unless it is obscene or disrespectful. Continue the activity for at least 5 to 10 minutes so that various ideas are generated. When the brainstorming session is complete, go back and eliminate any items that are too expensive or otherwise unrealistic—it is important that you select rewards that you can and will use (Hall & Hall, 1980). Some of the items on your final list will probably have more value than others. For example, some may cost money while others do not, some may cut into more class time than others, and some may require more time from school personnel than others. When you first implement your system, do not hesitate to start with rewards that have a fairly high value. The value of the reward should correlate with the effort involved to receive it (Skinner et al., 2009). Bigger rewards should be used for behaviors that students are least motivated (possibly because of difficulty) to display. The system should be exciting enough that most of the students feel it is in their best interest to improve their behavior. As students experience success, you will likely be able to use smaller rewards, or a system where earning the reward is less certain (intermittent), as students will begin shifting toward more intrinsically motivated behavior.

Set up the system so that student success is likely. Students must believe that they have a high probability of achieving success. If they think their chances of earning a reward are low, they are not likely to change their behavior—even if they really want the reward. (Think about the concept of Expectancy times Value = Motivation discussed in Task 1 of this chapter.)

One of the most critical considerations for any motivational system (and especially those that use rewards) is that students have the ability to exhibit expected behavior and that they clearly understand your expectations. When in doubt, pair the motivational system with increased structure and explicit teaching of expectations to ensure that students can in fact demonstrate the behaviors identified as goals of the system.

Another way to increase the probability of student success is to ensure that any time limits involved are short enough that students can meet your criteria (Alberto & Troutman, 2012;

> **One of the most critical considerations for any motivational system is that students have the ability to exhibit expected behavior and that they clearly understand your expectations.**

Walker et al., 1998). For example, a fifth-grade teacher implements a system in which the class earns one point for each day the entire class behaves responsibly. Students may reasonably believe that they will never earn any points because the chances are slim that they will make it through a full day without someone messing up. This system is likely to fail because the students will never feel motivated enough to make it work. The system would be stronger and probably more effective if it were set up so that the class earns a point for each hour, or even each half hour, that all students behave responsibly.

You can also help students believe that success is possible by making the cost of earning the rewards relatively inexpensive for the students. In other words, students initially need to see that they will get a reward relatively quickly when they meet your expectations (Alberto & Troutman, 2012; Scheuermann & Hall, 2008). Say you establish a system where your second graders can earn extra recess time by accumulating 25 points, but the most points they can earn in a day is five. At best, the students will have to work for a whole week before they get extra recess time. For second-grade students, this may be too long to wait for any payoff. When you choose your system, remember that if the students believe that it will take too long to earn the reward, their attitude may be, "Why bother?" In the second-grade example, the extra recess is more likely to motivate students if it costs 8 points rather than 25 points. The less mature your students are, the more immediately obtainable the rewards need to be for the system to be effective.

Once students are consistently behaving responsibly, you can and should make the time intervals longer or the rewards more expensive (or both) as part of the process of gradually fading the system. See Step 3 in this chapter for tips on effectively maintaining and fading a reward-based system.

Avoid systems with arbitrary time limits. A weakness of many reward-based systems is that they include an unnecessary and arbitrary time limit—the points must be earned within a certain time period in order for students to receive the reward. For example, consider a system in which a class can earn 5 points per day if everything goes extremely well. If the class earns 15 points by Friday, the students get the last 15 minutes of class as earned time with snacks. The arbitrary time limit in this system creates several potential problems. First of all, if students have trouble behaving well early in the week, they may know by Wednesday morning that they cannot possibly earn the reward that week. If they know they won't get the reward, they have no incentive to behave well on Wednesday afternoon, Thursday, and Friday. Or students might do so well that they have 15 points by the end of the day Wednesday. At least some of them are going to realize that they can misbehave all they want on Thursday and Friday because the reward has already been earned. Still another potential problem with a time limit is the difficult decision you face if the class earns 14 points by Friday afternoon. If you give them the reward because they came so close, they learn that you do not follow through on what you say (they cannot really trust you). However, if you do not give them the reward, meaning they start back at zero points on Monday, they may feel so discouraged they won't even want to try at all.

All of these potential problems can be eliminated by simply removing the time limit. The system in the above example would be much stronger if, as soon as the class earns 15 points, students get the last 15 minutes of class as earned time with snacks. They may earn the points in 3 days, or it may take a couple of weeks, depending on how well students manage their own behavior.

Carefully organize the entire system before you begin implementation. Many teachers rush to implement a motivation system when faced with behavior problems. However, to implement an effective system, you need to think carefully about your goals for the class's behavior and then develop a preliminary implementation plan in your mind. Once you create your mental plan, put it into writing. The act of writing out the procedures can help you identify possible weaknesses with the system and issues that need to be addressed (Scheuermann & Hall, 2008). As you identify those problems or issues, resolve them—make decisions.

For example, what will you do if one student repeatedly behaves in a way that prevents you from giving the point or reward to the entire group? You might plan to a) give the student a warning and tell them that continued misbehavior will not prevent the group from earning points, b) not allow the student to participate in any reward activities earned by the group, and c) if necessary, set up an individualized behavior management contract.

After you have a written plan that addresses all questions and issues you can think of, discuss the plan with a colleague. Speak to someone who is teaching or has taught the grade level you teach. Ask your colleague to listen to your proposed plan with a critical ear and encourage them to identify any weaknesses and unanswered questions in your plan.

Make sure your expectations for student behavior are clear and that you have adequate procedures for observing student behavior. Even a well-designed reward system can fail when the expectations for student behavior within the system are unclear (Conroy et al., 2008; Scheuermann & Hall, 2008). Without clearly defined behavioral expectations, you may be inconsistent in determining whether students have met the criteria for earning their reward (Anderson et al., 1980; Evertson & Emmer, 1982). That is, you may award points on a day when you are in a good mood, but the next day, when you are feeling more frustrated, you don't award any points, even though the students behaved the same way. This sort of inconsistency is very destructive to motivation because earning the reward is not contingent on the behavior students actually display. Students are likely to stop trying to meet expectations that are unclear and inconsistent (O'Leary & O'Leary, 1977).

In addition to clear expectations, you must have adequate procedures for observing student behavior (Conroy et al., 2008; Scheuermann & Hall, 2008). In fact, the only way you can reasonably implement a reward-based motivation system is if you can adequately observe student behavior. For example, if you have a system to address student behavior at recess—if everyone in the class follows the rules at recess, the class earns one point—you either need to be out with students during recess or have some way to get information from the playground supervisors at the conclusion of each recess. If there is some aspect of your students' behavior that you cannot adequately observe, that behavior should not be part of your system.

Teach the students how the entire system works. Before you implement any system, prepare one or more lessons to teach the students how the system works. When students don't understand all aspects of a system, there is very little chance it will motivate them—particularly the least mature students or those who struggle with understanding directions. If, when preparing the lessons, you find that the system seems too complicated for students to grasp, you should revise it. If you can't make it clear, concise, and easy to understand, you probably need a different system.

After you teach students how the reward system will work, verify that they understand. Ask questions to determine their level of understanding. Take special care to ensure that any

English language learners in your classroom understand your system. If specific aspects of the system are confusing, re-teach those aspects. In addition, you may want to give students an opportunity to suggest refinements or modifications. If students make suggestions that would strengthen the system—for example, rewards that would increase their interest in the system—try to incorporate those suggestions when possible.

Make sure you believe the system will help improve student behavior. Start with the assumption that your students will meet your expectations regarding the system. If you believe the system will work, the students will pick up on your optimism. Likewise, if you believe the system will probably fail, the students will sense that you do not expect them to be successful. It's in your best interest to be optimistic and maintain high expectations. Even if the system does not work initially, an optimistic attitude will lead you to try to identify refinements and modifications that will make the system work. On the other hand, with a pessimistic attitude you are likely to give up if the system does not produce immediate and drastic improvement in student behavior. Remember: Optimists are wrong just as often as pessimists; the big difference is optimists have a lot more fun.

STEP 3   *Determine how to maintain, modify, and fade a reward-based system.*

All reward-based systems require maintenance after they are up and running. It's like having a car. No matter how well engineered your vehicle is, you still have to put fuel in it and make sure it gets the occasional oil change, brake job, and tune-up. In fact, you wouldn't expect your car to run without gas and periodic mechanical work. Unfortunately, some teachers think that once a motivation system is in place, it should pretty much run by itself. It won't. Furthermore, in most cases a reward-based system should be a temporary measure that you employ to get the class into a pattern of successful behavior. Your eventual goal should be to fade it so that your students' intrinsic motivation maintains their responsible and enthusiastic behavior (Skinner et al., 2009).

The following information should help you maintain your system as long as necessary at one level as well as help you decide when and how to modify the system. If the system is not working, you should either modify it or select a new system. If the system is working well, you can make it incrementally more challenging for students and eventually fade it out altogether.

Keep your energy and enthusiasm about the system high. You are the fuel that keeps the system supplied with energy to run. If you don't "fill 'er up" with your excitement, interest, and support, students are very likely to lose interest, even if the rewards they are working toward are compelling. Convey your enthusiasm about how the classroom will function or the success you anticipate for students if they are able to meet the goals of the system.

Keep your focus on the students' behavior rather than the rewards they earn. The energy and excitement you invest in the system and in acknowledging student successes should be concentrated on what students do to earn the reward, not the reward itself (Horcones, 1992). That is, say to students "Look at what you did!" rather than "Look at what you get." By keeping your focus on the students' improved growth, maturity, and progress, you increase the chances that the students will begin working less for the reward and more for their sense of satisfaction in meeting expectations successfully (Jovanovic & Matejevic, 2014).

Continue to use other motivational strategies at a high level. A number of basic strategies for establishing and maintaining student motivation were presented in Chapters 3, 6, and earlier in this chapter. All the systems for boosting motivation discussed in this task require that you maintain your use of the following basic strategies:

- Present activities and tasks in a manner that induces student motivation.
- Use effective instructional practices and present tasks in interesting ways.
- Provide frequent noncontingent attention.
- Provide frequent positive feedback that is contingent, specific, descriptive, and age appropriate.
- Pay more attention to every student when they are engaged in responsible behavior than when they are engaged in misbehavior (minimally, a ratio of 3:1).
- Motivate students through non-reward-based strategies like stimulating interest and using goal-setting activities.

To increase the likelihood that students will continue to be successful, be prepared to increase your use of these strategies as you begin to fade back the use of the external reward system (Alberto & Troutman, 2012).

When a system has been successful for a period of time, start making it more challenging. Once student behavior improves to the point that your class is successfully meeting your expectations most of the time, modify the system to make it more challenging so students don't get bored with it. In addition, as students become more successful at meeting expectations, you will likely want to increase the standards for success.

Following are suggestions for making a system more challenging:

- Increase the time interval in which students need to demonstrate the appropriate behavior to earn a point (say, from 15 minutes to 20 minutes).
- Increase the number of points students need to earn a reward.
- Increase the number of behaviors being monitored; for example, make the target behavior "reduced disruptions" rather than "reduced blurt-outs" so that more behaviors are included within the definition.

EXAMPLES, IDEAS, AND TIPS

Let's say a third-grade class is implementing the Whole-Class Points (Time Interval) system using one of the point charts shown on page 325. Initially, the timer goes off every 15 minutes. If students have met expectations for responsible behavior during the 15-minute interval, the class earns a point and a circle is filled in. When the class earns ten points, they get one of the rewards. If the class is regularly earning a point during most intervals (more than 80% of the time), you need to make things slightly more challenging. The next time students earn a reward and the chart is reset, inform the class that after they earn the next reward, the system will change. Instead of a penguin chart, it will be a horse chart. Instead of 10 spaces to reach the goal, there will be 13 circles before the class reaches the goal. By increasing the difficulty, you make earning the next reward slightly more challenging.

It's important to give students plenty of advance notice before making this kind of modification. As you explain the increased number of spaces, emphasize to students that you are making the change because they have been successful. Be careful not to sound apologetic about this change and convey a sense of pride that students are becoming so responsible they have advanced to the next level of the system. If students complain, let them know that the system, like many things in life, is challenging and may increase in difficulty, but emphasize that they have the skills to still earn the reward quickly. Increasing the difficulty by requiring more points is the first of many steps you will take in fading the system. If your students enjoy video games, a video-game analogy about advancing to the next, more challenging level (i.e., "leveling up") might be effective.

Another way to make the system more challenging is to make the criteria for earning points harder.

With a point chart system, you might go from monitoring in 15-minute intervals to monitoring in 20-minute intervals. Or you could increase the number of behaviors being monitored. For example, you could add the behavior "treating everyone with respect" as an additional criteria for determining whether the class earns a point for a given interval.

The following shows how you can make gradual changes in a point chart system. These changes would be phased in over a period of several months.

15-minute intervals	10 points required for reward
15-minute intervals	13 points required for reward
20-minute intervals	13 points required for reward
20-minute intervals	18 points required for reward

"Treating everyone with respect" added to expectations

30-minute intervals	18 points required for reward
30-minute intervals	25 points required for reward
45-minute intervals	25 points required for reward
45-minute intervals	35 points required for reward
60-minute intervals	35 points required for reward

Remember, don't increase a system's difficulty until students have been consistently successful. If you make things too difficult before students feel somewhat in control of their own success, they may be inclined to give up and stop trying to meet the expectations.

By making changes like these gradually, you make the system increasingly lean—students demonstrate highly responsible behavior for relatively small extrinsic rewards (Freeland & Noell, 1999). Notice that in the preceding example, students started out working in 15-minute intervals and needing 10 points for a reward, so 150 minutes of responsible behavior earned students a reward. A few months later, the same class works in 60-minute intervals and needs 35 points for a reward—meaning 2,100 minutes of responsible behavior earns a reward.

Once a system is fairly lean, modify it to be based on intermittent rewards. Some of the systems in the menu that are identified as appropriate for medium-support classrooms involve the use of intermittent rewards—rewards that are given only on some occasions rather than every time performance criteria are met. Even if your classroom uses high levels of support, you should eventually shift to intermittent rewards once the students have learned and are consistently displaying the skill or skills that are the focus of your classwide system. Moving to intermittent rewards is important for two reasons:

- It is not practical for you to deliver rewards at a high rate over a long period of time (Freeland & Noell, 1999).
- Intermittent schedules of reinforcement have been shown to be most effective in maintaining student behavior over time (Alberto & Troutman, 2012; Cooper et al., 2007; Scheuermann & Hall, 2008).

Moving to intermittent rewards is another step in making your motivation system more challenging.

Once a class is working successfully for intermittent rewards, consider adding or switching to one of the goal-setting systems described in Task 2. Goal setting is one of the last steps in fading students from the support of extrinsic rewards to reliance on their intrinsic motivation. While you are still using a system of intermittent rewards, begin setting individual goals for each student (or have the students set their own goals) and help the class set a classwide goal. Then, make a point of providing frequent positive feedback to students for meeting the goals. Once you have motivated students to strive toward their individualized goals and you are maintaining high rates of positive feedback to individuals and the whole class, you will be very close to being able to abandon reward-based systems altogether (O'Leary & Becker, 1967).

When appropriate, have a class discussion about abandoning the use of the reward-based system. When the class seems ready—most students seem to take pride in behaving responsibly—arrange to conduct a whole-class discussion about whether students feel they can continue to behave responsibly without getting rewards. If the tone of the discussion suggests that most students think they can maintain their responsible behavior without a reward system, set a classwide goal such as:

We, the students in Room 14, can behave responsibly and we will strive to meet our Guidelines for Success without needing a reward system.

When students can agree to this kind of classwide goal, you can stop using a reward-based system. However, you do need to continue providing positive feedback and an occasional special treat when the class exhibits ongoing responsible behavior. (See Chapter 6, Task 4: Provide Intermittent Celebrations.)

Menu of Classwide Systems

The rest of this chapter describes a variety of classwide systems for increasing student motivation—a menu of procedures. Those appropriate for high-support classes are presented first, followed by those for medium-support classes. Read through the systems that fit the level of support your class needs (you will probably want to read others as well to gain some perspective), then choose the system or systems that you think will be practical to implement and will improve the motivation of your students. You can also use the ideas presented here as a basis for creating your own system, if you wish. Figure 7.2 (p. 324) lists the systems described in the menu in the order they appear.

Figure 7.2 *Menu of Classwide Support Systems*

For Classes Needing High Support	For Classes Needing Medium Support
• Whole-Class Points (Time Interval) • Economic Simulation • Reinforcement Based on Reducing Misbehavior • Good Behavior Game • Behavioral Grading	• 100 Squares • Group Response Cost • Lottery Tickets • Mystery Behavior of the Day • Public Posting (Classwide) • Self-Evaluation of On- and Off-Task Behavior • Target and Reward a Specific Behavior • Mystery Motivators: A Variation of "Target and Reward a Specific Behavior" • Team Competition with Response • Cost Lottery • Whole-Class Points (Intermittent)

Reward-Based Systems Appropriate for Classes Needing High Support

Whole-Class Points (Time Interval)

In this system you provide feedback, both positive and corrective, to the entire class at regular intervals. For each interval during which the behavior of the class meets your expectations, the group earns a point, or if you prefer, a range of points (for example, zero to three points). Once the group earns a predetermined number of points, the entire class gets a reward. This is an excellent system to use when you have quite a few immature students in the class. However, it is not a good choice when most of your class behaves well and one or two students are responsible for most of the misbehavior.

The first thing to determine when using this system is the duration of the interval—each hour, each half hour, or each quarter hour, for example. The more misbehavior your class exhibits, the shorter the intervals should be. For example, with a relatively immature group of students, you may need intervals as short as 15 minutes. Keep track of the duration using an alarm on your watch or phone, a kitchen timer, or a timer app that beeps at various intervals.

Next, have a class brainstorming session to identify possible rewards. Eliminate unreasonable suggestions and then set prices for how many points it will take to earn various reward items and activities. Your prices should be based in part on the length of the interval you are using—if you use 15-minute intervals, the rewards should cost more than if you use 60-minute intervals. Prices should also be based on the monetary, instructional, and personnel costs (the time that school personnel will spend providing the rewards) the various rewards entail. Thus, a 2-hour movie with popcorn will be more expensive than 5 minutes of extra recess.

The last consideration is how you will keep track of the points. This could be as simple as marking points in a small designated box on the board for that class period. Or you could make a simple chart with the goal at the top and color in the total number of points earned at the end of each period. Some kind of graphic representation on a bulletin board or flip chart is very effective. The downloadable materials (see p. 3) have a variety of reproducible forms (Reproducibles 7.4A-Q) that can be used for Whole-Class Point systems. The version you choose depends on how many points you plan to award and how quickly you want the class to receive the rewards. Note that if you start with a low number, students can earn the reward quickly and start a new chart. Then, once they become highly successful (they earn points on 90% of the intervals), you can move to a version of the chart with a different theme and more required points. The reproducible materials include full-color point charts for 5, 10, 15, 20, 25, 50, and 100 points, each with a different theme, which you can resize for an 11" x 17" poster.

Reproducible 7.4P is an example of how you can use the CHAMPS icons to create your own CHAMPS-themed point charts. Blank templates (Reproducibles 7.5A–H) are provided in the downloadable reproducible forms for you to start with. The templates are preprinted

Reproducibles 7.4F, 7.4I, 7.4K, 7.4O, 7.4P *Whole-Class Point Chart Examples*

with 5, 10, 15, 20, 25, 30, 50, and 100 stars to fill in as points are earned, with space for you to add your own slogan and artwork.

Instead of using the reproducibles provided, you could make a bulletin board display that relates the reward system to a subject the class is currently studying. For example, you might track points using a covered wagon on the way to Oregon or a whale migrating to Baja. Figure 7.3 shows this system with a whale migration motif.

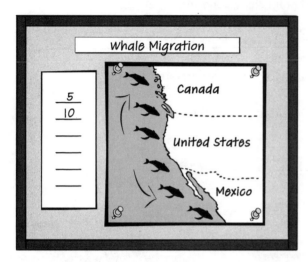

Figure 7.3 *Whale Migration Point Chart*

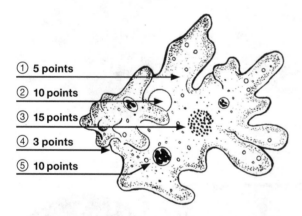

Figure 7.4 *Parts of a Cell Point Chart*

Figure 7.4 shows another graphic representation idea that might be appropriate for an intermediate or middle school science class. This chart shows a picture of the parts of a cell. Each part is labeled as soon as the class earns the specified number of points. The various labels cost different amounts—the cell wall costs five points, the chromosomes ten points, the cytoplasts three points, for example. When the entire cell has been labeled, the group earns the reward.

If you are a middle school teacher, use your own judgment about whether your students will be motivated by this kind of graphical point tracking. If you don't think they will be, simply devote a small corner of the chalkboard to recording the points (for example, "4th period: 6 points").

Once these decisions are made, implementation is fairly simple. At the conclusion of each interval (when the timer goes off after 30 minutes, for example), review the behavior of the entire class for the preceding 30-minute period. If students met your expectations, the group earns two points. If all but one or two students met your expectations, the group earns one point. If more than two students failed to meet expectations, the group earns zero points. If the group earns anything less than two points, describe the inappropriate behaviors that led to your assessment, but do not name the students who misbehaved. "Because I had to give several of you reminders about talking during quiet study time, the group does not get any points for this time period. However, I am resetting the timer, and I am sure that in the next 30 minutes you will be able to earn two points."

If student behavior does not improve, increase the amount of positive feedback you give to individual students and to the class during each interval. If improvement is still insufficient, consider using shorter intervals (15 minutes rather than 30). When the class earns a reward, begin the system again by having the class vote on the next reward. You can keep the system interesting for students by changing the theme periodically—you do not want to use a cell motif or penguin motif for more than a couple of weeks at a time.

A variation of this system is the Whole-Class Points (Intermittent) system. The intermittent system is described on page 337.

Economic Simulation

In an Economic Simulation system, you use pretend money and create a mini-economy in your classroom. Students are paid for their good behavior and can use the money to purchase a variety of items. This can be a useful system in grades 2 through 8 for reducing frequent but minor misbehavior such as off-task behavior, talking in class, put-downs, and so on.

You can make this type of system simple or complex. In its simplest form, it functions as a response cost type of system. Every student starts the week with a certain amount of money in the bank. During the week, you use a Misbehavior Recording Sheet (see Chapter 10, Task 1, Tool 3) to observe the inappropriate behavior of individual students. Each misbehavior costs the student who misbehaved one dollar. At the end of the week, you determine each student's payout. Any student who has had no recorded misbehaviors receives ten pretend dollars.

A student who misbehaved six times receives four dollars, and a student who misbehaved once receives nine dollars. Students can spend the money on items in a student store, such as pencils, stickers, erasers, and certificates for computer time. Plan to give bonuses (one or two extra dollars, for example) to individual students who have been following rules, striving toward the Guidelines for Success, or making progress toward their individual goals. Be careful not to be inadvertently discriminatory, though. Every student should get a bonus every now and then.

CHAMPS Bucks in one-, five-, and ten-dollar amounts are shown in Figure 7.5 below. These printable sheets of CHAMPS bucks (6 per page) are available in the downloadable materials. Reproducible 7.6A–C uses primary-level icons, Reproducible 7.7A–C uses intermediate-level icons, and Reproducible 7.8A–C uses pictograph icons. You can use these reproducible masters to mint your class money, or you may prefer to design your own money.

Figure 7.5 *CHAMPS Bucks (Samples from Reproducibles 7.6A, 7.7B, and 7.8C)*

In a slightly more sophisticated version of this system, students can also be "paid" for completing academic work or demonstrating responsible behavior. For example, you might give students two dollars for each assignment completed (more for major projects). If you want to incorporate something like this, you need to record the positive feedback you give students in addition to recording their misbehavior. See the information in the Behavioral Grading system (Chapter 3, Task 10) for suggestions on how to manage this kind of recording. Then have each student start each day with a certain number of dollars (say five). Throughout the day, they add one dollar for each positive behavior and subtract one dollar for each negative behavior. To start, students might be paid daily, but as they get familiar with the system, this can be modified to a weekly payday.

If you wish, once the basic system is running smoothly and showing positive effects, you can use it to teach students about how the real economy works. Every 2 weeks, add one of the following features:

- Establish savings accounts for students.
- Establish checking accounts for students.
- Charge students rent for their desks.
- Require students to buy certain supplies (e.g., pencils, art paper).
- Have students purchase certain privileges.
- Arrange to pay students extra for special projects (extra-credit assignments).
- Establish charitable foundations to which students can contribute.
- Assess taxes on the money students are paid.
- Give every student a paid class job. Examples include:
  - Managers of student store
  - Accountants (help you compute payments)
  - Bankers (manage savings accounts)
  - City council (paid from taxes collected)
  - Supply managers
  - Tutors or helpers who assist in kindergarten
  - Real estate agents (determine and collect rents for desks)
  - Zoologists (care for class animals)
  - Computer maintenance
  - Graphic artists (prepare bulletin boards and displays)

Reinforcement Based on Reducing Misbehavior

This system is designed to reward an entire class for significant reductions in the total number of misbehaviors that occur on any given day. It is particularly effective when many different students in the class exhibit a wide variety of misbehavior.

To implement the system, keep data on class misbehavior for at least 5 days by using either a daily or weekly Misbehavior Recording Sheet (see Chapter 10, Tool 3). Then determine the average number of misbehaviors per day that occurred during your 5-day baseline period (add the total number of misbehaviors you recorded and divide by five).

From the average number of incidents per day, build a sliding scale for awarding points. Create the scale so that if the average number of incidents (or more) occurs, students earn no points, but as progressively fewer incidents occur, they earn an increasing number of points that can be applied toward a reward.

If your baseline class average is 33 misbehaviors per day, your point scale might look like this:

More than 32 incidents	=	0 points
22–32 incidents	=	1 point
15–21 incidents	=	2 points
7–14 incidents	=	3 points
3–6 incidents	=	4 points
1–2 incidents	=	5 points
0 incidents	=	6 points

Post the chart and point out to students the number of incidents that occurred over the preceding 5 days. Explain your concern and inform the class that you are willing to provide them with some rewards if they work on reducing the amount of misbehavior that occurs each day. Then show students your scale of number of incidents and corresponding points. Next, have students brainstorm a list of class reward ideas.

Once you have a reasonable list, set prices for each of the possible rewards in terms of how many points will be required to get it. The prices need to be set by you, and you should base the prices on the instructional, personnel, and/or monetary costs of the items. Monetary cost is clear—the more expensive the item, the more points should be required to earn it. Instructional cost refers to the amount of instructional time lost or interrupted as the result of a particular reward—for example, an extra 10 minutes of recess means 10 minutes taken from instructional time. Any reward that results in the class missing academic instruction should cost more points than one that does not result in missed instruction, such as a reward the class can do during recess time. Personnel cost refers to the time required for you or other staff to give the reward. An extra recess that requires arranging for extra supervision costs more than playing music for students during an independent work period.

Have the class vote on the rewards. Students will work for the winning reward first. The items that come in second and third in the voting will be the second and third rewards that students have a chance to win.

Each day, keep a careful count of the number of incidents of misbehavior. At the end of the day, record the total number of misbehavior incidents and tell the class how many points they earned that day. Also let them know each day the total number of points they have accumulated to date. When the class has enough points, they get the designated reward. Then the system starts again, and they have zero points. Remind the class of the next reward they are working toward (the item that got the second most votes).

Good Behavior Game

The Good Behavior Game (Barrish et al., 1969) is a simple but effective system that has been used successfully in elementary classrooms. Divide the class into two or more teams and list each team on the board. Tell students that every time they misbehave (be sure to specify the behavior you are looking for), you will place a mark next to their team name on the board. The team with the fewest marks at the end of the day, or both teams if they each stay under five marks, receives a reward, such as first to line up or a couple of minutes of extra recess. In the original 1969 study, the Good Behavior Game was implemented in a fourth-grade classroom. The intervention resulted in decreases in disruptive behavior and was well liked by both the implementing teacher and the students. Since the 1969 study, versions of the game have been implemented in a variety of general and special education settings, primarily with students in first through sixth grade. Although the exact procedures implemented across studies vary, the core components include:

- Specifically teach expected and unacceptable behaviors.
- Divide the class into two or more teams to use peer influence to increase appropriate behavior and minimize problem behaviors.
- Reinforce appropriate behaviors by acknowledging social behavior successes and allowing students to earn rewards (Barrish et al., 1969).

The Good Behavior Game has resulted in decreased disruptive behaviors, increases in appropriate social behaviors, and improvements in students' work completion rates (Bowman-Perrott et al., 2016; Flower et al., 2014; Tankersley, 1995; Tingstrom et al., 2006).

Behavioral Grading

If you are using behavioral grading practices as described in Chapter 3, Task 10, you may also wish to combine the individual behavioral grades into a broader classwide system. Calculate the average percentage the class earns for behavioral grades each week. Add up the total number of points earned by all students in the behavioral grade category. Find the total number of points possible by multiplying the number of students in the class times the number of points each student can earn per week. Then divide the total points earned by total points possible to get the percentage.

Set a goal for the class to improve this percentage. For example, if the class is averaging 70% on their behavioral grade each week, set a goal that students will collectively earn 80% or 85%. If students achieve this goal the following week, they will earn a designated reward.

Reward-Based Systems Appropriate for Classes That Need Medium Support

100 Squares

100 Squares is a combination of tic-tac-toe and bingo. It uses intermittent rewards to acknowledge the behavior of the entire class. 100 Squares is especially useful when trying to improve student behavior regarding a specific rule ("Work during all work times," for example).

Draw a large 10-square by 10-square grid (100 spaces total) on a whiteboard or flip chart. Number each square from 1 to 100 (see Figure 7.6). Place the chart in a prominent place in the room. Get two containers (bowls or hats, for example) and 100 small tokens such as poker chips, small tag board squares, or Popsicle sticks. On each token, write a number from 1 to 100. Place all of them into one of the two containers.

Figure 7.6 *100 Squares Tokens and Chart*

On *some* occasions when the entire class is working well, stop what is going on and have a student draw one of the tokens from the full container. Identify the number written on the token, then fill in—initial or color—the space on the chart that has the same number. Put the token into the empty (second) container. When ten squares in a row—horizontally, vertically, or diagonally—have been filled in, the entire class gets one of the group rewards identified by you or by the class during a brainstorming session. Once a full line has been completed and a reward given, erase the filled-in squares or put up a new grid on the flip chart, and return all the drawn tokens to the original container. Identify the next reward students will work toward (you choose or have the class vote) and begin the system again.

NOTE: Be sure to clarify that the students who draw the numbers are doing so for a class, not an individual, reward.

Have a different student draw the number each time so that eventually every student has a chance. In the early stages of using the system, try to have at least ten drawings per day, but *do not* have a drawing unless everyone in the class is doing well at that particular moment.

Class, right now everyone is seated, with eyes on the board, and anyone who wants to talk is waiting for me to call on them. Micah, please draw a number from the bowl and tell me the numbered space that we will fill in.

After the class has earned at least six or more rewards, modify the system to make the chart an 11 by 11 grid with 121 spaces and add the additional tokens. This allows you to continue to hold frequent drawings, but it also means that it takes longer for students to earn a reward. As time goes on, if the system continues to have a positive effect on student behavior, you can make the chart a 12 by 12 grid with 144 spaces and eventually even a 15 by 15 grid with 225 spaces.

At some point, plan to have a class discussion to see whether students want to continue the system. If they think they can continue to behave responsibly without the system, let them know that you will periodically give them free time or other favorite rewards. If students want to continue the system, double the number of tokens in the container so that there are two tokens for each number. If a number is drawn and its space is already filled in, the token just goes into the second container. This doubling of tokens makes the actual reward harder to earn and moves students one step closer to working without the system.

Students find this system more interesting than simply filling in successive boxes because there is an element of chance—they hope, but can't be sure, that the number drawn is one that brings a row closer to completion.

Group Response Cost

Group Response Cost is a simple system that can be used very effectively to reduce one specific misbehavior that tends to be exhibited by several different students in the class. It is also effective in improving a group's behavior in terms of following directions and being efficient during transitions.

To use this system to reduce a common group misbehavior (for example, use of profanity), first set up a special time in the afternoon for a fun group activity—an extra 10 minutes of recess, for instance. Or, for middle school teachers, 10 minutes of social time at the end of the week. On index cards write times in 30-second intervals from 0 to 10 minutes—on one card write 0 seconds, on the next 30 seconds, on the next 1 minute, then 1 1/2 minutes, and so on until you reach 10 minutes. Tell students that each day the class will start out with 10 minutes of extra recess (or 10 minutes of social time at the end of the week), but if at any time you hear profanity, they will lose 30 seconds of that extra recess. Take your stack of cards (with the "10 minutes" card on top) and demonstrate how when you hear profanity, you will take the top card and move it to the bottom of the stack, leaving the "9 1/2 minutes" card on top. The time on the top card at recess time will show how much extra recess the class gets that afternoon.

When using this system to improve behaviors such as following directions and being efficient during transitions, make cards for 10 extra minutes of recess as described above. Let students know that when you give a directive for a transition ("Everyone get out your math books and a blank piece of paper"), they have a reasonable amount of time, say 1 minute, to complete the transition. Tell students that if it takes them more than 1 minute to complete the transition, that additional time will come off the 10 minutes of extra recess time. Then, after you give your first directive of the day, wait for 1 minute. If the class is ready, thank students for their efficiency. If students are not ready, hold up the stack of cards with the "10 minutes" card showing. Every 30 seconds, move the top card to the back of the stack. Continue this process, without saying a word, until all students are ready. After you give the next directive for a transition, wait the allotted time, and then pick up the stack of cards. After 30 seconds, move the top card (which now may say "9 minutes") to the back of the stack. Over the course of a day, each block of 30 seconds that students waste will cost them 30 seconds off the extra recess period.

Because Group Response Cost is predominately punitive (taking time away from the extra recess), you really need to make a concerted effort to provide students with frequent positive attention, positive feedback, and even intermittent rewards (see Chapter 6) when they behave appropriately. Too much focus on a negative behavior without frequent positive interactions can backfire on you—students may try to lose the 10 minutes quickly just to frustrate you and see what you will do next.

This system is most likely to work when more than three or four students exhibit one specific misbehavior. If only one, two, or three students are having difficulty exhibiting expected behavior, you are better off setting up individualized plans (both positive and corrective) with those students. The system is also unlikely to be powerful enough to be effective if your class frequently exhibits many different misbehaviors.

Lottery Tickets

A relatively simple but highly effective way to specifically encourage appropriate behavior or a specific positive behavior is to use an intermittent lottery reward system.

Each week on an unpredictable basis, present individual students who are following the rules or demonstrating responsible behavior with lottery tickets for a weekly drawing. Reproducibles 7.9A -B, shown below, are reproducible sheets of multiple lottery tickets available in the downloadable materials.

Reproducibles 7.9A–B *Lottery Tickets (Version 1) and CHAMPS Tickets (Version 2)*

When you give a ticket, have the student write their name and the date on it. Be sure to tell the student exactly why they are getting the ticket so they can write a brief description, such as "completed all homework." Have the student put the completed ticket into a container for a drawing that will occur at the end of the week. Each Friday before the drawing, identify two rewards you think students would like, perhaps a coupon for free ice cream or 15 minutes of computer time. At the time of the drawing, announce the first reward and draw a lottery ticket from the container. The student whose name is on that ticket receives the reward. Repeat the process for the second reward. Throw away or recycle the tickets that remain in the container. The next Monday, start giving out tickets for that week's drawing.

NOTE: This is a difficult system to use with very young primary students—they don't understand why one or two people get a reward and they don't.

With a Lottery Ticket system, it is especially important to watch that you are not being discriminatory. For example, it would be easy to inadvertently harbor a grudge toward individual students who have been especially troublesome during the current week or in the past and so not notice their positive behavior. It can also be easy to fall into the trap of noticing the small improvements of your more difficult students and the great leaps of your high achievers but not recognizing or acknowledging the ongoing, sustained effort of your average students. Finally, work to frequently evaluate whether biases related to race/ethnicity, religion, gender, proficiency with English, disability status, or other factors could be impacting the frequency with which you give lottery tickets to some students. All students should have frequent opportunities for positive recognition with this system.

> **Diversity, Equity, Inclusion, and Access**
>
> *Be careful when using lottery tickets and other reward-based systems that personal biases related to individual student characteristics, situations, or beliefs (e.g., race/ethnicity, LGBTQ+, socioeconomic status, religion, disability, etc.) do not affect the way in which you apply the system. The system should provide equitable opportunities for students to be successful and participate in corresponding rewards.*

Mystery Behavior of the Day

This simple and creative intermittent reward-based system was developed by Pat Gagnon, a fourth-grade teacher in Springfield, Oregon. Each morning Pat decides on a particular positive behavior or trait that she will look for that day—helping others, for example. The students know that she will be watching for some behavior, but she does not tell them what the day's behavior or trait is. During the day, she watches for and notes to herself examples of students exhibiting the Mystery Behavior. Toward the end of the day, she puts a small treat on the desks of the students she caught exhibiting the behavior. After the rewards are given, the class spends a few minutes guessing what the day's Mystery Behavior is. Whether or not students guess correctly, Pat tells them the behavior and lets them know that she will be looking for a different Mystery Behavior the next day.

You can add to the level of interest in this system by having a large envelope with the words Mystery Behavior of the Day prominently displayed in the room. Before the students arrive each morning, write the behavior or trait you will look for that day on a piece of paper and place it in the envelope. At the end of the day, after students discuss what they think the Mystery Behavior is, have one of the students who earned the reward that day draw the piece of paper from the envelope and announce

> *For teachers struggling with transitions or clean-up, a variation on the Mystery Behavior system is Mystery Items. In this system, the teacher secretly names an item in the classroom as the Mystery Item, and then sets a timer for clean-up time. The student who puts that item in its place within the time frame gets a prize.*

the behavior. You might even want to encourage the student to add a bit of fanfare—like an Academy Awards ceremony: "And, the Mystery Behavior for today is . . ."

When using this system, be sure to vary the Mystery Behavior so that every student gets recognized periodically. That is, be very careful that no student goes too long without being caught exhibiting one of the Mystery Behaviors.

Public Posting (Classwide)

When there is one specific behavior you want to increase (homework completion, for example) or decrease (use of student-to-student put-downs during class), you can overtly chart the overall class rate of that behavior in a place and in a way that all students can see it. This is especially useful when quite a few students in the class exhibit a specific problem as opposed to a problem that only a couple of students exhibit. Public posting makes everyone aware of how pervasive a problem is and gives the entire group positive feedback when the situation improves. Note that this is not posting each individual class member's rate in a public way, but involves posting the whole class's compiled rate of behavior. Periodically, when students demonstrate improvements or meet a class goal, provide a reward for the whole group and encourage them to keep up the good work.

EXAMPLES, IDEAS, AND TIPS

If a middle school class has trouble with frequent name-calling, laughing at peers' mistakes, and other forms of student-to-student disrespect, you could start by keeping a simple tally of the total number of disrespectful actions that occur each day for 3 days. Then post a chart with the data from those 3 days. Posting the chart serves as the impetus for holding a class discussion about the problem, the benefits of reducing the negative behavior, and strategies that individual students might employ to help reduce the problem. In this example, one strategy that you could share is that individuals should avoid laughing when someone calls someone else a name or otherwise puts somebody down. Each day, keep a simple count of the number of disrespectful incidents. At the end of the day, record the data on the chart. At least twice a week when you post the data, initiate a short discussion about whether the problem is getting better, getting worse, or staying about the same. If the situation is staying the same or getting worse, have students discuss other actions they can take to help reduce the problem.

As noted before, public posting can also be effective in helping you increase a positive behavior—daily work completion, for example. To use the system for this purpose, start by determining the class's daily percentage of completed work turned in on time for a period of 1 week. You can do this by simply counting the number of assignments turned in each day and dividing that number by the total number of assignments that should have been turned in that day. This figure is the class's percentage of work completion for that day. Record a week's worth of daily work completion percentages on a chart placed prominently in the room.

Use the initial record to prompt a discussion of the importance of work completion, the benefits to each individual of completing their work, and strategies individuals can use to help increase their own work completion. Then compute the class's daily percentage of work completion and plan to record it on the chart the next day. At least twice a week, preferably daily, discuss the data on the chart and whether the percentage of work completion is increasing, decreasing, or staying about the same.

Self-Evaluation of On- and Off-Task Behavior

In this system, students observe and record their own behavior. Meanwhile, you monitor their on-task and off-task behavior during instructional activities to determine whether the students' and your evaluations match. This system is particularly appropriate when your students do not exhibit a great deal of overt misbehavior but also do not use their work time well. That is, quite a few students in the class tend to sit and do nothing or converse instead of doing their work or participating actively in instructional activities.

> *With clear instruction and feedback, self-monitoring has been successfully used to improve academic and social behaviors.*

To use the system, it's important to first thoroughly teach students what on-task behavior looks and sounds like for teacher-directed instruction, independent work periods, and cooperative groups (see Chapter 4), which may take several weeks.

With clear instruction and feedback, self-monitoring has been successfully used to improve academic and social behaviors (Bruhn et al., 2015; Lan, 2005; Mooney et al., 2005; Zimmerman, 2002).

After students clearly understand the difference between on-task and off-task behavior, make copies of Reproducible 7.10, Self-Evaluation of On- and Off-Task Behavior (not shown), for each student. Set a timer at the beginning of each work period for anywhere from 1 to 30 minutes. When the timer goes off, each student evaluates whether they were on task or off task at that moment and then fills in the circle for the next number in the appropriate column of the recording sheet. After you give students an opportunity to do their recording, instruct them to get back to work and reset the timer. Vary the length of the timed period so that students never know exactly when they will be evaluating their behavior next.

Periodically monitor a few students (not always the same ones!) to see if they are recording accurately. If you disagree with a student's rating, discuss your assessment of the situation with the student. Avoid arguing, but do encourage students to be honest with themselves in their ratings. You can teach students in grades 5 and above how to calculate their own daily percentage (divide the total on-task numbers filled in by the total of both on-task and off-task numbers filled in). With younger students, you will probably have to calculate the percentage for them. Have each student keep a graph of their daily on-task percentage and encourage students to try to improve their performance from one day to the next. Use the procedure for a couple of weeks.

This procedure can be used with kindergarten and first-grade students by making the focus on "Being in the Right Place" versus "Being in the Wrong Place" and evaluating whether students are in their seats during seatwork time, on the rug during story time, in line when it is time to line up, and so on. With young students, however, it may be better to set the system up as a group count—how many students are in the right place when the timer goes off?

The group earns a point if everyone is in the right place when the beeper goes off. Reserve a place on a whiteboard or flip chart to record the students' accumulated point total. When the class earns a predetermined number of points, they get a treat or a special activity.

Target and Reward a Specific Behavior

This simple classwide behavior management system is useful when quite a few different students exhibit one specific behavioral problem, such as name-calling or put-downs. For a couple of days, count the number of times the targeted behavior occurs. Don't bother to count how many incidents any individual student has, just the total number of incidents for the class during the day or class period.

After 2 days, share the information you have collected with students and tell them they need to reduce the frequency of this misbehavior. Guide the class in the process of setting a realistic improvement goal—reducing the number of daily incidents from 40 to 32, for example. Students may be tempted to set an unrealistic goal, such as reducing the number of incidents from 40 per day to zero. Explain that if they set an unreasonable goal, it will be very difficult to achieve that goal. Explain that a realistic goal—say, no more than 32 incidents—increases their chances of success. Also tell them that once they achieve their initial (reasonable) goal, they can start setting more challenging goals for themselves.

Have the class generate a list of classwide rewards. Create a Grab Bag—write each reward on a small card and put all the cards into a container. On any day that the class meets the goal, one of the students gets to draw a card from the container. The class receives the reward written on the card. When you are ready to start fading the system, let students know that you have put some cards into the container that say, "Congratulations! Today you have the satisfaction of having attained your goal." Explain that when one of these cards is drawn, students will not get an actual reward that day. Instead, it will give them the opportunity to learn that people do many things in life not for any reward but simply for the satisfaction of doing something well. The more of these cards you add, the closer you move students toward eliminating the system completely.

Mystery Motivators: A Variation of "Target and Reward a Specific Behavior"

A variation of the previous system is called Mystery Motivators. This variation makes the system even more of a gamble, which may mean that it is more interesting and compelling for some classes. On a calendar for the next month, use an invisible-ink pen to mark an X on approximately 60% of the school days. (Invisible-ink pens are available at novelty stores or can be ordered from online retailers.) *The Tough Kid Tool Box*, available from Ancora Publishing, has many reproducible samples of Mystery Motivator forms that are fun and interesting.

Choose one of the rewards from the list generated by the class, write it on a card, then place the card in an envelope labeled Mystery Motivator. Do not tell students what reward is written on the card. On days when the class meets its behavior goal, one student gets to color in that day on the calendar to see if there is an X (previously invisible) in the square.

If there is an X, have another student open the Mystery Motivator envelope and announce which Mystery Motivator the class has earned. If there is no X when the calendar square is colored in, enthusiastically congratulate students on meeting their goal, but don't award or reveal the Mystery Motivator. On days when the class does not meet the goal because there were too many incidents of the misbehavior, students do not get to check to see whether there is an X. If the system is effective, you can begin fading it during the second month by putting fewer Xs on the calendar, thereby creating fewer chances to get an extrinsic reward.

Team Competition With Response Cost Lottery

A system that involves team competition (groups of students competing against each other) can be useful for reducing a minor but annoying behavior such as students blurting out or disruptions. Of course, whenever you do anything with teams—especially when the competition involves academic or behavioral performance—it's important to ensure that the teams themselves are as comparable as possible. Thus, you should assign students to teams rather than letting them self-select their teams, and you should make sure that no team is overloaded with students with excessive behavioral concerns or students who are extremely responsible.

To use this system, divide students into four to six teams. Have each team give itself a team name. At the beginning of each day, every team receives a certain number of tickets, perhaps ten. Have the students write their team's name on their tickets. Then, whenever a student misbehaves, take a ticket from that student's team. At the end of the day, collect the remaining tickets from each team and put them in a container for a lottery drawing. The team whose name is on the winning ticket earns the reward for the day. (The class can generate a list of desired rewards.) Start the system over again the following day.

Whole-Class Points (Intermittent)

An alternative to using whole-class points based on time intervals (see pp. 324–326) is to intermittently catch the class when everyone is behaving well and award one or more points. Use the time interval concept and a point chart (Reproducibles 7.A–Q) and have the class brainstorm various reward items and activities. You set the prices. Then, whenever you notice that everyone in the class is meeting expectations, you can announce that you are awarding one (or any number you wish) point.

The advantage to this variation is that the system is entirely under your control—you decide when to award points. The disadvantage is that without a specific interval (as marked by the timer going off or by the end of a work period), it is easy to forget about the system. Ironically, this is especially true if the students are behaving really well. So, if you are going to use this system intermittently, keep reminding yourself to catch the class and award points. If you do this well and students respond quickly with increased appropriate behavior, an easy way to begin fading this system is to use longer intervals (on average, because this is an intermittent system) between awarding points. For example, during the early days of using the system, you might catch the class 10 or 15 times a day. Later in the year, you catch the class only once or twice per day. Whole-Class Points (Intermittent) may be used with both medium- and high-support classes. For a high-support class, award points more frequently.

UPDATE YOUR CLASSROOM MANAGEMENT PLAN

ITEM 10: ENCOURAGEMENT PROCEDURES

If you have identified that one reward-based system or more may be beneficial for your class, update your Classroom Management Plan with the system(s) you plan to use and for what behaviors.

Conclusion

This chapter covered the nuts and bolts of motivation and use of non-reward and reward-based systems to boost motivation. Consider whether non-reward approaches, reward-based systems, or a combination of the two will prompt the most responsible behavior from your students. With any reward-based system carefully plan for how to implement, maintain, and fade the system.

CHAPTER 8

Correct Misbehavior Fluently

When you treat student misbehavior as an instructional opportunity and give fluent corrections, you give students the chance to learn from mistakes.

Chapter 8 addresses the C in STOIC—Correct misbehavior fluently. A certain amount of misbehavior is bound to occur in your classroom, no matter how well you organize your room or how effectively you communicate your behavioral expectations. If you have followed the suggestions in previous chapters, you have minimized much of the misbehavior that would have occurred without more proactive and positive strategies. However, it is also important to preplan for how you will correct students when they do engage in misbehavior. This chapter begins by providing information on how to establish and maintain high positive expectations for your students so that even when they misbehave, you maintain and communicate a positive vision for student success. The remaining tasks suggest ways to provide effective corrective feedback, corrective consequences, and interventions to address misbehavior.

As you are probably aware, there is no magical punitive consequence that will miraculously "cure" all student misbehavior. If there were, teachers would never have to consider other classroom management techniques! The purpose of corrective consequences is to reinforce rules and expectations designed to help students be successful in the classroom, but it is important to recognize that corrective consequences on their own are unlikely to change persistent challenging behavior. Many educators make the assumption that corrective consequences are the primary strategy used to change behavior, but consider this example outside of education.

If corrective consequences were the most powerful factor in changing behavior, a person who was speeding on the highway and received a ticket would never speed again. Clearly, many people who receive a ticket continue to periodically push the limits and speed. Why? Because there are other motivating factors for speeding—getting somewhere faster, a feeling of exhilaration, not having to drive behind someone else, and so on—some drivers will continue to speed even though they know the rules and why they are in place. For students, it is not enough to know the rules and receive corrective consequences when they misbehave. Teachers must work to motivate students to adhere to the rules more than other alternatives, and this usually does not occur only through corrective consequences.

If you find yourself asking, "What is the bigger, better punishment I can put in place?" especially with students who exhibit recurring or chronic misbehavior, remind yourself that you are unlikely to find the perfect corrective consequence that will work in the absence of more proactive and positive strategies. When you find yourself searching for that "magical corrective consequence," instead turn your attention to the S, T, O, and I variables in STOIC. No corrective consequence is so powerful that it will work to change behavior in 100% of the situations you encounter with your students.

Many teachers tend to react, rather than respond, to student misbehavior in ways that actually lead to more, rather than less, of the inappropriate behavior (Dreikurs et al., 1998; Lewis & Sugai, 1999). This chapter is based on the following ideas about corrections:

- When you treat student misbehavior as an instructional opportunity and give fluent corrections, you give students the chance to learn from mistakes (Conroy et al., 2008)
- While the C in STOIC (correct misbehavior fluently) is the weakest tool in your behavior management toolbox, you must plan your corrective feedback to ensure that it is given in an effective manner. Corrections may also inadvertently reinforce or prompt negative behaviors (Alberto & Troutman, 2012).
- If corrective interactions are not effectively delivered and carefully applied, it is entirely possible that they may damage the relational trust you have worked to establish (Gregory & Ripski, 2008).

Correcting student misbehavior effectively is surprisingly difficult to do well for a variety of reasons. A fundamental question to consider is: *What is an effective correction?*

What correction strategies are effective is a debatable topic. If a teacher reacts by communicating how angry he is to the student, he may feel better and think he has conveyed an effective correction. However, imagine that in this case the emotional reaction is actually reinforcing to the student. The student delights in demonstrating to other students her ability to press the teacher's buttons and make him upset. The teacher's emotional reaction makes him feel better in the short run, but it is not really effective because it increases the chance that the student will exhibit this behavior again. In fact, this attempt to punish the student is more closely analogous to giving the child a paycheck for misbehaving.

Some teachers may think removing a disruptive student from the classroom is an effective correction strategy. In some cases, it may be. However, in many cases, it isn't effective, and it carries significant risks. For a student who is struggling in the classroom environment, whether because of academic or social-emotional difficulties, sending the student out of the room may actually be viewed as a reward because she escapes an aversive environment. The more time the student spends outside of the classroom environment, the more she risks falling behind academically or further disengaging from peers and the teacher (Noltemeyer et al., 2015). The student may also be sent to an environment that is reinforcing because she gets one-on-one attention from someone like the principal or office staff, gets help on academic work during ISS, or gets sent home where she is unsupervised and gets to play video games.

So, if getting emotional with the student is not an effective correctional strategy, and sending a student out of class carries inherent risks, what is an effective correction? In the CHAMPS approach, an effective correction is one that:

- Changes the future occurrence of the misbehavior. The correction reduces the chance that the student will exhibit that behavior in that situation in the future.
- Does not disrupt other students. In other words, the correction is fluent. The teacher's response does not stop the flow of instruction and does not distract other students from the work they are doing at the time the student misbehaved.
- Treats the student who misbehaved with respect and honors their inherent dignity. As stated in the introduction to this book, teachers should never belittle their students.
- Does not reduce the student's motivation to exhibit positive behaviors. Imagine a high school coach who corrects athletes in a manner that makes students want to quit the team, as opposed to a coach whose corrections inspire all players to want to work even harder in the future.
- Does not jeopardize the positive relationship you have worked to establish with the student. The student should still perceive that the teacher likes her and has high expectations for her—both academically and behaviorally.

It is difficult to correct effectively, but it is absolutely essential. This is not just true for reducing misbehavior but also for providing necessary feedback for students to achieve their fullest potential. An important part of a teacher's role is to give students corrective information that will help them learn behaviors and habits that will help them be successful in any environment. If you do not correct students when they exhibit behaviors or attitudes that will cause them to struggle in future learning or job environments, you do the student a disservice by not helping them learn necessary skills. The absence of corrective feedback can be negligent at best and perhaps even discriminatory.

> *An important part of a teacher's role is to give students corrective information that will help them learn behaviors and habits to be successful in any environment.*

So it is to everyone's advantage that you correct misbehavior when it occurs. However, this must be done skillfully and with care. This chapter begins with a task designed to ensure that you have and convey high positive expectations for the success of all of your students. Corrective feedback should be designed to help students achieve those high and positive expectations of success. Other suggestions in this chapter help you correct misbehavior in a manner that helps the student whose behavior is problematic, reduces the degree to which the student's misbehavior interferes with the learning of others, and makes it easier for you to have a sense of efficacy about your role as teacher. You will learn ways to deliver effective corrective feedback and use a range of corrective strategies in class, as well as how to work with administrators and families regarding serious or chronic misbehaviors. This chapter also provides suggestions for when and how to begin moving toward proactive intervention planning when an individual student's misbehaviors are resistant to effective general classroom management and corrective techniques.

The six tasks presented and explained in this chapter are:

- Task 1: Maintain Positive Expectations
- Task 2: Provide Effective, Fluent Corrective Feedback
- Task 3: Develop a Menu of Corrective Consequences
- Task 4: Know When and When Not to Use Disciplinary Referral
- Task 5: Use Supportive Communication With Parents Regarding Student Misbehavior
- Task 6: Move Toward Proactive Intervention Planning with Individual Students Who Display Chronic Misbehavior

TASK 1

Maintain Positive Expectations

Ensure that you have, and that you convey, high positive expectations for the success of all your students.

• • • • •

Research has repeatedly demonstrated what common sense tells us: When a teacher has low expectations for students, they achieve less than if the teacher has high expectations (Jussim & Harmer, 2005; Peterson et al., 2016; Weinstein, 2009). In other words, your vision of student achievement and performance has a significant impact on the reality of your students' achievement and performance. Therefore, to be an effective teacher, you must have and convey high expectations for all your students in regard to both academic achievement and their ability to behave responsibly.

Low expectations = Low achievement
High expectations = Set the stage for high achievement

You should not wear rose-colored glasses or ignore the difficulties your students may have. Rather, you must foster high, albeit realistic, expectations for your students if you want them to accomplish what they are capable of accomplishing. To understand the difference, consider the following examples. Imagine that you have a student in your class who is permanently confined to a wheelchair due to a birth defect. Though it would be unrealistic to ignore the student's disability and pretend that she does not have different needs from the other students, it is both realistic and important for you to expect her to thrive and be successful academically in your classroom. It would be unrealistic to expect this student to get out of her chair and run with other students in PE class. However, you can and should expect her to participate actively and successfully in PE class if you get information on how to adapt the class to her needs.

For a more subtle example, imagine a student with a reputation for chronic and long-standing behavior problems. He is placed in your class at the beginning of a new school year.

To think that this student will never misbehave is unrealistic. However, it is important for you to expect that he will be able to learn to behave independently and responsibly in your classroom. This task is all about believing in the potential success of every student.

Implementing the following suggestions can help you to keep a positive attitude and high expectations for your students.

Be mindful of thoughts and statements that convey low expectations. The first step in ensuring that you have positive expectations for all students is to honestly and objectively consider the kinds of things you think to yourself and say to others about students. Whether or not you make disparaging remarks directly to students, you communicate low expectations when you let yourself think or talk about students in unproductive ways. Statements that indicate you may have low expectations for your students include:

Mission and Beliefs

Whether you are starting CHAMPS at the beginning of or during the school year, take the time to carefully consider this task. If you have low expectations for your students' behavior, they will live up to (or, perhaps more accurately, down to) your expectations. In order to successfully implement CHAMPS, you must have and communicate high expectations for the success of every student.

- *This student can really press my buttons.*
- *That kid has ADHD, so there's no way he can do it.*
- *What can you expect from a student like this?*
- *I just wish this student would move to a different school.*
- *I guess that kind of thing is expected with a student from that kind of a home.*

If you find that you have such thoughts or make such statements to others, realize that you need to stop. Try to identify specific alternate phrases that you can use that do not convey negative expectations. When you begin to think or speak negatively, force yourself to substitute a more positive way of thinking or speaking.

Even if you start the year with high expectations and positive feelings about your students, it can be difficult to sustain this mindset. It's easy to get so busy that you don't notice the negative thoughts and statements creeping in. Perhaps a particularly trying student or class wears you out and your expectations are inadvertently lowered. To alert yourself to possible negative changes, periodically make an honest evaluation of your attitude toward your students. Mark your calendar now with times during the year when you will thoroughly examine your thoughts and statements about students.

In addition, once school is in session, make a point of monitoring the statements you actually make to students themselves, especially when you are providing any sort of corrective feedback. At various times throughout the year, be honestly self-critical about whether you have been using statements such as:

- To a small group: *You students have to work with me because you can't work by yourself.*
- *I am not even going to bother to answer that question.*
- *Stop asking such stupid questions.*
- *Why don't you just grow up?*
- *You can't do that. It is too difficult for you. You better do this instead.*
- *Are you that thick that you can't figure it out?*
- *Why would you do something like that? Use your head.*

Remarks like these are not only damaging to students, they are unprofessional and unacceptable. All teachers need to make a commitment to never use this kind of language with students.

A college professor was once asked, "But what do you do about the kid you just don't like?" He wisely and calmly responded, "You can't dislike kids on company time." The point is that although you do not have to personally like every student, during the hours you are being paid, you must maintain high expectations for every student's success. You are not allowed to demonstrate dislike of any student at any time. The way you treat your students at school should have little to do with how much you like or dislike them, just as the quality of care your physician provides should not depend on her like or dislike of you. When you are feeling frustrated with a student or students, think before you speak. It is fine to address a misbehavior or problem with a statement such as, "Jill, the expectation is that you don't make lots of noise when people around you are trying to work." However, calling her names or otherwise passing judgment about her will in no way help make the situation better and will probably damage any trust she has in you.

Examine your biases. Also carefully consider whether you hold any biases about particular groups of students that may be lowering your positive expectations for those students. Examine whether you hold and convey different expectations for students who:

- Are of a different race/ethnicity than you
- Practice a particular religion
- Are identified with a disability
- Identify as LGBTQ+
- Come from situations of poverty

If you evaluate your expectations and realize that you have lower expectations for some students, engage in efforts to increase your awareness. As introduced in Chapter 1, becoming informed is the first phase of nurturing diversity, equity, inclusion, and access in schools. Becoming informed might involve reading books, seeking out colleagues with expertise, or participating in professional development sessions oriented around better serving students from particular groups. Once you are better informed, you can begin to engage in self-reflection (increasing sensitivity phase) and work towards integrating your knowledge and sensitivity into daily actions of teaching (changing practice phase).

Take care of yourself. You are more likely to maintain a positive mindset when you are in good health and a good frame of mind. Design a wellness program for yourself to ensure you are getting adequate rest and exercise and that you have activities and interests outside of your career. See Chapter 10, Task 2 for ideas for self-care.

Maintain a positive and realistic vision of student success. When problems occur, remind yourself of the vision of students behaving successfully. This is especially important when you are dealing with students who repeatedly behave poorly. Set aside a minute or two each day to visualize those students being successful.

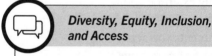

Diversity, Equity, Inclusion, and Access

Throughout the year, carefully consider whether you hold and convey different expectations for particular groups of students. If you realize you have lower expectations for some students, you must work to expand your awareness and sensitivity to address biases, then engage in intentional practices to communicate and support positive expectations for all students.

Don't take disrespectful behavior personally. If a student misbehaves, try to remain objective. If you are working to implement the strategies advocated in this book, you are likely not the cause of the problem, but you do offer the best hope of positively reaching the student. Remind yourself that you are a professional and that you can, eventually, solve any problem. Consider that when a student violates your rules, it is not an indictment of your character. It may mean that the rules or guidelines the student has learned about how to survive in other environments are at odds with the rules you are trying to teach them for school. They may not currently have the skills to exhibit expected behavior, or they may currently have reasons why misbehavior feels more rewarding or feasible than the behaviors you are expecting. Over time, you and the student can work together to find solutions.

> " *Don't take disrespectful behavior personally. If a student misbehaves, try to remain objective.* "

Make an overt effort to interact positively with every student. All students should feel that you notice and have positive regard for them. Say "hello" to them and show interest in them. When you try to make contact with every student as an individual, they know that you value them—and that reduces the likelihood that they will misbehave.

Consult with colleagues. If an individual student or group becomes particularly challenging, discuss your concerns with fellow staff members. Be careful not to communicate low expectations, but do describe the kinds of problems the student is having and seek ideas for ways to support the student. Collegial problem-solving is a powerful mechanism for getting ideas about ways to help students.

Implement the tasks described in this book. All of the tasks presented in this book are designed to help you develop an effective and comprehensive approach to managing student behavior. Keep trying different strategies until you find something that works for you.

It isn't enough to simply avoid having or communicating negative expectations about students. You also need to make a conscious effort to actively communicate high positive expectations to your students:

- Share your Guidelines for Success and tell students that you know they can achieve those guidelines.
- Remind students frequently that they are capable of achieving your classroom goals and any goal they set their minds to.
- Remember to treat all students with respect, honoring their inherent dignity.
- Interact with students in a friendly manner.
- Provide effective, fluent corrective feedback in a way that helps students meet your high expectations and achieve their full potential.

In summary, high positive expectations for students are a foundation upon which much of your Classroom Management Plan rests. They are critically important for guiding how you think about corrective interactions with students—your corrections should be designed to help students learn prosocial behaviors, learn from mistakes, and reach their full potential. Periodically evaluate whether you hold and convey high expectations for all of your students. Implement strategies to keep a positive attitude that will help you maintain these positive expectations across time.

TASK 2

Provide Effective, Fluent Corrective Feedback

Any time you are working to correct or change behavior through corrective feedback, use principles for providing effective, fluent corrections.

• • • • •

During the first week or so of school, plan to correct rule violations in an instructional manner—that is, correct the misbehavior by providing instruction about the rule and how to follow it (Darch & Kame'enui, 2004; Emmer et al., 1980, 2003; Evertson et al., 2003). Remember that your room is unique—a behavior that is unacceptable in your room may have been acceptable in the student's classroom last year. Therefore, you should view misbehavior, at least initially, as an honest error, not as an intentional or willful attempt to push the limits in your classroom. Correct these errors with informational corrections rather than corrective consequences.

After the first few weeks of school, and when you are sure students understand your rules, you should plan to move from informative early-stage corrections to mild corrective consequences that impose a penalty for breaking a rule. The next task in this chapter provides suggestions for choosing appropriate corrective consequences that help students learn that if they choose to engage in misbehavior, there is a cost associated with it.

Whether you are correcting in an instructional manner or imposing a mild penalty, there are some basic principles that should characterize all corrective feedback. The most effective error corrections are brief (Abramowitz et al., 1988), delivered consistently (Acker & O'Leary, 1988), matched to the severity of the problem (Epstein et al., 2008), and explicit in providing instruction about the behavior expectation or rule that was violated and the alternative behaviors the student should engage in instead (Colvin & Sugai, 1988). The rest of this task provides practical suggestions for implementing corrective consequences consistently, calmly, briefly, and privately.

NOTE: In addition to correcting rule violations, you will also be making a concerted effort to provide positive feedback when students are following the rules.

Plan to Implement the Corrective Consequence Consistently

For corrective consequences to reduce or eliminate misbehavior problems, especially purposeful or habitual misbehavior, they must be implemented consistently (Acker & O'Leary, 1988; Alberto & Troutman, 2012; Scheuermann & Hall, 2008). This means that any time a student exhibits a rule violation and it is observed, a corrective consequence must be applied. The corrective consequences can be something as mild as a gentle verbal reprimand or marking a tally on a recording sheet to something as severe as an office disciplinary referral (ODR) and administrator-assigned consequences.

Regardless of what the consequence is, when you implement a corrective consequence only some of the time, the consequence, no matter how severe, is unlikely to change the behavior. In fact, it may even make things worse than if there were no consequence at all (Barbetta et al., 2005). Any time a student is able to violate a rule and not receive the designated consequence, they are likely to feel a great sense of satisfaction. Getting away with misbehavior can be great fun, and the student may find they like to see how frequently they can engage in the behavior and not get caught.

Teachers tend to implement corrective consequences based on an accumulation of misbehavior. Teacher emotion sometimes controls classroom consequences, but corrections should be controlled by a series of rules. Let's say a student gets away with a misbehavior five times—but the sixth time is the last straw for the teacher, and they finally give the student a consequence. To the student, the consequence for the sixth time seems to happen out of the blue, only as a result of the teacher's emotion. After all, the student did the same thing five other times without receiving a corrective consequence. While this is understandable behavior on the part of the teacher and can happen to anyone, it will not create a disciplined environment in your class. To reduce misbehavior over time, you need to define specific behaviors that are not acceptable and then implement corrective consequences for them every time, regardless of how you feel about the behavior at the moment.

Make sure you have a clear definition of the difference between acceptable and unacceptable behavior. Your goal is to develop clear expectations about what behaviors are unacceptable so that you can be consistent with your students. If you are concerned about disruptions, specify the precise behaviors you consider disruptive and connect the concept of disruption to one of the positively stated rules. For example, if you have the rule "Work during work times," you can teach students which disruptive behaviors would violate that rule. Also be sure to provide positive examples of nondisruptive behavior and class participation so the class knows exactly what you expect. Let the students know that when you observe the negative behaviors, you will implement a corrective consequence from a menu of corrections (see the next task for how to develop a menu of corrective consequences).

When you don't implement consequences consistently, it becomes difficult for students to know what is and what is not acceptable behavior. If a student sometimes receives corrective consequences for a behavior and other times engages in the behavior without consequences from you, the line between acceptable and unacceptable behavior becomes blurred. It also leads to an environment in which students feel the teacher is being unfair and arbitrary, and perhaps picking on certain students, as in, "Everyone else is doing it too—why are you picking on me?"

Make sure the corrective consequence fits the severity and frequency of the misbehavior. One way to ensure consistency is to err on the side of milder rather than harsher corrective consequences. When deciding which corrective consequence to implement, choose one that matches the severity of the problem (Simonsen et al., 2008; Wolfgang & Glickman, 1986) and ensure that you are willing to apply that correction for every instance of the misbehavior. All too often, teachers pick a consequence that is so harsh they are unwilling to implement it when the occasion arises.

"LaVona, stop that because I do not want to have to give you a detention." This statement is an indication of inconsistency. In this case, you are letting the student get away with it, but in some cases you may give a correction. Choose a consequence that fits even the mildest example of the rule violation so that you will be comfortable implementing it every time the student exhibits an irresponsible behavior. Also consider how often the student or group of students is likely to exhibit the misbehavior. Based on that frequency, select corrections that can be applied every time the misbehavior occurs. For example, if students habitually use swear words several times during each period, you will not be able to be consistent in assigning lunch detention for every swear word. A milder consequence, such as 10 seconds of time owed at the end of class for each swear word, allows you to remain consistent. When determining the severity of a consequence, err on the side of making consequences too mild, because you may not follow through if the consequence is too harsh. It is better to implement mild corrective consequences consistently than to apply a bigger penalty that is inconsistently administered.

> *Whatever corrective consequence you choose, plan to implement it in the same way for all behavior within that category and with any student.*

Whatever corrective consequence you choose, plan to implement it in the same way for all behavior within that category and with any student who violates that rule. In other words, if you decide to deduct a point, all disruptive acts should result in the loss of one point. Do not create a situation in which some disruptive acts cost one point and some cost three. You will find yourself having to explain why you feel the acts are of different severities and deserve different penalties. If you decide to use time owed as a consequence for a student who tends to be disrespectful, have each infraction equal the same amount of time owed (for example, 10 seconds owed after class). Do not issue 10 seconds in some instances and several minutes in others.

Again, when you err on the side of mild consequences, you are much more likely to follow through than when the consequences are too harsh. Also keep in mind that a student may exhibit the misbehavior several times. If the consequence is fairly severe—a detention, for example—you probably cannot assign three detentions to the same student in one class period. On the other hand, if the student is disruptive three times, you can impose 15 seconds of time owed after class or during recess for each incident.

NOTE: Some flexibility is needed within your plan for corrective consequences. For example, if you realize that a student is acting out because he is upset after finding out his parents are divorcing, you might pull the student aside and tell him that his behavior is unacceptable but that you know he's having a hard time because of things outside of school. Tell him that you are here for him and willing to work with him to figure out how to make things OK for him at school, but that if the current negative behavior continues, a corrective consequence will be applied. By providing a bit of flexibility within your plan, you are also able to meet the individual needs of your students.

Plan to Implement the Correction Calmly

Some students have learned that there is a high probability they can make adults frustrated, hurt, or angry by misbehaving. For some students, this is virtually an invitation to misbehave as often as they can. If you get angry when correcting a student, your anger may reinforce the student's misbehavior (Alberto & Troutman, 2012). When a student is seeking a sense of power, seeing an adult frustrated or exasperated can be highly satisfying. For this student, getting an adult angry on a regular basis can provide a huge sense of power and control. You must strive to implement corrective consequences unemotionally so your reactions do not give any students the idea that they can have power over you by misbehaving (Dreikurs et al., 1998).

Angry and emotional reactions can be highly damaging to the relational trust you have intentionally worked to build with your students (Gregory & Ripski, 2008). For students who have experienced trauma, especially those students who have experienced emotional or physical abuse, reactions like yelling or any sort of physical posturing can be highly triggering (Craig, 2015). This can even occur for students who are simply observing the emotional interaction between you and another student. At their worst, angry and emotional reactions can cause some students to fear you. In other cases, students may feel a sense of worry or panic because you are demonstrating that you are not in control of yourself or the situation. Other students may be so used to hearing anger and frustration from other educators and their family members that they are totally unfazed by your attempts to use anger or disappointment to change their behavior. Your reactions just become background noise.

One additional reason to remain calm and emotionally neutral in your corrective interactions with students is that it can help defuse situations in which there is a risk of emotional escalation. Some students do not know how to calm themselves down when they begin to get upset. When additional emotion is infused into the situation by an adult's angry reactions, the student is likely to continue ramping up, sometimes to the point of physical violence or running from the classroom. If your interactions with the student are emotionally neutral, it demonstrates to the student that it is possible to control one's emotions. You demonstrate a powerful positive model through your behavior. You also convey a sense of calm for a student who may be feeling out of control.

Some students are virtually conditioned to respond to angry reactions from adults with more anger and aggression (think about the types of yelling matches you can observe on reality TV). By remaining calm even when the student is angry, you demonstrate that you are not going to get sucked into a ping-pong match of negative interactions with the student.

Use emotionally neutral corrective interactions. While it is easy to say that you should remain calm and emotionally neutral when students are misbehaving, this can be easier said than done! Chronic student misbehavior can be hugely triggering. You may even find that you exhibit physiological symptoms of distress (e.g., increased pulse rate, sweating, tight muscles, fast and shallow breathing) when you are entering into activities where students frequently struggle or when certain students walk into your room.

The following suggestions can help you remain calm (or at least act calm) when you know you might fall into the trap of emotional corrective interactions.

- Carefully consider what an emotionally neutral correction looks and sounds like. The easiest way to do this is to think about what you look like and what your voice sounds like when you are delivering an academic or content area correction. If a student made an error on a math problem, and you are telling the

Relational Trust

Avoid angry, emotional reactions to misbehavior like yelling, physical posturing, or even extreme disappointment, which can damage relational trust. Demonstrating calm and neutrality when students misbehave can enhance relational trust by demonstrating that you don't take mistakes personally and that you are in control of yourself even when students are struggling.

Logic Over Impulse

Remember your amygdala? In Chapter 1, you learned how student misbehavior can trigger emotional and physiological responses and lead you to react in impulsive and emotional ways. These types of reactions have a high probability of escalating negative situations. Use strategies to calm yourself down when students misbehave so you can rely on logic and reason rather than impulse and emotion as you respond to misbehavior.

student it is incorrect and how to fix it, what facial expression do you use? What is your tone of voice and voice level? What does your body language look like? Or, if you are a music teacher and you notice that a group of students is pitchy on a portion of a song, consider what you look and sound like when you are helping them correct this error. Identify your version of an emotionally neutral facial expression, body language, and tone of voice and voice level.

- Once you have identified *emotionally neutral*, practice delivering common corrections to misbehavior. It may seem silly, but practicing these interactions in a mirror or with a colleague or family member can help you apply calm interactional techniques at times when you may be feeling upset. You might even think through common misbehaviors or negative interactions you've had with students and script out how you could respond in the future. Then role-play these situations. The point of this practice is to be able to *act* calm in the moment of misbehavior with students, even if internally you are feeling upset or out of control.
- The one absolute in behavior management is that belittlement, humiliation, and ridicule of a student has no place in your behavioral repertoire. In any situations where you know you are likely to feel angry or seriously frustrated, be very careful to remember this principle and work to avoid any language or action that violates it.

Deliver gentle verbal reprimands. To use a gentle verbal reprimand (correction), simply go over to the student or students engaged in misbehavior and quietly remind or tell them what they should be doing at that moment. For example, you move over and quietly say to two students who are talking during a teacher-directed portion of a lesson, "Johanna, Alexander, if you have something to say, raise your hand and wait to be called on." If you are delivering a corresponding corrective consequence, you will deliver it through a gentle verbal reprimand such as, "Elias, that was inappropriate. I will need to call your mom after school to let her know what you said. I hope I can let her know that you participated appropriately for the rest of class." Effective verbal reprimands have the following features (Abramowitz et al., 1988; Jenson & Reavis, 1996; Matheson et al., 2005):

- They are short—one or two words or very short sentences.
- They cause only a very brief interruption in the lesson.
- They are given when you are physically near misbehaving students (approximately 2 to 3 feet)—not from across the room.
- Their tone and content are respectful.
- They are clear and unequivocal.
- They state the expected behavior, rather than accusing the student(s) of the misbehavior or asking them to behave for you (e.g., "Remember the CHAMPS expectation is . . ." vs. "You need to" or "I need you to").
- They are given in a way that creates the illusion of privacy. You don't want to try to make it truly secret or the other students will try to hear what you are saying to the misbehaving student, but you also do not want to make it seem that you are putting the student on public display.

Even if another corrective consequence is delivered (e.g., timeout, positive practice, detention, ODR), follow the suggestions above when delivering the reprimand and additional consequence. Avoid lecturing, making a public display of the correction by shouting across the room, and other missteps that commonly occur when delivering a correction.

Trauma-Sensitive Practice

Avoid approaching a student from behind to give a correction. Students who have been victims of abuse may become anxious or react negatively. Also avoid touching the student when providing a reprimand (e.g., don't touch the student's shoulder or hand), and avoid confrontational body language such as standing over the student or squaring off your shoulders with the student. The most effective corrections are usually delivered at eye level or slightly below the student by kneeling down and beside or diagonal to the student.

Plan to Interact With the Student Briefly, and Without Arguing, at the Time of the Misbehavior

When any student breaks a rule, your interaction with that student at that time should be brief (Abramowitz et al., 1988). Simply state the rule and the consequence. A common mistake is to explain and justify. The student may ask you for such information, but resist explaining yourself. Any explanations should already be self-evident from your instruction or can be analyzed in a discussion with the student later. Corrections should typically be no more than one short sentence or two, so we use the term *one liners* to refer to effective, brief corrections. For example, "Susan, please remember to keep your hands to yourself in class" or "Penny, Rule 2 says 'work during work times.'"

Sometime during the first few days of school, let the students know that if they ever want to speak to you about something they think is unfair, they can make an appointment to see you before or after school. Once you have made this clear, simply remind any student who tries to argue that they can make an appointment to see you, and then resume teaching. It is imperative that you don't let students draw you into explaining your actions, your consequences, or your reasoning. Doing so transfers the power to them and lets them know that they can disrupt class by misbehaving and by making you explain yourself. It also provides far too much attention to the misbehaving student, which can be gratifying for a student who loves attention and highly embarrassing for a student who does not.

Although keeping interactions brief may be a difficult habit to develop, you will find that it allows you to keep your focus where it belongs—on teaching and providing positive feedback to all students who are meeting your expectations. Remember that the frequency of your positive feedback must far outweigh your negative feedback. Think about the consequence you plan to use for a targeted misbehavior. If you cannot imagine implementing that consequence without lengthy explanations or negotiations at the time of the misbehavior, you should consider a different consequence.

Deliver Corrective Feedback in a Private Way as Much as Possible

Many corrections are far too public. They are shouted across the room or delivered in a loud voice in front of the entire class. For students who are seeking attention through misbehavior, these public displays provide them exactly what they want—attention. For other students, public corrections are highly embarrassing and can damage the student's positive regard and trust in you.

Instead of publicly correcting, try to deliver corrective feedback in a manner that creates an illusion of privacy. Work to minimize the audience to your interaction by moving close enough to the student that you can deliver feedback in a quiet voice while still respecting the student's physical space. Even if the student's voice is raised, continue to interact in a calm and private way. For example, with the two students who are quietly but inappropriately talking during an independent work time, you could walk calmly towards the students (but avoid making a beeline), possibly delivering some positive feedback to students who are working on your way. Once you reach the students, use a quiet voice and nonconfrontational body language to deliver corrective information. While this approach takes a few extra seconds, it is a much more effective technique.

In some circumstances, student misbehavior is so obvious and disruptive that other students may already be observing to see what happens. However, it still benefits you to continue to work to minimize the public display of your interaction with the student. By moving closer to the student and talking in a quiet voice, you demonstrate to the student that you don't want to put them on the spot or embarrass them. You also illustrate that you are not willing to get sucked into a public, argumentative display with the student.

Adopt Trauma-Sensitive Discipline Policies

A trauma-sensitive approach involves discipline policies that hold students responsible for their actions through fair and consistent responses to misbehavior delivered by supportive and caring adults (NASP, 2015). Reflect on whether any of the disciplinary practices commonly used within your building have the potential for contributing to re-traumatization and whether they might be replaced by other methods that promote skill-building. For example, timeout and seclusion procedures may trigger fear and remind a child of past experiences with isolation or abandonment. Instead of assigning a timeout, a teacher could prompt the student to take a "time-in"—having the student remain at their seat, but instructing them to put their head down on their desk and pay attention to their feelings and thoughts for the next 5 minutes. Afterward, the teacher checks in with the student to see how they are feeling, talks through any problem-solving that needs to occur, and praises the student for being able to calm down and manage their feelings.

Give Positive Feedback When Behavior Improves

Whichever correction strategy you use, be sure that when the students who engaged in the misbehavior begin to behave responsibly, you give them positive feedback. Students need to see that you notice positive behavior more than misbehavior (Gable et al., 2009). This is important because, generally, the behaviors that receive more attention increase while those that receive less attention decrease. Therefore, when you see a student re-engage in appropriate behavior, be sure to provide specific praise and acknowledgment for that behavior to increase the likelihood the student will engage in the expected behavior in the future. Also, remember that if one or more of these strategies does not solve the problem quickly, you will need to develop and implement an intervention plan based on a more thoughtful analysis of the misbehavior (Babkie, 2006; Sugai et al., 2000; Trussell, 2008).

NOTE: The corrective consequences that you include in your Classroom Management Plan are designed to address the vast majority of student misbehaviors. Some students may exhibit chronic misbehavior that will require planned interventions rather than just corrective consequences. Refer to the strategies in Task 6 of this chapter to address chronic misbehaviors from individual students. However, the strong foundation you build for implementing rules and consequences with the majority of your students will help ensure that techniques for chronic misbehavior remain individualized and manageable.

In summary, effective corrections are delivered in a way that is consistent, calm, brief, and private. It is also important to follow up with positive feedback when behavior improves. If any of these are currently difficult for you, make a note in your Classroom Management Plan in Correction Procedures for Misbehavior about how to deliver effective corrections. When you follow these principles of effective corrections, you are less likely to risk escalation or inadvertently reinforce the misbehavior. More importantly, effective corrections preserve your positive relationship with the student. The student never feels belittled, ridiculed, or humiliated by your interactions. The student knows that you are correcting because you have high expectations for their success.

TASK 3

Develop a Menu of Corrective Consequences

Calmly implement corrective consequences when rules are violated.

• • • • •

Having a range of corrective consequences in your management toolbox is important so that you can impose corrective consequences for rule violations that fit the nature and severity of the violation. At the earliest stages of seeing a particular behavioral concern, and especially at the beginning of the year, your corrections will be more instructional in nature. Strategies like proximity, gentle verbal reprimands, and discussion at a neutral time allow you to respond to rule violations with corrective techniques that clarify your rules and expectations.

Early-stage correctional techniques are especially important in the first 20 days of school and when new students enter your classroom. Chapter 9 provides more information about how to deliver early-stage corrections in the first month of school.

Once students fully understand your classroom procedures and classroom rules, you will use a range of corrective consequence strategies that allow you to respond consistently, unemotionally, and quickly to rule violations. Having a range of corrective consequences available also helps ensure that if one type of consequence is not working to change behavior, you can pull other strategies from the menu.

Once you have created a menu of possible corrective consequences, put careful thought into what the typical consequence for rule violations should be. While you should avoid being too rigid in saying that every time you see a particular misbehavior it must be paired with a specific corrective consequence, if you do not plan your likely response to common misbehaviors in advance, the probability is high that you may inadvertently reinforce misbehavior by being emotional or by giving too much attention to the misbehaving students (Alberto & Troutman, 2012). Identify what should happen when a student does not arrive on time with all materials. Identify an appropriate consequence for tardiness, speaking out of turn, and so on.

Corrective Consequences for the Classroom

The following pages contain descriptions of effective corrective consequences that can be implemented in your classroom. Each description includes a brief explanation of the consequence and how to use it. Remember that it is better to choose simple, mild consequences that you can apply consistently (i.e., every time the misbehavior occurs) than to use more severe penalties that you do not feel comfortable using when misbehavior is observed. Also remember to assign corrective consequences calmly, and keep the interaction with the student as brief and as private as possible.

Be Mindful of the "Weight" of Your Chosen Consequences

While in general there are milder and more severe consequences that indicate the degree to which student misbehavior was inappropriate, it is also important to recognize that individual students will respond differently to certain types of corrections. Some students may remain unfazed when you assign any consequence, while others may be much more sensitive to the correction procedure you use. Be mindful of your students' personalities and individual needs when choosing consequences. The corrective consequences you choose to use should be mild enough that the student won't feel bad or guilty for hours or days to come. The manner in which you deliver the consequence will also make a difference: Corrections that are delivered calmly, briefly, privately, and respectfully are less likely to embarrass or upset a student. This is especially true for students with internalizing behaviors (e.g., anxiety, depression, shyness) and students who may have experienced trauma.

In addition to these consequences, your school has a range of possible administrator-assigned consequences; however, it is beneficial to manage misbehavior as much as possible within your classroom setting. The next task provides information about when office involvement with misbehavior is appropriate, but it also describe some of the downsides of overreliance on administrator-assigned consequences to solve management concerns.

Proximity

In the classroom, proximity involves simply moving toward the students who are engaged in misbehavior. The proximity correction strategy is based on a principle of human behavior that is used very effectively by the highway patrol—most people, even those who tend to exceed the speed limit, are more likely to obey the speed limit when they see a patrol car. Students' misbehavior is likely to cease as you approach them because your proximity at that moment prompts them to stop exhibiting the misbehavior and start exhibiting the desired behavior. The more you move throughout your room in unpredictable ways, the better you can correct misbehavior through proximity (Colvin et al., 1997; Gunter et al., 1995).

For example, if you are presenting a lesson and a couple of students begin talking to each other instead of listening to you, start walking over to that part of the room while continuing to present the lesson. If the students quit talking while you are on the way, continue the lesson from where you are and then move to a different place in the room or back to the front. After a few minutes, make eye contact with the students who were talking. You may even want to compliment them for listening and participating (although in middle school this is inadvisable if you think it would embarrass them in front of peers).

Nonverbal Correction

Sometimes simply delivering a nonverbal cue, such as giving a hand signal to sit down or subtly shaking your head to indicate "no," can be an effective way to redirect the student's behavior. These are simple gestures that address the misbehavior without requiring a verbal response from the student. Gaining eye contact with a student can also increase compliance and redirect behavior (Kodak et al., 2007). A few seconds of eye contact communicate observance of behavior and can cue the student to stop a behavior or resume a designated task (Allday, 2011). Note that you should take cultural considerations into account when utilizing eye contact, as some cultures view eye contact between an adult and a child as disrespectful or threatening.

> **Diversity, Equity, Inclusion, and Access**
>
> *Expectations regarding when and how eye contact is appropriate differ greatly across cultures. Take these cultural considerations into account when using or expecting eye contact, especially during times of misbehavior.*

Another form of nonverbal correction is a simple direction or reprimand written on a sticky note and delivered to the student without any verbal interaction. This is a great way to deliver private corrective feedback to a student who may feel embarrassed by a verbal reprimand. It provides minimal attention to the misbehavior for students who may be attention seeking. If you are using the CHAMPS acronym and have students with limited reading skills, you can simply write down the letter you wish to address. For example, preteach to your students that if they are not following your expectations for conversation, you may write C on a sticky note and hand it to them. This will serve as their reminder to look at the CHAMPS poster and follow the posted expectations for conversation during the remainder of the activity or transition.

Provide a Group Redirect

Sometimes, rather than addressing an individual student, a group reminder about expectations can serve to get a student back on track. Avoid singling out an individual by directing the group's attention to what they should be doing. "Class, just a reminder to everyone, right now I should see your book open on page 119. At this point, you are either reading silently or beginning to write about the thinking prompts in your journal." Group redirects typically work best when a student's misbehavior is not hugely obvious to other students (e.g., quiet off-task behavior) or when multiple students or groups could use a reminder (e.g., several small groups have veered off track during a cooperative activity). If the inappropriate behavior is displayed by only one student and it is fairly obvious who the group redirect is for, it would be more effective to use a quiet gentle verbal reprimand with the individual student. For example, if Timothy is the only student out of his seat and you say, "Class, everyone needs to remember that the expectations are to ask for permission to move about the classroom," this very public reprimand could have a negative effect by singling Timothy out. Move closer to Timothy and quietly remind him about the expectation.

Redirect by Asking a Question or Providing an Offer of Help

It may seem counterintuitive, but in many cases, asking a question or providing an offer of help can be a highly effective correctional technique. While not punitive in nature, these interactions are corrective because the purpose of your question or offer for help is to get a student on track. It is also corrective in the sense that you are providing attention to the student at a time when they are not meeting your expectations. Imagine a student who is not working during work time. Rather than walking over and saying, "You need to get to work," try asking something like, "Do you have any questions before you get started?" or "Is everything OK?" With the first question, you communicate that you are confident the student will get started. You also open an opportunity for a student who is unsure of what to do to ask you for help. If you have a student who tends to resist directions from adults, this kind of interaction can be a less confrontational way to prompt the student. An offer of help, such as "Let's do the first two problems together" or "I see your pencil is broken. You can borrow mine," can provide a mild prompt and create a snowball effect that gets a student moving in the right direction.

If the student is truly upset about something, asking a question like "Are you OK?" demonstrates that you care about the student's well-being even if she is struggling to meet expectations. One teacher described a situation in which a student wasn't following directions, and instead of overtly reprimanding the student, the teacher used this technique. She said to the student, "Tanisha, I've noticed you seem upset today. Is everything OK?" The student, who often exhibited overt defiance and aggressive behavior, broke down in tears and explained that a close family member was seriously injured the night before and she wasn't sure if he was going to be OK. If the teacher had provided a direct reprimand in that particular moment, the student would have been highly likely to escalate because she had a history of escalation when distressed. Instead, the teacher was able to provide care and support for the student throughout the day. This allowed the student to participate appropriately, while also demonstrating that the teacher was there for her student in a time of difficulty. The teacher indicated that from that point, the student's behavior and motivation significantly improved, and the student would come to the teacher for support when she was struggling.

Note that the previous examples feature very different types of questions than asking whether the student was engaged in an inappropriate behavior or not. If two students are talking, and the teacher walks over and says, "Are you talking?" it is highly likely that some students will respond "no!" This invites a back-and-forth argument about whether the student was following expectations or not. If you know that students were not following expectations, simply go over to them and remind them of the rule or expectation, or ask a question like, "Can you tell me what you are supposed to be working on right now?"

The Power of Praise

While not a direct correctional technique, one strategy to prompt responsible behavior is to praise several students who are behaving responsibly and who are near a student who is not meeting expectations. If the student who is misbehaving is starved for attention, he will see that he can get your positive attention and feedback if he is following expectations by the time you reach him. If he is unsure of what the expectations are, your specific positive feedback cues the student in on what to do (e.g., "Katalei, thank you for turning right to page 382" or "Jacob, great job keeping your hands to yourself while lining up"). This strategy also helps to boost your positive ratios of interaction within your class, ensuring that you are in fact paying attention to those students who are meeting expectations.

The tricky thing with the strategy of praising other students to prompt a student who is not meeting expectations is to ensure that you are authentically interacting in positive ways with the other students, not just using them as a prop! Avoid looking at the student who is misbehaving while interacting positively with the other students. Ensure that you are praising something meaningful the other student is doing well.

Planned Discussion

Sometimes you may need to talk with a student about a misbehavior in a way that is more detailed and lengthy than a reprimand. For example, if a student makes a disrespectful comment as you are presenting a lesson, you may want to have a talk with the student about the importance of treating others respectfully. Provide a gentle reprimand immediately and let the student know that the behavior is serious enough that you want to discuss it later—after class.

Discussions that occur at a neutral time usually work best. In fact, there are several reasons why having a discussion immediately after a misbehavior tends to be ineffective. Think about the downsides of having a discussion with the student in the hallway as an immediate response to misbehavior:

- You leave the rest of the class waiting.
- You give the misbehaving student too much immediate attention.
- The student is likely to be defensive.
- You are likely to be somewhat frustrated or angry.

It is far more effective to wait until later, when the class is engaged in independent work, or even after class, and then privately discuss the situation with the student. During your meeting, be sure to discuss with the student better ways to handle similar situations in the future. Reproducible 8.1 is a form you can use to record a discussion with a student about an isolated incident of misbehavior. The What Happened? form guides you in discussing the event from the student's point of view as well as your own, discussing teacher actions and student actions that will be taken in the future to avoid a similar problem, and whether there should be a follow-up meeting.

If you have already had a discussion or two with a student in response to similar misbehaviors, consider whether subsequent discussions on their own will be beneficial or if additional strategies are needed. If these previous discussions were not effective in changing the student's behavior, additional discussions may not produce a different result without some other adjustment in your management approach. Continue having periodic planned discussions with the student to evaluate how things are going, but consider implementing other corrective techniques and STOIC strategies to help the student be successful. See Task 6 in this chapter for guidance on how to move towards intervention planning with students who have chronic behavioral concerns.

Count and Chart

If you have already discussed the problem behavior with the student but have seen no improvement, explain to the student that you are going to conduct a frequency count (or duration or latency recording for less frequent but lengthy behaviors). At the end of each day or period, the student will chart the amount of misbehavior to help her understand just how often the misbehavior is occurring. This strategy can also be used with a whole class.

Record the number of times the misbehavior occurs by writing tally marks on a recording sheet (e.g., tally the number of times the student disrupted or blurted out) or recording the length of time the misbehavior occurs (e.g., record the number of minutes of work refusal). Tell the student you will give her a signal every time you record an instance, or have the student do the recording when you signal. Explain that you will use the data to determine the student's progress and whether you need to talk with her parents or involve an administrator. One benefit of the Count and Chart strategy is it allows you to address each instance of misbehavior consistently but without providing much attention or emotional energy to each interaction. For a student who is unaware of the frequency or length of their misbehavior, or for student who is seeking attention through misbehavior, this can be a very powerful strategy.

Reproducible 8.2 is an example of a simple chart you could use to tally the number of misbehaviors recorded across a week.

Planned Ignoring

When verbal reprimands and other mild corrections haven't been effective, ask yourself whether the student (or class) may be seeking your attention through misbehavior. By providing corrections, you may inadvertently be reinforcing this need for attention. Planned ignoring can be an effective next step, but it should be implemented in a preplanned way. This strategy can teach the student that misbehaving to get attention is ineffective, but it also requires that you pay lots of attention to the student when they are not engaged in misbehavior. Ignoring a misbehavior does not mean you will ignore the student.

Reproducible 8.1 *What Happened?*

What Happened? — CHAMPS

STUDENT _____ DATE _____
TEACHER _____ GRADE/CLASS _____

Teacher's description of problem _____
_____
_____
_____

Student's description of problem _____
_____
_____

Teacher actions   Student actions
_____   _____
_____   _____
_____   _____
_____   _____
_____   _____

Does there need to be a follow-up meeting? ☐ Yes ☐ No

Date _____ Time _____ Participants _____
_____

© 2021 Ancora Publishing   REPRODUCIBLE 8.1

Reproducible 8.2 *Behavior Counting Form*

Behavior Counting Form — CHAMPS

STUDENT _____ GRADE/CLASS _____
TEACHER _____

WEEK OF: _____
Monday   ① ② ③ ④ ⑤ ⑥ ⑦ ⑧ ⑨ ⑩ ⑪ ⑫ ⑬ ⑭ ⑮ ⑯ ⑰ ⑱ ⑲ ⑳ 21 22 23 24 25
Tuesday   ① ② ③ ④ ⑤ ⑥ ⑦ ⑧ ⑨ ⑩ ⑪ ⑫ ⑬ ⑭ ⑮ ⑯ ⑰ ⑱ ⑲ ⑳ 21 22 23 24 25
Wednesday ① ② ③ ④ ⑤ ⑥ ⑦ ⑧ ⑨ ⑩ ⑪ ⑫ ⑬ ⑭ ⑮ ⑯ ⑰ ⑱ ⑲ ⑳ 21 22 23 24 25
Thursday ① ② ③ ④ ⑤ ⑥ ⑦ ⑧ ⑨ ⑩ ⑪ ⑫ ⑬ ⑭ ⑮ ⑯ ⑰ ⑱ ⑲ ⑳ 21 22 23 24 25
Friday   ① ② ③ ④ ⑤ ⑥ ⑦ ⑧ ⑨ ⑩ ⑪ ⑫ ⑬ ⑭ ⑮ ⑯ ⑰ ⑱ ⑲ ⑳ 21 22 23 24 25

WEEK OF: _____
Monday   ① ② ③ ④ ⑤ ⑥ ⑦ ⑧ ⑨ ⑩ ⑪ ⑫ ⑬ ⑭ ⑮ ⑯ ⑰ ⑱ ⑲ ⑳ 21 22 23 24 25
Tuesday   ① ② ③ ④ ⑤ ⑥ ⑦ ⑧ ⑨ ⑩ ⑪ ⑫ ⑬ ⑭ ⑮ ⑯ ⑰ ⑱ ⑲ ⑳ 21 22 23 24 25

Have a discussion with your class at a neutral time. Let students know that from this point forward you will ignore all instances of the specific misbehavior. When you see that a student is engaged in the expected behavior, you will give them lots of your attention and positive feedback. A classic example of a behavior that responds well to planned ignoring is blurting out. If a student blurts out without raising his hand, the reason is likely because you interact with him (at least occasionally) when he blurts out a response. If you ignore the student consistently when he is blurting out by calling on other students who have their hands raised (even if they provide the same answer the student was blurting out!), the behavior will be extinguished in a few days or weeks. Another classic behavior that responds well to planned ignoring is whining—teach students that whenever they use a whining tone of voice, you will act like you do not hear it. Model examples and non-examples of a whining versus appropriate tone. Let students know that as soon as they try again in a normal speaking voice, you will provide your full attention.

When implementing planned ignoring, do not acknowledge the behavior verbally or physically (including facial expressions and gestures). Also ensure that you are prepared to follow through with the plan to ignore, unless the student begins escalating into physically dangerous behaviors. It is likely that the student's misbehavior may get slightly worse for a short period of time as they work harder to try to get the attention you previously provided when they misbehaved. If you ignore the student but at some point get so annoyed or distressed that you end up interacting with them, you teach the student they only have to try harder to misbehave to get your attention.

Before you begin using planned ignoring, let your class know about your plan for ignoring the misbehavior so they do not think you are using different standards for behavior with different students. Let students know that they will see you ignoring certain misbehaviors as a way to help everyone learn to follow expectations and thrive in your classroom. Tell them that they should simply ignore these misbehaviors as well—they do not need to report them to you unless a student is engaging in something physically dangerous or harmful to another student.

Time Owed

When a student misbehaves and you have to intervene, some time is wasted. Therefore, a reasonable corrective consequence is to have the student lose time from an activity they value—recess or a fun activity, for example. Time owed is an appropriate and effective corrective consequence for misbehaviors that occur frequently (disruptions, talking during lessons, name-calling, disrespectful behavior) and for behaviors that tend to involve duration (a student is out of her seat for a period of time, or a student takes an excessive amount of time to comply with a direction). For a duration type of misbehavior, the time a student owes should be equal to the time spent misbehaving.

To use this corrective consequence, you will have to decide when the time owed will be paid back. The time should be deducted from an activity that the student values. For example, for an elementary student who likes recess, time owed from recess is an easy and logical choice. If your schedule does not include recesses, or if the misbehaving student prefers not to go to recess, possible alternatives are passing periods between classes or free-time activities. It is important that the payment of the time owed does not interfere with the student's time with another teacher. Thus, if keeping middle school students after class for more than 1 minute means that they won't be able to get to their next class on time, you should plan to keep any student for no more than 1 minute. Similarly, an elementary student should not be assigned to repay time owed during PE class if this reduces the time the student spends with the PE teacher.

Another decision you need to make is how much time will be owed for each infraction. As a general rule, keep the amount of time short enough that you will not hesitate to implement the consequence each time the student misbehaves. Also keep in mind the amount of time available for the penalty. Thus, elementary teachers might have students owe 30 seconds per infraction, while middle school teachers (who can't keep students after class for more than 1 minute) may use 10 seconds owed for each infraction. Although 10 seconds might sound almost silly, it is actually a pretty long time for an adolescent who wants to be in the hall talking with friends. And it allows you to assign the consequence for up to six infractions. Middle school teachers may need to establish a policy such as: "Each infraction will cost 10 seconds of time owed, and if there are more than six infractions, the student will be assigned to Lunchtime Detention."

When dealing with behaviors that last for a period of time, establish a minute-by-minute correspondence between the behavior and the consequence so that the number of minutes owed corresponds directly to the number of minutes the student engages in the misbehavior.

Finally, decide what the student will do when repaying the time owed. As a general rule, have the student do nothing. If it is their first time paying this consequence, you may wish to use the time to discuss the misbehavior and ways the student can behave more responsibly in the future. Do not do this regularly, however, as the one-on-one interaction time with you may become reinforcing to the student and actually serve to perpetuate the misbehavior.

Timeout (In Class)

When a student engages in misbehavior frequently, an in-class timeout communicates that taking part in class activities is a privilege. Considerable research suggests that in-class timeout can be a successful consequence strategy for reducing misbehavior (e.g., Brantner & Doherty, 1983; Clark et al., 1973).

Many people think that the purpose of timeout is to send the student to an aversive setting. That is not the case. The actual purpose of timeout is to remove a misbehaving student from the opportunity to earn positive reinforcement (Taylor & Miller, 1997). In other words, you communicate to the student that if they engage in the misbehavior, they will not get to participate in the interesting, productive, and enjoyable activities going on in the classroom. The obvious implication here is that instruction and classroom activities need to be interesting, productive, and enjoyable. If the student dislikes what is going on in the classroom, a timeout is unlikely to be effective, and it may actually be reinforcing because it allows the student to escape an environment or activity they dislike. Following are descriptions of four different types of timeouts that are appropriate for different situations and ages.

> " *The actual purpose of timeout is to remove a misbehaving student from the opportunity to earn positive reinforcement (Taylor & Miller, 1997).* "

- **Timeout from a favorite object (primary level).** When developing an intervention plan to correct a primary student with chronic misbehavior, ask the student if he would like to bring a favorite object, such as a stuffed animal, to class. Tell him that the stuffed animal is there to watch him work and follow the rules. Initially the object is placed on the student's desk. If the student misbehaves, the object is removed and placed on the teacher's desk facing away from the student. When the student begins behaving appropriately, the object is returned to the student's desk. Rhode et al. (2020) describe this as a Bumpy Bunny Timeout.

  If you are concerned that the student may play with the object, explain to the student that playing with the object means that the object goes to timeout on your desk. Another option is to place the object near the student initially, on a bookshelf near his desk, for example. If the student misbehaves, take the object to a different part of the room and place it facing away from the student. When the student begins to behave responsibly again, return the object to the shelf near the student so that it can "watch" the student behaving responsibly.

- **Timeout from small group instruction (elementary level).** If a student misbehaves during small group instruction, have the student push back her chair so that she is not physically part of the group. You should conduct the next minute or two of instruction in an especially fun and reinforcing manner so the student feels that she is missing out on the privilege of participating in something that is enjoyable and beneficial.

- **Timeout at desk (elementary level).** If a student misbehaves, ask him to put his head down on his desk and close his eyes for a short period of time—2 minutes, for example. This form of timeout is very mild but can be effective for relatively minor problems such as disruptions during instructional periods or independent seatwork.

- **Timeout in private area of the classroom (elementary and middle school levels).** In this option, you establish a timeout area in a low-traffic part of your classroom. The area can be as simple as a chair off to the side of the room or a screened-off area arranged so that you can see the student but he cannot see the majority of his classmates.

With all the above options, you should keep the timeout brief. Don't allow the student to take work to the timeout area. For primary students, a 2- or 3-minute timeout is best; for intermediate and middle school students, the optimal time is 5 minutes. When using this consequence, instruct the student to go to timeout, and the timeout period should begin when the student is in the area, seated and quiet.

If you think a student is unlikely to go to timeout and is old enough to understand the concept of time owed, establish the rule that when instructed to go to timeout, the student has 1 minute to get there and get settled. If it takes more than 1 minute for the student to go to timeout, they will owe time equivalent to that extra time—time owed will be deducted from recess or a fun activity. If the student is unlikely to understand time owed (as in the case of a kindergarten student or a student with cognitive deficits), plan to conduct a few practice sessions in which you model and have the student role-play going to timeout. If you conduct sessions like this, be sure the student knows they have not done anything wrong—you are just pretending so that the student learns how to go to timeout if it is necessary.

Timeout (In Another Class)

For students who are likely to misbehave during an in-class timeout (such as the student who clowns around to get a laugh from other students), it may be more effective to assign them to timeout in another class. To do this, you need to find a teacher with a room near yours who has a class with fairly mature students. It could be a younger grade or an older grade, but should probably not be your exact grade level.

If such a student misbehaves in your room, she is sent to the timeout teacher's room. This teacher should have a prearranged location for the student—perhaps a chair in a low-traffic area of the class—and should preteach his class to ignore the student when she enters. The timeout teacher should not be required to stop teaching his class or do problem-solving with the misbehaving student. The idea behind this procedure is simply that the student is less likely to show off for students in a different class, especially a class at a different grade level.

Unlike the in-class timeout options above, the student probably should have work to do so she does not get so bored that she begins to entertain herself by showing off for the other students. Both you and the timeout teacher must work out in advance how long the timeout period will last and how the student will transition from one room to the other. Ensure that you are able to fully observe the student as the transition occurs, so do not select a classroom that is in another hallway or part of the school. As with in-class timeout, keep timeout in another class relatively brief, no longer than 10-15 minutes.

We also strongly recommend that if you use this procedure, you should maintain records and/or records of these timeouts should be kept by administrators to ensure that the student is not missing too much class. For a student who chronically misbehaves, it is easy for this procedure to become an easy escape—for the student from a class in which they struggle, and for the teacher from a student who may usurp valuable class time through misbehavior. If the same student is assigned a timeout in another class several times in a relatively short period of time (e.g., within the same month), this corrective consequence is not working to change behavior. Alternative corrective consequences should be applied and proactive individual intervention planning should begin (see Task 6 for preliminary strategies).

NOTE: Avoid hallway timeouts. It is a common practice to send students into timeout in the hallway. Some teachers have a small desk outside of their door, and in other cases, the student sits on the floor outside their room. This practice is not recommended. Unless you plan to teach from your doorway, the student will be unsupervised during the timeout. During observations of schools, it is common to see students in these "timeouts" horsing around or having leisurely conversation with peers or adults who pass in the hallway. We even heard from a student in one school that students were having a competition to see how far they could sneak away from their classroom while on a timeout without being caught by their teacher!

Restitution

The goal of restitution is for a misbehaving student to learn that when their behavior causes damage, they need to repair that damage. If a student writes on a desk, he should have to wash that desk. If a student is rude to a guest speaker, she should be required to apologize in writing, on the phone, or in person to the guest speaker. If you use the restitution strategy, try to make it clear to the student that what you are asking them to do, such as apologize to the guest speaker, is not a punishment but a reparation—an attempt to repair any damage their rudeness may have caused in terms of the guest speaker's feelings or his opinion of students in the school.

If a student engages in behavior that causes damage, a logical consequence is that the student has to repair the damage. For example, if a student plugs a washroom sink with paper towels so that water runs all over the floor, requiring him to mop the floor is more logical than having the custodian clean up the mess. (You probably cannot have the student use chemicals such as disinfectants, but he can certainly use a mop and bucket.)

When this strategy is used with ongoing misbehavior, the "amount" of the restitution should increase with successive instances of misbehavior. Thus, when a student writes on a desk, you might have her wash the desk. If she does it a second time, have her wash all the desks in the class.

Positive Practice

If a student breaks a rule about a behavior that can easily be practiced correctly, positive practice (or overcorrection) is an appropriate corrective consequence. The major components of positive practice are rehearsal and attention to learning the task (Foxx & Bechtel, 1982). An obvious example is when a student runs in the halls, you ask them to go back and walk. A student who runs in the halls repeatedly might be required to spend time during recess or after school practicing walking in the halls.

Behavior Improvement Form

If students have mastered basic academic skills, one consequence is to have the misbehaving student complete a Behavior Improvement Form (see the next page for samples) so the student can reflect on her actions and avoid future problems. When a student misbehaves, calmly say, "That was an example of [blank]. Please think about what you did and fill out a Behavior Improvement Form." Reproducible 8.3A shows a very basic example of such a form. Reproducible 8.3B is a more complex form that can be used with older, more sophisticated students. Note that on the more sophisticated version of the form, the student is asked to describe how he thinks you, the teacher, would describe the incident. Reproducible 8.3C is a form specifically for classes and schools that use the CHAMPS acronym to guide behavior.

Reproducibles 8.3A–C *Behavior Improvement Forms (Versions 1–3)*

Behavior Improvement Form
(Version 1)

CHAMPS

STUDENT _____ GRADE/CLASS _____

TEACHER _____ PERIOD/TIME _____

1. What was your behavior?

2. What could you do differently?

3. Will you be able to do that?

© 2021 Ancora Pu...

Behavior Improvement Form
(Version 2)

CHAMPS

STUDENT _____ DATE _____

TEACHER _____ PERIOD _____ CLASS _____

1. Describe the incident.

2. Describe your behavior during the incident.

3. How would the teacher describe your behavior during the incident?

4. How could you have behaved in a different way?

5. If this happens again, how do you plan to behave or respond?

6. Are you willing to commit to making this effort?

7. How can we help you be successful?

© 2021 Ancora Publishing

REPRODUCIBLE 8.3B

Behavior Improvement Form
(Version 3)

CHAMPS

STUDENT _____ DATE _____ TIME _____ TEACHER _____

CHAMPS Practice

*C*onversation _____

*H*elp _____

*A*ctivity _____

*M*ovement _____

*P*articipation _____

*S*uccess _____

This form was developed by Maureen Gale, Behavior Coach for Orange County Public Schools in Florida.

I did not follow this CHAMPS expectation:

Next time, I will make a better choice. I will:

© 2021 Ancora Publishing

REPRODUCIBLE 8.3C

Response Cost—Loss of Points

Point systems are useful tools for promoting motivation and can also provide another corrective consequence option. If you use any kind of a point system in your class, establish a rule that certain infractions result in point "fines."

An example of a simple way to use a point system as a corrective consequence is to have the student start each day with 20 points. Every time you have to speak to him about the problem behavior, he loses a point. At the end of the day, you write the number of points he has remaining on a special note that he takes home. Each remaining point equals 10 minutes of television or video game time (or some other privilege the student enjoys) at home. The less the student misbehaves, the more points he has at the end of the day and the more television time he gets. Obviously, this system depends on family cooperation. Also, because your main interaction within the system is to give the student attention when he has misbehaved, you will need to make a concerted effort to pay attention to the student when he is not misbehaving to ensure that he always gets more attention for following the rules than for violating them.

Response Cost Lottery

Response cost lottery is a variation on a response cost consequence that can be used in situations where three or four students in class have challenging behaviors. You give those students, or even every student in the class, a certain number of tickets (ten, for example) at the beginning of each day, or each week for middle school level. Each time a student misbehaves, that student loses a ticket. At the end of the day or week, the students write their names on all their remaining tickets and place them in a container (hat, bowl, box) for a drawing. The name of the student on the drawn ticket gets a treat or a small reward. The more tickets a student has, the greater their chances of winning.

Humor

Humor can be a powerful and effective way to respond to misbehavior—especially with older students. For example, consider a situation in which a student makes a smart-aleck comment on the second day of school as the teacher is presenting a lesson. If the teacher is quick-witted enough, she might be able to respond to the student's comment in a way that will make the student himself laugh, and a tense moment will be diffused. However, please note that you should not use sarcasm or ridicule, which is at the expense of the student. The sensitive use of humor brings people closer together. Sarcasm or ridicule makes a student feel hostile and angry that you made a joke at his expense.

If you do use humor in response to a misbehavior, you should plan on talking to the student later to make sure that he understands that his behavior was not acceptable and that he knows you expect him to behave more responsibly in the future. In addition, you can check to see that you did not embarrass the student with your humorous comment.

Be extremely careful with the use of humor. If there is any concern that the student will misunderstand your attempt at humor, or if other students will not get it and think you are being mean or belittling the student, do not use this strategy.

EXAMPLES, IDEAS, AND TIPS

In a situation similar to the one in the previous paragraph, you might say something like: "Thomas, today in class you made a comment, and then I made a joke out of what you said. First, I want to make sure that I did not embarrass you. Good, I'm glad I didn't. I owe it to all students to treat them as respectfully as I expect them to treat me. If I ever do anything that feels disrespectful to you, please come and talk to me about it. Now, I need to remind you to raise your hand when you have something to say in class and to make an effort to see that your comments are respectful. I appreciate humor in the classroom, and I suspect that you will be someone who will not only contribute to our lessons, but also get us to see the humor in different situations as well. Thanks for taking the time to talk to me. I'm looking forward to seeing you in class tomorrow."

Emotional Reaction

Exhibiting an emotional reaction (such as anger) is a strategy that should be used very sparingly—only with a group of students, not more than twice a year, and not at all in the first 5 or 6 weeks with a new class. For example, say that most of the students in a class start acting silly while a guest speaker is in the room. Usually this class is respectful and a pleasure to teach. In this case, it might be helpful to let the class know that you are disappointed in them. If the class has never seen you angry before, it may have a bit of a shock effect and help improve the class's behavior in the future. This is especially effective when you have built a positive relationship with your students—if they don't like you very much, knowing they have disappointed you likely won't make too much of a difference!

Avoid using this particular strategy with an individual student, as you may be dealing with someone who is seeking power through his misbehavior. Angering an adult can be a powerful motivating force for this kind of student, and your negative response may be very reinforcing to the student (Alberto & Troutman, 2012). It can also be frightening or triggering for many students. Also avoid using this procedure at the beginning of the school year, because showing students anger or frustration too early in the year may encourage the class to act up more in the future—they may think it is fun or funny to see you get angry. Finally, avoid overusing the procedure, as it will lose any power it may have had. An emotional reaction will shock students only if they rarely see it (no more than twice a year). If students are used to seeing you get angry repeatedly, they are more likely to think, "There he goes again, blowing his stack over nothing."

Of course, an emotional reaction should also never be so extreme you lose control or appear to. If you would be embarrassed for another adult in the building to see you engaging in the reaction, it is probably too extreme. Something like yelling so that someone in the hallway could hear you or slamming an item down on your desk or across the room is not appropriate. Sparing use of an emotional reaction to express frustration or disappointment can be an effective technique, but you also need to remember that, no matter how frustrated you were with the class, it is your job to model appropriately managing emotions.

Revoke a Privilege

For some students, the reinforcing value of misbehavior may be so powerful and ingrained that other reinforcement and consequence strategies may not effectively motivate them to change their behaviors. In such cases, it may be useful to remove a highly valued privilege as a consequence for misbehavior (Bear, 2008).

When a student breaks a rule or does not meet an expectation for behavior, the student loses access to a predetermined privilege. To use this strategy, set up the privilege in advance and inform the student that if certain misbehaviors continue, the student will not earn the privilege. The privilege should be something relatively small, and the loss of the privilege should occur close to the time of the misbehavior (e.g., in a 24-hour period) so the student makes a connection between the misbehavior and the loss of the privilege. Do not, for example, take away the student's access to a field trip scheduled 2 weeks later or take away recess for days on end. It is more effective to restrict access to a privilege like 10 minutes of computer time for one day or the loss of recess on that day. The next day, the student is able to start over. If behavior is appropriate, they earn the privilege. If it is not, they lose the privilege for the day, but get to start fresh on the next day.

Detention

Detention is usually a schoolwide system where any teacher can assign any student who has misbehaved to spend a set amount of time (40 minutes, for example) in a nonstimulating setting. Most schools schedule their detention periods during lunch. Often, detention is structured so that students are required to do academic tasks during the detention period. One problem with detention is that students may find it reinforcing when they happen to have friends assigned to the same detention period. Or, if a student doesn't like lunch recess because she struggles with social interactions or gets overstimulated, a lunch or recess detention is unlikely to be effective. As with any corrective consequence you try, keep a written record of the detentions you assign. If you repeatedly assign the same student to detention across a period of weeks, this particular corrective consequence is not working for that student, and you should modify your correction plan to include a more effective consequence.

Demerits

Demerits represent negative points that, when accumulated, result in the loss of a privilege or the imposition of a negative consequence. Demerits can be used to soften a predetermined consequence that might otherwise be overly harsh for a single example of a misbehavior. For example, if the consequence for talking in class is lunchtime detention (which seems rather harsh for a single instance), the teacher is likely to respond to that behavior inconsistently—sometimes ignoring the behavior, sometimes threatening ("If you keep talking, I am going to have to give you a detention"), and maybe finally giving the detention. The use of demerits allows you to set up a more consistent policy. For example, a middle school teacher might tell students that each time he has to speak to a student about talking in class (or some other minor disruption), that student will get a demerit. If a student gets four demerits within 1 week, it equals a lunchtime detention. With this system, the teacher is more likely to intervene every time there is a disruptive behavior because the response for each single incident is reasonable, resulting in a more consistent policy. Note that the recording of demerits should be done in a private location such as a clipboard or notebook in your possession rather than in a public display like a posted chart or on the board.

Another way to use demerits, which may be especially useful for elementary teachers, is to establish a rule that all students who have no more than 5 demerits get to participate in a free-time activity at the end of the day, but those with 6 or more demerits do not get to participate. You could even arrange to give a special treat to each student who has no more than 1 demerit.

Jot It Down

The Jot It Down strategy is a way to slow down momentum if a student is overtly refusing to follow directions, is not responding to efforts to implement minor in-class corrective consequences, and is at risk of an ODR. If the student refuses to follow a direction, restate the direction, taking special care to make sure it is clear, observable, and immediate. For example, rather than saying, "AJ, take your seat," say "AJ, please sit down at your desk." In the first statement, the teacher's lack of clarity may invite a smart-alecky response like, "Take it where?"

If the student refuses to follow the direction a second time, tell the student that you are going to need to write down what is happening so that you have an accurate record of what is taking place. Say something like, "AJ, this is very serious. I'm going to need to take some notes so that I make sure I've got a clear record of what is happening here." Take out a piece of paper and write the direction and the student's inappropriate response on paper. This action breaks your eye contact with the student, and the act of writing slows the momentum down between you and the student, hopefully reducing the likelihood of more serious conflict. If during this time the student begins complying, thank the student for making a good choice and continue teaching. However, at a later time, have a neutral discussion with the student about how you can both work to prevent a similar conflict in the future. Let the student know that you will maintain the record of this incident.

If the student does not comply, you should probably write an ODR and include the written evidence of your direction and the student's refusal.

Use Nonprogressive Rather Than Progressive Consequence Systems

Progressive systems of consequences typically use a visual display or a series of cards representing the number of misbehaviors a student has engaged in during the period or day and the type of corrective consequence that will be applied for each progressive infraction. For example, each student has a set of colored cards contained in a pocket chart. The pocket chart is located in a prominent place in the classroom. When a student misbehaves, a card is pulled from their pocket. Each card is a different color, and the colors represent a progression of consequences. When the green card is pulled, it serves as a warning. When the yellow card is pulled, the student loses recess. When the orange card is pulled, there will be a parental contact. When the red card is pulled, the student is sent to the office.

In some cases, teachers use a chart on the wall, and each student has a clip on the chart that moves according to their number of infractions. Other teachers place student names on the board and add a series of checks, circles, or other marks to represent where the student is in the progression of consequences.

We do not recommend using progressive consequence systems for a variety of reasons. It is very difficult for a teacher to be consistent, day after day, in handing out progressive penalties, especially if that teacher is with the same children for the entire day. It's probably easier for a middle or high school teacher to implement a system of progressive consequences; however, this practice is still not recommended. For an elementary teacher, it can be almost impossible to use progressive consequences consistently. Consider the following scenario.

 CASE STUDY

Johnny absentmindedly begins to tap his pencil on his desk. He is not doing this purposefully to cause trouble. It's a habit that he is virtually unaware of. However, his action is disruptive to the lesson. The teacher issues a warning and pulls Johnny's green card from the pocket. Johnny stops immediately. Twenty minutes later, he starts up again. The teacher, who genuinely likes Johnny, pulls his yellow card. Now he's lost his recess. But he does stop the misbehavior.

Ten minutes go by—then Johnny starts up again. What does the teacher do now? Pull the orange card and call his parents? What if he taps his pencil another time? Would the teacher send him to the office?

At this point, the misbehavior is too trivial for the severity of the consequence, yet that is the progression. To be consistent, the teacher should pull the orange card—but she doesn't really want to send Johnny to the office for tapping his pencil four times. So instead, she looks him straight in the eye and says firmly, "Don't make me pull this card!"—a phrase that can only lead Johnny into thinking that he has the power to "make" his teacher do something she doesn't want to do. Or even worse, she says, "I really don't want to pull this card," leading Johnny to wonder what she does want to do and to continue the misbehavior just to find out.

• • • • •

The problem inherent in a progressive consequences system is that all misbehavior is addressed with the same increasingly severe penalties. However, misbehaviors are not equivalent. Tapping a pencil is not the same as pushing someone. Pushing someone while engaging in physical horseplay is not the same as pushing someone aggressively in anger. Each of these types of misbehaviors warrants a different type of corrective approach, so applying a range of nonprogressive consequences is far more effective.

If the teacher uses any sort of clip chart or visual display (e.g., names on the board), these systems are also far too public a display of a student's behavioral issues. They risk belittling and humiliating the student, and for students who seek attention through misbehavior, these systems can reinforce the student's need for attention.

> *The problem inherent in a progressive consequences system is that all misbehavior is addressed with the same increasingly severe penalties, even though misbehaviors are not equivalent.*

Instead of a progressive consequence system, you might devise a nonprogressive system that covers all misbehavior and helps you to categorize misbehaviors and potential responses. In this system, as part of your planning, identify four categories. The first category is misbehavior that receives no consequences at all, just reminders. This might be the case in kindergarten, for instance. Your young pupils simply forget that they are not supposed to shout out an answer. No need to issue a consequence when a simple reminder will do.

The second category is misbehavior that receives minor consequences—like Johnny with his pencil. This category is like a parking ticket—each misbehavior receives a parking ticket type of minor consequence, and the consequences remain on the same level. Every time Johnny taps, he owes 15 seconds.

For most teachers, these two categories will take care of 90% to 95% of the misbehaviors that occur. The final two categories deal with the other 5% to 10%.

The third category is more serious misbehavior that earns more serious consequences—examples include displays of disrespect and use of bad language. For these actions, you can devise a menu of consequences that all of your students know about and understand. When one of these misbehaviors occurs, you select a consequence from the menu—for example, time owed, timeout, detention, parental contact, or parent conference. The fourth category is misbehavior that violates your school's code of conduct or involves physical or emotional violence—for these you issue a major consequence, such as office referral or parental notification. See the next task for more information on office referrals.

Once again, you must make sure that your students understand your system. Teach them exactly what consequences apply to which behaviors.

A nonprogressive consequences system allows some flexibility between classrooms. Not every teacher needs to use the same classifications, with one exception—consequences for category four misbehaviors (disciplinary referral to the office—discussed in the next task) should be consistently implemented throughout the entire school.

UPDATE YOUR CLASSROOM MANAGEMENT PLAN

ITEM 11: CORRECTION PROCEDURES FOR MISBEHAVIOR

List the menu of corrective consequences you plan to use in your classroom. Make note of any implementation recommendations that you would like to highlight and remember.

TASK 4

Know When (and When Not) to Use Disciplinary Referral

Identify which situations warrant sending students to the office and which you should handle in your own classroom. Know how to write an effective disciplinary referral.

• • • • •

Severe misbehavior may require the involvement of the school administrator in charge of discipline. This may be the principal, or in larger schools an assistant principal or dean. Regardless of who this person is, as a teacher you must know their expectations regarding what types of behaviors you should handle on your own and what types warrant sending a notification and possibly the student to the office—known as an office disciplinary referral (ODR). Some behaviors should always be referred to the office, such as illegal acts or sexual harassment. Some behaviors may warrant an ODR but the student can and should remain in class. These ODRs can be thought of as notifications—the teacher is notifying the administrator about a concern, but immediate removal is not necessary. And many behaviors should be managed with in-class correctional techniques rather than requiring administrative involvement. In this task, you will learn how to get clarity on when and how to use an ODR.

Understand the Strengths and Weaknesses of ODRs and Administrator-Assigned Consequences

ODRs can serve several useful functions. Some students and families will respond to the gravity of having an administrator address the seriousness of behavior. This can lead to immediate positive changes in behavior for some students. Administrators can assign corrective consequences that are outside of the teacher's menu of corrective consequences, such as in-school suspension or certain restorative practices. For some students, these corrective consequences may be more potent for a student than some of the in-class procedures used by a teacher. ODRs can provide a useful record of serious incidents of misbehavior when chronic concerns warrant additional intervention planning or something like an evaluation for special education services. They are also essential when there are potential legal ramifications regarding the student's behavior.

Despite their important function, ODRs are often misused. Students receive ODRs for minor or moderate infractions. Students are sent to the office, missing valuable class time, when their behavior could have been addressed more effectively through classroom-based corrective action or when the student could have remained in class while an ODR was sent to the office. Remember that no "magical consequence" will correct all misbehavior on its own. ODRs and administrator-assigned consequences are unlikely to magically cure most chronic misbehavior.

When ODRs are overused, many negative things can occur. Administrators may be unable to deal effectively with severe and chronic misbehavior because they are inundated with referrals for mild and moderate misbehavior. Students miss out on valuable instructional time and may further disengage from their teacher or class community. Family members may become defensive or disenfranchised with the school. Cooperation between administrators and teachers breaks down as teachers feel like administrators aren't doing anything to support them. Administrators feel like teachers should be managing minor and moderate situations on their own. ODRs and administrative actions also lose much of their potency when they are overused, and teachers may inadvertently signal to their students that they are unable to manage classroom situations on their own.

It is important to recognize that for many students, getting sent to the principal's office is at best neutral, and at worst reinforcing. In addition, for students who have skill deficits (i.e., they do not know how to exhibit expected behavior), a visit to the principal's office or receiving in-school suspension is not likely to provide the skill instruction the student needs. Finally, for some students, frequent ODRs and administrative actions further reinforce students' perception that the school is against them, or that they are bad and cannot change.

Determine Which Behaviors Must Be Referred

To ensure that you appropriately use ODRs, you must first know what behaviors must be referred to the office. You should also find out which behaviors warrant immediately sending the student to the office versus sending an ODR but keeping the student in class. As much as possible, avoid immediately removing the student from the classroom setting unless the misbehavior is severe, meaning there was illegal activity, there was real danger of someone getting hurt, or the staff member was at real risk of losing total control of the situation.

Some behaviors require documentation but are not so severe the student must immediately be removed. There will also be times when you are uncertain whether behaviors warrant removal, but you can keep the student in class until you hear from your administrator. In these cases, you may write an ODR but not require immediate removal or assistance.

If the administrator has clarified her expectations during an inservice and you feel you understand her position, you may disregard the suggestions below. However, if you are at all unclear, make an appointment with the administrator to discuss the following issues.

Find out precisely what types of behaviors you should refer the first time they occur. For example, should you refer physically dangerous acts? The answer will probably be yes, but what exactly is a physically dangerous act? What discretion do you have to make judgments about the severity of such an act? For example, a very young child may not understand how much they can hurt others by pulling a chair out from under a classmate. If this happens but no one is hurt, it may be more effective to provide instruction to the student within class rather than sending them to the office. Some of the misbehaviors that you should clarify with your administrator and that we recommend should be sent to the office include:

- **Illegal acts that involve breaking of state or federal laws.** In all schools, these behaviors must be reported to administrators and authorities as appropriate.
- **Physically dangerous acts that pose a serious threat to physical safety or that cause significant physical harm to the student or others.** You will likely need to use some professional discretion to determine when these acts are serious enough to warrant administrative involvement. When in doubt, it is probably best to complete an ODR. However, if the student is back under physical and instructional control, you may be able to send the ODR to the office but keep the student in class while you wait for further instructions from your administrator.
- **Severe refusal to follow a reasonable adult direction.** This is also known as defiance or insubordination. but we recommend not using these terms because the concepts are so broad and subject to interpretation. For example, some staff think that eye rolling should be referred to the office, but if the student follows the adult direction within a reasonable amount of time, their negative attitude is better addressed through in-class approaches. Severe misbehavior within this category involves repeated refusal to follow a direction that is:

  - *Reasonable.* The direction is clear and related to an observable behavior (e.g., "Please use a Level 2 voice and school-appropriate language"), not something subjective or unclear (e.g., "Change your attitude" or "Shape up").
  - *Given three times in a calm and professional manner.* The second time you give the direction, we recommend emphasizing the seriousness of the student's choice. "Vivian, this is a direction. Please remember that one of our rules is to follow directions quickly." On the third time, you may wish to write the direction and the student's inappropriate response. See the Jot it Down strategy in the previous task for more information on how to use this technique to slow the momentum of conflict between you and the student.
  - *Immediate and significant.* You want the direction to be able to be carried out within a few minutes of being given. Do not refer a student for not following a long-term direction such as completing homework, as it is easy for students to forget or get

confused with long-term directions. Also be cautious in referring a student who passively refuses to complete their work. If the student's behavior is not disrupting others and the classroom is able to function despite the student's refusal, it may be more appropriate to continue instruction and let the student know you will talk with them later. At that time, you can determine whether it is appropriate to use an ODR, apply another classroom correctional technique, or use other proactive intervention supports.

- **Severe disruption.** Disruptive behavior should not involve removing a student from the class unless it is so severe that there is a loss of instructional control. If you can continue teaching and other students have been trained to ignore disruptive behavior, you should do what you can to keep the student in class and assign in-class consequences. You can determine if it is appropriate to send an ODR so the administrator is aware of the concern (i.e., send a notification but keep the student in class).

Other possible misbehaviors that you should discuss how to handle with your administrator include:

- Code of Conduct violations
- Misbehaviors related to district, state, and federal mandates
- Bullying and harassment, including racial and gender-based teasing
- Obscene language about or directed at someone

Be clear on the broad categories of behaviors that can result in ODRs, and find out your administrator's recommendations for specific examples that you are unsure about. Should they be handled with an ODR the first time they occur, or should you handle them with your classroom-based consequences and parental contacts? There is no right answer to what warrants an ODR and what does not—the key is that both you and the administrator are in agreement.

Think through how you would address each of the following situations. If you are unsure about how you should handle any of them, discuss what is expected with your administrator and other colleagues.

Physically dangerous acts
- One student hits another student, but no one is hurt.
- One student pushes a student in line, but no one is hurt.
- Two students are in a slugging fight.
- Two students are arguing, and one pushes the other.
- Two students are engaging in physical horseplay, and one gets a cut or bruise from getting knocked into something.
- One student pulls a chair out from another student.
- A student is tipping over desks.
- A student is throwing books.

Inappropriate comments
- A student makes a rude comment.
- A student directs an obscenity at the teacher.

- A student makes a disparaging remark about an assignment or about the teacher, but there is no obscenity.
- A student says something negative about a student of color and uses the phrase, "People like you . . ."

Threats
- A student threatens to damage materials.
- A student threatens violence toward another student or an adult.
- A student threatens to bring a weapon.

Refusal to follow directions
- A student says, "I am not going to . . .," but actually complies.
- A student says, "I am not going to . . .," and does not comply.
- A student puts their head down on the desk and will not respond to anything.

Classroom disruption
- A student is tapping a pencil.
- A student is screaming.
- A student is telling jokes.
- A student is repeatedly pounding on the desk.

Write Appropriate and Effective Referrals

Find out exactly what kind of referral form should be used in the event you do need to send a student to the office. Reproducible 8.4 is a sample referral adapted from *Foundations: A Positive Approach to Schoolwide Discipline* (Sprick et al, 2014; available from Ancora Publishing, ancorapublishing.com).

Note that this referral form includes a place where the teacher can specify if the referral is for a more moderate infraction—the student stays in the classroom but the referral form goes to the office, or for severe misbehavior—the student is immediately sent to the office along with the referral form. Ask your administrator if your school has provision for a referral in which the student is not removed from class, but administrative or counseling staff receive an incident report. The teacher can use this type of referral when a student's behavior may warrant a more serious, collaborative response but is not so severe as to warrant removing the student.

A well-written referral is important because it conveys essential information about what occurred, which can increase your administrator's ability to appropriately address the situation with the student. It also reduces the likelihood parents will misunderstand or get defensive about the incident.

Be sure to use objective language to describe the incident that led to the referral. The administrator needs an objective description in concrete terms that explains exactly what you saw and heard that prompted you to refer the student. The referral form should not contain responses that are based on jargon, labels, or judgments, all of which are conclusions about, rather than observations of, events. Conclusions can be biased depending on whether you are

Reproducible 8.4 *Behavior Referral Form Example*

Behavior Referral Form   *CHAMPS*

STUDENT _Jayden_____ GENDER: F ___ M _X_ NONBINARY ___ GRADE LEVEL _6_ DATE _11/3___

CLASS PERIOD __2_____ LOCATION ____Hall_____ (if classroom, indicate subject of class)

Moderate (Paper goes to office)	Severe (Student goes to office)
☐ Chronic misbehavior (e.g., late to class, homework, classwork, disruption)	☐ Illegal (e.g., threats, weapons, drugs, assault)
☒ Not following direction (but eventually complies)	☐ Physically dangerous
☐ Disrespect to an adult (low grade)	☐ Not following direction (even when direction is written)
☐ Name-calling, put-downs, or mild behavior that might be gender or racially based	☐ Gross insubordination
☐ Other _____	☐ Gender, racial, or other gross teasing
	☐ Other _____

Description of problem/situation:

#2 Hall
Jayden was running in the hallway after first period. I asked him to stop and show me how he is supposed to behave in the halls between classes. He responded by continuing down the hallway. I repeated the direction and he stopped and came back but said, "This is so stupid. Jerk."

Action taken by referring adult:

☐ Use a one-liner (e.g., "That is not OK. Keep your hands to yourself.")
☐ Instructional/verbal correction (e.g., for minor disrespect)
☐ State that you will follow up (e.g., "We'll talk later.")
☐ Parental contact
☒ Have student demonstrate or practice the rule
☐ Off-limits or otherwise restrict activity
☐ Stay with supervisor
☐ Assigned school-based consequence (e.g., detention)
☐ Restitution
☐ Other _____

Referring adult _Mr. Apo_____

Action taken by administrator:

REPRODUCIBLE 8.4

having a good day, whether you like the student, or even whether you have unconscious prejudices about ethnicity, gender, age level, or other issues.

Figure 8.1 shows the differences between objective and nonobjective descriptions of the same event that resulted in an office referral.

Figure 8.1 *Objective Versus Nonobjective Descriptions*

Objective Description	Nonobjective Description (Jargon/Label/Conclusion)
Kindra was pounding on her desk. When I asked her to stop, she loudly shouted, "You fat, ugly b_____."	Kindra was obscene and obnoxious.
During a cooperative group activity, Allen and Alphonso were disagreeing. As I made my way to that part of the room, Allen got out of his seat, grabbed Alphonso by the shirt, and threw him to the floor. I was able to intervene at that point.	Allen attacked Alphonso.
James was out of his seat, pulling students' hair and knocking work off their desks. When I told him to go to his desk and sit down, he kept running around the room, refusing to go to his seat. I repeated the instruction three times.	James's ADHD is out of control, and I can't take it any more!

Nonobjective responses tell very little about what actually took place. In some cases, as in James's example above, they tell more about the teacher than what the student actually did. The following are examples—taken from actual referral forms—of what not to write. Imagine you are the administrator who has to process these referrals. Imagine you are the parent who sees this on the copy of the referral that is sent home!

- *Straw—camel's back.*
- *This student needs to see a psychiatrist or at least be on some kind of medication. He's out of control.*
- *Student does his level best to trash my class's learning every day. Needs SUSPENSION. How can he be allowed to ruin others' chances to learn? I'm sick of writing him up only to learn he received a too-lenient punishment that encourages him to play the class clown.*
- *I'm done with this student.*
- *I told the student he needed to stop acting like a three-year-old, and he told me I was acting like a three-year-old. Incredibly disrespectful.*

Remember that referral forms are legal documents and may be used in due process mediation or hearing. Referral reforms can be reviewed and become evidence in a legal action. They should only be used to convey objective and nonemotional information to administrators and parents about what occurred leading to the referral. The example shown in Reproducible 8.4 (shown on the previous page) illustrates a form that is filled out appropriately.

A few additional recommendations for writing effective referrals include:

- Use appropriate spelling and syntax, and use legible handwriting. If you want others to respect your actions and comments, write professionally. Use correct spelling, grammar, and punctuation.
- NEVER prepare forms in advance for students who struggle with misbehavior. This sends the message that you *expect* the student to cause trouble. If you are tempted to do this, reread Task 1 of this chapter on maintaining high expectations. Evaluate how you can invigorate yourself so you view the student as one who is capable of meeting your positive expectations.
- Be specific and provide as much information as possible to help others (administrators, family members) understand what occurred. If the student has recurring problems with misbehavior, these records can help provide context so you can see if there are patterns in the student's behavior that may lead to logical intervention approaches.

Student Reentry After a Serious Behavioral Incident

It is very important to consider how you will reintegrate the student into the class after any severe incident that warranted the student's removal. The student may feel embarrassed or on edge upon their return and uncertain how you and their peers will react. If other students were witnesses or involved in the incident, they may also be feeling apprehension about the student's return to class. Successful reentry procedures accomplish the following goals:

- The student knows that you are not holding a grudge and that you are invested in their success.
- The class sees you giving a positive and welcoming greeting to the student.
- The student knows what is expected and to behave appropriately in the future.

If you need to have a conversation prior to the student's return to class so you can clarify expectations and reestablish your positive relationship with the student, work out a plan with your administrator for someone to watch your class for a short period while you and the student meet privately. Even if you do not feel the need for such a meeting, carefully consider whether the student would benefit from a one-on-one conversation to clear the air and help the student feel comfortable returning to class. If this is not necessary, ensure that you give the student a positive greeting as soon as they enter your class. Avoid statements that indicate you are upset with the student, are concerned they will continue behaving inappropriately, or have not moved on from the incident. For example, avoid statements like, "Juan, we had a rough morning this morning. I hope this afternoon is going to be better." Instead, say something like, "Juan, I'm glad to have you in class this afternoon. We are going to be continuing with our story. Let me know if you need anything before we start."

TASK 5

Use Supportive Communication With Parents Regarding Student Misbehavior

Communicate effectively with families when students misbehave and establish collaborative approaches with ongoing behavioral concerns.

• • • • •

Communicating behavioral and academic concerns to parents is an important part of a teacher's job. At the early stages of concerns, these family contacts can ensure that parents understand a teacher's expectations and are aware of the teacher's concern for the student's success. Some families will follow through with reinforcing or supporting school expectations from home. In other cases, you learn important information about how to support a student in overcoming challenges at school, or you may learn about circumstances that provide context for the student's struggles.

Make Initial Contact With a Family Regarding Behavioral Concerns

When making contact with the family regarding misbehavior, keep the following suggestions in mind:

- Provide an objective description of the behavior, not a judgment about the student. Consider the difference between "Tabatha didn't complete 6 out of 10 in-class assignments this week" and "Tabatha seems unmotivated and lazy in class."
- Suggest that it would be useful for the family to discuss the behavior with the student and communicate the expectation that the student behave more responsibly in the future.
- Avoid implying that the student should be punished at home or that the family should "make" the student behave. Simply communicate that you have a concern and will be working with the student to figure out ways for them to be successful in your class.
- Ask if the family has any insights that might help you work with the student and help them achieve their high potential in your class.
- Create a sense that you and the family can work as partners in helping the student reduce misbehavior and succeed.

Reproducible 8.5 outlines content to cover in an early-stage family contact. A fillable version is provided. When you prepare to contact a family member about behavioral concerns, fill out this worksheet in advance so that the call can be as focused and brief as possible. The sample shows a template that has been completed by a fifth-grade teacher.

Reproducible 8.5 *Early-Stage Problems—Family Contact Example*

Early-Stage Problems—Family Contact

CHAMPS

1. Introduce yourself and provide an appropriate greeting.

   Hello, Mrs. Thompson? This is Mr. McLemore, Rasheed's teacher. How are you today? I'll bet that new baby is keeping you very busy. How is she doing? May I take just a moment of your time?

2. Share with the family that you are calling to speak to them about a situation at school.

   I am calling because I wanted to speak with you about a situation that has been going on at school.

3. Describe the problem (avoid labeling or passing judgment on the child).

   For the last two days, Rasheed has not been doing his work in class. He sits at his desk and stares out the window, talks with his neighbor, and plays with his pencil. When I remind him to get to work, he will work if I am standing right there, but as soon as I go to do something else, he quits working again. Today he didn't finish any of his assignments.

4. Describe why the behavior is a problem (keep the focus on the student, not on yourself or the other students). Emphasize that you know the student can be successful.

   I am concerned because Rasheed is a very able student. I don't want him to develop the bad habit of wasting class time. To succeed at school, he will need to learn to keep his attention on his work.

5. If appropriate, ask whether the family has any insight into why the behavior is occurring. If they share with you, adjust the remainder of this call based on what you learn.

   One of the reasons I am calling is to find out if you know of anything that might be bothering Rasheed or that could be distracting him from his classwork.

6. Make suggestions about how the family might help the child.

   I am not calling so that you will punish Rasheed. I am just concerned about him and hope you will talk to him about the problem. I know that he is capable of being successful in my class, but he has to keep his attention focused and do his work. Please tell him I called and that I look forward to seeing him tomorrow. I will call you in a few days to let you know how he is doing. Feel free to call me as well. The best time to reach me is between 3:30 and 4:00 any afternoon but Tuesday.

Date of this contact: ___September 27___

Notes on the contact:

Mrs. Thompson couldn't tell me any particular reason that Rasheed has been so inattentive the last two days. She said she would talk to him, find out if anything is wrong, and encourage him to pay attention to his work.

REPRODUCIBLE 8.5

Diversity, Equity, Inclusion, and Access

Family involvement in school is influenced by a variety of factors, including culture, the family's past experiences with schooling, and circumstances like work schedules, mental and physical health, and access to transportation or technology. Continue to be consciously inviting and boost positive communication with the family while working with the student to address factors that are within your locus of control at school.

When you make initial contact with a student's family regarding behavioral concerns, remember that family involvement or lack thereof may be influenced by culture or a family's past experiences with schooling. Some families may also appear minimally responsive because of factors like conflicts with job schedules, limited proficiency in English, or mental health concerns. If you receive a muted response, or even if the family member responds negatively to your call, try to understand factors that may be contributing to this type of response. Consider ways to increase positive school-home communication to make school feel more welcoming and comfortable for the family.

Provide Follow-Up Communication

If you make an early-stage contact about behavioral concerns and notice improvements after the call, make sure to follow up as soon as possible to let the parent know about this success (i.e., within the same day). This positive communication is essential so that the student knows they are on the right track. If the student continues to demonstrate improvements, make efforts to periodically notify the family about the student's growth. These types of interactions demonstrate to the student and family that you are invested in the student's success. They also help you to maintain a positive ratio of interactions with the student and the family.

If the student does not demonstrate improvements after your initial call, continue to communicate ongoing concerns, but be careful not to inundate parents with lots of negative calls. Some parents begin to dread calls from their student's teacher because they occur so frequently and are always negative. Continue to maintain at least a 3:1 ratio of positive to corrective interactions with these families (see Chapter 6, Task 5). If this seems difficult because of the number of phone calls you must make to communicate a concern, begin working on intervention planning and also consider using a more regular feedback system such as a daily or weekly home note or daily monitoring system. These systems provide regular and consistent communication about both positive and negative aspects of the student's behavior. A number of programs formalize such communication systems, including *Connections*, a web-based Tier 2 and 3 daily behavioral grading intervention, and *The Tough Kid Electronic Home Notes*, both available through ancorapublishing.com. Reserve more direct communication such as phone calls and conferences with families to communicate about serious behavioral incidents and to provide positive feedback about student efforts and growth.

Remember that effective correctional techniques change the future occurrence of the misbehavior. If your initial one or two calls to parents did not result in behavioral change, this type of family contact is not working as a corrective consequence. Rather, the communication is designed to keep parents informed about your ongoing efforts to work with the student. It also is a way to ensure collaborative supports in cases where parents are willing and able to coordinate a plan with the school.

TASK 6

Move Toward Proactive Intervention Planning With Individual Students Who Display Chronic Misbehavior

For students with significant behavioral needs, modify your management plan and/or connect a student with additional intervention supports.

• • • • •

If you have written more than two referrals regarding an individual student's behavior, it is likely time to begin proactive intervention planning. Even if you have not written ODRs, if you find that a student has not responded to effective proactive and positive classroom management approaches, and corrective consequences are not working to change the student's behavior, it is time to begin moving toward individualized intervention planning for the student.

This does not necessarily mean that it is time to seek out intervention supports outside of your classroom, such as a counselor-led social skills group or referral for special-education evaluation. In many cases, relatively simple classroom-based interventions can be highly effective in providing needed supports for a student. It is also important to recognize that if the student exhibits concerning behavior in the classroom, classroom-based interventions and adaptations in the classroom environment will be essential even if the student requires additional supports outside of the classroom.

You cannot know whether a simple intervention will work or not unless you try it and implement it well. If the problem is resistant to simple interventions, you will progress to more detailed and intensive interventions, possibly including other school or community-based professionals at some point in the process. All interventions that are tried should have a long record of success, meaning there is a wide body of evidence documenting the intervention's positive effect in different settings and with different types of students. Any intervention that is tried should be based on respectful, noncoercive, and nonhumiliating procedures.

The information in this task is most useful for classrooms where student behavior is basically under control, but one or students misbehave frequently enough it concerns you. If your class has more than one or two students who chronically misbehave, do one or more of the following to refocus your efforts on increasing the level of classroom support:

- Increase the structure provided to students through the organization of your classroom environment and during classroom activities and routines where students are struggling (Chapters 2 and 3).
- Define and then clearly communicate your behavioral expectations (Chapter 4).
- Observe and supervise systematically (Chapter 5).
- Build positive relationships with your students and provide positive feedback when students meet expectations and demonstrate effort or growth (Chapter 6).
- Implement one or more non-reward-based and at least one high-structure classwide motivational systems approaches (Chapter 7).

STOIC Framework

If more than two students frequently struggle with misbehavior, problem-solve within the STOIC framework and make changes to your Classroom Management Plan to create greater stability for the class. This is more effective than trying to create and implement many different individualized behavior support plans.

Does the Student Already Have a BIP?

Before designing an intervention plan for a student, check with your school counselor, administrator, or special education staff to determine whether the student already has a behavior intervention plan (BIP). If she does, work with school personnel such as the special education department or your school psychologist to assist in implementing that plan. If the student does not have a BIP, consider the suggestions in this task and use any other evidence-based resources available to you. Work with colleagues who have expertise in the area of intervention supports to design a BIP.

- Analyze your corrective interactions and determine if one or more changes are required in the ways you provide corrective feedback and corrective consequences to students (Chapter 8).

In other words, if you have numerous students who are struggling with misbehavior, it may be too difficult to manage multiple individualized support plans. Do as much as possible to stabilize the class with effective classroom management techniques. If the totality of your management plan is not effective, the task of intervening with individual students will likely be overwhelming and probably relatively ineffective.

The suggestions in this task provide only a brief overview of some concepts related to behavioral intervention practices. If you realize you need more support and training, *Early-Stage Interventions: Behavior Strategies for Every Teacher* (available at ancorapublishing.com) is a resource designed for classroom teachers as a logical companion resource for CHAMPS. This book offers a set of simple, teacher-friendly interventions to use as a starting place in addressing an individual student's chronic behavioral concerns—disrespect, noncompliance, lack of motivation, bullying, aggression, and more. When a student doesn't respond to the teacher's general classroom management efforts, this book provides a protocol of classroom-based interventions that a classroom teacher can try with an individual student before (or while) accessing intervention supports outside the classroom.

Analyze and If Needed Adjust the Implementation of Your Basic Management Plan

In some cases, making adjustments to your management plan for an individual student who exhibits chronic misbehavior may be enough to help the student improve their behavior (Lewis & Sugai, 1999; Scheuermann & Hall, 2008). For example, moving the student's desk to a different location or providing more focused opportunities to talk to the student about your expectations and have them practice may help improve the situation.

To work through your management plan with an individual student in mind, carefully consider the questions on the Classroom Management Plan—Reflection for an Individual Student form (Reproducible 8.6). See the completed sample on pages 383–384, followed by a version (Reproducible 8.7) with bullet points for you to consider as you fill out your own form. Note that the ideas and suggestions on this form have been covered earlier in the book. You are now exploring how you can adjust the suggestions to help an individual student, just as you might do in differentiating instruction or providing accommodations for a student with academic support needs. Pay careful attention to the strategies in the I of STOIC, including building a positive relationship with the student and providing high rates of positive feedback for growth, effort, and appropriate behavior. Strategies that focus on positive interactions with students are some of the most important when working with students with chronic challenging behavior.

Reproducible 8.6 *Classroom Management Plan—Reflection for an Individual Student (p. 1) Example*

Classroom Management Plan— Reflection for an Individual Student (p. 1 of 2)

CHAMPS

STUDENT **Monique**   TEACHER **Ms. Bradford**   DATE **11/13**

Targeted Activities (activities in which the student is unmotivated and/or unsuccessful)	List the Student's Strengths
• *Coming to school regularly* • *Completing assignments in class* • *Completing homework*	• *Gets along well with others* • *Easily redirected* • *Enjoys nonacademic activities*

1. List three strategies you will use to provide noncontingent attention to the student every day.

   A. *I will give her a smile and/or compliment (e.g., "You look sharp this morning" or "My daughter has a pair of shoes like yours") every day as she enters the classroom.*

   B. *When I see her exhibiting appropriate social behavior when interacting with other students, I will establish eye contact and wink, smile, give a thumbs-up, etc.*

   C. *Every time she is absent, I will say to her on the day of her return something like, "I'm so glad you're back. It's just not the same without you here."*

2. For which targeted activities will you provide positive feedback to the student?

   A. *Beginning an assignment on time*
   B. *Following a direction or responding to a redirection*
   C. *Turning in her homework*

REPRODUCIBLE 8.6

Reproducible 8.6 *Classroom Management Plan—Reflection for an Individual Student (p. 2) Example*

Classroom Management Plan—Reflection for an Individual Student (p. 2 of 2)   *CHAMPS*

3. What will you do if the student doesn't respond well to positive feedback?

   Try a different method of providing the feedback, such as writing her a private note.

4. Identify two strategies for increasing your ratio of interactions with the student and describe how and when you will use them.

   A. *I will make a point to greet her every morning when she enters the room and will tell her at dismissal that I'm looking forward to seeing her the next morning.*

   B. *I will provide both positive feedback and noncontingent attention when she is appropriately interacting with other students.*

5. Which intermittent celebration(s) will you use to reinforce the student for showing appropriate behaviors and/or progress on the targeted activities? How will you select the celebration and when will you deliver it?

   A. *I will have her use a prepared checklist to identify her top five choices for celebrations.*

   B. *I will randomly provide the celebrations once or twice a week when she comes to school and when she submits her homework.*

REPRODUCIBLE 8.6

Reproducible 8.7 *Bulleted Classroom Management Plan—Reflection for an Individual Student (p. 1)*

Bulleted Classroom Management Plan— Reflection for an Individual Student (p. 1 of 2)

CHAMPS

STUDENT _____ TEACHER _____ DATE _____

Targeted Activities (activities in which the student is unmotivated and/or unsuccessful)	List the Student's Strengths
• Give specific examples—do not say "everything" • Identify each academic area • Consider study skills and work habits • Don't forget nonacademic activities (e.g., sports, singing, peer relationships, drawing)	Consider: • Academic strengths • Behavioral strengths • Social strenths • Interests

1. List three strategies you will use to provide noncontingent attention to the student every day.

> These strategies should be specific (e.g., verbal greetings, hand gestures like thumbs up or handshake, facial expressions like smile, head nod, or wink) that are delivered at specific times of the day (e.g., entering or leaving the classroom, during small group work) and whenever appropriate (e.g., seeing student in the hallway).

2. For which targeted activities will you provide positive feedback to the student?

> • Look at the student's strengths and consider using some of them as opportunities for providing positive feedback.
> • Positive feedback should also be given for behaviors that are new, difficult, or a source of pride for the student.
> • Remember to deliver verbal positive feedback calmly and quietly, and within 3 to 4 feet of student. Be brief, specific, and descriptive.

Reproducible 8.7 *Bulleted Classroom Management Plan—Reflection for an Individual Student (p. 2)*

Bulleted Classroom Management Plan—Reflection for an Individual Student (p. 2 of 2)   *CHAMPS*

3. What will you do if the student doesn't respond well to positive feedback?

> - Does the student feel embarrassed by the public display of positive feedback or not know how to accept positive feedback?
> - Ask yourself if you are being too public or too dramatic with the feedback.
> - Are you pausing expectantly after giving feedback so that the student feels compelled to respond verbally?
> - Adjust feedback delivery accordingly and revert to giving only noncontingent attention for several weeks if the student continues to reject positive feedback.

4. Identify two strategies for increasing your ratio of interactions with the student and describe how and when you will use them.

> The goal is to provide a ratio of at least three positive interactions when the student is behaving appropriately to one corrective interaction when the student is engaged in inappropriate behavior. Here are some ways to increase the ratio:
>
> - Identify the times of day when the student often behaves appropriately.
> - Schedule individual conference times.
> - Scan the room to identify reinforceable behaviors.
> - Give the student plenty of noncontingent attention when entering the room, at lunch, on playground, etc.
> - Use gestures (e.g., thumbs-up, head nod) to acknowledge appropriate behavior.
> - Post visual reminders to praise students on your plan book, wall, desk, or overhead.
> - Give students more opportunities to respond.
> - Publicly post examples of positive work by students.
> - After praising one student, find and praise another student who is displaying the same behavior.
> - Provide precorrections (quick reminders of how to behave appropriately when you anticipate students might have problems behaving appropriately).
> - Emphasize attending to positive behaviors after responding to misbehavior.

5. Which intermittent celebration(s) will you use to reinforce the student for showing appropriate behaviors and/or progress on the targeted activities? How will you select the celebration and when will you deliver it?

> - Provide a concrete reward or celebration when the student shows an important appropriate behavior. The reward or celebration must be meaningful to the student. Ask the student to identify rewards.
> - While delivering, make sure to provide specific positive feedback on what the student has done well. Also keep up the noncontingent attention.

REPRODUCIBLE 8.7

A general principle when designing individualized plans is to try the easiest things that have a likelihood of working first. Make some minor tweaks to your management plan or consider if you need to change aspects of how you implement the plan. If you are successful, you can turn a chronic problem into no problem. Be sure to keep your positive feedback at a very high level with this student, and tell the student's family that improvement is taking place. If these adjustments to your plan prove ineffective after a couple of weeks, add in additional layers to your intervention plan.

Implement Classroom-Based Individualized Interventions

When a student has not responded to tweaks to your management plan, implement one or more classroom-based individualized behavioral interventions (some examples follow).

Planned Discussion

An intentional, targeted discussion ensures that the student is aware of your perception of the problem and your expectations for what they should be doing instead. This simple intervention is often a logical starting place that can potentially resolve issues that result when a student doesn't know or fully understand your behavior expectations. If additional intervention is needed, you will continue having Planned Discussion meetings with the student to review progress and introduce new efforts. (See brief procedures in Box 8.1 (pp. 389-390) or detailed procedures in *Early-Stage Interventions*.)

Data Collection and Debriefing

Data collection and debriefing should occur in any case where you have tried some easy, simple interventions and realize that the behavior is complex and chronic enough that you may need to seek assistance (from a counselor, social worker, or school psychologist, for example) in designing a more intensive plan sometime in the near future. Data collection starts with defining the problem behavior in measurable terms and then deciding how to collect and report data on the problem. Involve the student and parents in reviewing data, discussing progress, and becoming "shareholders" in the process of improvements. In many cases, the act of collecting and reviewing data can resolve the problem on its own. If it does not, this intervention will become an essential part of any subsequent intervention plan, whether interventions take place primarily in the classroom or are delivered in another school- or community-based setting. (See detailed procedures in *Early-Stage Interventions*.)

Goal Setting

The process of setting goals encourages students to think about what they hope to accomplish in the future and how they can take steps to achieve their aspirations. By teaching goal-setting strategies as skills, you not only help a student change current behavior patterns, but also set the student on a path for developing more agency over future aspirations and successes. (Adapt procedures described in Chapter 7, Task 2 or see detailed procedures for Goal Setting with an individual student in *Early-Stage Interventions*.)

Meaningful Work

Many students who struggle with aspects of behavior or motivation can benefit from having a classroom job that gives them a sense of purpose and belonging, and provides opportunities for you (and others) to deliver lots of positive feedback. A classroom or school-based job can provide stimulation or a brief change of environment or focus that allows students who may get easily frustrated or bored a chance to move around and then refocus. This can be as simple as having a student pass out papers, erase the board, or sharpen pencils on a regular basis, or it can be as formalized as providing maintenance or updates on computers and tablets, running a classroom store, or designing bulletin boards in your room or in the hallways. One recommended resource that describes how to implement a school-based jobs program is *Meaningful Work*.

Structured Reinforcement

Structured reinforcement systems use external rewards to motivate students to increase positive behaviors or reduce inappropriate behaviors. It may be appropriate when a student needs extra motivation because of the high level of effort it takes to learn and use new behaviors, and it is also appropriate for students who do not currently express much value in school success or who find their needs are more fulfilled by engaging in inappropriate behavior than appropriate behavior. Some of the whole-class systems described in Chapter 7, Task 3 could be easily adapted for use with an individual student, such as:

- Economic Simulation (p. 327)
- Reinforcement Based on Reducing Misbehavior (p. 328)
- Group Response Cost (p. 331)
- Self-Evaluation of On-Task and Off-Task Behavior (p. 335)
- Target and Reward a Specific Behavior (p. 336)
- Mystery Motivators (p. 336)

Also see procedures described in *The Tough Kid Book* and *Interventions*, which provide recommendations and reproducible resources for setting up systems of reinforcement for individual students.

Managing Emotional Escalation

When a student escalates into serious acting-out behavior such as volatile or explosive behavior, verbal or physical outbursts, sustained disruptions or tantrums, running away, or physically dangerous behavior, these events are typically emotionally based and fueled by a series of events—often related to the student's interactions with others. Effective intervention for managing emotional escalation involves both teaching a student to manage their own behavior and learn to stay in control over the longer term, and learning to intervene and defuse potentially volatile confrontations in the shorter term. Although escalating behavior is expressed in different ways by different students, some distinct and readily identifiable patterns typically occur when a student goes through a cycle of emotional escalation. You can learn to recognize and pinpoint these patterns to prevent serious incidents of escalated behavior. See *Managing the Cycle of Acting Out Behavior in the Classroom* (2nd ed.) by Colvin and Scott for in-depth procedures for students who exhibit patterns of escalating behavior. This information is available in an abbreviated form in *Foundations* (3rd ed.)—*Module D*, and *Interventions: Support for Individual Students with Behavior Challenges*. All resources mentioned on this page are available at ancorapublishing.com.

Planned Discussion as an Early Intervention

Adapted from *Early-Stage Interventions: Behavior Strategies for Every Teacher*, available at ancorapublishing.com

Planned discussion is a simple but powerful early intervention that has the potential to have a positive impact on just about any behavior. If used effectively in the early stages of problem behavior, this intervention has the potential to eliminate the need for more time consuming and intensive intervention strategies. Even if the intervention on its own is unsuccessful in helping the student, this initial discussion sets the stage for subsequent interventions because it is a respectful, collaborative, and empowering way to involve the student in addressing concerning behavior. The purpose of the intervention is to demonstrate your concern in a way that the student truly understands it, to involve the student in brainstorming and coming up with a plan, and to let the student know with certainty that you are there to help them learn and grow.

Basic steps for implementing a Planned Discussion are:

Step 1. Plan to meet with the student.

Schedule the meeting for a neutral time that is as free from distractions and interruptions as possible. Make an appointment with the student in advance. Say something like, "Lillianna, let's meet tomorrow. I'm going to have Mr. Edwards stop in and watch the class while you and I go and chat. I've noticed that we've had some tense moments in the last few days when I've given you a direction and you've told me that you don't need to do it. I'd like us to talk and see if we can come up with some ideas for how we can work together. I care about your success and want to make sure we figure out a solution that works for both of us."

Identify a primary concern to discuss during the meeting, such as off-task behavior, poor work completion rate, difficulties interacting with other students. If the student has many problems, you will need to narrow the scope and focus your initial discussion on only the most pressing concern or two.

Also be prepared to begin and end the meeting with some discussion of the student's strengths or interests. This has two main benefits. It helps you reflect on the positive things the student brings (or can bring) to your class so that you don't enter the conversation solely focused on the student's weaknesses. It also ensures that the student sees that you are paying attention to them beyond their current challenges and that you are invested in their success. Starting the conversation with a simple authentic comment like, "Finn, I noticed yesterday that you really helped Bodhi calm down when he was frustrated. You really look out for your peers."

Step 2. Meet with the student.

Start on a positive note by mentioning something positive about the student or asking about an interest or recent experience ("Congratulations on making the varsity team. I know you've really been practicing" or "I liked your comment about dolphins during our group discussion yesterday. Your science camp at the aquarium sounds like fun").

Introduce your primary concern and encourage the student to share their perspective. Be careful that the discussion is framed in a way that sets it up as a joint problem-solving effort, not a lecture about what the student is doing wrong and must do differently. When discussing difficulties that you have observed, be clear in communicating that you are not attaching blame or labeling the student as "bad," but rather are looking to work with the student to figure out ways to handle situations appropriately in the future. Also keep a forward-looking orientation throughout the meeting. If previous behavior is mentioned, it is only from a perspective of figuring out the best way to ensure a positive outcome if something similar comes up in the future.

Develop a list of possible solutions. Work together to brainstorm actions that both you and the student can take to resolve the concern. Clarify that the goal of brainstorming is to develop ideas, not finalize a plan, so during brainstorming you will list all ideas, and then you and the student will work together to identify those that seem like the best initial approach.

Continued on next page ⟶

Box 8.1 continued

Once a number of ideas are on the table, select one or two ideas that seem manageable and most likely to lead to success. Formalize your action plan by keeping a written record. The Discussion Record (Reproducible 8.8) can be used to document this and any subsequent discussions.

Conclude the meeting by scheduling a follow-up meeting a few days to a week after the initial discussion. Scheduling this meeting in advance increases the likelihood that you and the student will follow through with your part of the plan. It also sends a message that this begins a sustained effort to resolve the problem, so if this particular plan isn't working, you and the student will continue working together until you find a solution. Conclude your discussion with words of encouragement: "Jian, I really appreciate your participation today. I know that you've felt frustrated in my class in the past. It means a lot that you're willing to discuss this and come up with suggestions that you can do and that I can do to help you stay focused and get your work done. If we work together, I'm confident that we can get things on track."

Reproducible 8.8 *Discussion Record*

Discussion Record — CHAMPS

STUDENT _____ TEACHER _____
GRADE/CLASS _____ DATE _____ OTHER PARTICIPANTS _____

1. Describe the problem. _____

2. Describe the general goal. _____

3. Brainstorm a list of possible solutions. _____

4. Set up an action plan. _____

Schedule a follow-up meeting: Date _____ Time _____
Participants _____

© 2021 Ancora Publishing — REPRODUCIBLE 8.8

Function-Based Intervention

When students with chronic behavioral or motivational concerns have not responded to simpler intervention strategies, the situation requires a more analytical and comprehensive plan. As described in Chapter 1, almost every behavior that occurs repeatedly serves some purpose, or function, for the student—whether it's gaining attention from peers by misbehaving in class, obtaining access to favorite playground equipment by bullying another student, or escaping classwork by wandering around the classroom. While teachers should not be expected to know how to conduct full-blown functional behavior assessments (these should be performed by trained professionals such as school psychologists and Board Certified Behavior Analysts), all teachers can learn basic principles about function so they can develop effective hypotheses about why behavior is happening and design intervention plans based on that guess. These interventions are designed with the understanding that chronic misbehavior occurs for a reason and that misbehavior is related to the environment in which it occurs. Effective function-based intervention, therefore, includes a variety of preventive, teaching, and corrective strategies that address both the context and the reason for chronic behavioral concerns. To review basic ideas related to function of behavior, go back to Chapter 1, Task 2 while considering this information in light of the concerns for one student who exhibits chronic misbehavior. Do you have a hypothesis about what function the behavior may be serving for the student? If so, how might this inform your selection of classroom-based interventions and supports for the student? For information on how you as a classroom teacher can learn to create function-based intervention plans, see *Early-Stage Interventions*, *Interventions*, or *Foundations* (3rd ed.) *Module F*, available at ancorapublishing.com. A series of free web modules, developed by Drs. Chris Borgmeier, Sheldon Loman, and Kathleen Strickland Cohen, train school professionals to develop effective Behavior Intervention Plans using function-based principles. These web modules are available at www.basicfba.com.

In summary, chronic misbehavior represents one of the greatest frustrations and challenges to classroom teachers (Lewis & Sugai, 1999; Walker et al., 1995). It is not necessary to update your Classroom Management Plan with these procedures, but ensure that you keep records of any intervention attempts and the corresponding data you collect for an individual student with challenging behavior. Keep the following general ideas in mind as you work with the student.

- In designing an intervention plan, always try the easiest strategy first. Try to use the strategy that is likely to have the biggest impact on the student's behavior. If more than one or two students are chronically misbehaving, work on the implementation of your overall Classroom Management Plan—trying to implement multiple individualized interventions while also teaching a class with 20 or 30 other students is too challenging for even the most skilled teacher. If one or two students are chronically misbehaving, first try an intervention that makes minor adjustments, tailored for that student or students, to your management plan. Pay careful attention to building a positive relationship with the student.

- If your original efforts are ineffective, begin collecting objective data and implement one or more other interventions that make sense based on the hypothesized function or cause of the behavior. Although function-based intervention planning is a great deal of work, a well-designed and implemented individualized intervention has the potential to bring about life-altering change for a student whose chronic behavioral concerns put them significantly at risk.

Conclusion

Correcting misbehavior is the weakest tool in your management toolbox; however, it is vitally important that every teacher (and every other staff member who has a role in correcting misbehavior at school) understands how to correct effectively. Periodically analyze your corrective interactions. Consider whether you consistently correct students in a way that conveys your high expectations and reduces the likelihood of similar misbehavior in the future. Analyze whether you equitably address all students in a consistent, calm, brief, and private manner. Consider whether you have an adequate menu of different classroom-based corrections so you can appropriately address mild to severe misbehaviors that occur in your classroom. Also consider the suggestions in this chapter for using and writing effective ODRs, communicating with families about problematic incidents, and moving toward intervention planning when one or two students exhibit chronic concerns. The strategies in this chapter help to reduce the risks of inadvertently reinforcing negative behavior, ruining relational trust with students, and using procedures that put the student at greater risk of falling behind academically or disengaging from the school system.

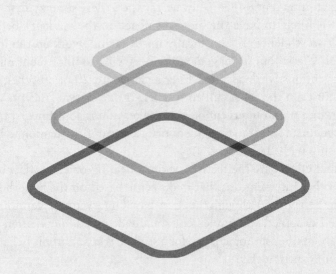

SECTION

3

Implementing, Sustaining, and Refining Your Classroom Management Plan

Imagine your dream vehicle . . .

What you could have if finances were no object. Whether you envision a luxury private jet, a "practically-perfect-in-every-way" family car, or a fun and efficient bicycle, that vehicle is going to need ongoing maintenance. Although maintenance is rarely part of the dream, it is always a necessity for our vehicle, our residence, our relationships, our careers, and our very selves.

Think of your Classroom Management Plan as the vehicle you have designed for your dream classroom. As you implement, you will need to (metaphorically speaking) change the oil, have regular tune-ups, wash the outside, and in the case of the family vehicle, remove food wrappers, toys, stains, dirt, and who-knows-what-else on the inside. If you do not do at least some of this maintenance, even the dream vehicle will be a pile of junk relatively quickly. In the following two chapters, you will consider ways to put your classroom management plan in place and continue to fine-tune and adjust you approach to achieve the goals of your dream classroom.

SECTION THREE

CHAPTER 9

Launch

Set the stage for a productive year by getting off to a good start.

By following the suggestions presented so far in this book, you have created the potential for a wonderful classroom. You have developed your classroom vision and organization and defined your CHAMPS expectations for student behavior.

This chapter offers suggestions for how you can implement all of the creative work you have done and make the first month of school a highly productive one, setting the stage for the rest of the year. The first month of school is an incredibly important time. It is essential to get students on board and behaving responsibly from the start because it can be very difficult (not impossible, but very difficult) to change negative behavior patterns later in the year. Research has shown that starting the year with an effective Classroom Management Plan results in increased appropriate behavior and improved academic performance (Emmer et al., 2009; Evertson & Anderson, 1979; Evertson & Emmer, 1982; Kounin, 1970). Also, student-rated "best" teachers focused more on teaching expectations and establishing guidelines for appropriate behavior from the first day of school (Moskowitz & Hayman, 1976).

The information and strategies in this chapter are primarily designed to ensure that during the first month of school you build positive relationships with students and communicate your expectations so clearly that you and your students are working productively as a team by the end of the first 4 weeks of school.

The first three tasks in this chapter are presented chronologically. They address final preparations you should make before school starts, what to do on the first day of school, procedures and considerations to deal with during the remainder of the first month, and preparations for special circumstances that may come up later. The fourth task provides suggestions for how to begin using the CHAMPS approach if you are starting your implementation midyear.

Task 1 reviews the most essential concepts from Chapters 1 through 8 to make sure you are ready for the first day of school. This task guides you through reviewing and summarizing information about your vision, classroom organization, and other aspects of your Classroom Management Plan.

Task 2 describes a few ideas that may help the first day of school run more smoothly. These include making it easy for students to find your classroom, planning for how you will get students into the room and settled down, and preparing to make effective use of the first 10 minutes of class. We also review how to use the three-step process for communicating expectations on the first day of school.

The third task in this chapter focuses on the process of communicating your behavioral expectations throughout the first month of school. You need to ensure that by the end of the first week, students have a thorough understanding of how to behave during each type of classroom activity and transition. In addition, if you are an elementary teacher, you should have coordinated with specialists (media, music, PE) so that your students know the behavioral expectations for these classes. During weeks two and three, continue to teach, monitor, and give feedback on your expectations. Eventually you will objectively verify student understanding of the expectations using a brief quiz or interviews with students. If you find that students do not fully understand what is expected of them, you will need to re-teach your CHAMPS expectations.

> **The best time to have an impact on student behavior is the first day of school.**

The best time to have an impact on student behavior is the first day of school. However, if it's not possible to have a plan in place at that time, the first day of second or third term or second semester is a good time to make major changes in your classroom. If you are beginning CHAMPS part way through the year, Task 4 provides suggestions for what may be the most effective way to approach working through the CHAMPS book and implementing strategies throughout the remainder of the year.

The four tasks presented and explained in this chapter are:

- Task 1: Make Final Preparations for Day One
- Task 2: Implement Your Plan on Day One
- Task 3: Implement Your Plan on Days 2 Through 20 (the First Four Weeks)
- Task 4: Begin CHAMPS Implementation Midyear

TASK 1

Make Final Preparations for Day One

Finalize your Classroom Management Plan and make final preparations to ensure an orderly, respectful, and comfortable first day for you and your students.

• • • • •

If you are fully prepared for the first day of school, you will be relaxed and ready to handle whatever takes place. In the previous chapters you identified the most essential preparation tasks, and in this task you will summarize and prepare to launch that information.

Review Your Completed Classroom Management Plan

If you have worked through each of the tasks in Section 2 and updated your Classroom Management Plan, review your completed plan to ensure it accurately reflects your best efforts to design a proactive and positive management approach.

If you have not yet completed the Classroom Management Plan, take some time to fill out each section of Reproducible 1.1. Use the bulleted Classroom Management Plan (Reproducible 1.2) shown on pp. 398–399 to assist you in filling out your vision of the Classroom Management Plan. This version provides suggestions for how to apply major considerations from tasks in Chapters 2–8 for each section of the plan.

The process of summarizing your vision, organization, and procedures in writing helps ensure that you are clear on your own plan. It also creates a document to share with building administrators and substitute teachers. When you've completed the document, ask your administrator to review it to ensure that they are comfortable with and supportive of your ideas, particularly the types of corrective actions you will take regarding misbehavior. This completed Classroom Management Plan can also be kept on file with the other information you leave for substitute teachers.

Add Information to Your Classroom Syllabus

For middle school teachers, consider adding information about your management plan into your classroom syllabus. The syllabus functions as a reference tool, making it easy to remind students about your policies, but you will still need to explicitly teach the components of your classroom plan. Each day during the first week of school, teach some portion of the syllabus in detail. If you are concerned that this may be overwhelming to students, you might instead provide a one-page overview on the first day of school and then one more page each subsequent day for the first week. This way you will cover a small amount of information at a time, but still cover everything necessary before getting too far along in the class (Bell, 1998; Lovitt, 1978).

Reproducible 1.2 *Bulleted Classroom Management Plan (pp. 1–3)*

Bulleted Classroom Management Plan (p. 1 of 6)   *CHAMPS*

TEACHER _____ SCHOOL YEAR _____ ROOM NO. _____ GRADE LEVEL/CLASS _____

The level of support I anticipate establishing is (check one): ☐ High ☐ Medium ☐ Low

ITEM 1 Guidelines for Success (*Chapter 2, Task 1; pp. 55–59*)

A. List 3–5 positive expectations—what students must do to be successful in school and in life.
- They don't need to be specific behaviors.
- They refer to habits, traits, or attitudes that teach students how to be successful.
- Refer to them when teaching, encouraging, and correcting.

B. Indicate where and how you will visually post the Guidelines for Success in your classroom.

ITEM 2 Posted Rules (*Chapter 2, Task 2; pp. 60–64*)

A. List 3–6 classroom rules.
- These should be positively stated, objective descriptions of specific behaviors.
- They should address the most frequent misbehaviors that occur in your classroom.
- Demonstrate and teach the rules at the start of the year and after major breaks.
- When rules are violated, plan to deliver corrective consequences calmly and consistently.

B. Indicate where and how you will visually post the classroom rules.

ITEM 3 Attention Signal (*Chapter 2, Task 4; pp. 75–76*)

Describe the attention signal you will use in your classroom. If you will use more than one signal (e.g., one inside and one outside of your room), describe each one and how it will be used.
- The signal should immediately capture the students' attention. It should be both auditory and visual.
- Teach students to stop talking, stop working, and establish eye contact with you within 5 seconds of hearing and/or seeing the attention signal. If needed, include a participatory component to ensure that students are paying attention.

ITEM 4 Beginning and Ending Routines (*Chapter 2, Task 5; pp. 77–88*)

1. Routine for entering class:

Describe procedures for how students will enter the room (GOAL: Students feel welcome and immediately go to their seats and start on a productive task.)
- Plan to greet students as they enter the room.
- Teach students how to enter the room and follow expectations for getting to their seats and beginning productive seatwork. Decide whether students can talk to whom, about what, how loud, and how long when they enter the room. Also decide whether they can get out of their seats. If so, for what?

© 2021 Ancora Publishing

Bulleted Classroom Management Plan (p. 2 of 6)   *CHAMPS*

2. Routine for opening activities:

A. Describe how students will be instructionally engaged while attendance is taken and business conducted. (GOAL 1: Opening activities are efficient, orderly, and keep students instructionally engaged. GOAL 2: Announcements and housekeeping tasks do not take too much time.)
- During attendance, provide an assignment to work on.
- Use assigned seats and take attendance by referring to the seating chart.
- Spend no more than a minute or two on announcements and housekeeping tasks.

B. Indicate the procedures you will use when students are tardy. (GOAL: Procedures for dealing with tardiness are effective and do not cause a loss of instructional momentum.)
- Ensure your procedures allow you to maintain instructional momentum when a tardy student enters the room. Teach what you expect students to do when entering the class so they don't disturb the class.
- Use a method for keeping accurate records of excused and unexcused tardies, such as having a tardy student sign a tardy notebook.
- Assign consistent corrective consequences for unexcused tardies.

3. Protocols for students not prepared with materials:

Indicate what procedures will be used when students arrive without materials needed for the day. (Goal: Procedures allow you to deal effectively with students who do not have materials or who are not prepared to participate in the class.)
- Make sure students know exactly what materials are needed each day.
- Make sure students coming from situations of poverty are able to access needed materials in a nonstigmatizing way.
- Create procedures for students who forget materials to get what they need without disrupting the teacher or the instruction. Options include having the student ask a neighbor, go to a specified spot in the room to borrow the materials (require the student to leave a "deposit" like a book bag so that the borrowed materials are returned), or return to their locker and receive a mild penalty such as 20 seconds of time owed after class or a tardy.

4. Protocols for students returning after an absence:

Describe how you will manage students who return from an absence (GOAL 1: Students are welcomed back to class. GOAL 2: Students can find out what they missed and get handouts and returned papers without consuming much of your time and energy.)
- Welcome students back to class and ensure they know their absence was noticed and they were missed.
- Consider monitoring and discussing attendance patterns across time. Students should attempt to have fewer than 5% of days absent in any time period.
- Set up a system that allows a student to collect work and assignments and delivers makeup work without taking your time. One effective system is to use two baskets, one labeled "Absent, What You Missed" and the other "Absent, Assignments In."
- Describe how many days students are allowed to make up missed work. Consider giving the same number of days to complete missed work as the number of days a student was absent from school.

REPRODUCIBLE 1.2

Bulleted Classroom Management Plan (p. 3 of 6)   *CHAMPS*

5. Procedures for end of class or period:

Describe how you will wrap up the end of the day or class (GOAL 1: Students organize their materials and complete any necessary cleanup tasks. GOAL 2: Procedures provide you with enough time to give students both positive and corrective feedback.)
- End class on a relaxed and positive note.
- Allow enough time for students to organize their materials and clean up, and for you to provide positive and corrective feedback and give any needed reminders.

6. Routine for dismissal:

Describe your routine for dismissing the class. (Goal: Students will leave the classroom when you dismiss them, not by the bell.)
- Establish the expectation that the teacher dismisses the class when the room is quiet and the ending routine is done. Explain to the students that the bell does not dismiss the class.
- Dismiss classes that need higher support by rows or table clusters. Lower-support classes may be excused all at once as long as they do not rush out of the room or crowd the door.

ITEM 5 CHAMPS Expectations for Classroom Activities and Transitions (*Chapter 2, Task 6 [pp. 89–101] & Chapter 3, Tasks 2–5 [pp. 121–153]; Forms 2.3 and 3.2*)

A. List the common activities and transitions that occur in your classroom.

B. Once you have completed the CHAMPS Worksheets (Reproducibles 2.3 or 3.2) for each activity and transition, attach them or include them in a binder with a paper record of your Classroom Management Plan, and/or include the filled-out digital versions in a file that contains your plan.
- Incorporate best practices for facilitating teacher-directed activities, independent work, and cooperative partner and group activities.

C. Indicate how you plan to visually display your expectations and describe ways you will teach and review them with students at the beginning of the year and at other times as necessary.

ITEM 6 Procedures for Family Contact (*Chapter 2, Task 8; pp. 104–114*)

Describe your family contact plan, including:
- Make initial contact with families at the beginning of the school year by sending a letter home, creating a video, making a phone call, or having a face-to-face introduction.
- Maintain contact with families throughout the year and invite and seek parental feedback.
- Keep track of your ongoing contacts with families.

© 2021 Ancora Publishing

REPRODUCIBLE 1.2

Reproducible 1.2 *Bulleted Classroom Management Plan (pp. 4–6)*

Bulleted Classroom Management Plan (p. 4 of 6)   *CHAMPS*

ITEM 7 Procedures for Managing Student Assignments (*Chapter 3, Task 6; pp. 154–164*)

1. Procedures for assigning classwork and homework:

> Indicate how you will have students keep track of their classwork and homework.
> - Design a permanent place where students can easily find information about work and assignments. Options include writing on board, class website, or having students record on an assignment sheet. Keep the assignment posted throughout the day.
> - Include daily reminders about short-term and long-term assignments (e.g. "Science project is due Monday, and you should have finished your first draft.").
> - Teach students how to record their assignments and keep the record in a consistent location (e.g. three-ring binder or agenda book). Show examples of how their assignment sheet should look.

2. Procedures for collecting completed work:

> Describe how you will collect completed work in ways that promote student responsibility for submitting work.
> - Whenever possible, personally collect each student's work. This allows you to quietly provide positive feedback and to know immediately who hasn't done the work. While collecting the work, make sure students are doing something worthwhile. For students who haven't completed their work, establish the procedure that they must talk to the teacher later about why the work isn't done.
> - Other options for responsible and self-motivated students include having them hand in work by rows or tables, asking a student helper to collect work, or having students place their completed work in a basket and check off their name on an assignment sheet or a wall chart.
> - Consider having students check off completed tasks on a daily assignment sheet or wall chart.

3. Procedures for returning completed work:

> Describe procedures for returning work to students in a timely manner.
> - For simple homework and in-class assignments, return it the next day whenever possible.
> - Avoid having students wait while you return graded work.
> - Maintain confidentiality when returning graded work.

4. Procedures for maintaining records and keeping students informed of their current grade status:

> Describe procedures for managing student assignments and providing regular feedback to students on their completed work and current grade status.
> - Students need regular weekly feedback on their work completion and current grade status. Options for keeping track of the student's work include using a computer grade book program and printing a weekly report for each student, and/or having students self-monitor their own grade records.
> - If a student is behind a specified number of assignments (e.g. three to five), send home a letter or call the family.
> - For high-support classes, consider using a chart illustrating the rate of work completion by the entire class. An intermittent class reward for improving or maintaining a certain rate of completion can be an effective reinforcement.

Bulleted Classroom Management Plan (p. 5 of 6)   *CHAMPS*

5. Procedures and policies for dealing with late and missing assignments:

> Indicate how you plan to address students with late and missing assignments.
> - Consider whether you plan to use a policy in which there is a mild penalty for late work (e.g., 10% reduction of points for late assignments or time owed outside of class to work on missing work).
> - If such a policy will be used, clearly communicate the policy to students and families and emphasize the importance of open communication if a student is struggling with work requirements.
> - Provide periodic reinforcement for students who turn in work on time.

ITEM 8 Procedures for Managing Student Technology Use (*Chapter 3, Task 7; pp. 164–171*)

A. If students will be using shared devices in class, describe expectations and how you plan to teach them to students.

> - Use the CHAMPS or ACHIEVE Classroom Transitions and Activity Worksheets to clarify how students should behave during technology-based activities.
> - Establish an electronics policy and teach students about acceptable use of technology in the classroom.
> - Evaluate and revise your attention signal as necessary to ensure you can quickly get all students' attention when they are on devices.
> - Provide clear instructions and learning objectives for tasks before students begin using devices.
> - Monitor technology use and provide positive and corrective feedback.

B. Describe the expectations and procedures you will use regarding students' personal devices in class.

> - If your school has a policy, ensure you are following the policy at all times with your students and your own personal devices.
> - If your school allows teachers to define their own policies, plan to communicate expectations with students and their families, and clearly teach and visibly post information about your policy in your classroom.

ITEM 9 Long-Range Goals (*Chapter 3, Task 8; pp. 172–174*)

> List 4–7 long-range goals for your class.
> - Long-range goals can be instructional or academic, behavioral or social, or a mixture.
> - Include long-range goals on your syllabus and share with students and families at the beginning of the year.

ITEM 10 Procedures for Interacting Positively With and Encouraging Students (*Chapter 6, Tasks 2–4 [pp. 264–285] & Chapter 7, Tasks 2–3 [pp. 301–337]*)

A. Describe specific ways in which you will build positive relationships with students; provide positive feedback and acknowledgment of student strengths, efforts, and accomplishments; and interact positively with students' families.

> - Strive to have at least 3 times more positive interactions with each student than corrective interactions (maintain at least a 3:1 ratio of positive to corrective interactions).
> - Provide noncontingent attention (verbal and nonverbal) to each student throughout the day regardless of their behavior. This can include greetings, showing interest, learning about cultures and personal identities, and identifying each student's strengths.
> - Provide lots of positive feedback to the student and the class when appropriate academic and/or behavioral performance is demonstrated. Feedback should be accurate, specific, descriptive, contingent, age appropriate, and delivered in a manner consistent with your personal style.
> - Provide intermittent celebrations by giving rewards when a student or the class demonstrates a particularly important behavior. The reward or celebration must be meaningful to the student(s) and delivered on an unpredictable schedule (not every day).
> - Provide frequent positive feedback to students' families about their strengths, efforts, and accomplishments.

REPRODUCIBLE 1.2

Bulleted Classroom Management Plan (p. 6 of 6)   *CH*

B. Describe how you plan to encourage students using classwide motivational strategies and systems.

> - Recognize that motivation is influenced by many factors, including how much students value the rewards that accompany success (whether intrinsic or extrinsic) and the degree to which they believe they can be successful. If a student demonstrates a lack of motivation, consider whether strategies influence value, expectancy, or both are needed.
> - Use non-reward-based strategies such as stimulating and fostering interest and goal setting to boost students' motivation to exhibit appropriate behavior or meet other academic or behavioral goals.
> - Consider whether one or more classwide reward systems would boost motivation and responsible behavior. If you plan to use a reward-based system, carefully plan for factors such as the system's goal (what you want to accomplish), highly desirable rewards, setting it up so success is likely, teaching students the expectations for behavior, and how you will monitor students behavior within the system. Make sure you believe the system will improve student behavior and model energy and enthusiasm throughout. As students demonstrate success, gradually make the reward criteria more challenging, and when students are ready, modify and fade the system.

ITEM 11 Correction Procedures for Misbehavior, both early-stage corrections and rule violation consequences (*Chapter 8, Tasks 2–3 [pp. 346–370]*)

A. List the menu of corrective consequences you plan to use in your classroom.

B. Make note of any implementation recommendations you would like to highlight and remember how to correct misbehavior fluently and effectively.

> - Maintain high positive expectations for student behavior and student success. Ensure that corrective procedures for misbehavior communicate that you believe students can learn and exhibit prosocial behaviors, learn from mistakes, and reach their full potential.
> - Ensure that all corrections are delivered in an effective and fluent manner, meaning they are given consistently, calmly, briefly, and privately (as much as possible). If student behavior improves after corrective procedures, make sure to follow up with positive feedback.
> - Establish protocols (specific steps) for how you will handle common misbehaviors such as sleeping in class or the use of personal electronic devices at inappropriate times.
> - Include a range of corrective consequences from mild to more severe penalties, but err on the side of milder consequences that you can implement consistently.
> - Ensure that your corrective interactions never belittle, humiliate, or ridicule a student.
> - Understand that office disciplinary referrals and administrator-assigned consequences are often misused and overapplied. When they are warranted, use objective language and professionalism when writing a referral and communicating concerns with parents.
> - When corrective consequences have been consistently and appropriately applied and the student's behavior is not improving, recognize that corrective consequences are not working. Begin moving toward individualized intervention planning, starting with relatively simple interventions and moving to more intensive supports as needed.

REPRODUCIBLE 1.2

Figure 9.1 shows a completed class syllabus for a highly structured class of eighth-grade students. Although you might not provide a handout to your students that includes this much detail, you need to know in advance what your procedures and policies are going to be. We recommend that your syllabus be as comprehensive as possible to prevent confusion and other issues in the future. If you have followed each task in the preceding chapters, much of this information is probably already at hand. The sample provided in Figure 9.1 is an example of how to organize and present information on grading, rules, expectations, and procedures within your syllabus.

Figure 9.1 *Class Syllabus (Example for an Eighth-Grade Remedial Reading Skills Class)*

WELCOME TO EXPANDING ACADEMIC OPPORTUNITIES
Teacher: Mrs. Hernandez

Classroom Goals

By the end of this class, you will be able to:

1. Read long multisyllable words.
2. Use strategies to understand and analyze what you read. These strategies include:

   - Paraphrasing
   - Visual imagery
   - Self-questioning
   - Learn to use new vocabulary words.
   - Read aloud smoothly and with expression.
   - Write complete sentences and well-organized paragraphs.

3. Learn study strategies so you can take reading tests with confidence and perform well on those tests.
4. Learn to self-manage and stay on task with classwork and homework.

Accomplishing these goals will require cooperation. Think of this class like a sport such as basketball or track. You will have to work hard independently, but you will also have to work effectively with other students and with me.

Guidelines for Success

Winners make their own luck. They achieve.

It takes:
- Preparation
- Responsibility
- Integrity
- Dedication
- Effort
to be successful!

Classroom Rules

Winners know the rules and follow them.

1. Come to class every day that you are not sick.
2. Arrive on time with your own pencil and paper.
3. Keep hands, feet, and objects to yourself.
4. Follow directions the first time.
5. Stay on task during all work times.

Activities

Winners participate and strive to be CHAMPS. The CHAMPS approach will teach you exactly what you have to do during each type of classroom activity. For now, just be aware that each activity below will include very specific information for you about how to be successful in this class.

Large Group Activities

- Teacher-directed instruction

Station Activities

- Partner fluency practice
- Mastery checks with teacher (Parents: Mastery checks involve each student reading to me so I can monitor progress. These will occur about every 2 weeks.)
- Partner vocabulary practice
- Computer practice
- Independent practice: Writing activities

Notice the word "practice." These activities are practice for you to improve your skills, just like an athlete, dancer, or musician does.

Grades

Winners know that you have to keep score. Your grades for each of the coming 9 weeks will be based on the following:

- 20% of your grade will come from your class participation and how well you follow the rules. There are 10 possible points per day, for a total of 450 points for the quarter.

  - You will start each day with 8 points, which is 80%, or a low B.
  - Strong effort and application will add 1 point. I will mark additional points earned in my grade book throughout class.
  - Each rule violation costs 1 point.

- Your written work is worth a total of 40%.
- Your performance on mastery checks is worth 40%.

Classroom Procedures

Entering the Classroom

1. Be in the room and seated at your desk before the bell rings.
2. Have your folder and writing implement ready.
3. Begin work on the activity that is on the board or on your desk.
4. Quietly work on this activity until I signal for your attention.

Tardy to Class

If you are in the classroom and seated before the bell rings, you are on time. If you enter after the bell rings or are wandering around the classroom 10 seconds after the bell, you are tardy and will lose 1 behavior point. When you are tardy, enter the room silently. Write your name and reason for being late on the clipboard by the door (attach an excused note if you have one), then immediately join in whatever activity the class is doing. All tardies are reported to the attendance office according to school policy.

Paper and Pencil

If you do not have a pencil, I keep golf pencils and stubs on my desk. Please return them when you are finished and donate pencils that you no longer intend to use. There is also extra notebook paper on my desk. Use it when you need to and replace it when you bring your own.

Continued on next page ⟶

Figure 9.1 continued

Daily Assignments

Each of you will have a folder with your name on it on the counter by the door. A weekly assignment sheet will be in this folder every Monday. This sheet will outline the tasks you will work on during the week.

> ***Turning In Assignments:*** Turn in your completed work by putting it in the tray labeled "Period Two," which is on the counter by the door.

> ***Returning Assignments:*** Graded work will be returned to your folder.

> ***Finding Out Grade Status in Class:*** A grade printout will be placed in your folder every week. This will show your current grade in the class, any missing assignments, and a progress report showing your current reading level.

> ***Your Responsibilities After an Absence:*** Any time you are absent, you will view a video of the large group activities you missed. You may do this during your study hall or before or after school. You will also need to complete independent practice and vocabulary assignments for the days missed.

> You will have the same number of days to make up your work as the number of days you were absent. If you were absent on Monday and Tuesday, you will have to finish your makeup work and turn it in on Friday. Always be in class unless you are seriously ill!

Communication Procedures With Parents or Guardians

Show your weekly grade printout to a parent or guardian each week. You will get 3 bonus points for each week you return a weekly grade printout with a parent or guardian's signature.

Ending Class

One minute before the end of class, I will ask you to return to your assigned seats for final announcements. You will be excused by rows, after the bell rings.

Consequences for Classroom Rule Violations

If you violate a rule, you may be assigned a consequence. Depending on the frequency and severity of the misbehavior, you may receive one or more of the following consequences:

- Loss of a behavior point
- Change in seating assignment
- Time owed after class
- Detention
- Office referral

If you ever feel that the enforcing of rules and consequences is unfair, you have the right to make an appointment with me to discuss the situation. I will be as neutral as I can in hearing your complaints or comments.

Consequences for Code of Conduct Violations

If you break a rule that is covered by the Code of Conduct in your student handbook (possession of illegal substances, abuse, etc.), I must refer the situation to the office for the administrator to make decisions on parent contacts, police involvement, and other matters. This is part of my job, and not my decision. If you violate a Code of Conduct rule, it will be handled out of class.

On the first day of the school year, you have the opportunity to communicate to students that your classroom will be interesting, organized, and fun—although students will work hard, the work will be relevant and will help them to be successful students. In this task, you will work through suggestions to ensure that you are ready on day one to implement all of the work you have prepared.

Develop a Modified Schedule for the First Day of School

In Chapter 3, Task 1, you learned about developing a well-thought-out daily class schedule. That schedule should be modified for the first day of school to allow the inclusion of the unique tasks and activities that must occur on the first day. Your goal is to have the day be as representative of a typical day as possible, but also include activities that will accomplish these important first-day functions:

- Help students feel comfortable and settled.
- Communicate your classroom goals, rules, guidelines, and expectations.
- Communicate any schoolwide rules and expectations.
- Deal with logistics such as distributing textbooks.

Elementary teachers will probably want to plan get-acquainted activities for the first day to help the class begin to function as a group. Be careful not to fill the entire first day with games, however. Students should leave at the end of the day feeling that the class provides a welcoming and enjoyable environment and fully aware that they will be expected to work and study to the best of their abilities.

At the middle school level, get-acquainted activities can be included in advisory or homeroom periods, but should not be a part of every class period. Imagine how you would feel if you had to play the "Get to Know the Names" game in six different class periods on the first day of school!

Before you create your Day One Schedule, find out from your building administrator whether you need to take into account any schoolwide activities (assemblies or testing, for example). Be sure to schedule the first few minutes of the day to go over your goals, classroom rules, Guidelines for Success, and other essential information. Other activities to consider in your scheduling include how and when to pass out books, assign storage space, and otherwise get students settled. Plan to allow more time than usual for each activity on the first day in order to acquaint students with your procedures. For example, something as simple as having second-grade students line up at the door for recess, which should eventually take no more than 30 seconds, may take anywhere between 2 and 5 minutes on the first day of school.

A sample Day One schedule as it might be posted for an elementary classroom might look like the following:

8:30	Welcome, goals & rules
8:45	Getting organized
9:00	Reading
9:45	Getting ready for recess

10:00   Recess
10:15   Math
11:00   Getting to know each other
11:30   Getting ready for lunch
11:45   Lunch
12:30   Spelling/Writing
1:15   Science (weather & climate)
2:00   Afternoon break
2:10   Getting to know each other
2:30   Wrap up and get ready to go
2:45   The end of a great school day!

A sample Day One schedule for a middle school classroom might look like the following:

10 min.   Welcome, goals & rules
10 min.   Grading & homework
15 min.   Activity to identify what you know about science (This is not graded, so relax!)
10 min.   Tips on being successful in this class
3 min.   Wrap-up and dismissal

Make a Sign for Your Room

Create an easy-to-read sign that you can place in the hall on or near the classroom door to help your students find your room. Include your name, your grade level or subject, and the room number. Be sure to print large enough that students will be able to see the information from a distance. Remember, your students are likely to be self-conscious about looking lost—a nice clear sign will keep them from having to go door to door looking at small room numbers or teacher names.

Consider Assigning Seats as Students Enter the Room

Establishing the structure of assigned seats from the first day can help students who don't know anyone settle into the classroom with ease while also establishing a productive structure right at the start of your class. Some possibilities for assigning seats include:

- Having student name tags ready on student desks when they enter the room (for elementary) and guiding students to the location of their seat as you greet them at the door
- Having a large number on the back of each seat and telling each student the number they should go to as they enter the room
- Having the seating chart projected on the screen and directing students to find their assigned seat

- Assigning seats according to the order in which students enter the room (e.g., student 1 goes to seat 1 in row 1, student 2 goes to seat 1 in row 2, student 3 goes to seat 1 in row 3, and so on)

Prepare an Initial Activity for Students to Work on When They Enter the Room

An initial activity serves several important functions. First, it gives students something to do while they wait for the bell to ring and for class to begin, reducing the self-consciousness that some students may feel about not having someone to talk to. In addition, having an activity to work on keeps students who do know each other from congregating and conversing in groups. Without an activity, groups of students may become so engrossed in conversations that when the bell rings, you must interrupt them or try to get them into their seats before you can begin class. If students have a task to work on when they enter the room, you can keep most of your attention on greeting all students as they arrive. Finally, an initial task communicates the expectation that when students are in your class, they will be actively engaged, not just sitting around (Ornstein & Lasley, 2004).

Choose any task that students can do independently—in other words, a task that will not require assistance from you. Ideally it should be reasonably short and somewhat open ended. Don't forget that students who enter the room first will have longer to work on the task than students who enter just before the final bell rings. Following are some suggestions for this initial first-day task.

At the kindergarten and first-grade levels, give students a coloring sheet and a couple of crayons.

At the second-grade level and beyond, have students fill out a general information form (name, phone number, address) such as that shown in Figure 9.2 (p. 406). Or have students write answers to one or two open-ended questions that will help you get to know them better.

For example, you might ask students in grades 2 through 5 to identify the two school activities or subjects they like most and why, and the two school activities they like the least and why. Middle school students could be asked to identify when (for what accomplishments) they like to receive public praise and when they prefer to get feedback in a more private manner.

Prepare a Plan for Responding to Families Who Want to Take Your Time on the First Day

This is an especially important consideration for teachers of primary students, kindergartners in particular. Families of young students often want to spend time helping their student adjust or telling you about the unique needs or interests of their child. Spending 5 minutes with the families of just three students, however, would cost you the first 15 minutes of school.

Schedule a classroom open house or family conference sessions before the first day of school. One way to prevent this problem is to pick a day during the week prior to the first day

Figure 9.2 *Sample First-Day Worksheet*

WELCOME TO ROOM 19, MR. JACOBI'S SCIENCE CLASS!

For my records and to help you learn as much as possible from this class, please fill out this form while waiting for class to begin.

Name: *Carlos Yturra*
Preferred pronoun: [x] he/him/his [ ] she/her/hers [ ] they/them/theirs
Name of parent or guardian: *Enrique and Janice Yturra*
Address: *1972 Oak St.*
Phone number: *555–1212*   E-mail address:

Please identify which type of classroom activity you think helps you learn most effectively:

   [ ] Lecture   [x] Hands-on Labs
   [ ] Cooperative Groups   [ ] Independent Study

Explain why: *Everything makes more sense when I get to do it myself.*

Identify two things for which you like to receive public praise and two things for which you would prefer to get feedback in a more private manner.

  Public praise: *getting an answer right, looking good*
  More private feedback: *work that needs improvement, grade problems*

of school and invite kindergarten (or primary) students and their families to visit the classroom and talk with you—something like an open house. These visits can be time consuming, but they can make the first day go much more smoothly. Another procedure is to hold conferences with families before school starts. Conferences can be even more time consuming but pay even bigger dividends in building relationships with your students and their families. You get to know each student as a unique individual and create a working relationship with the family; at the same time, you learn about the student's medical or behavioral issues, if any.

At the open house or conference, you can also explain how the first day of school will work, how the student will be dropped off by the family or arrive on the bus, how the student will get to the classroom, and other first-day details. In other words, you can work out how the child's care will be transferred from the family to you, the teacher. You can assure the family that the child will be supervised and supported in getting safely to class on the first day of school.

Distribute an orientation handout for parents and guardians. If time does not permit the suggestion above, and if families bring the student to your classroom, plan to have a prepared note that you can distribute to families who drop into the classroom on the first day. You can also send written or recorded video communication in advance of the first day that describes what drop off or arrival from the bus will look like and prepare family members for a smooth transition. Let families know that you would be happy to speak with them before or after the first day of school if they have questions or concerns. Indicate that you want to ensure that your attention is focused on helping students smoothly transition into your room on the first day of school, so during the morning transition, you will keep your conversations with families brief.

If you know that the families of several of your students speak a language other than English, see if you can arrange to have the note written in English on one side and in that language on the other side. For video-based communication, consider having a translator provide text you can use to subtitle your video, or ask a translator to record audio that can you dub over your own voice.

If you are a kindergarten teacher, you may also want to ask the school counselor (or someone else who has a more flexible schedule on the first day of school) to assist you in getting families to leave their students behind. You can interact with the student while the counselor gently escorts the student's family into the hall. "Hi, Mrs. Thompson, I am Mr. Verner, the school counselor. While Mrs. Morales helps Joanie find her desk, let's you and I go out in the hall. I can give you some information about Mrs. Morales's program and how you can get in touch with her."

You can plan a similar scenario with ELL families. They often have great and justifiable concerns about whether the first day of school will be difficult for their child because of language issues—especially if their son or daughter is the only one or one of few ELL students in the classroom. Teachers or their administrators should contact someone at the district level to help with orientation and translation. If your district does not have personnel who can do this, most communities have volunteers fluent in different languages who can provide translation services.

Diversity, Equity, Inclusion, and Access

Consider how to support ELL students and families for the first day of school. Work with administrators to see if someone can help with orientation and translation to ensure that students and their families experience a smooth transition.

In summary, the procedures suggested in this task are designed to ensure that the first day of school goes smoothly and that students feel comfortable and know what you want them to do from the moment they arrive at your classroom. Implementing these procedures will help you head into the first day feeling confident, organized, and prepared to guide your students toward responsible, motivated behavior.

TASK 2

Implement Your Plan on Day One

Be prepared to implement strategies that allow you to make a great impression on your students on the first day of school.

• • • • •

The first day of school is an important one for both you and the students. When the day is managed well, students leave thinking, "This teacher is organized and friendly, and expects a lot from us. This class will be a lot of work, but it should be exciting and fun. The teacher really wants to help me be successful!" Your goal is to conduct the first day of school in a manner that will make students feel welcome and will help them learn to behave responsibly from the beginning (Moskowitz & Hayman, 1976). The following strategies can help you do just that.

Welcome Students to Your Classroom

Your goal is to conduct the first day of school in a manner that will make students feel welcome and will help them learn to behave responsibly from the beginning (Moskowitz & Hayman, 1976). The following strategies will help you succeed in doing just that:

> *Your goal is to conduct the first day of school in a manner that will make students feel welcome and will help them learn to behave responsibly from the beginning.*

Post your Day One schedule. When students enter the room, they will want to know what the day or class period will be like. If students see a prepared schedule or agenda, they can get a sense for "what they are in for." In addition, a written schedule provides a subtle message that you are prepared and organized, and that you have a clear idea of how you want the day or period to go (Trussell, 2008). Middle school teachers who have different classes may want to put the first-day schedule information for each class on a separate page of a flip chart. Before class starts, flip to the appropriate page so students see only their class period schedule. (Obviously, for kindergarten and first-grade students, most of whom probably cannot read, it would be silly and even intimidating to have a written schedule, but you might consider using a picture schedule to provide a sense of the day for your students.)

Greet students individually as they enter your room. Exactly how you greet students depends on the amount of time you have before the bell rings. If the time period for students to enter your classroom is less than 10 minutes, arrange to be near the door so you can greet each student as they enter. Ask the students their names and introduce yourself. Then instruct (or help) them to take their seats and start on the task you prepared (coloring, filling out the information form, answering the questions). Then go back to greeting other entering students. By the time the bell rings, all students should be in their seats and quietly working on the task.

In schools where the building is open early, you may have some students enter the classroom up to 30 minutes before the opening bell rings. If this is the case, greet individual students as they enter the room, but realize that you probably cannot be at the door the entire time. Get the early arrivals seated and started on the initial task. Let the students know that if they complete the task, they can raise their hand and wait for you to give them something else to do. Decide in advance whether you will give these students other tasks to do quietly at their seats, chat with them in small groups, or have them assist you with last-minute classroom tasks. You may want to ask other teachers what they do to keep students occupied during a lengthy waiting period before the official beginning of the school day.

Get students' attention as soon as the bell rings. Use your attention signal to get students to focus on you (for example, raise your hand and say, "Class, your attention please"—see Chapter 2, Task 4). Even though students do not yet know your signal, it is likely to be effective because students will be working quietly at their seats. If students look at you, thank them for their attention and explain that regardless of whether they completed the task, they should put their pencils down and pay attention to you. If students fail to give you their attention, repeat the signal, but only one time. Wait with your hand up until everyone is quiet and looking at you. Even if this takes several minutes (it probably won't), simply maintain the visual aspect of the signal and wait quietly. Resist the urge to shout at the students to get their attention. If you start shouting for students' attention at the beginning of the year, you are likely to be shouting at them every day from then on. Also make sure that you do not begin talking over students when the majority of students are paying attention but a few are still not with you. If you begin throwing your voice over a few students, over time, fewer and fewer students will follow your attention signal when it is given.

Communicate the essential classroom information in the first 10 minutes. Once you have the full attention of all students, introduce yourself and tell the students one or two personal or interesting things about yourself. Do not go into great detail. Then describe your long-range goals for the year, both academically and behaviorally.

> *Thank you for giving me your attention. Please put your pencils down for now; you will be able to complete the questions later in the period. My name is Mr. Younce (write it on the board). I will be your teacher this year. Over the year we will get to know each other better. I am looking forward to getting to know all of you and learning about you and your interests. For now I just want to tell you a couple of things about myself. I have two children of my own. They are both older than you—my daughter is 13 and my son is 17. My hobby is bicycling, and I sometimes bike as many as 100 miles in a day. We will have a chance to learn more about each other as the year goes on.*

Next, explain to students what your Guidelines for Success and classroom rules are. As you share this information, involve the students in age-appropriate ways.

> *Give me a thumbs-up when you have an idea about why I might have a rule that says "Keep hands and feet and objects to yourself." Get ready to share your idea with the person sitting next to you.*

At the conclusion of the first 10 minutes, students should have a preliminary sense of who you are, what will be expected of them, and what they will learn. Do not spend more than 10 minutes on this orientation. If you talk too much or provide too many details, students may get overwhelmed or tune you out.

Teach your attention signal. Demonstrate the signal you will be using to get students' attention and tell them why the signal is important.

> *I appreciate how well all of you are keeping your attention on me while I am speaking. During class there will be times when I need you to stop what you are doing and look at and listen to me. At those times, I will say, "Class, your attention please," while I make this big circular motion with my arm. Then I will hold my hand in the air. When you hear me say those words or see me make that motion, stop whatever you are doing, stop talking or walking, look at me, and raise your own hand. When you raise your hand, it helps get the attention of other students who may not have seen or heard my signal.*

> *Stopping immediately when I give that signal is important. There will be many times when we need to start an activity together. Even if everyone is doing something different, like working at your seats or in the learning centers, or sharpening a pencil, I can give the signal and everyone will be quiet and paying attention within 5 seconds. Then we can all be together for the next activity. I'm going to show you my signal one more time and show you how long 5 seconds is. This is how quickly I expect the whole class to be quiet and looking at me.*

Demonstrate the signal and count the 5 seconds. Provide a few immediate practice opportunities. For example, after you have taught your signal, tell students they are going to demonstrate how well they understand this signal. Then give them a short partner task such as telling a person sitting next to them a few things they are hoping to learn in the class. Once students are engaged in the task, call for their attention. Use at least three of these immediate practice attempts, and provide positive and corrective feedback.

Orient students to the posted Day One schedule. Start by giving students a clear idea of what the day or class period is going to be like. For students in second grade and higher, point out the schedule you posted for the day or class period. Then, for each activity, use the three-step process for communicating expectations. This cycle, which was introduced in Chapter 4, is summarized again in Figure 9.3 with essential steps for implementing introduced next.

Figure 9.3 *Three-Step Process for Communicating Expectations*

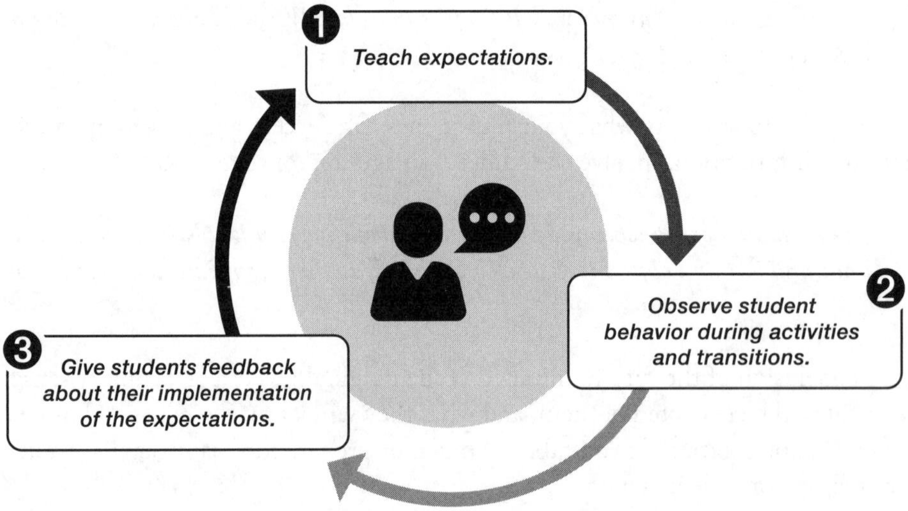

Use the Three-Step Process for Communicating Your Expectations

Just before students engage in any activity or transition, use the lessons you have developed (see Chapter 4, Task 2) to prepare students to exhibit the proper behavior during that activity or transition. It's important to note that you should teach your lesson for each particular activity or transition immediately before the activity or transition occurs. You do not want to teach the expectations for all (or even several) activities or transitions at one time.

STEP 1   *Teach your expectations.*

The first step in this process is teaching students what your expectations are. Just before students engage in any activity or transition, use the lessons you have developed (see Chapter 4, Task 2) to prepare students to exhibit the proper behavior during that activity or transition. It's important to note that you should teach your lesson for each particular activity or transition immediately before the activity or transition occurs. You do not want to teach the expectations for all (or even several) activities or transitions at one time.

Be prepared to spend as much time as necessary at the beginning of an activity or transition to ensure that students understand what is expected of them. If the lesson you have prepared involves modeling or practicing a behavior, you need to allow for more time than if you simply describe your expectations to students.

For example, say you have scheduled a 15-minute teacher-directed instructional period. It is possible that, on the first day, 5 to 7 of those 15 minutes will be spent explaining and modeling your expectations for student behavior during that activity. In other words, you should be prepared to spend anywhere from 20% to 50% of the time scheduled for a given activity on teaching your expectations for that activity during the first day(s) of school. If you think it likely that students will exhibit a particular misbehavior during the activity, you can precorrect and prompt desired behavior during the first week or so of school to minimize problem behaviors (Colvin, Sugai, & Patching, 1993; Darch & Kame'enui, 2004). Correct the error before it happens by explaining the potential problem and then reclarifying the positive expectation.

Some of you may feel that you do not have enough time to teach expectations because there is so much academic content to cover. However, taking the time to thoroughly teach your expectations makes such a positive difference in student behavior that you actually save time in the long run—there will be fewer disruptions and better on-task behavior for the rest of the year (Sugai & Horner, 2002). As a result, students will likely learn more. An established relation exists between high rates of student problem behavior and low rates of student learning (Brophy & Good, 1986; Martella et al., 2003; Sutherland & Wehby, 2001).

STEP 2   *Observe student behavior.*

The only way to know how well students are meeting your behavioral expectations for classroom activities and transitions is for you to observe their behavior in some way—the second step in the three-step process for effectively communicating expectations. Two of the most useful and efficient ways to observe student behavior during an activity or transition are to circulate among students and to visually scan all parts of the classroom (Colvin et al., 1997; DePry & Sugai, 2002; Gettinger & Ball, 2008; Pedota, 2007; Schuldheisz & van der Mars, 2001; Shores et al., 1993).

Circulating and scanning are two basic (but absolutely essential) strategies that allow you to know exactly what is going on at all times. You can use the information you gain from observing your class to help you make sound decisions about the type and frequency of feedback you should provide to students about their behavior. Circulating has an additional benefit in that your physical presence tends to reduce student misbehavior (Evertson, 1989)—it's human nature. Just as most drivers are more likely to adhere to the speed limit when they know a speed-detecting device is present, so too are students more likely to follow classroom rules and procedures when the teacher is physically close to them.

While circulating, frequently look around at other parts of the classroom. This is called scanning. Also scan frequently during those times you cannot circulate, such as when you are helping an individual student or working with a small group. Chapter 5, Task 1 provides further suggestions for the strategies of circulating and scanning.

Observing is an important component of communicating your expectations and is a critical tool regardless of the type of classroom support and structure your students need. You have to know what is going on in your classroom. A classroom that needs high support requires monitoring at all times. In fact, a line you sometimes hear from an experienced teacher with a high-support class is, "This class is so tough you can't take your eyes off them for a second." This is a teacher who understands that continuous monitoring is absolutely essential with students with high needs.

STEP 3   *Give students feedback on their implementation of expectations.*

The third step in the process of effectively communicating your behavioral expectations involves giving students (individually and as a class) clear feedback about their behavior. Both during and after each activity or transition, give students information about the degree to which they are behaving (and have behaved) as expected. As you observe students during an activity or transition, you are likely to notice examples of students who are meeting your expectations as well as examples of students who are not meeting your expectations. Both represent opportunities for you to continue to teach students how to meet your behavioral expectations by giving them positive and corrective feedback.

Provide positive feedback in the form of age-appropriate praise when students are meeting or have met your expectations. Provide corrective feedback—calmly, immediately, and consistently—when they are not meeting or have not met your expectations (Babkie, 2006; Emmer & Evertson, 2009; Greenwood et al., 1974; Mayer, 1995; Sugai & Tindal, 1993; Trussell, 2008). Positive feedback serves several vital functions—it gives students specific information about what they are doing correctly, and it gives them adult attention when they are behaving responsibly (Alberto & Troutman, 2012; Lewis & Sugai, 1999; Trussell, 2008). In addition, positive feedback serves as a prompt for misbehaving students and students who may be on the verge of misbehaving. Specific positive feedback to one or a few students provides a reminder to the class of the appropriate expected behavior.

Following are a few quick tips on providing effective positive feedback (Alberto & Troutman, 2012; Brookhart, 2017; Cooper et al., 2007; Hattie & Timperley, 2007). This information is a brief review of the more in-depth concepts you learned in Chapter 6.

- **Give feedback that is accurate.** Do not provide positive feedback unless the student (or class) has actually exhibited the responsible behavior. If you tell students that they have been responsible when they have not, you ruin your credibility and lead them to think (justifiably) that your positive feedback means nothing.
- **Give feedback that is specific and descriptive.** Tell the student or the group exactly what they are doing that is responsible and important. "Alex, Maria, Travis, you are keeping your attention focused on your work. That is a very important part of being successful in this class." Avoid a rote phrase like, "Good job."
- **Give feedback that is contingent.** Positive feedback provides useful information on important behaviors—that is, it is not simply a mindless compliment. For example, an experienced driver who receives a "Great right turn" compliment will probably be insulted. On the other hand, if this is the first time the driver has ever been behind the

wheel, receiving a compliment like, "Great right turn—you signaled and checked your blind spot," is probably useful information. Inform students how the positive behaviors they are demonstrating will contribute to their success and the success of the class. Also, praise students for demonstrating behaviors that are new or difficult.

- **Give feedback that is age appropriate.** Feedback for a kindergarten student should be presented differently than feedback for an eighth grader. With older students, it is more appropriate to focus on advanced behaviors, and it is important to present the feedback without embarrassing the student. If feedback is presented too publicly or enthusiastically, your efforts to encourage good behavior may backfire—the student may do anything to avoid getting any more embarrassing praise. When giving praise to older students, use a quiet voice, be brief, be somewhat businesslike, and avoid pausing and looking at the student for a response after you praise.

- **Give positive feedback immediately.** Immediacy is important because students need to know when they are doing something correctly. In addition, students who are starved for attention may start demanding attention through misbehavior if they get none for meeting expectations—they may feel that attention for behaving badly is better than none at all. Positive feedback is most effective when it occurs very soon after the behavior you are trying to encourage. With primary students in particular, waiting until later to give the feedback will not help to solidify the desired behaviors. By the time you praise them, the students will have forgotten exactly what it was they did.

- **Give positive feedback in a manner that fits your style.** The specific manner in which you give positive feedback does not matter—what is important is that you are specific and sincere. Thus, if you are a bubbly, happy person, your positive feedback should take that form. On the other hand, if you are a more serious and businesslike person, your positive feedback should be given in a more serious, businesslike manner.

When students (one or more) exhibit behavior that does not meet your expectations for the activity, you must correct the inappropriate behavior. Corrective feedback serves two vital functions—it lets students know that you are observing their behavior, and it communicates that you are serious and will be consistent about your expectations for student behavior (Barbetta et al., 2005).

To give the most effective correction, consider each instance when a student does not meet expectations as an instructional opportunity (Colvin, Kame'enui, & Sugai, 1993; Conroy et al., 2008). That is, consider students' behavioral errors as similar to errors they might make in math. Most math errors are a function of students not fully understanding a particular concept or all of the steps in a particular process. In these early-stage corrections, realize that the purpose is not to impose a penalty but rather to help students understand the lines between appropriate and inappropriate behavior in your classroom. Use instructional corrections such as gentle verbal reprimands, nonverbal corrections, proximity, discussion, and other mild techniques.

Effectively correcting errors in the early stages of misbehavior involves re-teaching the concept or steps. If students fail to meet your behavioral expectations, ask yourself, "Is it possible students did not understand what the expectations were? Is it possible they did not know how to meet the expectations?" If the answer to either of those questions is yes (or even a tentative maybe!), you need to re-teach your expectations or how students can meet them (or both). These two questions are especially important at the primary level and when you work with students with academic or behavior challenges, language or other communication delays, and with ELL students.

Following are a few tips on providing effective corrective feedback (Abramowitz et al., 1988, Acker & O'Leary, 1988; Alberto & Troutman, 2012; Cooper et al., 2007). More detailed information on using corrective feedback is provided in Chapter 8.

- **Correct the misbehavior immediately.** When students are not meeting behavioral expectations, let them know. Do not ignore the misbehavior and do not wait until the end of the activity, transition, or event to address it. Ignoring can be an effective strategy for responding to chronic misbehavior designed to elicit attention, but when you are trying to establish your expectations at the beginning of the year, students may interpret ignoring to mean, "She was not really serious about how she expects us to behave."
- **Correct the misbehavior calmly.** Correcting calmly shows students that you are serious and have high expectations, but also that you are completely in control and will not be rattled by their misbehavior. Emotional corrections, on the other hand, are more likely to give power to the misbehavior and put you in a position of seeming somewhat out of control. Students may think, "When I do this, look how frustrated and angry I can make the teacher." Be calmly assertive, but not strident, emotional, or aggressive.
- **Correct misbehavior consistently.** For the first several days of instruction, correct most misbehavior with mild verbal reprimands that focus on the behavior, not the person. Simply restate what the students should be doing at the time. Be direct. Communicate that you are firm and that the expectations are nonnegotiable. Saying something like, "Tina and Adam, you should be working quietly on your lab notebooks at this time," is more appropriate and effective than saying, "Tina and Adam, you are so immature. I should not have to remind you that this is a work period, not a time to socialize."

If it becomes necessary because of the severity or frequency of a misbehavior to use a prearranged corrective consequence, calmly state the misbehavior and the corrective consequence—and then follow through.

Early in the year, you should plan to end each activity or transition by giving students feedback about how well they collectively met your CHAMPS expectations. When an activity or transition is finished but before the next activity or transition begins, let the group know whether their behavior was appropriate. Did they behave as expected (the way they should for the rest of the year)? Or do they need to improve their behavior the next time that particular activity or transition occurs? When an activity goes perfectly, you have a wonderful opportunity to reinforce the class and begin establishing a sense of group pride.

Class, this work period went exactly the way a lab activity of this type should go. Everyone followed safe lab procedures. Conversations at the lab stations were quiet, and all the talking I heard as I was going around was focused on the lab activity. This is going to be a great class.

If an activity does not go well, describe the specific behaviors that need to be different (without singling out individuals) and set a goal for the next time you have that activity.

Class, during the teacher-directed portion of the math lesson that we just completed, there were several times I had to remind people to raise their hand if they had something to say. Please remember that whenever anyone is presenting to the class, whether it is me or a student, there should be no side conversations. Later this afternoon we will be having a science lesson.

During the time I am demonstrating an experiment, remember—no side conversations, and keep your attention focused entirely on the person who is speaking.

Avoid statements such as, "Almost everyone remembered the expectation about talking only when you raise your hand and I call on you." A statement of this type is not positive feedback; it serves only to make students wonder, "Which students did not meet the expectations?"

Some classroom teachers formalize the step of providing feedback at the end of an activity, transition, or event by posting a rating of how well students met expectations. See the procedures for using the CHAMPS Versus Daily Reality Rating Scale in Chapter 10, Task 1, Tool 1. Consider whether using a similar procedure by visually posting and completing a rating with students might help them make connections between expectations, their behavior, and the feedback you provide. For example, at the end of an activity, say something like:

Class, for the next few weeks, we are going to rate ourselves at the end of each activity to see how well we've done in meeting the CHAMPS expectations. To get us started, think about the expectations for Conversation. How did we do? Get ready to hold up a number from one to three showing how well we as a class met expectations for conversation today. If everyone followed the conversation expectations throughout the whole activity, hold up a one. If the class had to have quite a few reminders, but everyone seemed to get back on track once I gave a reminder, hold up a two. If many students struggled throughout much of the class period, hold up a three.

Yes, I can see most of you are holding up ones. I only had to provide a few reminders that you should use a Level 2 voice and talk only to your partners during this activity. After each reminder, everyone did a great job of following the expectations.

Look back at the expectation for Help. Get ready to hold up a number between one to three for how well we as a class followed the Help expectations . . .

Prepare Students for a Calm and Positive End to the Day or Period

Conclude the day or class period by orienting students to your end-of-day procedures (see Chapter 2, Task 5). On the first day of school, allow plenty of time for this activity. Remember that you may have to take time to help students identify their bus, review materials they need to bring the next day, and make sure they have all important papers to take home. Think about how to convey your enthusiasm for working with the students and communicating your vision for what you can accomplish together. You should put closure on this day in such a way that the students leave your classroom feeling comfortable and eager to return. They should leave with the sense that you are a teacher who will uphold high expectations for students to do their best but is also concerned about and interested in each of them as individuals.

The strategies presented in this task have been included because they will help you have a smooth first day of school, leading you and your class into a productive and rewarding school year. Remember, the information you present and the atmosphere you establish on Day One yields valuable dividends throughout the school year.

TASK 3

Implement Your Plan on Days 2 Through 20 (the First Four Weeks)

During the first month of school, continue to implement the three-step process for communicating expectations, and take the time to verify that your students understand what is expected of them.

• • • • •

No matter how clearly and carefully you communicate your CHAMPS expectations on the first day of school, few students will know exactly how they are supposed to behave after just one day. To make sure students truly learn your expectations, you'll need to continue the three-step communication process and verify student understanding throughout the first month of school.

Continue to Implement the Three-Step Process for Communicating Expectations

For the first two or three weeks, begin each activity and transition with a lesson on the expectations, observe student performance of the behaviors during the activity or transition, and give positive and corrective feedback during and after the activity or transition to both individuals and the class as a whole.

If you are a middle school teacher, remember that your students will be hearing about expectations from four to six other teachers. They are likely to get tired of hearing about expectations, but they are also likely to be confused about details such as which teachers let them talk during independent work and which teachers do not. Let them know that part of the reason you are spending a lot of time on expectations up front is that you know it can be confusing for students who work with 5–8 teachers during a day to remember all of the little details about each teacher's expectations. You want to make sure to set them up for success. Also let them know that this work up front will make sure that you don't end up spending lots of time nagging and reprimanding them! As you continue to present lessons on your CHAMPS expectations, be sure to vary the format of the lessons, and involve students as much as possible so that you are not just lecturing.

As the first month of school progresses, the lessons should become increasingly brief, and they should focus mainly on any specific expectations that have been problematic (students talking when the teacher is presenting, for example). You can also use the lesson time to set goals for student behavior. When students seem to fully understand and remember the expectation for an activity or transition, you can start to fade the lessons. For instance, you might introduce an activity by letting students know that because they have been so responsible, you do not need to review the expectation.

> *Class, next we have a 20-minute work period for you to get going on the math assignment. Since this type of work period has gone so well, I don't even need to review the expectations. Get started working on the assignment that is written on the board.*

Another option is to consider using an alternating pattern of lessons or teaching different expectations on different days. For example, during a math lesson on Monday, you present CHAMPS lessons on the teacher-directed and cooperative group portions of the lesson, but not on the independent work period. On Tuesday, you present a brief CHAMPS lesson on independent work and cooperative group activities, but not on teacher-directed instruction. Whenever a particular activity or transition has not gone as smoothly as you would like, plan to use the three-step process to reassert your expectations. If more than three students have not been meeting the expectations, plan on re-teaching your expectations to the entire class. If only one, two, or three students are having problems, focus on re-teaching those individuals. You might pull a few students aside to do additional teaching or review of expectations prior to an activity while other students are working independently or in small groups.

By gradually reducing the length and frequency of your CHAMPS lessons and by shifting your focus to individuals or small groups who may need more review than others, you gain more time for instruction. Before you cease all CHAMPS lessons for any given activity or transition, however, you should verify whether or not students fully understand your expectations for that activity or transition. The final part of this task provides suggestions for administering a quiz and conducting student interviews to determine the degree to which students understand your expectations.

The second step in the communication cycle for expectations—observing student behavior—should be maintained at a very high level throughout the year. If a class requires only a low-support management plan, you can get by with less direct monitoring than if the class needs medium or high support. Whatever the degree of support your students need, however, plan on continuing to circulate and visually scan during all activities and transitions throughout the year.

During the first several days of instruction, give students very frequent feedback on how they are (or are not) meeting your expectations—the third step in the communication process. In fact, you can consider feedback an ongoing monologue. With classes that can function well with a low-support management plan, you can begin to reduce the amount of positive feedback given to the class and to individual students as soon as any given activity or transition has gone well for several consecutive days. In addition, corrective feedback can be reduced to simply stating the name of a student who is not meeting your expectation. For example, if two students are talking when they should be listening to a lesson, you may be able to correct the error by saying the names of the two students, making brief eye contact, and getting on with your lesson. On the other hand, if your class needs medium or high support, you should probably keep the frequency of positive feedback and the descriptive clarity of corrective feedback at a very high level for a long time—at least for the entire first month of school.

Following is one example of how you might implement the three-step process for communicating expectations during the first month of school in response to your attention signal. In the downloadable files, you can also find samples for communicating expectations during independent work periods when you are otherwise occupied and for expectations for students' behavior when they are with specialists.

The basic process described can be used as is, or modified as appropriate, for communicating any and all of your expectations.

 CASE STUDY *Three-Step Communications Cycle*

For the first several days of school, frequently review with students your attention signal and your expectations for student behavior when you give the signal (teach expectations).

> *Class, remember that when I am going to call for your attention, I will raise my arm in the air like this and say, "Attention, please." When you see or hear that, stop what you are doing, turn your attention to me, and raise your hand in the air. Keep your hand raised until you see mine go down. Let's practice that one time before we get started with our first partner activity.*

Whenever you give the signal, check your watch or the clock (observe). If the students respond with silence, stillness, and attention in less than 5 seconds (and every student raised their hand), thank them for their cooperation (provide positive feedback).

> *Class, that took only 4 seconds. Some of you who were moving toward the back of the room stopped, turned around, and looked at me immediately. That was exactly the way to respond to this signal. The reason I need your attention is to let you know that . . .*

If the students do not respond appropriately within 5 seconds, do not repeat the signal and do not say anything. Simply wait with your hand raised, and make it obvious that you are looking at the time. If needed, say something like:

> *We've got about 80% of our class following the attention signal. Thank you for those of you with your hands raised, and let's keep them up until we have 100% of the class together.*

When the class is finally silent, provide corrective feedback.

> *Class, some students immediately stopped what they were doing and raised their hand. However, it took 18 seconds from the time I gave the signal until everyone stopped talking and looked at me. That is too long. By continuing to talk, you were being disrespectful to the students who gave me attention immediately because you wasted their time. Next time I give this signal, be respectful of your classmates and me. Stop what you are doing immediately. Now, the reason I need your attention is to let you know that . . .*

For several days, provide frequent positive feedback to students for following the signal. If students are taking too long to respond to the signal, provide additional instruction and practice opportunities. If, after a few days of this kind of positive and corrective feedback, students are still not responding quickly enough to your signal, inform the class that you are going to start implementing a corrective consequence for not paying attention to the signal. If only two to four students are not responding to the signal, assign those individuals time owed off recess (for elementary level) or after class (for middle school). If more than four students are not responding to the signal, have the entire class owe time. Make the time owed equal to the number of seconds wasted (the number of seconds beyond 5 after you gave the signal).

For example, if it takes the class 18 seconds to be fully compliant, they owe 13 seconds. Then, when it is time for recess or a break between classes, the entire class must wait quietly for 13 seconds. This procedure usually quickly generates enough peer pressure that students start responding to the attention signal within the 5-second limit.

For a class that is having a great deal of difficulty responding to the signal, you might consider adding a positive component. For example, you could let the class know that each time all students respond appropriately to the signal within the 5-second time period, the class earns a point. When they earn 10 points, the class gets 5 extra minutes of recess or some free time to socialize at the end of class.

Verify That Students Understand Expected Behaviors

During the second or third week of school, take some time to systematically determine whether your students really understand your expectations for their behavior. This information will help you decide whether you need to continue actively teaching your CHAMPS expectations or eliminate the lessons because students have mastered the content. If most of your students are able to accurately answer specific and detailed questions verbally or on paper about your CHAMPS expectations, you can rapidly fade the process of teaching and reviewing the expectations. However, if a significant percentage of students cannot answer your questions, or cannot answer them correctly, you should continue to conduct CHAMPS lessons on a reasonably regular basis.

Making the effort to determine students' understanding of your expectations by giving a quiz or conducting interviews (or both) does more than provide you with information on whether your students fully understand the expectations. By taking the time to give quizzes or conduct interviews, you further communicate to students the importance you place on their knowledge of the CHAMPS expectations. Two main procedures for verifying students' understanding (or lack of understanding) of expectations are:

- Give all students a short written quiz.
- Conduct one-on-one interviews with a few individual students.

You should use at least one of these procedures—and consider using both. On the following pages are directions and materials for giving a quiz and for conducting interviews on CHAMPS expectations.

Give a Quiz

A written quiz is a relatively simple way to get information from all students in your class or classes on their knowledge of your expectations. A major advantage of the quiz (as opposed to individual interviews with a few students) is that you can get information from all students in a relatively short period of time. The major disadvantage is that some of the students who do poorly on the quiz may actually know the expectations perfectly well but have trouble with reading or writing. For this reason, a quiz is probably not suitable for grades 2 and lower or for ELL students who are just beginning to learn English. If you know that students may struggle with reading the quiz, consider projecting it and reading each question aloud as students follow along and respond to each question. Follow these directions for giving a quiz on expectations:

1. *Decide on the format of the quiz.* The format of the quiz may be true/false, multiple choice, fill-in-the-blank, short essay, or some mix of these formats. Base your decision on both the type of format you typically use for academic purposes (a format your students are familiar with) and the type of format you think will yield the most useful information.

2. *Determine the specific content of the quiz.* Choose one or two activities and one or two transitions to be the focus of your quiz. You may get the most useful information by targeting those activities and transitions that have the most complex expectations and those that seem to be giving students the most difficulty. Examine your written CHAMPS worksheets (see Chapters 2 and 3) for details to ask students about. Your questions should target issues such as whether students can talk during the activity or transition, what kind of movement (if any) is allowed, and so on. Keep the quiz fairly short so that students can complete it in approximately 10 minutes.

3. *Prepare your students to take the quiz.* Explain to the students that the quiz will help you know whether the class understands some of your important expectations. Make sure they know they are not being graded, but the more errors there are on the quiz, the greater the likelihood that you will provide additional practice and explanation of expectations for student behavior.

Figure 9.4 is a sample quiz on expectations that might be used in a fifth-grade classroom.

Interview Students

Student interviews can provide more detailed and slightly more reliable information than a written quiz. If, during an interview, you are unsure from a student's answer whether she really understands a particular expectation, you can ask additional questions. The interview format also allows students who struggle with written tests to provide more accurate information about what they really know. The major disadvantage of interviews is that they are more time consuming—you can only do one interview at a time. Because of the time issue, you should probably interview just a representative sample of about six students. Follow these directions for interviewing students:

1. *Identify two major classroom activities and two major transitions that occur daily (or at least three times per week) in your classroom.* Choose activities and transitions that are complex or seem to be particularly troublesome for students. Classroom activities might include, for example, opening activities, teacher-directed instruction (whole class and small group), independent seatwork, class discussions, cooperative groups, and work in

Figure 9.4 *Sample Quiz on Expectations*

QUIZ ON EXPECTATIONS NAME __*Brandi*__
 DATE __*9-30*__

Circle the letter for the best answer to each question.

1. When you enter the classroom and begin working on the challenge problem:

    a. you should be completely silent from the moment you enter the room.
    (b.) you can talk quietly as you enter but must be silent when you take your seat.
    c. you can talk quietly about anything, but when the bell rings, you should be in your seat and then you can talk only about the challenge problem on the overhead projector.
    d. you can talk loudly about anything, but when the bell rings, you should get to your seat within two minutes and then get quiet.

2. During class, you can use the pencil sharpener:

    a. only before and after class.
    (b.) before and after class and during independent work periods.
    c. any time you need to.
    d. at no time without teacher permission.

3. When the teacher gives the attention signal and says, "Class, your attention please," you should:

    a. be silent and have your eyes on the teacher within 5 seconds.
    (b.) be silent and have your eyes on the teacher within 10 seconds.
    c. be silent and have your eyes on the teacher within 20 seconds.
    d. loudly tell other students to be quiet and pay attention to the teacher.

4. During the time the teacher is speaking to the class, you may:

    a. talk quietly to someone near you and get out of your seat only to sharpen your pencil.
    b. talk quietly to someone near you and not get out of your seat for any reason.
    c. talk only if you have been called on by the teacher and get out of your seat only if you need a drink of water or supplies.
    (d.) talk only if you have been called on by the teacher. You may not get out of your seat without permission.

5. Active participation while the teacher is presenting lessons should look and sound a certain way. Circle the items that describe active participation. There are six correct answers.

    a. Sit up straight or lean forward.
    (b.) Raise your hand if you have something to say.
    (c.) Answer questions when called on.
    d. Write notes to your friends.
    (e.) Write notes to keep in your binder that will help you study for tests.
    f. Tell people who are talking that they need to be quiet and listen.
    g. Have things on your desk that will help entertain you during the lesson.
    h. Keep your eyes on the person speaking or on the class notes you are writing.
    i. Let your mind wander.
    j. Talk while the teacher is talking.
    (k.) Be respectful toward the teacher and other students in what you say and how.
    l. Call out answers to questions.
    (m) Be vocal with your opinion.
    (n.) Actively discuss the lesson.

Continued on next page ⟶

Figure 9.4 continued *Sample Quiz on Expectations*

---

6. **When you return after an absence, you should:**

   a.   ask the teacher, "Did I miss anything while I was gone?"
   b.   ask another student for his or her notes.
   (c.) go to the file by the drinking fountain and find the folder for this class period; then take the copied pages for the days you were absent.
   d.   go to the teacher's desk and open her plan book to the dates you missed, and copy all the important information.

7. **In the parentheses after each of the following statements, put a T if the concept is true and an F if the concept is false about the weekly points you earn for behavior and effort.**

   a.   Every student starts the week with 10 out of 20 possible points. (*F*)
   b.   Every reminder the teacher gives you about your behavior or effort in class costs 1 point. (*T*)
   c.   Every compliment the teacher gives you about your behavior or effort in class adds 1 point. (*T*)
   d.   These points are added into the grade book and are part of your academic grade. (*T*)
   e.   The teacher will take points away without informing you about each incident. (*F*)
   f.   For severe misbehavior, you can have a choice between an office referral or a loss of points. (*F*)
   g.   g. You can make an appointment to discuss anything you do not understand or think is unfair about this system. (*T*)

---

learning centers or lab stations. Transitions might include coming into the room at the beginning of the day or period, handing in materials, moving to and from small group work, going to the library, cleaning up the classroom, getting books out and open to a particular page, and getting ready for dismissal.

2. *Develop interview questions that address specific aspects of the CHAMPS expectations for the two classroom activities and two transitions that you have selected.* You may wish to use Reproducible 9.2 to organize your interviews. A completed sample of this reproducible with one teacher's interview questions appears on the next page. As suggested for the quiz items, base your questions on the issues covered in the CHAMPS worksheets that you completed in Chapter 2 and 3.

3. *Identify a representative sample of students.* Choose about six students to interview. Select three students who are academically average or higher and three who are academically lower or have demonstrated some misbehavior.

4. *Decide on a time and format for conducting the interviews.* Identify a time when you will be free to conduct the interviews. If you cannot be completely free of supervising your class, plan to conduct the interviews while the class is doing independent work or working in cooperative groups. Because the interviews will take about 5 minutes per student, it may take more than one day to complete them. You may wish to work with a colleague and interview each other's students.

5. *Prepare students for the interviews. The whole class:* Describe what you will be doing and why. Emphasize that no one is in trouble—rather, you want to see how clear you have been in communicating what students need to do to be successful. Let them know that

Reproducible 9.2 *Student Interview*

Student Interview

CHAMPS

STUDENT _____ PERIOD _____ DATE _____

CLASSROOM ACTIVITY: *Teacher-directed work*

Questions:

- *Can you talk to another student while I am teaching?*
- *What should you do if you have a question or don't understand something?*
- *When I say, "Work on the problem," what should you do?*
- *Can you get out of your seat for any reason?*
- *How do you show that you are actively participating in the lesson?*

Student Responses:

CLASSROOM ACTIVITY: *Independent seatwork in math*

Questions:

- *Can you talk to another student while you are working? About what? How loud a voice?*
- *What should you do if you need help?*
- *Can you get out of your seat for any reason?*
- *How do you show that you are actively participating in this part of the lesson?*

Student Responses:

CLASSROOM ACTIVITY: *Beginning class, before and after bell*

Questions:

- *What should you do when you come into the room and are waiting for the bell to ring?*
- *Where should you be when the bell rings?*
- *While we are going through calendar, sharing, etc.:*
  - *Can you get out of your seat?*
  - *Can you talk to people at your table?*
- *What should you do if you want to say something to the class?*

Student Responses:

CLASSROOM ACTIVITY: *Getting book out and open*

Questions:

- *When I say get your math book out and open, how do you know which page?*
- *What should you do if you ever do not have your book?*
- *How long should it take for everyone to have books open and ready?*
- *Is it OK to talk to your neighbor as you are finding the page? Why not?*

Student Responses:

REPRODUCIBLE 9.2

you would like to be able to meet with all the students to talk about this, but because of time constraints, you can meet with only a few.

The individual students you are interviewing: Identify the activity or transition and then proceed with your questions. "Each day during math, I begin the lesson by presenting information on the board. I'm going to ask you some questions about what you and the other students should be doing during that time. Imagine we had a new student in class—what you would tell her about how we do things? For example, what should a student do when they have a question? What should a student do . . ."

If you find a significant number of errors on the quiz or in interviews, continue the three-step process of teaching expectations, monitoring behavior, and providing positive and corrective feedback with the whole group or individuals. If the students understand your procedures and expectations, you can begin to eliminate the teaching of expectations. Always remember to keep monitoring, however, by circulating and scanning and work to provide a 3:1 ratio of positive to corrective feedback to students to keep students aware that you are observing their behavior and maintaining high expectations.

TASK 4

Begin CHAMPS Implementation Midyear

Adjust your approach for reading and implementing aspects of CHAMPS depending on the time of year you get started.

• • • • •

Ideally, you will be able to read the book and work through each of the tasks before school begins. However, if you begin learning about the CHAMPS approach in the middle of the year, this task provides some suggestions for how to organize your approach. These suggestions will allow you to work through priority tasks and make manageable adjustments to your current management approach during the current school year. Later, you can do more in-depth work in preparation for the next school year.

Begin at the Start of a New Term or Semester

The best time to have an impact on student behavior is the first day of school. However, if it's not possible to have a plan in place at that time, the first day of second semester is a good time to make needed changes. Review the tasks in the Table of Contents for Chapters 1 through 8, and go directly to tasks that may have suggestions that may be of immediate benefit to your classes. Then work to skim through the chapters and as you have time read any content that seems particularly relevant for starting a new term or semester.

You can view the start of each new term, semester, or return from a major break as a chance to make more significant adjustments to your classroom approach. This is especially true if you are a specials or secondary school teacher who will see new groups of students during these transition times. If you will see new groups of students during the year, read and work through Tasks 1–3 of this chapter for launching your plan with a new class. Apply them to each new group of students you work with during the year.

Everyone has probably picked up a book that you intend to read, but then it sits on the shelf. To increase the likelihood this doesn't happen with your work to implement a positive and proactive classroom management approach, place reminders in your calendar for when you plan to work through tasks in the *CHAMPS* book. For example, you might set an intention to read at least 3 tasks that address a pressing area of need at least once a month. Each month, you can identify three of the tasks that seem most beneficial for your current classroom needs, and calendar in when you will work through these tasks. You might also identify one chapter that you will focus on during each grading or teacher work day. Plan to work through all of the chapters during the summer to be completely prepared for the first day of school next fall.

Begin in the Middle of a Term or Semester

If you begin the book somewhere in the middle of the year, plan to start by reading:

- Chapter 2: Task 6: Design Procedures for Managing Common Transitions
- Chapter 3: Task 2: Clarify Expectations for the Common Instructional Activities That Occur in Your Classroom
- Chapter 4: Teach Students to Meet Expectations
- Chapter 6: Build Positive Relationships With Students and Provide Positive Feedback

These chapters and tasks will provide ideas that can make an immediate difference with your students without requiring major reorganization of existing structures and routines. In addition, use the Table of Contents to identify tasks and suggestions that can help you address specific problems. Plan to work through the complete book over the summer, as suggested above.

Conclusion

This chapter offered suggestions for how you can launch the implementation of your Classroom Management Plan. The first month of school is an incredibly important time. It is essential to get students behaving responsibly right away because it can be very difficult to change negative behavior patterns later in the year. The four tasks covered the final preparations you should make before school starts, what to do on the first day of school, procedures and considerations to deal with during the remainder of the first month, and what to do if you are beginning CHAMPS implementation midyear.

The next chapter provides information for how to use a cycle of continuous improvement to guide your decision-making throughout the year and from year to year.

CHAMPS Notes

CHAPTER 10

Maintain a Cycle of Continuous Improvement

Engage in activities to ensure sustained implementation of effective management practices and ongoing improvements.

I n this chapter, you will learn how to engage deeply in the process of continuous improvement. Why is continuous improvement so important? Let's continue using a healthcare analogy. If you have to go to a hospital, you probably don't want to go to one whose staff decided 10 years ago they are so good they no longer need to continue reading medical journals, attending conferences and seminars, or discussing clinical cases with qualified colleagues. You would hope they are not saying when a new, better type of surgical equipment comes out that they don't need to try it because their procedures are just fine as is. You also don't want to go to a hospital whose staff decided 10 years ago that they are so bad there is no hope of improving! You want a hospital that is continuously striving to provide better care for its patients. Likewise, all teachers (and other school staff) should be working to continuously improve their own practices so they can provide better care and education for their students.

In Task 1, you will learn more about the Improvement Cycle, which was previewed in Chapter 5. You will also learn how to use seven different data tools to gather objective information about how well your classroom is functioning across a variety of dimensions, including student behavior, student engagement, and teacher behavior (e.g., ratio of interactions). Task 2 presents ideas for maintaining professionalism as a teacher and ways to engage in critical self-care if you find you are struggling with too much stress or are at risk of burnout. The final task provides ideas for maintaining your process of continuous improvement through a variety of strategies for ongoing learning and reflection. The information in this task is important so that the CHAMPS approach doesn't become something you learned one time a few years ago, but instead becomes a valuable and ongoing part of your lifelong development process as a teacher.

The three tasks presented and explained in this chapter are:

- Task 1: Use Data to Monitor and Adjust Your Classroom Management Plan
- Task 2: Maintain Awareness of Professionalism and Engage in Self-Care
- Task 3: Engage in Ongoing Learning and Professional Development

TASK 1

Use Data to Monitor and Adjust Your Classroom Management Plan

Once or twice a month, use observation tools to collect data that can help you adjust your management plan.

•••••

In Chapter 5, Task 3, you learned about the Improvement Cycle. In this ongoing cycle, you use data to observe what is occurring in the classroom, prioritize goals based on that data, revise your Classroom Management Plan to address those goals, and implement changes to your management approach. It is a continuous cycle because the process of evaluating how things are going in your classroom and making adjustments is never finished. The most effective teachers are those who are willing to engage in this process throughout each year, and from year to year, continually refining and adjusting their practices to fit the needs of the students they are currently working with. A teacher who is highly effective with one group of students may find that the next group presents new and unique challenges that require the teacher to seek new strategies to address particular areas of need. This is one of the great challenges but also one of the most exciting parts of teaching—it is never boring because each group of students and each individual have unique strengths and needs!

In this task, you will learn more about how to use data snapshots within the Improvement Cycle, and we present a variety of tools for collecting and evaluating objective information (data) about what is actually occurring in your classroom. Without accurate information, your decisions are likely to be based on hunches, guesses, or whatever feels right at the moment. As a professional, you should be making informed decisions based on objective information (Alberto & Troutman, 2012; Scheuermann & Hall, 2008).

The information-gathering tools in this chapter are designed to give you objective information about the overall health of your current Classroom Management Plan, essentially a snapshot of your class at a particular point in time. They include:

- **Tool 1: CHAMPS Versus Daily Reality Rating Scale.** This tool allows you to look at each major activity and transition during your day and evaluate (on a three-point scale) how well students meet your CHAMPS expectations for that activity or transition.
- **Tool 2: Ratio of Interactions Monitoring Form.** There are actually three different versions of this tool for determining whether you have fallen into the Criticism Trap—that

is, you are inadvertently paying so much attention to student misbehavior that you may actually be perpetuating some of it.

- **Tool 3: Misbehavior Recording Sheet.** Keeping a systematic record of your students' misbehavior for one day (elementary teachers) or one week for a particular class period (middle school teachers) can help you determine whether your management plan's level of support needs adjusting or whether one or more of your students, or the whole class, would benefit from a targeted behavior management plan or classwide motivation system.

- **Tool 4: Grade Book Analysis Worksheet.** An up-to-date grade book is a wealth of data. You can compile and analyze the existing data in your grade book to determine whether individual students are exhibiting chronic problems with absenteeism, tardiness, work completion, or assignment failure.

- **Tool 5: On-Task Behavior Observation Sheet.** This simple tool can be used to determine your class's average rate of on-task behavior during independent work times.

- **Tool 6: Opportunities to Respond Observation Sheet.** This tool can be used to examine the degree to which you actively engage students in your lesson. How frequently do students have the opportunity to respond during instruction as opposed to being passive recipients of the lesson content?

- **Tool 7: Family/Student Satisfaction Survey.** Just as many businesses find it worthwhile to look at customer satisfaction, you can benefit from knowing how satisfied your students and their families are with your classroom. Tool 7 is a short survey that can be given to families to discuss with their children at the end of the year or during the year (or both).

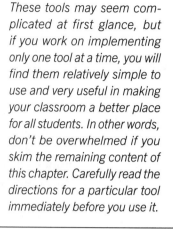

These tools may seem complicated at first glance, but if you work on implementing only one tool at a time, you will find them relatively simple to use and very useful in making your classroom a better place for all students. In other words, don't be overwhelmed if you skim the remaining content of this chapter. Carefully read the directions for a particular tool immediately before you use it.

Apply the Improvement Cycle

The Improvement Cycle is a way for data to be used in your classroom for meaningful decision-making and improvements that will help your classroom feel good to you while boosting student success. There are four steps within the cycle, which are explained in detail below.

STEP 1 *Review*

Use data snapshots to understand the current conditions in your classroom.

During the **Review** portion of the Improvement Cycle, collect and analyze different types data of data in your classroom to identify priorities for improvement. There may be times where your subjective perceptions guide you to collect data on one or more aspects of your classroom. For example, if you feel like the amount of misbehavior is increasing as you near a major break, you might begin tallying misbehaviors and tracking trends to see if adjustments are needed in your management plan.

REVIEW
Collect and analyze data.

IMPLEMENT
Monitor and motivate staff and students.

PRIORITIZE
Set priority goals for improvement.

REVISE
Develop proposed policies or procedures to address priority goals.

While efforts to review a specific data source can occur at any time, we also recommend using data snapshots to provide a picture of your classroom at a specific point in time during the school year. These snapshots should take place with some regularity in your classroom. At minimum, try to collect and analyze data focusing on one aspect of student behavior, student engagement, or teacher behavior once or twice a month. Chapter 5, Task 3 suggested adding prompts in your calendar for when to collect data using different tools. Later in this chapter, these tools are described in detail with accompanying forms.

Data-Driven Processes

Use data snapshots throughout the school year so you can get a clear picture of your classroom. Collect data on student behavior, student engagement, or teacher behavior at least once or twice a month, and rotate which tools are used to provide different views of your classroom.

When reviewing each data snapshot, ask yourself questions such as:

- What aspects of my Classroom Management Plan are working well for all students and should be maintained and celebrated?
- Are there one or two problem areas that indicate I should make adjustments to my plan?
- Are concerns occurring for the whole group, or are certain students or particular demographic groups struggling with the current approach?
- Are there patterns or trends based on times, day of the week, or type of activity?
- Should I maintain or revise the overall level of classroom support I am providing for students?

STEP 2   *Set Priorities for Improvement*

Use collected data to determine priorities for improvement.

In the **Prioritize** step, you will use data that you've just reviewed to identify aspects of your Classroom Management Plan that are priorities for improvement. Determine your improvement priorities and set goals by utilizing one of the following approaches.

Use Basic 5 Benchmarks as a general guide.

The Basic 5 Benchmarks, Reproducible 10.1, provide general guidance for the minimum standard that should be met in any classroom for the following indicators: ratio of interactions, opportunities to respond, disruptions, on-task behavior, and alignment with expectations.

These benchmarks allow you to analyze your classroom data with clear goals in mind, such as having students on task at least 90%–100% of the time, maintaining at least a 3:1 ratio of positive to corrective interactions, and having fewer than five disruptions in a 10-minute period across your whole class. However, if you collect data and find you are already reaching these goals, remember that the broader goal is continuous improvement. Continue to look for ways to tweak your classroom management practices to continue maximizing student success.

Each benchmark is categorized using three classifications:

- Level 3 (immediate changes to the Classroom Management Plan are necessary)
- Level 2 (caution—changing or augmenting current management practices is recommended)
- Level 1 (classroom management skills are functioning at a high level and may not require changes)

Use data to set a measurable goal for improvement.

If your classroom data indicate reason for concern, set a measurable goal for improvement, such as, "We will have fewer than 5 disruptions across class during 10 minutes of teacher-directed instruction." If you are far from that goal at the outset of this process—for example, the class is currently averaging 25 disruptions in a 10-minute period—set reasonable short-term goals, such as:

Reproducible 10.1 *The Basic 5 Behavior Benchmarks*

Basic 5 Behavior Benchmarks   CHAMPS

Level 3 = Stop (do something different)
Level 2 = Caution (intervention recommended)
Level 1 = Keep going (keep doing what you're doing)

BENCHMARK	LEVEL 3	LEVEL 2	LEVEL 1	FORM TO USE
Ratio of Interactions (positive to corrective)	Less than 1:1 or less than 1 interaction per minute	At least 1:1 consistently	At least 3:1 consistently	*Ratio of Interactions Monitoring Form* (Reproducible 10.4 to 10.6) • 30-minute recording time • Any activity • Use for individual or classwide monitoring
Opportunities to Respond (per 10-minute interval)	Fewer than 10	10–40	More than 40	*Opportunities to Respond Observation Sheet* (Reproducible 10.13) • 10-minute recording time • Use during teacher-guided instruction • Use for individual or classwide monitoring
Disruptions (per 10-minute interval)	More than 10	5–10	Fewer than 5	*Misbehavior Recording Sheet* (Reproducible 10.7 to 10.10) • Use for duration of one activity or entire period • Any activity • Use for classwide monitoring
On-Task Behavior	Less than 80%	80%–89%	90%–100%	*On-Task Behavior Observation Sheet* (Reproducible 10.12) • 5-minute recording time • Any independent work time • Use for classwide monitoring
Alignment with Expectations	Less than 80%	80%–89%	90%–100%	*CHAMPS Versus Daily Reality Scale* (Reproducible 10.3) • Use for duration of one activity or entire period • Any activity • Use for classwide monitoring

© 2021 Ancora Publishing   REPRODUCIBLE 10.1

- In 2 weeks, we will average no more than 15 disruptions in a 10-minute period.
- In a month, we will average no more than 5 disruptions in a 10-minute period.

The goal is to describe the goal for improvement in a way that you or any other third-party observer can easily make judgments about progress towards the goal when observing the classroom. The goal should relate to specific behaviors you can see or hear and refer to measurable outcomes.

STEP 3   *Make Revisions to Address Priorities*

Analyze your Classroom Management Plan and STOIC variables to reach your classroom goals.

In the **Revise** step, you will prepare to revise your Classroom Management Plan and other aspects of your classroom to address the priorities that were identified in the Review and Prioritize steps of the Improvement Cycle. During this step, if the data indicate that things are going, you will make a plan for maintaining and preserving aspects of your current management plan. If there are one or more problems, you will make decisions about whether to make minor tweaks, major adjustments, or a complete overhaul of aspects of your management plan.

REVIEW
Collect and analyze data.

PRIORITIZE
Set priority goals for improvement.

REVISE
Develop proposed policies or procedures to address priority goals.

IMPLEMENT
Monitor and motivate staff and students.

Use additional data sources to deepen understanding of areas of concern.

In some cases, you may look at the data you collect and realize that you need a more nuanced understanding of what is causing a particular concern or leading to inequitable practices or results in your classroom. Ask yourself whether you have enough data to allow you to understand *why* the class or particular groups of students are not achieving the benchmarks, your long-term goals, or the overarching vision of success in your classroom.

If you cannot point to evidence based on existing data in response to these questions, collect more data. Use different types of data sources, such as perception data (anecdotal notes, surveys, interviews, rating scales), observation data, or historical data to see if you can get a better understanding of the conditions in your classroom and with your students. These clarifying data are critically important so that you do not make changes to your classroom practices based on incorrect assumptions or subjective judgments.

Data-Driven Processes

If data indicate changes are warranted, consider whether you need more information about why the class is struggling. You may need to use different data sources, such as surveys and interviews, to gain a clear understanding about what changes are needed.

Use STOIC as a problem-solving framework.

Brainstorm a variety of strategies that might be used to meet the goals you set in Step 2: Set Priorities for Improvement. We suggest that you use STOIC as a problem-solving framework for variables that you can manipulate. Work through each variable and try to list multiple possibilities in each category. Review suggestions in Chapters 2–8 as needed to prompt additional ideas. You will narrow your focus and select a manageable number of changes in the next step of this process. Consider a range of strategies in the categories of:

- *Structure.* Can you modify structural elements of the setting? Can you modify the organization, orchestration, or predictability brought to behavioral or academic considerations in your classroom? (See Chapters 2 and 3 for ideas relating to structure.)
- *Teach.* Can you modify how you teach behavioral expectations to students? Do you need to re-teach expectations or bring effective instructional techniques to how you teach your behavioral expectations? (See Chapter 4 for ways to teach expectations to students.)
- *Observe.* Can you modify supervisory elements within your classroom, such as how you circulate, scan, or collect and present data to students? (See Chapter 5 for observational strategies.)
- *Interact positively.* Can you modify how you interact with students—by building intentional positive relationships with them and increasing the amount of positive feedback you provide when they are meeting expectations or demonstrating growth? (See Chapters 6 and 7 for ideas for building positive relationship and providing positive feedback and encouragement.)
- *Correct fluently.* Can you modify how you correct misbehavior in the moment, correcting fluently? Can you begin planning simple interventions when individual students require individualized supports? (See Chapter 8 for ways to effectively correct misbehavior.)

One critical question you want to ask as you examine possibilities for revising your Classroom Management Plan is whether the level of support you are currently using for students is appropriate. Should the current level of support be maintained, or do your students require higher support and structure to be successful? Or are your students demonstrating they are mature and responsible enough that you can gradually release responsibility to them by lowering your levels of support? The further your class is from meeting the Basic 5 Benchmarks, the more carefully you should consider adjusting the level of support.

In some cases, you may wish to have students help you brainstorm possible supports and solutions for the class to reach its goal. This input can be valuable in helping you understand unmet needs or concerns the students may have as you plan for improvements.

The STOIC Problem-Solving Worksheet (Reproducible 10.2) shown on page 434 can be used to brainstorm ideas across each of the STOIC variables once you identify a particular concern as a priority for improvement.

Select strategies and update your management plan if necessary.

From your brainstormed list of possible changes, identify a manageable number of strategies that you think are likely to help your class meet the goal for improvement. If you plan to make relatively minor changes, such as re-teaching existing expectations for a particular activity, you may not need to make revisions to your Classroom Management Plan. However, if you plan to make substantial changes. such as significantly altering the procedures for the activity, teaching these new expectations to students, and using a structured reinforcement system to motivate students to follow the new procedures, put these decisions in writing so that you have a detailed description of all changes to your procedures.

STEP 4   *Implement Your Plan*

Launch your revised plan, evaluate its effectiveness, and maintain over time.

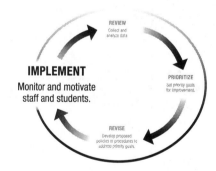

In the **Implement** step, launch any changes identified in Step 3 and monitor the efficacy of those changes. Make decisions about whether to finalize and maintain the plan or make further adjustments.

Introduce newly adopted changes to staff, students, and families as appropriate.

If other staff members will be involved in implementing the revised plan, provide adequate time prior to launching the plan to get all staff members on board. For example, if you have instructional assistants who provide supports in your classroom and you will be rolling out new procedures for group work, plan to spend some time orienting them to the new plan and answering their questions. You want to ensure that all of the adults in the room are on the same page prior to rolling out any changes with students.

STOIC Worksheet
For Revising Aspects of Your Management Plan (p. 1 of 3)

CHAMPS

Use this worksheet to clarify your revision process.

ACTIVITY, TRANSITION, OR PROCEDURE _____

S — **Structure for success.** Identify and modify variables that positively influence student behavior. These variables include the physical setting, schedule, orchestration of routines and procedures, and purpose of the activity/transition/procedure.

T — **Teach expectations.** Teach students the specific skills and behavioral expectations that will result in their success.

O — **Observe and monitor.** Use effective supervisory techniques, such as circulating and visually scanning the area. Use objective data to make decisions and monitor trends over time.

I — **Interact positively.** Model the core belief that all students must be treated with respect. Provide positive attention and specific descriptive feedback on behavior when students behave responsibly. Maintain a high ratio of positive to corrective interactions.

C — **Correct fluently.** React to misbehavior calmly, consistently, briefly, and immediately.

STRUCTURE FOR SUCCESS
Read or review Chapters 2–3

1. What goal related to the activity, transition, or procedure do you hope to achieve?

2. Identify problematic structural and organizational variables related to the activity, transition, or procedure:

Structural/Organizational Variable	Problem Created	Possible Solutions

© 2021 Ancora Publish

Reproducible 10.2 *STOIC Worksheet for Revising Aspects of Your Management Plan*

STOIC Worksheet for Revising Aspects of Your Management Plan (p. 2 of 3)   *CHAMPS*

3. Define expectations for adult behavior: What adult behaviors will prompt responsible behavior during the activity, transition, or procedure?

TEACH EXPECTATIONS
Read or review Chapter 4

4. Define student behavioral expectations for the activity, transition, or procedure:

student behavioral expectations for the activity, transition, or procedure.
op lesson plans. Use techniques common to good instruction:

- ationale and objectives
- odel, lead, test formats
- ts of practice

- Active engagement
- Role-play—students modeling only the *positive* behaviors
- Assess

mine how and when lessons will be taught:

tially to all students _____

taught to all students _____

OTE: Keep teaching behavioral expectations until students *consistently* meet expectations.

new students who arrive after Day One _____

-taught to students who chronically misbehave _____

substitutes and other teachers _____

ther _____

ora Publishing   REPRODUCIBLE 10.2

STOIC Worksheet for Revising Aspects of Your Management Plan (p. 3 of 3)   *CHAMPS*

OBSERVE AND MONITOR STUDENT BEHAVIOR
Read or review Chapter 5

6. Define how you will monitor and supervise the students during the activity, transition, or procedure. Include formal data collection procedures at regular intervals throughout the year.

INTERACT POSITIVELY WITH STUDENTS
Read or review Chapters 6–7

7. Identify encouragement procedures. Include one liners that are the positive opposite of your misbehaviors of concern, strategies to prompt yourself to interact positively, and possible motivation/reinforcement systems to address specific concerns:

CORRECT MISBEHAVIOR FLUENTLY
Read or review Chapter 8

8. Identify correction procedures. Include some one liners, alternatives to correction, and a range of corrective consequences:

© 2021 Ancora Publishing   REPRODUCIBLE 10.2

If significant changes will occur in the classroom, consider what information should be shared with students, families, and other adults in the building who may provide supports for your classroom. For example, if you will be rolling out a new set of CHAMPS expectations that differ from what was shared with your administrator and families at the beginning of the year, send an update about the changes. Convey your enthusiasm that the revised procedures will be beneficial for improving outcomes, and introduce new procedures with a positive focus on student success. Plan to provide adequate time to introduce students to any major changes, providing rationale, modeling and practice opportunities, and time for students to ask questions.

Monitor data to evaluate efficacy of changes.

As you implement new procedures, collect data to evaluate the impact of recently adopted changes. Consider whether you can take continuous data for a period of time (e.g., tally your ratio of positive to corrective interactions each day for 2 weeks) or if you will take data at periodic times (e.g., take 10 minutes of on-task data 2 times a week).

After a few weeks, use the data to make decisions:

> *As you implement new procedures, collect data to evaluate the impact of recently adopted changes.*

- If the new procedures, interventions, or supports are having a positive impact, provide positive feedback to students and parents, and as appropriate to staff involved in implementation. Plan to maintain new procedures.
- If the adopted changes are having a negative (or neutral) impact, determine whether quality of implementation is a problem.

  - If the plan is not being implemented as it was designed, determine whether you need additional training or support to implement the new plan. For example, some teachers find when they are first working to improve their ratio of interactions, they need to give themselves a support such as a randomly vibrating timer to prompt them to give positive feedback. Or if you struggle to remain consistent with your expectations, see if there is a coach or mentor teacher within the building who can observe and work with you on strategies for maintaining consistency. If you find yourself unable to implement the changes even after seeking support, you may need to go back to Step 3: Revise and select a different set of strategies that are more manageable.
  - If you are implementing the plan as it was designed and it is not working, go back to Step 3: Revise, and come up with an alternate plan. Tweak the existing plan by making minor or moderate changes or by adding a few additional STOIC strategies. In some cases (e.g., students beginning to exhibit unsafe behavior after you implemented revised procedures), you may need to abandon the revised plan and come up with an entirely new plan. However, recognize that making too many major changes in quick succession can be destabilizing for students and lead to increased resistance and behavior problems. Whenever possible, identify aspects of your plan that can be maintained to provide some sense of stability as you make any other major changes.

Maintain new procedures.

Once data indicate that you have found a plan that is helping your class reach desired outcomes and goals, work to maintain these procedures across time. Some creative ways to keep implementation alive include:

- Place reminders in your calendar at various times that remind you to boost your enthusiasm, provide reminders to students, and celebrate successes related to the adopted procedures.
- Check in with your students to see how things are going—informally through brief check-ins, and more formally through something like a feedback survey.
- Celebrate accomplishments and provide updates to families and other staff. For example, send pictures home of students successfully engaging in the activity that was previously difficult for the class. Share data with your administrator to celebrate your class's efforts.
- Reward yourself with something fun or something you have been wanting to treat yourself to when your class meets short-term goals for improvement or meets Basic 5 Benchmarks.

Continue to periodically monitor the data to ensure that you and the class are maintaining positive improvements across time. If the data become concerning at any point, make decisions about whether the current plan is still working but requires reminders and increased energy and enthusiasm, or whether you will need to return to the Improvement Cycle to make changes.

CHAMPS Tools for Data Collection

Procedures for using each of the seven data collection tools are described below, including the tool's purpose, when to use each tool, and how to accurately collect information.

TOOL 1: CHAMPS VERSUS DAILY REALITY RATING SCALE

Determine the degree to which student behavior during daily activities and transitions matches your CHAMPS expectations.

WHY
- To help you decide whether you need to re-teach your CHAMPS expectations
- To help you decide whether your current level of support fits the needs of your class
- To help you decide whether you might need some kind of classwide system to increase students' motivation to behave responsibly

WHEN
- During the fourth or fifth week of school
- Shortly after major vacations (e.g., winter and spring breaks)

HOW
1. Print a copy (or copies) of the reproducible form (Reproducible 10.3).

Reproducible 10.3 *CHAMPS Versus Daily Reality Rating Scale*

CHAMPS Versus Daily Reality Rating Scale *CHAMPS*

TEACHER **Mrs. McNealy**

CLASS PERIOD _____ DATE _____

Percentage of Students Who Met Expectations	**1** = 90% to 100%
	2 = 80% to 89%
	3 = Less than 80%

Conversation	①	2	3
Help	①	2	3
Activity: *Before the Bell*			
Movement	①	2	3
Participation	①	2	3
Success			

Conversation	1	2	③
Help	①	2	3
Activity: *Cooperative Groups*			
Movement	①	2	3
Participation	①	2	3
Success			

Conversation	①	2	3
Help	①	2	3
Activity: *Attendance/Opening*			
Movement	①	2	3
Participation	①	2	3
Success			

Conversation	①	2	3
Help	①	2	3
Activity: *Getting Ready for Independent Work*			
Movement	①	2	3
Participation	①	2	3
Success			

Conversation	①	2	3
Help	①	2	3
Activity: *Teacher-directed instruction*			
Movement	①	2	3
Participation	①	2	3
Success			

Conversation	①	2	3
Help	①	2	3
Activity: *Independent Work*			
Movement	①	2	3
Participation	①	2	3
Success			

Conversation	1	②	3
Help	①	2	3
Activity: *Getting into Cooperative Groups*			
Movement	①	2	3
Participation	①	2	3
Success			

Conversation	①	2	3
Help	①	2	3
Activity: *Clean-Up/Closing*			
Movement	①	2	3
Participation	①	2	3
Success			

ANALYSIS:

Only one activity (Cooperative Groups) and one transition (Getting into Cooperative Groups) have ratings of 2s and 3s. The main problem during these times is that students are talking too loudly, making the noise level in the room excessive. The classroom level of support can remain as it is—low support—because students are doing great at meeting most expectations. However, I will re-teach behavioral expectations with emphasis on how the students in each cooperative group monitor and manage the voice levels within their group.

REPRODUCIBLE 10.3

2. Identify activities and transitions. Use your plan book, daily schedule, or the CHAMPS Classroom Activity and Transitions worksheets you filled out in Chapters 2 and 3 (Reproducibles 2.3 and 3.2) to identify the major activities and transitions that occur during a typical school day. Write each activity and transition on the "Activity" line in one of the form's rating boxes. (See Reproducible 10.3).

   • Elementary teachers may need several pages and may wish to spread this evaluation activity across several days. For example, one day evaluate the morning activities and transitions, and the next day evaluate the afternoon activities.
   • Middle school teachers should complete a rating scale for each of their classes. You may want to spread this across several days. For example, one day conduct the evaluation for first and second periods; the next day, for third and fourth periods; and the third day, for fifth and sixth periods.

3. Before each activity or transition, briefly review your CHAMPS expectations with students, if necessary. Then, immediately after completing the activity or transition, use the following scale to rate the degree to which students met your expectations:

   1 = 90%–100% of students met expectations
   2 = 80%–89% of students met expectations
   3 = Less than 80% of students met expectations

4. Review the data you collected and determine which activities or transitions require re-teaching of expectations. See Reproducible 10.3 on the previous page for an analysis of a sample completed form. Consider each activity and transition separately as you make decisions. Consider the following as you interpret your data.

   • If all variables within the activity or transition are rated a 1, keep doing what you are doing in your general management approach. The fact that over 90% of your students are meeting expectations indicates that your Classroom Management Plan and procedures for the particular activity or transition are working at a Tier 1 level. If one or two students are having difficulty meeting expectations, use individualized procedures such as those described in Chapter 8, Task 6 to help the students meet expectations for behavior. If you wish to give your class an extra boost, consider implementing one or more of the non-reward-based approaches in Chapter 7, Task 2.
   • If some of the CHAMPS variables were rated a 2, it may be a good idea to implement one or more of the classwide motivation systems appropriate for a medium-support classroom (see Chapter 7, Task 3). Analyze aspects of STOIC to determine if minor adjustments are needed in your management plan during the problematic activity or transition. For example, if students are struggling to maintain a 0 voice level during independent work, consider adjusting the seating arrangement or altering your CHAMPS expectations to minimize excessive movement that may prompt students to talk to one another during the activity. If the behavior of one or two students is of particular concern, you may need to consider individual behavior management plans (see Chapter 8, Task 6).

- If some of the CHAMPS variables were rated a 3, you should probably implement one or more of the classwide motivation systems appropriate for a high-support classroom (see Chapter 7, Task 3). Also analyze aspects of STOIC to determine what adjustments are needed in your management plan. Consider whether students require more structure and support to be successful.

NOTE: If you find that you have ratings of 3 in numerous activities and transitions (less than 80% of the students are meeting CHAMPS expectations), you should implement one of the classwide systems for a high-support class and at least two systems appropriate for a medium-support class (see Chapter 7). Analyze aspects of STOIC to determine what adjustments are needed in your management plan. Students likely require more structure and support to be successful.

> *Some teachers may want to involve students in the CHAMPS rating process. If you choose to do so, explain the purpose and procedures to students ahead of time. Be sure to tell students that their input should have no references to individual students who did not meet expectations. A reproducible master of an enlarged rating form is provided in the downloadable forms (Reproducible 10.3 Enlargement, not shown). It can be used if you plan to involve your class in the rating process.*

TOOL 2: RATIO OF INTERACTIONS MONITORING FORM(S)

Determine whether you are interacting with students at least three times more often when they are behaving responsibly than when they are misbehaving.

WHY
- To help you evaluate whether you have fallen into the Criticism Trap—that is, whether you are responding so frequently to misbehavior that the behavior stops in the short run but is actually increasing over time
- To help you decide whether you need to increase the number of positive interactions you have with students when they are behaving appropriately
- To help you identify if you are maintaining equitable ratios of interactions with students from different demographic groups

WHEN
- During the second month of school
- In early to mid-February
- Any time you sense that you are responding to misbehavior too frequently

HOW
1. Print a copy (or copies) of the appropriate forms provided for download:

   - Reproducible 10.4: Ratio of Interactions Monitoring Form (During a Particular Time of Day)
   - Reproducible 10.5: Ratio of Interactions Monitoring Form (With a Particular Student)
   - Reproducible 10.6: Ratio of Interactions Monitoring Form (For a Particular Behavior)

Reproducible 10.4 *Ratio of Interactions Monitoring Form (During a Particular Time of Day)*

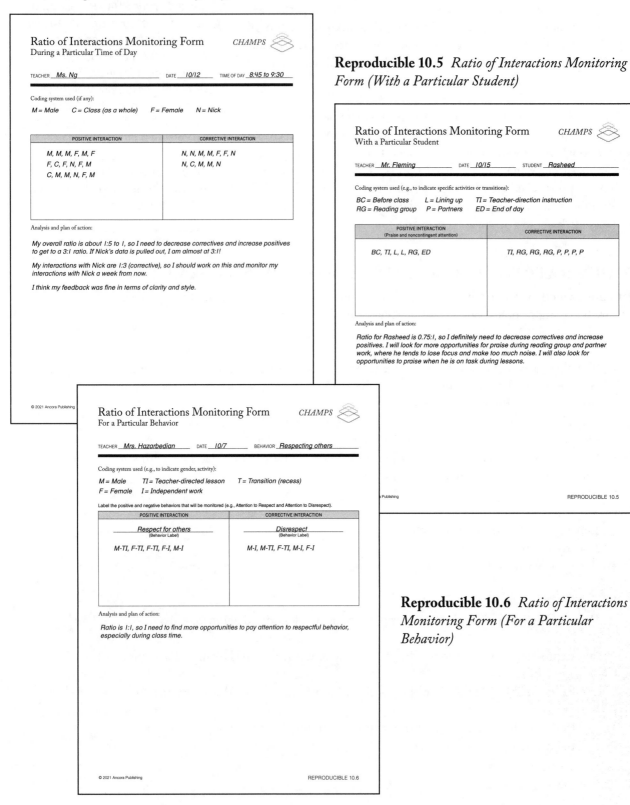

Reproducible 10.5 *Ratio of Interactions Monitoring Form (With a Particular Student)*

Reproducible 10.6 *Ratio of Interactions Monitoring Form (For a Particular Behavior)*

2. Make sure you thoroughly understand the difference between positive interactions with students and corrective interactions with students. Review the following:

- It is the student behavior that prompts the interaction (or the behavior that is occurring at the time the interaction is initiated), not the tone of the interaction, that determines whether an interaction is positive or corrective. When you interact with a student who is or has just engaged in appropriate (or desirable) behavior, the interaction is counted as a Positive Interaction. You are giving the student attention when they are engaged in a positive behavior.

 EXAMPLES   *Positive Interactions*

Praise: "Owen, you have been using this work time very efficiently and have accomplished a great deal."
Nonverbal: thumbs-up, high-five, give the student a sticker
Noncontingent attention: "Charlene, how are you today?"
Implementing a positive system: "Both Teresa and Ming earned a marble in the jar for the class. They worked out a disagreement without needing my help." (This example is counted as two positive interactions because the teacher gave attention to two different students.)

• • • • •

- When you interact with a student who is or has just exhibited an inappropriate (or undesirable) behavior, the interaction is recorded as a Corrective Interaction. You are giving the student attention when they are engaged in inappropriate behavior, and you providing some sort of attention to prompt the student to do something different.

EXAMPLES   *Corrective Interactions*

Prompts: The student is not working and you say, "You did a great job staying focused yesterday. I'm looking forward to seeing your work today."
Reminders: "Cody, right now it is work time. Please keep a 0 voice level."
Reprimands: "Khadijah, keep your hands to yourself."
Corrections: "Amar, I don't think you need to tell me about that because I think you can handle it on your own."
Warnings: "Jennifer, if I have to speak to you again about talking in class, I will need to call your mother."
Consequences: "Javier, that is disruptive. You owe 15 seconds off recess."

• • • • •

3. Determine a time of day (approximately 30 minutes) when you seem to have the most trouble being positive with students. Arrange to record (either audio or video) that time period for one day.

4. Listen to (or watch) the recording and mark your interactions on the Ratio of Interactions Monitoring Form.

   Make a tally mark under Positive Interaction for each interaction you had with a student (or the class) when the behavior was responsible. Make a tally mark under Corrective Interaction for each interaction you had with a student (or the class) when the behavior was irresponsible. Do not mark instructions to the group—for example, "Class, open your books to page 133." However, do count an instruction to an individual student ("Beth, please turn out the lights") as positive if the student was behaving responsibly at the time and negative if the student was misbehaving.

   If you wish to get more detailed information, consider using codes instead of simple tally marks for each interaction.

EXAMPLES *Codes*

M, F, NB = Brief attention to an individual male, female, or nonbinary student
W, B, API, AI, HL = Brief attention to a White, Black, Asian/Pacific Islander, American Indian/Alaska Native, or Hispanic/Latino student
C = Brief attention to the class or a group
F/15 = Attention to an individual female lasting approximately 15 seconds
NC = Noncontingent attention to an individual (e.g., "Good morning!")
NV = Nonverbal attention (e.g., a reassuring smile or a threatening look)

•••••

5. Calculate your ratio of positive interactions with students to corrective interactions with students (i.e., divide number of positive interactions by number of corrective interactions). If you coded your interactions—by gender, type of instructional activity, or type of attention, for example—calculate separate ratios for each category.

6. Analyze your data.

   • Evaluate whether you achieved an overall 3:1 ratio of positives to correctives.
   • Evaluate whether your ratio of positives to correctives varied by category (for example, it's lower with students who have identified disabilities than students without).
   • Evaluate the overall style of your interactions (corrections too harsh, praise too friendly or insincere sounding) and whether or not you are comfortable with it.
   • Evaluate the quality of positive feedback you gave to individual students—was it specific and descriptive, accurate, age appropriate, contingent, and delivered immediately?
   • Evaluate whether one or two individuals received most of the corrective interactions. If so, plan to use Reproducible 10.5, Ratio of Interactions Monitoring Form (With a Particular Student).
   • Evaluate whether you had to correct a particular category of behavior (for example, off-task talking) more frequently than other problems. If so, use Reproducible 10.6, Ratio of Interactions Monitoring Form (For a Particular Behavior).

7. Plan a course of action.

　　If your overall interactions or any subset of interactions do not reflect a 3:1 (positive to corrective) ratio, use the strategies suggested below and make an effort to both decrease attention to negative behavior and increase attention to positive behavior. After approximately 2 weeks, monitor your interactions again to see if you have achieved the desired 3:1 ratio.

　　Once you have successfully modified your ratios, check for an improvement in student behavior. If students are behaving better, congratulate yourself and keep up the good work. If they are not, plan to read and implement the suggestions about increasing motivation in Chapters 6 and 7 to see if there are any variables regarding student motivation that you have not implemented. Determine whether a classwide motivation system might be appropriate.

Strategies for increasing the frequency of positive interactions include:

- Each time you give a corrective interaction, remind yourself that you "owe" three positives.
- Identify specific times during each day that you will give individual students or the whole class positive feedback on some aspect of their behavior or class performance. For example, at the beginning of the math lesson, you might compliment five or six students.
- Use individual conference times, such as the first few minutes of periods during which the class is working on an independent assignment, to compliment individual students on their performance.
- Frequently scan the room and search for important reinforceable behaviors.
- Identify particular events that occur during the day—a student getting a drink of water, for example—that will serve as a prompt to observe the class and identify a reinforceable behavior.
- Reduce the amount of attention (time and intensity) students receives for misbehavior. Increase the amount of attention (time and intensity) students receives when not engaged in misbehavior.
- Interact with students frequently with noncontingent positives.

Strategies for decreasing the frequency of corrective interactions include:

- Identify whether you might modify aspects of the physical setting, schedule, organization, and so on to reduce the probability that students will misbehave. For example, if some students push others in the rush to get out the door, excuse the students by rows or table groups.
- Try precorrecting a misbehavior before it occurs (Colvin, Sugai, & Patching, 1993, Colvin et al., 1997). For example, if you anticipate that students will push each other while leaving the classroom, give a prompt like, "Remember to keep your hands and feet to yourself as you are leaving the room when I excuse the class."
- Try praising someone who is behaving the "right way" and intervene only if the misbehaving student does not change the behavior.

TOOL 3: MISBEHAVIOR RECORDING SHEET

Determine whether you need to implement an intervention plan or plans to deal with specific types of student misbehavior.

NOTE: Some teachers use this tool every day as an integral part of their Classroom Management Plan.

WHY

- To help you identify how often and for what reason you are intervening with students regarding their inappropriate behaviors
- To help you detect any patterns to students' misbehavior (for example, times of day, day of week, individual students who never misbehave)
- To give you specific and objective information about the behavior of individual students that you can share with the students and their families, if necessary
- To help you decide whether you might need a classwide system to increase students' motivation to behave responsibly

WHEN

- During the early part of the third month of school
- In mid to late January
- Midway through the semester or term (middle school)
- Anytime you notice a frequent amount of misbehavior

HOW

1. Choose one of the following four reproducibles and print it. You may wish to design your own form:

   - Reproducible 10.7: Misbehavior Recording Sheet (Daily by Student Name). This form is a daily record of misbehavior by hour, organized by student name. This form is appropriate for an elementary teacher. If you wish, you can change the headings (1st hour, 2nd hour) to reflect particular activities (math, reading). The idea is for the columns to reflect meaningful divisions in the school day so you can analyze whether certain times or subjects have a greater preponderance of misbehavior.
   - Reproducible 10.8: Misbehavior Recording Sheet (Weekly by Student Name). This is a weekly record of misbehavior by day, organized by student name. This form is probably most appropriate for a middle school teacher, who would need one form for each class that will be monitored. Note that the week runs from Friday through Thursday so that you don't have to wait over a weekend to give feedback. If you give students feedback about the previous five days on Friday, it is much more immediate, and they will see Friday as the beginning of a new chance to be successful.
   - Reproducible 10.9: Misbehavior Recording Sheet (Daily by Seating Chart)
   - Reproducible 10.10: Misbehavior Recording Sheet (Weekly by Seating Chart)

   The last two forms are daily and weekly records of misbehavior, organized by student seating when desks are arranged in rows. Each square represents a desk. Elementary teachers should use the daily form and note individual class activities on the horizontal lines within a square. Middle school teachers should use the weekly form (one form

Reproducible 10.7 *Misbehavior Recording Sheet (Daily by Student Name)*

Misbehavior Recording Sheet
(Daily by Student Name) CHAMPS

DATE 11/3   REMINDERS on Wednesday, remind about test on Friday

Name	1st Hour	2nd Hour	3rd Hour	4th Hour	5th Hour	Total
Ayala, Ramon	T					1
Barker, Stella						
Bonhoffer, Courtney						
Camargo, Damian		T				1
Cho, Suenn						
Dixon, Dakota			T			1
Durbin, Takesia						
Eng, Stacy		O		T		2
Fox, Kylisha						
Garger, Lily						
Galarraga, Alejandro		DT		O	D	4
Horner, Brady		T				1
Iwanaga, Jen						
Kraft, DaWayne						
LoTurco, Mandy						
Madison, M'shell						
Montoya, Graciela				T		1
Norton, Max						
O'Neill, Nora						
Papandrea, Elias		TT	O			3
Pedroso, Jamie						
Robinson, Hassan						
Singh, Ranjiv						
Sotomayor, Javier	O	TT	O			
Vincent, Kate						
Warren, Aleyshia						
Yates, Carla			T	T		

CODES: *D = Disruption, O = Off task, T = Talking*

© 2021 Ancora Publishing   REPR

Reproducible 10.8 *Misbehavior Recording Sheet (Weekly by Student Name)*

Misbehavior Recording Sheet
(Weekly by Student Name) CHAMPS

DATE 11/4   REMINDERS on Wednesday, remind about test on Friday

Name	Friday	Monday	Tuesday	Wednesday	Thursday	Total
Anderson, Chantel			T			1
Baena, Ruben						0
Bell, Justin						0
Carraza, Melinda		T		T		2
Cummings, Teresa						0
Demalier, Lee			T			1
Diaz, Margo						0
Etienne, Jerry						0
Fujiyama, Kim		O			T	2
Grover, Matthew						0
Henry, Scott	DDT	DO		DT	T	8
Isaacson, Chris						0
Kaufman, Jamie				D		1
King, Mark						0
LaRouche, Janel						0
Morales, Maria		T				1
Nardon, Jamayla						0
Neely, Jakob	T		T			2
Nguyen, Trang						0
Ogren, Todd	TTD	D	OO	T	TT	9
Pallant, Jared						0
Piercey, Dawn		T	O	T		3
Reeves, Rashawn						0
Thomason, Tony	TT		T	T	TT	6
Vandever, Aaron						0
Wong, Charlene						0
Yamamoto, Junko		T		T		2

CODES: *D = Disruption, O = Off task, T = Talking*

© 2021 Ancora Publishing   REPRODUCIBLE 10.8

Reproducible 10.9 *Misbehavior Recording Sheet (Daily by Seating Chart)*

Reproducible 10.10 *Misbehavior Recording Sheet (Weekly by Seating Chart)*

per class period for the week) and note the days of the week on the horizontal lines within a square. Create your own form if desks are arranged in clusters or a U-shape.

2. Put the appropriate Misbehavior Recording Sheet on a clipboard. Plan to keep the clipboard close by for the entire day if you are an elementary teacher or for 5 days of a particular class period if you are a middle school teacher.

3. Explain to students that for the entire day or the next 5 class periods, you will be recording any time you have to speak to someone or the whole class about inappropriate behavior.

4. Whenever you correct a student about a misbehavior, note the specific misbehavior on the form using a coding system. Build your code so that you have a different letter for each type of major misbehavior you think is likely to happen. For example:

> O = Off-task
> H = Hands/feet/objects bothering others
> T = Talking
> D = Disruption
> S = Out of seat at wrong time
> A = Arguing

> **For Middle School Teachers and Elementary Specialists**
>
> *Decide whether to use a Misbehavior Recording Sheet in one, two, or all of your classes. You should record misbehavior with all classes for at least 1 full week. However, you might try it initially for a week with just one class (probably the class with the most misbehavior). If you find the information useful, you can plan how and when to use the tool with the rest of your classes.*

5. Analyze the data and determine a plan of action.

- You may find that the behavior of some students improves simply because you are keeping records. If so, consider using the Misbehavior Recording Sheet on an ongoing basis. This data will be very useful for discussing behavior with students and their families, determining citizenship grades, and making decisions about your Classroom Management Plan.
- Make a decision regarding your level of concern about the amount of misbehavior that is occurring. If you are unconcerned (the amount of misbehavior is so low that it is not interfering with student learning), do not bother making any changes.
- If you are concerned about the amount of misbehavior in your class, analyze the data from the Misbehavior Recording Sheet further. First, consider whether misbehavior is a problem for the entire class or just exhibited by a few students. Identify the three students who had the most frequent incidents of misbehavior and calculate the percentage of the total class misbehavior attributed to those students (divide the total number of misbehaviors exhibited by the three students by the total number of misbehaviors exhibited by the entire class). For example, if the three students' total for two days is 45 and the total for the entire class is 61, divide 45 by 61 to get 74%.
- Once you identify the percentage of misbehavior exhibited by the top three misbehaving students, use the following criteria to determine the most appropriate action.

- If more than 90% of the total classroom misbehavior can be attributed to the three individual students, keep your level of support and procedures as they are. For the one, two, or three individuals with the most misbehavior, consider implementing individual behavior management plans. See Chapter 8, Task 6 for ideas for intervening with individual students.
- If 60% to 89% of the total classroom misbehavior can be attributed to the three individuals, review your level of classroom support, consider adjustments you can make within the STOIC variables, and implement one or more classroom motivation systems appropriate for medium support (see Chapter 7). In addition, consider individual behavior management plans for the students whose behavior is the most problematic.
- If less than 60% of the misbehavior can be attributed to the three individuals (that is, the problem is classwide), review and implement all the suggestions for high-support classrooms in Chapters 2 through 8. Carefully read the information in Chapter 7 and arrange to implement one or more of the classwide systems appropriate for high-support classrooms.

TOOL 4: GRADE BOOK ANALYSIS WORKSHEET

Determine whether student attendance, punctuality, in-class work completion, homework completion rates, and academic work are satisfactory.

WHY
- To help you decide whether you need to implement a plan to improve one or more area of concern with your class, a small group of students, or individuals
- To help you determine how the grade book variables may interact

WHEN
- During the third month of school
- In early to mid-March
- Prior to the end of each grading period

HOW
1. Gather relevant data.

   In your computerized grading system, determine whether and how the program provides you data for:

   - Attendance rates (percentage)
   - Punctuality/tardiness rates (percentage)
   - Percentage of in-class work completion
   - Percentage of homework assignments completed
   - Current grade status (to identify students who may need targeted academic assistance)

   If your computerized grading system does not automatically report the rates and percentages above, calculate data for each student in your class.

2. Print a copy or copies of Reproducible 10.11, Grade Book Analysis Worksheet, and enter data for each student.

Reproducible 10.11 *Grade Book Analysis Worksheet*

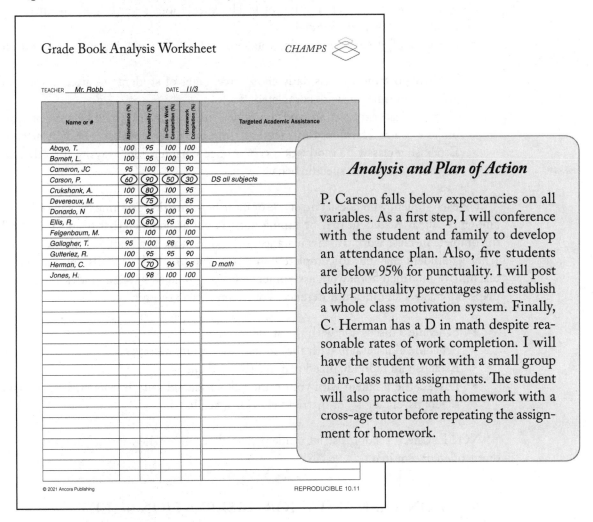

Grade Book Analysis Worksheet   CHAMPS

TEACHER __Mr. Robb__   DATE __11/3__

Name or #	Attendance (%)	Punctuality (%)	In-Class Work Completion (%)	Homework Completion (%)	Targeted Academic Assistance
Abayo, T.	100	95	100	100	
Barnett, L.	100	95	100	90	
Cameron, JC	95	100	90	90	
Carson, P.	(60)	(90)	(50)	(30)	DS all subjects
Crukshank, A.	100	(80)	100	95	
Devereaux, M.	95	(75)	100	85	
Donardo, N	100	95	100	90	
Ellis, R.	100	(80)	95	80	
Felgenbaum, M.	90	100	100	100	
Gallagher, T.	95	100	98	90	
Gutteriez, R.	100	95	95	90	
Herman, C.	100	(70)	96	95	D math
Jones, H.	100	98	100	100	

© 2021 Ancora Publishing   REPRODUCIBLE 10.11

Analysis and Plan of Action

P. Carson falls below expectancies on all variables. As a first step, I will conference with the student and family to develop an attendance plan. Also, five students are below 95% for punctuality. I will post daily punctuality percentages and establish a whole class motivation system. Finally, C. Herman has a D in math despite reasonable rates of work completion. I will have the student work with a small group on in-class math assignments. The student will also practice math homework with a cross-age tutor before repeating the assignment for homework.

3. Under targeted academic assistance, record any unsatisfactory grade and the related subject.

4. Analyze your results. Use the following suggested benchmarks for reference:

- *Attendance.* Students should have at or above 95% attendance, missing no more than 2 or 3 days per quarter or 4 to 5 days per semester. This combines excused absences, unexcused absences, and absences related to misbehavior (e.g., ISS, OSS).
- *Punctuality.* Students should be at or above 95% punctuality.
- *In-class work completion.* Students should be at or above 95% in-class work completion.
- *Homework completion.* Students should be at or above 95% homework completion.
- *Targeted academic assistance.* Students should be passing all academic subjects.

If three or more students fail to meet one of the benchmarks above, consider implementing a whole class action plan. For example, you might:

- Revise and/or re-teach your CHAMPS expectations for independent work periods to increase work completion rates, or teach expectations regarding attendance or punctuality. See Chapters 3 and 4.
- Review and, if necessary, revise your procedures for managing work completion. See Chapter 3.
- Publicly post and discuss daily class percentages of students in attendance, students arriving on time, or work completed.
- Communicate expectations and classwide concerns to family members and ask for ideas on how you and families can partner to improve homework rates or daily attendance.
- Establish a classwide motivation system. See Chapter 7 for ways to directly motivate students to improve specific behaviors.

For each student who doesn't meet one or more benchmarks, examine the interrelationships among the data. A student may be failing due to poor attendance that results in an inability to complete in-class work. In this instance, the student needs a plan to improve attendance. Another student may fail to complete homework due to a lack of skills and may need pre-teaching or modified homework assignments. Once problems have been identified, proactive plans can make a significant difference. For example, you might:

- Schedule a discussion with the student.
- Schedule a discussion with the student and family members.
- Establish an individualized plan for the student.
- Discuss the problem with your principal, special education teacher, school counselor, school psychologist, or district behavior specialist.

NOTE: Check school/district guidelines to determine when formal intervention is recommended or required.

TOOL 5: ON-TASK BEHAVIOR OBSERVATION SHEET
Determine how effectively your students use independent work time.

WHY
- To help you decide whether you need to re-teach students your CHAMPS expectations for independent work periods
- To help you identify the possible cause of poor work completion rates and misbehavior during independent work periods

WHEN
- During the fourth month of school
- In mid to late February
- Midway through the semester or term (middle school)
- Any time you notice a frequent amount of off-task behavior

HOW

1. Print a copy (or copies) of Reproducible 10.12, On-Task Behavior Observation Sheet.

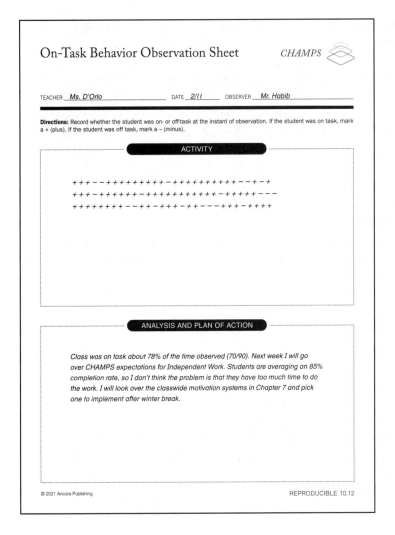

Reproducible 10.12 *On-Task Behavior Observation Sheet*

2. Identify the independent work periods that you wish to monitor. Middle school teachers should target any class or classes that are having trouble completing work or those with frequent misbehavior.

3. Determine whether you will conduct your own observation or have a colleague observe (you reciprocate at another time).

Having a colleague collect the data has several advantages. First, you will be available to do whatever you usually do during this work period—for example, teach a small group or circulate and help students who have questions. Second, a colleague is likely to be slightly more objective. You may have an unconscious tendency to make students look better or worse than they really are. Third, exchanging classroom observations with a colleague gives the two of you a great opportunity to share ideas about how to help students improve their overall rate of on-task behavior.

4. During the observation period, whoever is collecting data should use the following method of data collection:

- Position yourself away from high-traffic areas and in a place where you can easily see students working at their seats. Use the On-Task Behavior Observation Sheet (Reproducible 10.12) and a pen or pencil to record data.

- Decide on an observation pattern that allows you to observe each student in the class a minimum of three times. For example, if students are in rows, start with the student in the front row to the left. Then look at the next front-row student to the right, and then the next student in the front row, and so on until you have observed each student in the front row. Move to students in the second row next, moving from left to right; then the third row; and so on. After observing the last student in the back row, repeat this pattern at least two more times. Note that it is important to keep a consistent, unchanging pattern—if you skip around, the data will be less accurate.

- When observing an individual student, look at that student for only an instant—almost like taking a mental snapshot. Then look down at your paper and asks whether the student was on- or off-task at the instant of observation. If the student was on task, mark a + (plus). If the student was off task, mark a – (minus). Repeat this for every student, following the pattern established in the step above. The idea is for the observer to set up a rhythm with a quick pace, spending no more than 3 to 5 seconds on each student. Look, think, mark. Next student: Look, think, mark. Note that the mark should reflect what the student is doing at the moment of being observed—not what they were doing a moment before the observation or what they do a moment after (even if they are off task).

- The observer should work through the whole pattern at least three times so that every student is observed a minimum of three times. When finished, the Observation Sheet should look something like sample Reproducible 10.12 on the previous page (from a class with 30 students).

- Notice that no effort is made to record which individual students were on or off task. The point of this tool is to look at a class average.

5. Determine the percentage of on-task behavior by dividing the total number of on-task marks (pluses) by the total number of marks (pluses and minuses).

    In the sample, this would be 70 divided by 90, meaning that during the observation period the class was on task approximately 78% of the time.

6. Analyze the data and, if necessary, determine a plan of action.

- If the class had an on-task rate of 90% or more, provide positive feedback (including telling them how they did) and encourage them to keep up the good work. If you feel that the percentage does not accurately reflect their typical behavior (they were more on task because they knew they were being observed), let them know that you are pleased with what they demonstrated they could do and that you want them to strive to behave every day the way they did when observed. If you know that only one or two students exhibited all of the off-task behavior, arrange a private discussion with those individuals. Use the time to set improvement goals for the students and, if necessary, to develop individualized management plans to help them learn to manage work times more responsibly.

- If the class had an on-task rate of between 80% and 89%, tell them the percentage and let them know that although they did well, there is room for improvement. Together with the students, identify strategies that individual students can use to monitor and improve their own on-task behavior.
- If the class had an on-task rate of less than 80%, tell them what the percentage was and explain that improvement needs to occur. Review your CHAMPS expectations for independent work periods, placing special emphasis on what constitutes appropriate participation. At a later time, examine your grade book. If, despite their high rates of off-task behavior, the class has high rates of work completion (above 95%), consider the possibility that you are giving students too much class time to do their assignments. If both on-task behavior and work completion are low, you may want to establish a classwide system to motivate students to improve both their work completion and on-task behavior (see Chapter 7). Also consider whether the material is too difficult or too easy for students, leading to off-task behavior due to boredom or students' lack of expectancy of success. Remember, if students are on task less than 80% on average, too much valuable instructional time is being lost, and you need to intervene.

> **Overt Monitoring**
>
> *If the process of overt monitoring seems to improve student behavior (that is, the act of observing motivates students to be more on task than usual) and if you are working with students in grades 4 and above, consider teaching the students how to record this kind of data. Then, periodically ask an individual student (not always the same person) to observe and record. Give the class feedback at the end of the work period. Use this procedure a couple of times per week until the class is consistently on task 90% or more of the time.*

TOOL 6: OPPORTUNITIES TO RESPOND OBSERVATION SHEET

Determine the degree to which your students are engaged during teacher-directed instruction parts of your class.

WHY
- To help you decide whether you need to modify your instructional methods to create more active student involvement
- To help you identify the possible causes of poor work completion rates and misbehavior during teacher-directed lessons

WHEN
- During the fourth month of school
- In mid to late February
- Midway through the semester or term (middle school)
- Any time you notice low levels of student engagement or high rates of misbehavior during teacher-directed instruction

HOW

1. Print copies of Reproducible 10.13, Opportunities to Respond Observation Sheet.

2. Identify the teacher-directed lessons that you wish to observe. Target a time when students have trouble staying focused or exhibit frequent misbehavior during lessons.

3. Determine whether you will observe yourself using video or whether a colleague will observe your lesson.

    Analyzing your own lesson on video has several advantages. Taking video of the class is less threatening to your students than having someone else watch you teach. In addition, you will learn a great deal about your own teaching by observing students during your lesson. The major disadvantage is that students may behave differently when you film them than they would for a neutral party. Another disadvantage is that there may be restrictions on taping students without getting parental permission (check with your administrator).

    Having a colleague collect the data has other advantages. A colleague is more likely to be objective. You may have an unconscious tendency to make students look better or worse than they really are. Exchanging classroom observations with a colleague gives the two of you an opportunity to share ideas about how to create lessons that facilitate the active engagement of your students.

4. During the observation period, plan to focus on three or four specific students.

    If you are recording, set the camera to the side of the room toward the back. Inform students that you are filming your teaching so you can improve the quality of your lessons. Focus the camera on a group of four students, preferably four who represent different ability levels, so you can see them making verbal, written, or action responses. If you are having a colleague observe, arrange for them to sit to one side of the room toward the back. Have them observe four students of different ability levels.

    Whoever does the observation—you or your colleague—should record the start time of the lesson, mark a V on the observation sheet each time any of the target students makes a verbal response, a W each time any of the target students makes a written response, and an A each time a target student makes an action response.

    At the end of the teacher-directed portion of the lesson, record the stop time and the length of the lesson. If you have an observer who is not available for the entire class period, have them record the length of the observation.

5. Determine the average number of responses per minute.

    First, calculate the average number of responses per student by adding the total number of Vs, Ws, and As and dividing by four. Then, divide the average number of responses per student by the total number of minutes observed. This figure is the average responses per minute.

6. Analyze the data and, if necessary, determine a plan of action.

Look at the data and determine whether all students who were being observed had a response rate that demonstrated high levels of engagement with your teacher-directed instruction. If there were few opportunities to respond, or if three students had only one response or no responses, and one student had many, this indicates you need to work on delivering opportunities to respond that engage all learners.

Research with primary-level students determined that learning was maximized when students were responding between 4 and 6 times per minute with 80% accuracy during instruction on new material and between 9 and 12 times per minute with 90% to 95% accuracy during drill and practice work (CEC, 1987; Stichter et al., 2009).

There is little research, however, on what represents optimal response rates for intermediate and middle school students with more complex tasks and with different types of activities such as discussion and lecture. Therefore, you (and your colleague if you had an observer) need to determine whether the number of student responses is optimal for your class. Recognize that the more students are doing something that engages them with the lesson content, the greater the chances are that they are learning the essential content (Brophy & Good, 1986; Engelmann & Becker, 1978).

If students seemed overly passive during your lesson, explore with colleagues or instructional supervisors and department chairs how to get students to participate more actively. More active response methods could include whole group choral responses, whole group physical responses (for example, "Stand up if the statement is true. Stay seated if it's false"), copying notes, and quick ungraded quizzes.

Reproducible 10.13 *Opportunities to Respond Observation Sheet*

Opportunities to Respond Observation Sheet   *CHAMPS*

TEACHER __Mrs. Montoya__   ACTIVITY __Math class__   DATE __12/4__
OBSERVER __Mrs. Nguyen__   LESSON: START TIME __12:50__   END TIME __1:30__   OBSERVATION LENGTH __10__

Mark a "V" for each verbal response, a "W" for each written response, and an "A" for each action response.

Student 1	Student 2	Student 3	Student 4
V, V, W, A, V, V, V, V, V	W, W, W, A, V, V, V, W, V, V, A	V, W, W, W, V, V, V, V, A, W, V, A, V, V	V, V, V, A, W, V, V, W, W, V, A, V, W

Total number of responses __48__ divided by 4 equals __12__ (average number of responses)

Average number of responses divided by number of minutes equals __1.2__ (average responses per minute)

Notes on subjective perception of the degree of student engagement in the lesson:

All but one student seemed attentive during presentation of new material. One student appeared to be reading a different assignment and did not respond to most group questions.

Analysis and plan of action:

Work on adding opportunities to respond when presenting new material to keep students engaged. Try to move around the classroom more during instruction to keep students focused on the lesson.

© 2021 Ancora Publishing   REPRODUCIBLE 10.13

TOOL 7: FAMILY/STUDENT SATISFACTION SURVEY

Determine how your students and their families perceive various logistical and organizational features of your classroom.

WHY

- To help you identify those aspects of your classroom program that are working well and those that may need modification
- To help you identify whether there are aspects of your classroom program that you need to communicate more clearly to students and their families

WHEN

- Last two weeks of school
- (Optional) Midyear

For Middle School Teachers

Discuss with colleagues whether to have a schoolwide survey that goes to all families as opposed to individual teachers doing their own surveys. If too many individual teachers give their own surveys, a family with two students in the school could end up having to complete over ten surveys!

HOW

1. Print copies of the two-page Reproducible 10.14, Student/Family Satisfaction Survey A Spanish-language version is also available for download (Reproducible 10.14 ES).

   NOTE: The survey can and should be modified to reflect your classroom program and any areas of concern that you may have. Also note that giving a survey of this type can be feel very threatening when you receive critical feedback. As you examine the results, remind yourself that you cannot take critical information personally. Rather, you are looking for patterns of information that will help you fine-tune your classroom program.

2. Determine how you will let families know they will be receiving the survey, and determine the logistics of how they will receive and return the survey.

   For example, you could have students take the surveys home and return them to school. Or, if your school can budget for postage, send the surveys by mail with pre-addressed, postage-paid return envelopes enclosed.

3. When all surveys have been returned, analyze the results.

   Keep in mind that although the information is subjective opinion, it can help you identify aspects of your classroom that may require further review. For example, if 50% of the families respond that students do not have enough homework, you should carefully consider whether the amount of homework you assign is sufficient. On the other hand, if 60% say the amount of homework is about right, 20% say it's too much, and 20% say it's not enough, you can probably assume that the amount of homework matches the average family's perception of what is appropriate.

In summary, this task should help you continue to periodically monitor data to ensure you and your classes are maintaining positive improvements across time. If the data from a mid-year survey indicates there are concerns, you can make decisions about whether the current plan is still working but requires reminders and increased energy and enthusiasm, or whether you should make changes. If the data from an end-of-year survey indicates there are concerns, you can use this information to make changes that create improvements for your incoming students in the next school year.

TASK 2

Maintain Awareness of Professionalism and Engage in Self-Care

A few times a year, self-assess your level of professionalism and whether you are providing adequate self-care to be at your best.

• • • • •

Congratulations on embarking on (and continuing) the exciting adventure of being a teacher! Teaching holds many rewarding and memorable experiences. The CHAMPS approach can assist you in ensuring that your classroom management and organizational strategies make this experience as positive as possible. However, being a teacher can also include many intimidating and difficult moments. For early-career teachers, you will encounter some of the most challenging situations of your career because so many situations will be new to you—understanding how to work within your grade-level team and school campus, trying to meet the needs of all of your students, and even something as mundane as figuring out your district's expectations about insurance! For veteran teachers who have been in the field for 10, 20, or even 30 years, you may find that your student population and school community has changed so much across time that classroom management approaches that previously worked for your classes are no longer sufficient to meet your students' needs. Whether you are a first-year teacher or have been in the field for many years, it is important to periodically evaluate whether you are behaving and communicating in a manner that is warranted in this important career as a professional.

Effective teachers understand that it is important to behave in a manner that communicates professionalism. Imagine you go to see a professional—a physician, architect, or attorney—and find he is sloppily dressed and acts hesitant or unsure, or arrogant and condescending. During your discussion, he does not actively listen to you or make eye contact. He appears distracted by other responsibilities. Later, you discover he talked about your personal issues with members of your community. How would you feel about engaging this person's services? What opinion would you form about his level of expertise? Would you trust this person? Would you feel a rapport with him? It is doubtful that you would have much confidence in him. Consequently, he probably wouldn't be very effective in helping you, nor would you willingly seek his advice when you needed it. An effective teacher is a professional who works to assist all staff, students, and students' families in a manner that leaves them informed, reassured, and hopeful. An effective teacher goes the extra mile in building relationships with students and everyone who has a vested interest in the students.

A professional can be defined as one who works in a position that requires specialized knowledge and often long academic preparation and who exhibits a courteous, conscientious, and generally businesslike manner in the workplace. Teachers who fail to demonstrate characteristics of professionalism tend to have more difficulty managing the behavior of their students, so it is appropriate to include tips on professionalism in a book about classroom management. Professionalism alone will not ensure that your students don't misbehave—its's not that simple. However, there is no doubt that if you lack professionalism, you can cause some behavioral situations to be worse. You, your students, their families, and your colleagues will benefit if you maintain a vision of yourself as a professional and demonstrate professionalism at all times. This task provides suggestions for how to look, think, and behave like a professional. It also provides suggestions for how to engage in essential self-care that will allow you to be at your best as a professional. When you are exhausted, stressed, and at the end of your rope, it is likely that aspects of professionalism will suffer, and you may find yourself questioning yourself or your profession as a teacher.

While this task is primarily geared towards early-career teachers (those who are just about to begin or are within their first few years of teaching), the suggestions in this chapter serve as good reminders for veteran teachers as well. People naturally can become complacent about certain aspects of their profession, and if you are experiencing any frustration or lowered morale for any reason (personally or professionally), it is important to consider what you can do to maintain professionalism and self-care. Read the suggestions below, discuss them with mentors or colleagues, and reflect on whether you are exhibiting professional qualities. Keep this information in mind, and periodically evaluate each year how you are doing at maintaining professionalism and engaging in self-care.

Build a Professional Relationship With Each of Your Students

> *Building positive relationships with students is a foundational component of any successful Classroom Management Plan.*

Students need to believe you have their best interests at heart and that you will do everything in your power to help them succeed in your class and throughout school. Building positive relationships with students is a foundational component of any successful Classroom Management Plan. We have explored many strategies throughout this book to achieve this goal. The first step is to learn each student's name (and learn to pronounce it correctly!), and use their names to greet them each day. Greeting each student by name demonstrates that you are aware of and interested in each student as an individual.

Beyond this first step of using students' names, the concept of building relationships gets a little less clear-cut. Building a relationship with your students is like being a great tour guide. Imagine that you arrange a group tour in a foreign country where you cannot speak or read the language and the culture is very different from your own. Your ideal tour guide will have enough leadership abilities and organizational skills to keep your group together and safe and to take you where you want to go, ensuring that everyone has a good time in the process. This tour guide's main responsibility is to be a leader, not a friend. However, while keeping things organized and keeping you all safe, she will make you feel that she is interested in you, that she enjoys your company, and she has your best interests at heart. So, be a good tour guide for your students—be a positive leader. Organize your classroom, orchestrate student behavior to the degree necessary for all students to be successful, and let every student know their success and well-being is important to you.

Building positive relationships with students does not mean that you should cut them a break by being lenient with your rules and corrective consequences, or by lowering your expectations of what they can accomplish. Avoid any effort to be a friend or peer, to be cool or trendy. The students need you to be their professional guide on this journey you take together. Always enforce your rules in a consistent, calm, pleasant, professional, and nonnegotiable manner. Students need the structure and safety of your organized and consistent Classroom Management Plan.

To build and maintain positive relationships with all of your students, avoid shutting down on a student who has misbehaved or been disrespectful to you—no matter how badly or how often. Don't take student misbehavior or lack of motivation personally. Some students may even actively strive to push you away. Remember that you are the adult (and leader) in this daily adventure. Even the student who seriously misbehaved on Tuesday needs a friendly greeting and a fresh start on Wednesday morning.

Logic Over Impulse

Don't take student misbehavior personally! While it can be easy to become emotional or shut down on a student who exhibits repeated misbehavior, continue to lead in a professional and positive manner.

Keep in mind that you are modeling how to build a positive relationship for your students. As an educator, you are not only building and maintaining your relationships, but you are also showing your students how to build relationships with others, including their peers and the adults on campus, other people they may interact with who are in positions of authority, and even possibly their family members. If you find you are struggling to either build or maintain a positive relationship with one student, or perhaps several students, try these suggestions:

- Sponsor after-school activities or attend activities outside of school that your students are involved in.
- Take a walk and have a conversation with a group of students about something unrelated to their class work or efforts.
- Implement class meetings.
- Find out more about your students through the use of interest inventories or reinforcement menus.
- Celebrate the good times.
- Ask a colleague to join you for a home visit.
- Invite a small group of students to have lunch with you.
- Read a book, watch a movie or show, or listen to music recommended by students and then share your opinion with them.
- Greet students verbally, with handshakes, or with high-fives.
- At dismissal, use specific praise with students' names for a job well done.

Part of building professional and positive relationship with students is making efforts to learn where your students are coming from—literally, economically, and culturally. Values, beliefs, and behaviors may not be the same as yours, so be aware of these differences. For example, the way competition is viewed differs greatly across cultures. In some cultures, it is inappropriate to try to be better than others—to want a better grade, to want to be the best,

Diversity, Equity, Inclusion, and Access

Learn where your students are coming from and how their values, beliefs, and behaviors are shaped by their culture, background, and personal circumstances. Use this information to honor and acknowledge differences, better understand and connect with your students, and provide any needed supports.

to win the race. If students are more motivated by progress of the group than by competition, you could use more whole class praise and whole class rewards instead of systems that focus on individuals.

Be respectful of differences in background or culture while teaching your students how to be successful in your classroom. Work to skillfully and respectfully guide your students toward successful classroom behaviors, while being careful not to devalue other beliefs, customs, practices, and social behaviors. If the expected classroom behaviors are new or different for the student, it is simply "the way we do it in Ms. Johnson's classroom."

Some additional tips for getting to know students and their background and culture include:

- Ask age-appropriate questions in surveys, essay prompts, or discussions, such as:

  How many siblings do you have?
  What are your responsibilities around the house?
  What do you like to do when you are not at school?
  What free-time activities do you like the most when you are at school?
  Who do you spend your free time with?

- Create a culture jar. Have students write something about their culture on a card and put it in the jar. During sharing time or every once in a while at the beginning or end of class, pull one of the culture cards. You can also look at the cards to get ideas for decorating your classroom and creating special lessons or connections to students' culture in existing curricular content.

Remember the I in STOIC—positive interactions build positive relationships! Teachers who exhibit professionalism make efforts to engage their students frequently in positive ways. See Chapter 8, Task 1 for more tips on how to keep your expectations positive. By teaching high expectations and helping students set and work towards goals, you help students from all backgrounds develop skills and attitudes that will help them throughout their lives. In some cases, you may be the first person to tell students they can attain goals. Review Chapters 6 and 7 for ideas on how to keep your expectations high, build strong relationships, and ensure that the majority of your feedback remains positive.

Build Professional Relationships With Your Students' Families

Plan ahead to build a professional relationship with each student's family. Strategies for working effectively with families are included in more detail in Chapter 2, Task 8; Chapter 4, Task 5; Chapter 6, Task 5; and Chapter 8, Task 5.

Families do not want you to be their friend or their child's friend. They want you to guide their child on their journey, to use the metaphor from above, to successfully learn the essential skills and competencies of your grade level or subject. They expect you to keep the child's best interests at heart. Keep families informed about their child's progress throughout this journey.

Building positive relationships and connecting with families supports not only them but also your students, your class, and your school community. To collaborate with and support the families of your students, keep the following strategies in mind:

Relational Trust

To build and maintain relational trust with families, communication is key. Keep families informed about student progress and be open to family input. Strive to maintain higher rates of positive communication than corrective so families feel that you are in their child's corner.

- Establish a rapport and positive communication.
- Respect the confidentiality of information you have regarding their children.
- Provide reassurance.
- Be open to family input.
- Be compassionate and communicate with families often.
- Give families the benefit of the doubt that they want the best for their child and are doing the best with the skills and resources they have available to them. Avoid making judgments about students' families.

If you have to talk to the family about a misbehavior their child has exhibited, keep the focus of the discussion on objective descriptions of the behavior and how that behavior is interfering with their child's academic or behavioral progress. When you focus on the child and working to figure out solutions to help the child be successful, the family will be far more responsive to supporting you than if you talk about how the child's behavior affects you or the other students in the class. Avoid getting defensive if the family is critical of you. Ask a colleague, mentor, or your administrator to join you for a family conference if you are unsure how to proceed. Remember that you are the professional—keep the focus on what can be done to help the student be successful. Also remember that families need to hear about successes and growth, not just misbehavior. Strive to maintain a 3:1 ratio of positive to corrective interactions with families across time.

Build Professional and Collaborative Relationships With Your Colleagues

Every school has numerous social structures. There are formal relationships such as grade-level or departmental colleagues as well as informal structures of friends and other alliances. In some schools you may find cliques or groups who do not like or respect other groups. If you are a new staff member in a school, be careful not to get caught up in these alliances. If you have been on a staff for a while, periodically evaluate whether you are playing a role in any negative social structures that exist on your campus and work to change your behavior patterns if you identify involvement in any relationships with colleagues that exhibit a lack of professionalism. Gossip, badmouthing colleagues, and exclusionary behaviors are common examples of unprofessional behaviors that can creep into the daily social interactions of school staff.

Treat everyone with respect, honoring their dignity: teachers, administrators, and clerical, custodial, and food service staff. You are a member of a vitally important community, and it is important that everyone in that community feels honored and valued. Act with humility as you interact with others but be an active participant. Ask questions, volunteer to assist committees as your time allows, and be flexible, cooperative, prompt, and optimistic—all professional qualities. If you work toward building positive relationships with colleagues, they will be more open to planning with you and you will learn more from each other.

If you are new to the staff, avoid criticizing institutional traditions that you don't understand or that existed before you began teaching. Avoid gossip, and don't get pulled into negative, unproductive groups. As you get to know the staff, seek out mentors—people you feel comfortable going to for advice and assistance. Seek out those who have the best relationships with their students, who love their work, and who are committed to ongoing learning and improvement to their practice despite being good teachers already.

If you have a student who consistently misbehaves and your efforts to help them improve their behavior have been ineffective, you should not hesitate to ask a fellow teacher for additional ideas. Seeking collegial assistance is a sign of professional strength, not weakness. This may be most clearly demonstrated by professionals in the field of medicine. When faced with a puzzling situation, most physicians discuss the case with other physicians. Teachers can and should exhibit this same level of collegial problem-solving.

TIPS FOR THE FIRST-YEAR TEACHER

Shelley Jones, coauthor of the Read Well curriculum, offers these tips on collaboration for first-year teachers.

Most of the young or first-year teachers that I've worked with as a mentor or supervising teacher expressed great appreciation for my support, help, and collaboration with both the details of running a classroom and big issues such as discipline and lesson plans. Some of the questions these young teachers asked were:

- How and where do I get posters and decorations to put on my walls?
- How do I use the district computer system for reporting grades?
- What do I do at staff meetings? (I see some people grading papers at the meeting. Is that OK?)
- Do I have a budget for printing?
- How do I get copies of assignments for my students?
- What do I do when my students have no materials?
- What do I do if my students need counseling?
- What do I do if I think a student is being abused?

As a result of my experiences, I would say the following five things are really important for a first-year teacher:

1. **Request (or find) your own mentor.**
   A mentor is another teacher or someone else in the education field who can help you plan for your class, offer tips and advice, answer questions, and provide you with supplemental materials. Ideally your mentor teaches in your school at your grade level.

Trading observations and evaluations with your mentor can be valuable training. Your mentor can observe you teach and write an evaluation, and you should be asked to do the same for your mentor. Observe, evaluate, and talk with each other as often as possible—perhaps weekly to begin with, and then monthly.

A small number of new teachers seem to think they know it all. I've found they can be the most difficult to help, and yet they often need the most assistance. More than anything they need a strong mentor presence.

2. **Attend a CHAMPS training.**
   Attend a CHAMPS training prior to the start of the school year. If it's not offered in your district, actively seek out a training opportunity. Take your mentor along with you. If you are unable to attend a training, create your own. Ask your mentor to guide you through the *CHAMPS* book and see if other relatively new teachers or other first-year teachers in your building want to form a CHAMPS work group. Use the Peer Discussion questions in Task 3 of this chapter as a guide to working through each chapter.

3. **Invite your principal into your classroom on a regular basis.**
   Tell your principal that you welcome their informal and formal observations. Most inexperienced teachers think I'm crazy when I make this suggestion. However, frequent visits to your classroom allow your principal to get familiar with your teaching style and to know what kinds of training they can offer privately or during staff meetings to meet your needs. It's a wonderful feeling to know that your principal is invested in your future and wants you to succeed as a teacher! Also, your comfort level with being observed will increase at every visit.

4. **Get out of your classroom and observe.**
   Whenever possible, take the time (yes, even prep time) to get out of your own classroom and observe other teachers. There is nothing more powerful than seeing a master teacher at work! Once again, involve your mentor and principal. They should be able to identify master teachers in both your building and district.

5. **Ask questions. Ask for help.**
   ASK, ASK, ASK! No one knows you need help unless you ask. No question is too silly or dumb. Every question is an opportunity to learn. You will undoubtedly make mistakes in your first year of teaching—turn those mistakes into learning opportunities. Ask your mentor how you can improve and constantly strive for success.

• • • • •

Your professional and collaborative relationships will also benefit if you respect the confidentiality of both students and colleagues. You should not discuss your students outside of school, especially if you live in the community where you teach. In addition, unless you are participating in a school-sponsored problem-solving procedure, avoid talking about school business or the concerns of your coworkers.

For example, imagine that another teacher is not giving you the help and support you need regarding a student who both of you teach. The most professional response is to go to this person, discuss your concerns, and ask for more assistance. It would be highly unprofessional to discuss the problem with other teachers or talk about the problem during a family-teacher conference. Again, look at the medical profession as an example. A physician can and should discuss cases confidentially with colleagues at work. However, it is unprofessional and inappropriate for her to talk about a patient or colleagues at a dinner party. As a teaching professional, you owe your students and fellow staff members the same level of professionalism that they expect and deserve from their doctors. As many of you are aware, in some schools discussions in the faculty room may border on being unprofessional—you may hear teachers discussing students in a hostile, rude, or sarcastic manner. You may hear some teachers making disparaging remarks about their administrator or other teachers. Regardless of the behavior of others, maintain your high level of professional behavior.

Act in a Professional Manner

The definition of how to act in a professional manner is somewhat subjective, but a good model for professional behavior is, for example, a physician or attorney. Think about the demeanor you want and expect from your doctor or lawyer. Most of us probably prefer someone who seems knowledgeable, confident, and comfortable—but not haughty or arrogant. We are generally uncomfortable with someone who seems hesitant or insecure, doesn't seem to like their job, or complains about their working conditions. We may not trust someone who doesn't make eye contact, and we may find it hard to interact with someone who mumbles when they talk to us.

A teacher should try to project a relaxed and confident manner. You do not need to be relaxed and confident at all times (very few of us are capable of this!), but you should act relaxed and confident. In fact, there are probably times when you are unsure of yourself or unsure how to handle a situation. While it is not necessary to give the impression that you know what to do when you really don't, do keep in mind that you are a professional. You provide a valuable service to your students and the community, and you can solve any problem—eventually. Ask yourself whether you would rather go to a physician who bluffs and blusters when he is unsure, or one who confidently says, "I am unsure what the best course of action is, but I assure you I will work until I find out."

Locus of Control

When you encounter a problem, work to assess it and take responsibility for making changes that are within your locus of control. Rather than blaming others or saying that a problem is not your concern because it relates to factors that are outside of your control, be an active problem solver with those variables you can control. Seek out support from other professionals as needed.

Be an active problem-solver. When faced with a problem—for example, the student is not behaving responsibly or is not making adequate academic progress—the teacher who demonstrates professionalism analyzes the problem and takes responsibility for seeking and implementing a solution. On the other hand, a teacher who is not acting professionally tends to blame the problem on someone else or feels that someone else should solve the problem (or both). The teacher who is demonstrating professionalism continues to try until a solution is found—they never give up. Even if the situation eventually requires involving other professionals to ensure the student has the support they need, the professional remains involved and invested in the student's success. Keep Eleanor Roosevelt's words in mind: "We have never failed unless we have ceased to try."

Professionalism includes dependability. As a professional, you need to arrive at work and meetings on time, fulfill your various duties (for example, supervising a bus loading area for 2 weeks) without needing reminders, attend staff meetings and give your full attention to the proceedings (for example, avoid grading papers or doing other work during meetings), and complete attendance and grade reports on time.

You should also work to present a professional appearance and select an appropriate level of formality for your school attire. In general, make sure your dress is neat and clean, but the specifics of what considered is appropriate varies greatly from community to community. When you are new to a school, speak with your administrator, mentor, or veteran, respected teaching colleagues to determine what is an appropriate level of professional dress.

Engage in Self-Care

Working with a classroom full of students can be an exhausting and challenging endeavor, especially when dealing with ongoing student misbehavior or lack of motivation. Acting professionally and implementing any of the other strategies in this book requires that you be at your best—fresh, positive, optimistic, and willing to persevere as long as it takes to find workable solutions for you and your students. Relaxation and stress management techniques are beneficial for any teacher, but they are absolutely critical if you find yourself frequently stressed or on the verge of burnout. If you find yourself thinking or making any of the following statements, give special attention to the ideas that follow:

- *I am always exhausted.*
- *I just don't like this kid. He's never going to change.*
- *How can I be expected to do any more? I have 29 students in the room.*
- *They make me so mad. It's impossible to remain calm.*
- *I just want that student out of my room!*

The following are brief descriptions of stress reduction and self-care techniques to consider when you're dealing with the daily pressures of teaching (these are adapted from *Early-Stage Interventions*, available at ancorapublishing.com, which provides more detailed information about each technique). These strategies can help you keep the challenges of teaching in perspective, enjoy your job more, and maintain high positive expectations for your students and optimism for their success. Consider which strategy or combination of strategies will work for you, and seek out additional resources as needed.

Practice deep muscle relaxation.

Deep muscle relaxation is an important strategy that addresses the physical state of tension that your body is likely to go into when you are stressed and feeling the pressures of teaching. Tension is typically associated with a state of mind, but it also relates to the physical state of your body, which in turn affects your state of mind. The more physically tense you get in response to the pressures of the day, the more your physical tension can drain your energy and lead to a sense of feeling "wound" and about to snap. The strategy of deep muscle relaxation involves triggering two opposites ends of the continuum of tension and relaxation so that you can learn to keep your muscles in a relaxed state. While it may seem like this wouldn't make much of a difference, learning to keep your muscles in a relaxed state can help you in many areas of your life: teaching, taking care of routine tasks, taking care of your own children or family members, engaging with friends and colleagues, and participating in activities outside of school.

To get an introduction to deep muscle relaxation, try the following 30-second exercise:

> *Begin by tensing as many muscle groups as you can. Tense the muscles in both feet. Tense your legs and buttocks. Tense your torso, arms, and neck, and ball your hands into tight fists. Tense all of the muscles in your face, squeezing your eyes tight shut, and tightening all of the muscles in your mouth. While keeping your entire body tense for 15 seconds, visualize a child engaging in a highly annoying or frustrating behavior. Imagine how you might handle the problem. Then, reverse this process. Relax all the muscles you were tensing, and keep working to deepen that relaxed state for 15 seconds while you imagine effectively handling the problem with the student.*

To do daily practice with deep muscle relaxation, schedule 3- to 5-minute sessions. During each session, start with one muscle group (e.g., start with your hands or your feet), and tighten the muscle group for 5 seconds. Slowly release the muscles. Concentrate on feeling how your muscles feel before, during, and after you tense them. Progressively work through each muscle in your body, including feet, calves, thighs, buttocks, hands, arms, shoulders and neck, jaw, and the rest of your face.

Keep a confidential journal.

Schedule a few minutes at the end of each school day or before you go to bed to write in a journal. Write in a stream-of-consciousness mode, and allow yourself to include challenges, frustrations, concerns, doubts, questions, and also successes.

This process can help you sort out problems and provides an emotional release. If you make sure to focus at least part of your writing each day on successes, it can help you recognize that even when things are really tough, there are also wins in each day. This writing process gives closure to the day, allowing you to put aside anything that happened for the rest of the evening or as you go to sleep.

Make sure that your journal is confidential, so do not write during school hours, on school grounds, or on a school computer. You don't want to worry about being diplomatic or objective in your journal writing—this is a place for you to express your feelings, doubts, and frustrations. However, if you engage in journaling on school grounds or devices, the document could be considered an official record, not a personal reflection. Write your journal at home and keep it there.

Cultivate a balanced lifestyle.

Although many teachers take immense pride in their profession and view a large part of their identity as being defined as a teacher, it is important to maintain a balanced lifestyle. Although total immersion might seem beneficial given how critically important this job is, when teachers don't work to maintain some balance, they can easily become overwhelmed and burned out. When problems occur, which they inevitably will at one point or another, these problems can easily feel severe and debilitating when you don't have other things to give you a sense of fulfillment.

A balanced lifestyle involves three aspects of life—your career, your relationships with others, and your relationship with yourself. If you find you are lacking balance, see if you can provide focused attention to fostering the areas that may have been neglected. For example, if a teacher is so wrapped up in work that they neglect their family, this can lead to strife and turmoil at home. If this continues, this unhealthy commitment to work at the expense of their family can lead to reduced effectiveness on the job because the teacher is distressed about their home life.

Promote positive self-talk.

People often underestimate the power of their internal monologue. Negative thinking often turns into a self-fulfilling prophecy where each negative thought provides one more piece of evidence that a situation is hopeless. In contrast, positive self-talk can help you develop positive expectations and reframe every experience, whether positive or negative, as a learning experience or opportunity for growth. At first, reframing negative thoughts into positive ones may feel a bit forced, but if your keep practicing, you can actually begin to think and act in ways that reduce tension and increase your ability to persist through challenges.

> *Positive self-talk can help you develop positive expectations and reframe every experience, whether positive or negative, as a learning experience or opportunity for growth.*

To restructure your own self-talk, be conscious of your internal monologue, especially in challenging moments or when you are feeling particularly stressed. Actively practice taking negative internal statements and turning them around. Rather than stating what can't be done, focus on what you do have control over. Instead of expressing pessimism about situations, acknowledge the reality of where things are now, but work to express optimism about where they can be in the future. For example, instead of "I just don't know what to do," reframe as "I don't know what to do right now, but I will find a solution." Instead of "This behavior is driving me nuts and I'm going to lose it one day," tell yourself, "This behavior is annoying, but I'm an adult and can stay calm."

As with any new skill, consider scheduling daily practice until positive self-talk becomes more natural. Try to begin each school day by saying or writing a few positive thoughts. Other natural times might include breaks, as students are lining up, before students return from lunch, as the day ends, and prior to going home. You might wish to incorporate this practice in writing if you are using the journaling method described previously.

Practice visualization.

Visualization practice involves mentally rehearsing a new or difficult skill such as how to respond effectively to student misbehavior. If you repeatedly visualize yourself successfully handling a complex situation or one in which you know you tend to get tense and overly emotional, you are more likely to handle the real-life situation effectively. You can use visualization to reduce your stress about how to handle student misbehavior, how to talk to a difficult colleague, or how to interact with your partner or children.

If you are having difficulty working with a group of students or an individual, mentally rehearse successful responses to various situations:

- Identify situations that have caused problems in the past.
- Mentally rehearse how to handle these situations in the future.
- Visualize each situation in its entirety in as much detail as possible.
- If your visualization begins to veer toward a negative outcome, rewind the mental image and begin again.

Identify strengths—yours as a teacher and your students' strengths.

Simply reminding yourself about your strengths as a teacher or person and your students' strengths can help you realize there are positive features within a situation to build on. Feelings of hopelessness contribute greatly to stress. The very act of focusing on strengths will reduce any tendency on your part to view the situation as hopeless.

If you have a student or group of students with whom your interactions have begun to be adversarial, or if their challenges are making you feel it is next to impossible for things to change, begin focusing on their strengths. Student maturity and self-discipline often improve when you help students foster their strengths and abilities. See Chapter 6, Task 2 for suggestions for identifying, acknowledging, and providing opportunities to build off students' strengths. In addition, if you are having difficulty identifying student strengths, ask others to help you. It can be difficult to see past students' problems when you are dealing with misbehavior, but other teachers, an administrator, or students' families can often give great insights that help you get a sense of your students' strengths and abilities.

If you struggle to identify your own strengths as a teacher, take some time to think about the parts of teaching that you don't have to think about much. Maybe you are someone who cares deeply about the success of your students. Maybe you are extremely organized and clear in your content area instruction. Perhaps you are a highly creative individual who comes up with unique and stimulating activities, or you are very good at helping your students develop positive social relationships. Whatever those strengths are, if you can remind yourself of them when you are feeling stressed about some aspect of your classroom, it can help you reframe your current challenges as a momentary thing that you will be able to overcome. Reach out to supportive colleagues who can help you maintain a positive outlook—about your own abilities and about the general situation.

Engaging in self-care through relaxation and stress management strategies can help you reduce the tension and anxiety you may sometimes feel when dealing with the daily pressures of the classroom. When you have to work with students who exhibit significant challenging behavior, it is essential that you continually work to be at your best so you can continue engaging in positive and professional ways with your students and families. Learning to relax does not automatically change the problem behavior of your students, but in conjunction with the other strategies advocated in this book, your efforts to support yourself will increase the probability you are effective with your students. It will also increase your job satisfaction and hopefully encourage you to stay in this incredibly important profession.

In summary, this task offered considerations to reflect on in assessing whether you are exhibiting professional qualities and taking care of yourself as you tackle the many responsibilities of being a teacher. Keep this information in mind, and periodically evaluate how you are doing at maintaining professionalism and engaging in self-care throughout the year.

TASK 3

Engage in Ongoing Learning and Professional Development

For continuous improvement, engage in opportunities to strengthen your knowledge and practice of effective classroom management.

• • • • •

Because CHAMPS is an approach, not a program, and because a good management plan is fluid (for example, more highly structured in the last month of school than the second-to-last month of school), teachers should develop a mindset that emphasizes continuous improvement. Any professional, such as the physician you trust with your health, should be a lifelong learner of the craft of medicine. No matter how skilled the teacher, every classroom has some students who can learn to behave more responsibly or increase their motivation, so every teacher should take opportunities to strengthen their knowledge and reflect on their practice. Periodically assessing your Classroom Management Plan and how it is addressing the needs of individual students is critical to avoid mediocrity, which comes from maintaining the status quo. This task covers suggestions for deepening your understanding and implementation of the CHAMPS approach. Note that these different suggestions can be combined in creative ways to keep you thinking and talking about CHAMPS as a continuous improvement model.

Attend Initial Inservice Training Opportunities at the Building or District Level

The implementation of CHAMPS can be enhanced with engaging, practical, and clear inservice. If the inservice is provided directly by Safe & Civil Schools, you will not receive training from a graduate student or someone who has never worked with kids! All Safe & Civil Schools consultants are seasoned former teachers with years of personal experience successfully implementing the CHAMPS approach, and many also have other experience as building or district administrators, or other roles within schools.

If your district provides CHAMPS training, take the opportunity to attend. If you attended a CHAMPS training years ago, consider attending another so that you can listen and reflect with the benefit of having already implemented some of the practices. If CHAMPS training is not available to you through your district, see if there are web-based inservices, public presentations, or inservice available in another district that you could attend. Safe & Civil Schools typically offers web-based and public conferences several times throughout the year (see safeandcivilschools.com for information about upcoming in-service opportunities).

Self-assess your knowledge and practice.

If you have not already done so, use Reproducible 1.2: CHAMPS Bulleted Classroom Management Plan to keep track of the tasks you are successfully implementing and which still need work. This form provides an overview of the major concepts and practices within CHAMPS tasks. You can use it as you complete each task or chapter, and you can also use it to periodically remind yourself of recommended practices without rereading the whole book. This form also serves as an easy way to identify tasks that you might want to reread to address a current concern in your classroom.

Imagine the teacher who has used the same attention signal successfully for years. When she initially attended a CHAMPS training and read the book, she didn't need to change her attention signal because it was working great (remember, one principle in the CHAMPS approach is "don't fix it if its not broken"!). However, this teacher now has a very challenging group of students who have not been responding to her attention signal. She has tried re-teaching and providing lots of corrective feedback, but it's just not working. When she uses the CHAMPS Bulleted Classroom Management Plan, she realizes she should review the task on developing an effective attention signal (Chapter 2, Task 4). Use this resource once or twice a year (e.g., once partway through the fall and once at the end of the year) to reflect on your knowledge and practice.

In addition to the Bulleted Classroom Management Plan, make sure to use the data collection tools from Task 1 of this chapter to guide your continuous improvement process.

Engage with colleagues in ongoing activities for growth.

There are numerous options for engaging with your colleagues to strengthen your collective knowledge and implementation of effective classroom management techniques. The following is an overview of three such approaches.

Create a book club. With this approach, work through the *CHAMPS* book across the course of the year with your colleagues. Assign one or two chapters a month and meet to discuss and reflect on the content. Your book club could meet before or after school, during an extended lunch on a grading or teacher work day, or even on a weekend at a coffee shop or someone's home. Peer Discussion Worksheets (Reproducible 10.15A–J) can be used to create these professional exchanges of ideas. This is a highly effective approach for your first year of CHAMPS implementation. It can also be beneficial if you have been using the CHAMPS approach for a number of years and would like a refresher, but are unable to attend a CHAMPS inservice. Meet once or twice a month.

Use peer observation and coaching. It is always beneficial to receive observational data about your classroom so you can identify areas of strength and weakness and goals for improvement. Observation also tends to elevate implementation by creating a sense of urgency. It is easy to fall into old habits if there is no accountability. If you change the way in which you deliver corrective feedback or you circulate more when your colleague is observing, for example, this probably indicates that these are practices you should focus on implementing on a regular basis. Periodically ask teaching colleagues, your administrator, and others in your building (e.g., counselor, coach) to observe in your classroom using one of the CHAMPS data tools.

If your school/district has an instructional or behavioral coach, invite them to observe and provide observational feedback. In some cases, you may also wish to enlist these colleagues or another teacher in the school to assist you in ideas for implementing an aspect of CHAMPS that is particularly challenging for you. For example, some teachers find it very difficult to achieve a 3:1 ratio of positive to corrective interactions, while this is more natural for other teachers in the building. If you take your own data or receive observational feedback from others that

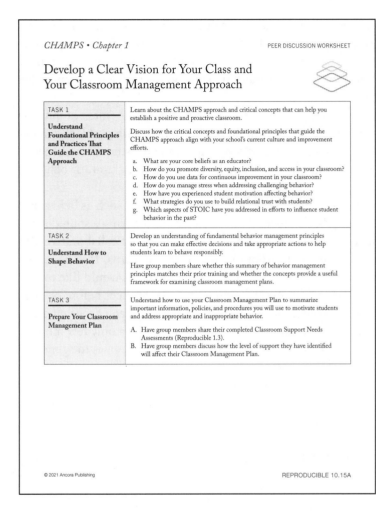

Reproducible 10.15A
Chapter 1 Peer Discussion Worksheet

Downloads

The Chapter 1 Peer Discussion Worksheet only is shown. Peer Discussion worksheets for all chapters are available to download.

indicates you are struggling to achieve a positive ratio despite your best efforts, you might ask another teacher to mentor you in this aspect of your practice. Or enlist the help of the coach in your building. In most fields, coaching and mentoring is viewed as the mark of someone's value to a company—the company is willing to invest in the employee's professional development and continuous improvement. Take up these opportunities if they are available to you.

Engage in collaborative problem-solving. The old adage "two heads are better than one, four heads are better than two" can certainly be true when it comes to behavioral and motivational concerns. When students are misbehaving, it can be difficult to objectively problem-solve on your own because of the concern, emotional intensity, or stress you may be feeling about the misbehavior. Others may be able to view the situation in a more objective light, or they may bring a different and beneficial skillset to the table that is valuable in helping address the problem.

While most schools have some sort of intervention team to discuss ways to support individual students who are struggling (e.g., Student Support Team [SST], Intervention Support Team [IST]), these teams are often overwhelmed by the number of requests for assistance they receive. It is common for these teams to meet only once or twice a month, and each time there are far more students on their list than they can reasonably get to in a one- or even several-hour meeting. If you refer a concern to such a team, it is reasonable to assume in some schools that you might not receive assistance for several months or more. In addition, these teams typically do not work to address whole class concerns because they focus on individual student interventions. Therefore, it is important to consider additional ways to engage in collaborative problem-solving with colleagues.

Reach out to individual colleagues who have expertise in classroom management or individualized intervention. Some of the individuals who might be able to help with problem-solving include other general education teachers, a paraprofessional who knows the student well, special education teachers, counselor, social worker, school psychologist, administrator, or behavior specialist or coach.

In some schools, established teacher-to-teacher problem-solving teams, such as behavioral Professional Learning Communities (PLCs), meet a few times a month during a shared planning period. Similar to academic PLCs, these groups engage in a process of collaborative idea generation and problem-solving to address classroom management concerns. If your school does not have a similar structure, consider whether one or more colleagues would like to join you in creating such a group. Similar to a book study group, you could meet before or after school, during a shared prep period, or a few times a month during lunch. Each time you meet, one or two teachers bring a classwide or individual student concern. Spend a only few minutes describing the concern and what has been done about it already. The tendency is to spend the majority of the time describing the problem, but it is more important to focus the discussion on possible solutions. Spend no more than 5 minutes of a 25- or 30-minute problem-solving session discussing the problem. Then spend most of the remaining time brainstorming ideas and then helping the teacher craft an implementation plan for one or more of them. For classwide concerns, consider using the STOIC Problem-Solving Worksheet (Reproducible 10.2) described in Task 1 of this chapter.

Whenever you engage in collaborative problem-solving with a colleague or group of colleagues, actively work to avoid some of the pitfalls commonly associated with discussions about student behavioral or motivational concerns, including:

Locus of Control

Be careful to focus on problem solving, not "problem admiring," when speaking with colleagues. Spend your time discussing solutions that are within your locus of control.

- *Too much time spent on problem admiring, not problem solving.* Push yourself (and your colleagues) to move beyond just describing problems and discussing all of the things that are outside of your control or the things that can't be done (e.g., "If only the principal would . . . " or "If she had different parents, then . . ."). There is a point where someone should say, "Now we know the concerns, so what are we going to do about them?"
- *A focus on reactive consequences and punishment rather than proactive procedures.* If you find the discussion begins cycling to primarily discussing which corrective consequences should be used, remind yourself (and colleagues) that corrective consequences are the weakest tool in your management toolbox. Spend only a few minutes of a 25- or 30-minute collaborative problem-solving session discussing which corrective consequences might be consistently and effectively applied. Spend the majority of the time on what positive and proactive procedures will make a difference (the STOI of STOIC).

- *A never-ending discussion or meeting.* Set time limits for your discussions. If you plan to engage a colleague in an informal problem-solving discussion, set a time limit in advance: "Mary, I'm wondering if you've got 15 minutes so I can pick your brain for ideas about something I'm dealing with in my fourth-period class." If you are meeting in a more formal, collaborative problem-solving group, plan to devote about 25 to 30 minutes to discuss one person's classwide or individual student concern. If you have a 1-hour meeting scheduled, two people in the group could bring their classroom concern. Give yourself reasonable time limits for each portion of the problem-solving discussion. For example, you might devote up to 10 minutes to describing and analyzing the problem (e.g., looking for trends in when, where, and why the problems might be occurring), 10–15 minutes to brainstorming possible solutions, and 5 minutes to identifying a plan (e.g., strategies for the teacher to implement and data that will be collected to monitor the plan).

In summary, this task encourages you to develop a professional mindset that emphasizes continuous improvement, ongoing learning, and self-reflection. By attending training opportunities, engaging in regular self-assessment, and/or collaborating with colleagues, you will be able to take your efficacy as a classroom manager to the next level.

Conclusion

Professionals in any field are expected to continually learn and grow in their chosen fields. For example, most physicians do some things differently today than when they first started practicing. Most people probably hope that if they are going in for surgery, their surgeon is well versed with the most up-to-date, evidence-based practices and is not using antiquated techniques from 30 years ago. Professional development requires both keeping up to date on new information in your field and being willing to look at your own behavior with a critical eye: "What am I doing that is working effectively? What is not working effectively?" After identifying strategies and techniques that are not working effectively, the true professional is always looking for a better way—from peers, from staff development, from professional books, and from the research literature.

The information in this book will help you examine and, as necessary, modify your behavior management practices. The tasks in this chapter included numerous resources that you can use to facilitate professional development as you work on your own and with colleagues to use the skills and procedures suggested in this book. Remember that whether you work with a whole staff, a small study group or partner, or even just yourself, you can be an active participant in considering how the skills and procedures in this book can help you on your journey as a lifelong learner committed to continuous improvement. In discussions with colleagues, recognize that there are no dumb questions and that collaboration around difficult classroom management concerns pushes everyone to learn and try new things. Most importantly, enjoy the ongoing puzzle and adventure of managing student behavior and motivating students so they are able to achieve their full potential!

Implementing CHAMPS in Virtual Learning Environments

This section contains one chapter to provide guidance in applying content from the first three sections to a virtual learning environment. If you teach in a virtual learning environment for some or all of the time, this chapter specifically discusses which tasks in the preceding chapters can be applied as is, which tasks apply but may need some adaptation, and which tasks are not relevant in the virtual classroom. Additionally, this chapter presents specific tools that are well suited for the virtual leaning environment and strategies teachers can use to create a positive and productive virtual classroom experience, increase student attendance and engagement, and build relationships with students from a physically distant role.

CHAPTER 11

CHAMPS in the Virtual Classroom

Develop a Classroom Management Plan specifically for virtual teaching.

Although your virtual Classroom Management Plan will have many similarities to one for face-to-face learning, there will be some important differences. If you are in a hybrid situation, you may wish to have two different Classroom Management Plans, one for face-to-face learning and one for virtual.

First, let's briefly explore some background and clarify some terminology. In March of 2020, schools in the United States rapidly transitioned to distance and virtual learning environments due to the COVID-19 pandemic. Over the course of the next year, schools adopted a variety of models to try to accommodate the demands of the moment, and teachers had to rapidly learn how to effectively educate their students when they were not connecting with them face to face in the school building. While this created incredible challenges, it also illustrated that good instruction is good instruction! Whether you are working with students in person or through a virtual learning platform, teachers can implement many effective practices, such as those in this book, to promote responsible behavior, increase student motivation and engagement, and help students experience academic success. This chapter is designed to help educators who are instructing students in a virtual learning model. Determine which strategies you can put in place to help all your students thrive.

While this chapter is written for teachers who educate their students in a virtual or hybrid learning model, a large number of the principles and strategies in the rest of the CHAMPS book are highly relevant. In some cases, approaches in Chapters 1–10 are even more important in virtual learning settings. For example, it important to intentionally work to create a positive relationship and build relational trust with your students no matter what the environment; however, a teacher in a virtual learning environment may need to preplan and bring more intentionality to this practice because it is more difficult to connect through a computer screen. We have structured this chapter as a guide for how to read and use the content in CHAMPS to boost your management approach while providing specific examples of how to adapt and implement CHAMPS strategies for virtual learning. This chapter also provides an increased focus on strategies to boost attendance and engagement during synchronous learning sessions, which are two prominent concerns about student behavior in virtual learning.

Clarifying Terminology

In this chapter, we use the following terms to refer to different activities that occur in virtual learning environments:

Synchronous: Any activity during which students are logged into a virtual learning platform at the same time as the teacher and interact in learning activities in real time. Synchronous activities include class sessions that occur on learning platforms such as Zoom, Microsoft Teams, and Google Meets, among others.

Asynchronous: Any activity that occurs on students' own time outside of real-time meetings with the teacher. Examples of asynchronous activities include watching prerecorded videos and completing assignments related to the videos, posting responses on an online discussion board after attending a synchronous class session, and completing homework activities. Common platforms that host and organize asynchronous activities include Canvas, Seesaw, and Schoolology.

While these terms are used throughout this chapter, with students and parents we recommend you use simpler terms such as *class time* and *independent work*.

How to Use This Chapter

This chapter references each of the tasks in Chapters 1–10 in order. You will be directed to "Read this task and implement as is" for tasks in Chapters 1–10 that apply to the virtual setting with minimal adaptation. Read these tasks and take notes about how you plan to incorporate the strategies and concepts in your virtual classroom.

Some tasks direct you to "Read this task and implement with the following adaptations and considerations." Start by reading the main task from Chapters 1–10. These tasks provide information about mindset, purpose, and many of the nuances of implementation. Then read the corresponding content for the task in this chapter. This information will give specific examples of how to implement the task in a virtual setting. While it may be tempting to just read the content in this chapter, do not skip the main task because those sections will provide far more understanding about *how* to effectively implement the examples given in this chapter.

A few tasks will indicate that the content from the main CHAMPS task is not relevant in the virtual setting. For these tasks, you will skip the main task and read only the modified content in this chapter.

CHAPTER 1, TASK 1

Understand Foundational Principles and Practices That Guide the CHAMPS Approach

Read the task on pages 14–32 and implement as is.

CHAPTER 1, TASK 2

Understand How to Shape Behavior

Read the task on pages 32–39 and implement as is.

CHAPTER 1, TASK 3

Prepare Your Classroom Management Plan

Read the task on pages 40–49 and implement with the following adaptations and considerations.

Reproducible 11.1 is a modified Classroom Management Plan for use in the virtual classroom. A completed version appears as Figure 11.6 later in this chapter (pp. 553–557). Developing a plan that summarizes your major classroom management decisions will help you identify the rituals, routines, rules, and corrective and motivational techniques you can use to set the stage for a productive learning environment. You will adapt and modify your plan across time to meet the needs of your class. A blank fillable version of Reproducible 11.1 is available for download (see p. 3). Complete each section as you read this chapter.

The Virtual Classroom Management Plan is similar to the one introduced in Chapter 1, but some sections increase emphasis on considerations that will need to be clarified for virtual instruction. For example, you will be prompted to list procedures for motivating students to attend virtual class and procedures for actively engaging students in virtual instruction. If your classroom uses a hybrid model (e.g., students spend some time in virtual learning environments and some time physically in the school building), consider completing both a virtual and traditional Classroom Management Plan, but work to create as much consistency across the two learning environments as possible.

Determine Whether You Need Low, Medium, or High Support in the Virtual Learning Environment

We recommend using a high-support management plan for the virtual classroom, especially when the virtual setting is a new model for you and your students. If you have been teaching in a virtual setting for longer and your students are highly responsible and self-motivated, consider how to release some of the structure and support provided in different activities.

For example, in a high-support class, you may:

- Use an attention signal that requires a student response (e.g., all students raise their hand) to demonstrate that they are in fact paying attention. On a computer screen, it can be more difficult to determine if students are paying attention when there is not a participatory component.
- Keep your behavioral expectations posted at all times. Later in this chapter are options for visually posting Guidelines for Success, rules, and expectations throughout your virtual class session.
- Turn off the option for private chat among students. Most virtual platforms have settings that you can change to allow students to chat privately with the host (you) but not with each other.
- Explicitly teach expectations for use of the chat box, such as, "You can use the chat box to type questions to the group about the current activity. You will use it to respond to teacher questions or prompts. You should not use the chat box at any other time. I will monitor and address off-topic conversations and use of the chat box."
- Plan for shorter activities interspersed with teacher-directed instruction or guided practice. For example, rather than having students do 20 minutes of uninterrupted independent work, break the task into smaller 5-minute portions. Have students complete one part, then come back as a group to check understanding, discuss questions, and share ideas and student work before moving to the next part.
- Clearly define roles in any small group or partner activity and carefully consider group composition and which students will work productively together in each room.
- Closely monitor breakout rooms and active participation from all students. Follow recommendations in Chapter 3, Task 5 for ways to manage partner and small group work times, and see suggestions later in this chapter for ways to collect data on active participation in the virtual environment.
- Use fewer rather than more features of the technology (e.g., limit number of concurrent apps running, amount of toggling back and forth, and use of different features such as chats, polls, breakout rooms, and so on). As students gain proficiency with the features you are using regularly during instruction, you can explicitly teach them how to use one additional feature at a time. Recognize that some students may need additional instruction or support to understand how to use specific features, especially if they have had less access to technology in their home.

In contrast, in a class that needs lower support, you might:

- Use an attention signal, but not require a participatory response from students.
- Teach and display behavioral expectations up front, but continuous posting may not be necessary.
- Allow use of the group chat feature without specific directions (e.g., student can ask peers for help while you are providing instruction). We recommend that you keep private chat turned off, even with classes that are mature and responsible. Even mature, responsible adults in professional development sessions tend to get off task chatting with colleagues when the private chat feature is turned on!

- Plan for longer partner or group activities. For example, during a 1-hour class, students might engage in a 20–30 minute cooperative activity while you move between breakout rooms.
- Periodically monitor breakout rooms and active participation from all students.
- Integrate more technology options.

CHAPTER 2, TASK 1

Develop and Display Guidelines for Success

Read the task on pages 55–59 and implement with the following adaptations and considerations.

Guidelines for Success are especially important in the virtual learning environment because they become a defining way in which you can motivate and encourage your students. When you make efforts to link the habits, skills, and attitudes students demonstrate in their virtual classroom with success in life outside of school, it can help them develop a vision of success and a sense of pride in their efforts: "Evelyn, you've been showing up on time to each of our virtual sessions. That level of dependability, our third Guideline for Success, is something that I know will serve you so well in any job that you want to have in the future."

> **Guidelines for Success are especially important in the virtual learning environment because they become a defining way in which you can motivate and encourage your students.**

Your Guidelines for Success provide the *why* when some students struggle with motivation or question the value of what they are doing in the virtual classroom. When used effectively as the basis of a positive, encouraging, and supportive classroom culture, the Guidelines for Success can provide a powerful link for why students should attend and engage productively in virtual learning opportunities.

Visually Display Guidelines for Success

In a physical classroom setting, guidelines are posted in a prominent place where everyone can see them. This is also recommended for the virtual class so that the guidelines become a vehicle for frequent celebrations of effort and progress, corrective feedback, and building the culture of your virtual class. Some possibilities for visual posting and communicating Guidelines for Success to students and parents include:

- Create a physical poster and position it in the background of your camera view so that students can see the poster to the left or right of your face on the screen.
- Create a digital version of your poster and include it on a virtual background that is continuously behind you during class.

- If you use a class bitmoji—a graphical image of a classroom with hyperlinked resources—include in the image a "poster" of your Guidelines for Success. Link to videos or activities related to your guidelines as appropriate.
- Include your Guidelines for Success in your classroom syllabus, website, and communication to students and families.
- Send home a small display such as poster or trifold card that can be placed in the student's workspace as a visual reminder during class sessions.

UPDATE YOUR CLASSROOM MANAGEMENT PLAN

ITEM 1: GUIDELINES FOR SUCCESS

- List 3–5 Guidelines for Success for your classroom.
- Indicate where and how you will visually post the Guidelines for Success in your virtual classroom and whether they will be shown periodically or continuously throughout class.

CHAPTER 2, TASK 2
Develop and Display Classroom Rules

Read the task on pages 60–64 and implement with the following adaptations and considerations.

Select 3–6 positively stated rules that refer to observable behaviors in the virtual environment. Classroom rules should address the misbehaviors that present the greatest concerns for the productivity and learning of your students when on a virtual platform. These behaviors may be different than those most common in a physical classroom setting. For example, many teachers report that incidents of disruption are less frequent on the virtual platform, but students may have a greater tendency to be off task or to refuse to participate in active engagement activities. Some possibilities for rules in the virtual environment include:

- Arrive on time and remain throughout class on every day you are not seriously ill.
- Follow directions quickly.
- Work during all work times.
- Demonstrate participation throughout class.
- Use respectful, school-appropriate language.
- Use school- and work-appropriate language and topics.
- Keep negative comments to yourself.

- Remain with the screen in your view unless given permission to exit.
- Stay at your work space during meeting times.
- Listen and pay attention while others talk.
- Use online tools and functions as instructed.
- Mute your microphone when others are talking.
- Use only approved virtual backgrounds and keep one throughout the class period.
- Use the chat box only for conversations related to class (e.g., asking a question, communicating a concern, replying to instructions).
- Use real names (or get permission from teacher to change) in your login and when addressing others.

When creating rules for your virtual classroom, incorporate the recommendations in Chapter 2, Task 2 about how to design rules.

Carefully Consider Issues of Equity and Home and Personal Circumstances When Designing Rules

It is important to carefully consider the ramifications of certain rules in the virtual environment. Because rules form the basis of corrective consequences—if a rule is violated, a corrective consequence is imposed—you must carefully consider whether each rule is reasonable and just in the virtual environment. You might feel that some rules help you run your classroom effectively, but you must also recognize that the rules are being imposed in students' home settings and so are different than rules applied in a physical classroom. Some rules can be thought of as "implicit shaming policies" that punish students because they don't take into account differing levels of access to resources or home circumstances (DuBose & Gorski, 2020). Even a rule as simple as "Arrive on time" could punish a student whose parent has to use a shared device for work purposes, thus making the student late to your class. Policies that implicitly shame students can create more distance between students and their teacher as the student feels unsupported and punished for being unable to meet expectations due to circumstances beyond their control. Before using rules in your virtual classroom, share them with your principal and a few teaching colleagues and students, and discuss whether they are equitable, have any unforeseen negative consequences, or raise other concerns.

Diversity, Equity, Inclusion, and Access

Carefully consider ramifications of each of your rules in the virtual environment. Rules imposed in students' homes need to be carefully vetted from an equity and access perspective so that students are not penalized for circumstances that are beyond their control or when rules are in conflict with other rules that may be in place in the student's home setting.

One rule that you should be cautious in implementing or avoid altogether is requiring students to keep their cameras on during synchronous learning sessions. Many teachers like to include such a rule because they believe it helps them connect with their students and monitor engagement. However, rules regarding cameras on are problematic for numerous reasons. Many students have home environments they are embarrassed for others to see, or they may fear something like a parent or other person in their home appearing in the background looking unkempt, not fully dressed, or under the influence of alcohol or drugs. While teaching students to use a virtual background or hang a sheet behind their workspace can alleviate these concerns for some students, others will still be highly anxious or even avoid coming to class if they are required to keep their camera on. Some students may feel highly uncomfortable about their own image being viewed on the screen. For example, a student who has an eating disorder may be triggered when viewing their own image for hours on end, or a student who has struggled with cyberbullying may be concerned that peers will take a screenshot or video of them and use it to further bullying behaviors. Students who have limited bandwidth may find that turning their camera off allows them to participate more fully because the session doesn't freeze. Furthermore, simply because a student has their camera on does not mean they are getting a meaningful connection with the teacher or engaging in instruction.

Instead of requiring that cameras remain on, consider strongly recommending that they do and provide rationale for why it is beneficial (e.g., "It helps us build community when we can see others' faces," "It lets me see when you all look confused or are starting to fade so I can modify my instruction!" etc.). Let students know that you understand there may be times when they are unable to have their cameras on, and that if they are unable to have them on for a period of time, you would like them to speak with you about why.

Provide instruction in how to use features of the synchronous platform that can provide workarounds for students who do not want others to see their background or who do not like seeing their own image. For example, provide mini lessons on how to use a virtual background feature and how to turn off self-view in a student's settings.

If a student regularly requests to have their camera off during the group session and you hope to connect with more than a blank screen, consider the following options:

- Ask the student to select a photo of themselves or their favorite activity that they can use as their screen image.
- Let the student know that you will be closely monitoring their active engagement since you can't see if they look like they're paying attention. For example, each time students are directed to type a response into the chat box, mark a tally when you see the student's response. Calculate the student's rate of participation and ensure that the student is actively participating throughout instruction.
- See if you can schedule several meetings to connect individually with the student for a few minutes and have them turn their camera on. This can occur during synchronous class time by joining a breakout room with the student, or by scheduling a separate meeting with the student—during office hours, for example.

If you plan to include a rule about arriving on time, needing certain materials, or attending each day a student is not seriously ill, ensure that you include procedures for students and families to communicate why a student cannot meet that expectation because of family circumstances or technology problems. For example, tell students and parents something like, "If your student cannot meet this rule on a given day because a family member needs to use the computer for a meeting or similar circumstances, please email me with information about why the student was late or absent that day. You can also reach me by phone or leave a message at 555-1212." Also use strategies such as needs assessments (e.g., surveying or interviewing students or parents) at the beginning of the year to determine what students may require to be able to engage productively in your classroom. When possible, help facilitate access by connecting the student and family to resources in the district or community. When it is not possible to increase access, consider how to adapt learning materials, activities, or expectations to ensure that all students are able to learn within the constraints of their circumstances.

Rules regarding eating during class and expected clothing should be discussed with your principal. Some teachers find it perfectly acceptable for students to eat during class if needed, while others find this highly distracting. Some teachers are OK with students wearing pajamas as long as they don't have profanity, while others prefer that their students dress according to a certain dress code. However, more restrictive rules can become unreasonable and seem aimed to force compliance—e.g., it is probably not justifiable to require students to wear shoes during a virtual math class! Because students are engaging in learning in their home settings, restrictive rules regarding eating or dress code should be approached with caution and consideration about students' home circumstances.

Post Rules and Provide Them to Students

Just as posting rules serves as a visual reminder of your expectations in a physical class setting, it can create a similar sense of importance in the virtual class. See recommendations for visually posting Guidelines for Success in the previous section and use these ideas to determine how you will visually post and communicate your classroom rules to students and families.

UPDATE YOUR CLASSROOM MANAGEMENT PLAN

ITEM 2: CLASSROOM RULES

List 3–6 classroom rules. Double-check that each rule:

- Is stated positively.
- Refers to specific, observable behaviors.
- Is applicable throughout the entire class period (is never negated).
- Is appropriate given that students are working in their home settings.

Indicate where and how you will visually post the classroom rules in your virtual classroom and whether they will be periodically or continuously posted.

CHAPTER 2, TASK 3

Design a Positive Physical Space

Skip reading the referenced task and only read modified content introduced in this chapter. Most of the strategies in Chapter 2, Task 3 do not apply to the virtual setting. They relate to factors such as optimizing the classroom desk arrangement, making sure you have physical and visual access to the classroom, and whether and how to assign seats. Skip Chapter 2, Task 3, and read the suggestions below for how to design a positive physical space in your own virtual teaching environment and how to help students and families create a productive home learning environment.

A virtual classroom encompasses many different physical spaces where instruction and learning take place. There's the physical space from which you plan and deliver instruction. For some teachers, this means delivering instruction from a physical classroom, while for others it may mean working from home or another designated office space. There's also the physical space from which each of your students participates in your class. For some students, this means working in a living or dining room, for others in their bedroom, and for some students in a community center with access to the Internet.

Having an optimal workspace where you are teaching can help increase your effectiveness and job satisfaction while teaching in a virtual model. Helping students and families to optimize the environment where students will be working at home can increase their productivity and attention, reduce distractions and barriers to learning, and increase their motivation to participate. However, because many recommendations about designing an optimal work environment hinge on access to resources and relate to home circumstances, the suggestions in this section are designed to guide your thinking about how to do the best with what you have. The general rule when it comes to designing physical space is to change what you can and make the best out of what you cannot change. This is especially important when it comes to communicating about recommendations for students' working environments at home. It is perfectly acceptable to provide ideas about how students and families can create an optimal working environment; however, be careful not to require or in any way shame students who are unable to change any of these conditions within their home.

Locus of Control

The general rule when designing physical space (for your own workspace and making recommendations for students' workspaces) is to do the best with what you have. Make sure to communicate this message to families when discussing recommendations for the home work environment.

Designing an Optimum Teacher Workspace

To increase comfort and productivity within your own physical workspace, use the Teacher Workspace Self-Assessment Checklist, Reproducible 11.2, to identify optimal conditions for your own environment. See recommendations and considerations below for each item on the checklist.

A. DESIGNATED WORKSPACE

A designated workspace helps you get into the mindset of teaching and prepares you for the time you will spend with your students. It also allows you to distinguish between work and family time, which is hard to differentiate when working from home. As much as possible, your designated workspace should be free of distractions, quiet, and set up appropriately so you can teach your class. A designated space could be a desk in an office or bedroom, an area partitioned off by curtains in a shared living space, or even a converted garage or attic space. When possible, try to designate a space that will not be used for other activities throughout the day so that you can keep the space organized for class activities.

B. CAMERA

The placement of your camera is extremely important. This is how students see you and is the first point of access to the content. Position your primary monitor at eye level. If your monitor is below eye level, you may experience neck strain after several hours of teaching. Boxes or books are inexpensive ways to raise your monitor, while desks that can convert to a raised or standing position provide another option. The camera should face you directly as this gives students a better viewpoint of you (they don't have to stare up your nostrils throughout class!).

Reproducible 11.2 *Teacher Workspace Self-Assessment Checklist*

Teacher Workspace Self-Assessment Checklist — CHAMPS

	Yes	No
A. Do you have a designated workspace? If no:	☐ Yes	☐ No
B. Is your camera at eye level? If no:	☐ Yes	☐ No
C. Can you see your students? If no:	☐ Yes	☐ No
D. Is lighting adequate for students to see you? If no:	☐ Yes	☐ No
E. Is sound conducive to virtual teaching? If no:	☐ Yes	☐ No
F. Is your workspace comfortable? If no:	☐ Yes	☐ No
G. Is your workspace as free from distractions as possible? If no:	☐ Yes	☐ No
For example: • If working from home, is your teaching schedule posted for family members? If no:	☐ Yes	☐ No
• Do you have a Do Not Disturb sign or other way of communicating to family members that you are engaged in teaching activities in your workspace? If no:	☐ Yes	☐ No
H. Do you have materials nearby (e.g., power cord, pens, paper, whiteboard, marker, eraser, sticky notes)? If no:	☐ Yes	☐ No
I. Does your school or home have adequate bandwidth to ensure a reliable and stable internet connection while teaching classes?	☐ Yes	☐ No

© 2021 Ancora Publishing — REPRODUCIBLE 11.2

C. COMPUTER SETUP

Not only is it important for the students to see you, but it is equally important for you to see all of your students. Online teaching may limit how many students you see on your screen, and the number may be even more limited when you share your screen. If you have access to a secondary monitor or can find a way to acquire one for free or with minimal expense, consider using one so you can easily see your students, your course materials, and the chat box. If you are unable to acquire an inexpensive secondary monitor, spend some time experimenting with the settings on your virtual learning platform to see if there are ways to optimize the space on your screen. For example, some platforms allow you to drag and resize your shared screen or classroom gallery view of your students. If you are less familiar with how to customize the view and other features of the platform, connect with others in your district who have experience with the platform, or watch video tutorials online.

D. LIGHTING

Even with your camera set up properly with optimal angles, too much or too little lighting can interfere with your students' ability to view you on their screens. Test out your lighting before class begins. If possible, choose a designated workspace that has window lighting and be sure that there isn't too much light when you are teaching. It is best to have the window to one side of your workstation. Try to avoid having a window behind you—your camera will adjust to the bright light and you will appear as a silhouette. A window directly in front of you can be so bright that you can't adequately see your own screen, and a window directly behind you can cause a reflection off your screen that can damage your eyes.

If your workspace doesn't have a window, consider placing a desk lamp to the side of your computer to light yourself. Inexpensive and adjustable LED desk lamps can be easily adjusted to create nice light to illuminate you for your students. A light 30° to 45° off center will create the most flattering light while not blinding you while you are trying to teach.

E. SOUND

Make sure that you can hear your students and that they can hear you. As much as possible ensure that your workspace does not have loud sounds that will distract from the lesson. If your workspace is facing the front lawn, which gets mowed every week at the same time as your lesson, consider whether you can use a different location as your designated workspace. If possible, headphones with a built-in microphone and noise cancellation features can help reduce background noise. Corded headphones/microphone headsets can be less expensive than wireless, and they don't run out of battery life.

F. COMFORTABLE WORKSPACE

You may be teaching for many hours back to back with minimal opportunities to stretch or take a break. You will need to have a comfortable workspace. Consider whether you will be more comfortable sitting or standing while teaching, or being able to switch between the two. Whether you choose to sit at a table or desk or stand at a counter or with a raised computer, the following considerations will apply.

- Try to have your keyboard at a height where your arms are at 90° while typing. If you have elevated your laptop, consider using a secondary keyboard and mouse. If you are seated, try to use a chair and desk or table that position your arms at 90° while typing.
- If you are sitting, choose a chair that allows your feet to touch the ground. If your feet do not touch the ground, use a foot rest or a stack of books so your knees bend at a 90° angle. Your chair should allow you to sit upright without slouching. Consider adding a lumbar pillow for additional support.
- If you are standing, use cushioned shoes or inserts, or see if you can access an anti-fatigue mat like those commonly used in work environments where people stand for long periods of time.

G. DISTRACTION-FREE ENVIRONMENT

A distraction-free environment is important not only for your students but for you as well. While this is not always possible, especially if you are teaching from your home environment (and even more so if there are kids in that home environment!), consider ways to minimize distractions and interruptions as much as possible.

Make sure others in your home or work environment know when you are teaching (synchronous classes and recording asynchronous lesson content) and when you are available. If you are working from home, set up a schedule, share it with your family, and post it so they can refer back to it. When you are teaching a lesson, consider posting a Do Not Disturb sign or other visual (e.g., "Teaching! Get me in an emergency. Otherwise ask Dad!"). Include a time when you will be available along with the name of someone family members can get help from while you are working. A sign that indicates when you are actively engaged in instruction can also be beneficial if you are teaching in a classroom. The sign can help ensure that a colleague does not inadvertently interrupt you when you are 20 minutes into a video lesson.

In your home workspace, consider whether other ground rules would help you teach more effectively. For example, can you specify a maximum allowable volume on the television while you are teaching or recording class videos? Do you expect your children to complete certain chores or classwork while you are engaged in teaching? Do you need to clarify that people should not remove the pens or other materials you have placed in your workspace? Would you prefer that roommates or household members avoid flushing the toilet in the bathroom next to your teaching space and instead use one in another part of the house? Consider which STOIC variables can be applied to establish effective habits and routines with your children and others in your household while you are engaged in teaching activities.

H. MATERIALS

Make sure that you have all of the office materials you will need within reach—for example, your computer charger, a whiteboard and whiteboard pens, eraser, sticky notes, pens, pencils, paper, etc. As much as possible, keep materials that you will need for each class session readily available in your workspace so that you do not have to hunt for them before a class begins.

You may also want to consider other materials that will enhance your lesson, such as a document camera that can interface with your computer. If you teach multiple different class sessions that all have different logins, keep a printed sheet with login information at your workspace as well as a digital copy that is easily accessible on your computer.

I. INTERNET CONNECTION

Anticipate your home or school's Internet usage. In most cases, home Internet isn't as robust as office networks, so you may have to upgrade or troubleshoot how to keep a stable connection while teaching. For example, if all of your family members are streaming movies and playing games, you might experience bandwidth issues. Set expectations for limiting Internet use that will cause your connection to drop or slow down while you are teaching. In schools, if you find you are struggling to maintain a stable connection, communicate with your administrator and school or district technology specialists to discuss options.

Help Students and Families Create Positive Routines and a Designated Workspace at Home

To help your students optimize their work environment at home, you can provide information to families and discuss with students the importance of establishing routines and a dedicated workspace at home. However, be very mindful and considerate of the fact that this might look very different in each of your students' homes. Be careful not to convey that your recommendations are requirements or that there is only one way to implement these ideas. Also be careful to provide a range of strategies that can be implemented with little or no cost rather than focusing on solutions that require families to buy equipment, furniture, or technology that may be outside their reach. Focus on the overarching goals of a good workspace (e.g., is relatively quiet, minimizes distractions, keeps classroom materials that have been provided organized, and helps you focus on learning).

Diversity, Equity, Inclusion, and Access

Rather than indicating there is only one "best" way for families to set up a student's work environment at home, focus on communicating the overarching goals of a productive work space.

Discuss ways to develop routines to help students show up prepared for learning. For example, some students may benefit from a posted schedule of their daily activities in their workspace, as shown in Figure 11.1. Many students may benefit from the self-reinforcement of checking off the activities as they complete them (e.g., if using a laminated schedule sheet and erasable marker) or using something like a paper clip that they move for each time period throughout the day. This can help students have a mental map of their day so they can remain focused and feel a sense of accomplishment as they complete their daily schedule.

Figure 11.1 *Sample Daily Schedules for an Elementary School and a Middle School*

▪ Elementary School Schedule
Ellie, Monday

8:00	Breakfast
8:30–9:15	Reading (live session)
9:15–9:35	PE (independent video session)
9:35–10:00	Recess (play time)
10:00–10:45	Math (live session)
10:45–11:45	Science and health (independent work)
11:45–12:45	Lunch/Recess
12:45–1:45	Continue completing any unfinished work/reading on own

▪ Middle School Schedule
Jonah, Monday

7:30	Breakfast
8:00–8:50	Math (live session)
9:00–9:50	Science (live session)
9:50–10:20	Break
10:20–11:00	Work on Independent/Homework
11:00–11:50	Social Studies (live session)
11:50–1:00	Lunch/Break
1:00–1:50	Spanish (live session)
2:00–2:50	English Literature (live session)
2:50–3:30	Break
3:30–5:00	Any remaining work

For students who struggle with time management or organization, you may find it helps to encourage students' parents or the students themselves to set a recurring alarm on their phone or other devices to go off 5 to 10 minutes before they are supposed to attend any synchronous class sessions. Encourage parents to teach their children that as soon as the alarm goes off, they should begin preparing for their class session. This can help them arrive on time and ready to learn. Also consider designing a checklist of the actions and items students will need to prepare before class begins. List any materials that students will require on a regular basis, such as their computer or tablet and charger, a pencil and paper, class notes, and class text. See Figure 11.2 for a sample Before-Class Checklist.

Figure 11.2 *Sample Before-Class Checklist*

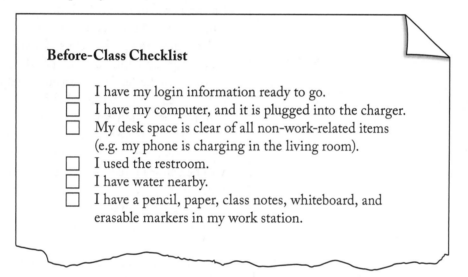

Before-Class Checklist

- ☐ I have my login information ready to go.
- ☐ I have my computer, and it is plugged into the charger.
- ☐ My desk space is clear of all non-work-related items (e.g. my phone is charging in the living room).
- ☐ I used the restroom.
- ☐ I have water nearby.
- ☐ I have a pencil, paper, class notes, whiteboard, and erasable markers in my work station.

While such a checklist may seem somewhat elementary for middle school students, it can help some students learn organizational skills necessary for success. Students who frequently have to leave the class session to search for a charger or gather needed materials may need help learning routines and strategies for self-management when instruction occurs in a student's home environment.

When discussing possibilities for creating an optimal workspace with students and families, consider the ideas in the Student Workspace Self-Assessment Checklist, Reproducible 11.3, and determine which recommendations for each element might be helpful. Note that many of the elements on the student checklist are similar to those in the teacher checklist, but the language of the recommendations for each item on the checklist has been slightly modified to give you more student- and parent-friendly descriptions. Remember that your students may have differing levels of access to material resources, quality Internet, and parent supervision at home. Access to computers and the Internet is not distributed equally, and some families cannot afford traditional learning resources (e.g., pencils, paper, art supplies, books). Unless your school is able to provide them, students will not have access, so expectations will need to be adjusted. Provide ideas for setting up the home learning environment with these factors in mind.

Diversity, Equity, Inclusion, and Access

Remember that students will have differing levels of access to material resources, quality Internet, and parent supervision. Provide ideas for setting up the home environment with this consideration in mind.

Reproducible 11.3 *Student Workspace Self-Assessment Checklist*

Student Workspace
Self-Assessment Checklist

CHAMPS

A. Is there a regular workspace with a desk or table? Is your workspace as free from distractions as possible? (TV is off, other electronic devices are put away, the view around your workspace is limited so you can focus on class, etc.)
   ☐ Yes ☐ No
   If no:

B. Do you have a comfortable chair?
   ☐ Yes ☐ No
   If no:

C. Is your camera at eye level?
   ☐ Yes ☐ No
   If no:

D. Is lighting adequate for the teacher and your peers to see you?
   ☐ Yes ☐ No
   If no:

E. Is your workspace quiet enough for virtual learning? Or do you have headphones and a microphone?
   ☐ Yes ☐ No
   If no:

F. Is your class schedule posted for other family members?
   ☐ Yes ☐ No
   If no:

   Do family members know not to disturb you during your class time as much as possible?
   ☐ Yes ☐ No
   If no:

G. Do you have materials ready (e.g., power cord, pens, paper, notebook)?
   ☐ Yes ☐ No
   If no:

© 2021 Ancora Publishing   REPRODUCIBLE 11.3

A. REGULAR WORKSPACE

Having a regular workspace is important for students who are working from home and attending class sessions online. This helps them get into a mindset for learning and helps separate school and family time, which can be difficult when school is occurring from home.

While students may prefer to sit on a couch or bed, discourage them from using these as workspaces for class time, if possible, and even during their independent work times. These spaces tend to not be conducive to learning and may have lots of distractions. Encourage students to sit at a desk, kitchen counter, or table. Hard surfaces help students keep computer screens from moving around too much and can improve their ability to complete written assignments and keep class materials organized. If students will be using a tablet or phone for class, provide ideas or create and send home materials for students to make a cardboard stand to prop their device up throughout class. This will ensure that the student will not need to hold the device throughout class. Search "DIY cardboard tablet/phone stand" on your web browser for multiple ways to create a simple stand.

As much as possible, the student's workspace should be free from distractions, relatively quiet, and set up with what the student needs to attend and engage productively in class. Encourage students to turn off TVs and other devices, or make sure their workspace is away from these potential distractions. If a student's home does not have a location that can be set up specifically for student learning, consider ways to make a dining table or counter a space where the student can focus and be comfortable throughout class time. For example, if multiple siblings will be working at a dining room table, consider creating cardboard dividers or "cubby" spaces that create an illusion of privacy and prevent distractions. One school in Oregon shared that when teachers were able to send home trifold science board-type stations to students, the stations greatly improved student focus during class sessions (thank you to Jodi Ketchum and Jennifer Vaught for sharing this idea).

If a student does not have a suitable background, teach them to use a virtual background or position their work station so that there is a wall directly behind them. Virtual backgrounds are available in Zoom and Microsoft Teams. Ask that students choose a relatively simple background that is not distracting, or provide students with a few approved school-appropriate options to select from.

B. COMFORTABLE CHAIR

Encourage students to use a chair that allows their feet to touch the ground. If their feet do not touch the ground, suggest they use a footrest or a stack of books so their knees bend at a 90° angle. The chair should allow students to sit upright without slouching. Provide ideas for adding a lumbar pillow or rolled-up sweatshirt for additional support. Students who get fidgety during hours of work on the computer may prefer to stand, so provide ideas for ways to prop their computer up while they stand.

C. CAMERA

Teach students to position their device or web camera at eye level so the teacher can see the student's entire face. The teacher should be centered on the screen and take up most of the screen. If the student's monitor is below eye level, they will experience neck strain and may not watch the screen. Boxes or books are inexpensive ways to raise a monitor.

D. LIGHTING

Even when cameras are set up correctly, too much or too little lighting can interfere with the student's learning. Have students test out the lighting in their workspace before class begins. If possible, students should work in a space with window lighting, but be sure that there isn't too much light. It is best to have the window to one side of the computer. Students should avoid sitting with a window right in front of or right behind them so they don't appear as a silhouette or get blinded from glare off their screen. If the workspace doesn't have a window, place a desk lamp to the side of the computer. A light 30° to 45° off center will create the most flattering light without blinding the student.

E. SOUND

The teacher should be able to hear the student and the student be able to hear the teacher. Try to ensure the workspace is quiet enough that the student feels comfortable unmuting and participating in discussions or asking questions. Loud sounds will be audible to other students on the video platform and will distract them from the lesson. To prevent this, one possibility is for students to use headphones with a built-in microphone. This allows the teacher to hear students and minimizes outside noise. It also reduces reverberation. Corded headphones are inexpensive and can help with noise issues. If students are unable to purchase these materials, schools should consider what options they have for creating an audio headset lending program or seeking donations from community members or organizations so that all students have their own headset or earbuds with built-in microphone.

F. POSTED SCHEDULE

Posting a schedule in the student's workspace as well as in a family common area or on the door to the workspace can help everyone know when the student is supposed to be focused on class work or a live class session. Families can set up their own expectations for how family members such as siblings and parents can help the student remain focused on class. For example, they might discuss expectations for noise level, disruptive activities to avoid, and how to avoid interrupting the student unless it is absolutely necessary. Some families will use something like a Do Not Disturb or Quiet, I'm in Class sign when the student is in class. While some students may need to help facilitate schooling for younger siblings and interruptions inevitably occur, establishing ground rules can help students remain as focused and engaged as possible.

The school may also need to consider accommodations for students who must manage competing responsibilities, such as allowing them to view a recorded video of the class session and submitting a participation record such as class notes.

G. MATERIALS

> *Instructional time is limited, so students need to be well prepared for class.*

Instructional time is limited, so students need to be well prepared for class. Encourage families to stock the workspace with anything their student may need—paper, pencils, pens, erasers, etc. If the student does not have access to required supplies in the home, schools should consider how to assess students' needs and provide necessary materials. If the school is unable to provide need materials to students, classroom activities and expectations will need to be modified to ensure that a student does not fall behind because of limited resources in the home.

CHAPTER 2, TASK 4
Select an Attention Signal

Read the task on pages 75–76 and implement with the following adaptations and considerations.

In the virtual setting, you need an attention signal to signal the beginning of class time after students appear in the platform and to prompt students to move between whole group learning, cooperative group or partner work in breakout rooms, and independent work periods. For example, if students are engaged in a 5-minute independent activity while in the whole group virtual meeting, consider how you plan to draw their attention back at the conclusion of the 5 minutes. Identify and consistently use an attention signal such as:

- A verbal signal such as "Class, let's come back together" or "Attention everyone."
- An auditory sound such as ringing a bell or playing three to five tones on a xylophone (this can be done with physical instruments in your workspace or a recorded sound on your computer).

In a physical classroom setting, an effective attention signal is auditory and visual, portable, and may have a participatory element so students can demonstrate they are paying attention. Consider which of these elements are needed in your virtual class. For some classes, just an auditory signal may be sufficient. In others, additional elements may help students meet your expectations. Ask yourself if a visual component such as raising your hand in the air or a 1–2 second video (e.g., fireworks or confetti) would help draw your students' attention to their screens. If you will be teaching from different parts of your physical classroom or workspace, or may be a few feet away from your computer keyboard while you are demonstrating something, does your signal need to be portable? Would a participation component (e.g., having students raise their hand in the air) help you monitor that they are engaged and ready to move forward?

If you select a signal and find that you are struggling to gain students' attention, consider which elements might help. As with in-person instruction, you will need to teach your signal and your expectations for how students will demonstrate appropriate participation in response to the signal. Develop a plan for providing both positive and corrective feedback to students regarding their response to the signal.

In addition to an effective signal, use a countdown timer for cooperative activities and independent activities to help students monitor their time. While you might use an egg timer or timer on your own device, having something that students can see on their screens is even better. Free timer apps can be found with a web search, and some computers or virtual platforms may have this feature already built in. It is also helpful to give periodic prompts about time (e.g., while students are in breakout rooms for a 20-minute activity, broadcast a message when students have 10 minutes of work time left, 5 minutes, and 2 minutes). Be sure to provide a warning when students have 1–2 minutes left before the conclusion of an activity or when getting ready to return from a break.

UPDATE YOUR CLASSROOM MANAGEMENT PLAN

ITEM 3: ATTENTION SIGNAL

Describe the attention signal you will use in your classroom. Double-check that it takes no more than 5 seconds to gain all students' attention. Additional features to consider are whether the signal:

- Can be given from any location
- Has an auditory and visual component
- Involves active participation from the students to ensure they are all paying attention (optional but recommended for classes requiring high support)

CHAPTER 2, TASK 5

Design Effective Beginning and Ending Routines

Read the task on pages 77–88 and implement with the following adaptations and considerations.

As with in-person instruction, the way that a teacher structures beginning and ending routines in the class can make a huge difference. In the example scenario below, you can see how these activities set the tone for the rest of the class time, and they can be highly efficient and engaging or highly inefficient and lead to students checking out. Teacher A put procedures in place to ensure an efficient and positive start to class. He pretaught expectations to students and designed beginning routines to ensure he is not wasting students' time or valuable instructional minutes.

 CASE STUDY

Consider the following two scenarios:

Teacher A logs into the virtual class session approximately 10 minutes before class time. He has a waiting room set up in the virtual platform so he can take care of last-minute organizational details and check in with individual students. Today, he notices that one student who has been absent for a few days has joined the meeting early. He lets the student into the main session so he can say how glad he is to see the student in class and ask if the student needs any help or clarification about what she missed. Three minutes before the start of class time, Teacher A lets the rest of the students into the main session and warmly greets each student as they come into view. On the screen, students see a slide with their starting bell work activity, a timer showing how long they have to complete the assignment before instruction begins, and a list of the materials they will need for the session. The teacher plays upbeat music in the background. At the official start of class time, the teacher begins entering attendance while students continue their bell work. Within 1 minute of the start of class, the teacher uses his attention signal to secure the attention of the class and start teaching. A few students enter class late, and the teacher welcomes them to class in the chat box while continuing instruction and directing them to follow preestablished procedures for entering class late. The students know these procedures, which are designed to ensure that the teacher can keep accurate records and that the class is not disrupted. He quickly continues with instruction after welcoming the students.

Teacher B typically logs into the class meeting at the posted class time or up to 3 minutes late. As students enter the virtual platform, the teacher pulls up slides and organizes class materials, so students sit staring at the screen or looking at their phones until she is ready. The teacher begins marking student attendance while the students wait. When the teacher begins instruction, she lets students know they will need their textbooks. Numerous students leave their screens so they can search for the books elsewhere in their house. When they return, the teacher prompts them to be more responsible in the future. Five minutes after the posted start of class time, the teacher begins teaching. Across the next 10 minutes, three students arrive late. Each time, the teacher stops teaching to find out if the students have a reasonable excuse for being late and to update the attendance record. The other students stare at the screens, listening to the exchange between the teacher and the tardy students. Some students send text messages or do other non-class-related activities until the teacher is ready to continue.

The following provide specific recommendations for establishing effective beginning and ending routines in the virtual classroom. Use these in conjunction with the recommendations in Chapter 2, Task 5.

Entering the Virtual Space

Establish a regular routine for when students enter the virtual class session. The goal is for students to feel welcome, make sure they have needed materials, and immediately begin working on a productive task. Consider the following ideas for your entry routine:

- When possible, use a waiting room for before class time so you can connect with individual students. Randomly select a student each session, or systematically work through your class to ensure you connect with each student multiple times throughout the term or semester.
- Greet each student by name and offer other forms of noncontingent attention as time allows (e.g., ask about outside-of-school activities or interests, inquire about family members). If a student enters late to the virtual platform, still make an effort to offer a warm greeting so they know you are glad they came to class. However, be careful not to take too much time from the class or call too much attention to the student. "Antonio, great to see you today" or a simple message in the chat box is sufficient.
- Use music to provide a comfortable background while students enter and are engaged in an independent starting activity. Look for energizing, upbeat music, or music that creates a calming atmosphere. Of course, music will need to be school appropriate, so look for acoustic covers of popular songs or search for school-appropriate renditions. Periodically ask students to suggest opening music they would like you to play.
- Include an opening slide or other visual that displays exactly which materials students will need for the day. Teach students to use the minute or two before class starts to double-check that they have all needed materials and gather anything they need before the "bell" rings.
- Because digital assignments can be problematic for all students to access (e.g., some students can open a PDF file from the chat box, but others may need to access the content via an email or on a shared drive), make an effort to provide any necessary assignments and digital materials in a variety of ways (e.g., email, chat box, class website, shared drive). When possible, share materials at least 10 minutes before class starts and again as needed during instruction to ensure that all students have needed reading materials or other digital assignments for class.
- On the first slide or visual, provide an opening task for students to work on that is instructionally relevant and takes no more than 2 to 5 minutes. This gives students something to do while they wait for class to start and for you to take care of attendance. Use a countdown timer or other visual to indicate the time when they will be expected to be finished with the bell work/starter activity.

A special thank you to Ms. Jeffries in Alief ISD (Texas) for providing many of the above suggestions for creating a positive and productive entry routine in the virtual classroom.

Conducting Opening Business and Activities

Opening activities should be efficient and orderly, and keep students instructionally engaged while you take attendance. Announcements and housekeeping tasks should also be efficient and not take too much time. Consider the following ideas for conducting opening business and activities in the virtual space:

- Use your attention signal right at the start of class time. This will serve like the bell at the beginning of a classroom in a physical building, signaling to students that class has officially started.
- Take attendance immediately or take a screenshot so you have a record of which students arrived right on time (the next section provides suggestions for taking attendance and monitoring which students come and go throughout class).
- Provide positive feedback to students who are working on the entry task or who have already submitted their completed entry task. Also provide positive feedback to students who arrived on time and/or with necessary materials.
- When possible, send a brief email or text message or make a quick phone call (while muted for the rest of the class) to students who haven't arrived in class and haven't sent a reason for their absence. Let them know that you hope you will see them in class today and will follow up later if you have not heard from them.
- When you are ready to begin, display and briefly discuss your agenda and any housekeeping items for the day.
- Provide information about any necessary technology considerations or troubleshooting suggestions that apply to the class, but avoid spending too much time troubleshooting with an individual student. When conversations about individual concerns take more than a minute and cause the rest of the class to sit and wait, it can lead to problems with boredom and disengagement. If the concern cannot be addressed in less than a minute, let the student know that you will work to help them as soon as possible once you get other students started on an independent or cooperative task and that they should sit tight for the time being. Another possibility is to have a student helper who is highly proficient with technology see if they can assist the other student in a breakout room or through the chat box while you resume teaching the rest of the class.

Taking Attendance and Monitoring Attendance Throughout Class

Attendance can be difficult to monitor on a virtual platform. It is easier for students to come and go than in a physical classroom. Without good procedures for monitoring attendance throughout class, some students will abuse this fact, leaving class early or dropping off for periods of time. Other students may drop in and out of sessions because of Internet connectivity issues. When a teacher has good attendance procedures that enable them to notice a student's sporadic attendance, the teacher may be better able to help the student troubleshoot or connect the student with resources in the school or district to address the concern.

We recommend that you take attendance several times during a virtual class session, using the suggestions that follow. Later in this chapter are suggestions for monitoring collected attendance data across time and using the data to inform your implementation of positive and corrective strategies to address class attendance and each student's individual attendance record.

Take attendance immediately at the beginning of class while students are working on their starting activity. Take attendance again at least one more time in the first half of the class session and again within the last 5 minutes of class. It may help to set a vibrating timer on your watch or phone to remind you to take attendance a few times during class, but avoid taking it at exactly the same times every day. Some students will figure out if attendance is taken according to a specific pattern.

Simple ways to take attendance on a virtual platform include:

- Use the screenshot feature on your computer to take a screenshot of the participant list. Usually the list is in alphabetical order, so you can quickly use it with your roll sheet to identify any students who were absent or missing for part of the class.
- Enlist a student helper whose job it is to take attendance and submit the list of present and absent students to you. Consider one at the beginning of class and a different student at the end of class.
- Use times when students are engaged in independent work or breakout rooms to compare students present with your class roster. Independent work times provide some of the best opportunities for taking attendance because you will not need to physically circulate around the classroom as you would in a traditional class setting.
- Use polls, chat box responses, or other active engagement tools to monitor which students are present and participating in class. For example, a poll that is not anonymous should provide you with a record of attendance because it will display each student's response. If you direct students to type a response into the chat box, you should have a record of each student in the chat. If you plan to use this method, make sure to let students know that you will be using their responses to monitor attendance. Students who choose not to participate in a chat or poll should be aware that it could cause them to be marked as absent.

Procedures for Responding to Students Who Enter Late and Exit Early

Offer a brief greeting whenever a student enters class, even if they are late. Be sure to avoid lecturing or expressing frustration if they enter late or drop out of the class and then return. While you will have procedures in place to address tardiness and in some cases corrective consequences will apply, it is important not to shame students or ignore them if they arrive late to the virtual environment. When students are working from home, entering late or exiting early may be due to circumstances beyond their control. Furthermore, if you ignore students who arrive late to make a point, it can imply that a student is not welcome and should have just skipped the whole class instead. Make sure your interactions emphasize that students are welcome in class and their attendance is appreciated: "Shai, it's nice to have you in class today.

We were just getting started discussing the reading from last night, and I look forward to hearing your thoughts. Once we get everyone started on the next task, you and I can touch base."

After you offer a brief greeting, ask the student to wait for further instruction or prompt the student to follow pretaught procedures for updating you about the cause of tardiness. Once other students are engaged in an independent or cooperative task, you can connect with the student through the chat box or in a private breakout room and catch the student up on any important information they missed. Also update your attendance record to reflect that the student is in class, and mark a tardy if the student did not have a legitimate excuse for being late.

Most schools do not have anything in their record-keeping that is similar to a tardy but indicates that a student left a virtual class session before the end of class. It would not be appropriate to mark the student fully absent if they were in fact present for part of the class period. However, it is also important that leaving early does not become a chronic problem simply because the attendance record-keeping system does not provide a clear way to monitor and identify when this occurs. Consider keeping your own record of students who leave class early or come in and out of synchronous sessions.

For students who exit early, the important thing is to ensure that they know you notice when it occurs and, if it occurs regularly, you will put corrective consequences or intervention procedures in place. Whenever a student leaves class early and does not return, check in with the student sometime after class (e.g., via email or a phone call) or in a brief private chat the following day. If tardiness, dropping in and out of the session, or leaving early becomes a chronic issue, plan to re-teach your attendance expectations and connect with the student's family to see if any causes or barriers need to be addressed to help the student. If there are no causes or barriers to attendance, implement corrective consequences as appropriate (see pp. 545–550 on corrective consequences in the virtual environment) and use strategies to motivate and encourage the student to come to class (see pp. 539-545 for procedures for motivating and engaging students).

Protocols for Students Returning After an Absence

As with in-person instruction, there are two goals for when students return from an absence from virtual learning:

1. Students are welcomed back to class.
2. Students can find out what they missed and get any necessary class materials without consuming too much of your time and energy.

If you notice that a student who has been absent is back in class, make sure to greet them by name and say something like, "Xena, we missed you the last few days. I hope everything is all right. It's great to have you back in class."

If you use a waiting-room feature and notice that the student has arrived a few minutes early, make an effort to let the student into the main session to chat with you briefly before you admit the other students. The purpose of this conversation is not to put the student on the spot or force an uncomfortable discussion about why the student was gone. It is simply to connect in a positive way with the student and let them know you are glad to have them in class.

If the student has problems with chronic absenteeism, a brief interaction before or after class is likely not the time to address these concerns. But it can provide a starting place for you to express caring for the student's well-being and concern about the absenteeism: "Liz, I've noticed that you've missed several days in the last month. I'm concerned that this could cause you to fall behind, and you are always so helpful to your peers when you are here. Let's set up a time to meet and talk about how I can support you to come to class every day. We can explore options together until we find a solution."

Consider ways to help students who have been absent find out what they missed and get any handouts or returned papers. One option is to use the chat box or a private breakout room to briefly explain any necessary details to the student; however, this requires that you can carve out the time immediately upon a student's return. Another possibility is to send an email update or message the student via your class platform to indicate what they missed and what they will need to do to catch up. A final option that could be used on its own for highly responsible groups of students or in combination with either of the previous two options is to update the class website or a shared drive with the latest class information to support students and families when students have been absent. This strategy can foster student independence and organization, but it may be too hands-off for students with limited maturity or organizational skills or who do not have lots of parental involvement in their virtual schooling.

Some teachers record synchronous class sessions and make them available for students who have been absent. This can be a great way to get students caught up with all relevant course material; however, it also carries some risks. Some students may decide that it's easier to view the video on their own time than to engage in the class session. Double-check with your principal if you plan to use this procedure and think through policies and contingency plans for encouraging students to attend synchronous class sessions in real time.

Procedures for End of the Class Period

In the virtual environment, the goal for the end of the class period is to ensure that students organize their materials and understand the expectations for any asynchronous work so they are prepared for the next class period. Procedures should also give you enough time to give students positive and corrective feedback.

Initially, schedule up to 10 minutes for closing tasks. Set a timer or assign a student the job of reminding you when the class is nearing the end of the period. Stop instruction or student work and briefly review the daily agenda while celebrating accomplishments and providing positive feedback. If students struggled with any expectations, provide brief corrective feedback about what should happen differently in the next class session. Make a note for yourself to plan extra time in the next class for re-teaching any expectations that were difficult for students.

In the chat box or on a slide, post any asynchronous work that students will be expected to complete outside of your class session. Review the work expectations and next steps, and provide time for questions. You may wish to check for understanding of the expectations using a poll, the chat box, or another form of participation (e.g., reaction feature on platform, indicate level of understanding using a gesture). Make sure to frequently offer assistance and extended support, such as offering to schedule one-on-one meetings or phone calls and reminding students about office hours if they are available.

Dismissing Students

Similar to the face-to-face classroom, teach students that they should leave when you dismiss them. Use a consistent signal or phrase to indicate the class session is over. Plan to remain in the session for a few minutes if possible to accommodate any needs or requests for individual support or just to connect with students who need a little noncontingent attention.

UPDATE YOUR CLASSROOM MANAGEMENT PLAN

ITEM 4: BEGINNING AND ENDING ROUTINES

Describe your beginning and ending routines. Double-check that your procedures are designed in a such a way that you increase the likelihood students meet the goal listed for each routine. Describe your classroom routines for:

- **How students will enter the virtual space.** *Goal:* Students feel welcome, check that they have needed materials, and start on a productive task.
- **How students will be instructionally engaged while you take attendance and conduct opening business.** *Goal 1:* Opening activities are efficient and orderly, and keep students instructionally engaged while you take attendance. *Goal 2:* Announcements and other housekeeping tasks do not take up too much time.
- **How you will take attendance at the beginning of class and during the virtual class session.** *Goal:* Procedures do not interrupt instruction and allow you to monitor student attendance throughout the class session.
- **Managing situations when students arrive late or leave class early.** *Goal:* Procedures for dealing with tardiness, students coming in and out of the meeting, and students leaving early are effective and do not cause a loss of instructional momentum.
- **When students return from an absence.** *Goal 1:* Students who have been absent are welcomed back to class. *Goal 2:* Students can find out what assignments they missed and get any handouts and returned papers without consuming much of your time and energy.
- **Wrapping up the end of day/class.** *Goal 1:* Students organize their materials and understand the expectations for any asynchronous work. *Goal 2:* Procedures provide you with enough time to give students both positive and corrective feedback.
- **Dismissal.** *Goal:* Students do not leave the classroom until you dismiss them.

CHAPTER 2, TASK 6

Design Procedures for Managing Common Transitions

Most strategies in Chapter 2, Task 6 are not applicable in the virtual setting because there are fewer transitions, and transitions may present fewer problems than when there are 20–35 students physically in a classroom. Consider the following situations to determine whether to read and how to apply the strategies in Chapter 2, Task 6.

Identify transitions that will occur during your virtual class. In some classes, you may not require transitions and can skip this task, or you may find that students are successful in engaging in transitions without too much direction. Other classes may require additional structure and clarity during transitions. Some examples of possible transitions in the virtual classroom include:

- Getting out a book and opening to a particular page
- Moving into and returning from breakout rooms
- Transitioning into and returning from independent work time
- Opening and logging into other applications while on the virtual class session
- Opening and dismissal routines

If your students would benefit from additional support and clarity of expectations when transitioning, read and apply the suggestions in Chapter 2, Task 6. Use Reproducible 11.4, CHAMPS Virtual Classroom Transition Worksheet, to clarify expectations such as whether students should be muted or unmuted during the transition and whether they should use the group chat for any reason. One important thing to clarify for A, Activity, is how long the transition should reasonably take if all students follow all other expectations.

Reproducible 11.4 *CHAMPS Virtual Classroom Transition Worksheet*

CHAMPS Virtual Classroom
Transition Worksheet

CHAMPS

TRANSITION _____

CONVERSATION
Can students use the microphone? ☐ muted ☐ unmuted
Can students use group chat during the transition?

HELP
How do students get questions answered? How do students get your attention?

If students have to wait for help, what should they do while they wait?

ACTIVITY
Explain the transition. What will be different afterward (e.g., change in the virtual format, use of different materials)?
What is the time criteria (how long should the transition take)?

MOVEMENT
Does the transition involve movement away from the virtual platform?
If yes, what kind of movement is allowed for the transition?

PARTICIPATION
What behaviors show that students are transitioning fully and responsibly?

What behaviors show that a student is not participating appropriately during the transition?

SUCCESS
Success comes from following the expectations.

REPRODUCIBLE 11.4

UPDATE YOUR CLASSROOM MANAGEMENT PLAN

ITEM 5: CHAMPS EXPECTATIONS FOR TRANSITIONS

- On your Classroom Management Plan, list the common transitions that occur in your virtual classroom (if there are any).
- Once you have completed CHAMPS Transition Worksheets (Reproducible 11.4) for each transition, attach them or include them in a binder with a paper record of your Classroom Management Plan, and/or include the filled-out digital versions in a file that contains your Classroom Management Plan.

CHAPTER 2, TASK 7

Prepare for Common Areas and Special Circumstances

Most strategies in Chapter 2, Task 7 are not applicable in the virtual setting. Skip to page 103 and read suggestions for preparing a plan for working with substitutes. Apply the suggestions in this section as appropriate.

CHAPTER 2, TASK 8

Establish and Maintain Family Contact

Read the task on pages 104–114 and implement with the following adaptations and considerations.

Establishing and maintaining productive family contacts are essential in any classroom environment. In the hybrid and virtual classroom, positive communication and collaboration with students' families take on special importance since the student will be learning from home. Virtual learning provides a unique opportunity to invite family members to partner even more deeply with the school in supporting their child's learning. Consider the strategies in Chapter 2, Task 8 for effective initial contact and productive ongoing communication. In this section, we expand on that content by discussing four opportunities for productive school/family partnerships:

1. Building mutual trust and accountability by providing more personalized, two-way communication between schools and families
2. Building each family's capacity and confidence to support their child's learning by modeling effective practices and sharing resources and tools

3. Focusing on learning by leveraging available resources from school and home and honoring the skills, beliefs, and background that families bring to the table
4. Engaging with the greater community to help meet the basic needs of families in ways that are compassionate and culturally responsive

Focus on Two-Way Communication

Two-way communication moves away from treating parents and families as passive receivers of information toward treating them as collaborative equals who can provide ideas, insights, and supports that can help students in their educational experience. In virtual learning environments, effective two-way communication can help build mutual trust and accountability between teachers and caregivers.

One of the first steps in fostering two-way communication is to find out from families their preferred method of communication and who you should engage with when seeking ideas or sharing information. How will you best communicate with and engage family members who will be supporting distance learning in the home, which may include parents, grandparents, extended family members, caregivers, and others? Recognize that some students will have a caregiver at home who can provide support for learning throughout the day, while other students will not have supervision or support while they are in classes or working on asynchronous work. In both cases, it is important to consider ways to communicate with and engage the student's family to support the student's learning experience.

Consider creating a spreadsheet for each of your classes. Include each student's name and the primary adult responsible for distance learning support. See Figure 11.3 for a sample communication spreadsheet.

Figure 11.3 *Sample Family Communication Spreadsheet*

Student	Distance Support Adult	Preferred Mode of Communication	Other Trusted School Contact
Raquel Baldwin	Macie Baldwin	Email	
Gregory Hernandez	Lydia Vaught	Email or text	
Charline Galarza	Edgar Galarza	Text	
Trang Sheehan	Hoa Sheehan	Email or phone	Eliza
Kevin Land	Jafari Land	Text	
Rosette Rau	Maryanne Rau	Phone	Principal Garcia

Use surveys, intake interviews, or other conversations with families to learn the best way to communicate with them. On your spreadsheet include any information you gather from families about their preferred mode of communication and the best time to engage them with questions, concerns, general information, or celebrations of success. As much as possible, try to use their preferred communication methods with your families. This may require that you send information out in a few different formats or use a more personalized form of communication; however, these efforts will go a long way in maintaining effective communication with each family.

Relational Trust

For each student, determine if the student and family have a positive, established relationship with any other staff members. If you have any difficulty connecting with particular families, it can be beneficial to work with another staff member who already holds the family's trust as you work to establish positive communication.

If the student and family have a positive, established relationship with an individual in the school other than you, the teacher, add this person's name to your spreadsheet. This might be a coach, specialist, counselor, mentor, or other teacher. See if you can enlist this person to be a part of communication efforts with the family, especially in situations where concerns must be discussed. If translation is required for communication, include on your spreadsheet information about who will assist with translation or how it will take place.

In addition to finding the best way to communicate with the family, make a plan for how you will frequently invite parents to bring questions and provide ideas and insights about their student's learning experience. Encourage joint decision-making by giving parents and students a voice in the learning process. On your spreadsheet, identify tools that you will put in place to learn about the family's hopes and concerns regarding their child's learning. For example, you might indicate that you will invite families to record video or audio, or send you a letter introducing their student and suggesting ways you might develop a positive connection or motivate the student. You might note that you will plan to hold Family Office Hours every other week where parents or other caregivers can join and ask you questions or discuss concerns. Some teachers may choose to use anonymous feedback surveys to solicit information throughout the term about how the design of their course is meeting students' learning needs and whether families have insights that might help their student better learn in the virtual environment. The important thing to remember is to be consciously inviting and to provide frequent reminders to families that you view them as important partners in the learning process.

Model Effective Practices and Share Resources and Tools

Modeling effective teaching practices and helping families build their knowledge base about how to support their student can go a long way when students are learning in the home setting. Consider ways to build each family's capacity and confidence to support their student's learning experience. Some possibilities for modeling and sharing resources include:

- Think out loud and describe what you are doing as you provide instruction. For example, if you are demonstrating how to fill out a graphic organizer, talk out loud about your thought processes: "Next I'm going to think about how to expand on my second topic. I'm going to look back at this section of the book to see which details I highlighted . . ." Modeling the learning process can benefit students and their family members.
- Help family members understand the *why* behind distance learning assignments and critical student behaviors like regular attendance and participation. Use short information videos, memos, and meetings or calls with families to provide information about why what their students are doing is important for short-term success in your course and for longer term success in school and beyond.
- Share the CHAMPS approach and how families can use CHAMPS to establish clear expectations for things like independent schoolwork, homework, and even

non-school-related activities like dining in a restaurant or riding in the car on a long road trip.

- Provide tips and information about organizational, technological, and social-emotional skills that may help students be successful. For example, you might record a video and send home a short letter providing information about how to help students establish productive daily routines for home learning. Or you could provide a short tutorial with strategies for relaxation and anxiety management. Some families might benefit from learning how to use goal-setting procedures, as described in Chapter 7, Task 2, with their student.

Periodically ask your families what they would like to learn and understand. Ask if they are looking for strategies to address any particular issues that you might help with. Consider including these strategies in your communications with families or pointing them to resources to address their concerns.

Leverage Available Resources in the Home

Focus on learning by leveraging available resources in the home setting and honoring the skills, beliefs, and background that families bring to the table. When possible, find ways to connect learning experiences to families' home lives, interests, and identities.

Identify interests, skills, and strengths that families have to offer. Just as every student has strengths that should be acknowledged and fostered, every family has strengths that can become a powerful point of connection to build on. While some families may be able to provide consistent supervision and have skills to help the student stay on track in their coursework, other families may have particular experiences from their background that connect to an element of the course and provide valuable insights. For example, you might share course topics with parents and invite them to take part in a class session that aligns with their work or area of interest. Seek ways to connect to families' beliefs, backgrounds, and cultural identities in ways that enhance engagement and connectivity. As you get to know your students and their families, consider ways to learn about these strengths, and when possible connect to them during your course or in your communication with them.

Connect Communities

Engaging with the greater community to help meet the basic needs of families in ways that are compassionate and culturally responsive is not the sole responsibility of a classroom teacher. However, you can play an important role in opening lines of communication to identify areas of need and begin creating points of connection. Work to learn about the supports that are available within your school, district, and broader community. If your school or district has a coordinator for school and community partnerships, reach out to learn about their role and recommended practices for connecting families and the community. If this is not a defined role, consider whether a group of educators in your school would be interested in creating a

Diversity, Equity, Inclusion, and Access

When students are struggling due to factors like food insecurity, housing insecurity, inadequate medical care, or lack of access to reliable technology or other materials, you can play an important role in opening lines of communication and creating points of connection between families and broader school and community supports.

task force to research community organizations, leaders, businesses, and so on to enlist as partners with the school.

Carefully consider how to connect with families about any critical needs they may need support with before their student can effectively engage in learning from home. On your spreadsheet, list information about when and how you will reach out to families about these needs. At the beginning of the year and at periodic points during the year, make an effort to communicate that families can (and should) connect with you or someone else from the school (e.g., administrator, counselor, school psychologist, family engagement coordinator) if the student does not have access to food, clothing, housing, supervision, medical services, reliable technology or Internet, or school supplies. The family should be aware that they can (and should) communicate if they have concerns about the student's social-emotional well-being; issues of depression, anxiety, or substance abuse; or development of social skills such as anger management, conflict resolution, and social entry skills.

While you may not always be the primary person who will work with the family to address these areas of need, you can open lines of communication to connect the family with available supports. Use needs assessments and conversations with families to find out any physical or emotional support needs that the family may need help with. Even if families do not express needs directly to you, be consciously inviting in letting them know that the school would like to partner with them to address any areas of need that may make it difficult for the student to learn and grow. In your communication with families, frequently advertise contact information for a variety of different personnel in the school and district who can work with families to meet these needs.

UPDATE YOUR CLASSROOM MANAGEMENT PLAN

ITEM 6: FAMILY CONTACT

Describe your family contact plan, including:

- Procedures for making initial contact with families at the beginning of the school year
- Procedures for maintaining contact with families throughout the year
- Procedures for:
  - Focusing on two-way communication
  - Modeling effective practices and sharing resources and tools
  - Leveraging available resources from school and home
  - Connecting the family to community supports

CHAPTER 3, TASK 1

Establish an Efficient Daily Schedule

Read the task on pages 116–121 and implement with the following adaptations and considerations.

Many aspects of students' daily schedules in virtual or hybrid-learning models are not under a teacher's control. Decisions such as how many minutes students will spend in synchronous versus asynchronous learning are made at the school or district level, and teachers must comply with these decisions. Individual states and teaching organizations, such as the National Board of Professional Teaching Standards, have proposed guidelines for the minimum and maximum number of minutes students should spend in online instruction. These recommendations suggest that elementary students should have around 1–2 hours a day of online instruction, middle school students should have 2–3 hours, and high school students 3–4 hours (e.g., Illinois State Board of Education, 2020; Oregon Department of Education, 2021). No matter the age of the students, these hours should be broken up into reasonable amounts that take into account the length of time students can sustain their attention in the virtual platform.

Within a synchronous class period, make sure to have a reasonable balance of activities (see suggestions in Chapter 3, Task 1). Also work to create frequent "state changes" in which students see a different view (e.g., switch from a shared screen to gallery view) or move their bodies (e.g., stand to signal agreement or to indicate they are finished with a brief independent task).

Creating a Balance of Synchronous and Asynchronous Learning

If you will use a mix of synchronous and asynchronous activities, following are ideas for how best to use these models to support learning. While there is a lack of high-quality research directly comparing synchronous learning with asynchronous learning, many advocate for shifting the discussion from trying to determine the best medium to developing a better understanding of when, why, and how to use different forms.

Synchronous learning that occurs in real time includes activities such as videoconferencing to offer a lesson to a class of students and chatting or hosting discussion. It is best used to foster two-way communication and interaction in learning activities by creating opportunities for collaboration, brainstorming, student input, and immediate responses to questions. Teachers can use synchronous instruction to hold breakout groups (if the platform has this feature), poll students, conduct live assessments of mastery, and host fun sessions that provide students an opportunity to socialize. In a survey of educators, synchronous instruction was found to be most useful for holding virtual office hours, team decision-making and brainstorming activities, community building, and dealing with technical issues (Branon & Essex, 2001). When planning for synchronous sessions, keep these benefits in mind and work to integrate activities that capitalize on them.

One of the greatest challenges with synchronous instruction is getting students to log in at a particular time. Students may have competing priorities. such as family responsibilities or work schedules, and may face challenges related to Internet connectivity, especially if multiple people within a household are using the Internet at the same time. Asynchronous activities can eliminate these challenges. Asynchronous learning involves a delay between when you send or post instructional information and when the learner engages with the content. Activities such as discussion boards, prerecorded lessons and learner response activities, and email messaging are examples of asynchronous instruction and communication.

Asynchronous activities are best for one-way communication where feedback can be provided after the fact or no feedback is needed, such as short, recorded lessons or tutorials from the teacher, viewing presentations recorded by students, and posting assignments that students can complete and upload for instructor feedback. Asynchronous learning provides more flexibility for individual student pacing and progress and can offer students significantly more time to reflect on material they are learning. This can increase the likelihood they understand it more thoroughly. In a survey of educators, asynchronous communication was reportedly useful for:

- Encouraging in-depth, more thoughtful discussion and higher-level cognitive processing
- Offering instructions and setting deadlines
- Communicating with temporally diverse students
- Holding ongoing discussions where archiving is required
- Allowing all students to respond to a topic (Branon & Essex, 2001)

> **Because synchronous and asynchronous models both have benefits and limitations, consider ways to use the models to complement each other.**

While asynchronous learning activities have numerous possible benefits, they also pose limitations, such as a lack of immediate feedback, students not checking in often enough, students feeling a sense of isolation, and requiring students to be fairly focused and have good time management skills (Brannon & Essex).

Because synchronous and asynchronous models both have benefits and limitations, consider ways to use the models to complement each other. Together they support several ways for learners and teachers to exchange information, collaborate on work, and get to know each other. Higher learning outcomes have also been shown to occur when students are provided with a combination of asynchronous and synchronous forms of communication. Synchronous videoconferencing can offer immediate social interaction and co-construction of knowledge while asynchronous text communication can allow for deep, reflective thinking. Research supports the notion that both synchronous and asynchronous communication tools offer advantages to learners in a distance education environment (Cao et al., 2009; Chou, 2002; Gillies, 2008; Hiltz & Goldman, 2005; Hrastinski & Keller, 2007; Mabrito, 2006; Skylar, 2009).

CHAPTER 3, TASK 2

Clarify Expectations for the Common Instructional Activities That Occur in Your Classroom

Read the task on pages 121–131 and implement with the following adaptations and considerations.

Identify the major types of activities that your students will engage in on a daily (or regular) basis. Your list might include:

- Opening/attendance routines
- Teacher-directed instruction
- Whole group discussion
- Small group instruction (you work with a small group while others work independently or in breakout rooms)
- Small group work (breakout rooms)
- Partner work (breakout rooms)
- Independent work while in virtual class
- Viewing multimedia, videos, etc.
- Assessments
- Independent work while not in virtual class (homework)

Once you have identified your major classroom activities, use the CHAMPS Virtual Classroom Activity Worksheet (Reproducible 11.5 shown in Figure 11.4 on p. 515) to clarify your behavioral expectations for students for each separate activity. Reproducible 11.6, the ACHIEVE Virtual Classroom Activity Worksheet (not shown), is also available for download.

Additional guidance for teacher-directed instruction, independent work periods, and cooperative partner/group activities are included in Tasks 3–5 of this chapter. As you complete CHAMPS Virtual Classroom Activity Worksheets for these common classroom activities, read through the corresponding task to ensure that your procedures set students up for success in meeting the goals for your classroom.

UPDATE YOUR CLASSROOM MANAGEMENT PLAN

ITEM 5: CHAMPS EXPECTATIONS FOR CLASSROOM ACTIVITIES

- On Reproducible 3.1, list all common instructional activities for which you will complete CHAMPS Virtual Classroom Activity Worksheets.
- Once you have completed CHAMPS Virtual Classroom Activity Worksheets (Reproducible 11.5) for each activity, attach them or include them in a binder with a paper record of your Classroom Management Plan, and/or include the filled-out digital versions in a file that contains your Classroom Management Plan.

CHAPTER 3, TASK 3

Design Procedures for Managing Teacher-Directed Activities

Read the task on pages 132–140 and implement with the following adaptations and considerations.

Teacher-directed activities in the virtual platform can include direct instruction, reading content aloud, facilitating viewing of video content, facilitating a whole group discussion, and so on. Box 11.1 includes guidance and examples to consider in structuring teacher-directed activities in a virtual platform. Consider the functions available in the virtual platform your school uses as you define your expectations for teacher-directed activities.

Best Practices for Facilitating Teacher-Directed Activities

Follow the recommendations in Chapter 3, Task 3 for implementing effective instructional practices. In addition, consider the recommendations discussed below.

Recognize that most students' attention span is roughly 10 minutes, and after that their attention begins to wane. Some students may struggle to sustain attention for 10 minutes on the virtual platform, so consider ways to break down instruction into smaller pieces that are easier for students to digest. Use logical sequencing of content that guides students through the learning process. For example, if you are showing a video to students, break the video into a series of 5–7 minute segments with opportunities to discuss and reflect on the information, and use active participation strategies to rehearse and review information so it becomes better committed to their long-term memory.

BOX 11.1

Structuring Teacher-Directed Activities

Conversation: In activities in which students are expected to be quietly working or listening, have students remain muted, but ensure that all students are prepared to quickly unmute if called upon. Younger students who struggle with technology may need explicit instruction and practice opportunities to be able to mute and unmute quickly.

Consider students' maturity and ability to make relevant comments or questions when defining expectations for use of a chat box feature. A classroom requiring high support may benefit from more restrictive expectations, such as, "Only use the chat box for private questions to the teacher or when directed to comment to the whole group," whereas a classroom needing lower support might be able to handle looser expectations, such as, "Use the chat box to pose content or technology questions to the whole group or to make comments relevant to the current topic."

Help: Define how students should get help for technology-related questions and for questions that relate to the current subject content. It may be beneficial to use a different signal for each so that you can determine in which order to take questions based on your instructional flow. Some possible ways for students to signal they need help in a virtual class include:

- Raising hand if video is on (using different hand signals such as a 1 or 2 to show whether it's a technology or a content question)
- Using emoticons available in the platform, such as a raised hand or clapping icon
- Typing a question into the whole group chat (most appropriate when peers may be able to help, for example, with technology-related questions)
- Typing a question privately into chat to the teacher
- Unmuting and waiting for an appropriate moment (when speaker finishes their thought) to ask a question

- Sending a text message to the teacher (numerous sites and applications allow you to send text messages to and from students without sharing your actual phone number)
- Using a shared document with a "parking lot" where students can pose questions in real time

When you are considering which help methods to use, consider factors such as whether all students will have their cameras on (and a backup method for seeking help if they will not), your ability to monitor the chat box while you provide instruction, and students' comfort with using multiple features of technology.

Activity: Similar to in-person instruction, be cautious that students do not become inattentive when teacher-directed activities run too long or are devoid of active engagement strategies. Indicate ways that you plan to assess student understanding throughout the teacher-directed activity, such as:

- Using thumbs up/thumbs down, standing up/sitting down, or another gesture (e.g., raise hand, fist to five, etc.) to indicate true/false, yes/no, or a multiple-choice response
- Have students use whiteboards or response cards to show their response to a whole group question. You can purchase inexpensive individual whiteboards, or create simple whiteboards using plastic plates or a clear plastic folder with a piece of white card stock inside. Response cards can include colored cards used to indicate different responses (e.g., red and green to indicate agreement/disagreement, true/false responses), or a sheet of paper with different multiple choice responses that students can hold up and point to their response.
- Use a polling feature in the virtual platform or a separate application to quickly assess student understanding or levels of agreement.

Continued on next page ⟶

Box 11.1 continued

- Randomly call on individuals using popsicle sticks, a random name generator app, or selecting a pattern based on the order in which students appear on your screen (e.g., call on the person in the top right corner, then the person in the bottom right corner, and so on). When using a random method to call on students, be careful to ensure that this strategy does not put students who struggle academically, have limited English proficiency, or who struggle with self-esteem or anxiety in an uncomfortable situation. You might call on these individuals for questions you already know they have the answer to or give them the option to pass but come back to them to share a good idea they heard from someone else.
- Have students free write, brainstorm, or work on a series of independent questions and be prepared to type a response into the chat box if you randomly call on them. Another option is to have students submit their compiled responses from a variety of active participation prompts to you at the end of the class session.
- Have students type short responses into the chat box. Be cautious about using this procedure or asking students to type lengthy responses when they may struggle with writing or typing skills. Some students may not participate if they fear being made fun of by peers for poor grammar or poor spelling. For these students, consider giving them the option to submit responses privately to you in the chat, and then you can periodically read their responses to the group or call on them to verbally share what they wrote.
- Provide students with fillable notes, worksheets, or graphic organizers and have them submit copies or screenshots of completed notes to you at the end of the day or week.

One way to think about virtual instruction is to consider the types of verbal, written, and action responses that can be used throughout in-person instruction. Identify engagement strategies that can be used as is in a virtual environment, those that can be applied with adaptations, and those that may not be useful or feasible. Consider whether the virtual platform provides some opportunities for engagement that might have been more difficult in a physical classroom, such as polls or having students quickly research a topic online and report out their findings. Regardless of the methods you select, ensure that teacher-directed activities are highly engaging and encourage frequent participation from all students.

Movement: Clarify whether students are allowed to move away from the screen, and for what reasons. Indicate whether students need to get your attention or permission to do so. Some teachers may tell students they can get up to use the restroom, get a drink of water, or get needed materials without needing permission from the teacher, but they should do so sparingly. Others may require students to get permission by typing a request privately into the chat box, while others may plan short breaks from the screen that are frequent enough that students should not need to leave their workspace during teacher-directed portions of the class.

Also clarify whether students can move around while still in proximity of their screen. Can they stand up, walk around, stretch? Should they turn their cameras off while doing this so as not to distract others, or would you prefer that cameras remain on as much as possible? Allowing students to move or change positions (from seated to standing, for example) can help them remain focused and engaged if they are expected to be on their computers for long periods of time.

Participation: Provide clarity about what student behaviors will demonstrate they are paying attention and participating throughout teacher-directed activities, and what common off-task behaviors should be avoided. Expected behaviors may include things like answering when called on, using reactions and chat box when directed, sharing answers on a whiteboard or response card, and taking notes. For young students, one anticipated difficulty is students wanting to move around to different locations in their home setting throughout class or switching between virtual backgrounds. Provide as much clarity as possible around these and other anticipated concerns.

One beneficial technique with large groups on a virtual platform is to have students state their name first when they unmute and say something to the group. This will help ensure that everyone knows who is talking. Explicitly clarify that students should turn TVs off, close all windows and applications on their computer that do not directly relate to your course, and put their phones out of reach.

Success: Identify specific ways you will provide encouragement and positive feedback to students during teacher-directed activities. See the section expanding on Chapter 6 for ways to provide positive feedback in the virtual learning environment.

Figure 11.4 shows a sample completed CHAMPS Virtual Classroom Activity Worksheet for a first-grade class needing high levels of support.

CHAMPS Virtual Classroom Activity Worksheet

CHAMPS

A
Teacher-Directed Instruction, High Support

ONLINE LEARNING ACTIVITY __*Teacher-Directed Instruction (1st grade)*__

CONVERSATION
Can students use the microphone? ☒ muted ☐ unmuted *Unless directed by teacher to unmute*
Can students use group chat? *No (we will not use group chat except for help)*
Parents/guardians can private message me
Can students chat privately with each other?
No (will turn this feature off on platform)

HELP
How do students indicate that they need help: With technology? *In chat, type T*

With subject content? *In chat, type S*

ACTIVITY
What types of learning structure will be used (e.g., read aloud, direction instruction, video, breakout rooms, etc.)?
Direct instruction, read aloud, group discussion
Do you plan on assessing student progress for this activity? *Yes* If yes, how will you assess? *Individual check-ins, choral responses (muted but watching mouths), thumbs up/down, Hold-ups (whiteboards)*

MOVEMENT
Can students move away from the screen if needed (restroom, etc.)? *No—will create formal times for restroom and movement breaks*
Can students move around if needed (stand up, walk around, etc.)? *Yes, but if on screen, minimally distracting (will teach examples/non-examples)*
Do students need to get your attention before moving? *Yes* If yes, how should students get your attention? *Only for out of meeting range, use "clapping"*

PARTICIPATION
How will students show active participation (video, audio, chat, etc.)? *Answer when called on; use reactions/gestures/whiteboards*

What behaviors do you expect students to display through their screen? *Screen is recommended but not required, if on screen show eyes.*

What are your expectations for students when talking (e.g., do they say their name first)? *Comments must relate to topic (will teach examples and non-examples)*

What are your expectations for using other technology and reducing other distractions? *Phones/TV/other chats and windows away (no multitasking)*

SUCCESS
What words of encouragement and connection will you use with students? *Greet students by name at start; praise attendance and participation with verbals, typed feedback, and meetings with individuals (aim for 5 per week).*

REPRODUCIBLE 11.5

Figure 11.4 *CHAMPS Virtual Classroom Transition Worksheet (Reproducible 11.5), Example A*

Use a variety of content delivery methods and learning activities to keep students engaged. Consider ways to mix kinesthetic or tactile methods in addition to visual and auditory modalities. For example, if students are learning about origami in an art class, a mix of learning activities might include:

- Reading about the history of origami and other elements of Japanese culture
- Watching a video of master origami artists
- Watching the teacher provide a synchronous demonstration of how to fold simple origami shapes
- Creating origami art using these techniques

Multimedia options such as videos, illustrations, graphs, and text provide ways to keep instruction interesting and relevant to different learners. However, when using lots of multimedia, be cautious to ensure it is easily accessible to all students. Consider ways to embed multimedia into a single platform or hyperlinked slides. If students have to navigate to many different sites or open a variety of documents in different formats, you may lose students along the way as they struggle to navigate across platforms and documents.

In addition, use frequent opportunities to respond to engage learners. Engagement strategies in the virtual environment should focus on the function of engagement, not just the tools (Fisher, Frey, & Hattie, 2020). Carefully consider how different tools on a virtual platform will engage learners, help them apply or solidify learning, and help you assess their level of understanding. For example, a brief poll can be useful to gauge students' level of understanding with new content or to see if they are retaining previously learned material. Even for young students, you could use simple agree/disagree or true/false responses and read them the question on a simple poll. This immediate feedback can help you determine whether to move on or take additional time to clarify areas of confusion. The chat box feature can be effectively used to have students pose extension questions, brainstorm ideas as a whole group, or share a short individual experience or idea. However, it would not make sense to use the chat box to share the answer to a question with a single correct answer. As soon as the first few students type their responses, other students can simply copy the response, so this will not help you gauge student understanding. Instead, use a multiple-choice poll or have students write their responses on whiteboards and hold them up to the camera at the same time.

Help students cross the gap of knowing and doing by embedding application activities into each lesson. When you provide effective instruction with new information, student actions should follow to help them apply and retain information and skills. Student actions might include:

- Participating in an online discussion forum
- Creating their own examples or scenarios
- Solving a problem
- Writing a short essay or opinion piece
- Having a conversation on- or offline
- Taking notes or journaling
- Answering teacher questions. Short questions can be helpful for engagement or rehearsal of factual information. Open-ended questions are beneficial for activating higher-level reflection and deep thinking.

Embedding frequent opportunities to respond and application activities throughout instruction allows students to practice and apply concepts, while giving you the opportunity to provide immediate positive and corrective feedback. A high rate of opportunities to respond during synchronous learning provides lots of opportunities to praise correct academic responses and appropriate manners of response. It also gives you the opportunity to immediately correct areas of student misunderstanding.

CHAPTER 3, TASK 4

Design Procedures for Managing Independent Work Periods

Read the task on pages 141–145 and implement with the following adaptations and considerations.

Independent work activities can be broken into two different time periods. The first relates to independent work that is done while students are logged into a synchronous class session. For example, there may be times when you direct students to work for 5–15 minutes on their own while they are still with you on the virtual platform. Students can ask you questions in real time, and you can check in with individual students in a breakout room while others are working. Students also engage in independent work when they complete asynchronous assignments and activities at home. This section provides recommendations for how to facilitate and provide recommendations for each of these times. Box 11.2 (pp. 518–519) covers considerations for structuring independent work times.

Best Practices for Facilitating Independent Work Periods During Synchronous Class Time

Follow the recommendations in Chapter 3, Task 4 for effectively structuring independent work periods. In addition, consider the following recommendations:

- Use a visual countdown timer on the screen to help students monitor the amount of time they have to complete their independent work.
- Post a slide or other visual continuously throughout the work time that provides explicit directions for the task and the outcomes students will be expected to complete by the end of the work time. Also include CHAMPS expectations or another visual posting (e.g., looks like/sounds like chart) for students' behavior during the independent work period.
- Ensure that all students have the materials needed to complete independent work, including access to assignments, reading materials, technology, and anything else necessary for the work. Consider ways to get students needed materials or adaptations to accommodate students who may not have access. See "Managing Student Assignments" later in this chapter for ideas on how to ensure materials are accessible for all students.

Structuring Independent Work Periods During Synchronous Class Time

Conversation: During independent work, a 0 voice level is appropriate.

Help: Consider how students will indicate they need help in ways that are minimally distracting to the class. Options include typing "help" into the chat box, placing a sticky note over their camera that says "assistance needed," or using a verbal signal.

If you will remain in the main room throughout students' independent work time, the simplest way for a student to get help is to unmute and indicate they need your help. This way, if you are not directly monitoring the chat or look away from the screen, the student will not need to wait for you to notice a message. The downside of this practice is that if any students are embarrassed by asking for help, a verbal signal is very public. Consider having an alternate private signal for students who wish to ask for help without everyone in the class hearing. If the student poses the question verbally on the whole group meeting, also consider whether the conversation will be distracting to other students.

After a student gains your attention through a signal, consider the best way for the student to pose the question and for you to respond. You and the student might privately chat in the text box or over a text messaging application. Some teachers allow students to call them on their office phone or a dedicated phone line, and the teacher can mute their computer microphone while answering the student's question. Another option is for you and the student to move to a breakout room if this feature is available on the virtual platform you use. This method should probably not be used with highly immature groups and those who struggle to remain focused and on task. If you have any concerns that students will bully others or engage in inappropriate behaviors while you are "out of the room," you should probably plan to use another method. If you use this method, make sure to explicitly teach students your expectations for what they will work on while you meet with an individual student, and periodically check in with individuals when you return to see their progress while you were out of the room. Also work to ensure that you are not out of the main room for more than a few minutes. If the student's question will require longer to answer, you should return to the main room every few minutes to check on the class, or schedule a separate time to work with the individual student.

Consider whether you will allow students to use the chat to pose questions to their peers. You might designate a few highly responsible students as "technology experts" and "content experts" who can help answer peer questions in the chat box or who you can move into a breakout room with another student to answer their question. Students might preface their questions with T for questions about technology and C for questions about the content or expectations for the assignment.

Activity: Independent work activities while logged into a synchronous class can include things like conducting research, working on a paper or presentation, reading and taking notes from a textbook or website, completing comprehension or computation problems, and brainstorming, among others. When students are first learning how to do something or when they are engaging in a particularly complex independent task, consider having them do the work while they are logged into class rather than making these asynchronous independent activities. Students may benefit from opportunities for real-time feedback and asking questions. If you notice that numerous students are struggling with the task, this provides you the opportunity to adjust and provide in-time instruction. Once you are sure students can be successful with the tasks in an asynchronous format, you can reserve the majority of your synchronous class time for teacher-directed and cooperative activities.

Carefully consider how you plan to evaluate student participation during independent work time. While some students may do well with submitting their work to you at the end of a work period, other students will need brief check-ins during a work period to ensure they are in fact doing the work and also to see if they have any questions or areas of understanding that need clarification. Some teachers will have all students submit their work at the end of each work period, while others will spot-check randomly selected individuals.

Movement: Independent work time provides an opportunity for students to stretch, use the restroom, or get a drink of water without missing class instruction or engagement with peers. However, some students may fail to complete independent tasks if movement expectations are too loose. For classes that require more structure and support, consider requiring teacher permission for movement to other locations off screen, or provide an official break before students start independent work so they do not need to move away from the screen during the work time. If students will have their camera off during work time, make sure students know that you will periodically check in with individuals to see how their work is progressing and ensure they are still at their workspace.

Participation: Provide clear expectations for what appropriate participation looks and sounds like for the particular activity. If you were looking over students' shoulders, what would they be doing to participate? What would they not be doing? The higher the support needs of your students, the more definition you should provide, giving examples and non-examples. Consider what common off-task misbehaviors you expect students to avoid (e.g., text messaging with friends), and which on-task behaviors you expect to see (e.g., looking at materials for the task, completing each direction, asking questions when you are stuck).

Figure 11.5 is a sample of the CHAMPS Virtual Classroom Activity Worksheet for a seventh-grade teacher's math class that needs medium levels of support.

CHAMPS Virtual Classroom Activity Worksheet

CHAMPS

B
Independent Work, Medium Support

ONLINE LEARNING ACTIVITY *Independent Work (7th Math)*

Conversation

Can students use the microphone? ☒ muted ☐ unmuted
Can students use group chat? *No*

Can students chat privately with each other? *No*

Help

How do students indicate that they need help: With technology? *Type "Tech" in the chat box. Type question to group if you can. Anyone can respond. If not, wait for my help and continue working on what you can.*
With subject content? *Unmute and pose your question to the group if others might benefit from clarification or ask in chat if you can call me on office line for an individual question about content.*

Activity

What types of learning structure will be used (e.g., read aloud, direction instruction, video, breakout rooms, etc.)?
Completing problem sets, reading text, researching

Do you plan on assessing student progress for this activity? *Yes* If yes, how will you assess? *Students submit work at end of session. Call on a few students randomly to share work, or students will partner up to discuss responses.*

Movement

Can students move away from the screen if needed (restroom, etc.)? *Yes, but only one time per period*

Can students move around if needed (stand up, walk around, etc.)? *Yes, but must remain working during that time*

Do students need to get your attention before moving? *Yes* If yes, how should students get your attention?
For moving away from workspace, type privately in chat box

Participation

How will students show active participation (video, audio, chat, etc.)? *Responding quickly when I give a direction, completing independent task*

What behaviors do you expect students to display through their screen? *None (cameras not required)—will submit work progress whenever directed*

What are your expectations for students when talking (e.g., do they say their name first)? *No talking during independent work*

What are your expectations for using other technology and reducing other distractions? *Phones away, TVs and other applications off, only task windows open if on computer. If task off computer, only direction slide showing*

Success

What words of encouragement and connection will you use with students? *Check in with a few students (e.g., have them submit response to their last completed question). Provide praise for working and staying focused. Type compliments to several students for on time, growth, exceptional effort*

 REPRODUCIBLE 11.5

Figure 11.5 *CHAMPS Virtual Classroom Transition Worksheet (Reproducible 11.5), Example B*

Recommendations for Asynchronous Independent Work Periods

Be cautious about the information you provide about expected student behaviors during asynchronous work periods for factors like conversation and movement. Students' parents or guardians and the students themselves will be responsible for monitoring these work times, and it is not appropriate to dictate what must happen or not happen in the student's home when you are not facilitating a live session. However, you should provide some information, such as:

- **How students can reach you with questions and the time frame in which you will commit to replying.** Students should not expect an immediate response, but you should make an effort to respond to all questions in a timely fashion (e.g., within 24 hours). Some options for reaching you outside of class time include: during office hours, by email, or through a class discussion platform or class social media page. You should probably define only one or two ways for students to reach you so that you do not have to monitor multiple different locations.
- **What students should do while waiting for a response.** Should they continue working on other tasks or portions of the task? Should they try to seek help from peers or someone in their home?
- **Explicit directions for each independent work task.** Include completed work samples, rubrics, and other information that can help students successfully meet independent work expectations.
- **What you will be looking for as evidence that students have appropriately participated during independent work periods.** This will likely be related to the work products they produce, but it may also include things like self-assessments of on-task behavior and effort, or periodic check-ins with family members who are supporting the student's learning. Also clarify the supports that might be put in place if a student is struggling to meet expectations for independent work activities. For example, if a student falls below 90% work completion, let the student and family know some of the ways you might work with them to boost the student's work completion rates.

Instead of defining each aspect of CHAMPS, consider providing possibilities and recommendations to students and their family members that might help students be successful, such as:

- How families can use the CHAMPS acronym to clarify their expectations for students during independent work. Provide some samples of completed CHAMPS visuals for students' independent work outside of the virtual class meeting. In addition to defining expectations for the student, families may wish to clarify expectations for siblings and others who might inadvertently distract the student.
- Making a to-do list with all independent work tasks the student should complete each day and crossing off each item as it is completed.
- Making sure that the student turns off and removes all distractions from their work space prior to beginning independent work tasks.
- Having the student use the restroom, get water, and gather all needed materials prior to getting started.
- Setting a goal for the amount of time or the amount of work the student will complete in each sitting. Make sure the student takes a 10-minute stretch and screen break approximately each hour, and more often if needed. However, set a goal for a reasonable

amount of time that the student should stay focused (e.g., at least 15 minutes and then a 3-minute break). Use timers to monitor work and break time as needed.

 CASE STUDY *Example from the Field*

When we had to transition to virtual instruction in March 2020 due to the COVID pandemic, my son was in first grade. Each Sunday, my son's teacher would send home a list of the schedule (all asynchronous assignments and class meeting times) for each day during the week. We would print out this list and put the page for the day right next to the computer in his workspace. Each day, as my son completed his assignments or finished a class meeting, he delighted in getting to highlight or cross off the part he just finished. This was such a helpful way to keep him on task and motivated throughout each day! He could see his accomplishments and celebrate how much he was learning. —Jessica Sprick

CHAPTER 3, TASK 5

Design Procedures for Managing Partner and Cooperative Group Work

Read the task on pages 146–153 and implement with the following adaptations and considerations.

Virtual platforms with breakout rooms provide opportunities for teachers to facilitate partner and small group cooperative work. Teachers who don't have access to a breakout room feature might have students set up their own small group meetings for extended work periods. Skip this task if you do not have breakout rooms or your district does not allow their use, or if you don't plan to facilitate partner or group work in the virtual environment because of concerns about student age, maturity, or ability to focus in a breakout room.

If you do plan to use partner and small group activities, read the information in Chapter 3, Task 5, then consider how to adapt CHAMPS expectations and best practices for cooperative work for the virtual environment. Box 11.3 (pp. 522–523) provides structural considerations.

Best Practices for Facilitating Partner and Small Group Work Periods

Follow the recommendations in Chapter 3, Task 4 for effectively structuring independent work periods. In addition, consider the following recommendations:

- Form groups of 3–6 students for all cooperative activities. If students are placed in dyads (partners) and one student does not join the breakout room in a timely way or a student is absent, the other student is left with nothing to do. A triad increases the likelihood

BOX 11.3

Structuring Partner and Cooperative Group Activities in the Virtual Setting

Conversation: In partner or small group activities, it is helpful if all students unmute throughout the cooperative work period. When students are muted and must unmute to speak, it can stall conversation and create uncomfortable silences that break down communication. If all students are unmuted, conversation is likely to flow much more naturally. However, if students have excessive background noise in their home environment, they may need to remain muted and unmute only when speaking. Specify that students should be unmuted in partner or breakout rooms unless absolutely necessary due to background noise.

Help: Consider providing a few ways for students to get help from you or from other groups while in a breakout room or separate meeting. Some platforms provide an "ask for assistance" button that calls the host to join a breakout room. Give students a number they can call or text (e.g., through your computer, not your personal cell phone). Consider designating one student in each group as the "help seeker" who can return to the main room to ask you a question or request that you join a particular breakout room. If students are responsible enough to call each other and provide focused assistance, consider ways to create partners across groups who can call each other if necessary. For example, each group might have one student who shares their number with a peer in another group. If the group has a question, the student can text or call the partner from the other group to seek assistance.

Activity: Carefully consider how to use partner and group activities. Because transitioning to and from breakout rooms can be somewhat time consuming, you may wish to err on the side of slightly longer cooperative work periods (e.g., 5–30 minutes) than you would in a physical class setting. When students are seated right next to each other, you can use frequent,

brief turn-and-talk activities. In a virtual setting, these brief cooperative activities may be more difficult.

However, if you are planning for longer cooperative work times, consider your students' ability to focus and demonstrate appropriate social skills in breakout rooms with limited supervision. While you may be moving in and out of different rooms to observe the groups' progress, you will not be providing supervision 100% of the time as you would in a physical class setting. If activities in breakout rooms are too long, students may get off track or struggle to work collaboratively. If students are highly immature and struggle with appropriate peer interactions, you may need to find alternatives to partner and small group work while you work across time to teach the skills they will need to work collaboratively. One alternative is to have students engage in partner and small group work through asynchronous formats, such as participating in threaded discussions on a discussion board, recording video or audio responses to one another, or providing individual contributions to a small group project.

Movement: It is probably best to indicate that during cooperative work time students should not leave their workspace for any reason except for emergencies. Students should not leave peers waiting while they use the restroom or get a drink. It may help to provide a short break right before and/or after cooperative activities. Let students know they should take care of personal needs during that time and remain fully engaged with their partner or small group during work time.

Participation: Because you will not be present in every breakout room, provide explicit expectations for student participation. If you were present, what would you expect students to look and sound like as they are demonstrating appropriate participation? Strongly encourage students to turn their cameras on during cooperative work times, as this can help peers feel a better sense of connection. If a student is unable or unwilling to turn their camera on for any reason, ensure that they understand there will be an even greater expectation that they participate throughout cooperative activities.

Figure 11.6 is a sample CHAMPS Virtual Classroom Activity Worksheet for a fifth-grade class needing low levels of support.

CHAMPS Virtual Classroom Activity Worksheet

CHAMP

C
Small Group Work, Low Support

ONLINE LEARNING ACTIVITY __Small Group Work (5th grade)__

CONVERSATION

Can students use the microphone? ☐ muted ☒ unmuted *Stay unmuted unless lots of background noise*
Can students use group chat? *Yes for on-topic comments and questions*

Can students chat privately with each other? *No (will turn this feature off on platform)*

HELP

How do students indicate that they need help: With technology? *Pose question to group. If unable to solve, return to main room for help from teacher.*
With subject content? *Send one "question asker" to main room to seek help from teacher, or press "ask for help" button*

ACTIVITY

What types of learning structure will be used (e.g., read aloud, direction instruction, video, breakout rooms, etc.)? *Brainstorming, group project prep*

Do you plan on assessing student progress for this activity? *Yes* If yes, how will you assess? *Students submit work/report on progress at end of session, be prepared to copy/paste work in chat, share screen, or report if called on.*

MOVEMENT

Can students move away from the screen if needed (restroom, etc.)? *No, only for emergencies*

Can students move around if needed (stand up, walk around, etc.)? *Yes, but must remain working during that time*

Do students need to get your attention before moving? *No* If yes, how should students get your attention?

PARTICIPATION

How will students show active participation (video, audio, chat, etc.)? *Everyone contributes ideas: chat, verbally, taking notes. Each person will have a defined role (TBD).*

What behaviors do you expect students to display through their screen? *Cameras strongly recommended. If not on screen, must frequently contribute.*

What are your expectations for students when talking (e.g., do they say their name first)? *Listen to others while they are talking.*

What are your expectations for using other technology and reducing other distractions? *Put away/turn off all distractions. Be a positive group member.*

SUCCESS

What words of encouragement and connection will you use with students? *Spend time in each room. Provide specific positive feedback to individuals and home group. Provide some during session and some as a follow-up.*

© 2021 Ancora Publishing   REPRODUCIBLE 11.5

Figure 11.6 *CHAMPS Virtual Classroom Transition Worksheet (Reproducible 11.5), Example C*

that at least two members of the group are present and able to work. Groups larger than six may struggle to remain focused and ensure that all students have an active role.

- Consider using a "base group" structure to provide consistency, support, and social connection throughout a term or semester. With this practice, teachers assign students to a cooperative group that meets at least a few times a week (and in some classes on a daily basis) for a few minutes. During each base group meeting, students might respond to an ice breaker question, share ideas for a challenge problem related to course content, or summarize their main points of understanding from the previous session or class reading. Sometimes you can structure these meetings with a prompt and an expected outcome (e.g., "Each group member will summarize and submit a discussion thread with the main takeaways from their base group members"). Other times, you might provide some open-ended time for students to give one another academic or personal support or just get to know one another. Students will be involved in other cooperative groups for course projects or in-class activities, but the base group provides a consistent peer group that can help students develop positive relationships and receive encouragement and assistance.

- If the majority of students are able to manage working in breakout rooms without the teacher, but you have a few students who may lack the maturity or social skills to handle the lack of direct teacher supervision, consider having a small group work in the main room with you present while other students work in separate breakout rooms. This can allow you to directly teach necessary collaborative skills, monitor student interactions, and provide positive and corrective feedback. As these students gain cooperative skills, begin placing them in groups with highly responsible and mature peers for partner or small group activities.

CHAPTER 3, TASK 6

Design Procedures for Managing Student Assignments

Read the task on pages 154–164 and implement with the following adaptations and considerations.

In addition to helping students keep track of assignments, you will need to come up with a clear and consistent method or methods for assigning and delivering materials necessary for classwork and independent work in the virtual learning environment. Consider your virtual alternatives that are similar to a bulletin board space for recording assignments, such as:

- Updated listing on your class website
- A shared "class assignments" document, like a Google doc, that is continuously updated
- Post assignments and materials on a slide at the beginning and end of class, or on the classroom bitmoji background
- Share on a classroom social media account
- Email to the class list

At a minimum, ensure that you share classwork and independent work assignments and provide due date reminders verbally and visually during class sessions and in one other medium (e.g., website, Google doc, social media, or class email).

Ensure That Students Can Access Needed Materials

At the beginning of the term or semester and at least once midway through the grading period, conduct a needs assessment to determine whether all students have access to needed materials. This assessment should include things like checking that the student has a reliable and functioning computer or tablet and consistent access to the Internet with sufficient bandwidth for class meetings and assignments. Also assess whether students have access to materials that are not provided by the school but that may be needed for class, such as writing utensils and paper, a printer and paper, and so on. If you have students who lack access to materials, work with your school to find ways to provide what is necessary, or adapt assignments so the student can be successful without them.

For virtual class meetings and independent work, ensure that all students can access the course materials they need to participate. If students will use documents for reading or note-taking, use several methods to provide access. For example, you might email links and materials to the class list prior to the start of class, put the links and materials into the chat box, and post them on your class website. Use a response like thumbs up/thumbs down or a brief poll to verify that all students were able to access the materials.

If a textbook or other print material is required, be sure to tell students what they will need in advance of class. At the close of each class period, let students know what they need to bring the following day. Consider sending an email reminder each morning or at least 30 minutes before class begins reminding them to bring books or other necessary materials. Also consider what you will do if some students do not have the materials for the day. You might have a backup scanned copy of any required pages, or students might be directed to complete an alternate assignment that does not require use of the book. Or you might put the student in a breakout room with a partner or small group who can read the material out loud. If a student frequently comes to class without needed materials, see suggestions in Chapter 2, Task 5.

Collect Completed Work

Give some thought to how you will collect completed classwork and independent work completed outside of class time. Consider what will be easiest from a student perspective but also what is manageable for your time and organization. For example, students may find it is easiest to submit all assignments via email; however, if you have 200 students and they are all submitting daily assignments, this could quickly become an organizational nightmare!

Another possibility is to set a regular routine during class entry or closing procedures for students to upload completed assignments for the day into the meeting chat. This allows you to immediately see which students have submitted work but also requires you to take the time to download each assignment before you log off the platform. If you have tight transition times between classes, this may not be feasible. If you use a platform like Canvas or Seesaw, you can post assignments and have students submit completed work within that assignment posting. This may be easier and more manageable than the previous two options, but this feature may not be available on your district's learning platform.

Whatever method you use, provide clear instruction to students and their families about how you will assign and collect completed work. Monitor students' work submissions carefully and provide timely feedback about student work. If some students fall behind in their work submissions, make sure to check in as soon as possible to see if they are having difficulty with the procedures you are using to collect work or if they are struggling with the work itself. Provide supports as necessary. Also make an effort to provide positive written or verbal feedback to students who turn in work on time.

Follow the recommendations in Chapter 3, Task 6 for returning graded work to students, maintaining records, keeping students informed of their current grade status, and dealing with late or missing assignments.

UPDATE YOUR CLASSROOM MANAGEMENT PLAN

ITEM 7: PROCEDURES FOR MANAGING STUDENT ASSIGNMENTS

Describe procedures for managing student assignments, including:

- Assigning classwork and homework/asynchronous work
- Collecting completed work
- Returning graded work to students
- Maintaining records and keeping students informed of their current grade status
- Late or missing assignments

CHAPTER 3, TASK 7

Design Procedures for Managing Student Technology Use

Read the following sections in Chapter 3, Task 7: "Establish an electronics policy and teach students about acceptable use of technology in the classroom" (pp. 166–167) and "Define expectations for use of personal devices in class" (pp. 169–171). Implement with the following adaptations and considerations.

In addition to an electronics policy for personal devices, consider what expectations must be established for students who are using school devices. Some students may fail to treat these devices with appropriate care if they are not given explicit directions for their use. Consider teaching and including expectations in the electronics policy about:

- How to carry the device from one location to another within the home.
- How to pack and carry the device outside of the home (e.g., if the student is going from one parent's house to another). If a student does not have a padded case, determine if there are ways to provide one so the device does not get scratched or damaged in transit.
- Double-checking that they have the charger and any necessary accessories such as headphones before taking the device to another location.
- Keeping liquids and food away from the device. If a student will be drinking near the device, they should use a cup with a lid and straw or a water bottle.

UPDATE YOUR CLASSROOM MANAGEMENT PLAN

ITEM 8: PROCEDURES FOR MANAGING STUDENT TECHNOLOGY

Describe procedures for managing student technology, including:

- Expectations for use of school devices
- Expectations for use of personal devices in class

Once you have developed a written electronics policy to share with students, attach a copy of it to your Classroom Management Plan.

CHAPTER 3, TASK 8
Develop Long-Range Classroom Goals

Read the task on pages 172–174 and implement as is.

UPDATE YOUR CLASSROOM MANAGEMENT PLAN

ITEM 9: LONG-RANGE GOALS

List 4–7 long-range goals for your class.

CHAPTER 3, TASK 9

Understand Considerations for Developing Effective Grading Practices

Read the task on pages 174–182 and implement as is.

CHAPTER 3, TASK 10

Develop a Grading System That Creates a Relationship Between Student Effort, Growth, and Success

Read the task on pages 182–199 and implement as is.

CHAPTER 4, TASK 1

Teach Your Guidelines for Success and Classroom Rules

Read the task on pages 203–209 and implement as is.

CHAPTER 4, TASK 2

Prepare Visuals and Lessons to Communicate Your CHAMPS Expectations

Read the task on pages 209–219 and implement with the following adaptations and considerations.

Consider how you will organize and display your expectations for students in major instructional activities. For classes that require higher support, visual displays that use the CHAMPS or ACHIEVE acronym help create consistency and clarity. See Figures 11.4 and 11.5 for samples of expectations visuals in the virtual class. Determine whether your students will respond best to visuals with text only, icons only, or both text and icons. While the reproducible materials include visuals for you to choose from, these icons were not specifically developed for the virtual environment. You may need to supplement with your own icons or visuals, from pictures or clip art, to create your virtual CHAMPS or ACHIEVE visuals.

With classes that require high support, consider ways to keep the visuals continuously posted throughout class. For example, you might have the visual posted in the corner of each slide that relates to that activity structure, or you could have physical CHAMPS posters in your workspace that are visible on students' screens. Consider sending home copies of your expectations visuals so that students can flip to them when you change to different activities. For example, if each student has a set of CHAMPS expectations cards on a binder ring, when

Figure 11.4a and 4b *Sample Expectations for Teacher-Directed Instruction with Young Students*

a.

- I will raise my hand when I want to talk.

- It is my turn when I see my name or I am called on.
- I will listen when it is someone else's turn.

- I stay at my workspace when I am using my computer.
- I am gentle with my screen and keyboard.

b.

C

H

A
- Math
- (–)
- 10 minutes

M

P

S
Subtract 2 digits ...
(learning target/objective)

CHAMPS for our Online Meetings

C Make sure your microphone is on mute and only turn it on when it is your turn to talk. I will make sure everyone gets a chance to talk.

H If you need help, you can type questions in the chat box. I will call on individuals to share one at a time.

A The activity will be active listening, some speaking, some typing, and some note-taking, so have your journals ready with something to write with.

M Stay at your computer with the camera on. Time will be limited, so go to the bathroom before session starts and have all materials ready.

P Participating includes asking questions, typing comments, and questions in the chat box, and keeping good notes. Again, we have limited time online, so please stay on task.

Figure 11.5 *Sample CHAMPS Expectations (thanks to Kenneth Reever, Fifth-Grade Teacher in Wichita, Kansas)*

it is time for independent work you can direct them to flip to the card for independent work. When it is time to return to teacher-directed instruction or whole group discussion, have students flip to the appropriate card while you review the slide showing the expectations. For classes that are fairly mature and responsible, it may be enough to show your visual display at the beginning of each activity and then take it down unless you need to refer to it for positive or corrective feedback.

CHAPTER 4, TASK 3

Teach Behavioral and Social-Emotional Skills

Read the task on pages 219–225 and implement with the following adaptations and considerations.

Consider those behavioral and social-emotional skills that may take on special importance when students are learning in a virtual environment. Decide whether to use a formal curriculum or design your own lessons to teach students skills like:

- Time management
- Self-discipline and goal setting for work completion
- Organizational skills (e.g., monitoring due dates, materials management, organizing digital content)
- Avoiding cyberbullying behavior and how to respond if you are targeted or a bystander
- Digital citizenship skills
- Awareness and balance of media and screen use
- Connecting with community without face-to-face interaction
- Managing feelings of isolation and loneliness

CHAPTER 4, TASK 4

Clarify Behavioral Expectations for Common Areas and Special Circumstances

Skip the content on teaching expectations for common areas, emergency situations, and unique events because it applies to situations in physical school environments. Read and apply the suggestions for teaching expectations to new students (starting on p. 228), paying special attention to "Create a 'Welcome to Our Class' Video."

CHAPTER 4, TASK 5

Clarify Behavioral Expectations With Parents and Guardians

Read the task on pages 233–235 and implement with the following adaptations and considerations.

Make a special effort to communicate with parents and guardians regarding your expectations for student behavior when they are engaged with you in a class session and for things like rates of work completion and putting in their best effort with independent work. At the same time, make this communication consciously inviting in seeking parental input and communicating a desire to make situations workable for all families.

For example, you may emphasize the importance of regular student attendance during live class sessions as those are your most important way to build community, make connections with your students, assess understanding, and provide real-time assistance. At the same time, let families know that you understand how difficult regular attendance can be and that many families have circumstances that may require flexibility and assistance in meeting the goal of regular attendance. Ask families to communicate with you early and often if their student is struggling to meet any of your expectations. Convey a willingness (and follow through!) to work with the family to find ways to help a student meet challenging expectations while also adjusting expectations and finding work-arounds when necessary to accommodate individual circumstances. For example, while attendance may be incredibly important in your class, if a student is making earnest efforts to attend each day but his Internet drops out when his parent is on important work-related video conferences, set up a plan that allows the student to view recorded class videos when absolutely necessary.

For students who will be directly supervised by an adult while they are working, it may be helpful to clarify what adults should do to provide supervision and support. Some teachers prefer that supervising adults do not correct students who are engaging in misbehavior. These teachers view it as their job as the teacher to correct misbehavior. Other teachers would love it for parents or caregivers to step in to gently correct a student who is getting off track. Some teachers appreciate it when a parent provides help to a student who is not performing an academic task correctly, while other teachers prefer that parents not provide this kind of feedback. The more clarity you can provide to families about what is beneficial in your class, the better. However, be careful not to imply that families who are unable to supervise or oversee their students' work are in the wrong—honor each family's individual circumstances and contributions.

> *Make a special effort to communicate with parents/guardians regarding your expectations for student behavior when they are in a class session.*

CHAPTER 5, TASK 1

Scan All Sections of the Classroom Continuously and Circulate Whenever Possible

Most strategies in Chapter 5, Task 1 are not for the virtual setting. These strategies include visual and auditory scanning and physically circulating to monitor student behavior and academic work. Read the suggestions below for how to use engagement strategies and visual cues to stay in touch with the students in your virtual classroom.

At the beginning of the shift to virtual instruction in March of 2020, a student shared with one of the authors that in one of his virtual classes, he would frequently take a screenshot of himself looking like he was paying attention. He would then make the screenshot his profile picture and go do other things without the teacher noticing he was no longer in the session. This went on for several months before the teacher noticed what was going on!

This is an extreme example and likely related to the demands of shifting to virtual instruction without warning during the pandemic. However, even in the best of situations, the virtual environment makes it difficult to monitor student engagement, and some students may be minimally engaged if teachers do not consciously work to monitor and enhance engagement. In a physical class setting, a teacher can frequently circulate around the room, looking over students' shoulders, visually scanning across the classroom to see if students are on or off task, and listening for auditory cues like students talking too loudly or about inappropriate topics. In the virtual setting, teachers can and should monitor students on their screens, but even with their cameras on, students can look engaged when they are in fact tuning out, looking at non-course-related material, or even messaging with friends. Teachers will need to carefully solicit and monitor students' active participation, providing praise for appropriate participation and correcting when students do not participate.

Consider something like the following:

Print a copy of the Opportunities to Respond Observation Sheet in Chapter 10, Task 2, Tool 6 for a selected class period. Randomly select four students each day who you will monitor throughout class, or select four students for the first half of class and four different students for the second half. When you provide an opportunity to respond, such as having students gesture, use a reaction on the screen, or type a response in the chat box, look for the responses from each of the four students. If the student responded, mark a + in the appropriate box. When possible, provide positive feedback to the student: "Hannah, thanks for being with me and responding!" If the student did not respond, mark a – and follow up with a verbal or written prompt to solicit the student's attention: "Jonathan, I look forward to seeing your response in the chat box over the next 2 minutes."

If you use this procedure regularly, not only will you be able to identify which students are participating regularly and which students are struggling, it will prompt you to distribute positive and corrective feedback across your class. Students will learn that they are accountable for participating and that you will notice if they are not engaged. You might also periodically calculate rates of engagement by adding up the number of pluses and dividing by the total opportunities to respond (pluses and minuses). You can report these rates of engagement to students, letting them know that you are selecting different students each day but not telling them who you monitored. Set a goal with the class for the rates of engagement the class will maintain each day.

An alternative is to use your class roster and mark tallies next to student names when you notice their participation. While it is probably not possible to tally every student every time they participate, especially if you are using lots of whole group responses, you can start to identify any students who you have not seen participate. As the class session progresses, monitor those students who do not have tally marks next to their names more closely, and find ways to prompt them to participate.

CHAPTER 5, TASK 2

Understand Why and How to Use Data for Continuous Improvement in Your Classroom

Read the task on pages 241–253 and implement as is.

CHAPTER 5, TASK 3

Use Data Snapshots to Monitor and Adjust Your Management Plan

Read the task on pages 253–256 and implement as is.

CHAPTER 6, TASK 1

Strive to Provide a High Ratio of Positive Interactions

Read the task on pages 258–264 and implement as is.

Recognize that maintaining a ratio of positive interactions of at least 3:1 is just as important in the virtual environment as it is in a physical classroom setting, but it may require more intentionality and thought. When you see students in a school building, many positive interactions occur in casual remarks in the hallway or common areas or when circulating around the classroom. In the virtual environment, these kinds of natural interactions may feel more forced, especially at first. Therefore, it is important to create a plan for monitoring and boosting your positive interactions with students using strategies in the following sections of this chapter.

CHAPTER 6, TASK 2

Build Positive Relationships With Students With Noncontingent Attention

Read the task on pages 264–272 and implement with the following adaptations and considerations.

Consider how to convey warmth, trust, nurturance, and acceptance of students when your primary interaction occurs through a computer screen. How will you build positive relationships with students and provide attention that is not contingent on any specific accomplishments or efforts the students display? Consider how to apply noncontingent strategies used in a traditional classroom environment in the virtual classroom, including:

- Greeting students by name as they enter the virtual platform
- Learning how to correctly identify your students and pronounce their names
- Showing an interest in students' work and other interests
- Learning more about students' cultures and other aspects of their personal identities they would like to share
- Using trust generators to build rapport with students
- Identifying, honoring, and fostering student strengths
- Inviting students to ask for assistance
- Having a conversation with a student or a group of students
- Making a special effort to greet or provide other forms of noncontingent attention with any student you've recently interacted with regarding a misbehavior

It is important to think through times when you can have authentic noncontingent interactions with students. Use times before and after class to meet with individual students or open the class up for discussion about topics not related to your course content. Use virtual office hours or Q & A sessions to connect. Create periodic times during your class to get to know your students. This can occur with the whole group, or by pulling a small group or individual into a breakout room while others are working independently.

In addition to creating times for noncontingent interactions, consider the different forms noncontingent attention can take in the virtual environment. Interactions can be verbal through meetings and discussion with students on the virtual platform and phone calls. They can be nonverbal through the chat box, text messaging, and email. Apply specific strategies like the following to connect with your students:

- Learn about and acknowledge milestones (e.g., birthdays, special holidays or cultural rituals, sports or other extracurricular accomplishments).
- Learn about students' favorite music and create a virtual playlist that you can use when students enter the classroom, during class breaks, and at other appropriate times.
- Make an effort to periodically send individualized messages to students through the chat box or email with brief messages like: "I hope you are well. It's good to see you

today," "Thinking about you and hoping that everything went OK with your mom's surgery," and "I heard that your music recital went really well. I'd love for you to tell me about it at some point this week."

- Use short games and brain teasers to have fun with your class.
- Use GIF and emoji check-ins. For example, have students select a GIF that represents how they are feeling on a particular day and submit it to you with a brief description of why they selected it. Invite individual students to share with the group if they would like, but do not randomly call on students or force any individuals to share.
- Share something interesting that happened to you or a fun fact students don't know about you, then invite a few students to share their own interesting experience or fun fact.
- Give students a chance to write about or record a short video about three things they would like you to know about them. Keep this open ended. One student might let you know about their hobbies and interests while another student might let you know he is struggling because his parents are going through a divorce.
- Have "sharing" time a few times a week and select two or three students who you will notify in advance that it will be their sharing time at the next class session. Rotate through the class so everyone gets opportunities to share.
- Smile at students and position windows on your screen so that your eyes look like you are making eye contact. Convey enthusiasm and interest through your facial expressions and tone of voice.
- Schedule brief Planned Discussion meetings with each student—weekly in the first few weeks of school and then less frequently for most students. For students who have lower attendance or work completion rates, continue to have these meetings throughout the semester. You might schedule appointments or pull students into these one-on-one meetings during group work breakout room time.
- Be honest with students about your adjustment to virtual learning. Ask for feedback from students about things that are working and things that aren't.
- Set up virtual office hours for students to drop in with questions and concerns.
- Set up an optional lunch video session for students to join and socialize with each other.
- Set up a discussion board with a thread for students to use to communicate with you (you can ask students to use this board first before directly emailing you so that other students can view common questions and answers) and a thread for students to use to communicate with each other (you can monitor this board but not participate).

 UPDATE YOUR CLASSROOM MANAGEMENT PLAN

ITEM 10: INTERACT POSITIVELY

List specific ways you plan to provide noncontingent attention to students (e.g., learn to pronounce each student's name correctly, greet at least six students as they enter the virtual platform, etc.).

Provide Positive Feedback With Contingent Attention

Read the task on pages 272–280 and implement with the following adaptations and considerations.

Positive feedback in the virtual classroom should be frequent and given to the whole group and to individual students. Follow the six hallmarks for contingent positive feedback outlined in Chapter 6, Task 3. It should be accurate, specific and descriptive, contingent, age appropriate and nonembarrassing, given immediately, and given in a manner that fits your style.

While most of the recommendations for these hallmarks apply without adaptation, you will need to give special consideration to providing nonembarrassing positive feedback in the virtual setting. In a traditional classroom setting, it is easy to give positive feedback in ways that do not put students on display because you can easily stand right next to them. In the virtual platform, any positive verbal feedback you provide will automatically be a public display, which may be embarrassing for some students and cause them to shut down or act inappropriately.

At the start of the year, consider asking each student whether they feel comfortable receiving positive feedback verbally or publicly in the chat box during your class meetings or if they would prefer to receive the feedback privately. If they express that it is OK to praise them publicly, make sure that the feedback is brief and businesslike: "Salomon, you were making a really solid connection in the breakout room," "Veronica, nice job following the expectations for independent work." If students would prefer to receive feedback privately, consider other methods for delivering feedback, such as typing feedback privately into the chat box, sending a brief email, or making a quick phone call to the student while you are muted and other students are working. While it may have less impact, you can also provide positive feedback more generally to the group, as in: "I noticed several of you have been doing a great job responding each time I give a prompt for participation. You are showing lots of responsibility. Keep up the good work." You could then follow up with a quick private message, "Kendra—I meant you! Thanks for participating."

Strategies for Providing Feedback in a Virtual Classroom

Specific ways to provide positive feedback in the virtual classroom include:

- Provide brief verbal praise.
- Type positive feedback privately or publicly into the chat box.
- Use reaction features available on the virtual platform, such as a thumbs-up or clapping.
- Send a positive email or written note or postcard home.
- Use a physical gesture like a wink, thumbs-up, head nod, or clapping.
- Make a positive phone call.
- Meet one-on-one with the student in a breakout room, before or after class, or during office hours.

- Display exemplary work in class, on your website, in social media posts, or in email messages. Remove identifying information as appropriate.
- Make a positive referral—share information about something the student is doing well with your administrator or another staff member (e.g., counselor, special education case manager, mentor) who can reach out to the student or family and provide positive feedback.
- Identify a Student of the Week who has demonstrated one or more of your Guidelines for Success.
- Give students jobs that allow you to provide praise and acknowledgment for helping you or the class. For example, one student might be the class Note Taker who takes notes for students who were absent from class. Another student might be the Chat Monitor, who lets you know when there is a question or important comment in the chat box. Additional ideas for virtual jobs are included later in this chapter.
- Use intermittent celebrations or structured reinforcement systems to acknowledge growth and achievements (see suggestions in the next tasks in this chapter).

> **Getting Creative With Positive Feedback**
>
> *One teacher in Oregon shared with us that she periodically tells her students that when she randomly calls on a student and they get a correct answer during instructional activities or when they are participating appropriately, she will put a sticker on her face. Over the course of the activity, she adds more and more stickers. She said, "I will do anything to get my kids to laugh, even if I look silly! We all love it, and it makes class so fun!" Many thanks to Bailey Watson for sharing this fun way to connect with students while providing positive feedback.*

UPDATE YOUR CLASSROOM MANAGEMENT PLAN

ITEM 10: INTERACT POSITIVELY

List specific ways you plan to provide contingent attention to students.

CHAPTER 6, TASK 4

Provide Intermittent Celebrations

Read the task on pages 281–285 and implement with the following adaptations and considerations.

Use intermittent celebrations of success in the virtual environment to acknowledge when students reach academic goals or improve performance, demonstrate your Guidelines for Success, or exhibit important behaviors such as regular attendance or active participation. These celebrations can occur with individual students and with groups of students or the whole class to acknowledge their progress and success.

In the virtual setting, the main adaptation to how you provide intermittent celebrations is the rewards that you provide. Following are examples of rewards that can be given in the virtual setting.

- Play a virtual game such as Pictionary using the virtual whiteboard, a Rock/Paper/Scissors tournament, or Two Truths and a Lie using polls or chat to vote
- Students submit song recommendations for class entry, exit, or work time
- Students vote (poll) on song selections for class entry, exit, or work time
- Invite a guest speaker (principal, counselor, outside speaker)
- Pajama day
- Dance party (mail students glow sticks in advance and have students turn down their lights)
- Play a funny sound throughout a lesson when students do a certain behavior (like some restaurants ring a bell when someone leaves a tip, play a duck quacking or other funny noise when someone contributes a great idea or the group has been focused and participating for a period of time)
- Write a collaborative story—each student provides an idea
- Have a Crazy ___ Day (hair, face paint, costume) or theme day (Talk-Like-a-Pirate Day, Backward Day, Opposite Day)
- Positive letter or postcard mailed home
- Positive phone call home from the teacher or principal
- Watch a movie as a class with popcorn (popcorn bags are mailed home to each student)
- Small individual raffle items that can be mailed home (nail polish, Gak/Silly Putty, school shirt/hat/bumper sticker)
- Free homework pass
- Make teacher do or wear something wacky (ice bucket challenge, dye hair with temporary color, funny makeup, clown nose/hair, shave head)
- Students provide recommendations of funny or inspiring YouTube or other videos (teacher reviews in advance and selects appropriate ones) to share with peers
- Let students choose a modified or independent assignment
- Leave class a few minutes early

UPDATE YOUR CLASSROOM MANAGEMENT PLAN

ITEM 10: ENCOURAGEMENT PROCEDURES

List ideas for how you plan to intermittently reinforce individuals and groups of students who demonstrate growth, effort, or achievement (e.g., identify at least two students who will receive certificates in the mail every month, play a funny 2- to 3-minute video when the class makes improvements on a goal they are working on, etc.).

CHAPTER 6, TASK 5

Maintain a Positive Ratio of Interactions With Parents and Guardians

Read the task on pages 286–288 and implement as is.

CHAPTER 6, TASK 6

Maintain Positive Communication With Colleagues

Read the task on pages 288–293 and implement as is.

CHAPTER 7, TASK 1

Understand Student Motivation

Read the task on pages 296–300 and implement as is.

CHAPTER 7, TASK 2

Use Non-Reward-Based Strategies to Increase Motivation and Responsible Behavior

Read the task on pages 301–309 and implement with the following adaptations and considerations.

In addition to using non-reward-based strategies such as stimulating interest and using goal-setting strategies with students, consider procedures to put in place for motivating students to attend virtual class and actively engaging students in virtual instruction.

Procedures for Motivating Students to Attend

Regular attendance can be one of the greatest challenges in the virtual classroom. Using STOIC strategies as described in this book and applying them specifically to attendance can greatly enhance the likelihood that students attend virtual sessions. Consider the following ideas for boosting student attendance:

- Provide rationale to students and parents about how attendance is important for their success and is essential for creating an effective classroom community. Consider using brief informational videos and letters emphasizing the importance of attendance, the goal of regular attendance—students attending at least 95% of the time—and your willingness to work with students and families to address any barriers and challenges that may make attending regularly a struggle. Avoid coming off as punitive or threatening, but express your positive hopes and expectations.

- Work to build a culture of attendance by regularly emphasizing it through your Guidelines for Success (e.g., "Class, you are demonstrating so much responsibility and integrity by showing up each day"), or consider creating an attendance motto or slogan that you use frequently in communication with students and parents ("Attendance matters!").

- When communicating your rationale for regular attendance, gently caution students and families about potential negative effects that can occur when a student is frequently absent. For example, the student may fall behind, peers may not want to work with the student because they have to frequently help the student get caught up, and you end up spending lots of time figuring out how to get the student caught up rather than planning effective instruction for the class. Have students brainstorm positive effects that can happen for individuals and the classroom community when they attend regularly as well as negative effects that can happen when they miss too much school.

- Provide frequent positive feedback for regular attendance or attendance improvements. Send letters home or make positive phone calls acknowledging students and families who attend at least 95% of the time, provide attendance certificates to students who have regular attendance each month, or make positive referrals to the administrator. For students who make attendance improvements from one month to the next, make an effort to provide acknowledgment to the student and family through positive calls or emails, and encourage the student to continue attending regularly.

- Greet and welcome students back from absences to show that you notice students, value when they attend class, and miss them when they are gone.

- Encourage students to contact their peers and encourage them to attend when they notice they are missing from class. Something as simple as a text message from a friend saying the student was missed in class can go a long way to encourage the student to come the next day.

- Use goal-setting strategies with individuals or the whole class related to improving attendance or maintaining a 95% or better attendance rate.

- Provide intermittent celebrations or use one or more individual or classwide reward systems (described in the next section) based on students' attendance rate.

- When a student has been gone for more than a day, make a brief phone call or send an email indicating that the student is missed and you hope to see them in class soon.

- When you notice that a student's attendance is consistently falling below the 95% mark, work with the student and family to identify and put supports in place to address any barriers or challenges that may cause the student to miss class. In some cases, this will involve bringing in other school personnel or community agencies to work with the family on solutions, but you play an important role in identifying the concern and starting productive communication with the student and family.

If you have significant concerns with attendance in your virtual classroom, *The Teacher's Guide to Tackling Attendance Challenges*, available through Ancora Publishing, provides a comprehensive guide for implementing strategies in the classroom to boost your students' attendance. While this resource was written for teachers in a traditional classroom setting, the majority of the strategies can be effectively used in the virtual environment as well.

Procedures for Actively Engaging Students in Virtual Instruction

Throughout this book, you have learned about ways to engage students in instruction. In this chapter, we provide tips for engaging students in virtual settings. On your Virtual Classroom Management Plan, summarize the ways that you will intentionally work to engage students, such as:

- Use frequent opportunities to respond during teacher-directed instruction that engage all learners. Use a variety of verbal, written, and action responses to keep things interesting.
- Use an effective presentational style—demonstrating energy and enthusiasm, conveying high positive expectations, varying the tone of your voice when providing instruction, and looking at your camera to make eye contact.
- Provide positive feedback and acknowledgment to students who are contributing and demonstrating effort in class.
- Create opportunities for social interaction and peer engagement through partner and small group breakout work, fun activities, and open discussion times. Clearly define parameters for appropriate social interaction and teach and monitor students' social interaction skills.
- Increase students' expectancy of success using effective instructional techniques and providing adaptations and accommodations as needed to ensure that all students can be successful in your classroom.
- Provide regular breaks during longer class sessions (e.g., at least one break per hour).

UPDATE YOUR CLASSROOM MANAGEMENT PLAN

ITEM 10: ENCOURAGEMENT PROCEDURES

- List ways you plan to motivate your students using non-reward-based methods.
- Describe specific ways you plan to stimulate interest and/or use goal-setting strategies with your students.
- Describe specific procedures you will use to motivate students to attend and engage them in virtual instruction and classroom activities.

CHAPTER 7, TASK 3

Employ One or More Classwide Reward Systems to Increase Motivation and Responsible Behavior

Read the task on pages 310–338 and implement with the following adaptations and considerations.

A classwide reward system may be appropriate in a virtual classroom under a variety of circumstances. Consider using one or more classwide systems when:

- The behavior of many students is challenging in many different ways (e.g., students not following directions, low attendance, students not participating in class activities, students disrupting instruction, students using technology to bully other students).
- Students are for the most part responsible but quite a few students have a problem with one specific behavior, such as work completion or not paying attention during instructional times.
- Your class behaves responsibly enough but students have grown apathetic or do the bare minimum to get by.

When designing and implementing a reward-based system in your virtual classroom, follow the steps and recommendations in Chapter 7, Task 3:

Step 1: Identify problems, goals, level of support needed, and the type of system you will use.

Step 2: Select a classwide system and prepare to implement it.

Step 3: Determine how to maintain, modify, and fade a classwide system.

One additional consideration that you should carefully analyze is whether the goals of the system are equitable and whether all students are capable of meeting the goals of the system. For example, basing a system around a goal of "arrive on time" is appropriate only when all students are fully capable of meeting this goal. Unlike a traditional classroom where tardies throughout the day are typically due to students dawdling in the hallway and socializing with peers, there may be circumstances in the home that are beyond a student's control and may cause them to be late (e.g., if a student has to share a computer with a sibling and their class times overlap). Work with the student, family, and your school to overcome these access barriers (e.g., in the previous example, to procure an additional device for the family). When this is not possible, you might need to modify the expectations of your system (e.g., remove the individual student from the group system and design an individualized way for that student to earn the same rewards as the class). Or do not use a reward-based system and simply encourage students to meet the goal as often as they can based on their personal circumstances.

When setting up the system, also consider potential threats to students' expectancy of success that are specific to the virtual environment, such as spotty Internet, lacking appropriate technology, not having the skills to use features of the technology required for participation, lacking needed materials in the home (e.g., no printer), competing responsibilities (e.g., helping watch younger siblings), not being able to adequately hear due to the home environment, or lacking prerequisite skills for typing or otherwise engaging. These factors should be considered in your selection and design of a reward-based motivational system.

For example, imagine your goal is for students to increase active participation, and one of the primary ways you work to engage students is by having them type responses in the chat box. If not all students have strong typing, spelling, and other writing skills, some students may refuse to engage for fear of embarrassment or because they know they cannot adequately express their ideas through the chat. One way to increase probability of success is to use the chat box primarily for shorter responses (e.g., one or two words) and have students submit longer responses privately to you. You can then read or paraphrase student responses for the class or randomly call on individuals to share their answers. This strategy could also be used with some individuals who would prefer not to have peers view their typed responses. While the rest of the class engages more publicly with the chat box, you have worked out a plan for the individual student to submit responses only to you. Another way to increase probability of success is to teach the class or certain individuals how to use a voice-to-text application to dictate their response verbally and then copy the text into the chat box. Some students might also write responses by hand, take a picture, and send it to you, or even audio record a response and send you the audio file. Whenever you identify a threat to students' expectancy of success, consider ways to alter the expectations or provide accommodations or other supports that increase their capability and confidence to meet the goals of the system.

You will also need to determine how to best take data on how students are meeting the goals of the system. This can be somewhat more challenging in the virtual environment than it is for systems based in the physical classroom. Consider the following examples and ideas for how to record data:

- For disruptions or other misbehaviors, keep a frequency count throughout the virtual class using a tally on a piece of paper or a golf counter.
- For attendance, have certain times when you identify students who are missing from the class or calculate the percentage of the class in attendance (e.g., at the beginning of class, in the middle, and at the end).
- For participation, mark down the number of students who respond to each poll or whole group response like a whiteboard or hold-up response. Randomly select certain opportunities to respond in the chat box and calculate the percentage of the class that participated.

Examples of Classwide Systems

Most of the systems described in Chapter 7, Task 3 can be used in the virtual classroom with minimal adaptations. The following are examples of a few specific systems that could be used to boost attendance, work completion, or participation.

Whole-Class Points for Attendance or Work Completion

Calculate the current average attendance or work completion rate for your class. Set a goal for improvement that is one or two students above your current average (e.g., if one or two more students attended or turned in their work each day). For example, if you currently average 22 out of 30 students in attendance each day, set a goal for 23 students in attendance. For each day students meet the goal, they earn a point. Celebrate with students when they meet their goal: "Class, we had 25 students in attendance today. Thank you all for showing that our work here matters!" Once the class earns a predetermined number of points, they receive a reward. Over time, as students are consistently meeting the initial goal, gradually increase the goal by one student at a time. Follow the remaining suggestions in Chapter 7, Task 3 for using a whole class point system.

Lottery Tickets for Attendance, Work Completion, Participation, Following Rules, or Meeting Guidelines for Success

Lottery tickets are an easy way to encourage a variety of appropriate behaviors. One possibility is to randomly select days in advance to award lottery tickets for a specific goal such as attending or completing work. Let students know that you have marked days on your calendar when you will award lottery tickets to those in attendance or those who completed all work for the day or week. Mark tallies on your class roster to keep track of how many lottery tickets each student earned. On the day of the drawing (e.g., each Friday or every other Friday), fill out the correct number of lottery tickets for each student or enter student entries into a computerized drawing. Select student names during the class period. Each student whose name is drawn earns the reward. This approach could also be used for participation—randomly select a few active participation responses during your classes. Each student who participated appropriately receives a tally indicating they earned a lottery ticket.

Another possibility is to use the lottery ticket approach to encourage appropriate behaviors such as those in your classroom rules or Guidelines for Success. For example, when you notice a student has demonstrated exceptional effort or was highly responsible throughout class, let them know that you will be marking a lottery ticket tally next to their name.

Target and Reward a Specific Behavior: Participation

To encourage all students to participate throughout class, count the number of students who are not participating during each time you present an opportunity to respond. For example, if you release a poll and 26 out of 30 students complete the poll, count 4 students not participating. If the next response is a reaction to give a thumbs-up/thumbs-down on screen or a Yes/No reaction button for students off screen, count the number of students who did not give a reaction. If two students did not react, add this to your count (4 + 2 = 6). If the next opportunity to respond is for students to type an idea into the chat box, quickly count the number of responses. If 22 students typed responses, count 8 students not participating and add it to your total (4 + 2 + 8 = 14). After 2 days, share the information you have collected with students and tell them they need to increase their frequency of participation. Guide the class in setting a realistic goal—reducing nonparticipation across the class from 30 times a period to 24, for example—and provide a randomly selected reward on each day students meet the goal. Follow the remaining suggestions in Chapter 7, Task 3 for implementing a system to Target and Reward a Specific Behavior.

UPDATE YOUR CLASSROOM MANAGEMENT PLAN

ITEM 10: ENCOURAGEMENT PROCEDURES

If you have identified that one or more reward-based systems may be beneficial for your class, update your Classroom Management Plan with the systems you plan to use and for what behaviors.

CHAPTER 8, TASK 1

Maintain Positive Expectations

Read the task on pages 342–345 and implement with the following adaptations and considerations.

In addition to maintaining positive expectations with your students, maintaining positive expectations with families is of particular importance when students are learning from home. In the same way that low expectations can set the stage for low achievement with students, low expectations with families can set the stage for ineffective communication and low engagement. While high and positive expectations for students set the stage for high achievement, high and positive expectations for parents and families create a foundation for mutual respect and collaboration. Apply the suggestions in Chapter 8, Task 1 using a lens for how you consider and communicate your high positive expectations and regard for students and their family members.

CHAPTER 8, TASK 2

Provide Effective, Fluent Corrective Feedback

Read the task on pages 346–353 and implement with the following adaptations and considerations.

Effective corrective feedback in the virtual classroom is delivered consistently, calmly, briefly, and, as much as possible, privately. The following are additional suggestions for implementing these principles in the virtual classroom.

Consistent

In any classroom, corrective consequences should fit the severity and frequency of the misbehavior, and it is better to err on the side of milder rather than harsher corrective consequences. In the virtual classroom, a limited number of corrective consequences can be implemented, so be very cautious that you do not jump too quickly to more severe consequences. It is better to use milder consequences consistently and move more quickly to intervention planning than to apply a more severe consequence that is harsher than the misbehavior being displayed.

For example, one severe corrective consequence that is often used too early or too often is removing the student from the virtual class meeting. This correction is the virtual equivalent of removing a student to the office, so it should be used only in the most extreme circumstances and with the most severe misbehavior. This corrective consequence is appropriate only when class cannot continue because the student's misbehavior is so severely disruptive or an incident is so emotionally harmful that the class cannot continue to function while the student is present. For example, this consequence might be appropriate if the student repeatedly unmutes and shouts disrespectfully and continually over the teacher or peers, or the student makes a threat of violence towards the teacher or class. It is not appropriate if the student makes a disrespectful comment but then sits passively and quietly for the remainder of class, or if the student refuses to participate but is logged into the session.

For most misbehavior, select milder corrective consequences that you will be comfortable using every time the student exhibits the misbehavior. See the next section of this chapter for a menu of corrective consequences that can be used in the virtual classroom.

Calm

Unless you use the chat box to deliver corrective feedback, your corrections in a synchronous class session will be public and on display for the rest of the class. Because most corrections will be highly visible to the student's peers, it is even more important to implement corrections for misbehavior in a calm and unemotional way. Your corrections should be emotionally neutral and matter of fact, short, respectful, and clearly refer to expectations or rules that have been pretaught. Consider how to apply the suggestions for delivering calm corrections in Chapter 7, Task 3.

Brief

Keeping corrective interactions brief at the moment of misbehavior is extremely important because of the public nature of corrections in the virtual classroom. Use one liner corrections that refer to your pretaught rules or explanations. Tell any student who needs or wants to discuss a concern further that you will make an appointment with them at the end of class. Then continue with instructional activities with the class.

Private

When possible, deliver corrective feedback privately through the chat box or by getting other students to work independently for a few minutes while you move with the individual student into a breakout room to deliver corrective feedback.

Remember to give positive feedback when behavior improves. If the student's behavior improves after your correction, privately send them brief specific praise in the chat box or find an unobtrusive way to let them know you acknowledge their improved behavior. Be careful not to deliver effusive public praise, especially with students who might be embarrassed or think it is uncool to look like they complied with your expectations. If you are unable to deliver private positive feedback after the student's misbehavior, make sure to follow up after the class with an email, positive phone call home, or other way to let the student know you noticed their efforts prior to your next class session with the student.

CHAPTER 8, TASK 3
Develop a Menu of Corrective Consequences

Many of the corrective consequences in menu in Chapter 8, Task 3 are not applicable or must be significantly adapted for use in the virtual classroom. Read the introductory content for Chapter 8, Task 3 on pages 353–354, then read the suggestions below for developing a menu of virtual corrective techniques.

Corrective Consequences for the Virtual Classroom

Proximity/Forced Change of View

In a physical classroom, many teachers use a strategy of moving toward students who are engaged in misbehavior as an early-stage approach for getting students to change inappropriate behavior. In the virtual classroom, you cannot physically move toward students, but it may be possible to change the direction of their attention through a forced change of view. Using this strategy involves changing the view on the screen so that students' attention might be drawn back into the current classroom activities. For example, if you have been screen-sharing slides for an extended period of time, exiting out of screen sharing so that students are looking at a gallery or speaker view can draw students back in. Or showing a quick video can break students' attention from off-task or disruptive behavior.

In other cases, proximity is implied by including all students in the conversation and dialogue. For example, frequently use your students' names in instructional examples: "If Tanisha was exploring in the Amazon and . . .," "When Dani and Gabriella shared their ideas about the reading, it made me think . . ." Call on students or use student names from a variety of locations on your screen, or find out if the images will shuffle on your screen when you briefly turn your camera view on and off.

Nonverbal Correction

To deliver a nonverbal cue like a hand signal or subtly shaking your head "no," you will need to gain the student's attention first. This can be done by saying the student's name and then delivering the cue.

Another form of nonverbal correction is a simple direction or reprimand delivered through the chat box. This is a great way to deliver private corrective feedback, but it carries the risk that the student may not immediately see the correction if they are not looking at their chat box. Consider verbally telling the student something like, "Habib, I just wrote you a quick message in the chat. Give me a thumbs-up on screen or an OK in the chat once you've seen it." If you use this strategy, make sure that you periodically use a similar verbal message to let students know when you have written positive feedback in the chat so that students don't start to associate this procedure with reprimands.

Provide a Group Redirect

Sometimes a group reminder about expectations can serve to get a student back on track. Avoid singling out an individual by directing the group's attention to what they should be doing. "Class, just a reminder to everyone, right now you should be typing ideas into the chat box." Group redirects typically work best when a student's misbehavior is not hugely obvious to other students (e.g., quiet off-task behavior,) or when multiple students could use a reminder (e.g., several students have not responded to a participation prompt). If the inappropriate behavior is displayed by only one student and it is fairly obvious who the group redirect is for, it would be more effective to use a brief individual correction with the student.

Planned Discussion

Sometimes you may need to talk with a student about a misbehavior in a way that is more detailed and lengthier than a reprimand. For example, if a student makes a disrespectful comment as you are presenting a lesson, you may want to have a private talk with the student about the importance of treating others respectfully. Provide a gentle reprimand immediately and let the student know that the behavior is serious enough that you want to discuss it later—after class, during office hours, or before the next class meeting.

If you have a discussion with the student in a breakout room during the class period, ensure that all other students are engaged in an independent or cooperative group activity that does not require your immediate supervision and help. Also ensure that the conversation does not go longer than 2 to 5 minutes so that you are not away from your class for too long. If the conversation looks like it may require more time, schedule a follow-up meeting.

NOTE: If you have already had a discussion or two with a student about similar misbehaviors, continue having periodic planned discussions with the student to evaluate how things are going, but consider implementing other corrective techniques and STOIC strategies to help the student be successful.

Count and Chart

If you have already discussed a problem behavior with a student but have seen no improvement, explain to the student that you are going to conduct a frequency count (or duration or latency recording for less frequent but lengthy behaviors). At the end of each day or period, the student will chart the amount of misbehavior to help them understand just how often the misbehavior is occurring. This strategy can also be used with a whole class.

Record the number of times the misbehavior occurs by writing tally marks on a recording sheet (e.g., tally the number of times the student disrupted or blurted out) or recording the length of time the misbehavior occurs (e.g., record minutes of work refusal). Tell the student you will give her a signal every time your record an instance, or have the student do the recording when you signal. Tell the student you will use the data to determine her progress and whether you need to talk with her parents or involve an administrator. One benefit of the Count and Chart strategy is that it allows you to address each instance of misbehavior consistently but without providing much attention or emotional energy to each interaction. For a student who is unaware of the frequency or length of their misbehavior, or for a student who is seeking attention through misbehavior, this can be a very powerful strategy.

Loss of Point

If you use the behavior grading procedures presented in Chapter 3, you have already set your class up so that certain infractions result in the loss of a point. Point systems can provide another corrective consequence option. If you use any kind of point system in your class, establish a rule that certain infractions result in point fines. In this system, each student starts the beginning of the week with a preestablished number of points—say, 15 out of a possible weekly total of 20. During the week, each singled-out example of positive behavior adds a point and each rule violation subtracts a point from the student's total.

Behavior Improvement Form

A Behavior Improvement Form prompts students to reflect on their actions and avoid future problems. When a student misbehaves, calmly say, "That was an example of [*blank*]. Please think about what you did and fill out a Behavior Improvement Form." Reproducible 8.3 (Version 2) on p. 364 shows an example of such a form. The Behavior Improvement Form requires students to think about their actions, begin assuming responsibility, and learn how to take control by identifying more acceptable ways of handling similar situations. On this form, the student is asked to describe how he thinks you, the teacher, would describe the incident. Reproducible 8.3 (Version 3) on p. 364 is a form specifically for classes and schools that use the CHAMPS acronym to guide behavior.

Restitution

The goal of restitution is for a misbehaving student to learn that when her behavior causes damage, she needs to repair that damage. If a student is rude to a guest speaker, she should be required to apologize in writing or via the phone or video chat to the guest speaker. If you use the restitution strategy, try to make it clear to the student that what you are asking her to do, such as apologize to the guest speaker, is not a punishment but a reparation—an attempt to repair any damage her rudeness may have caused in terms of the guest speaker's feelings or his opinion of students in the school.

If a student engages in behavior that causes damage, a logical consequence is that the student has to repair the damage. For example, if the student damages school-provided equipment, the student needs to pay to fix it. If the student is unable to afford the repair, the student might need to do school-related jobs to compensate for the damage.

Humor

Humor can be a powerful and effective way to respond to misbehavior—especially with older students. For example, consider a situation in which a student makes a smart-aleck comment on the second day of school as the teacher is presenting a lesson. If the teacher is quick-witted enough, she might be able to respond to the student's comment in a way that will make the student himself laugh, and a tense moment will be diffused. However, please note that you should not use sarcasm or ridicule, which is at the expense of the student. The sensitive use of humor brings people closer together. Sarcasm or ridicule makes a student feel hostile and angry that you made a joke at their expense.

If you do use humor in response to a misbehavior, you should plan on talking to the student later to make sure that he understands that his behavior was not acceptable and that he knows you expect him to behave more responsibly in the future. In addition, you can check to see that you did not embarrass the student with your humorous comment. Be extremely careful with the use of humor. If there is any concern that the student will misunderstand your attempt at humor, or if other students will not get it and think you are being mean or belittling the student, do not use this strategy.

Removal from the Class Session

As previously mentioned, sending a student out of the class should be reserved for only the most severe misbehavior. Students whose misbehavior may be occurring because they are attempting to cover up for an academic or social skills deficit may find removal from class highly reinforcing. Removal from class will not work for students who are unable to demonstrate the expected behavior because they don't understand expectations, are unaware they are exhibiting misbehavior, or currently lack skills to demonstrate expected behavior. It also has the potential to demonstrate to some students that they are not a valued member of the class community. Finally, students who are removed from class often fall further behind, which can lead to a cycle of misbehavior due to confusion or frustration, leading to further exclusion.

Any time this strategy is used, you must write an ODR and include written evidence of the misbehavior(s) that occurred. If the student exhibits severe misbehavior that warrants removal from class more than once, you must begin intervention planning to determine what individualized strategies are needed to prevent misbehavior from occurring in the future. See suggestions later in this chapter for ideas for intervention planning.

UPDATE YOUR CLASSROOM MANAGEMENT PLAN

ITEM 11: CORRECTION PROCEDURES FOR MISBEHAVIOR

List the menu of corrective consequences you plan to use in your classroom. Make note of any implementation recommendations that you would like to highlight and remember.

CHAPTER 8, TASK 4
Know When (and When Not) to Use Disciplinary Referral

Read and implement the task on pp. 370–377 as is. It may be beneficial to discuss specific examples of moderate and severe misbehaviors that occur in the virtual setting with your administrator or whole staff to determine which situations warrant administrator involvement and which you should handle.

CHAPTER 8, TASK 5

Use Supportive Communication With Parents Regarding Student Misbehavior

Read and implement the task on pp. 378–380 as is.

CHAPTER 8, TASK 6

Move Toward Proactive Intervention Planning With Individual Students Who Display Chronic Misbehavior

Read and implement the task on pp. 381–391 with the following adaptations and considerations.

Chapter 8, Task 6 provides recommendations for when you should consider beginning proactive intervention planning rather than relying on the idea that corrective consequences alone are going to resolve the problem. In the virtual setting, begin proactive intervention planning sooner rather than later, especially when you have concerns about inconsistent attendance and limited engagement. These problems are unlikely to respond to purely punitive approaches. The reality is that teachers and schools cannot punish most students and families into being motivated to attend or participate!

Therefore, consider classroom-based interventions and supports outside of the classroom that can help the student to be successful. See the examples of classroom-based interventions in Chapter 8, Task 6. For the Meaningful Work intervention, the following are sample jobs that could be used in a virtual classroom to meet student needs such as competence, purpose, and attention:

- Music Master (chooses opening and closing music)
- Timekeeper (early sign-on with responsibilities)
- Mute monitor
- Go Noodle Break leader
- Calendar or weather leader
- Attendance monitor
- Chat monitor
- Daily newscaster
- Cultural/Holiday monitor
- Mindfulness leader—leads relaxation lesson
- Tally keeper for participation, etc.
- Greeting Question/Question of the Day
- Have the student read the daily announcements
- Tech specialist
- Link/Instructions checker
- Small group discussion facilitator
- Specific tasks for project work (researcher, graph maker, etc.)

Thank you to educators in IMESD, HDESD, and CGESD in Oregon who provided some of these job ideas.

- Demonstrator
- Assignment checker—make sure teacher has posted the assignment
- Summarizes directions or provides recap of key points of understanding
- Agenda minder—checks off when each item is completed
- Classroom greeter—greets peers as they enter
- Teacher's aide for the class—helps other students who need help
- Sound engineer
- Brain Break leader
- Student translator
- Compliment/Encouragement giver
- Recorder of classroom instructions

CHAPTER 9, TASK 1

Make Final Preparations for Day One

Read the task on pages 397–407 and implement with the following adaptations and considerations.

Review Your Completed Classroom Management Plan

Figure 11.6 shows a completed Virtual Classroom Management Plan for a virtual sixth-grade classroom that requires high levels of support.

Develop a Modified Schedule for the First Day of School

Follow the majority of the suggestions in Chapter 9, Task 1 for developing a modified schedule for the first day. Obviously, you will not need to design a sign for your classroom, but it may be beneficial to send out a reminder email 10 minutes or so before class starts reminding students how to log in, providing the meeting link, and letting students know you look forward to seeing them shortly. Create a welcoming slide that will be on the screen when students enter, and prepare an initial independent activity that students can work on when they enter the room. You want to ensure that students don't feel awkward and uncomfortable immediately upon entering your class while they are waiting for the class to begin. Create a one-page orientation handout for families that you can provide in advance of the first day or that you can overview with your students on Day 1 and send to families immediately after the first class.

If you anticipate that some students will have a parent or caregiver sitting next to them on the first day of class, consider preparing welcoming remarks, and include clear expectations for those who might want to usurp your time during the first class. For example, you might welcome family members by saying, "Thank you so much to those parents and caregivers who are here with us today. I look forward to meeting you and partnering with you across the course of this year! For today, my goal is to get our class up and running and for me to start getting to know your children, so if you have questions or things I need to know about, hold on to

Figure 11.6 *Virtual Classroom Management Plan (Reproducible 11.1) Example*

Virtual Classroom Management Plan (p. 1 of 5)   *CHAMPS*

TEACHER *Mr. Hernandez*   SCHOOL YEAR *2022*   GRADE LEVEL/CLASS *Sixth-grade ELA*

LINK TO MEETING ROOM _____

The level of support I anticipate establishing is (check one): ☒ High   ☐ Medium   ☐ Low

ITEM 1 Guidelines for Success (*pp. 481–482*)

Winners make their own luck. They achieve. It takes:

- *Preparation*
- *Responsibility*
- *Integrity*
- *Dedication*
- *Effort*

to be successful!

ITEM 2 Posted Rules (*pp. 482–485*) *Winners know the rules and follow them.*

1. *Come to class every day that you are not sick. (Communicate with the teacher when there are circumstances out of your control that make it so you cannot attend).*
2. *Arrive on time with all class materials. (Communicate with the teacher when there are circumstances out of your control that make it so you cannot arrive on time or cannot access needed materials).*
3. *Keep negative comments to yourself or discuss concerns with the teacher.*
4. *Follow directions the first time.*
5. *Stay on task during all work times.*

These will be posted continuously behind me on a bulletin board throughout class.

ITEM 3 Attention Signal (*pp. 494–495*)

I will play a chime on my computer to call attention. Students should put down their writing utensil or anything else in their hands and raise one arm to show they are paying attention. If they have their camera off, they should use the "hand raise" icon.

ITEM 4 Beginning and Ending Routines (*pp. 496–502*)

1. Routine for how students will enter the virtual space:

    I will greet each student as they enter the room. I will play music and have an introductory slide available.

    For students entering the classroom:
    1. *Check that you have your computer/tablet and it is plugged in prior to class starting.*
    2. *Be logged in and seated at your personal workspace before the posted start of class time.*
    3. *Have your folder and writing implement ready. Double-check the screen to see if any other materials are needed for the day.*
    4. *Begin work on the activity that is on the screen.*
    5. *Quietly work on this activity until I signal for your attention.*

2. Routine for how opening business is conducted:

    I will have a buzzer on my phone for our start time. When it goes off, I will use my attention signal to get the class started. While I take attendance, students should be working on the challenge problem/journal entry. I will try to provide at least 3 students with positive feedback. I will send a quick text or email to any student who has not arrived

REPRODUCIBLE 11.1

Figure 11.6 continued *Virtual Classroom Management Plan (Reproducible 11.1) Example*

Virtual Classroom Management Plan (p. 2 of 5)   *CHAMPS*

3. Routine for taking attendance and monitoring at different points during the virtual class:

   Take a screenshot of participant list right at start of class and enter attendance into the school system while students are working. Midway through class, take another screenshot, and again in the final 2 minutes of class. After students exit, update my personal spreadsheet to record students who were not present during portions of class.

4. Routine for students who enter late and exit early:

   Teach students: If you are in the virtual meeting and seated before I ring our starting bell, you are on time. If you enter after the bell rings or are wandering around to get the materials you need for class, you are tardy and will lose 1 behavior point. When you are tardy, enter the room silently. Type in the chat and provide your reason for being late (attach an excused note if you have one), then immediately join in whatever activity the class is doing. All tardies are reported to the attendance office according to school policy. If you have to leave early, submit the reason to me in the chat box before exiting, or send me an email within the same day.

5. Routine for students returning after an absence:

   Any time students are absent, they will view a video of the large-group activities missed. Students and families will need to determine when they can work this into their schedule. Students will also need to complete independent practice and vocabulary assignments for the days missed.
   They will have the same number of days to make up work as the number of days they were absent. If students are unable to make up the work in a timely way, the student and I will meet with parents/guardians to work out a plan. I will teach: Always be in class unless you are seriously ill!

6. Routine for wrapping up at the end of day/class:

   Share a closing slide with final thoughts, work students will need to complete outside of class time, and materials needed for next class. Provide positive and corrective feedback. Close with a positive quote, joke, or wacky activity of the day.

ITEM 5   CHAMPS Expectations for Classroom Activities and Transitions *(pp. 503–504 & 511–524; Forms 11.4 & 11.5)*

Forms are completed for Teacher Instruction, Independent Work (computer work, independent writing activities), Tests, and small group work. I will provide a sample and a video overview for families about how they can clarify expectations with their student for independent work outside of class time.

REPRODUCIBLE 11.1

Figure 11.6 *Virtual Classroom Management Plan (Reproducible 11.1) Example*

Virtual Classroom Management Plan (p. 3 of 5)   *CHAMPS*

ITEM 6   Procedures for Family Contact (*pp. 504–508*)

At the beginning of the year, I will send home an initial letter to all families, and I will also use available email to send the letter. With the letter, I will have a quick video where I talk to families about my class, what students will learn, and my hope they will communicate openly with me about successes and concerns. I will use a communication and needs survey to find out more about my families. Throughout the year, I will make ongoing efforts to reach out to families via email, phone, and office hours (other methods as needed based on indications by families). I will host a monthly parent/guardian information and Q & A session. I have marked my calendar with points when I will make sure to reach out to families to connect and see how things are going—some will be whole group and I will rotate through with more personalized contacts.

ITEM 7   Procedures for Managing Student Assignments (*pp. 524–526*)

1. Procedures for assigning classwork and homework/asynchronous work:

    Every 2 weeks, students will receive a folder in the mail with their name on it and materials they will be using for the next 2 weeks. It will include a weekly assignment sheet that outlines the tasks that will be worked on for the next 2 weeks. We will review the assignment sheet each day, and I will keep the class website updated.

2. Procedures for ensuring all students can access needed materials:

    All print materials will be included in the student's folder. We will use a poll to make sure all students received their materials, and if any students do not receive items mailed home, we will work out an individualized plan. I will share digital materials in three ways: emailed in advance of class, on the class website on the section for the day, and in the chat box.

3. Procedures for collecting completed work:

    Students will submit work by uploading it to the class website by going to the date the assignment is due, clicking on the assignment, and following the upload instructions. We will go over exact details for how to do this several times during the first weeks of class. I will also record an instructional video that will be on the website and emailed to all students/families.

4. Procedures for keeping records and providing feedback to students:

    A grade printout will be sent home every 2 weeks. On the in-between weeks, I will provide an emailed version to parents/guardians and I will give each student a digital copy in class that they will review and use to set goals for the next week. This will include current grade in the class, any missing assignments, and a progress report showing current level of mastery of course objectives. Students can receive 3 bonus points each week they submit their grade report with a parent signature or upload a brief video of the parent/guardian saying they have viewed the grade report. For students who are beginning to fall behind with either work or learning objectives (less than 90% work completion or 75% mastery), I will set up a meeting with them to work together to come up with a plan for support.

5. Procedures and policies for dealing with late and missing assignments:

    When students are missing an assignment, they will fill out and submit a digital "missing assignment slip." If the assignment is late without valid communication and reason, the student will receive a 2-point reduction in participation points for the day the assignment was due. I will not accept late assignments during the final week of class. If a student has more than three missing assignments, or they are missing any major long-term assignment, I will set up a meeting with the student and family so we can come up with a plan.

       REPRODUCIBLE 11.1

Figure 11.6 continued *Virtual Classroom Management Plan (Reproducible 11.1) Example*

Virtual Classroom Management Plan (p. 4 of 5)　　　　　　　　　　*CHAMPS*

ITEM 8 Procedures for Managing Student Technology Use (*pp. 526–527*)

See attached technology contract that I will distribute to students and families. I will teach about the contract in the first week of school and send home a recorded video discussing each of the contract items.

ITEM 9 Long-Range Goals (*p. 527*)

By the end of this class, students will be able to:

- *Read long multisyllable words.*
- *Use strategies to understand and analyze what they read. These strategies include: a) Paraphrasing, b) Visual imagery, c) Self-questioning.*
- *Learn to use new vocabulary words.*
- *Read aloud smoothly and with expression.*
- *Write complete sentences and well-organized paragraphs.*
- *Learn study strategies so they can take ELA tests with confidence and perform well on those tests.*
- *Learn to self-manage and stay on task with class work and homework.*

Accomplishing this will require cooperation. Teach students to think of this class like a sport such as basketball or track. They will have to work hard independently, but they will also have to work effectively with other students and with me.

ITEM 10 Procedures for Interacting Positively With and Encouraging Students (*pp. 534–545*)

1. Procedures for motivating students to attend virtual class:

   Emphasize the importance of attendance in bi-weekly mini lessons about how attendance impacts success in school and work. Use a daily visual posting of the percentage of the class that attended and the percentage of work completion across the class. Set short-term goals and use intermittent or structured reinforcement for meeting improved attendance goals. Use an interest inventory on Day One to find out how to get students excited to attend—connecting to their interest, playing preferred music, doing goofy activities as a class.

2. Procedures for interacting positively and building a positive relationship with students:

   Greet students by name when they enter. Spend 10 minutes of each class each week connecting with individuals in a breakout room and/or inviting individuals to office hours so I can get to know them. Acknowledge student successes, efforts, and growth by giving positive verbal feedback through chat box, sending a quick email or written note, and making positive phone calls. I will spend 5 minutes at the end of the day on Tuesday and Friday making a few calls or writing a few notes.

3. Procedures to build social engagement/interaction among students:

   At first, create small group teacher-directed opportunities where I can observe and facilitate each small group by having the class work on independent work while I go with a small group to a breakout room. As students are successful with these procedures, I can start having multiple small group in breakout rooms at a time and I will bounce between them. Assign each student a classroom buddy who will provide encouragement, contact if their buddy is missing from class, and do "pen pal" writing activities.

　　　　　　　　　　REPRODUCIBLE 11.1

Figure 11.6 *Virtual Classroom Management Plan (Reproducible 11.1) Example*

Virtual Classroom Management Plan (p. 5 of 5) *CHAMPS*

4. Procedures for actively engaging students in virtual instruction:

Include fillable notes in students' bi-weekly packet so they fill out responses during class. Use whiteboards and response cards for vocabulary and responding to comprehension questions. Use polls for formative tests of understanding. Have students chorally read (with microphones muted) but monitoring lips moving. If students do not have their cameras on, I will have them periodically record a short passage reading for me and submit it. Randomly call on students using popsicle sticks. I will ask individuals that if they find this highly aversive (e.g., anxiety, worried about academic level), we will find an alternate way to have them respond, such as I will type a question privately to them in the chat and they can voice record or type a response and submit to me.

ITEM 11 Correction Procedures for Misbehavior, both early-stage corrections and rule violation consequences (*pp. 545–550*)

1. Procedures for responding to misbehavior in the moment:

Direct the student to look at the chat box. Type private corrective feedback in the chat. After a redirect, if the student continues to not follow directions, the student will lose a behavior point. Depending on the frequency and severity of the misbehavior, they may also: have a discussion with me and/or parents, complete a behavior improvement form or goal-setting contract, owe additional time outside of class (e.g., detention during office hours), or an office referral. Let students and families know that if they ever feel enforcement of rules and consequences is unfair, they can make an appointment with me to discuss the situation. I will be as neutral as possible in hearing complaints or comments. If there is a Code of Conduct violation as listed in the Student Handbook (possession of illegal substances, harassment, etc.), I must refer the situation to the office. This is part of my job and not my decision. Code of Conduct violations will be handled out of class by the administrator, who will make decisions about parent contacts, police involvement, and other matters.

2. Procedures for partnering with families regarding misbehavior:

Use the Early-Stage Family Contact form to guide initial conversation with a family member about concerns. Seek the family's insight and try to establish a collaborative rapport so we can partner to support the student. If the student improves after the contact, follow up the next day to thank them. If the concern is ongoing, continue to reach out with positive communication about growth and efforts, and provide regular objective information about what is occurring in class. Periodically analyze whether my communication conveys my commitment to and belief in the student.

REPRODUCIBLE 11.1

them during today's class. You can type a note to me in the chat box or send me an email and I'll try to get back to you later today with a response, or you can join the parent office hours that I have posted. Today our goals for class are..."

CHAPTER 9, TASK 2

Implement Your Plan on Day One

Read the task on pages 407–416 and implement with the following adaptations and considerations.

Adapt the strategies in Chapter 9, Task 2 for the virtual setting. For example, greet students individually as they arrive to the virtual platform. Refer to the directions for the opening task on the screen, and let them know that you will bring everyone together at the posted start time. Rather than posting the Day One schedule on the board, you will likely put the schedule on a slide or perhaps on a flip chart positioned to one side of you but in your camera view.

With the three-step process for communicating your expectations, you will need to communicate both behavioral and academic expectations for each activity or transition as described in Chapter 9. One additional consideration is how to teach expectations and provide clear instruction on use of the virtual platform or other technology and applications for the next activity. Do not assume that all students will know how to do things like mute and unmute their microphone, turn their camera on and off, use screen sharing features, or open the chat box. Make the assumption for every activity that at least one student will need you to provide step-by-step instructions and practice opportunities for any technology that will be used.

CHAPTER 9, TASK 3

Implement Your Plan on Days 2 Through 20 (the First Four Weeks)

Read and implement the task on pages 416–424 with the following adaptations and considerations.

Continue to follow the suggestions for the three-step process for communicating expectations for behavior, but also use the process for instruction and review of how to use technology features. While some students will already know or easily pick up how to use expected features, applications, and so on, others will continue to need more explicit instruction and opportunities to practice before they are able to use them fluently.

To verify that students understand expected behavior, use active participation techniques, and consider giving students a quiz during the second or third week of school. Figure 11.7 is a modified example of a quiz on expectations that could be delivered via a poll or by posting the questions and having student submit the answers to you.

Figure 11.7. *Sample Quiz on Expectations*

QUIZ ON EXPECTATIONS

Circle the letter for the best answer to each question.

1. When you enter the classroom and look at the screen, you should:

   a. sit quietly and do nothing.
   b. chat with peers until the teacher signals the start of class.
   c. say a quick hello to the teacher and peers, check the slide for needed materials and get anything you don't have, and begin working independently on the challenge problems.
   d. you can talk about anything, but when the bell rings, you should start looking for the materials you need and be ready to within 2 minutes.

2. During class, you can get up to get a drink of water or use the restroom:

   a. only before and after class.
   b. before and after class and during independent work periods.
   c. any time you need to.
   d. at no time without teacher permission.

3. When the teacher gives the attention signal and says, "Class, your attention please," you should:

   a. be silent and have your eyes on the teacher within 5 seconds.
   b. be silent and have your eyes on the teacher within 10 seconds.
   c. be silent and have your eyes on the teacher within 20 seconds.
   d. loudly tell other students to be quiet and pay attention to the teacher.

For young students, consider using a simplified version of the quiz by using true/false questions, verbally delivering questions to students, and having them indicate their response using thumbs up/down, whiteboards, or true/false response cards.

4. During the time the teacher is speaking to the class, you may:

   a. have the TV on.
   b. send text messages to peers.
   c. talk only if you have been called on by the teacher and get out of your seat only if you get permission.
   d. unmute any time you have a comment or question for the class.

5. Active participation while the teacher is presenting lessons should look and sound a certain way. Circle the items that describe active participation. There are six correct answers.

   a. Sit up straight or lean forward.
   b. Raise your hand or use the "raise hand" icon if you have something to say.
   c. Answer questions when called on.
   d. Chat with your friends in the chat box.
   e. Write notes to keep in your workspace that will help you study for tests.
   f. Critique other people's responses in the chat box.
   g. Have things on your desk that will help entertain you during the lesson.
   h. Keep your eyes on the person speaking or on the class notes you are writing.
   i. Let your mind wander.
   j. Work on other work or send emails while the teacher is talking.
   k. Be respectful toward the teacher and other students in what you say and how.
   l. Unmute any time and call out answers to questions.
   m. Participate in any responses as directed by the teacher (e.g., type in chat, write on your paper, be prepared to be called on, hold up a response card).

Continued on next page ⟶

Figure 11.7 continued *Quiz on Expectations*

6. **When you return after an absence, you should:**

   a. ask the teacher, "Did I miss anything while I was gone?"
   b. ask another student for their notes.
   c. go to the file on the website for this class period, view the class video, and complete related coursework.
   d. send the teacher an email asking for notes.

7. **In the parentheses after each of the following statements, put a T if the concept is true and an F if the concept is false about the weekly points you earn for behavior and effort.**

   a. Every student starts the week with 10 out of 20 possible points. ( )
   b. Every reminder the teacher gives you about your behavior or effort in class costs 1 point. ( )
   c. Every compliment the teacher gives you about your behavior or effort in class adds 1 point. ( )
   d. These points are added into the grade book and are part of your academic grade. ( )
   e. The teacher will take points away without informing you about each incident. ( )
   f. For severe misbehavior, you can have a choice between an office referral or a loss of points. ( )
   g. You can make an appointment to discuss anything you do not understand or think is unfair about this system. ( )

CHAPTER 9, TASK 4

Begin CHAMPS Implementation Midyear

Read and implement the task on pages 424–425 as is.

CHAPTER 10, TASK 1

Use Data to Monitor and Adjust Your Classroom Management Plan

Read and implement the task on pages 428–457 with the following adaptations and considerations.

In Chapter 10, Task 1, you learned about how to use specific data collection tools to provide data snapshots to guide your process of continuous improvement. This section provides ideas for how to use each tool in the virtual class environment and provides suggestions for a few additional tools that may be beneficial.

The Improvement Cycle

Follow the suggestions in Chapter 10, Task 1 for gathering data snapshots and applying the four steps of the improvement cycle:

Step 1: **Review.** Use data snapshots to understand the conditions in your classroom.

Step 2: **Set priorities for improvement.** Use collected data to determine priorities for improvement.

Step 3: **Make revisions to address priorities.** Analyze your Classroom Management Plan and STOIC variables to reach your classroom goals.

Step 4: **Implement your plan.** Launch your revised plan, evaluate its effectiveness, and maintain over time.

TOOL 1: CHAMPS VERSUS DAILY REALITY RATING SCALE

Implement as is.

TOOL 2: RATIO OF INTERACTIONS MONITORING FORM(S).

Because it is so important to intentionally use positive interactions to build your positive relationship with students when you are not physically in a room with them, plan to use this tool the first time no later than the second to fourth week of each new term. Also plan to use once at some time during the second half of the term.

If you have many interactions with students through email, office hours, and other times outside of the synchronous class session, plan to collect the data across several days and include these interactions in your calculations.

It is probably easiest to simply record tallies for positive and corrective interactions in real time during the session, but if you plan to use a recording to collect data, ensure that you are in compliance with your district policy regarding recordings of class sessions.

In *The Distance Learning Playbook*, Fisher et al. (2020) recommend monitoring your interactions with students in the virtual classroom by selecting three students and asking yourself the following questions:

- *Did I greet the student by name when they entered the classroom?*
- *How many times did I use their name (not as a correction) during the session?*
- *Did I ask them a critical-thinking question related to the content?*
- *Did I ask them a personal question?*
- *Did I pay them a compliment?*
- *How many times did I provide them with praise for learning performance?*

If you use a procedure like this several times throughout the term, it can help ensure that you are using a variety of different techniques to connect with students and ensure that they feel like valuable members of the class community.

TOOL 3: MISBEHAVIOR RECORDING SHEET

Use the Misbehavior Recording Sheet in the virtual classroom for times when you need to speak to an individual or the whole class about inappropriate behavior (e.g., verbally or through the chat box), but also for concerns that may be observed and not corrected in the moment, such as students arriving late, leaving early, or popping in and out of the session. Because these might not be misbehaviors and could be related to something like spotty Internet, you likely would not address them through something like a verbal reprimand and would instead follow up with the student at a later time. However, carefully monitoring these concerns can help you determine when you should connect with a student and provide necessary supports.

Examples of common behavioral concerns and codes that might be used in the virtual class include:

- Not participating = NP
- Off-topic comments/questions = OT
- Inappropriate language = IL
- Late arrival/early leaving = T
- Incomplete work = IW
- Blurt out (unmuting without permission) = B
- Out of seat/offscreen without permission (OS)

Another possibility would be to code using CHAMPS, so if a student did not follow your expectations for Help, mark an H. If the student moved to a different location at an inappropriate time, mark an M.

TOOL 4: GRADE BOOK ANALYSIS WORKSHEET

Follow the suggestions in Chapter 10 for analyzing grade book data such as attendance, punctuality, in-class work, homework, and passing grades. In-class work includes any work done while present in the synchronous class, and homework includes any asynchronous work completed outside the live session.

TOOL 5: ON-TASK BEHAVIOR OBSERVATION SHEET

Consider whether this tool is applicable in the virtual class as it is much more difficult to observe whether students are on-task or off-task during independent work times when you are not in the room with them. If you plan to use this tool, you may need to use work formats that allow you to see students completing assignments in real time. This can be accomplished with shared documents, intelligent tutoring system (ITS), or other applications that allow you to see student progress.

TOOL 6: OPPORTUNITIES TO RESPOND OBSERVATION SHEET

Opportunities to respond are essential in the virtual class to increase engagement. Frequent opportunities to respond also allow you to monitor student understanding and provide immediate positive and corrective feedback. Because this is so important in the virtual class, consider collecting this data fairly early on during each term (e.g., sometime during the first month of school).

Determine whether you can observe the data for three to four specific students in real time. Whenever you provide an opportunity to respond (e.g., type in the chat, gesture or use a response button to indicate agreement, randomly call on a student), mark a tally in the correct column for all of the targeted students who provided a response. If it does not seem feasible to do this at the time of instruction, ask a colleague to observe your class and take the data, or consider recording the session and reviewing the chat transcript to mark each student's participation.

TOOL 7: FAMILY/STUDENT SATISFACTION SURVEY

Reproducible 11.7 is a modified version of the Family/Student Satisfaction survey for virtual learning environments:

Reproducible 11.7 *Family/Student Satisfaction Survey*

Family/Student Virtual Class Satisfaction Survey

CHAMPS

Independent Work (Outside of Live Class)

1. The amount of independent work has been:
   ☐ way too much   ☐ a bit too much   ☐ about right   ☐ not enough

2. Independent work has been:
   ☐ way too difficult   ☐ a bit too difficult   ☐ about right   ☐ not difficult enough

3. Most of the time I felt that the independent work was:
   ☐ irrelevant   ☐ boring   ☐ OK   ☐ interesting   ☐ fun

Classwork (During Live Class)

4. The amount of classwork has been:
   ☐ way too much   ☐ a bit too much   ☐ about right   ☐ not enough

5. Classwork has been:
   ☐ way too difficult   ☐ a bit too difficult   ☐ about right   ☐ not difficult enough

6. Most of the time I felt that classwork was:
   ☐ irrelevant   ☐ boring   ☐ OK   ☐ interesting   ☐ fun

7. The activity I like *most* is:
   ☐ whole class teacher-guided activities
   ☐ small group activities in breakout rooms
   ☐ independent activities while in class
   Please explain why:

8. The activity I like *least* is:
   ☐ whole class teacher-guided activities
   ☐ small group activities in breakout rooms
   ☐ independent activities while in class
   Please explain why:

9. What suggestions do you have to make virtual learning more helpful or engaging?

REPRODUCIBLE 11.7

CHAPTER 10, TASK 2

Maintain Awareness of Professionalism and Engage in Self-Care

Read the task on pages 457–468 and implement as is.

CHAPTER 10, TASK 3

Engage in Ongoing Learning and Professional Development

Read the task on pages 469–473 and implement as is.

Conclusion

This chapter was designed to assist you in developing a Classroom Management Plan specifically for virtual teaching. Your virtual plan should include the same core features of any well-designed Classroom Management Plan, but the specific strategies will be tailored to the technology you use in virtual teaching and the logistics of having your students learning from their home environment. Good instruction is good instruction and, with a little preparation, effective teaching practices can transcend the walls of a physical classroom.

References

Abramowitz, A. J., O'Leary, S. G., & Futtersak, M. W. (1988). The relative impact of long and short reprimands on children's off-task behavior in the classroom. *Behavior Therapy, 29*(2), 243–247.

Acker, M. M., & O'Leary, S. G. (1988). Effects of consistent and inconsistent feedback on inappropriate child behavior. *Behavior Therapy, 19*(4), 619–624.

Alberto, P. A., & Troutman, A. C. (2012). *Applied behavior analysis for teachers* (9th ed.). Pearson.

Allday, R. A. (2011). Responsive management: Practical strategies for avoiding overreaction to minor misbehavior. *Intervention in School and Clinic, 46*(5), 292–298.

Allday, R. A., & Pakurar, K. (2007). Effects of teacher greetings on student on-task behavior. *Journal of Applied Behavior Analysis, 40*(2), 317–320.

Alter, P., & Haydon, T. (2017). Characteristics of effective classroom rules: A review of the literature. *Teacher Education and Special Education, 40*(2), 114–127.

American Psychiatric Association. (2013). *Diagnostic and statistical manual of mental disorders* (5th ed.). Washington, DC: American Psychiatric Association.

Anderson, L., Evertson, C., & Emmer, E. (1980). Dimensions in classroom management derived from recent research. *Journal of Curriculum Studies, 12*, 343–356.

Appleton, J. J., Christenson, S. L., & Furlong, M. J. (2008). Student engagement with school: Critical conceptual and methodological issues of the construct. *Psychology in the Schools, 45*(5), 369–386.

Arain, M., Haque, M., Johal, L., Mathur, P., Nel, W., Rais, A., Sandhu, R., & Sharma, S. (2013). Maturation of the adolescent brain. *Neuropsychiatric Disease and Treatment, 9*, 449.

Archer, A. L., & Hughes, C. A. (2011). *Explicit instruction: Effective and efficient teaching*. Guilford Press.

Arlin, M. (1979). Teacher transitions can disrupt time flow in classrooms. *American Educational Research Journal, 16*, 42–56.

Babkie, A. (2006). 20 ways to be proactive in managing classroom behavior. *Intervention in School and Clinic, 41*, 184–187.

Bain, A., Houghton, S., & Williams, S. (1991). The effects of a school-wide behaviour management programme on teachers' use of encouragement in the classroom. *Educational Studies, 17*(3), 249–260.

Baker, S., Lesaux, N., Jayanthi, M., Dimino, J., Proctor, C. P., Morris, J., Gersten, R., Haymond, K., Kieffer, M. J., Linan-Thompson, S., & Newman-Gonchar, R. (2014). *Teaching academic content and literacy to English learners in elementary and middle school* (NCEE 2014-4012). http://ies.ed.gov/ncee/wwc/publications_reviews.aspx

Bandura, A. (1977). *Social learning theory*. Prentice Hall.

Barbetta, P. M., Norona, K. L., & Bicard, D. F. (2005). Classroom behavior management: A dozen common mistakes and what to do instead. *Preventing School Failure: Alternative Education for Children and Youth, 49*(3), 11–19.

Bargh, J. A. & Schul, Y. (1980). On the cognitive benefits of teaching. *The Journal of Educational Psychology 73*, 593–604.

Barrett, P., Davies, F., Zhang, Y., & Barrett, L. (2015). The impact of classroom design on pupils' learning: Final results of a holistic, multi-level analysis. *Building and Environment, 89*, 118–133.

Barrish, H. H., Saunders, M., & Wolf, M. M. (1969). Good behavior game: Effects of individual contingencies for group consequences on disruptive behavior in a classroom 1. *Journal of Applied Behavior Analysis, 2*(2), 119–124.

Barron, B., & Darling-Hammond, L. (2008). *Teaching for meaningful learning: A review of research on inquiry-based and cooperative learning* [book excerpt]. George Lucas Educational Foundation. (ERIC ED539399)

Batsche, G., Elliott, J., Graden, J. L., Grimes, J., Kovaleski, J. F., & Prasse, D. (2005). *Response to intervention: Policy considerations and implementation*. National Association of State Directors of Special Education.

Baumeister, R. F., Bratslavsky, E., Finkenauer, C., & Vohs, K. D. (2001). Bad is stronger than good. *Review of General Psychology, 5*(4), 323–370.

Beaman, R., & Wheldall, K. (2000). Teachers' use of approval and disapproval in the classroom. *Educational Psychology, 20*(4), 431–446.

Bear, G. G. (2008). Classroom discipline. In A. Thomas & J. Grimes (Eds.), *Best practices in school psychology V* (pp. 1403–1420). National Association of School Psychologists.

Bear, G.G., Whitcomb, S.A., Elias, M.J., & Blank, J.C. (2015). SEL and schoolwide positive behavioral interventions and supports. In J. A. Durlak, C. E. Domitrovich, R. P. Weissberg, & T. P. Gullotta (Eds.), *Handbook of social and emotional learning: Research and practice*. Guilford.

Beland, L. P., & Murphy, R. (2016). Ill communication: Technology, distraction & student performance. *Labour Economics, 41*, 61–76.

Bell, K. (1998). In the beginning: Teacher created a positive learning environment. *Teaching Elementary Physical Education, 9*, 12–14.

Bennett, N., & Blundell, D. (1983). Quantity and quality of work in rows and classroom groups. *Educational Psychology, 3*(2), 93–105.

Blatchford, P., Kutnick, P., Baines, E., & Galton, M. (2003). Toward a social pedagogy of classroom group work. *International Journal of Educational Research, 39*(1–2), 153–172.

Blum, R. W. (2005). A case for school connectedness. *Educational Leadership, 62*(7), 16–19.

Boekaerts, M. (2002). *Motivation to learn* [Educational Practice Series]. https://unesdoc.unesco.org/ark:/48223/pf0000128056

Bouygues, H. L. (2019). *Does educational technology help students learn? An analysis of the connection between digital devices and learning.* https://reboot-foundation.org/wp-content/uploads/_docs/ED_ TECH_ANALYSIS.pdf

Bowman-Perrott, L., Burke, M. D., Zaini, S., Zhang, N., & Vannest, K. (2016). Promoting positive behavior using the Good Behavior Game: A meta-analysis of single-case research. *Journal of Positive Behavior Interventions, 18*(3), 180–190.

Brafman, O., & Brafman, R. (2010). *Click: The forces behind how we fully engage with people, work, and everything we do.* Crown Publishing.

Branon, R. F., & Essex, C. (2001). Synchronous and asynchronous communication tools in distance education. *TechTrends, 45*(1), 36.

Brantner, J. P., & Doherty, M. A. (1983). A review of timeout: A conceptual and methodological analysis. In S. Axelrod (Ed.), *Effects of punishment on human behavior* (pp. 87–132). Academic Press.

Brookhart, S. M. (2017). *How to give effective feedback to your students.* ASCD.

Brophy, J. (1981). Teacher praise: A functional analysis. *Review of Educational Research, 51*, 5–32.

Brophy, J. (1983). Classroom organization and management. *The Elementary School Journal, 83*(4), 265–285.

Brophy, J. (1985). Classroom management as instruction: Socializing self-guidance in students. *Theory Into Practice, 24*(4), 233–240.

Brophy, J. (1986). Teacher influences on student achievement. *American Psychologist, 41*(10), 1069.

Brophy, J. (1996). *Teaching problem students.* Guilford Press.

Brophy, J. E., & Good, T. L. (1986). Teacher behavior and student achievement. In M. C. Whitrock (Ed.), *Handbook of research on teaching* (3rd ed., pp. 328–375). Macmillan.

Bruhn, A., McDaniel, S., & Kreigh, C. (2015). Self-monitoring interventions for students with behavior problems: A systematic review of current research. *Behavioral Disorders, 40*(2), 102–121.

Bryk, A. S., & Schneider, B. (2003). Trust in schools: A core resource for school reform. *Educational Leadership, 60*(6), 40–45.

Buck, G. H. (1999). Smoothing the rough edges of classroom transitions. *Intervention in School and Clinic, 34*(4), 224–235.

Bureau of Exceptional Education and Student Services (2006). *Grading policies for students with disabilities* (Technical Assistance Paper). http://www.fldoe.org/core/fileparse.php/7571/urlt/0086206-y2006-11.pdf

Caldarella, P., Larsen, R. A., Williams, L., Downs, K. R., Wills, H. P., & Wehby, J. H. (2020). Effects of teachers' praise-to-reprimand ratios on elementary students' on-task behaviour. *Educational Psychology, Advance online publication.* https://doi.org/10.1080/01443410.2020.1711872

Cameron, J., & Pierce, W. (1994). Reinforcement, reward, and intrinsic motivation: A meta-analysis. *Review of Educational Research, 64*, 363–423.

Cantrell, S. (2003). *Pay and performance: The utility of teacher experience, education, credentials, and attendance as predictors of student achievement at elementary schools in LAUSD.* Los Angeles Unified School District, Program Evaluation and Research Branch.

Cao, Q., Griffin, T. E., & Bai, X. (2009). The importance of synchronous interaction for student satisfaction with course web sites. *Journal of Information Systems Education, 20*(3), 331–338.

Cardenas, A. (2017). *A cell phone policy that works.* Mud and Ink Teaching. https://www.mudandinkteaching.org/news/2017/11/22/a-cell-phone-policy-that-actually-works

Carnine, D., Silbert, J., Kame'enui, E., & Tarver, S. (2004). *Direct instruction reading* (4th ed.). Pearson.

Carr, E. (1993). Behavior analysis is not ultimately about behavior. *The Behavior Analyst, 16*, 47–49.

Carr, J., Coriaty, S., Wilder, D., Gaunt, B., Dozier, C., Britton, L., Avina, C., & Reed, C. (2000). A review of "noncontingent" reinforcement as treatment for the aberrant behavior of individuals with developmental disabilities. *Research in Developmental Disabilities, 21*, 377–391.

Carr, J. E., & Sidener, T. M. (2002). On the relation between applied behavior analysis and positive behavioral support. *The Behavior Analyst, 25*(2), 245–253.

Carter, S. P., Greenberg, K., & Walker, M. S. (2017). The impact of computer usage on academic performance: Evidence from a randomized trial at the United States Military Academy. *Economics of Education Review, 56*, 118–132.

CASEL. (2020). *CASEL's SEL framework: What are the core competence areas and where are they promoted?* https://casel.org/wp-content/uploads/2020/12/CASEL-SEL-Framework-11.2020.pdf

Cayanus, J. L., & Martin, M. M. (2008). Teacher self-disclosure: Amount, relevance, and negativity. *Communication Quarterly, 5.*

CEC (Council for Exceptional Children). (1987). *Academy for effective instruction: Working with mildly handicapped students.* Author.

Centers for Disease Control and Prevention. (2009). *School connectedness: Strategies for increasing protective factors among youth.* U.S. Department of Health and Human Services.

Chaffee, R. K., Briesch, A. M., Johnson, A. H., & Volpe, R. J. (2017). A meta-analysis of class-wide interventions for supporting student behavior. *School Psychology Review, 46*(2), 149–164.

Chalk, K., & Bizo, L. (2004). Specific praise improves on-task behavior and numeracy enjoyment: A study of year four pupils engaged in the numeracy hour. *Educational Psychology in Practice, 20*, 335–351.

Cheng, S. C., & Lai, C. L. (2020). Facilitating learning for students with special needs: A review of technology-supported special education studies. *Journal of Computers in Education, 7*, 131–153. https://doi.org/10.1007/s40692-019-00150-8

Chou, C. C. (2002, January). A comparative content analysis of student interaction in synchronous and asynchronous learning networks. In *Proceedings of the 35th annual Hawaii international conference on system sciences* (pp. 1795–1803). IEEE.

Christenson, S., & Godber, Y. (2001). Enhancing constructive family-school connections. In J. N. Hughes, A. M. LaGreca, & J. C. Conoley (Eds.), *Handbook of psychological services for children and adolescents* (pp. 455–476). Oxford University Press.

Christenson, S., Reschly, A., Appleton, J., Berman-Young, S., Spanjers, D., & Varro, P. (2008). Best practices in fostering student engagement. In A. Thomas & J. Grimes (Eds.). *Best practices in school psychology V* (pp. 1099–1119). National Association of School Psychologists.

Clark, H. B., Rowbury, T., Baer, A. M., & Baer, D. M. (1973). Timeout as a punishing stimulus in continuous and intermittent schedules. *Journal of Applied Behavior Analysis, 6*(3), 443–455.

Colvin, G., Kame'enui, E. J., & Sugai, G. (1993). Reconceptualizing behavior management and school-wide discipline in general education. *Education and Treatment of Children, 16*(4), 361–381.

Colvin, G., & Sugai, G. (1988). Proactive strategies for managing social behavior problems: An instructional approach. *Education and Treatment of Children, 11*, 341–348.

Colvin, G., Sugai, G., Good, R.H., III, & Lee, Y. (1997). Using active supervision and precorrection to improve transition behaviors in an elementary school. *School Psychology Quarterly, 12*, 344–361

Colvin, G., Sugai, G., & Patching, B. (1993). Pre-correction: An instructional approach for managing predictable problem behaviors. *Intervention in School and Clinic, 28*, 143–150.

Conroy, M. A., Sutherland, K. S., Snyder, A. L., & Marsh, S. (2008). Classwide interventions: Effective instruction makes a difference. *Teaching Exceptional Children, 40*(6), 24–30.

Cook, C. R., Fiat, A., Larson, M., Daikos, C., Slemrod, T., Holland, E. A., Thayer, A. J., & Renshaw, T. (2018). Positive greetings at the door: Evaluation of a low-cost, high-yield proactive classroom management strategy. *Journal of Positive Behavior Interventions, 20*(3), 149–159.

Cook, C. R., Grady, E. A., Long, A. C., Renshaw, T., Codding, R. S., Fiat, A., & Larson, M. (2017). Evaluating the impact of increasing general education teachers' ratio of positive-to-negative interactions on students' classroom behavior. *Journal of Positive Behavior Interventions, 19*(2), 67–77.

Cooper, M.A. (1999). Classroom choices from a cognitive perspective on peer learning. In A. M. O'Donnell & A. King (Eds.), *Cognitive perspectives on peer learning* (pp. 215–234). Erlbaum.

Cooper, J. O., Heron, T. E., & Heward, W. L. (2007). *Applied behavior analysis* (2nd ed.). Pearson.

Craig, S. E. (2015). *Trauma-sensitive schools: Learning communities transforming children's lives, K–5.* Teachers College Press.

Darch, C., & Kame'enui, E. (2004). *Instructional classroom management: A proactive approach to behavior management.* Pearson/Prentice Hall.

Deal, T. E., & Peterson, K. D. (2010). *Shaping school culture: Pitfalls, paradoxes, and promises.* John Wiley & Sons.

Deno, S. L. (2005). Problem-solving assessment. In R. Brown-Chidsey & K. D. Andren (Eds.), *Assessment for intervention: A problem-solving approach* (pp. 10–40). Guilford.

DePalma, R. (2010). *Language use in the two-way classroom: Lessons from a Spanish-English bilingual kindergarten* (Vol. 76). Multilingual Matters.

De Pry, R.L., & Sugai, G. (2002). The effect of active supervision and pre-correction on minor behavioral incidents in a sixth grade general education classroom. *Journal of Behavioral Education, 11*, 255–264.

Dicintio, M. J., & Gee, S. (1999). Control is the key: Unlocking the motivation of at-risk students. *Psychology in the Schools, 36*(3), 231–237.

Dishion, T. J., & Stormshak, E. A. (2007). *Intervening in children's lives: An ecological, family-centered approach to mental health care.* American Psychological Association.

Doabler, C. T., Nelson, N. J., & Clarke, B. (2016). Adapting evidence-based practices to meet the needs of English learners with mathematics difficulties. *Teaching Exceptional Children, 48*(6), 301–310.

Downs, K. R., Caldarella, P., Larsen, R. A., Charlton, C. T., Wills, H. P., Kamps, D. M., & Wehby, J. H. (2019). Teacher praise and reprimands: The differential response of students at risk of emotional and behavioral disorders. *Journal of Positive Behavior Interventions, 21*(3), 135–147.

Dreikurs, R., Grunwald, B., & Pepper, C. (1998). *Maintaining sanity in the classroom: Classroom management techniques* (2nd ed.). Taylor and Francis.

DuBose, M. & Gorski, P. (2020). *Equity literacy during the COVID19 crisis.* Equity Literacy Institute. https://08a3a74a-dec5-426e-8385-bdc09490d921.filesusr.com/ugd/38199c_c355c89c7634495584ead8f230c0d25b.pdf

Dueck, M. (2014). *Grading smarter, not harder: Assessment strategies that motivate kids and help them learn.* ASCD.

Durlak, J. A., Weissberg, R. P., Dymnicki, A. B., Taylor, R. D., & Schellinger, K. B. (2011). The impact of enhancing students' social and emotional learning: A meta-analysis of school-based universal interventions. *Child Development, 82*(1), 405–432.

Dweck, C. S. (2008). *Mindset: The new psychology of success.* Ballantine.

Emmer, E. T., & Evertson, C. M. (2009). *Classroom management for middle and high school teachers* (8th ed.). Pearson.

Emmer, E. T., Evertson, C. M., & Anderson, L. M. (1980). Effective classroom management at the beginning of the school year. *The Elementary School Journal, 80*(5), 219–231.

Emmer, E., Evertson, C., & Worsham, M. (2003). *Classroom management for elementary teachers.* Pearson.

Engelmann, S., & Becker, W. (1978). Systems for basic instruction: Theory and applications. In A. C. Catania & T. A. Brigham (Eds.), *Handbook of applied behavior analysis* (pp. 326–377). Irvington.

Engelmann, S., & Carnine, D. (1982). *Theory of instruction: Principles and applications*. Irvington Publishers.

Epstein, J. L. (2018). *School, family, and community partnerships: Preparing educators and improving schools*. Routledge.

Epstein, M., Atkins, M., Cullinan, D., Kutash, K., and Weaver, R. (2008). *Reducing behavior problems in the elementary school classroom: A practice guide* (NCEE #2008-012). http://ies.ed.gov/ncee/wwc/publications/practiceguides.

Erwin, J. C. (2004). *The classroom of choice: Giving students what they need and getting what you want*. ASCD.

Escueta, M., Quan, V., Nickow, A. J., & Oreopoulos, P. (2017). *Education technology: An evidence-based review* (No. w23744). National Bureau of Economic Research.

Esler, A., Godber, Y., & Christenson, S.(2008). Best practices in supporting school-family partnerships. In A. Thomas & J. Grimes (Eds.), *Best practices in school psychology V* (pp. 917–936). National Association of School Psychologists.

Evans, G., & Lowell, B. (1979). Design modification in an open-plan school. *Journal of Educational Psychology, 71*, 41–49.

Evertson, C. M., & Emmer, E. T. (1982). Effective management at the beginning of the school year in junior high classes. *Journal of Educational Psychology, 74*(4), 485–498.

Evertson, C. M., Emmer, E. T., & Worsham, M. (2003). *Classroom management for elementary teachers* (6th ed.). Allyn & Bacon.

Fairbanks, S., Simonsen, B., & Sugai, G. (2008). Classwide secondary and tertiary tier practices and systems. *Teaching Exceptional Children, 40*(6), 44–52.

Fairbanks, S., Sugai, G., Guardino, D., & Lathrop, M. (2007). Response to intervention: Examining classroom behavior supports in second grade. *Council for Exceptional Children, 73*, 288–310.

Fan, X., & Chen, M. (2001). Parental involvement and students' academic achievement: A meta-analysis. *Educational Psychology Review, 13*(1), 1–22.

Feather, N. T. (1982). *Expectations and actions: Expectancy-value theories in psychology*. Erlbaum.

Fedewa, A. L., & Erwin, H. E. (2011). Stability balls and students with attention and hyperactivity concerns: Implications for on-task and in-seat behavior. *American Journal of Occupational Therapy, 65*(4), 393–399.

Feldman, J. (2014). Do your grading practices undermine equity initiatives? *Leadership, 47*(2), 8–11. http://crescendoedgroup.org/wp-content/uploads/2014/03/Equitable-grading-Leadership-Mag_NovDec.pdf

Feldman, J. (2019). Beyond standards-based grading: Why equity must be part of grading reform. *Phi Delta Kappan, 100*(8), 52–55.

Felitti, V. J., Anda, R. F., Nordenberg, D., Williamson, D. F., Spitz, A. M., Edwards, V., & Marks, J. S. (1998). Relationship of childhood abuse and household dysfunction to many of the leading causes of death in adults: The Adverse Childhood Experiences (ACE) study. *American Journal of Preventive Medicine, 14*(4), 245–258.

Ferguson, E., & Houghton, S. (1992). The effects of contingent teacher praise, as specified by Canter's assertive discipline programme, on children's on-task behaviour. *Educational Studies, 18*, 83–93.

Ferrara, N. C., Vantrease, J. E., Loh, M. K., Rosenkranz, J. A., & Rosenkranz, J. A. (2020). Protect and harm: Effects of stress on the amygdala. In *Handbook of Behavioral Neuroscience* (Vol. 26, pp. 241–274). Elsevier.

Fisher, C., Fibly, N., Marliave, R., Cahen, L., Dishaw, M., More, J., & Berliner, D. (1978). *Teaching behaviors, academic learning time, and student achievement* (Report of Phase III-B, Beginning Teacher Evaluation Study. Tech. Rep. V-1). Far West Laboratory for Educational Research and Development.

Fisher, D., Frey, N., & Hattie, J. (2020). *The distance learning playbook, grades K-12: Teaching for engagement and impact in any setting.* Corwin Press.

Floress, M. T., Jenkins, L. N., Reinke, W. M., & McKown, L. (2018). General education teachers' natural rates of praise: A preliminary investigation. *Behavioral Disorders, 43*(4), 411–422.

Flower, A., McKenna, J. W., Bunuan, R. L., Muething, C. S., & Vega, R. (2014). Effects of the Good Behavior Game on challenging behaviors in school settings. *Review of Educational Research, 84*, 546–571. doi:10.3102/0034654314536781

Foxx, R., & Bechtel, D. (1982). Overcorrection. In M. Hersen, R. Eisler, & P. Miller (Eds.), *Progress in behavior modification* (pp. 227–288). Academic Press.

Fredericks, J. A., Blumenfeld, P. C., & Paris, A. H. (2004). School engagement: Potential of the concept, state of the evidence. *Review of Educational Research, 74*, 59–109.

Freeland, J. T., & Noell, G. H. (1999). Maintaining accurate math responses in elementary school students: The effects of delayed intermittent reinforcement and programming common stimuli. *Journal of Applied Behavior Analysis, 32*(2), 211–215.

Freer, P., & Watson, T. S. (1999). A comparison of parent and teacher acceptability ratings of behavioral and conjoint behavioral consultation. *School Psychology Review, 28*, 672–684.

Fuchs, D., Fuchs, L., Dailey, A., & Power, M. (1985). The effect of examiner's personal familiarity and professional experience on handicapped children's test performance. *Journal of Educational Research, 78*, 141–146.

Fuchs, L. S., & Fuchs, D. (1986). Effects of systematic formative evaluation: A meta-analysis. *Exceptional Children, 53*, 199–208. https://doi.org/10.1177/001440298605300301

Fuchs, L. S., Fuchs, D., & Deno, S. L. (1985). Importance of goal ambitiousness and goal mastery to student achievement. *Exceptional Children, 52*, 63–71.

Gable, R. A., Hester, P. H., Rock, M. L., & Hughes, K. G. (2009). Back to basics: Rules, praise, ignoring, and reprimands revisited. *Intervention in School and Clinic, 44*(4), 195–205.

Gathercoal, F. (1997). *Judicious discipline* (4th ed.). Caddo Gap Press.

Gersten, R., & Baker, S. (2000). *Practices for English language learners: An overview of instructional practices for English language learners: Prominent themes and future directions.* National Institute for Urban School Improvement.

Gersten, R., Baker, S. K., Shanahan, T., Linan-Thompson, S., Collins, P., & Scarcella, R. (2007). *Effective literacy and English language instruction for English learners in the elementary grades.* (NCEE 2007–4011). Institute of Education Sciences, U.S. Department of Education.

Gersten, R., & Brengelman, S. (1996). The quest to translate research into classroom practice: The emerging knowledge base. *Remedial and Special Education, 17*, 67–74.

Gersten, R., & Jimenez, R. (2002). Modulating instruction for English-language learners. In E. J. Kame'enui, D. Carnine, R. Dixon, D. Simmons, & M. Coyne (Eds.), *Effective teaching strategies that accommodate diverse learners* (2nd ed.). Merrill/Prentice Hall.

Gest, S. D., & Rodkin, P. C. (2011). Teaching practices and elementary classroom peer ecologies. *Journal of Applied Developmental Psychology, 32*(5), 288–296.

Gettinger, M., & Ball, C. (2008). Best practices in increasing academic engaged time. In A. Thomas & J. Grimes (Eds.), *Best practices in school psychology V* (pp. 1043–1058). National Association of School Psychologists.

Gillies, D. (2008). Student perspectives on videoconferencing in teacher education at a distance. *Distance Education, 29*(1), 107–118.

Good, R., & Brophy, J. (2000). *Looking in classrooms* (8th ed.). Longman.

Gortmaker, V., Warnes, E. D., & Sheridan, S. M. (2004). Conjoint behavioral consultation: Involving parents and teachers in the treatment of a child with selective mutism. *Proven Practice, 5*, 66–72.

Granström, K. (1996). Private communication between students in the classroom in relation to different classroom features. *Educational Psychology, 16*(4), 349–364.

Greenwood, C. R., Hops, H., Delquadri, J., & Guild, J. (1974). Group contingencies for group consequences in classroom management: A further analysis. *Journal of Applied Behavior Analysis, 7*, 413–425.

Gregory, A., & Ripski, M. B. (2008). Adolescent trust in teachers: Implications for behavior in the high school classroom. *School Psychology Review, 37*(3), 337–353.

Gresham, F. M. (1998). Social skills training with children. In T. S. Watson & F. M. Gresham (Eds.), *Handbook of Child Behavior Therapy* (pp. 475–497). Plenum.

Gresham, F. M. (2002). Best practices in social skills training. In A. Thomas & J. Grimes (Eds.), *Best practices in school psychology* (pp. 1029–1040). National Association of School Psychologists.

Gresham, F. M., Watson, S. T., & Skinner, C. H. (2001). Functional behavioral assessment: Principles, procedures, and future directions. *School Psychology Review, 30*, 156–172.

Guardino, C. A., & Fullerton, E. (2010). Changing behaviors by changing the classroom environment. *Teaching Exceptional Children, 42*(6), 8–13.

Gueldner, B., & Merrell, K. (2019) Supporting students with internalizing challenges. In R. Sprick, C. Coughlin, M. Garrison, & J. Sprick (Eds.), *Interventions: Support for individual students with behavior challenges* (pp. 469–540). Ancora Publishing.

Gunter, P. L., Shores, R. E., Jack, S. L., Rasmussen, S. K., & Flowers, J. (1995). On the move using teacher/student proximity to improve students' behavior. *Teaching Exceptional Children, 28*(1), 12–14.

Guskey, T. R. (2002). Professional development and teacher change. *Teachers and Teaching, 8*(3), 381–391.

Gutiérrez, K. D. (2008). Developing a sociocritical literacy in the third space. *Reading Research Quarterly, 43*(2), 148–164.

Hall, R., & Hall, M. (1980). *How to select reinforcers.* H&H Enterprises.

Hall, R. V., Lund, D., & Jackson, D. (1968). Effects of teacher attention on study behavior. *Journal of Applied Behavior Analysis, 1*, 1–12.

Hammond, Z. (2014). *Culturally responsive teaching and the brain: Promoting authentic engagement and rigor among culturally and linguistically diverse students.* Corwin Press.

Hamre, B. K., & Pianta, R. C. (2001). Early teacher–child relationships and the trajectory of children's school outcomes through eighth grade. *Child Development, 72*(2), 625–638.

Haring, T., Roger, B., Lee, M., Breen, C., & Gaylord-Ross, R. (1986). Teaching social language to moderately handicapped students. *Journal of Applied Behavior Analysis, 19*, 159–171.

Harmer, J. (2007). *The practice of English language teaching.* Pearson Longman.

Harrop, A., & Swinson, J. (2003). Teachers' questions in the infant, junior and secondary school. *Educational Studies, 29*(1), 49–57.

Hattie, J. (2012). *Visible learning for teachers: Maximizing impact on learning.* Routledge.

Hattie, J., & Timperley, H. (2007). The power of feedback. *Review of Educational Research, 77,* 81–112.

Hawkins, R. O. (2010). Introduction to the special issue: Identifying effective classwide interventions to promote positive outcomes for all students. *Psychology in the Schools, 47*(9), 869–870. https://doi.org/10.1002/pits.20510

Haydon, T., Macsuga-Gage, A. S., Simonsen, B., & Hawkins, R. (2012). Opportunities to respond: A key component of effective instruction. *Beyond Behavior, 22*(1), 23–31.

Heckman, J. J., & LaFontaine, P. A. (2010). The American high school graduation rate: Trends and levels. *The Review of Economics and Statistics, 92*(2), 244–262.

Helfrich, S. R., & Bosh, A. J. (2011, July). Teaching English language learners: Strategies for overcoming barriers. In *The Educational Forum* (Vol. 75, No. 3, pp. 260–270). Taylor & Francis Group.

Heller, P., & Hollabaugh, M. (1992). Teaching problem solving through cooperative grouping. Part 2: Designing problems and structuring groups. *American Journal of Physics, 60*(7), 637–644.

Henderson, A., & Mapp, K. (2002). *A new wave of evidence: The impact of school, family, and community connections on student achievement.* National Center for Family and Community Connections with Schools, Southwest Educational Development Laboratory.

Henricsson, L., & Rydell, A. M. (2004). Elementary school children with behavior problems: Teacher-child relations and self-perception. A prospective study. *Merrill-Palmer Quarterly, 502,* 111–138.

Herman, K. C., Reinke, W. M., Dong, N., & Bradshaw, C. P. (2020). Can effective classroom behavior management increase student achievement in middle school? Findings from a group randomized trial. *Journal of Educational Psychology.* Advance online publication. https://doi.org/10.1037/edu0000641

Hershfeldt, P. A., Rosenberg, M. S., & Bradshaw, C. P. (2010). Function-based thinking: A systematic way of thinking about function and its role in changing student behavior problems. *Beyond Behavior, 19*(3), 12–22.

Hilberg, R. S., Waxman, H. C., & Tharp, R. G. (2004). Introduction: Purposes and perspectives on classroom observation research. In H. C. Waxman, R. G. Tharp, & R. S. Hilberg (Eds.), *Observational research in U.S. classrooms: New approaches for understanding cultural and linguistic diversity* (pp. 1–20). Cambridge University Press. https://doi.org/10.1017/CBO9780511616419.001

Hiltz, S. R., & Goldman, R. (Eds., 2005). *Learning together online: Research on asynchronous learning.* Erlbaum.

Hintze, J. M., Volpe, R. J., & Shapiro, E. S. (2008). Best practices in the systematic direct observation of student behavior. In A. Thomas & J. Grimes (Eds.), *Best practices in school psychology V* (pp. 996–1003). National Association of School Psychologists.

Hirn, R., & Scott, T. M. (2012). *Academic and behavior response to intervention project.* University of Louisville.

Ho, V. (2019, August 28). Teenage hangups: the drastic plans to keep high schoolers off their phones. *The Guardian.* https://www.theguardian.com/education/2019/aug/27/highschoolers-phones-yondr-distraction

Hofmeister, A., & Lubke, M. (1990). *Research into practice: Implementing effective teaching strategies.* Allyn & Bacon.

Horcones, C. L. (1992). Natural reinforcement: A way to improve education. *Journal of Applied Behavior Analysis, 25*(1), 71.

Horner, R. H., Dunlap, G., Koegel, R. L., Carr, E. G., Sailor, W., Anderson, J., Albin, R., & O'Neill, R. E. (1990). Toward a technology of "nonaversive" behavioral support. *Journal of the Association for Persons With Severe Handicaps, 15*(3), 125–132.

Houghton, S., Wheldall, K., Jukes, R., & Sharpe, A. (1990). The effects of limited private reprimands and increased private praise on classroom behaviour in four British secondary school classes. *British Journal of Educational Psychology, 60,* 255–265.

Howell, K. W., & Nolet, V. (2000). *Curriculum-based evaluation: Teaching and decision making.* Wadsworth/Thomson Learning.

Hrastinski, S., & Keller, C. (2007). Computer-mediated communication in education: A review of recent research. *Educational Media International, 44*(1), 61–77.

Hudson, P., & Miller, S. P. (2006). *Designing and implementing mathematics instruction for students with diverse learning needs.* Allyn and Bacon.

Huston-Stein, A., Friedrich-Cofer, L., & Susman, E. J. (1977). The relation of classroom structure to social behavior, imaginative plan, and self-regulation of economically disadvantaged children. *Child Development, 48,* 908–916.

Illinois State Board of Education (2020). *Remote learning recommendations during COVID-19 emergency.* https://www.isbe.net/Documents/RL-Recommendations-3-27-20.pdf

Ingersol, R. M., Merrill, E., Stuckey, D., & Collins, G. (2018). *Seven trends: The transformation of the teaching force* (CPRE Research Report# RR 2018-2). Consortium for Policy Research in Education.

Jacobsen, B., Lowery, B., & DuCette, J. (1986). Attributions of learning disabled children. *Journal of Educational Psychology, 78*(1), 59.

Jarzabkowski, L. M. (2002). The social dimensions of teacher collegiality. *Journal of Educational Enquiry, 3*(2), 1–20.

Jenkins, L. N., Floress, M. T., & Reinke, W. (2015). Rates and types of teacher praise: A review and future directions. *Psychology in the Schools, 52*, 463–476.

Jenson, W. R., & Reavis, H. K. (1996). Reprimands and precision requests. In H. Reavis, M. Sweeten, W. Jenson, D. Morgan, D. Andrews, & S. Fister (Eds.), *Best practices: Behavioral and educational strategies for teachers* (pp. 49–55). Sopris West.

Jenson, W. R., Rhode, G., & Williams, N. A. (2020). *The tough kid tool box* (3rd ed.). Ancora Publishing.

Johnson D. W., & Johnson, R. (1989). *Cooperation and competition: Theory and research.* Interaction Book Company.

Johnson, D., & Johnson, R. (1991). *Learning together and alone: Cooperative competitive and individualistic learning* (3rd ed.). Prentice Hall.

Johnson, D. W., Johnson, R. T., & Holubec, E. J. (2008). *Cooperation in the classroom* (8th ed.). Interaction Book Company.

Johnson, L., Graham, S., & Harris, K. (1997). The effects of goal setting and self-instruction on learning a reading comprehension strategy: A study of students with learning disabilities. *Journal of Learning Disabilities, 30*, 80–91.

Jones, V., & Jones, L. (2007). *Comprehensive classroom management: Creating positive learning environments* (8th ed.). Allyn & Bacon.

Jovanovic, D., & Matejevic, M. (2014). Relationship between rewards and intrinsic motivation for learning–Researches review. *Procedia-Social and Behavioral Sciences, 149*, 456–460.

Jussim, L., & Harmer, K. D. (2005). Teacher expectations and self-fulfilling prophecies: Knowns and unknowns, resolved and unresolved controversies. *Personality and Social Psychology Review, 9*(2), 131–155.

Kame'enui, E., & Carnine, D. (1998). *Effective teaching strategies that accommodate diverse learners.* Merrill/Prentice Hall.

Kame'enui, E. J., Carnine, D. W., Dixon, R. C., Simmons, D. C., & Coyne, M. D. (2002). *Effective teaching strategies that accommodate diverse learners* (2nd ed.). Merrill Prentice Hall.

Kame'enui, E. J., & Simmons, D. C. (1990). *Designing instructional strategies: The prevention of academic learning problems.* Macmillan.

Kame'enui, E., & Simmons, D. (1999). *Toward successful inclusion of students with disabilities: The architecture of instruction.* Council for Exceptional Children.

Katzell, R. A., & Thompson, D. E. (1990). Work motivation: Theory and practice. *American Psychologist, 45*(2), 144.

Kazdin, A. (1977). Assessing the clinical or applied importance of behavior change through social validation. *Behavior Modification, 1*, 427–451.

Keith, T., Keith, P., Quirk, K., Sperduto, J., Santillo, S., & Killings, S. (1998). Longitudinal effects of parent involvement on high school grades: Similarities and differences across gender and ethnic groups. *Journal of School Psychology, 36*, 335–363.

King, A. (2002). Structuring peer interaction to promote high-level cognitive processing. *Theory into Practice, 41*, 33–40.

Klem, A. M., & Connell, J. P. (2004). Relationships matter: Linking teacher support to student engagement and achievement. *Journal of School Health, 74*, 262–273.

Kluger, A. N., & DeNisi, A. (1996). The effects of feedback interventions on performance: A historical review, a meta-analysis, and a preliminary feedback intervention theory. *Psychological Bulletin, 119*(2), 254–284.

Kodak, T., Northup, J., & Kelley, M. (2007). An evaluation of the types of attention that maintain problem behavior. *Journal of Applied Behavior Analysis, 40*, 167–171.

Kohli, R., & Solórzano, D. G. (2012). Teachers, please learn our names! Racial microaggressions and the K–12 classroom. *Race Ethnicity and Education, 15*(4), 441–462.

Konrad, M., Joseph, L. M., & Eveleigh, E. (2009). A meta-analytic review of guided notes. *Education and Treatment of Children, 32*(3), 421–444.

Kounin, J. (1970). *Discipline and group management in classrooms.* Holt, Rinehart, & Winston.

Kuznekoff, J. H., & Titsworth, S. (2013). The impact of mobile phone usage on student learning. *Communication Education, 62*(3), 233–252.

Lan, W. (2005). Self-monitoring and its relationship with educational level and task importance. *Educational Psychology, 25*, 109–127.

Lee, M., Goodman, C., Dandapani, N., & Kekahio, W. (2015). *Review of international research on factors underlying teacher absenteeism* (REL 2015-087). U.S. Department of Education, Institute of Education Sciences, National Center for Education Evaluation and Regional Assistance, Regional Educational Laboratory Pacific.

Leverson, M., Smith, K., McIntosh, K., Rose, J., & Pinkelman, S. (2016). *PBIS cultural responsiveness field guide: Resources for trainers and coaches.* Office of Special Education Programs Technical Assistance Center on Positive Behavioral Interventions and Supports.

Lewis, T. J., & Sugai, G.(1999). Effective behavior support: A systems approach to proactive schoolwide management. *Focus on Exceptional Children, 31*(6), 1–24.

Lloyd, J., Forness, S., & Kavale, K. (1998). Some methods are more effective than others. *Intervention in School and Clinic, 33*, 195–200.

Locke, E. A., & Latham, G. P. (2006). New directions in goal-setting theory. Current *Directions in Psychological Science, 15*(5), 265–268.

Lomos, C., Hofman, R. H., & Bosker, R. J. (2011). Professional communities and student achievement—A meta-analysis. *School Effectiveness and School Improvement, 22*(2), 121–148.

Lou, Y., Abrami, P. C., Spence, J. C., Poulsen, C., Chambers, B., & d'Apollonia, S. (1996). Within-class grouping: A meta-analysis. *Review of Educational Research, 66*(4), 423–458.

Lovitt, T. C. (1978). *Managing inappropriate behaviors in the classroom.* Council for Exceptional Children.

Lubit, R., Rovine, D., Defrancisci, L., & Eth, S. (2003). Impact of trauma on children. *Journal of Psychiatric Practice, 9*(2), 128–138.

Luiselli, J. K., Putnam, R. F., Handler, M. W., & Feinberg, A. B. (2005). Whole-school positive behavior support: Effects on student discipline problems and academic performance. *Educational Psychology, 25*(2–3), 183–198.

Mabrito, M. (2006). A study of synchronous versus asynchronous collaboration in an online business writing class. *The American Journal of Distance Education, 20*(2), 93–107.

Mace, F., Belfiore, P., & Shea, M. (2001). Operant theory and research on self-regulation. In B. Zimmerman and D. Schunk (Eds.), *Learning and academic achievement: Theoretical perspectives* (pp. 39–65). Lawrence Erlbaum.

Maggin, D. M., Pustejovsky, J. E., & Johnson, A. H. (2017). A meta-analysis of school-based group contingency interventions for students with challenging behavior: An update. *Remedial and Special Education, 38*(6), 353–370.

Malone, B. G., & Tietjens, C. L. (2000). Re-examination of classroom rules: The need for clarity and specified behavior. *Special Services in the Schools, 16*, 159–170.

Marshall, M. (2001). *Discipline without stress, punishments or rewards: How teachers and parents promote responsibility and learning.* Piper.

Martella, R., Marchand-Martella, N., Miller, T., Young, K., & Macfarlane, C. (1995). Teaching instructional aides and peer tutors to decrease problem behaviors in the classroom. *Teaching Exceptional Children, 27*, 53–56.

Martella, R. C., Nelson, J. R., & Marchand-Martella, N. E. (2003). *Managing disruptive behaviors in the schools.* Allyn & Bacon.

Martin, S. H. (2002). The classroom environment and its effects on the practice of teachers. *Journal of Environmental Psychology, 22*(12), 139–156.

Marx, A., Fuhrer, U., & Hartig, T. (1999). Effects of classroom seating arrangements on children's question-asking. *Learning Environments Research, 2*(3), 249–263.

Marzano, R. J. (2003). *What works in schools: Translating research into action.* ASCD.

Marzano, R. J., & Heflebower, T. (2011). Grades that show what students know. *Educational Leadership, 69*(3), 34–39.

Marzano, R. J., Marzano, J. S., & Pickering, D. (2003). *Classroom management that works: Research-based strategies for every teacher.* ASCD.

Matheson, A., Starkweather, A., & Shriver, M. D. (2005). Training teachers to give effective commands: effects on student compliance and academic behaviors. *School Psychology Review, 34*, 202–219.

Mayer, G. (1995). Preventing antisocial behavior in the schools. *Journal of Applied Behavior Analysis, 28*, 467–478.

McCurdy, M., Skinner, C., McClurg, V., Whitsitt, L., & Moore, T. (2020). Bonus rewards for everyone: Enhancing mathematics performance with supplemental interdependent group contingencies. *Preventing School Failure: Alternative Education for Children and Youth, 64*(1), 77–88.

McGinnis, E., & Goldstein, A. (1994). *Skillstreaming the elementary schoolchild* (Rev. ed.). Research Press.

McLeod, J., Fisher, J., & Hoover, G. (2003). *The key elements of classroom management: Managing time and space, student behavior, and instructional strategies.* ASCD.

Merrett, F., & Wheldall, K. (1990). *Positive teaching in the primary school.* Paul Chapman.

Merritt, J. M. (2014). Alternative seating for young children: Effects on learning. *Journal of American International Journal of Contemporary Research, 4*(1), 12–18.

Miller, D., & Kraft, N. (2008). Best practices in communicating with and involving parents. In A. Thomas & J. Grimes (Eds.), *Best practices in school psychology V* (pp. 937–951). National Association of School Psychologists.

Miller, R. (2012). *Teacher absence as a leading indicator of student achievement: New national data offer opportunity to examine cost of teacher absence relative to learning loss.* Center for American Progress.

Mooney, P., Ryan, J. B., Uhing, B. M., Reid, R., & Epstein, M. H. (2005). A review of self-management interventions targeting academic outcomes for students with emotional and behavioral disorders. *Journal of Behavioral Education, 14*, 203–221.

Moskowitz, G., & Hayman, M. (1976). Success strategies of inner-city teachers: A year-long study. *Journal of Educational Research, 69*, 283–389.

Nafpaktitis, M., Mayer, G..R., & Butterworth, T. (1985). Natural rates of teacher approval and disapproval and their relation to student behavior in intermediate school classrooms. *Journal of Educational Psychology, 77*, 362–367.

NASP (National Association of School Psychologists). (2015). *Creating trauma-sensitive schools: Supportive policies and practices for learning* [Research summary]. Author.

NCES (National Center for Education Statistics). (2020). U.S. Department of Education. Public high school graduation rates. *The Condition of Education 2020* (NCES 2020-144). https://nces.ed.gov/programs/coe/indicator_coi.asp

Noltemeyer, A. L., Ward, R. M., & McLoughlin, C. (2015). Relationship between school suspension and student outcomes: A meta-analysis. *School Psychology Review, 44*(2), 224–240.

O'Connor, K. (2017). *How to grade for learning: Linking grades to standards.* Corwin Press.

O'Leary, K. D., & Becker, W. C. (1967). Behavior modification of an adjustment class: A token reinforcement program. *Exceptional Children, 33*(9), 637–642.

O'Leary, K. D., & O'Leary, S. G. (1977). *Classroom management: The successful use of behavior modification.* Pergamon.

O'Neill, R. E., Horner, R. H., Albin, R. W., Sprague, J. R., Storey, K., & Newton, J. S. (1997). *Functional assessment and program development for problem behavior: A practical handbook* (2nd ed.). Brooks/Cole.

Olive, M. L. (2004). Transitioning children between activities: Effective strategies for decreasing challenging behavior. *Beyond Behavior, 14*, 11–16.

Oregon Department of Education. (2021). *Comprehensive distance learning.* https://www.oregon.gov/ode/students-and-family/healthsafety/Documents/Comprehensive%20Distance%20Learning%20Guidance.pdf

Ornstein, A., & Lasley, T. (2004). *Strategies for effective teaching* (4th ed.). McGraw Hill.

Paine, S. C., Radicchi, J., Rosellini, L. C., Deutchman, L., & Darch, C. B. (1983). *Structuring your classroom for academic success.* Research Press.

Park, H. S. L., & Lynch, S. A. (2014). Evidence-based practices for addressing classroom behavior problems. *Young Exceptional Children, 17*(3), 33–47.

Payne, R. (2018). *A framework for understanding poverty* (6th ed.). Aha! Process.

Pedota, P. (2007). Strategies for effective classroom management in the secondary setting. *The Clearing House: A Journal of Educational Strategies, Issues and Ideas, 80*(4), 163–168.

Pergande, K., & Thorkildsen, T. A. (1995). From teachers as experimental researchers to teaching as moral inquiry. In J. G. Nicholls & T. A. Thorkildsen (Eds.), *Reasons for learning: Expanding the conversation on student-teacher collaboration* (pp. 21–35). Teachers College Press.

Peterson, E. R., Rubie-Davies, C., Osborne, D., & Sibley, C. (2016). Teachers' explicit expectations and implicit prejudiced attitudes to educational achievement: Relations with student achievement and the ethnic achievement gap. *Learning and Instruction, 42,* 123–140.

Phelan, P., Yu, H., & Davidson, A. (1994). Navigating the psychosocial pressures of adolescence: The voices and experiences of high school youth. *American Educational Research Journal, 31,* 415–447.

Pianta, R. C., Hamre, B., & Stuhlman, M. (2003). Relationships between teachers and children. In W. M Reynolds & G. E. Miller (Eds.), *Handbook of Psychology* (pp. 199–234). John Wiley and Sons.

Posny, A., personal communication, September 7, 2010.

Rader, L. A. (2005). Goal setting for students and teachers: Six steps to success. *Clearing House: A Journal of Educational Strategies, Issues, and Ideas, 78*(3), 123–126.

Reeves, D. B. (2004). The case against the zero. *Phi Delta Kappan, 86*(4), 324–325.

Reinke, W. M., Herman, K. C., Stormont, M. (2013). Classroom level positive behavior supports in schools implementing SWPBIS: Identifying areas for enhancement. *Journal of Positive Behavior Interventions, 15,* 51–60.

Repp, A., Nieminen, G., Olinger, E., & Brusca, R. (1988). Direct observation: Factors affecting the accuracy of observers. *Exceptional Children, 55,* 29–36.

Reyes, M. R., Brackett, M. A., Rivers, S. E., White, M., & Salovey, P. (2012). Classroom emotional climate, student engagement, and academic achievement. *Journal of Educational Psychology, 104*(3), 700.

Rhode, G., Jenson, W. R., & Williams, N. A. (2020). *The tough kid book* (3rd ed.). Ancora Publishing.

Rhodes, R., Ochoa, S., & Ortiz, S. (2005). *Assessing culturally and linguistically diverse students: A practical guide.* Guilford Press.

Richards-Tutor, C., Baker, D. L., Gersten, R., Baker, S. K., & Smith, J. M. (2016). The effectiveness of reading interventions for English learners: A research synthesis. *Exceptional Children, 82*(2), 144–169.

Rimm-Kaufman, S. E., La Paro, K. M., Downer, J. T., & Pianta, R. C. (2005). The contribution of classroom setting and quality of instruction to children's behavior in kindergarten classrooms. *The Elementary School Journal, 105*(4), 377–394.

Rones, M., & Hoagwood, K. (2000). School-based mental health services: A research review. *Clinical Child and Family Psychology Review, 3*(4), 223–241.

Ronfeldt, M., Farmer, S. O., McQueen, K., & Grissom, J. A. (2015). Teacher collaboration in instructional teams and student achievement. *American Educational Research Journal, 52*(3), 475–514.

Roorda, D. L., Koomen, H. M., Spilt, J. L., & Oort, F. J. (2011). The influence of affective teacher–student relationships on students' school engagement and achievement: A meta-analytic approach. *Review of Educational Research, 81*(4), 493–529.

Rosenfield, P., Lambert, N. M., & Black, A. (1985). Desk arrangement effects on pupil classroom behavior. *Journal of Educational Psychology, 77*(1), 101–108.

Rosenshine, B. (1986). Synthesis of research on explicit teaching. *Educational Leadership, 43*, 60–69.

Rosenshine, B. (1997). Advances in research on instruction. In J. W. Lloyd, E. J. Kame'enui, & D. Chard (Eds.), *Issues in education students with disabilities.* Lawrence Erlbaum.

Rosenshine, B. (2012). Principles of instruction: Research-based strategies that all teachers should know. *American Educator, 36*(1), 12.

Rosenshine, B., & Stevens, R. (1986). Teacher behavior and student achievement. In M. C. Whitrock (Ed.), *Handbook of research on teaching* (3rd ed., pp. 376–391). Macmillan.

Rowan, B., Camburn, E., & Correnti, R. (2004). Using teacher logs to measure the enacted curriculum: A study of literacy teaching in third-grade classrooms. *The Elementary School Journal, 105*(1), 75–101.

Salend, S., & Sylvestre, S. (2005). Understanding and addressing oppositional and defiant classroom behaviors. *Teaching Exceptional Children, 37*, 32–39.

Saxe, G. B., Gearhart, M., Note, M., & Paduano, P. (1993). Peer interaction and the development of mathematical understanding. *Charting the agenda: Educational activity after Vygotsky*, 107–144.

Scheuermann, B., & Hall, J. A. (2008). *Positive behavioral supports for the classroom.* Pearson Education.

Schiefele, U. (2009). Situational and individual interest. In K. Wentzel & A. Wigfield (Eds.), *Handbook of motivation at school* (pp. 197–222). Routledge.

Schilling, D. L., & Schwartz, I. S. (2004). Alternative seating for young children with autism spectrum disorder: Effects on classroom behavior. *Journal of Autism and Developmental Disorders, 34*(4), 423–432.

Schilling, D. L., Washington, K., Billingsley, F. F., & Deitz, J. (2003). Classroom seating for children with attention deficit hyperactivity disorder: Therapy balls versus chairs. *American Journal of Occupational Therapy, 57*(5), 534–541.

Schraw, G., & Lehman, S. (2001). Situational interest: A review of the literature and directions for future research. *Educational Psychology Review, 13*(1), 23–52.

Schuldheisz, J. M., & van der Mars, H. (2001). Active supervision and students' physical activity in middle school physical education. *Journal of Teaching in Physical Education, 21*, 75–90.

Schunk, D. H., Meece, J. R., & Pintrich, P. R. (2012). *Motivation in education: Theory, research, and applications.* Pearson Higher Ed.

Shah, M. (2012). The importance and benefits of teacher collegiality in schools—A literature review. *Procedia-Social and Behavioral Sciences, 46*, 1242–1246.

Sheets, R. H., & Gay, G. (1996). Student perceptions of disciplinary conflict in ethnically diverse classrooms. *NASSP Bulletin, 80*(580), 84–94.

Sheridan, S. M., Kratochwill, T. R., & Bergan, J. R. (1996). *Conjoint behavioral consultation: A procedural manual.* Plenum Press.

Shinn, M., & Bamonto, S. (1998). Advanced applications of curriculum-based measurement: "Big ideas" and avoiding confusion. In M. R. Shinn (Ed.), *Advanced applications of curriculum-based measurement* (pp. 1–31). Guilford Press.

Shores, R., Gunter, P., & Jack, S. (1993). Classroom management strategies: Are they setting events for coercion? *Behavioral Disorders, 18*, 92–102.

Silver-Pacuilla, H., & Fleischman, S. (2006). Research Matters/Technology to help struggling students. *Educational Leadership, 63*(5), 84–85.

Simmons, C. (2020). Pacing lessons for optimal learning. *Educational Leadership, 77*, 46–52.

Simmons, K., Carpenter, L., Crenshaw S., & Hinton, V. M. (2015). Exploration of classroom seating arrangement and student behavior in a second grade classroom. *Georgia Educational Researcher, 12*(1), 51–68.

Simonsen, B., Fairbanks, S., Briesch, A., Myers, D., & Sugai, G. (2008). Evidence-based practices in classroom management: Considerations for research to practice. *Education and Treatment of Children, 31*, 351–380.

Skinner, B. F. (1953). *Science and human behavior.* Basic Books.

Skinner, C. H., Skinner, A. L., & Burton, B. (2009). Applying group-oriented contingencies in the classroom. In A. Akin-Little & S. Little (Eds.), *Behavioral interventions in schools: Evidence-based positive strategies* (pp. 157–170). American Psychological Association.

Skylar, A. A. (2009). A comparison of asynchronous online text-based lectures and synchronous interactive web conferencing lectures. *Issues in Teacher Education, 18*(2), 69–84.

Smith, D., Fisher, D., & Frey, N. (2015). *Better than carrots or sticks: Restorative practices for positive classroom management.* ASCD.

Souers, K., & Hall, P. (2016). *Fostering resilient learners: Strategies for creating a trauma-sensitive classroom.* ASCD.

Spencer, V. G. (2006). Peer tutoring and students with emotional or behavioral disorders: A review of the literature. *Behavioral Disorders, 31*(2), 204–222.

Sprick, R. (2017). *Start on Time!* (2nd ed.). Ancora Publishing.

Sprick, R. S., Booher, M., Isaacs, S. J., Sprick, J., & Rich, P. (2014). *Foundations: A proactive and positive behavior support system* (Modules A–F). Ancora Publishing.

Sprick, R., Coughlin, C., Garrison, M., & Sprick, J. (2019). *Interventions* (3rd ed.). Ancora Publishing.

Sprick, R., Sprick, J., M. Sprick, & Coughlin, C. (2020). *Early stage interventions: Behavior strategies for every teacher.* Ancora Publishing.

Sprick, R., Sprick, J., Coughlin, C., & Edwards, J. (2021). *Discipline in the Secondary Classroom* (4th ed.). Jossey Bass.

Stage, S. A., & Quiroz, D. R. (1997). A meta-analysis of interventions to decrease disruptive classroom behavior in public education settings. *School Psychology Review, 26*, 333–368.

Stapp, A. (2018). Alternative seating and students' perceptions: Implications for the learning environment. *Georgia Educational Researcher, 14*(2), Article 4. doi: 10.20429/ger.2018.140–204

Stichter, J. P., Lewis, T. J., Whittaker, T. A., Richter, M., Johnson, N. W., & Trussell, R. P. (2009). Assessing teacher use of opportunities to respond and effective classroom management strategies: Comparisons among high-and low-risk elementary schools. *Journal of Positive Behavior Interventions, 11*(2), 68–81.

Stokes, T., & Baer, D. (1977). An implicit technology of generalization. *Journal of Applied Behavior Analysis, 7*, 599–610.

Stormont, M., Smith, S., & Lewis, T. (2007). Teacher implementation of precorrection and praise statements in Head Start classrooms as a component of a program-wide system of positive behavior support. *Journal of Behavioral Education, 16*, 280–290.

Streeck-Fischer, A., & van der Kolk, B. A. (2000). Down will come baby, cradle and all: Diagnostic and therapeutic implications of chronic trauma on child development. *Australian and New Zealand Journal of Psychiatry, 34*(6), 903–918.

Stronge, J. H., Ward, T. J., & Grant, L. W. (2011). What makes good teachers good? A cross-case analysis of the connection between teacher effectiveness and student achievement. *Journal of Teacher Education, 62*(4), 339–355.

Sugai, G., & Horner, R. H. (2002). The evolution of discipline practices: School-wide positive behavior supports. *Child and Family Behavior Therapy, 24*, 23–50.

Sugai, G., & Lewis, T. (1996). Preferred and promising practices for social skill instruction. *Focus on Exceptional Children, 29*, 1–16.

Sugai, G., & Tindal, G. (1993). *Effective school consultation: An interactive approach.* Brooks/Cole.

Sulzer-Azaroff, B., & Mayer, G. R. (1991). *Behavior analysis for lasting change.* Holt, Rinehart, & Winston.

Sutherland, K. S., & Wehby, J. H. (2001). Exploring the relationship between increased opportunities to respond to academic requests and the academic and behavioral outcomes of students with EBD: A review. *Remedial and Special Education, 22*, 113–121.

Sutherland, K. S., Wehby, J. H., & Copeland, S. R. (2000). Effect of varying rates of behavior specific praise on the on-task behavior of students with EBD. *Journal of Emotional and Behavioral Disorders, 8*, 2–8.

Sweeney, W., Ehrhardt, A., Gardner, R., Jones, L., Greenfield, R., & Fribley, S. (1999). Using guided notes with academically at-risk high school students during a remedial summer social studies class. *Psychology in the Schools, 36*, 305–318.

Tamim, R. M., Bernard, R. M., Borokhovski, E., Abrami, P. C., & Schmid, R. F. (2011). What forty years of research says about the impact of technology on learning: A second-order meta-analysis and validation study. *Review of Educational Research, 81*(1), 4–28.

Tankersley, M. (1995). A group-oriented contingency management program: A review of research on the Good Behavior Game and implications for teachers. *Preventing School Failure, 40,* 19–24.

Thapa, A., Cohen, J., Guffey, S., & Higgins-D'Alessandro, A. (2013). A review of school climate research. *Review of Educational Research, 83*(3), 357–385.

Tilly, W. D. (2008). The evolution of school psychology to science-based practice: Problem solving and the three-tiered model. In A. Thomas and J. Grimes (Eds.). *Best practices in school psychology V* (Vol. 1, pp. 17–36). National Association of School Psychologists.

Tingstrom, D. H., Sterling-Turner, H. E., & Wilczynski, S. M. (2006). The Good Behavior Game: 1969–2002. *Behavior Modification, 30,* 225–253.

Trussell, R. P. (2008). Classroom universals to prevent problem behaviors. *Intervention in School and Clinic, 43*(3), 179–185.

Tuan, L. T., & Nhu, N. T. K. (2010). Theoretical review on oral interaction in EFL classrooms. *Studies in Literature and Language, 1*(4), 2948.

Tubbs, M. E. (1986). Goal setting: A meta-analytic examination of the empirical evidence. *Journal of Applied Psychology, 71*(3), 474.

van den Berg, Y. H., Segers, E., & Cillessen, A. H. (2012). Changing peer perceptions and victimization through classroom arrangements: A field experiment. *Journal of Abnormal Child Psychology, 40*(3), 403–412.

van den Bogert, N., van Bruggen, J., Kostons, D., & Jochems, W. (2014). First steps into understanding teachers' visual perception of classroom events. *Teaching and Teacher Education, 37,* 208–216.

van der Kolk, B. (2003). The neurobiology of childhood trauma and abuse. *Child and Adolescent Psychiatric Clinics of North America, 12*(2), 293–317.

Vangrieken, K., Dochy, F., Raes, E., & Kyndt, E. (2015). Teacher collaboration: A systematic review. *Educational Research Review, 15,* 17–40.

Varlas, L. (2001). Succeeding with substitute teachers. *Association for Supervision and Curriculum Development, 43*(7), 45.

Walker, H. (1983). Application of response cost in school settings: Outcomes, issues, and recommendations. *Exceptional Education Quarterly, 3*(4), 4–55.

Walker, H., Colvin, G., & Ramsey, E. (1995). *Antisocial behavior in school: Strategies and best practices.* Brooks/Cole.

Walker, H., Horner, R., Sugai, G., Bullis, M., Sprague, J., Bricker, D., & Kaufman, M. J. (1996). Integrated approaches to preventing antisocial behavior patterns among school-age youth. *Journal of Emotional and Behavioral Disorders, 4,* 193–256.

Walker, H. M., Ramsey, E., & Gresham, F. (2004). *Antisocial behavior in schools: Evidence-based practices* (2nd ed.). Wadsworth.

Walker, H. M., Severson, H. H., Feil, E. G., Stiller, B., & Golly, A. (1998). First step to success: Intervention at the point of school entry to prevent antisocial behavior patterns. *Psychology in the Schools, 35,* 259–269.

Walsh, J. (2018). Associations between 24 hour movement behaviours and global cognition in U.S. children: A cross-sectional observational study. *The Lancet Child & Adolescent Health, 2*(11). https://doi.org/10.1016/S2352-4642(18)30278-5

Wan, Y. (2017). Did I say your name correctly? Strategies for creating a culture of respect. *Perspectives, 40*(1), 6–13.

Wang, M. T., & Degol, J. L. (2016). School climate: A review of the construct, measurement, and impact on student outcomes. *Educational Psychology Review, 28*(2), 315–352.

Wannarka, R., & Ruhl, K. (2008). Seating arrangements that promote positive academic and behavioural outcomes: A review of empirical research. *Support for Learning, 23*(2), 89–93.

Warger, C. (1999). *Positive behavior support and functional assessment.* ERIC Clearinghouse on Disabilities and Gifted Education.

Watkins, C. L., & Slocum, T. A. (2004). The components of direct instruction. *Journal of Direct Instruction, 3,* 75–110.

Webb, N. M., Baxter, G. P., & Thompson, L. (1997). Teachers' grouping practices in fifth-grade science classrooms. *The Elementary School Journal, 98*(2), 91–113.

Weinstein, C. (1977). Modifying student behavior in an open classroom through changes in the physical design. *American Educational Research Journal, 14,* 249–262.

Weinstein, C. S. (1979). The physical environment of the school: A review of research. *Review of Educational Research, 49,* 577–610.

Weinstein, R. S. (2009). *Reaching higher.* Harvard University Press.

Weiss, H. B., Lopez, M. E., & Rosenberg, H. (2010). *Beyond random acts: Family, school, and community engagement as an integral part of education reform.* National Policy Forum for Family, School, & Community Engagement. Harvard Family Research Project. https://sedl.org/connections/engagement_forum/beyond_random_acts.pdf

Wentzel, K. R. (2002). Are effective teachers like good parents? Teaching styles and student adjustment in early adolescence. *Child Development, 73*(1), 287–301.

Wentzel, K. R., & Miele, D. (2016). *Handbook of motivation at school*. Routledge.

Wigfield, A., & Eccles, J. S. (1992). The development of achievement task values: A theoretical analysis. *Developmental Review, 12*(3), 265–310.

Winger, T. (2005) Grading to communicate. *Educational Leadership, 63*(3), 61–65. http://www.ascd.org/publications/educational-leadership/nov05/vol63/num03/Grading-to-Communicate.aspx

Wolfgang, C. H., & Glickman, C. D. (1986). *Solving discipline problems: Strategies for classroom teachers* (2nd ed.). Allyn & Bacon.

Wong, H. K., & Wong, R. T. (2009). *The first days of school: How to be an effective teacher* (4th ed.). Harry K. Wong Publications.

Woodward, J. (2001). Using grades to assess student performance. *Journal of School Improvement, 2*, 44–45.

Wu, W. L., Wang, C. C., Chen, C. H., Lai, C. L., Yang, P. C., & Guo, L. Y. (2012). Influence of therapy ball seats on attentional ability in children with attention deficit/hyperactivity disorder. *Journal of Physical Therapy Science, 24*(11), 1177–1182.

Ysseldyke, J. E., & Christenson, S. L. (1987). Evaluating students' instructional environments. *RASE, 8*, 17–24.

Ysseldyke, J., Thurlow, M., Wotruba, J., & Nania, P. (1990). Instructional arrangements: Perceptions from general education. *Teaching Exceptional Children, 22*, 4–8.

Zheng, B., Warschauer, M., Lin, C.-H., & Chang, C. (2016). Learning in one-to-one laptop environments: A meta-analysis and research synthesis. *Review of Educational Research, 86*(4), 1052–1084.

Zimmerman, B. J. (2002). Becoming a self-regulated learner: An overview. *Theory into Practice, 41*(2), 64–70.

Zimmerman, J. (2020, March 26). Reviving the original purpose of pass-fail. *Inside Higher Ed.* https://www.insidehighered.com/views/2020/03/26/reviewing-history-pass-fail-reminds-us-how-we-should-consider-option-today-opinion